Employment Discrimination

Selected Cases and Statutes – 2011

Employment Discrimination

Selected Cases and Statutes – 2011

Michael J. Zimmer

Professor of Law
Loyola University Chicago
&
Professor of Law Emeritus
Seton Hall University

Charles A. Sullivan

Professor of Law
Seton Hall University

Rebecca Hanner White

Dean and J. Alton Hosch Professor of Law
University of Georgia

Wolters Kluwer
Law & Business

To contact Customer Service, e-mail customer.service@wolterskluwer. com, call 1-800-234-1660, fax 1-800-901-9075, or mail correspondence to:

>   Wolters Kluwer Law & Business
>   Attn: Order Department
>   PO Box 990
>   Frederick, MD 21705

Printed in the United States of America.

1 2 3 4 5 6 7 8 9 0

ISBN 978-1-4548-0808-4

ISSN: 1529-7691

About Wolters Kluwer Law & Business

Wolters Kluwer Law & Business is a leading global provider of intelligent information and digital solutions for legal and business professionals in key specialty areas, and respected educational resources for professors and law students. Wolters Kluwer Law & Business connects legal and business professionals as well as those in the education market with timely, specialized authoritative content and information-enabled solutions to support success through productivity, accuracy and mobility.

Serving customers worldwide, Wolters Kluwer Law & Business products include those under the Aspen Publishers, CCH, Kluwer Law International, Loislaw, Best Case, ftwilliam. com and MediRegs family of products.

CCH products have been a trusted resource since 1913, and are highly regarded resources for legal, securities, antitrust and trade regulation, government contracting, banking, pension, payroll, employment and labor, and healthcare reimbursement and compliance professionals.

Aspen Publishers products provide essential information to attorneys, business professionals and law students. Written by preeminent authorities, the product line offers analytical and practical information in a range of specialty practice areas from securities law and intellectual property to mergers and acquisitions and pension/benefits. Aspen's trusted legal education resources provide professors and students with high-quality, up-to-date and effective resources for successful instruction and study in all areas of the law.

Kluwer Law International products provide the global business community with reliable international legal information in English. Legal practitioners, corporate counsel and business executives around the world rely on Kluwer Law journals, looseleafs, books, and electronic products for comprehensive information in many areas of international legal practice.

Loislaw is a comprehensive online legal research product providing legal content to law firm practitioners of various specializations. Loislaw provides attorneys with the ability to quickly and efficiently find the necessary legal information they need, when and where they need it, by facilitating access to primary law as well as state-specific law, records, forms and treatises.

Best Case Solutions is the leading bankruptcy software product to the bankruptcy industry. It provides software and workflow tools to flawlessly streamline petition preparation and the electronic filing process, while timely incorporating ever-changing court requirements.

ftwilliam.com offers employee benefits professionals the highest quality plan documents (retirement, welfare and non-qualified) and government forms (5500/PBGC, 1099 and IRS) software at highly competitive prices.

MediRegs products provide integrated health care compliance content and software solutions for professionals in healthcare, higher education and life sciences, including professionals in accounting, law and consulting.

Wolters Kluwer Law & Business, a division of Wolters Kluwer, is headquartered in New York. Wolters Kluwer is a market-leading global information services company focused on professionals.

Contents

Preface   *xi*
Acknowledgments   *xiii*

Case Supplement

Chapter 1:   Individual Disparate Treatment Discrimination   3
Chapter 2:   Systemic Disparate Treatment Discrimination   42
Chapter 3:   Systemic Disparate Impact Discrimination   51
Chapter 4:   The Interrelation of the Three Theories of
             Discrimination   65
Chapter 5:   Special Problems in Applying Title VII, Section 1981,
             and the ADEA   107
Chapter 6:   Disability Discrimination   159
Chapter 7:   Procedures for Enforcing Antidiscrimination Laws   215
Chapter 8:   Judicial Relief   256
Chapter 9:   Managing Risks in Employment Discrimination
             Disputes   265

Statutes

Age Discrimination in Employment Act
    29 U.S.C. §§621-633a   275

Americans with Disabilities Act
  Table of Contents, Title I, Title II, and Title V
    42 U.S.C. §§12101-12102, 12111-12117, 12131-12134,
    12201-12213   292
Americans with Disabilities Act Amendments Act of 2008
  Pub. L. No. 110-325; 122 Stat. 3553   313
Civil Rights Act of 1991
  Pub. L. No. 102-166, 105 Stat. 1071   320
Congressional Accountability Act
  2 U.S.C. §§1301-1302, 1311-1313, 1317, 1361   332
Equal Pay Act
  29 U.S.C. §206(d)   339
Fair Labor Standards Act
  29 U.S.C. §§216-217   340
Family and Medical Leave Act of 1993
  29 U.S.C. §§2601, 2611-2619, 2651-2654   342
Federal Arbitration Act
  9 U.S.C. §§1-16   360
  42 U.S.C. §1981   366
  42 U.S.C. §1981a   367
  42 U.S.C. §1983   370
  42 U.S.C. §1985(3)   371
  42 U.S.C. §1988   372
  42 U.S.C. §2000d-7   374
Genetic Information Nondiscrimination Act of 2008
  Title II   375
Immigration Reform and Control Act
  8 U.S.C. §1324b   393
Lilly Ledbetter Fair Pay Act of 2009
  Pub. L. No. 111-2; 123 Stat. 5   400
National Labor Relations Act
  29 U.S.C. §§151-169   403
Portal-to-Portal Act
  29 U.S.C. §§255, 256, 260   424
Rehabilitation Act of 1973
  29 U.S.C. §§705, 791, 793, 794, 794a   426
Religious Freedom Restoration Act
  42 U.S.C. §2000bb   432
Residual Statute of Limitations
  28 U.S.C. §1658   434
Title VI of the Civil Rights Act of 1964
  42 U.S.C. §§2000d, 2000d-1, 2000d-3, 2000d-4(a)   435
Title VII of the Civil Rights Act of 1964
  42 U.S.C. §§2000e-2000e-17   437
Title IX of the Education Amendments of 1972
  20 U.S.C. §§1681-1688   462

Regulations

Regulations to Implement the Equal Employment Provisions of the
    Americans with Disabilities Act
    29 C.F.R. Part 1630   469
Interpretive Guidance on Title I of the Americans with
    Disabilities Act
    Appendix to Part 1630   486
Part 1635 — Genetic Information Nondiscrimination Act of 2008   554

Table of Cases   *573*
Table of Selected Secondary Authorities   *581*

Preface

The publication of the Seventh Edition in 2008 reflected a growing maturity in the field of Employment Discrimination, with no meaningful new legislation having been passed in a number of years and a quiet, incremental (if often not hospitable) development in the courts. But things were about to change — in both directions. On the legislative front, the passage of the Americans with Disabilities Act Amendments Act of 2008 and the Lilly Ledbetter Fair Pay Act in 2009 were dramatic legislative developments as was, although perhaps to a lesser extent, the enactment of GINA, the Genetic Information Nondiscrimination Act. The Supplement reflects the changes wrought by these three laws in some detail, and the text of all three statutes is reproduced in this work, as are the EEOC's final ADAAA regulations and final GINA regulations.

While Congress was busy expanding the reach of the employment discrimination laws, the Court was busy contracting them in some major ways. Most dramatic were the Supreme Court's 2009 decision in *Ricci v. DeStefano* and its 2011 decision in *Wal-Mart Stores, Inc. v. Dukes.* Some believe that *Ricci* marks the end of the disparate impact theory but even if that is too gloomy a prediction, disparate impact is in the process of being reinvented in the post-*Ricci* era. As for *Wal-Mart,* the Court dealt what may well be a deathblow to large-scale employment discrimination class actions and, in the process, may also have significantly weakened the systemic disparate treatment theory itself, at least outside of the government enforcement context. Rounding out the trio of blockbuster restrictive High Court decisions, *Gross v. FBL Financial Services,* decided in 2009, required plaintiffs in individual ADEA cases to prove that age was a but-for cause of the adverse employment action they challenged. The extent to which *Gross* controls other statutes (such as the ADA and antiretaliation provisions) remains unclear.

While these three cases would warrant a respectable Supplement by themselves, they are by no means the only Supreme Court employment discrimination decisions handed down since the Seventh Edition, and they include some notable wins for plaintiffs. For example, the Supreme Court's recent retaliation cases have resulted in plaintiff victories. *Thompson v. N. Am. Stainless, LP* approved of third party standing to assert retaliation claims, at least in some cases, and *Crawford v. Metropolitan Government* held that responding to an employer's internal investigations was protected conduct, and several other decisions also applied the antiretaliation principle broadly. Moreover, this year, in *Staub v. Proctor*

Hospital, the Court addressed the "cat's-paw" question, holding for the plaintiff but also importing into antidiscrimination law the amorphous notion of proximate cause, which may not turn out to be so pro-plaintiff when the dust settles.

Other Supreme Court cases since 2008, a mixed bag on the ideological spectrum, addressed a wide variety of issues, including: the burden of persuasion for the reasonable factors other than age defense to ADEA claims; "me too" evidence; age specifications in pension eligibility; the continuing effects of pre-Pregnancy Discrimination Act denials of seniority credit for pensions; and the appropriate statute of limitations for disparate impact claims. And in the arbitration arena alone, the Court issued several important opinions that are likely to reinforce the shift toward less court involvement in discrimination disputes.

In short, a lot has changed since 2008 when the Seventh Edition appeared, and this Supplement deals with all of the changes, as well as tracking major decisions in the lower courts and new scholarship in the field.

And, if you're wondering, yes—we're hard at work on a new edition!

In most respects, the Supplement proceeds by the usual mechanism of inserting principal cases and new notes at appropriate points. With respect to Chapter 6, however, the ADAAA required revising the material in the main volume; therefore, many of the changes there reflect wholesale replacement of the original text to make it easier for both professor and student. To a lesser extent, this is also true with respect to Chapter 7, Procedures, where we have replaced the *Ledbetter* principal case with text considering the effects of the overriding Lilly Ledbetter Fair Pay Act.

MJZ
CAS
RHW

August 2011

Acknowledgments

Professor Sullivan offers his heartfelt thanks to his research assistants, who contributed in so many ways to work on this Supplement over the last three years, all the more so because my RAs often worked under unreasonable deadlines and had to put up with occasional authorial missteps. They are:

Katherine Planer and Tara Touloumis, Seton Hall class of 2009;
Elizabeth Losey, class of 2010;
Mariel Belanger, Anthony Marroney Noto, and Daniel McGrady, class of 2011;
Mark Heftler, Temi Kolarova, Renee Levine, and Caitlin Petry, class of 2012; and
Ezra Alter, Jinkal Pujara, Liana Nobile, and Kaitlyn Stone, class of 2013.

And then there's Beth Krauzlis, Professor Sullivan's assistant, who not only provided much help with parts of this Supplement but also kept the rest of his life more or less on track while this Supplement was being finished.

Rebecca White thanks her research assistants Amy Smith (UGA 2010), Jason McCoy (UGA 2009), and Brandon Moulard (UGA 2009), as well as Rachel Hinckley (UGA 2011).

Employment Discrimination

Selected Cases and Statutes – 2011

Case Supplement

1 Individual Disparate Treatment Discrimination

B. The Elements of an Individual Disparate Treatment Case

1. Intent to Discriminate

Page 7. Add to end of carryover Note 6, *Acting on Stereotypes*:

Tying together this scholarship with the holding in *Slack,* Michael J. Zimmer argues in *A Chain of Inferences Proving Discrimination,* 79 U. COLO. L. REV. 1243, 1279-80 (2008):

> [E]vidence of stereotypical thinking supports an ultimate inference of intent to discriminate precisely because it is an unconscious expression of bias. . . . [Pohasky's statement] is powerful evidence that he made his decision as to who would do cleaning based on race. In other words, he may not have been conscious that his statements reflected bias, but, by being so forthcoming with a statement as to his actual state of mind that was biased, that statement constituted strong support for a finding of discriminatory intent

Page 7. Add at end of second paragraph of Note 7, *The Extent of the Phenomenon*:

Even those paragons of rationality, law students, seem to be subject to such influences. Justin D. Levinson & Danielle Young, *Implicit Gender Bias in the Legal Profession: An Empirical Study,* 18 DUKE L. GENDER L. & POL'Y 1 (2010), report that law students tended to associate judges with men, not women, and women with the home and family. However, they also found that study participants were frequently able to resist their implicit biases and make decisions in gender-neutral ways. *See also* Laura Giuliana, David I. Levine, & Jonathon Leonard, *Manager Race and the Race of New Hires,* 27 J. LAB. ECON. 589 (2009) (using data from a large retailer with frequent employee turnover, the study finds that non-black managers hire more whites and fewer blacks than do African American managers; in areas with large Hispanic populations, Hispanic managers hire more Hispanics and fewer whites than white managers).

Page 8. Add at end of carryover paragraph in Note 7, *The Extent of the Phenomenon*:

See also Gregory Mitchell, *Second Thoughts*, 40 McGeorge L. Rev. 687 (2009) ("considerable evidence exists that individuals often naturally engage in self-correction and that situational pressures often encourage self-correction to overcome biased judgments, decisions, and behavior"); Gregory Mitchell & Philip E. Tetlock, *Facts Do Matter: A Reply to Bagenstos*, 37 Hofstra L. Rev. 737 (2009) (arguing that Bagenstos "misconstrued our scientific arguments and has accepted at face value empirically unsubstantiated claims about the power of millisecond-reaction-time measures to predict behavior in workplaces"); Amy L. Wax, *The Discriminating Mind: Define It, Prove It*, 40 Conn. L. Rev. 979, 984-85 (2008) (while decisions caused by unconscious mental processes are as actionable as those that are the product of deliberate awareness, it does not follow that discrimination is widespread; even assuming that tests such as the IAT establish unconsciously biased mental associations, there may not be unlawful discrimination. "Biased thinking and attitudes, and mental processing of stimuli and concepts, are not the same as unlawful discrimination.").

Page 8. Add at end of second paragraph in Note 8, *Is "Unconscious Discrimination" an Oxymoron?*:

Cf. Katharine T. Bartlett, *Making Good on Good Intentions: The Critical Role of Motivation in Reducing Implicit Workplace Discrimination*, 95 Va. L. Rev. 1893, 1900 (2009) (agreeing that "Title VII already prohibits unconscious as well as conscious race and gender discrimination," the article "cautions against approaches to unconscious discrimination—whatever its prevalence and whatever the inadequacies of existing law—that rely principally on stronger legal coercion as the primary tool to fight implicit discrimination" because of the potential negative effects on internalization of nondiscrimination norms).

Page 8. Add before contra *Selmi* cite in last paragraph in Note 8, *Is "Unconscious Discrimination" an Oxymoron?*:

See also Patrick Shin, *Liability for Unconscious Discrimination? A Thought Experiment in the Theory of Employment Discrimination Law*, 62 Hastings L. J. 67 (2010) (assuming that implicit bias exists and can be proven to have caused an adverse employment action, the article examines whether making such conduct illegal is normatively desirable).

Page 9.   Add at end of Note 11, *The Bad Old Days*:

Ralph Richard Banks & Richard Thompson Ford, *(How) Does Unconscious Bias Matter?: Law, Politics, and Racial Inequality*, 58 EMORY L. REV. 1053, 1055 (2009) ("the findings of the IAT are ambiguous. The test could just as plausibly be thought to measure racial bias that is simply covert, known to oneself yet intentionally concealed from researchers. On this interpretation, the IAT reveals not that individuals are more biased than they realize, but that they are more biased than they want others to know").

Page 13.   Add at end of first paragraph of carryover Note 2 *"But for motivation"*:

But see Michael J. Zimmer, *A Chain of Inferences Proving Discrimination*, 79 U. COLO. L. REV. 1243, 1257 (2008) ("While it is possible that the defendant had only one motivation for its action, it is not the only possible scenario. Most importantly, a showing of 'but-for' linkage can result in liability without proof that *only* the employer's discrimination motivated the employer's action. In other words, liability can be made out using the 'but-for' test even if some additional reason, such as the employer's explanation, played a role it its decision.").

2.   *Terms, Conditions, or Privileges of Employment*

Page 20.   Delete new Note 2; replace with the following:

2. *Materiality* As *Minor* suggests, the lower courts have generally required more than a mere showing that the employer discriminated in order for its conduct to be actionable. They have required an "adverse employment action," which they have usually defined to require some material effect on the terms and conditions of employment. Obviously, "ultimate employment actions" — hiring and firing— suffice, and meaningful changes in compensation have also been held actionable. *E.g., Leibowitz v. Cornell Univ.*, 584 F.3d 487 (2d Cir. 2009) (loss of a position constituted an adverse employment action regardless of whether it was labeled "non-renewal," "lay off," or "termination,"); *Wilkerson v. New Media Tech. Charter Sch. Inc.*, 522 F.3d 315, 320 (3d Cir. 2008) ("The failure to renew an employment arrangement, whether at-will or for a limited period of time, is an employment action"); *Farrell v. Butler Univ.*, 421 F.3d 609, 614 (7th Cir. 2005) (while denial of bonuses is not an adverse employment action, denial of a raise can be, and the denial to plaintiff of a regularly-conferred award resulting in any recipient getting a permanent increase in base salary is best characterized as a raise). *See also*

Crawford v. Carroll, 529 F.3d 961 (11th Cir. 2008) (denial of merit raise actionable if discriminatory, even if the denial was later reversed by the employer).

When it comes to less directly economic effects on employees' lives, however, the lower courts decisions are confused. A few examples illustrate the problem in cases where there was not sufficient adversity:

- mid-range evaluation, *Primes v. Reno*, 190 F.3d 765 (6th Cir. 1999), or even negative evaluation when future prospects were hindered, *Davis v. Town of Lake Park, Fla.*, 245 F.3d 1232, 1242-1243 (11th Cir. 2001). *See also De la Rama v. Ill. Dep't of Human Servs.*, 541 F.3d 681 (7th Cir. 2008) (no adverse employment action when employer left unauthorized absences on plaintiff's record, at least when it assured her that they would not be used in any disciplinary proceeding).
- lateral transfer usually defined to mean no reduction in pay or title or any diminution in pay "indirect and minor," *Williams v. Bristol-Myers Squibb Co.*, 85 F.3d 270 (7th Cir. 1996), even though the transfer might be to a distant location, *Reynolds v. Ethicon Endo-Surgery*, Inc., 454 F.3d 868 (8th Cir. 2006); *see also Lucero v. Nettle Creek Sch. Corp.*, 566 F.3d 720 (7th Cir. 2009) (reassignment of teacher from 12th grade/Honors/AP English classes to seventh grade English class was not adverse action, despite contention that teaching junior high students is less prestigious than teaching seniors, where plaintiff continued to teach same subject in same building under same conditions). *But see Barone v. United Airlines, Inc.*, 355 F. App'x 169 (10th Cir. 2009) (asking plaintiff to choose between resignation and reassignment several states away from her current assignment was an adverse emp-loyment action); *Hrisinko v. N.Y. City Dep't of Educ.*, 369 F. App'x. 232 (2d Cir. 2010) (transfer to substitute teacher position was adverse employment action even though salary and benefits did not change, where it was less distinguished, had diminished responsibilities, and eliminated plaintiff's opportunity for tenure); *Beyer v. County of Nassau*, 524 F.3d 160, 164 (2d Cir. 2008) (denial of a transfer from a unit with little chance of advancement to one that was "both highly desirable and objectively preferable" for pursuing a career in police forensics was actionable).
- investigation of plaintiff, *Mazumder v. Univ. of Mich.*, 195 F. App'x 320 (6th Cir. 2006), even when plaintiff put on paid administrative leave, *Joseph v. Leavitt*, 465 F.3d 87 (2d Cir. 2006).
- family-oriented questions asked only of female job applicant, *Bruno v. City of Crown Point*, 950 F.2d 355 (7th Cir. 1991);
- failure to provide plaintiff with a computer, *Enowmbitang v. Seagate Tech.*, 148 F.3d 970, 973 (8th Cir. 1998).

These decisions are often fact-sensitive, and some courts see more harm in actions with little direct economic effect.

1. Individual Disparate Treatment Discrimination

3. Linking Discriminatory Intent to the Employer's Treatment of Plaintiff

Page 29.   Add to end of the first paragraph of Note 3, *Direct Evidence Not a Prerequisite to Motivating Factor Proof*:

See Michael J. Zimmer, *A Chain of Inferences Proving Discrimination*, 79 U. Colo. L. Rev. 1243, 1254 (2008).

Page 30.   Add in Note 5, *Back to Costa*, in second to last line after "to discharge her":

See also DeCaire v. Mukasey, 530 F.3d 1, 18 (1st Cir. 2008) (a district court's finding in a mixed motive case that there was gender discrimination required the court to find liability; "in such a case, it is plaintiff's remedies, not the employer's liability, that are limited.").

Page 43.   Add at end of Note 4, *Mixed Motive vs. Pretext*:

But see EEOC v. Con-Way Freight, 622 F.3d 933 (8th Cir. 2010) (direct evidence of racial bias not sufficient to create a jury question in light of pre-existing employer policy disqualifying applicants with theft-related convictions) See Marcia McCormick, *Twisting and Turning Towards Summary Judgment*, http://lawprofessors.typepad.com/laborprof_blog/2010/09/twisting-and-turning-towards-summary-judgment.html/.

C. Proving the Discrimination Element

Page 44.   Add to end of carryover of Note 5, *Two Distinct Proof Methods?*:

See Michael J. Zimmer, *A Chain of Inferences Proving Discrimination*, 79 U. Colo. L. Rev. 1243 (2008).

Page 44.   Add at end of second paragraph of Note 6, *Direct Evidence Is Still Important*:

See Darchak v. City of Chi. Bd. of Educ., 580 F.3d 622 (7th Cir. 2009) (evidence that supervisor made derogatory remarks about ethnicity, including calling plaintiff a "stupid Polack," created a fact issue as to the reason for her discharge by that supervisor even though the decision to terminate her happened several months later; *Van Voorhis v. Hillsborough County Bd. of County Comm'rs*, 512 F.3d 1296, 1300 (11th Cir. 2008) (statements such as that supervisor's statement that he did not want to hire an old pilot "are direct evidence of age discrimination. The import of the alleged statements 'could be nothing other than to discriminate on the basis of age'").

Page 45. Add before *but see Barner* **cite in carryover Note 7,**
** *An Evidence Primer*:**

Simple v. Walgreen Co., 511 F.3d 668, 672 (7th Cir. 2007) (remark by person involved in the decision-making process that a store "was possibly not ready to have a black manager" made because he would not have been "very happy working there," was made within the scope of her employment and therefore admissible; together with another admission to plaintiff by that person that race played a role in the denial of a promotion, it was direct evidence of discrimination);

Page 45. Add after title of Note 8(b), *Does the Statement Show Illegitimate*
** *Considerations?*:**

Some remarks seem to be pretty obviously pejorative on racial grounds, *King v. Hardesty*, 517 F.3d 1049, 1059 (8th Cir. 2008) (reversing district court in §1981 case because supervisor's comment to black teacher—that "white people teach black kids . . . better than someone from their own race"—was "evidence that may be viewed as directly reflecting Hardesty's alleged discriminatory attitude"). *See also Sanders v. Southwestern Bell Tel., L.P.*, 544 F.3d 1101 (10th Cir. 2008) (plaintiff's testimony that supervisor said she was discharged because of her age was direct evidence barring summary judgment for employer since reasonable jury that credited it could conclude that age caused her discharge). But a more refined analysis is sometimes necessary.

Page 46. Add before *But see Putman* **after extract:**

See also Bailey v. USF Holland, Inc., 526 F.3d 880 (6th Cir. 2008) (continued use of the word "boy" after plaintiffs had objected and after the racial implications had been explained at sensitivity training sessions was part of a pattern of racial harassment).

Page 47. Add in Note 9, *Expert Testimony on Stereotyping*
** after** *see generally*:

Susan T. Fiske, Eugene Borgida, *Providing Expert Knowledge in an Adversarial Context: Social Cognitive Science in Employment Discrimination Cases*, 4 ANN. REV. LAW SOC. SCI. 123 (2008).

Page 49.   Delete all material until *McDonnell Douglas* on p. 50; replace with:

As for the hierarchical model, it is now clear that, if the decisionmaker is the one acting with discriminatory intent, the employer is liable. But what if the decision-maker is innocent of such intent but is influenced with someone who does have intent to discriminate? This is the "cats-paw" problem that the Supreme Court recently addressed.

Staub v. Proctor Hosptial
131 S. Ct. 1186 (2011)

Justice SCALIA delivered the opinion of the Court.

We consider the circumstances under which an employer may be held liable for employment discrimination based on the discriminatory animus of an employee who influenced, but did not make, the ultimate employment decision.

I

Petitioner Vincent Staub worked as an angiography technician for respondent Proctor Hospital until 2004, when he was fired. Staub and Proctor hotly dispute the facts surrounding the firing, but because a jury found for Staub in his claim of employment discrimination against Proctor, we describe the facts viewed in the light most favorable to him.

While employed by Proctor, Staub was a member of the United States Army Reserve, which required him to attend drill one weekend per month and to train full time for two to three weeks a year. Both Janice Mulally, Staub's immediate supervisor, and Michael Korenchuk, Mulally's supervisor, were hostile to Staub's military obligations. Mulally scheduled Staub for additional shifts without notice so that he would "'pa[y] back the department for everyone else having to bend over backwards to cover [his] schedule for the Reserves.'" She also informed Staub's co-worker, Leslie Sweborg, that Staub's "'military duty had been a strain on th[e] department,'" and asked Sweborg to help her "'get rid of him.'" Korenchuk referred to Staub's military obligations as "'a b[u]nch of smoking and joking and [a] waste of taxpayers['] money.'" He was also aware that Mulally was "'out to get'" Staub.

In January 2004, Mulally issued Staub a "Corrective Action" disciplinary warning for purportedly violating a company rule requiring him to stay in his work area whenever he was not working with a patient. The Corrective Action included a directive requiring Staub to report to Mulally or Korenchuk "'when [he] ha[d] no patients and [the angio] cases [we]re complete[d].'" According to Staub, Mulally's justification for the Corrective Action was false for two reasons: First, the company rule invoked by Mulally did not exist; and second, even if it did, Staub did not violate it.

On April 2, 2004, Angie Day, Staub's co-worker, complained to Linda Buck, Proctor's vice president of human resources, and Garrett McGowan, Proctor's chief operating officer, about Staub's frequent unavailability and abruptness. McGowan directed Korenchuk and Buck to create a plan that would solve Staub's "'availability' problems." But three weeks later, before they had time to do so, Korenchuk informed Buck that Staub had left his desk without informing a supervisor, in violation of the January Corrective Action. Staub now contends this accusation was false: he had left Korenchuk a voice-mail notification that he was leaving his desk. Buck relied on Korenchuk's accusation, however, and after reviewing Staub's personnel file, she decided to fire him. The termination notice stated that Staub had ignored the directive issued in the January 2004 Corrective Action.

Staub challenged his firing through Proctor's grievance process, claiming that Mulally had fabricated the allegation underlying the Corrective Action out of hostility toward his military obligations. Buck did not follow up with Mulally about this claim. After discussing the matter with another personnel officer, Buck adhered to her decision.

Staub sued Proctor under the Uniformed Services Employment and Reemployment Rights Act of 1994, 38 U.S.C. §4301 *et seq.*, claiming that his discharge was motivated by hostility to his obligations as a military reservist. His contention was not that Buck had any such hostility but that Mulally and Korenchuk did, and that their actions influenced Buck's ultimate employment decision. A jury found that Staub's "military status was a motivating factor in [Proctor's] decision to discharge him" and awarded $ 57,640 in damages.

The Seventh Circuit reversed, holding that Proctor was entitled to judgment as a matter of law. The court observed that Staub had brought a "'cat's paw' case," meaning that he sought to hold his employer liable for the animus of a supervisor who was not charged with making the ultimate employment decision.[1] It explained that under Seventh Circuit precedent, a "cat's paw" case could not succeed unless the nondecisionmaker exercised such "'singular influence'" over the decisionmaker that the decision to terminate was the product of "blind reliance." [Buck had looked beyond Mulally and Korenchuk's statements so their statements were not a "singular influence." even though her "investigation could have been more robust"].

II

[USERRA bars discrimination in employment on the basis of membership or an obligation to perform service in a uniformed service. §4311(a). It has a

---

1. The term "cat's paw" derives from a fable conceived by Aesop, put into verse by La Fontaine in 1679, and injected into United States employment discrimination law by [Judge] Posner in 1990. In the fable, a monkey induces a cat by flattery to extract roasting chestnuts from the fire. After the cat has done so, burning its paws in the process, the monkey makes off with the chestnuts and leaves the cat with nothing. A coda to the fable (relevant only marginally, if at all, to employment law) observes that the cat is similar to princes who, flattered by the king, perform services on the king's behalf and receive no reward.

structure similar to Title VII's 703(m) in that an employer is considered to have violated the statute when uniformed service membership is "a motivating factor in the employer's action, unless the employer can prove that the action would have been taken in the absence of such membership." §4311(c)].

The central difficulty in this case is construing the phrase "motivating factor in the employer's action." When the company official who makes the decision to take an adverse employment action is personally acting out of hostility to the employee's membership in or obligation to a uniformed service, a motivating factor obviously exists. The problem we confront arises when that official has no discriminatory animus but is influenced by previous company action that is the product of a like animus in someone else.

In approaching this question, we start from the premise that when Congress creates a federal tort, it adopts the background of general tort law. See *Burlington Industries, Inc.* v. *Ellerth* [reproduced at p. 384]. Intentional torts such as this, "as distinguished from negligent or reckless torts, . . . generally require that the actor intend 'the *consequences*' of an act,' not simply 'the act itself.'" *Kawaauhau* v. *Geiger*, 523 U.S. 57 (1998).

Staub contends that the fact that an unfavorable entry on the plaintiff's personnel record was caused to be put there, with discriminatory animus, by Mulally and Korenchuk, suffices to establish the tort, even if Mulally and Korenchuk did not intend to cause his dismissal. But discrimination was no part of Buck's reason for the dismissal; and while Korenchuk and Mulally acted with discriminatory animus, the act they committed—the mere making of the reports—was not a denial of "initial employment, reemployment, retention in employment, promotion, or any benefit of employment," as liability under USERRA requires. If dismissal was not the object of Mulally's and Korenchuk's reports, it may have been their result, or even their foreseeable consequence, but that is not enough to render Mulally or Korenchuk responsible.

Here, however, Staub is seeking to hold liable not Mulally and Korenchuk, but their employer. Perhaps, therefore, the discriminatory motive of one of the employer's agents (Mulally or Korenchuk) can be aggregated with the act of another agent (Buck) to impose liability on Proctor. Again we consult general principles of law, agency law, which form the background against which federal tort laws are enacted. See *Burlington*. Here, however, the answer is not so clear. The Restatement of Agency suggests that the malicious mental state of one agent cannot generally be combined with the harmful action of another agent to hold the principal liable for a tort that requires both. See Restatement (Second) Agency §275, Illustration 4 (1958). Some of the cases involving federal torts apply that rule. But another case involving a federal tort, and one involving a federal crime, hold to the contrary. Ultimately, we think it unnecessary in this case to decide what the background rule of agency law may be, since the former line of authority is suggested by the governing text, which requires that discrimination be "a motivating factor" *in the adverse action*. When a decision to fire is made with no unlawful animus on the part of the firing agent, but partly on the basis of a report prompted (unbeknownst to that agent) by discrimination, discrimination might perhaps be called a "factor" or a "causal factor" in the decision; but it seems to us a considerable stretch to call it "a motivating factor."

Proctor, on the other hand, contends that the employer is not liable unless the *de facto* decisionmaker (the technical decisionmaker or the agent for whom he is the "cat's paw") is motivated by discriminatory animus. This avoids the aggregation of animus and adverse action, but it seems to us not the only application of general tort law that can do so. Animus and responsibility for the adverse action can both be attributed to the earlier agent (here, Staub's supervisors) if the adverse action is the intended consequence of that agent's discriminatory conduct. So long as the agent intends, for discriminatory reasons, that the adverse action occur, he has the scienter required to be liable under USERRA. And it is axiomatic under tort law that the exercise of judgment by the decisionmaker does not prevent the earlier agent's action (and hence the earlier agent's discriminatory animus) from being the proximate cause of the harm. Proximate cause requires only "some direct relation between the injury asserted and the injurious conduct alleged," and excludes only those "link[s] that are too remote, purely contingent, or indirect." *Hemi Group, LLC* v. *City of New York*, 559 U.S. 1, ___, (2010) (internal quotation marks omitted).[2] We do not think that the ultimate decisionmaker's exercise of judgment automatically renders the link to the supervisor's bias "remote" or "purely contingent." The decisionmaker's exercise of judgment is *also* a proximate cause of the employment decision, but it is common for injuries to have multiple proximate causes. See *Sosa* v. *Alvarez-Machain*, 542 U.S. 692, 704 (2004). Nor can the ultimate decisionmaker's judgment be deemed a superseding cause of the harm. A cause can be thought "superseding" only if it is a "cause of independent origin that was not foreseeable." *Exxon Co., U.S.A.* v. *Sofec, Inc.*, 517 U.S. 830, 837 (1996) (internal quotation marks omitted).

Moreover, the approach urged upon us by Proctor gives an unlikely meaning to a provision designed to prevent employer discrimination. An employer's authority to reward, punish, or dismiss is often allocated among multiple agents. The one who makes the ultimate decision does soon the basis of performance assessments by other supervisors. Proctor's view would have the improbable consequence that if an employer isolates a personnel official from an employee's supervisors, vests the decision to take adverse employment actions in that official, and asks that official to review the employee's personnel file before taking the adverse action, then the employer will be effectively shielded from discriminatory acts and recommendations of supervisors that were *designed and intended* to produce the adverse action. That seems to us an implausible meaning of the text, and one that is not compelled by its words.

---

2. Under the traditional doctrine of proximate cause, a tortfeasor is sometimes, but not always, liable when he intends to cause an adverse action and a different adverse action results. See Restatement (Second) Torts §§435, 435B and Comment *a* (1963 and 1964). That issue is not presented in this case since the record contains no evidence that Mulally or Korenchuk intended any particular adverse action other than Staub's termination.

1. Individual Disparate Treatment Discrimination

Proctor suggests that even if the decisionmaker's mere exercise of independent judgment does not suffice to negate the effect of the prior discrimination, at least the decisionmaker's independent investigation (and rejection) of the employee's allegations of discriminatory animus ought to do so. We decline to adopt such a hard-and-fast rule. As we have already acknowledged, the requirement that the biased supervisor's action be a causal factor of the ultimate employment action incorporates the traditional tort-law concept of proximate cause. See, *e.g.*, *Anza* v. *Ideal Steel Supply Corp.*, 547 U.S. 451, 457-458, 126 (2006); *Sosa*. Thus, if the employer's investigation results in an adverse action for reasons unrelated to the supervisor's original biased action (by the terms of USERRA it is the employer's burden to establish that), then the employer will not be liable. But the supervisor's biased report may remain a causal factor if the independent investigation takes it into account without determining that the adverse action was, apart from the supervisor's recommendation, entirely justified. We are aware of no principle in tort or agency law under which an employer's mere conduct of an independent investigation has a claim-preclusive effect. Nor do we think the independent investigation somehow relieves the employer of "fault." The employer is at fault because one of its agents committed an action based on discriminatory animus that was intended to cause, and did in fact cause, an adverse employment decision.

Justice Alito claims that our failure to adopt a rule immunizing an employer who performs an independent investigation reflects a "stray[ing] from the statutory text." We do not understand this accusation. Since a supervisor is an agent of the employer, when he causes an adverse employment action the employer causes it; and when discrimination is a motivating factor in his doing so, it is a "motivating factor in the employer's action," precisely as the text requires. Justice Alito suggests that the employer should be held liable only when it "should be regarded as having delegated part of the decisionmaking power" to the biased supervisor. But if the independent investigation relies on facts provided by the biased supervisor—as is necessary in any case of cat's-paw liability—then the employer (either directly or through the ultimate decisionmaker) will have effectively delegated the factfinding portion of the investigation to the biased supervisor. Contrary to Justice Alito's suggestion, the biased supervisor is not analogous to a witness at a bench trial. The mere witness is not an actor in the events that are the subject of the trial. The biased supervisor and the ultimate decisionmaker, however, acted as agents of the entity that the plaintiff seeks to hold liable; each of them possessed supervisory authority delegated by their employer and exercised it in the interest of their employer. In sum, we do not see how "fidelity to the statutory text," requires the adoption of an independent-investigation defense that appears nowhere in the text. And we find both speculative and implausible Justice Alito's prediction that our Nation's employers will systematically disfavor members of the armed services in their hiring decisions to avoid the possibility of cat's-paw liability, a policy that would violate USERRA in any event.

We therefore hold that if a supervisor performs an act motivated by antimilitary animus that is *intended* by the supervisor to cause an adverse employment action,[3] and if that act is a proximate cause of the ultimate employment action, then the employer is liable under USERRA.[4]

III

Applying our analysis to the facts of this case, it is clear that the Seventh Circuit's judgment must be reversed. Both Mulally and Korenchuk were acting within the scope of their employment when they took the actions that allegedly caused Buck to fire Staub. A "reprimand . . . for workplace failings" constitutes conduct within the scope of an agent's employment. *Faragher* v. *Boca Raton*. As the Seventh Circuit recognized, there was evidence that Mulally's and Korenchuk's actions were motivated by hostility toward Staub's military obligations. There was also evidence that Mulally's and Korenchuk's actions were causal factors underlying Buck's decision to fire Staub. Buck's termination notice expressly stated that Staub was terminated because he had "ignored" the directive in the Corrective Action. Finally, there was evidence that both Mulally and Korenchuk had the specific intent to cause Staub to be terminated. Mulally stated she was trying to " 'get rid of ' " Staub, and Korenchuk was aware that Mulally was " 'out to get' " Staub. Moreover, Korenchuk informed Buck, Proctor's personnel officer responsible for terminating employees, of Staub's alleged noncompliance with Mulally's Corrective Action, and Buck fired Staub immediately thereafter; a reasonable jury could infer that Korenchuk intended that Staub be fired. The Seventh Circuit therefore erred in holding that Proctor was entitled to judgment as a matter of law.

[The Court reversed and remanded for Seventh Circuit to consider whether the jury instructions, which required a finding only of motivating factor, were harmless error.]

Justice KAGAN took no part in the consideration or decision of this case.

Justice ALITO, with whom Justice THOMAS joins, concurring in the judgment.

I agree with the Court that the decision of the Court of Appeals must be reversed, but I would do so based on the statutory text, rather than principles of agency and tort law that do not speak directly to the question presented here.

---

3. Under traditional tort law, " 'intent' . . . denote[s] that the actor desires to cause consequences of his act, or that he believes that the consequences are substantially certain to result from it." *Id.*, §8A.

4. Needless to say, the employer would be liable only when the supervisor acts within the scope of his employment, or when the supervisor acts outside the scope of his employment and liability would be imputed to the employer under traditional agency principles. See *Burlington Industries, Inc.* v. *Ellerth.* We express no view as to whether the employer would be liable if a co-worker, rather than a supervisor, committed a discriminatory act that influenced the ultimate employment decision. We also observe that Staub took advantage of Proctor's grievance process, and we express no view as to whether Proctor would have an affirmative defense if he did not. Cf. *Pennsylvania State Police* v. *Suders* [reproduced at p. 384].

1. Individual Disparate Treatment Discrimination

. . . For present purposes, the key phrase [in the governing statute] is "a motivating factor in the employer's action." A "motivating factor" is a factor that "provide[s] . . . a motive." See Webster's Third New International Dictionary 1475 (1971) (defining "motivate"). A "motive," in turn, is "something within a person . . . that incites him to action." *Ibid.* Thus, in order for discrimination to be "a motivating factor in [an] employer's action," discrimination must be present "within," *i.e.*, in the mind of, the person who makes the decision to take that action. And "the employer's action" here is the decision to fire petitioner. Thus, petitioner, in order to recover, was required to show that discrimination motivated *that* action.

The Court, however, strays from the statutory text by holding that it is enough for an employee to show that discrimination motivated *some other action* and that this latter action, in turn, caused the termination decision. That is simply not what the statute says.

The Court fears this interpretation of the statute would allow an employer to escape liability by assigning formal decisionmaking authority to an officer who may merely rubberstamp the recommendation of others who are motivated by antimilitary animus. But fidelity to the statutory text does not lead to this result. Where the officer with formal decisionmaking authority merely rubberstamps the recommendation of others, the employer, I would hold, has actually delegated the decisionmaking responsibility to those whose recommendation is rubberstamped. I would reach a similar conclusion where the officer with the formal decisionmaking authority is put on notice that adverse information about an employee may be based on antimilitary animus but does not undertake an independent investigation of the matter. In that situation, too, the employer should be regarded as having delegated part of the decisionmaking power to those who are responsible for memorializing and transmitting the adverse information that is accepted without examination. The same cannot be said, however, where the officer with formal decisionmaking responsibility, having been alerted to the possibility that adverse information may be tainted, undertakes a reasonable investigation and finds insufficient evidence to dispute the accuracy of that information.

Nor can the employer be said to have "effectively delegated" decisionmaking authority any time a decisionmaker "relies on facts provided by [a] biased supervisor." A decisionmaker who credits information provided by another person—for example, a judge who credits the testimony of a witness in a bench trial—does not thereby delegate a portion of the decisionmaking authority to the person who provides the information.

This interpretation of §4311(c)(1) heeds the statutory text and would provide fair treatment for both employers and employees who are members of the uniformed services. It would also encourage employers to establish internal grievance procedures similar to those that have been adopted following our decisions in [*Ellerth* and *Faragher*]. Such procedures would often provide relief for employees without the need for litigation, and they would provide protection for employers who proceed in good faith.

The Court's contrary approach, by contrast, is almost certain to lead to confusion and is likely to produce results that will not serve the interests of either employers or employees who are members of the uniformed services. The Court's holding will impose liability unfairly on employers who make every effort to comply with the law, and it may have the perverse effect of discouraging employers from hiring applicants who are members of the Reserves or the National Guard. In addition, by leaving open the possibility that an employer may be held liable if it innocently takes into account adverse information provided, not by a supervisor, but by a low-level employee, see n. 4, the Court increases the confusion that its decision is likely to produce.

[While disagreeing with the majority's interpretation, the concurrence agreed that the Seventh Circuit must be reversed in light of "sufficient evidence to support a finding that at least Korenchuk was actually delegated part of the decisionmaking authority in this case."].

NOTES

1. *The Holding vs. the Opinion.* The Court summarizes its analysis in a handy sentence: "We therefore hold that if a supervisor performs an act motivated by antimilitary animus that is *intended* by the supervisor to cause an adverse employment action, and if that act is a proximate cause of the ultimate employment action, then the employer is liable. . . ." (emphasis in original). But does the Court's analysis support this statement? How do you reconcile the earlier paragraph: "When a decision to fire is made with no unlawful animus on the part of the firing agent, but partly on the basis of a report prompted (unbeknownst to that agent) by discrimination, discrimination might perhaps be called a 'factor' or a 'causal factor' in the decision; but it seems to us a considerable stretch to call it 'a motivating factor.'"

2. *Back to the Meaning of Intent.* In footnote 3, Scalia writes: Under traditional tort law, "'intent' . . . denote[s] that the actor desires to cause consequences of his act, or that he believes that the consequences are substantially certain to result from it." Maybe that's true of "traditional tort law," but haven't we learned that intent requires something more in the discrimination context—a result sought *because* not merely in spite of the prohibited characteristic? *See* Personnel Administrator v. Feeney, p. 155. If Buck assigned Staub to report to Mulally and Korenchuk, being "substantially certain" that they would find a way to recommend his discharge, would the employer be liable when that happened? Surely, Justice Scalia is not using a footnote in *Staub* to redefine a core concept of antidiscrimination law? On the other hand, Professor Zimmer believes the Court did just that in *Ricci. See* p. 101 of this Supplement.

3. *Whose Intent?* Given the Court's continued focus on intent for individual disparate treatment cases, it is not surprising for the majority to hold that, "to find an entity has discriminated," we must "look[ ] to the intent of particular individuals within that entity." Whether such a requirement is inevitable is another question—since the "intent" of a collective body is sometimes used without any connection to any particular human actor, as in "legislative intent." *See* Richard W. Murphy, *NeuroCongress*, 37 SETON HALL L. REV. 221 (2006). But, of course, individual human beings did have such an intent in *Straub* and, according to the Court

they not only intended to discriminate but they intended to have such discrimination result in an adverse employment action.

4. *Intent Plus.* For the majority, actions with intent to cause an adverse employment action are necessary for liability but not sufficient, and that's true even if the discriminatory act does result in an adverse employment action. That's because, regardless of ordinary principles of tort law, the motivating factor language of Title VII commands otherwise. See Note 1.

Are you clear why, to quote the Court, this is "a considerable stretch"? Title VII bars discrimination by "employers" and does not impose individual liability. If intentionally discriminatory actions within a corporate employer result in an adverse action, wouldn't "motivating factor" describe them?

5. *Why Concur?* Looking to dictionary definitions, Justice Alito writes "in order for discrimination to be "a motivating factor in [an] employer's action," discrimination must be present "within," *i.e.*, in the mind of, the person who makes the decision to take that action. And "the employer's action" here is the decision to fire petitioner. Thus, petitioner, in order to recover, was required to show that discrimination motivated *that* action." However, Title VII does not textually make it illegal for a supervisor to do anything. What has to be wrongly motivated is the adverse action taken by the "employer," and Title VII offers no direct guidance on when discriminatorily motivated decisions by someone in the company can be attributed to the employer. That's an agency question, and one not answered by the text of the statute.

But if both opinions find "motivating factor" to require something beyond discrimination causing an adverse action, why is there a need for two opinions? Justice Alito seems to be arguing that an employer may avoid liability by what some lower courts have labeled an "independent investigation," but his approach would require the court to decide when a lower-level supervisor is being "delegated" decision-making power as opposed to being credited merely as a witness. Is the concurrence really drawing a bright line easily administrable by the lower courts?

6. *Co-workers and Cats-paws.* In footnote 4, the Court confines its opinion to situations where a supervisor's actions would be imputed to the employer under traditional agency principles. Further, it did not pass on "whether the employer would be liable if a co-worker, rather than a supervisor, committed a discriminatory act that influenced the ultimate employment decision." In this context, "co-worker" probably includes someone higher in the corporate hierarchy but not above the plaintiff in her chain of command. That's because anyone outside that chain would not normally trigger imputed liability under agency law. Suppose another worker, maybe even a higher level employee but not a supervisor, reported that Staub had left his station and made the report for discriminatory reasons in order to have Staub fired. Actionable if all other facts are the same?

7. *Causation.* Justice Scalia's approach in *Staub* adds a "proximate cause" dimension to causation in antidiscrimination law. What, other than confusion, does "proximate cause" add to the law? In tort law, proximate cause sets a limit on the extent of liability even though cause in fact can be established. How would that work in limiting an employer's liability for discrimination?

8. *Is an Internal Grievance Necessary?* We will see that, in the harassment area, an employer may sometimes avoid imputed liability if the victim failed to resort to

internal remedies. Footnote 4 also noted "Staub took advantage of Proctor's grievance process, and we express no view as to whether Proctor would have an affirmative defense if he did not." If he had not, what result?

Page 56. Add in second line from top of carryover of Note 3(a),
**   *Not by the Numbers*, before *See generally*:**

E.g., Ward v. Int'l Paper Co., 509 F.3d 457, 460 (8th Cir. 2007) ("In cases involving a reduction-in-force (RIF), a plaintiff makes a prima facie case by establishing: (1) he is over 40 years old; (2) he met the applicable job qualifications; (3) he suffered an adverse employment action; and (4) there is some additional evidence that age was a factor in the employer's action.").

Page 57. Add at end of carryover Note 1(a), *Not by the Numbers*:

See Ruiz v. County of Rockland, 609 F.3d 486 (2d Cir. 2010) (a defendant claim of serious misconduct by plaintiff does not bar his making out a prima facie case when his performance evaluations showed satisfactory work: "the step at which the court considers such evidence is important" because "no amount of evidence permits a plaintiff to overcome a failure to make out a prima facie case"); *Lake v. Yellow Transp., Inc.*, 596 F.3d 871, 874 (8th Cir. 2010) (a plaintiff is not required to disprove the asserted reason for firing him at the prima facie stage of the analysis since to do so would collapse the defendant's burden of production into the prima facie case; thus, plaintiff carried its burden by showing that he met the employer's expectations "other than the tardiness and unavailability Yellow offers as its reasons for firing him.").

Page 58. Add at end of first paragraph in Note 6, *The Third Step:*
**   *Proving Pretext*:**

Upshaw v. Ford Motor Co., 576 F.3d 576, 586 (6th Cir. 2009) (promotion of white candidates based on faulty performance ratings was nevertheless a legitimate, nondiscriminatory reason for failing to promote an African-American). *See generally* Ernest F. Lidge, III, *Disparate Treatment Employment Discrimination and an Employer's Good Faith: Honest Mistakes, Benign Motives, and Other Sincerely Held Beliefs*, 36 Okla. City U.L. Rev. 45 (2011) (exploring the honest belief rule and other situations where the employer's good faith is at issue).

Page 59. Add at end of carryover Note 6, *The Third Step: Proving Pretext*:

See also Natasha T. Martin, *Pretext in Peril*, 75 Mo. L. Rev. 313, 401 (2010).

1. Individual Disparate Treatment Discrimination

Page 59.   Add at end of Note 7, *Pretext for Discrimination*:

Perhaps because the jury is to focus on the ultimate issue of discrimination vel non, the trial court did not abuse its discretion by choosing not to explicitly instruct the jury in pretext terms. *See Browning v. United States*, 567 F.3d 1038 (9th Cir. 2009). *Contra Townsend v. Lumbermens Mut. Cas. Co.*, 294 F.3d 1232 (10th Cir. 2002).

Page 61.   Add at end of Note 10, *A Mixed Motive Case?*:

Michael J. Zimmer, *A Chain of Inferences Proving Discrimination*, 79 U. COLO. L. REV. 1243, 1257 (2008), argues against characterizing *McDonnell Douglas* cases as "single-motive" cases:

> The problem with calling *McDonnell Douglas* a "single-motive" approach is that demonstrating "but-for" linkage always involves mixed-motives until the fact finder accepts the employer's explanation or finds discrimination. It may continue to involve mixed-motives even if the plaintiff carries her burden of proving but-for linkage [since a] showing of "but-for" linkage can result in liability without proof that *only* the employer's discrimination motivated the employer's action. In other words, liability can be made out using the "but-for" test even if some additional reason, such as the employer's explanation, played a role in its decision.

Page 64.   Add at end of Note 1, *Comparators as Proof of Pretext*:

Madden v. Chattanooga City Wide Serv. Dep't, 549 F.3d 666 (6th Cir. 2008) (discharge for setting off firecrackers could be found a pretext for discrimination when white workers had engaged in the same conduct without being fired or even disciplined).

Page 65.   Add to end of carryover Note 2, Ash *as an Equal Treatment Case*:

See Michael J. Zimmer, *A Chain of Inferences Proving Discrimination*, 79 U. COLO. L. REV. 1243, 1274 (2008) ("[I]n an important and deep sense, all discrimination cases involve a violation of equal treatment. At the broadest, the question is whether the employer treated the plaintiff unfavorably because of race, creed, sex, religion, national origin, age, disability, or other characteristic protected against discrimination. Thus, the true issue is whether the employer would have treated the plaintiff more favorably if she was not within one of those protected classifications." ').

Page 66.   Add at end of Note 4(b), *Defendant's Stats*:

Risch v. Royal Oak Police Dep't, 581 F.3d 383 (6th Cir. 2009) (triable pretext issue existed when plaintiff's composite score on a test was higher than two male counterparts selected for promotion; the department claimed the promoted males had better scores in certain respects, but adverse comments about the capabilities of female officers, degrading remarks about women, and expressions of opinion that females would never be promoted to command positions provided additional evidence of pretext);

Page 67.   Add at end of carryover Note 4, *Failure to Follow Procedures*:

See also Medlock v. UPS, Inc., 608 F.3d 1185 (10th Cir. 2010) (no pretext shown for employer's refusal to reinstate plaintiff for not taking responsibility for his prior infraction even though its practice of rehiring drivers who admitted misconduct was not formal policy)

4(d). *"Unreasonable" Decision vs. Business Judgment.* Courts have often recognized that the more unusual and idiosyncratic a decision is — in terms of the way business is normally conducted — the more appropriate it is to infer discrimination. This principle is in obvious tension with what has sometimes been called the "business judgment" rule, which is that courts should not second-guess business decisions. One illustration of the conflict is *White v. Baxter Healthcare Corp.*, 533 F.3d 381, 394 (6th Cir. 2008) (2-1), where the majority reaffirmed that "the plaintiff may also demonstrate pretext by offering evidence which challenges the reasonableness of the employer's decision 'to the extent that such an inquiry sheds light on whether the employer's proffered reason for the employment action was its actual motivation'" (citation omitted). It went on:

> [O]ur Circuit has never adopted a "business-judgment rule" which requires us to defer to the employer's "reasonable business judgment" in Title VII cases. Indeed, in most Title VII cases the very issue in dispute is whether the employer's adverse employment decision resulted from an objectively unreasonable business judgment, i.e., a judgment that was based upon an impermissible consideration such as the adversely-affected employee's race, gender, religion, or national origin. In determining whether the plaintiff has produced enough evidence to cast doubt upon the employer's explanation for its decision, we cannot, as Judge Gilman [in dissent] does, unquestionably accept the employer's own self-serving claim that the decision resulted from an exercise of "reasonable business judgment." Nor can we decide "as a matter of law" that "an employer's proffered justification is reasonable." The question of whether the employer's judgment was reasonable or was instead motivated by improper considerations is for the jury to consider. . . .

Page 67.   Delete Note 5; replace with the following:

5. *Several Nondiscriminatory Reasons.* When defendant has more than one supposed legitimate nondiscriminatory reason, some courts have required the plaintiff to put in evidence of the pretextual nature of all the reasons. *See Crawford v. City of Fairburn*, 482 F.3d 1305, 1308 (11th Cir. 2007); (plaintiff must rebut each reason proffered by defendant); *Kautz v. Met-Pro Corp.*, 412 F.3d 463 (3d Cir. 2005) (summary judgment against employee who could not show that all of employer's

non-discriminatory reasons were pretextual). Other courts believe that proof that any reason is pretextual will usually permit the jury to infer that the pretext conceals a discriminatory motive. *E.g.*, *Tomasso v. Boeing Co.*, 445 F.3d 702, 704 (3d Cir. 2006) (plaintiff sufficiently challenged the defendant's "primary rationales" for the layoff and "a rational factfinder could dismiss the secondary reasons as pretextual, not because they played no role in Tomasso's layoff but because they cannot explain the layoff sufficiently."); *Jaramillo v. Colo. Judicial Dep't.*, 427 F.3d 1303, 1310 (10th Cir. 2005) ("Something less than total failure of the employer's defense is sufficient to create a genuine issue of fact in a number of situations). *See generally* Lawrence D. Rosenthal, *Motions for Summary Judgment When Employers Offer Multiple Justifications for Adverse Employment Actions: Why the Exceptions Should Swallow the Rule*, 2002 UTAH L. REV. 335.

Of course, sometimes an employer's multiple reasons will conflict, thus providing another basis to infer pretext. *Juarez v. AGS Gov't Solution Group*, 314 F.3d 1243 (10th Cir. 2003) (proof that manager's evaluation contained fraudulent data and the employer's conflicting reasons for discharge is sufficient to establish pretext in a race discrimination case). Along these lines, a change in defendant's rebuttal over time can be fatal to it. *See Jones v. Nat'l Am. Univ.*, 608 F.3d 1039 (8th Cir. 2010) (a change in the employer's reasons for its action between those offered the EEOC and those adduced at trial can be evidence of pretext sufficient to uphold a jury verdict, at least in the context of other evidence of age bias); *Zaccagnini v. Chas. Levy Circulating Co.*, 338 F.3d 672 (7th Cir. 2003) (jury could reasonably refuse to credit employer's explanation for not rehiring employee due to lack of reference by union since that explanation differed from its original stated reason that he was not rehired because of company policy of not rehiring laid off employees).

Page 71.   Delete Note 3; replace with:

3. *Comparator Cases.* It's possible to cast *Santa Fe* in the *McDonnell Douglas* mold, but to do so one has to say that the prima facie case is established not by any of the usual multi-element steps but rather by unequal treatment of people who are alike but for their race (or other prohibited classification). Another way to view cases like *Santa Fe* is as literal "disparate treatment" cases: plaintiff prevails by proving that she was treated differently than a "comparator" (a similarly situated person of the other sex or a different race). And that difference in treatment supports the inference that the different treatment was because of race. Most lower courts try to frame the analysis in *McDonnell Douglas* terms rather than as only literal disparate treatment. *Fields v. Shelter Mut. Ins. Co.*, 520 F.3d 859 (8th Cir. 2008) (comparators analyzed under a version of the *McDonnell Douglas* prima facie case); *Gates v. Caterpillar, Inc.*, 513 F.3d 680 (7th Cir. 2008) (same).

In any event, the problem is less the label than how close a comparator must be in order to count. Some lower courts seem to require the comparator to be "nearly identical" to the plaintiff, which is strange if the point of the inquiry is to infer a racial motivation from a difference in treatment. For example, in *Roland v. United States Postal Serv.*, 2006 U.S. App. LEXIS 25415, 12-14 (11th Cir. 2006), plaintiff, claiming that whites engaged in similar conduct to hers were not discharged, was found not "nearly identical" to a comparator. The differences included that the whites "worked in a different facility [and] reported to a different supervisor." Nor is *Roland* a mere outlier, as other circuits have imposed a "nearly identical" standard. *E.g., Johnson v. Ready Mixed Concrete Co.*, 424 F.3d 806 (8th Cir. 2005) (black truck driver who was discharged for lying in report about damage to his truck was not similarly situated to undisciplined white truck drivers who had not voluntarily reported similar damage to their trucks but did not make misrepresentations in a report).

However, *Crawford v. Ind. Harbor Belt R.R. Co.*, 461 F.3d 844, 846 (7th Cir. 2006), disapproved of a trend "to require closer and closer comparability between the plaintiff and the members of the comparison group." It explained:

> The requirement is a natural response to cherry-picking by plaintiffs. . . . If a plaintiff can make a prima facie case by finding just one or two male or nonminority workers who were treated worse than she, she should have to show that they really are comparable to her in every respect.
>
> But if as we believe cherry-picking is improper, the plaintiff should have to show only that the members of the comparison group are sufficiently comparable to her to suggest that she was singled out for worse treatment. Otherwise plaintiffs will be in a box: if they pick just members of the comparison group who are comparable in every respect, they will be accused of cherry-picking; but if they look for a representative sample, they will unavoidably include some who were not comparable in every respect, but merely broadly comparable. The cases that say that the members of the comparison group must be comparable to the plaintiff in all material respects get this right.

See also White v. Baxter Healthcare Corp., 533 F.3d 381, 395 (6th Cir. 2008) (While the employer's explanation was adequate to carry its burden of production, it was "self-serving and conclusory," and had to be viewed in the context of proof that plaintiff was more qualified than his successful competitor).

The cases that require the same supervisor may make more sense than others requiring near identity precisely because they focus is on the intent of the individual decisionmaker. The argument is that supervisor A's intent can't be inferred from what Supervisor B did. So if A thinks tardiness is a firing offense for an African American, the fact that B allows her white workers to be tardy does not prove that A had any discriminatory intent. This issue is treated in more detail in Note on Special Issues of Proof at p. 107.

Putting that aside, however, the better view of the comparator question is that the case should go to the jury unless no reasonable factfinder could find unequal

1. Individual Disparate Treatment Discrimination

treatment. That a jury might find in *Roland* that the differential treatment was explained by reasons other than race does not mean that the situations of the two workers were not alike enough to find a violation from the inequality of treatment. *See* Charles A. Sullivan, *The Phoenix from the Ash: Proving Discrimination by Comparators*, 60 ALA. L. REV. 191 (2009). *See also* Ernest F. Lidge III, *The Courts' Misuse of the Similarly Situated Concept in Employment Discrimination Law*, 67 MO. L. REV. 831 (2002). *But see* Suzanne Goldberg, *Discrimination by Comparison*, 120 YALE L.J. 728, 742 (2011) ("for all of the judgment avoidance and other instrumental values that comparators may bring to discrimination analysis, courts put too much faith in them. The judicial default to comparators crowds out not only other heuristics, but also other more textured conceptions of discrimination, all of which is to the detriment of discrimination jurisprudence and theory.").

Page 74. Add at end of page:

Abdullahi v. Prada USA Corp., 520 F.3d 710, 712 (7th Cir. 2008) (favoring the "loose" meaning of race for §1981 cases for Iranians "especially if they speak English with an Iranian accent," because, "though not dark-skinned" they may be "sufficiently different looking and sounding from the average American of European ancestry to provoke the kind of hostility associated with racism.").

Page 75. Add at end of Note 6, *Colorism*:

Joni Hersch, *Profiling the New Immigrant Worker: The Effects of Skin Color and Height*, 26 J. LAB. ECON. 345 (2008) (immigrants with the lightest skin color earn on average 17 percent higher wages than comparable immigrants with the darkest skin color, taking into account Hispanic ethnicity, race, country of birth, education, English language proficiency, family background, and occupation in the source country); Joni Hersch, *Skin Color, Discrimination, and Immigrant Pay*, 58 EMORY L.J. 357 (2008) (the penalty to darker skin color is not a spurious consequence of omitted variables bias. Instead, discrimination on the basis of skin color is the most likely explanation of the findings.).

Page 75. Add at end of Note 7, *Discrimination by Mistake*:

Craig Robert Senn, *Perception Over Reality: Extending the ADA's Concept of "Regarded as" Protection Under Federal Employment Discrimination Law*, 36 FLA. ST. U.L. REV. 827 (2009).

Page 76. Add at end of carryover of Note 8, *Relationship-Based Discrimination*:

See also Holcomb v. Iona College, 521 F.3d 130 (2d Cir. 2008) (discrimination because a white man was married to an African-American woman was actionable under Title VII); *Ellis v. UPS, Inc.*, 523 F.3d 823, 828 (7th Cir. 2008) (recognizing that application of an anti-fraternization policy more harshly to interracial associations than to intraracial ones would be actionable).

Page 77. Add before *Mlynczak* cite in top line:

Coulton v. Univ. of Pa., 237 F. App'x 741 (3d Cir. 2007) (African-American decision makers and predictions by a manager that a white would have problems working in a department where the overwhelming majority of his co-workers were African-American did not suffice to prove discrimination against white plaintiff where he could not show that similarly situated African-American employees were treated more favorably);

Page 77. Add before "see generally" towards end of last full paragraph:

See also Humphries v. Pulaski County Special Sch. Dist., 580 F.3d 688, 694 (8th Cir. 2009) (evidence that an employer followed an affirmative action plan in a consent decree in taking a challenged adverse employment action "may constitute direct evidence of unlawful discrimination").

Page 87. Add at end of carryover Note 2, *Rejecting the "Pretext-Plus Rule:*

See also Torgerson v. City of Rochester, 605 F.3d 584 (8th Cir. 2010) (where rankings were significantly impacted by the subjective interview process, which accounted for 40 percent of the final score, the fact that the plaintiffs were ranked lower than the successful candidates did not bar the establishment of a prima facie case); *Merritt v. Old Dominion Freight Line, Inc.*, 601 F.3d 289 (4th Cir. 2010) (a plaintiff raised factual question of pretext regarding her failing of a physical fitness test by a combination of factors, including prior biased comments in other positions, the fact that the employer ordered the test to assess a minor, temporary injury, the test did not directly evaluate her injury, its use was atypical in the industry, and the reasons she failed were not related to the injury that triggered the test).

Page 92. Add at end of Note 8(a), *Motions to Dismiss*:

In *Ashcroft v. Iqbal*, 129 S. Ct. 1937 (2009), the Supreme Court confirmed that *Twombly* applied to all complaints in federal court, not merely antitrust complaints, thus suggesting a more demanding standard for discrimination cases. However, *Iqbal* did not cite *Swierkiewicz*, and *Twombly* itself apparently saw no inconsistency with that opinion's rejection of any requirement that the plaintiff allege at least a *McDonnell Douglas* prima facie case. It remains unclear, therefore, what the effect of *Twombly/Iqbal* will be on pleading under the antidiscrimination laws. Some commentators see evidence of a greater rate of dismissals since *Twombly/Iqbal*, Joseph A. Seiner, *After* Iqbal, 45 WAKE FOREST L. REV. 179, 194 (2010); Joseph A. Seiner, *Pleading Disability*, 51 B.C. L. REV. 95 (2010); Suzette M. Malveaux, *Front Loading and Heavy Lifting: How Pre-Dismissal Discovery Can Address the Detrimental Effect of* Iqbal *on Civil Rights Cases*, 14 LEWIS & CLARK L. REV. 65, 82 (2010); Suja A. Thomas, *The New Summary Judgment Motion: The Motion to Dismiss Under* Iqbal *and* Twombly, 14 LEWIS & CLARK L. REV. 15 (2010); Joseph A. Seiner, *The Trouble with* Twombly: *A Proposed Pleading Standard for Employment Discrimination Cases*, 2009 U. ILL. L. REV. 101. But others see no such phenomenon. Joe S. Cecil, George W. Cort, Margaret S. Williams & Jared J. Bataillon, *Motions to Dismiss for Failure to State a Claim After* Iqbal, http://www.fjc.gov/public/pdf.nsf/lookup/motioniqbal.pdf/$file/motioniqbal.pdf.

A number of circuit courts have rejected Rule 12(b)(6) challenges under the new standard. For example, the Third Circuit seemed to believe that *Swierkiewicz* was overruled sub silentio although it nevertheless upheld the plaintiff's pleading. *Fowler v. UPMC Shadyside*, 578 F.3d 203, 212 (3d Cir. 2009) (ADA disability claim stated). *See also Sepúlveda-Villarini v. Dep't of Educ. of P.R.*, 628 F.3d 25, 30 (1st Cir. 2010) (Justice Souter) (finding a claim stated for violation of the ADA's duty of reasonable accommodation); *Tamayo v. Blagojevich*, 526 F.3d 1074 (7th Cir. 2008) (plaintiff had sufficiently alleged sex discrimination and her allegations of political motivation for the actions taken against her were not sufficient to plead her out of court). *But see Williams v. Temple Univ. Hosp.*, 400 F. App'x 650, 653 (3d Cir. 2010) ("Williams's complaint did not plausibly identify an impairment, allege a limitation, or otherwise indicate how she might be substantially limited in a major life activity. It merely states that she was injured at work but was later 'sent back to work' on 'full duty status.' Her complaint therefore does not allege facts sufficient to give rise to a plausible claim for relief.").

Even assuming *Twombly/Iqbal* do reject at least the broader readings of *Swierkiewicz* and that the more extreme possible meanings of "plausible pleading" are the governing standard for such cases, plaintiffs could still survive a motion to dismiss in several ways: first, by alleging facts that would, if proven, constitute a prima facie case under the *McDonnell Douglas* standard, *Swierkiewicz's* rejection of any such requirement notwithstanding; second, by pleading "direct evidence" of discrimination; third, by pleading the existence of an appropriate "comparator"; and, fourth, and most radically, pleading not merely "adjudicative facts," those facts unique to the particular dispute that triggered the lawsuit, but also "legislative facts," the kind of more generalized factual predicates that will "nudge[] . . . claims across the line from conceivable to plausible" as *Twombly/Iqbal* require. Charles A. Sullivan, *Plausibly Pleading Employment Discrimination*, 52 WM. & MARY L. REV. 1613, 1622 (2011).

Page 92. Add at end of Note 8(b), *Summary Judgment Motions*:

See also Eisenberg, Theodore and Lanvers, Charlotte, *Summary Judgment Rates Over Time, Across Case Categories, and Across Districts: An Empirical Study of Three Large Federal Districts*(2008). Cornell Law Faculty Publication, Paper 108, http://scholar-ship.law.cornell.edu/lsrp_papers/108 (civil rights cases had consistently higher summary judgment rates than other cases, and summary judgment rates were modest in non- civil rights cases).

Page 94. Add a new Note 9:

9. *Intersectionalism.* Some cases have explored the phenomenon of "intersec-tionality," when discrimination occurs not because of one protected trait (such as race) but rather because of two (such as race and sex). In *Lam v. University of Hawaii*, 40 F.3d 1551, 1562 (9th Cir. 1994), the court acknowledged that a claim brought by an Asian woman might be based upon multiple factors: "rather than aiding the decisional process, the attempt to bisect a person's identity at the intersection of race and gender will often distort or ignore the particular nature of the plaintiff's experiences." *See also Hafford v. Seidner*, 183 F.3d 506 (6th Cir. 1999) (district court should consider at trial whether harassment was based on race and religion, because plaintiff was a black Muslim). *See generally* Minna J. Kotkin, *Diversity and Discrimination: A Look at Complex Bias*, 50 Wm. & Mary L. R. 1439, 1440 (2009) ("Despite the common sense notion that the more different a worker is, the most likely she will encounter bias, empirical evidence shows that multiple claims — which may account for more than 50% of federal court discrimination actions — have even less chance of success than single claims. [This is in part because] the more complex the claimant's identity, the wider the evidentiary net must be cast to find relevant comparative, statistical and anecdotal evidence"); D. Aaron Lacy, *The Most Endangered Title VII Plaintiff?: Exponential Discrimination Against Black Males*, 86 Neb. L. R. 552 (2008); Nicole Buonocore Porter, *Sex Plus Age Discrimination: Protecting Older Women Workers*, 81 Denv. U. L. Rev. 79 (2003).

D. *Implementing* Desert Palace *and* Reeves

Page 95. Add before *Rachid*:

Gross v. FBL Financial Services, Inc.
129 S. Ct. 2343 (2009)

Justice Thomas delivered the opinion of the Court.

The question presented by the petitioner in this case is whether a plaintiff must present direct evidence of age discrimination in order to obtain a mixed-motives jury instruction in a suit brought under the Age Discrimination in

1. Individual Disparate Treatment Discrimination

Employment Act of 1967 (ADEA). Because we hold that such a jury instruction is never proper in an ADEA case, we vacate the decision below.

I

[At trial, plaintiff Jack Gross "introduced evidence suggesting that his reassignment was based at least in part on his age. FBL defended its decision on the grounds that Gross' reassignment was part of a corporate restructuring and that Gross' new position was better suited to his skills." The district court instructed the jury to deliver a verdict for Gross if he proved, by a preponderance of the evidence, that his "age was a motivating factor" in FBL's decision to demote him. The jury was, however, also instructed to find for FBL if it proved by the preponderance of the evidence that it would have demoted Gross regardless of his age. The jury decided in favor of Gross, awarding him $46,945.

FBL challenged the jury instructions, and the court of appeals ordered a new trial. Viewing Justice O'Connor's opinion in *Price Waterhouse v. Hopkins* as controlling, it found that Gross needed to present "[d]irect evidence . . . sufficient to support a finding by a reasonable fact finder that an illegitimate criterion actually motivated the adverse employment action." For the circuit court, the "jury instructions were flawed because they allowed the burden to shift to FBL upon a presentation of a preponderance of *any* category of evidence showing that age was a motivating factor — not just 'direct evidence' related to FBL's alleged consideration of age. Because Gross conceded that he had not presented direct evidence of discrimination, the Court of Appeals held that the District Court should not have given the mixed-motives instruction."]

II

The parties have asked us to decide whether a plaintiff must "present direct evidence of discrimination in order to obtain a mixed-motive instruction in a non-Title VII discrimination case." Before reaching this question, however, we must first determine whether the burden of persuasion ever shifts to the party defending an alleged mixed-motives discrimination claim brought under the ADEA.[1] We hold that it does not.

A

Petitioner relies on this Court's decisions construing Title VII for his interpretation of the ADEA. Because Title VII is materially different with respect to the

---

1. Although the parties did not specifically frame the question to include this threshold inquiry, "[t]he statement of any question presented is deemed to comprise every subsidiary question fairly included therein."

relevant burden of persuasion, however, these decisions do not control our construction of the ADEA.

In *Price Waterhouse,* a plurality of the Court and two Justices concurring in the judgment determined that once a "plaintiff in a Title VII case proves that [the plaintiff's membership in a protected class] played a motivating part in an employment decision, the defendant may avoid a finding of liability only by proving by a preponderance of the evidence that it would have made the same decision even if it had not taken [that factor] into account." But as we explained in *Desert Palace,* Congress has since amended Title VII by explicitly authorizing discrimination claims in which an improper consideration was "a motivating factor" for an adverse employment decision.

This Court has never held that this burden-shifting framework applies to ADEA claims. And, we decline to do so now. When conducting statutory interpretation, we "must be careful not to apply rules applicable under one statute to a different statute without careful and critical examination." *Federal Express Corp. v. Holowecki,* 552 U.S. 389, 393 (2008). Unlike Title VII, the ADEA's text does not provide that a plaintiff may establish discrimination by showing that age was simply a motivating factor. Moreover, Congress neglected to add such a provision to the ADEA when it amended Title VII to add §§20002-2(m) and §20002-5(g)(2)(B) even though it contemporaneously amended the ADEA in several ways, see Civil Rights Act of 1991, §115, 105 Stat. 1079; *id.,* §302, at 1088.

We cannot ignore Congress' decision to amend Title VII's relevant provisions but not make similar changes to the ADEA. When Congress amends one statutory provision but not another, it is presumed to have acted intentionally. Furthermore, as the Court has explained, "negative implications raised by disparate provisions are strongest" when the provisions were "considered simultaneously when the language raising the implication was inserted." As a result, the Court's interpretation of the ADEA is not governed by Title VII decisions such as *Desert Palace* and *Price Waterhouse.*[2]

B

Our inquiry therefore must focus on the text of the ADEA to decide whether it authorizes a mixed-motives age discrimination claim. It does not. . . . The ADEA

---

2. Justice Stevens argues that the Court must incorporate its past interpretations of Title VII into the ADEA because "the substantive provisions of the ADEA were derived *in haec verba* from Title VII," and because the Court has frequently applied its interpretations of Title VII to the ADEA. But the Court's approach to interpreting the ADEA in light of Title VII has not been uniform. In *General Dynamic Land Systems, Inc. v. Cline,* 540 U.S. 581 (2004), for example, the Court declined to interpret the phrase "because of . . . age" to bar discrimination against people of all ages, even though the Court had previously interpreted "because of . . . race [or] sex" in Title VII to bar discrimination against people of all races and both sexes. And the Court has not definitively decided whether the evidentiary framework of *McDonnell Douglas* utilized in Title VII cases is appropriate in the ADEA context. In this instance, it is the textual differences between Title VII and the ADEA that prevent us from applying *Price Waterhouse* and *Desert Palace* to federal age discrimination claims.

provides, in relevant part, that "[i]t shall be unlawful for an employer . . . to fail or refuse to hire or to discharge any individual or otherwise discriminate against any individual with respect to his compensation, terms, conditions, or privileges of employment, *because of* such individual's age."

The words "because of" mean "by reason of: on account of." 1 Webster's Third New International Dictionary 194 (1966); see also 1 Oxford English Dictionary 746 (1933) (defining "because of" to mean "By reason *of,* on account *of*" (italics in original)); The Random House Dictionary of the English Language 132 (1966) (defining "because" to mean "by reason; on account"). Thus, the ordinary meaning of the ADEA's requirement that an employer took adverse action "because of" age is that age was the "reason" that the employer decided to act. See *Hazen Paper Co. v. Biggins* [reproduced at p. 9] (explaining that the claim "cannot succeed unless the employee's protected trait actually played a role in [the employer's decision-making] process *and had a determinative influence on the outcome*") To establish a disparate-treatment claim under the plain language of the ADEA, therefore, a plaintiff must prove that age was the "but-for" cause of the employer's adverse decision. See *Bridge v. Phoenix Bond & Indemnity Co.*, 553 U.S. , (2008) (recognizing that the phrase, "by reason of," requires at least a showing of "but for" causation); *Safeco Ins. Co. of America v. Burr*, 551 U.S. 47, 63-64, and n. 14 (2007) (observing that "[i]n common talk, the phrase 'based on' indicates a but-for causal relationship and thus a necessary logical condition" and that the statutory phrase, "based on," has the same meaning as the phrase, "because of" (internal quotation marks omitted)); cf. W. Keeton, D. Dobbs, R. Keeton, & D. Owen, Prosser and Keeton on Law of Torts 265 (5th ed. 1984) ("An act or omission is not regarded as a cause of an event if the particular event would have occurred without it").[3]

It follows, then, that under §623(a)(1), the plaintiff retains the burden of persuasion to establish that age was the "but-for" cause of the employer's adverse action. Indeed, we have previously held that the burden is allocated in this manner in ADEA cases. See *Kentucky Retirement Systems v. EEOC,* 554 U.S. 135 (2008); *Reeves v. Sanderson Plumbing Products, Inc.* [reproduced at p. 78]. And nothing in the statute's text indicates that Congress has carved out an exception to that rule for a subset of ADEA cases. Where the statutory text is "silent on the allocation of the burden of persuasion," we "begin with the ordinary default rule that plaintiffs bear the risk of failing to prove their claims." *Schaffer v. Weast*, 546 U.S. 49, 56 (2005); see also *Meacham v. Knolls Atomic Power Laboratory*, 554 U.S. 84, 92 (2008) ("Absent some reason to believe that Congress intended otherwise, . . . we will conclude that the burden of persuasion lies where it usually falls, upon the party seeking relief.") We have no warrant to depart from the general rule in this setting.

Hence, the burden of persuasion necessary to establish employer liability is the same in alleged mixed-motives cases as in any other ADEA disparate-treatment action. A plaintiff must prove by a preponderance of the evidence (which

---

3. Justice Breyer contends that there is "nothing unfair or impractical" about hinging liability on whether "forbidden motive . . . play[ed] a role in the employer's decision." But that is a decision for Congress to make. . . .

may be direct or circumstantial), that age was the "but-for" cause of the challenged employer decision.[4]

III

Finally, we reject petitioner's contention that our interpretation of the ADEA is controlled by *Price Waterhouse*, which initially established that the burden of persuasion shifted in alleged mixed-motives Title VII claims.[5] In any event, it is far from clear that the Court would have the same approach were it to consider the question today in the first instance. Cf. *14 Penn Plaza LLC v. Pyett*, (declining to "introduc[e] a qualification into the ADEA that is not found in its text"); *Meacham*, (explaining that the ADEA must be "read . . . the way Congress wrote it").

Whatever the deficiencies of *Price Waterhouse* in retrospect, it has become evident in the years since that case was decided that its burden-shifting framework is difficult to apply. For example, in cases tried to a jury, courts have found it particularly difficult to craft an instruction to explain its burden-shifting framework. See, *e.g., Tyler v. Bethlehem Steel Corp.*, 958 F.2d 1176, 1179 (C.A.2 1992) (referring to "the murky water of shifting burdens in discrimination cases"); *Visser v. Packer Engineering Associates, Inc.*, 924 F.2d 665, 661 (C.A.7 1991) (en banc) (Flaum, J., dissenting) ("The difficulty judges have in formulating [burden-shifting] instructions and jurors have in applying them can be seen in the fact that jury verdicts in ADEA cases are supplanted by judgments notwithstanding the verdict or reversed on appeal more frequently than jury verdicts generally"). Thus, even if *Price Waterhouse* was doctrinally sound, the problems associated with its

---

4. Because we hold that ADEA plaintiffs retain the burden of persuasion to prove all disparate-treatment claims, we do not need to address whether plaintiffs must present direct, rather than circumstantial, evidence to obtain a burden-shifting instruction. There is no heightened evidentiary requirement for ADEA plaintiffs to satisfy their burden of persuasion that age was the "but-for" cause of their employer's adverse action and we will imply none. . . .

5. Justice Stevens also contends that we must apply *Price Waterhouse* under the reasoning of *Smith v. City of Jackson*. In *Smith*, the Court applied to the ADEA its pre-1991 interpretation of Title VII with respect to disparate-impact claims despite Congress' 1991 amendment adding disparate-impact claims to Title VII but not the ADEA. But the amendments made by Congress in this same legislation, which added the "motivating factor" language to Title VII, undermine Justice STEVENS' argument. Congress not only explicitly added "motivating factor" liability to Title VII, but it also partially abrogated *Price Waterhouse*'s holding by eliminating an employer's complete affirmative defense to "motivating factor" claims. If such "motivating factor" claims were already part of Title VII, the addition of §2000e-5(g)(2)(B) alone would have been sufficient. Congress' careful tailoring of the "motivating factor" claim in Title VII, as well as the absence of a provision parallel to §2000e-2(m) in the ADEA, confirms that we cannot transfer the *Price Waterhouse* burden-shifting framework into the ADEA.

application have eliminated any perceivable benefit to extending its framework to ADEA claims.[6]

IV

We hold that a plaintiff bringing a disparate-treatment claim pursuant to the ADEA must prove, by a preponderance of the evidence, that age was the "but-for" cause of the challenged adverse employment action. The burden of persuasion does not shift to the employer to show that it would have taken the action regardless of age, even when a plaintiff has produced some evidence that age was one motivating factor in that decision. Accordingly, we vacate the judgment of the Court of Appeals and remand the case for further proceedings consistent with this opinion.

It is so ordered.

Justice STEVENS, with whom Justice SOUTER, Justice GINSBURG, and Justice BREYER join, dissenting.

The Age Discrimination in Employment Act makes it unlawful for an employer to discriminate against any employee "because of" that individual's age. The most natural reading of this statutory text prohibits adverse employment actions motivated in whole or in part by the age of the employee. The "but-for" causation standard endorsed by the Court today was advanced in Justice Kennedy'S dissenting opinion in *Price Waterhouse*, a case construing identical language in Title VII. Not only did the Court reject the but-for standard in that case, but so too did Congress when it amended Title VII in 1991. Given this unambiguous history, it is particularly inappropriate for the Court, on its own initiative, to adopt an interpretation of the causation requirement in the ADEA that differs from the established reading of Title VII. I disagree not only with the Court's interpretation of the statute, but also with its decision to engage in unnecessary lawmaking. I would simply answer the question presented by the certiorari petition and hold that a plaintiff need not present direct evidence of age discrimination to obtain a mixed-motives instruction.

---

6. Gross points out that the Court has also applied a burden-shifting framework to certain claims brought in contexts other than pursuant to Title VII, citing, *inter alia* *NLRB v. Transportation Management Corp.*, 462 U.S. 393, 401-403 (1983) (claims brought under the National Labor Relations Act (NLRA)); *Mt. Healthy City Bd. of Ed. v. Doyle*, 429 U.S. 274, 287 (1977) (constitutional claims)). These cases, however, do not require the Court to adopt his contra statutory position. The case involving the NLRA did not require the Court to decide in the first instance whether burden shifting should apply as the Court instead deferred to the National Labor Relation Board's determination that such a framework was appropriate. And the constitutional cases such as *Mt. Healthy* have no bearing on the correct interpretation of ADEA claims, which are governed by statutory text.

I

... The ADEA provides that "[i]t shall be unlawful for an employer ... to fail or refuse to hire or to discharge any individual or otherwise discriminate against any individual with respect to his compensation, terms, conditions, or privileges of employment, *because of* such individual's age." As we recognized in *Price Waterhouse* when we construed the identical "because of" language of Title VII, the most natural reading of the text proscribes adverse employment actions motivated in whole or in part by the age of the employee. ... [4]

Today, however, the Court interprets the words "because of" in the ADEA "as colloquial shorthand for 'but-for' causation." That the Court is construing the ADEA rather than Title VII does not justify this departure from precedent. The relevant language in the two statutes is identical, and we have long recognized that our interpretations of Title VII's language apply "with equal force in the context of age discrimination, for the substantive provisions of the ADEA 'were derived *in haec verba* from Title VII.'" *Trans World Airlines, Inc. v. Thurston*, 434 U.S. 575, 584 (1978). For this reason, Justice KENNEDY'S dissent in *Price Waterhouse* assumed the plurality's mixed-motives framework extended to the ADEA, and the Courts of Appeals [including *Rachid v. Jack In The Box, Inc.*] to have considered the issue unanimously have applied *Price Waterhouse* to ADEA claims.

[The dissent distinguished *Hazen Paper Co.* and *Reeves* as "non-mixed-motives ADEA cases" following] the standards set forth in non-mixed-motives Title VII cases including *McDonnell Douglas* and *Burdine*. This by no means indicates, as the majority reasons, that *mixed-motives* ADEA cases should follow those standards. Rather, it underscores that ADEA standards are generally understood to conform to Title VII standards.

II

... Because the 1991 Act amended only Title VII and not the ADEA with respect to mixed-motives claims, the Court reasonably declines to apply the amended provisions to the ADEA. But it proceeds to ignore the conclusion compelled by this interpretation of the Act: *Price Waterhouse*'s construction of "because of" remains the governing law for ADEA claims.

Our recent decision in *Smith v. City of Jackson* is precisely on point, as we considered in that case the effect of Congress' failure to amend the disparate-impact provisions of the ADEA when it amended the corresponding Title VII

---

4. We were no doubt aware that dictionaries define "because of" as "by reason of" or "on account of." Contrary to the majority's bald assertion, however, this does not establish that the term denotes but-for causation. The dictionaries the Court cites do not, for instance, define "because of" as "*solely* by reason of" or "*exclusively* on account of." In *Price Waterhouse,* we recognized that the words "because of" do not mean "*solely* because of," and we held that the inquiry "commanded by the words" of the statute was whether gender was a motivating factor in the employment decision.

provisions in the 1991 Act. Noting that "the relevant 1991 amendments expanded the coverage of Title VII [but] did not amend the ADEA or speak to the subject of age discrimination," we held that "*Wards Cove*'s pre-1991 interpretation of Title VII's identical language remains applicable to the ADEA." If the *Wards Cove* disparate-impact framework that Congress flatly repudiated in the Title VII context continues to apply to ADEA claims, the mixed-motives framework that Congress substantially endorsed surely applies.

Curiously, the Court reaches the opposite conclusion, relying on Congress' partial ratification of *Price Waterhouse* to argue against that case's precedential value. It reasons that if the 1991 amendments do not apply to the ADEA, *Price Waterhouse* likewise must not apply because Congress effectively codified *Price Waterhouse*'s holding in the amendments. This does not follow. To the contrary, the fact that Congress endorsed this Court's interpretation of the "because of" language in *Price Waterhouse* (even as it rejected the employer's affirmative defense to liability) provides all the more reason to adhere to that decision's motivating-factor test. . . .

III

Although the Court declines to address the question we granted certiorari to decide, I would answer that question by following our unanimous opinion in *Desert Palace*. I would accordingly hold that a plaintiff need not present direct evidence of age discrimination to obtain a mixed-motives instruction.

[Assuming *Price Waterhouse* controlled, the dissent found that a majority of justices in that case had rejected any limitation of burden-shifting to direct evidence. It recognized that source of the direct-evidence debate was Justice O'Connor's opinion concurrence and that many courts treated her opinion as controlling for both Title VII and ADEA mixed-motives. However, *Marks v. United States*, 430 U.S. 188, 193 (1977), commands that "[w]hen a fragmented Court decides a case and no single rationale explaining the result enjoys the assent of five Justices, 'the holding of the Court may be viewed as that position taken by those Members who concurred in the judgments on the narrowest grounds.'" The dissent argued that] *Price Waterhouse* garnered five votes for a single rationale: Justice White agreed with the plurality as to the motivating-factor test, he disagreed only as to the type of evidence an employer was required to submit to prove that the same result would have occurred absent the unlawful motivation. Taking the plurality to demand objective evidence, he wrote separately to express his view that an employer's credible testimony could suffice. Because Justice White provided a fifth vote for the "rationale explaining the result" of the *Price Waterhouse* decision, his concurrence is properly understood as controlling, and he, like the plurality, did not require the introduction of direct evidence. . . .

Justice BREYER, with whom Justice SOUTER and Justice GINSBURG join, dissenting.

I agree with Justice Stevens that mixed-motive instructions are appropriate in the Age Discrimination in Employment Act context. And I join his opinion. The

Court rejects this conclusion on the ground that the words "because of" require a plaintiff to prove that age was the "but-for" cause of his employer's adverse employment action. But the majority does not explain why this is so. The words "because of" do not inherently require a showing of "but-for" causation, and I see no reason to read them to require such a showing.

It is one thing to require a typical tort plaintiff to show "but-for" causation. In that context, reasonably objective scientific or commonsense theories of physical causation make the concept of "but-for" causation comparatively easy to understand and relatively easy to apply. But it is an entirely different matter to determine a "but-for" relation when we consider, not physical forces, but the mind-related characterizations that constitute motive. Sometimes we speak of *determining* or *discovering* motives, but more often we *ascribe* motives, after an event, to an individual in light of the individual's thoughts and other circumstances present at the time of decision. In a case where we characterize an employer's actions as having been taken out of multiple motives, say, both because the employee was old and because he wore loud clothing, to apply "but-for" causation is to engage in a hypothetical inquiry about what would have happened if the employer's thoughts and other circumstances had been different. The answer to this hypothetical inquiry will often be far from obvious, and, since the employee likely knows less than does the employer about what the employer was thinking at the time, the employer will often be in a stronger position than the employee to provide the answer.

All that a plaintiff can know for certain in such a context is that the forbidden motive did play a role in the employer's decision. And the fact that a jury has found that age did play a role in the decision justifies the use of the word "because," *i.e.*, the employer dismissed the employee because of his age (and other things). I therefore would see nothing wrong in concluding that the plaintiff has established a violation of the statute [subject to the affirmative defense recognized in *Price Waterhouse*.] The law permits the employer this defense, not because the forbidden motive, age, had no role in the *actual* decision, but because the employer can show that he would have dismissed the employee anyway in the *hypothetical* circumstance in which his age-related motive was absent. And it makes sense that this would be an affirmative defense, rather than part of the showing of a violation, precisely because the defendant is in a better position than the plaintiff to establish how he would have acted in this hypothetical situation. I can see nothing unfair or impractical about allocating the burdens of proof in this way. . . .

NOTES

1. *The Holding.* The Court decided that in all ADEA individual disparate treatment age discrimination cases, plaintiff must carry the burden of production and of persuasion that age was the but-for cause of the adverse employment action that is challenged. However, the circuit courts have so far read *Gross* not to affect the application of *McDonnell Douglas* analysis in ADEA cases in carrying that burden. *E.g., Jones v. Okla. City Pub. Schs*, 617 F.3d 1273 (10th Cir. 2010) ("Although

we recognize that *Gross* created some uncertainty regarding burden-shifting in the ADEA context, we conclude that it does not preclude our continued application of *McDonnell Douglas* to ADEA claims."); *Smith v. City of Allentown*, 589 F.3d 684, 691 (3d Cir. 2009) ("*Gross* stands for the proposition that it is improper to shift the burden of persuasion to the defendant in an age discrimination case. *McDonnell Douglas*, however, imposes no shift in that particular burden" since it shifts only a burden of production). They have also continued to look to something like "direct evidence" — not as a burden-shifting device but rather as a reason to find that age was a determinative factor. *E.g., Mora v. Jackson Mem'l Found., Inc.*, 597 F.3d 1201 (11th Cir. 2010); *Baker v. Silver Oak Senior Living Mgmt. Co.*, 581 F.3d 684 (8th Cir. 2009).

2. *Three-Step Rationale.* The first step toward the majority's holding in *Gross* was that the amendment of Title VII in the 1991 Act to add the "a motivating factor" standard of liability in §703(m) did not apply to the ADEA. Given the decision in *Smith v. City of Jackson* that the 1991 amendment to Title VII to codify disparate impact analysis did not apply in age discrimination cases, this step is not surprising.

The second step, however, is startling. The Court held that the burden-shifting approach established for Title VII in *Price Waterhouse* did not apply. Not only was this issue was not included in the question presented but the majority's approach seems directly at odds with the Court's methodology in *Smith v. City of Jackson*, which held that Title VII's disparate impact analysis, as developed by the Court in *Wards Cove* before the 1991 amendments, controlled the ADEA. If treated analogously, the pre-1991 jurisprudence of Title VII, as established in *Price Waterhouse*, would seem to apply to individual disparate treatment cases.

The third step was even more bizarre: *Gross* appeared to overrule *Price Waterhouse* even though it had just found it inapplicable to the ADEA and, as to Title VII, it had already been superseded by the 1991 amendments to Title VII. If there is a point to this, it might be to foreclose the application of *Price Waterhouse* to §1981 and, perhaps, to retaliation cases under Title VII that are not explicitly subject to §703(m). *See generally* Michael C. Harper, *The Causation Standard in Federal Employment Law*: Gross v. FBL Financial Services, Inc., *and the Unfulfilled Promise of the Civil Rights Act of 1991*, 58 BUFFALO L. REV. 69, 107 (2010); Martin J. Katz, Gross *Disunity*, 114 PENN ST. L. REV. 857 (2010); David Sherwyn & Michael Heise, The Gross Beast of Burden of Proof: Experimental Evidence on How the Burden of Proof Influences Employment Discrimination Case Outcomes, 42 ARIZ. ST. L.J. 901.

3. Gross's *Effect on Other Antidiscrimination Statutes.* *Desert Palace* and *Gross* create separate analytic regimes for Title VII and the ADEA respectively. What about other laws? Some have argued that *Gross* will not apply to ADA cases because that statute incorporates Title VII procedures and remedies by reference. *See* Melissa Hart, *Procedural Extremism: The Supreme Court's 2008-2009 Employment and Labor Cases*, 13 EMP. RTS. & EMP. POL'Y J. 253 (2010). *See also* Catherine T. Struve, *Shifting Burdens: Discrimination Law Through the Lens of Jury Instruction*, 51 B.C. L. REV. 279 (2010) (predicting *Gross* will govern retaliation claims under Title VII and the ADEA). The circuits are so far split. *Serwatka v. Rockwell Automation, Inc.*, 591

F.3d 957 (7th Cir. 2010) (*Gross* requires holding that determinative factor causation applies under ADA since the ADA's cross-reference to Title VII remedies does not explicitly cross-reference §703(m)). *Contra Smith v. Xerox Corp.*, 602 F.3d 320, 327-332(5th Cir. 2010) (2-1) (despite *Gross*, retaliation cases under Title VII are subject to Title VII's motivating factor analysis for burden-shifting, and direct evidence of discrimination is not necessary). *See also Ford v. Mabus*, 629 F.3d 198 (D.C. Cir. 2010) (in a federal employee suit under ADEA §633a, plaintiffs need show only that age was a factor in the employer's decision in order to prevail as to liability).

4. *Mixed vs. Single Motive Cases.* Both Justice Thomas and Justice Stevens assume that there is a category of individual disparate treatment cases involving mixed-motives that is distinct from another category, presumably single-motive cases (although Stevens refers to them as "nonmixed-motive.") In some ways this simply reiterates *Hazen Paper*—a mixed-motive case requiring the plaintiff to prove age was the determinative factor in the decision. Presumably, but-for causation is also required for single-motive cases but such claims are viewed in either/or terms: either discrimination caused the action or it did not, which makes the but-for question inherent in the finding of liability. Perhaps needless to say, however, this underscores the unreality of a scheme that depends on finding only one motive to explain human interactions.

5. *Adverse Employment Action.* Plaintiff Gross was reassigned to a new position, but his compensation stayed the same. The Court appears to assume that this amounted to an adverse employment action because, in plaintiff's view, it was a demotion since some of his former responsibilities were reallocated to another employee. Does this suggest a broader version of the adverse employment action doctrine than we've seen to this point?

6. *Trying Title VII and Age Act Issues in One Case.* Following *Gross*, plaintiffs claiming both age and, say, sex discrimination will now have two very different sets of instructions to the jury (or standards of liability for the trial judge). While direct and/or circumstantial evidence apparently can be used to support both claims, plaintiff must prove her age claim with evidence strong enough to support drawing the inference that age was the but-for cause of the action. Failing to establish that means there is no liability under the ADEA. But, even if the factfinder finds but-for linkage as to age, plaintiff might still also prevail if the factfinder is convinced that sex was also "a motivating factor." It is logically possible to find sex was implicated even though age was the but-for reason since a but-for finding allows other reasons to be implicated.

Page 96.   Delete in *Rachid* opinion from "III. Discussion" through carryover paragraph on p. 98; replace with:

[The Eighth Circuit decided *Rachid* prior to the Supreme Court's decision in *Gross v. FSB Financial Services*, holding, contrary to what *Gross* would later decide, that ADEA claims should be analyzed identically to Title VII claims. While that portion of the opinion was overruled by *Gross*, the *Rachid* analysis of what it called a merger of *Price Waterhouse* and *McDonnell Douglas* presumably remains viable for Title VII.]

**Page 101.   Delete Note 1, Desert Palace *Applies to ADEA Claims*;
                      replace with:**

1. *Gross.* Contrary to a portion of *Rachid's* holding, *Gross v. FBL Fin. Servs.*, 129 S. Ct. 2343 (2009), reproduced at p. 26 of this Supplement, rejected applying §703(m) to the ADEA and even rejected the direct evidence/substantial factor analysis of *Price Waterhouse* for such cases.

**Page 103.   Add at end of carryover paragraph in Note 3,
                      Other Courts' Approaches:**

See also Natalie Bucciarelli Pedersen, *A Legal Framework for Uncovering Implicit Bias*, 79 U. Cin. L. Rev. 97, 102-03 (2010) (advocating using "the motivating factor framework at the summary judgment phase; using this analysis will ultimately change employers' behavior. Although judges are hesitant to attempt to detect employers' implicit biases, through the use of the motivating factor framework, judges can encourage an employer to self-reflect when making employment decisions).

Page 105.   Add at end of carryover Note 3(d), *Or Just a Grab-bag?*:

In *Brady v. Office of the Sergeant at Arms*, 520 F.3d 490, 494 (D.C. Cir. 2008), without mentioning *Desert Palace*, the court rejected any need for a lower court to focus on the *McDonnell Douglas* prima facie case:

> Lest there be any lingering uncertainty, we state the rule clearly: In a Title VII disparate-treatment suit where an employee has suffered an adverse employment action and an employer has asserted a legitimate, non-discriminatory reason for the decision, the district court need not — and should not — decide whether the plaintiff actually made out a prima facie case under *McDonnell Douglas*. Rather, in considering an employer's motion for summary judgment or judgment as a matter of law in those circumstances, the district court must resolve one central question: Has the employee produced sufficient evidence for a reasonable jury to find that the employer's asserted non-discriminatory reason was not the actual reason and that the employer intentionally discriminated against the employee on the basis of race, color, religion, sex, or national origin?"

Page 106.   Add at beginning of Note 4, *Academic Response to* Desert Palace:

William R. Corbett, *Fixing Employment Discrimination Law*, 62 SMU L. Rev. 81 (2009) (arguing for a unified proof structure for disparate treatment cases over the various antidiscrimination cases that would retain motivating factor proof for all such cases including reverse discrimination cases but would change the effect of a "same decision" defense); Michael J. Zimmer, *A Chain of Inferences Proving Discrimination*, 79 U. COLO. L. REV. 1243 (2008);

Page 107.   Add after parenthetical following *Waldron* cite in third paragraph:

But see Fitzgerald v. Action, Inc., 521 F.3d 867, 877 (8th Cir. 2008) ("Under different circumstances, the remarks attributed to Easley might create an inference of discrimination. In this instance, however, they are insufficient to overcome the presumption created by the fact Action hired Fitzgerald at age fifty" when it fired him at 52).

Page 108.   Add at end of first full paragraph:

See also Natasha T. Martin, *Immunity for Hire: How the Same-Actor Doctrine Sustains Discrimination in the Contemporary Workplace*, 40 CONN. L. REV. 1117, 1121 (2008) ("[T]he same-actor principle constitutes an untenable analytical paradigm that fails to comport with the realities of the contemporary American workplace, specifically, its complexities in structural, cultural and managerial terms.").

Page 108.   Delete *Same Supervisor* section; replace with new section:

Same Supervisor. A second recurring situation arises when plaintiff attempts to bolster her case by adducing evidence of discrimination against other members of her class. While there is no doubt that such evidence is often admissible, and may be very probative, there has been considerable resistance to its use when the alleged discrimination was by a different supervisor than the one accused of discriminating against plaintiff. In *Sprint/United Management Co.* v. *Mendelsohn*, 552 U.S. 379 (2007), a reduction in force case, plaintiff wanted to call as witnesses five other older workers who claimed that they, too, were discriminated against because of their age in the downsizing. Defendant objected because none of the other potential witnesses worked under the same supervisor as the plaintiff. The trial court excluded the testimony, and the jury found for the defendant. The court of appeals reversed because, as it saw it, the district court had relied on a *per se* rule of exclusion of all such so-called me too evidence.

The Supreme Court, in a unanimous opinion by Justice Thomas, vacated the judgment finding the evidence admissible and remanded the case to the district court to determine admissibility on a case-by-case basis since "such evidence is neither *per se* admissible nor *per se* inadmissible." *Id.* at 381. Emphasizing the broad discretion accorded trail courts' evidentiary rulings—reviewable under a deferential abuse of discretion standard—the trial court should make the admissibility determination: "With respect to evidentiary questions in general [including relevance under Federal Rule of Evidence 401 and the possibility of excluding even relevant evidence because of the risk of undue prejudice under Rule 403 in particular] the district court virtually always is in the better position to assess the admissibility of the evidence in the context of the case before it." *Id.* at 387. Discrimination cases are well suited to this generally applicable approach since

> [t]he question whether evidence of discrimination by other supervisors is relevant in an individual ADEA case is fact based and depends on many factors, including how closely related the evidence is to the plaintiff's circumstances and theory of the case. Applying Rule 403 to determine if evidence is prejudicial also requires a fact-intensive, context-specific inquiry.

Id. at 388. In fact, discrimination cases may be especially fact sensitive. The whole focus on "insular individualism" of supervisors and managers is inconsistent with how workplaces operate in practice, with any particular decision being influenced by a web of other decisions and practices, sometimes influencing individual actors in ways they do not themselves understand. Tristin Green, *Insular Individualism: Employment Discrimination Law After* Ledbetter v. Goodyear, 43 HARV. C.R.-C.L. L. REV. 353 (2008).

The significance of *Mendelsohn* will, of course, ultimately depend on how the district courts apply their discretion. The battle over admissibility will continue, but at the trial level rather than as a question for summary judgment. Given the abuse of discretion standard for appellate review, few of these questions of admissibility, however determined by the trial court, will be appealed. If plaintiff is assuming the RIF policy is neutral as to age, what is the relevance of the testimony that she sought to introduce of how other older workers were treated by their supervisors? One possibility is that such proof shows that the RIF policy, though age neutral on its face and, perhaps, in its intent, allowed for age discrimination in its application. The supervisors making the decisions had broad discretion and, in using that discretion, could discriminate because of age, either consciously or unconsciously.

That might be true, but doesn't the question remain whether plaintiff's supervisor discriminated? If A, B, and C are each separate decision makers, how could the fact that B discriminated show that A did? Even if there is some umbrella policy that allowed each of them freedom to make decisions? *See Mattenson v. Baxter Healthcare Corp.*, 438 F.3d 763, 770-71 (7th Cir. 2006) (in a division of 7,000 employees with hundreds of executives, the fact that some may dislike old workers and even fire old workers because of their age is weak evidence that a particular older employee was fired because of his age; absent proof of a pervasive culture of prejudice, such evidence may be excluded under Rule 403, although it not reversible error to admit it). And what about C? Can the employer put in evidence that C (and maybe D and E) did not discriminate?

Is the real problem in *Mendelsohn* the "same supervisor" rule in *Aramburu?* While it is true that the unexplained unequal treatment by the same supervisor is a strong basis to draw the inference of discrimination, is evidence that different supervisors enforced the same employer rule more leniently as to other workers without *any* probative value for plaintiff? *See Lee v. Kan. City S. Ry. Co,* 574 F.3d 253, 261 (5th Cir. 2009) (for comparator proof "[i]t is sufficient that the ultimate decisionmaker as to the employees' continued employment is the same individual, even if the employees do not share an immediate supervisor"). Couldn't one argue that, when institutional norms cut one way (for example, tolerating tardiness), the fact that a single supervisor violates those norms with respect to a protected class member is at least some evidence of bias? After *Reeves,* should that evidence be admissible unless no jury could reasonably rely on it to build a chain of inferences leading to a finding of discrimination? *See generally* Nicholas Soltman, Comment, *What About "Me (Too)"? The Case for Admitting Evidence of Discrimination against Non-parties,* 76 U. CHI. L. REV. 1875 (2009) (while "me too" evidence will almost always clear the low relevancy bar set by Rule 401, Rule 403 is likely to pose a more serious problem).

Page 109.   Add at end of last full paragraph:

Ramlet v. E.F. Johnson Co., 507 F.3d 1149 (8th Cir. 2007) (one and five years' age difference insufficient to establish a prima facie case).

Page 110.   Add after *Privirotto* cite:

See also Vincent v. Brewer Co., 514 F.3d 489, 491 (6th Cir. 2007) ("To establish a prima facie case of gender discrimination, however, a plaintiff who can prove that she was replaced by a member of the opposite sex need not show that she possesses qualifications similar to those of her replacement.");

Page 111.   Delete from first full paragraph up to Problem 1; replace with:

Elizabeth Hirsh, *Settling for Less? Organizational Determinants of Discrimination-Charge Outcomes,* 42 LAW & SOC'Y REV. 239 (2008) (complainants alleging race discrimination are less likely to prevail as compared to those alleging sex discrimination, perhaps because of the prevalence of harassment claims for sex discrimination); Kevin M. Clermont & Stewart J. Schwab, *Employment Discrimination Plaintiffs in Federal Court: From Bad to Worse,* 3 HARV. L. & POL'Y REV. 103, 126, 111 (2009) ("Over the period of 1979–2006 in federal [district] court, the plaintiff win rate for job cases (15%) was much lower than for non-job cases (51%)," and appellate courts reverse plaintiffs' wins far more than the defendant's wins below")

   If it is true that plaintiffs have a very hard time winning discrimination cases, why do you think that is? One possible explanation is that the really strong plaintiffs' cases settle early and so never get to trial or, maybe, even into the courts. *See* Minna J. Kotkin, *Outing Outcomes: An Empirical Study of Confidential Employment Discrimination Settlements,* 64 WASH & LEE L. REV. 111 (2007) (empirically analyzing settlement outcomes, this article finds that employment discrimination litigation results in a mean recovery of $54,651, which means that plaintiffs achieve "a reasonable degree of success, measured against their lost wages."). *See also* Laura Beth Nielsen, Robert L. Nelson, & Ryon Lancaster, *Individual Justice or Collective Legal Mobilization? Employment Discrimination in the Post Civil Rights United States*, 7 J. EMP. STUD. 175 (2010) (Where settlement amounts were available, the median settlement was $30,000; if the plaintiff survived summary judgment, the median rose to $40,000"). Another possible explanation is that many discrimination cases are brought by the plaintiff pro se, so the failure to have professional representation may take its toll. A third explanation may be that plaintiffs' cases are weak, at least in light of the difficulty posed in litigating them successfully. Might that be because, in the world of at-will employment, claiming discrimination is one of the few hooks employees have when they feel that they have been mistreated by their employers? Are there other reasons you can think of for the low success rate?

Will the developing jurisprudence based on *Reeves* and *Desert Palace* make any difference? Professor Charles Sullivan predicts that the litigation scorecard will not change because judges and jurors underestimate the amount of discrimination that continues to occur and are, therefore, reluctant to find defendants discriminated, no matter how the case is presented to them. *See* Charles A. Sullivan, *Disparate Impact: Looking Past the* Desert Palace *Mirage*, 47 WM. & MARY L. REV. 911 (2006).

2 Systemic Disparate Treatment Discrimination

C. Patterns and Practices of Discrimination

Page 121.   Add before last sentence in carryover Note 4, *A BFOQ?*:

Even for pilots subject to FAA rules, the age 60 limit was moved to 65 by new legislation. Pub. L. 110-135 (2007).

Page 121.   Add at end of Note 5, *Does Discrimination Require Animus or Stereotype?*:

You might want to reconsider the question of animus in light of *Kentucky Retirement Systems v. EEOC*, 544 U.S. 135 (2008), where a 5-4 majority of the Court held that a benefit scheme that facially differentiated on the basis of age was not necessarily impermissible, wholly without reference to any statutory exception. The dissent leaned heavily on *Manhart* in viewing the decision as very wrong. See p. 157-58 of this Supplement.

Page 139.   Add at end of page in Note 6, *Systemic Age Cases*:

See also Thompson v. Weyerhaeuser Co., 582 F.3d 1125 (10th Cir. 2009) (pattern and practice claims may be brought under the ADEA despite the absence of explicit language authorizing such suits in that statute).

Page 140.   Add at end of carryover Note 6, *Systemic Age Cases*:

And in *Aliotta v. Bair*, 614 F.3d 556, 566 (D.C. Cir. 2010), the court rejected a class systemic disparate treatment and disparate impact attack because plaintiffs' statistical evidence was lacking. Their expert combined the effects of the involuntary terminations with the effects of the voluntary retirements to find an age effect, but the court found this inappropriate: "class members cannot include as evidence of discrimination the statistics of a group of employees who, because they voluntarily accepted a buyout, suffered no adverse employment action." Does this make sense to you when the question in the first instance is whether the employer acted adversely to the class of older workers? It's one thing to say that potential class members have waived their rights by accepting the employer's buyout and another thing to say that older workers weren't targeted or adversely affected by the riffing. *See generally* Jason Bent, *The Telltale Sign of Discrimination: Probabilities, Information Asymmetries, and the Systemic Disparate Treatment Theory,* U. of MICH. J. OF L. REFORM (forthcoming 2011).

Page 140.   Add new Note 8:

8. *Goodbye Systemic Disparate Treatment Theory?* In *Wal-Mart Stores, Inc. v. Dukes,* 131 S. Ct. 2541 (2011), the Supreme Court decided a significant case involving class actions. See p. 230 of this Supplement for the opinion and its treatment of the Rule 23 issues. *Wal-Mart* involved whether to certify a class of about a million and a half women workers claiming pay and promotion discrimination because of sex. The Court reversed the Ninth Circuit *en banc* decision that the class should be certified. The Court was split 5-4 on the central question of whether plaintiffs had established a the common question required by Rule 23(a). Justice Scalia wrote the majority opinion, and Justice Ginsburg (joined by Justices Breyer, Sotomayor, and Kagen) dissented. While ostensibly a procedural decision, *Wal-Mart* may have dramatic effects on the substantive law of systemic disparate treatment, discussed here, and systemic disparate impact discussed in Chapter 2.

The basic thrust of plaintiffs' claim was that Wal-Mart's policy of granting unstructured and unreviewed discretion to store managers to make pay and promotion decisions was a practice of systemic disparate treatment discrimination. All the women store employees of Wal-Mart faced the risk of discrimination in pay and promotion because the central management of Wal-Mart kept data about the pay and promotion practices of all the store managers but did not intervene despite the clear evidence of discrimination by the store managers. In footnote 7, the Court cited *Teamsters* in its description of the prior law: "In a pattern-or-practice case, the plaintiff tries to "establish by a preponderance of the evidence that . . . discrimination was the company's standard operating procedure[,] the regular rather than the unusual practice." One way to proceed is by challenging a "biased testing procedure," presumably under the disparate impact theory for "every applicant or employee who might have been prejudiced by the test." More relevant here, however, was another possibility:

> Second, "[s]ignificant proof that an employer operated under a general policy of discrimination conceivably could justify a class of both applicants and employees if the discrimination manifested itself in hiring and promotion practices in the same general fashion, such as through entirely subjective decisionmaking processes." We think that

statement precisely describes respondents' burden in this case. The first [possibility] obviously has no application here; Wal-Mart has no testing procedure or other company-wide evaluation method that can be charged with bias. The whole point of permitting discretionary decisionmaking is to avoid evaluating employees under a common standard.

The second [possibility] requires "significant proof" that Wal-Mart "operated under a general policy of discrimination." That is entirely absent here. Wal-Mart's announced policy forbids sex discrimination the company imposes penalties for denials of equal employment opportunity. The only evidence of a "general policy of discrimination" respondents produced was the testimony of Dr. William Bielby, their sociological expert. Relying on "social framework" analysis, Bielby testified that Wal-Mart has a "strong corporate culture," that makes it " 'vulnerable' " to "gender bias." He could not, however, "determine with any specificity how regularly stereotypes play a meaningful role in employment decisions at Wal-Mart. At his deposition . . . Dr. Bielby conceded that he could not calculate whether 0.5 percent or 95 percent of the employment decisions at Wal-Mart might be determined by stereotyped thinking. . . . If Bielby admittedly has no answer to that question, we can safely disregard what he has to say. It is worlds away from "significant proof" that Wal-Mart "operated under a general policy of discrimination."

The only corporate policy that the plaintiffs' evidence convincingly establishes is Wal-Mart's "policy" of *allowing discretion* by local supervisors over employment matters. On its face, of course, that is just the opposite of a uniform employment practice that would provide the commonality needed for a class action; it is a policy *against having* uniform employment practices. It is also a very common and presumptively reasonable way of doing business — one that we have said "should itself raise no inference of discriminatory conduct,"

To be sure, we have recognized that, "in appropriate cases," giving discretion to lower-level supervisors can be the basis of Title VII liability under a disparate-impact theory — since "an employer's undisciplined system of subjective decisionmaking [can have] precisely the same effects as a system pervaded by impermissible intentional discrimination." But the recognition that this type of Title VII claim "can" exist does not lead to the conclusion that every employee in a company using a system of discretion has such a claim in common. To the contrary, left to their own devices most managers in any corporation — and surely most managers in a corporation that forbids sex discrimination — would select sex-neutral, performance-based criteria for hiring and promotion that produce no actionable disparity at all. Others may choose to reward various attributes that produce disparate impact — such as scores on general aptitude tests or educational achievements, see *Griggs* v. *Duke Power Co.* And still other managers may be guilty of intentional discrimination that produces a sex based disparity. In such a company, demonstrating the invalidity of one manager's use of discretion will do nothing to demonstrate the invalidity of another's. A party seeking to certify a nationwide class will be unable to show that all the employees' Title VII claims will in fact depend on the answers to common questions.

Respondents have not identified a common mode of exercising discretion that pervades the entire company — aside from their reliance on Dr. Bielby's social frameworks analysis that we have rejected. In a company of Wal-Mart's size and geographical scope, it is quite unbelievable that all managers would exercise their discretion in a common way without some common direction. Respondents attempt to make that showing by means of statistical and anecdotal evidence, but their evidence falls well short.

2. Systemic Disparate Treatment Discrimination

The statistical evidence consists primarily of regression analyses performed by Dr. Richard Drogin, a statistician, and Dr. Marc Bendick, a labor economist. Drogin conducted his analysis region-by-region, comparing the number of women promoted into management positions with the percentage of women in the available pool of hourly workers. After considering regional and national data, Drogin concluded that "there are statistically significant disparities between men and women at Wal-Mart . . . [and] these disparities . . . can be explained only by gender discrimination." Bendick compared work-force data from Wal-Mart and competitive retailers and concluded that Wal-Mart "promotes a lower percentage of women than its competitors."

Even if they are taken at face value, these studies are insufficient to establish that respondents' theory can be proved on a class wide basis. In *Falcon*, we held that one named plaintiff's experience of discrimination was insufficient to infer that "discriminatory treatment is typical of [the employer's employment] practices." A similar failure of inference arises here. . . . A regional pay disparity, for example, may be attributable to only a small set of Wal-Mart stores, and cannot by itself establish the uniform, store-by-store disparity upon which the plaintiffs' theory depends.

Even if it established (as it does not) a pay or promotion pattern that differs from the nationwide figures or the regional figures in *all* of Wal-Mart's 3,400 stores, that would still not demonstrate that commonality of issue exists. Some managers will claim that the availability of women, or qualified women, or interested women, in their stores' area does not mirror the national or regional statistics. And almost all of them will claim to have been applying some sex-neutral, performance-based criteria—whose nature and effects will differ from store to store. In the landmark case of ours which held that giving discretion to lower-level supervisors can be the basis of Title VII liability under a disparate-impact theory, the plurality opinion *conditioned* that holding on the corollary that merely proving that the discretionary system has produced a racial or sexual disparity *is not enough*. "[T]he plaintiff must begin by identifying the specific employment practice that is challenged." *Watson.*

Other than the bare existence of delegated discretion, respondents have identified no "specific employment practice"—much less one that ties all their 1.5 million claims together. Merely showing that Wal-Mart's policy of discretion has produced an overall sex-based disparity does not suffice.

Respondents' anecdotal evidence suffers from the same defects, and in addition is too weak to raise any inference that all the individual, discretionary personnel decisions are discriminatory. . . .

In beginning the discussion of the substantive law underpinning plaintiffs' claim, Justice Scalia sets up a dichotomy between an employer using employment tests versus it having a general policy of discriminating. In doing so, he overlooks a third option—that a policy neutral on its face nevertheless operates in a way that is discriminatory. In *Teamster's* terms, the claim is that the employer has a practice of discriminating even in absence of an express policy of discrimination. Presumably, in *Teamsters* the practice of discriminating was based on the aggregation of the individual decisions of individual managers who assigned drivers either to the city or to the over-the-road jobs. Of course, there the practice resulted in the "inexorable zero" of minority representation while in *Wal-Mart* not all women were discriminated in pay and promotion. But *Hazelwood* seemingly solved that problem through the use of sophisticated statistical evidence from which an inference of discriminatory intent behind the statistics could be drawn, exactly the kind of evidence plaintiffs used in *Wal-Mart*. Is the Court's ostensibly procedural decision one that really overturns systemic disparate treatment theory as it has been understood for more than three decades?

Justice Scalia never cites the statistical evidence that raises the question whether the policy of letting store managers who were, after all, agents of Wal-Mart make the decisions that could be aggregated to support drawing the inference that the company's "standard operating procedure" included a considerable amount of discrimination. That unchallenged statistical evidence, cited by Justice Ginsburg in dissent, was that 70 percent of the hourly employees but only 33 percent of the managerial employees at the stores were women and that women were paid less than men with the salary gap widening over time even for men and women hired into the same jobs. This dramatic shortfall for women in promotion and pay does not, by itself, prove intentional discrimination, but surely it raises the real possibility that the statistical profile is, at least partially, due to discrimination by managers.

If *Teamsters* and *Hazelwood* applied, the next step would be to determine whether this shortfall was because of sex. In *Teamsters*, the "inexorable zero" of African-American over-the-road drivers as compared to black city drivers sufficed because alternative explanations were so implausible. *Hazelwood*, however, relied on a more sophisticated statistical technique to draw the inference that the statistical underrepresentation of African American teacher was sufficiently unlikely to have occurred had race not been a factor that it could be found that race explained the stats. More precisely, the Court used a binomial distribution to reject the null hypothesis that race and hiring were not related; with the null hypothesis of no correlation disproved, it was appropriate to draw the inference that the absence of African-American teachers was because of race.

In *Wal-Mart*, plaintiffs relied on multiple regression studies to reject the null hypothesis that the operation of the unstructured and unreviewed discretion in setting pay and making promotions by store managers was not related to sex. Further, there was Dr. Bielby's testimony that the use of discretion allowed for stereotyping because of sex. Finally, as in *Teamsters*, there was anecdotal evidence that individual women had been the victims of pay and promotion discrimination. Rather than complete the approach envisioned by the *Teamsters* Court, Justice Scalia short-circuited that analysis by conflating what is a practice that is intentional disparate treatment and an employment practice that may not be intentionally discriminatory but nevertheless has a disparate impact on groups protected by Title VII.

In short, what happened to systemic disparate treatment, at least absent a facially discriminatory policy? Does the Court's apparent undermining of systemic disparate treatment discrimination result from its belief that whatever discrimination may exist is committed by a few bad apple store managers. A revealing statement of the Court's mindset that discrimination is limited to a few individual wrongdoers is a statement completely unsupported by the facts of the case or, perhaps anywhere else: "left to their own devices most managers in any corporation –and surely most managers in a corporation that forbids sex discrimination—would select sex-neutral, performance-based criteria for hiring and promotion that produce no actionable disparity at all."

2. Systemic Disparate Treatment Discrimination

This individualized conception of discrimination has been the subject of scholarly discussion in anticipation of the Court's decision in *Wal-Mart. See* Tristin K. Green, *The Future of Systemic Disparate Treatment Law*, 32 BERK. J. OF EMPLOY. & LAB. L. (forthcoming 2011)(the individualistic model of wrongdoing by corporations has led to under-theorizing, even mistheorizing,of entity responsibility for systemic disparate treatment); Michael Selmi, *Theorizing Systemic Disparate Treatment Law*, 32 BERK. J. OF EMPLOY. & LAB. L. (forthcoming 2011) (rejecting the argument that the pattern or practice claim of systemic disparate treatment is merely an aggregation of individual claims, and instead suggesting that the statistics prove a more subtle form of discrimination that would not be evident if one focused solely on individual claims). Leslie Wexler, Wal-Mart *Matters*, 46 WAKE FOREST L. REV. 95 (2011) (arguing that discrimination can persist at firms like Wal-Mart because of various market failures, despite the company's relentless pursuit of efficiency).

All of this Court's analysis took place in the context of the procedural question of whether plaintiffs had satisfied the commonality requirements of Rule 23 and, therefore, it does not necessarily indicate that *Wal-Mart* would apply in a substantive systemic disparate treatment case. Should the lower courts use *Wal-Mart* to determine those substantive claims? In any event, given that the circuits have generally banned the systemic theory in individual suits, does it matter? Large class actions will be few and far between in the wake of *Wal-Mart*.

Page 144.   Add after third full paragraph:

See Jason Bent, in *The Telltale Sign of Discrimination: Probabilities, Information Asymmetries, and the Systemic Disparate Treatment Theory*, U. OF MICH. J. OF L. REFORM (forthcoming 2011) draws upon economic models of optimal allocation of burdens of proof in civil litigation and the application of Bayesian probability analysis, to argue that the proper extent of the systemic disparate treatment theory depends on three critical considerations: (1) the background prevalence (or prior probability) of the type of discrimination alleged; (2) the relative strength of the evidentiary signal provided by the proffered statistical evidence; and (3) the parties' relative access to evidence on the element of discriminatory intent. The problem with the Bayesian approach is that there must be some way to determine the background prevalence of discrimination and raising that issue would expand the scope of the litigation to determine such general and abstract question before it would be possible to use statistical techniques in the case to be decided.

Page 154, Add at end of last full paragraph:

A recent article, D. James Greiner, *Causal Inference in Civil Rights Litigation*, 122 HARV. L. REV. 534 (2008), argues that multiple regression analysis should be rejected in favor of a "potential outcomes" approach, which is similar to the but-for standard of causation used in torts and elsewhere. This approach asks the expert to decide what treatment the employees would have received if they were of the opposite sex or race and compares that with the treatment they actually received.

It requires the expert to determine what characteristics the employees had that were relevant to employment *before* the employer perceived their race or sex or were otherwise clearly independent of manipulation by the employer. *But see* Steven Willborn & Ramona Paetzold, *Statistics Is a Plural Word*, 122 HARV. L. REV. 48 (2000) (agreeing that potential outcomes is a useful technique but arguing that Professor Greiner overemphasizes both the deficiencies of multiple regression and the advantages of potential outcomes).

D. Defenses to Disparate Treatment Cases

1. Rebutting the Inference of Discriminatory Intent

Page 167. Add at end of page:

See also Tristin K. Green & Alexandra Kalev, *Discrimination-Reducing Measures at the Relational Level*, 59 HASTINGS L.J. 1435, 1435 (2008) (discrimination-reducing measures should be broadened to address the relational sources of discrimination—social interactions and relations at work that operate to reinforce stereotypes and bias); *see also* Franita Tolson, *The Boundaries of Litigating Unconscious Discrimination: Firm- Based Remedies in Response to a Hostile Judiciary*, 33 DEL. J. CORP. L. 347, 347 (2008) (firms that have been previously exposed to extensive employment discrimination litigation use their market power to force their smaller competitors to adopt a new diversity norm, which Delaware law then memorializes in its case law, thus "transitioning the norm into a rule of law enforceable through the duty to monitor (a species of the duties of care and loyalty)").

2. Bona Fide Occupational Qualifications

Page 183. Add before Buchanan cite in carryover Note 4, *BFOQ Based on Privacy*:

But see Breiner v. Nev. Dep't of Corr., 610 F.3d 1202 (9th Cir. 2010) (risk of sexual abuse of inmates by male officers did not satisfy BFOQ requirements for prison policy restricting certain promotions to females NDOC's policy limiting correctional lieutenant positions at women's prison to female officers because the employers' "acknowledged leadership failure falls far short of providing 'a factual basis for believing that all or substantially all [men] would be unable to safely and effectively perform the duties of the job,' or that it would be "impossible or highly impracticable to determine job fitness"—here, the ability to enforce workplace rules prohibiting sexual misconduct—'on an individualized basis.'"); *But see Henry v. Milwaukee County*, 539 F.3d 573, 581 (7th Cir. 2008) (sex-based shift assignments in juvenile corrections facility violated the statute when the employer could not establish that it was impossible to "rearrange job responsibilities to eliminate or minimize the conflict between the inmates' privacy, security and rehabilitation interests and the employees' rights under Title VII").

Page 183.   Add in Note 5, *BFOQ for Race?* after first sentence:

See Chaney v. Plainfield Healthcare Ctr., 612 F.3d 908 (7th Cir. 2010) (holding that a honoring a patient's request for white caregivers was not a justification for discrimination in job assignments, even if the employer had a good faith belief that it was required by state law to honor such requests).

Page 183.   Add at end of in Note 6, *No Adverse Employment Action*:

In *Breiner v. Nev. Dep't of Corr.*, 610 F.3d 1202, 1208 (9th Cir. 2010), the rejected employer's argument that its reserving several promotions for women had only a "de minimis" impact on the plaintiffs and thus did not violate Title VII; "[i]t is beyond dispute that the denial of a single promotion opportunity such as the one here at issue is actionable under Title VII."

3.   *Voluntary Affirmative Action*

Page 184.   Add at end of first extract:

See generally Kenneth R. Davis, *Wheel of Fortune: A Critique of the "Manifest Imbalance" Requirement for Race-Conscious Affirmative Action*, 43 GEORGIA L. REV. 993 (2009) (critiquing "manifest imbalance as it is currently constructed).

Page 200.   Add a new Note 6:

6. *Is Avoiding Disparate Impact Permissible?* In *Ricci v. DeStefano*, 129 S. Ct. 2658 (2009), reproduced at p. 67 of this Supplement, the Court held that an employer could invalidate a test with disparate impact only if it had a strong basis in evidence for believing that it was in fact illegal, i.e., that it was not justified by business necessity or job relation. Otherwise, reliance on disparate racial impact to reject a test would be actionable disparate treatment.

While Ricci did not expressly discuss the validity of affirmative action cases under the Weber/Johnson analysis, there is at least considerable tension between its analysis and that of the earlier cases. *See* Sachin S. Pandya, Detecting the Stealth Erosion of Precedent: Affirmative Action After *Ricci*, 31 BERKELEY J. EMP. & LAB. L. 2 (2011).

In *United States v. Brennan*, 2011 U.S. App. LEXIS 9455 (2d Cir. May 5, 2011), the Second Circuit distinguished between the affirmative action defense under *Weber/Johnson* and *Ricci's* "strong basis in evidence" defense: the threshold determination is now "whether the race- and sex-conscious action constitutes an affirmative action plan at all." *Id.* at 83. In its view

> when an employer, acting ex ante, although in the light of past discrimination, establishes hiring or promotion procedures designed to promote equal opportunity and eradicate future discrimination, that may constitute an affirmative action plan. But where an employer, already having established its procedures in a certain way — such as through a seniority system — throws out the results of those procedures ex post because of the racial or gender composition of those results, that constitutes an individualized grant of employment benefits which must be individually justified, and not affirmative action

Id. at 99-100. It went on:

> We therefore hold that § 703(a), like § 706(g), draws a distinction between affirmative action plans, which are intended to provide ex ante benefitalics to all members of a racial or gender class, and make-whole relief, which is intended to provide ex post benefitalics to specified individuals who have suffered discrimination. And where this latter form of benefitalics is at issue, the employer may not invoke the "affirmative action" defense of *Johnson* and *Weber.*

Id. at 105.

Page 204.   Add after *Petit* citation in second full paragraph:

See also Martinez v. City of St. Louis, 539 F.3d 857, 860-61 (8th Cir. 2008) (denying any monetary relief in a reverse discrimination suit when the actions of the city were taken pursuant to a constitutionally valid degree).

Page 204.   Add after *But see* citation in second full paragraph:

Rothe Dev. Corp. v. DOD, 545 F.3d 1023, 1040 (Fed. Cir. 2008) ("we will hold in any event that [six statistical] studies do not provide a substantially probative and broad-based statistical foundation necessary for the 'strong basis in evidence' that must be the predicate for nationwide, race-conscious action").

Page 204.   Add at end of second full paragraph:

Angela Onwuachi-Willig, Emily Houh & Mary Campbell, *Cracking the Egg: Which Came First — Stigma or Affirmative Action?*, 96 CAL. L. REV. 1299 (2009) (an empirical study of students at seven state law schools showing "1) minimal, if any, internal stigma felt by minority law students, regardless of whether their schools practiced race-based affirmative action; 2) no statistically significant difference in internal stigma between minority students at affirmative action law school and non-affirmative action law schools; and 3) no significant impact from external stigma").

3 Systemic Disparate Impact Discrimination

A. The Concept of Disparate Impact

Page 212.   Add at end of Note 1, The Backstory:

See also Susan D. Carle, *A Social Movement History of Title VII Disparate Impact Analysis*, 63 FLA. L. REV. 251 (2011).

Page 213.   Add at end of first paragraph of Note 5, *The Scope of Practices Subject to the Disparate Impact Theory:*

See also United States v. Brennan, 2011 U.S. App. LEXIS 9455, 171-74 (2d Cir. May 5, 2011) (rejecting the argument that word-of-mouth recruiting, and limited advertising are not prohibited by Title VII even if they cause a disparate impact because § 703(a)(2), which makes it illegal for an employer "to limit, segregate, or classify his employees or applicants for employment in any way which would deprive or tend to deprive any individual of employment opportunities," does not refer to recruiting, because people who don't even apply for a job because of recruiting discrimination are not even "applicants for employment.").

Page 213.   Add at the end of Note 5, *The Scope of Practices Subject to the Disparate Impact Theory***:**

In *Wal-Mart Stores, Inc. v. Dukes*, 131 S. Ct. 2541 (2011), the Supreme Court decided a significant case involving class actions. that raises significant questions about the continuing viability of *Watson*. See p. 60 of this Supplement (this Chapter) and p. 230 (Chapter 7F) and

Page 222.   Add at end of Note 5, *Clash Between Disparate Treatment and Disparate Impact*:

Revisit this issue when you read *Ricci v. DeStefano*, 129 S. Ct. 2658 (2009), reproduced at p. 67 of this Supplement.

Page 228.   Add at end of first paragraph of Note 1, *Rehashing an Old Title VII Debate*:

However, there continue to be debates about this under the ADEA even after it became clear that the disparate impact theory applies under that statute. *See EEOC v. Allstate Ins. Co.*, 528 F.3d 1042 (8th Cir. 2008) (no rehire policy for former agents was more like an employment practice than like a hiring practice under the provisions of the ADEA paralleling (a)(1) and (a)(2)).

Page 229.   Delete Note 3; replace with:

3. What Policy Produced the Impact? The employer policy at issue in *City of Jackson* was designed to create salary "parity" with other public employers in comparable communities the Southeast. To do that, defendant set up salary comparison groups among its employees and then compared the salaries of its workers in those groups with the salaries of comparable employees of other employers. Salaries were then raised to bring Jackson in line with the comparison groups. The result was that most workers under age 40 received wage increases over 10 percent while fewer than half of those over age 40 did. But, given that the older workers typically earned more, the older workers may well have received larger dollar increases than younger workers, even though the percentage was less.

In this scenario, isn't the Court wrong to say that the plaintiffs did not identify a specific employment policy here? While the ultimate source of the age impact is in the pay structures of other employers, modeling pay on the pay of those other employers seems like a specific practice. How could it be more specific? *See also Allen v. Highlands Hosp. Corp.*, 545 F.3d 387, 404 (6th Cir. 2008) ("the plaintiffs have at best alleged that HHC desired to reduce costs associated with its highly paid workforce, including those costs associated with employees with greater seniority. But the plaintiffs have not established that this corporate desire evolved into an identifiable practice that disproportionately harms workers who are at least 40 years old.").

One possibility is compensation and benefits are simply not the kind of employment practice that should be subject to disparate impact attack. In *Finnegan v. Trans World Air Lines, Inc.*, 967 F.2d 1161 (7th Cir. 1992), the court found that changes in fringe benefits were not subject to attack even though they caused an adverse impact on older workers. After all, any percentage reduction/increase in compensation or certain types of fringe benefits, such as the vacation pay in *Finnegan*, will necessarily have an impact. Is the employer required to use equal percentage wage increases to avoid causing disparate impact on older workers? While doing that would cause an adverse impact on younger workers, they are not protected against by the ADEA if they are younger than age 40. Further, after *Cline,* workers over age 40 are not protected if the benefit flows to workers older than them. *See also* Jonah B. Gelbach, Jonathan Klick & Lesley Wexler, *Passive Discrimination: When Does It Make Sense to Pay Too Little?*, U. CHI. L. REV. 797 (2009) (employers can, either intentionally or not, use fringe benefit structures that sort employees by race and sex "as long as groups systematically differ in their preferences for various employment terms and conditions" in ways that regulators will find hard to prevent).

Page 230.   Delete Note 6; renumber Notes 7, 8, 9 as 6, 7, 8.

Page 231.   Add new principal cases at end of section A:

Meacham v. Knolls Atomic Power Laboratory
128 S. Ct. 2395 (2008)

Justice SOUTER delivered the opinion of the Court.

A provision of the Age Discrimination in Employment Act of 1967 (ADEA) creates an exemption for employer actions "otherwise prohibited" by the ADEA but "based on reasonable factors other than age" (RFOA). §623(f)(1). The question is whether an employer facing a disparate-impact claim and planning to defend on the basis of RFOA must not only produce evidence raising the defense, but also persuade the factfinder of its merit. We hold that the employer must do both.

I

The National Government pays private companies [such as Knolls] to do some of the work maintaining the Nation's fleet of nuclear-powered warships. The demands for naval nuclear reactors changed with the end of the Cold War, and for fiscal year 1996, Knolls was ordered to reduce its work force. Even after a hundred or so employees chose to take the company's ensuing buyout offer, Knolls was left with thirty-some jobs to cut. Petitioners (Meacham, for short) are among those laid off in the resulting "involuntary reduction in force." In order to select those for layoff, Knolls told its managers to score their subordinates on three scales, "performance," "flexibility," and "critical skills."[2] The scores were summed, along with points for years of service, and the totals determined who should be let

---

2. The "performance" score was based on the worker's two most recent appraisals. The "flexibility" instruction read: "Rate the employee's flexibility within the Laboratory. Can his or her documented skills be used in other assignments that will add value to current or future Lab work? Is the employee retrainable for other Lab assignments?" The "critical skills" instruction read: "How critical are the employee's skills to continuing work in the Lab? Is the individual's skill a *key* technical resource for the [Naval Reactors] program? Is the skill readily accessible within the Lab or generally available from the external market?" (emphasis in original).

go. Of the 31 salaried employees laid off, 30 were at least 40 years old.[3] Twenty-eight of them sued. . . . To show a disparate impact, the workers relied on a statistical expert's testimony to the effect that results so skewed according to age could rarely occur by chance;[4] and that the scores for "flexibility" and "criticality," over which managers had the most discretionary judgment, had the firmest statistical ties to the outcomes.

[The Court granted certiorari after the Court of Appeals had, based on *City of Jackson*, held for Knolls.]

II

A

The ADEA's general prohibitions against age discrimination, 29 U.S.C. §§623(a)(c), (e), are subject to a separate provision, §623(f), creating exemptions for employer practices "otherwise prohibited under subsections (a), (b), (c), or (e)." The RFOA exemption is listed in §623(f) alongside one for bona fide occupational qualifications (BFOQ): "It shall not be unlawful for an employer . . . to take any action otherwise prohibited under subsections (a), (b), (c), or (e) . . . where age is a bona fide occupational qualification reasonably necessary to the normal operation of the particular business, or where the differentiation is based on reasonable factors other than age. . . ." §623(f)(1).

Given how the statute reads, with exemptions laid out apart from the prohibitions (and expressly referring to the prohibited conduct as such), it is no surprise that we have already spoken of the BFOQ and RFOA provisions as being among the ADEA's "five affirmative defenses," *Trans World Airlines, Inc.* v. *Thurston*, 469 U.S. 111, 122 (1985). After looking at the statutory text, most lawyers would accept that characterization as a matter of course, thanks to the familiar principle that "[w]hen a proviso . . . carves an exception out of the body of a statute or contract those who set up such exception must prove it." *Javierre* v. *Central Altagracia*, 217 U.S. 502, 508, (1910) (opinion for the Court by Holmes, J.). That longstanding convention is part of the backdrop against which the Congress writes laws, and we respect it unless we have compelling reasons to think that Congress meant to put the burden of persuasion on the other side.

We have never been given any reason for a heterodox take on the RFOA clause's nearest neighbor, and our prior cases recognize that the BFOQ clause establishes an affirmative defense against claims of disparate treatment. *See, e.g.,* *City of Jackson*; *Western Air Lines, Inc.* We have likewise given the affirmative defense construction to the exemption in the Equal Pay Act of 1963 for pay differentials

---

3. For comparison: after the voluntary buyouts, 1,203 out of 2,063 salaried workers (or 58%) were at least 40 years old; and of the 245 who were at risk of involuntary layoff, and therefore included in the rankings scheme, 179 (or 73%) were 40 or over.

4. The expert cut the data in different ways, showing the chances to be 1 in 348,000 (based on a population of all 2,063 salaried workers); 1 in 1,260 (based on a population of the 245 workers at risk of layoff); or 1 in 6,639 (when the analysis was broken down by sections of the company).

based on "any other factor other than sex," *Corning Glass Works* v. *Brennan*, 417 U.S. 188, 196 (1974); and there, we took account of the particular weight given to the interpretive convention already noted, when enforcing the Fair Labor Standards Act of 1938 (FLSA). This focus makes the principle of construction the more instructive in ADEA cases: "[i]n enacting the ADEA, Congress exhibited both a detailed knowledge of the FLSA provisions and their judicial interpretation and a willingness to depart from those provisions regarded as undesirable or inappropriate for incorporation," *Lorillard* v. *Pons*, 434 U.S. 575, 581 (1978). And we have remarked and relied on the "significant indication of Congress' intent in its directive that the ADEA be enforced in accordance with the 'powers, remedies, and procedures' of the FLSA." *Id.* As against this interpretive background, there is no hint in the text that Congress meant §623(f)(1) to march out of step with either the general or specifically FLSA default rules placing the burden of proving an exemption on the party claiming it.

With these principles and prior cases in mind, we find it impossible to look at the text and structure of the ADEA and imagine that the RFOA clause works differently from the BFOQ clause next to it. . . .

If there were any doubt, the stress of the idiom "otherwise prohibited," prefacing the BFOQ and RFOA conditions, would dispel it. [The Court then cited an earlier ADEA case involving employee benefit plans, *Employees Retirement System of Ohio v. Betts*, 492 U.S. 158 (1989), where it had read the provision at issue not to be an affirmative defense. Congress responded by enacting the Older Workers Benefit Protection Act, Pub. L. 101-433, 104 Stat. 978, avowedly to "restore the original congressional intent" that the ADEA's benefits provision be read as an affirmative defense, §101.] What is instructive on the question at hand is that, in clarifying that §623(f)(2) specifies affirmative defenses, Congress not only set the burden in so many words but also added the phrase "otherwise prohibited" as a part of the preface (just as in the text of §623(f)(1)).[11] Congress thus confirmed the natural implication that we find in the "otherwise prohibited" language in §623(f)(1): it refers to an excuse or justification for behavior that, standing alone, violates the statute's prohibition. The amendment in the aftermath of *Betts* shows that Congress understands the phrase the same way we naturally read it, as a clear signal that a defense to what is "otherwise prohibited" is an affirmative defense, entirely the responsibility of the party raising it.

B

Knolls ventures that, regardless, the RFOA provision should be read as mere elaboration on an element of liability. Because it bars liability where action is taken

---

11. Congress surely could not have meant this phrase to contradict its express allocation of the burden, in the same amendment. But that would be the upshot of Knolls's suggestion that the only way to read the word "otherwise" as not redundant in the phrase "otherwise prohibited under subsection (a), (b), (c), or (e)" is to say that the word must refer only to §623(f)(1) itself, implying that §623(f)(1) must be a liability-creating provision for which the burden falls on the plaintiff. Besides, this argument proves too much, for it implies that even the BFOQ exemption is not an affirmative defense.

for reasons "other than age," the argument goes, the provision must be directed not at justifying age discrimination by proof of some extenuating fact but at negating the premise of liability under §623(a)(2), "because of age."

The answer to this argument, however, is *City of Jackson*, where we confirmed that the prohibition in §623(a)(2) extends to practices with a disparate impact, inferring this result in part from the presence of the RFOA provision at issue here. We drew on the recognized distinction between disparate-treatment and disparate-impact forms of liability, and explained that "the very definition of disparate impact" was that "an employer who classifies his employees without respect to age may still be liable under the terms of this paragraph if such classification adversely affects the employee because of that employee's age." (plurality opinion); *id.* (Scalia, J., concurring in part and concurring in judgment) (expressing agreement with "all of the Court's reasoning" in the plurality opinion, but finding it a basis for deference to the EEOC rather than for independent judicial decision). We emphasized that these were the kinds of employer activities, "otherwise prohibited" by §623(a)(2), that were mainly what the statute meant to test against the RFOA condition: because "[i]n disparate-impact cases . . . the allegedly 'otherwise prohibited' activity is not based on age," it is "in cases involving disparate-impact claims that the RFOA provision plays its principal role by precluding liability if the adverse impact was attributable to a nonage factor that was 'reasonable.'" (plurality opinion).

Thus, in *City of Jackson*, we made it clear that in the typical disparate-impact case, the employer's practice is "without respect to age" and its adverse impact (though "because of age") is "attributable to a non-age factor"; so action based on a "factor other than age" is the very premise for disparate-impact liability in the first place, not a negation of it or a defense to it. The RFOA defense in a disparate-impact case, then, is not focused on the asserted fact that a non-age factor was at work; we assume it was. The focus of the defense is that the factor relied upon was a "reasonable" one for the employer to be using. Reasonableness is a justification categorically distinct from the factual condition "because of age" and not necessarily correlated with it in any particular way: a reasonable factor may lean more heavily on older workers, as against younger ones, and an unreasonable factor might do just the opposite.[13]

---

13. The factual causation that §623(a)(2) describes as practices that "deprive or tend to deprive . . . or otherwise adversely affect [employees] . . . because of . . . age" is typically shown by looking to data revealing the impact of a given practice on actual employees. *See, e.g., City of Jackson* (opinion of the Court); cf. *Wards Cove Packing Co.* v. *Atonio*, (under Title VII, "specific causation" is shown, and a "prima facie case" is "establish[ed]," when plaintiff identifies a specific employment practice linked to a statistical disparity); *Watson* v. *Fort Worth Bank & Trust* (plurality opinion) (in Title VII cases, "statistical disparities must be sufficiently substantial that they raise . . . an inference of causation"). This enquiry would be muddled if the value, "reasonableness," were to become a factor artificially boosting or discounting the factual strength of the causal link, or the extent of the measured impact. It would open the door to incoherent undershooting, for example, if defendants were heard to say that an impact is "somewhat less correlated with age, seeing as the factor is a reasonable one"; and it would be overshooting to make them show that the impact is "not correlated with age, and the factor is reasonable, besides."

III . . .

[A]lthough we are now satisfied that the business necessity test should have no place in ADEA disparate-impact cases, we agree with the Government that this conclusion does not stand in the way of our holding that the RFOA exemption is an affirmative defense. . . .

Although *City of Jackson* contains the statement that "*Wards Cove*'s pre-1991 interpretation of Title VII's identical language remains applicable to the ADEA," *City of Jackson* made only two specific references to aspects of the *Wards Cove* interpretation of Title VII that might have "remain[ed] applicable" in ADEA cases. One was to the existence of disparate-impact liability, which *City of Jackson* explained was narrower in ADEA cases than under Title VII. The other was to a plaintiff-employee's burden of identifying which particular practices allegedly cause an observed disparate impact, which is the employee's burden under both the ADEA and the pre-1991 Title VII. Neither of these references, of course, is at odds with the view of RFOA as an affirmative defense. . . .

[To apply both business necessity and RFOA] tests, however, would force the parties to develop (and the court or jury to follow) two overlapping enquiries: first, whether the employment practice at issue (based on a factor other than age) is supported by a business justification; and second, whether that factor is a reasonable one. Depending on how the first enquiry proceeds, a plaintiff might directly contest the force of the employer's rationale, or else try to show that the employer invoked it as a pretext by pointing (for example) to alternative practices with less of a disparate impact. See *Wards Cove* ("first, a consideration of the justifications an employer offers for his use of these practices; and second, the availability of alternative practices to achieve the same business ends, with less racial impact"). But even if the plaintiff succeeded at one or the other, [under this approach] the employer could still avoid liability by proving reasonableness.

. . . At the very least, developing the reasonableness defense would be substantially redundant with the direct contest over the force of the business justification, especially when both enquiries deal with the same, narrowly specified practice. It is not very fair to take the remark about *Wards Cove* in *City of Jackson* as requiring such a wasteful and confusing structure of proof. . . .

IV

As mentioned, where *City of Jackson* did get help from our prior reading of Title VII was in relying on *Wards Cove* to repeat that a plaintiff falls short by merely alleging a disparate impact, or "point[ing] to a generalized policy that leads to such an impact." *City of Jackson*. The plaintiff is obliged to do more: to "isolat[e] and identif[y] the *specific* employment practices that are allegedly responsible for any observed statistical disparities." *Ibid.* (quoting *Wards Cove*). The aim of this requirement, as *City of Jackson* said, is to avoid the "result [of] employers being potentially liable for 'the myriad of innocent causes that may lead to statistical imbalances.'" (quoting *Wards Cove*). And as the outcome in that case shows, the requirement has bite: one sufficient reason for rejecting the employees' challenge was that they "ha[d] done little more than point out that the pay plan at issue [was] relatively less generous to older workers than to younger workers," and "ha[d] not identified any specific test, requirement, or practice within the pay plan that ha[d] an adverse impact on older workers." *City of Jackson*.

Identifying a specific practice is not a trivial burden, and it ought to allay some of the concern raised by Knolls's *amici*, who fear that recognizing an employer's burden of persuasion on an RFOA defense to impact claims will encourage strike suits or nudge plaintiffs with marginal cases into court, in turn inducing employers to alter business practices in order to avoid being sued. It is also to the point that the only thing at stake in this case is the gap between production and persuasion; nobody is saying that even the burden of production should be placed on the plaintiff. And the more plainly reasonable the employer's "factor other than age" is, the shorter the step for that employer from producing evidence raising the defense, to persuading the factfinder that the defense is meritorious. It will be mainly in cases where the reasonableness of the non-age factor is obscure for some reason, that the employer will have more evidence to reveal and more convincing to do in going from production to persuasion.

That said, there is no denying that putting employers to the work of persuading factfinders that their choices are reasonable makes it harder and costlier to defend than if employers merely bore the burden of production; nor do we doubt that this will sometimes affect the way employers do business with their employees. But at the end of the day, *amici*'s concerns have to be directed at Congress, which set the balance where it is, by both creating the RFOA exemption and writing it in the orthodox format of an affirmative defense. We have to read it the way Congress wrote it.

[The Court remanded for a determination of whether the outcome would be different when the burden of proving RFOA was placed on the employer.]

[Justice BREYER took no part in the case, and Justice SCALIA concurred because of the deference he thought due to the EEOC's view that the RFOA provision "is an affirmative defense on which the employer bears the burden of proof," and that, in ADEA disparate-impact suits, "that provision replaces the business-necessity test of *Wards Cove Packing Co.* v. *Atonio*." Justice THOMAS, concurring in part and dissenting in part, reaffirmed his position in *City of Jackson* that disparate-impact claims are not cognizable under the ADEA; he further disagreed with the Court that the RFOA exception "is principally relevant in disparate-impact cases." He concurred, however, because "I agree that the RFOA exception is an affirmative defense—when it arises in disparate-treatment cases."]

NOTES

1. *Jury Trial.* You might have noticed that the jury made the determination of disparate impact in *Meacham*. That is because the ADEA does not distinguish between judge and jury trials on the basis of the theory being litigated. In Title VII cases, however, disparate impact is for the judge to decide. See Note 9, p. 265.

2. *The Significance of the Decision.* *Meacham* resolves two questions: the burden of proof issue on RFOA and the relationship of RFOA to business necessity. *City of Jackson* had left both questions up in the air. *Meacham* takes a plaintiff-friendly

reading of the first question, but the significance of its answer to the second question is less clear. On principle, the substance of the rule would seem to be the more important issue: although the placement of burdens of persuasion can affect the outcome of close cases, the standard actually applied is more important to all cases. *Meacham*, like *City of Jackson*, was greeted by many as a plaintiff-oriented decision. Are you so sure it is?

3. *Comparing the Standards.* Under *Wards Cove*, assuming plaintiffs proved an employment practice had a disparity of impact, defendant would have had to put into evidence its business necessity. At that point, plaintiff would have to bear the burden of persuasion that (1) the practice didn't "serve[], in a significant way, the legitimate employment goals of the employer" or (2) other practices "without a similarly undesirable" age effect would be "equally effective" in meeting the employer's legitimate interests. See p. 218.

That burden is now out the window: plaintiff need not prove anything beyond the impact. Rather, the defendant must prove that the practice is a reasonable factor other than age. But what makes a factor "reasonable"? Is it that it serves the employer's legitimate goals? In a significant way? And what about alternative business practices? Is a practice nevertheless "reasonable" if it serves legitimate goals even though another equally effective alternative would also do so?

The only thing that seems clear after *Meacham* is that, whatever the problems with the business necessity defense, the RFOA defense is even vaguer. Of course, if RFOA essentially recapitulates *Wards Cove*-style business necessity analysis under another name, the decision will be plaintiff-friendly because *Meacham* will have shifted the burden on that issue from plaintiff to defendant. But if the notion of "reasonableness" is less demanding than showing a business necessity (which seems likely linguistically), the net result will be fewer successful ADEA disparate impact cases. *See generally* Judith J. Johnson, *Reasonable Factors Other Than Age: The Emerging Specter of Ageist Stereotypes*, 33 SEATTLE UNIV. L. R. 49 (2009).

4. *Proposed EEOC Regulations.* The EEOC has promulgated proposed regulations to clarify the meaning of the RFOA defense. http://edocket.access.gpo.gov/2010/2010-3126.htm. The operative language would amend 29 C.F.R. §1625.7. One thrust of the regulation is to ensure that the factor is truly "other than age." Thus, it cautions that "When disparate impact results from giving supervisors unchecked discretion to engage in subjective decision making, however, the impact may, in fact, be based on age because the supervisors to whom decision making was delegated may have acted on the bases of conscious or unconscious age-based stereotypes." §1625.7(b)(2). Assuming that the factor is other than age, the regulations address what makes such a factor reasonable. Such a factor

is one that is objectively reasonable when viewed from the position of a reasonable employer (i.e., a prudent employer mindful of its responsibilities under the ADEA) under like circumstances. To establish the RFOA defense, an employer must show that the employment practice was both reasonably designed to further or achieve a legitimate business purpose and administered in a way that reasonably achieves that purpose in light of the particular facts and circumstances that were known, or should have been known, to the employer.

§1625.7(b)(1). This suggests a kind of "industry practice" approach, which is confirmed by a list to relevant factors, including "(i) Whether the employment practice and the manner of its implementation are common business practices." Other factors in the reasonableness inquiry focus on the employer's effort to define the practice, apply it fairly, and assess its impact on older workers. The proposed regulations would also take a kind of sliding scale approach to reasonableness; thus, another factor looks to

> (v) The severity of the harm to individuals within the protected age group, in terms of both the degree of injury and the numbers of persons adversely affected, and the extent to which the employer took preventive or corrective steps to minimize the severity of the harm, in light of the burden of undertaking such steps;

A factor final looks to "(vi) Whether other options were available and the reasons the employer selected the option it did."

B. The Structure of Disparate Impact Law after the 1991 Civil Rights Act

1. Plaintiff's Proof of a Prima Facie Case

a. A Particular Employment Practice

Page 234. Add to end of Note 1 *Employer Practices Subject to Disparate Impact.*

In *Wal-Mart Stores, Inc. v. Dukes,* 131 S. Ct. 2541 (2011), the Supreme Court decided a significant case involving class actions. See p. 230 of this Supplement for the opinion and its treatment of the Rule 23 issues. The basic thrust of plaintiffs' claim was that Wal-Mart's policy of granting unstructured and unreviewed discretion to store managers to make pay and promotion decisions was a practice of systemic disparate treatment discrimination. There was also some discussion of systemic disparate impact law. Writing for the Court in a 5-4 decision (with Justice Ginsburg joined by Justices Breyer, Sotomayor, and Kagen in dissent), Justice Scalia rejected plaintiffs' attempt to have the action certified as a class action. In deciding the class action issues, he indicated that the substantive bases for the claim were relevant to determining the class action issues:

> "[C]lass determination generally involves considerations that are enmeshed in the factual and legal issues comprising the plaintiff's cause of action." . . . In this case, proof of commonality [for class action purposes] necessarily overlaps with respondents' merits contention that Wal-Mart engages in *a pattern or practice* of discrimination.

Quoting *General Telephone Co. of Southwest* v. *Falcon,* 457 U.S. 147, 156 (1982), Justice Scalia then identified e two factual patterns where a claim of pattern or practice discrimination could support a finding of commonality sufficient to establish a class action:

First, if the employer "used a biased testing procedure to evaluate both applicants for employment and incumbent employees, a class action on behalf of every applicant or employee who might have been prejudiced by the test clearly would satisfy the commonality and typicality requirements of Rule 23(a)." Second, "[s]ignificant proof that an employer operated under a general policy of discrimination. . . . The first manner of bridging the gap obviously has no application here; Wal-Mart has no testing procedure or other company-wide evaluation method that can be charged with bias. The whole point of permitting discretionary decisionmaking is to avoid evaluating employees under a common standard.

Presumably using such a "testing procedure" would be an employment practice implemented by agents of the employer pursuant to the employer's established policy. In *Wal-Mart,* the policy of permitting discretionary decisionmaking does result in its agents exercising discretion in making individual pay and promotion decisions. Nevertheless, the Court concluded that Wal-Mart's authorizing its agents to use discretion is not "a common standard." Why is the company-wide policy and subsequent use of discretion by individual managers not an "evaluation method?" Or is delegated discretion "an evaluation method" that cannot be the basis of a class action challenge to its use because the method does not produce test scores?

Justice Scalia then turned to explicit systemic disparate treatment analysis what he identified as the second type of factual pattern — "an employer operated under a general policy of discrimination." See Chapter 2C for further discussion. Instead of applying the analyses of systemic disparate treatment claims established in *Teamsters* and *Hazelwood,* Justice Scalia then appears to loop back to disparate impact analysis. While correctly concluding that a policy of using discretion to make employment decisions is not, by itself, an express policy of discrimination Justice Scalia then acknowledges that the administration of a policy that does not discriminate on its face can be subject to disparate impact analysis if plaintiffs identify a "specific employment practice":

In the landmark case of ours [*Watson*] which held that giving discretion to lower-level supervisors can be the basis of Title VII liability under a disparate-impact theory, the plurality opinion conditioned that holding on the corollary that merely proving that the discretionary system has produced a racial or sexual disparity *is not enough.*" [T]he plaintiff must begin by identifying the specific employment practice that is challenged."That is all the more necessary when a class of plaintiffs is sought to be certified. Other than the bare existence of delegated discretion, respondents have identified no "specific employment practice" — much less one that ties all their 1.5 million claims together. Merely showing that Wal-Mart's policy of discretion has produced an overall sex-based disparity does not suffice.

Did Justice Scalia use disparate impact theory to cut off plaintiffs' systemic disparate treatment claim? Regardless, what is his basis for concluding that a policy of delegated discretion is not an "employment practice" for purposes of establishing a systemic disparate impact claim?

An important question is what, if any, impact *Wal-Mart* has on *Watson.* Justice Ginsberg's dissent stressed that in *Watson* four different supervisors rejected plaintiff's repeated attempts to be promoted to a number of different job openings, and yet she successfully brought an individual discrimination claim based on a disparate impact theory. Would Watson have been precluded from bringing a class action claiming disparate impact discrimination even though the Court upheld her individual claim of disparate impact discrimination? In other word, is *Wal-Mart* only about class action law and not about disparate impact law?

If a potential client asks you to represent her because her employer, a large company, had a policy of giving discretion to lower-level managers who had exercised that discretion by denying her attempts to be promoted and that the general use by managers of that discretion had an adverse impact on women, would you advise her that:

1. Subjective employment decisions made pursuant to a policy allowing discretion cannot be challenged using disparate impact theory;
2. Subjective employment decisions made pursuant to a policy allowing discretion can be challenged in an individual disparate impact case but is not the basis for a class action; or
3. A company policy authorizing the use of subjective decisionmaking by managers insulates the decisions of those managers from challenge under any systemic theory of discrimination?

Page 236.   In Note 5, *Volitional Exception?*, replace SSRN cite for Peter Siegelman article with:

Contributory Disparate Impacts in Employment Discrimination Law, 49 Wm. & Mary L. Rev. 515, 568 (2007) ("not all disparities are the same: there are some instances in which plaintiffs could eliminate or reduce disparities at a reasonable cost to themselves. When this is possible, the law should encourage them to do so");

Page 242.   Add at end of Note 3, *Choice of Labor Market as a Particular Employment Practice*:

EEOC v. Allstate Ins. Co., 528 F.3d 1042 (8th Cir. 2008) (no-rehire policy of former agents could be analyzed by looking to (1) the total number of employees subject to the rehire policy ages 40 and older compared to the total number of employees under 40 who were subject to the rehire policy; (2) the employees subject to the rehire policy with Allstate's overall workforce; and (3) the average age of employees subject to the rehire policy with those not subject to the policy, i.e., the rest of Allstate's general workforce).

Page 244.   Add at end of Note 6, *Incapable of Separation for Analysis*:

McClain v. Lufkin Indus., 519 F.3d 264, 279 (5th Cir. 2008) (no error in analyzing several employment practices as one where the seniority system was subject to considerable managerial discretion, as was the treatment of absenteeism).

Page 245.   Add new Note 8(a):

8(A). *Is Disparate Impact Constitutional?* In *Ricci v. DeStefano*, 129 S. Ct. 2658 (2009), reproduced at p. 67 of this Supplement, the employer, the City of New Haven, administered a civil service test for promotions in its fire department. The results showed a disparate impact against minorities, leading the city to invalidate the test and refuse to make any promotions based on it. White firefighters sued under both Title VII and the Equal Protection Clause, claiming that the decision was racially motivated. The district court, and a badly divided Second Circuit, found that there was no actionable conduct: the need to avoid practices with a disparate impact justified the city's action. The Supreme Court, while it agreed that avoidance of disparate impact liability could sometimes justify disparate treatment, required a "strong basis in evidence" for disparate impact liability. Finding no such basis, the majority granted summary judgment to the white firefighters, which allowed it to avoid the equal protection question. However, Justice Scalia, concurring, questioned whether the theory would survive constitutional scrutiny. *See* Sullivan, *The World Turned Upside Down*, Note 8 *supra*. *See also* Richard Primus, The Future of Disparate Impact, 108 MICH. L. REV. 1341 (2010) Kenji Yoshino, The New Equal Protection, 124 HARV. L. REV. 747 (2011).

Page 253.   Add at end of carryover paragraph:

See also Stagi v. AMTRAK, 391 F. App'x 133 (3d Cir. 2010) (approving disparate impact challenge to requirement that union-represented employees work at least one year in their current position before they could be considered for promotion to a management job; in so doing, the court found a showing of "statistical significance" regarding the sex impact of the challenged rule to be sufficient to avoid summary judgment and rejected any further requirement of "practical significance").

2.   *Defendant's Options*

b.   Business Necessity and Job Relation

Page 263.   Add before *IBEW* cite in Note 4, *The Business Necessity Standard and Lanning II*:

Shollenbarger v. Planes Moving & Storage, 297 F. App'x 483 (6th Cir. 2008) (while a prima facie case was established by the employer's decision to confine a reduction in force to female-heavy departments and not male-heavy ones, employer had legitimate business justification for selecting those departments for RIF, because they dealt directly with customers and were more affected by declining business while predominantly male departments were staffed largely with seasonal workers who had already left at end of peak summer season);

Page 266. Add a new Note 15:

15. There has recently been renewed debate concerning the application of the disparate impact theory to state licensing requirements. Direct suits against the licensing agencies because their practices had a disparate impact on racial grounds have been uniformly unsuccessful. *E.g., Haddock v. Bd. of Dental Exam'rs,* 777 F.2d 462 (9th Cir. 1985); *Fields v. Hallsville Indep. Sch. Dist.,* 906 F.2d 1017 (5th Cir. 1990); *George v. New Jersey Bd. of Veterinary Med. Exam'rs,* 794 F.2d 113 (3d Cir. 1986). Until recently, the major exception to this is where the requirements are imposed by a state agency that the court views as essentially an employer because its rules apply only to public, as opposed to private, schools. *Association of Mexican Am. Educators v. California,* 231 F.3d 572, 582 (9th Cir. 2000) (en banc) (state agency had an indirect employment relationship based on "the state's high level of involvement in the operation of local public schools").

More recently, however, the Second Circuit held that a city board of education would have to validate a test with a disparate impact even though the test was required by state law for "permanent" city teachers. *Gulino v. N.Y. State Educ. Dep't,* 460 F.3d 361 (2d Cir. 2006). The argument can be framed as whether Title VII preempts state law that would require discrimination in employment by the use of practices with a disparate impact. *See* 42 U.S.C. §2000e-7 ("This title does not affect any law of any State or political subdivision "other than any such law which purports to require or permit the doing of any act which would be an unlawful employment practice" under Title VII). See the debate between Professors Masinter and Bagenstos on Workplace Prof Blog, December 5, 2007, http://lawprofessors.typepad.com/laborprof_blog/2007/12/masinter-on-gul.html.

C. Section 703(h) Exceptions

Page 281. Add at end of Note 5, *Differential Validation*:

In *Ricci v. DeStefano,* 129 S. Ct. 2658 (2009), reproduced at p. 67 of this Supplement, the Court adverted to §703(l): "If an employer cannot rescore a test based on the candidates' race, §2000e-2(l), then it follows *a fortiori* that it may not take the greater step of discarding the test altogether to achieve a more desirable racial distribution of promotion-eligible candidates — absent a strong basis in evidence that the test was deficient and that discarding the results is necessary to avoid violating the disparate-impact provision." This validates the *Billish* approach.

4 The Interrelation of the Three Theories of Discrimination

A. The Interrelationship of Individual and Systemic Disparate Treatment

Page 298.   Delete Note 3; replace with:

3. *Why Isn't* Baylie *a Systemic Case?* The Seventh Circuit does not explicitly address the issue, but *Baylie* implies that systemic disparate treatment can be invoked only in the context of a class action or a government enforcement action. These are, in fact, the two situations in which the theory has been applied by the Supreme Court in *Teamsters/Hazelwood* and *Franks*. Some courts have explicitly held that systemic disparate treatment is limited to these settings. *E.g., Davis v. Coca-Cola Bottling Co. Consol.*, 516 F.3d 955, 967 (11th Cir. 2008); *Celestine v. Petroleos de Venezuella SA*, 266 F.3d 343, 355-56 (5th Cir. 2001); *Gilty v. Oak Park*, 919 F.2d 1247, 1251 (7th Cir, 1991). The rationale appears to be that systemic treatment is a class concept and therefore applicable only in class actions. Some older cases, however, hold that a burden shift is appropriate even in an individual case where plaintiff can prove a pattern or practice of discrimination. *See Davis v. Califano*, 613 F.2d 957 224 (D.C. Cir. 1979). In the present era, there is certainly judicial skepticism towards class actions of any kind. Is this another example? What policy is served by truncating the use of class approaches in litigation? Does *Wal-Mart Stores v. Dukes*, see pp. 43, 60, and 230 of this Supplement, cast light on the question?

Page 298.   In Note 5, *Non-statistical Systemic Proof*, correct *Sun v. Bd. of Trs.* cite; replace with:

Sun v. Bd. of Trs., 473 F.3d 799, 813 (7th Cir. 2007)

Page 299. In carryover of Note 6, *Same Decision Maker?*, delete from Mendelsohn cite to end of paragraph; replace with:

See Mendelsohn v. Sprint/United Mgmt. Co., 552 U.S. 379, 387-388 (2008) (it would have been an abuse of discretion to apply excluding "me too" evidence since such rulings should be made in the context in which they arise, taking into account both relevance and the risk of unfair prejudice).

B. *The Relationship Between Individual Disparate Treatment and Disparate Impact*

Page 299. Correct the Seicshnaydre citation in first sentence of last paragraph as follows:

See Stacy Seicshnaydre, *Is the Road to Disparate Impact Paved with Good Intentions?: Stuck on State of Mind in Antidiscrimination Law*, 42 WAKE FOREST L. REV. 1141 (2008),

Page 300. Add at end of first paragraph:

See also Lopez v. Pacific Maritime Association, 636 F.3d 1197 (9th Cir. 2011) (plaintiff did not establish a disparate impact on drug addicts from defendant's "one-strike rule," which disqualified all job applicants who tested positive for drug use, regardless of whether they were addicted).

C. *The Relationship Between Systemic Disparate Treatment and Disparate Impact*

2. *Intent to Discriminate: The Dividing Line Between the Two Systemic Theories*

Page 302. Delete first full paragraph; replace with the following:

Raytheon reinforces the intent notion and sets out a litmus test: An employer cannot intentionally discriminate on the basis of a particular trait if it does not know of the trait. Obviously, the absence of knowledge is more likely where many disabilities are concerned than for race, age, or sex, but *Raytheon* has application even in such cases (as where a higher-level manager makes a decision without knowing the race of those affected). *See McDowell v. T-Mobile USA, Inc.*, 307 F. App'x 531, 533 (2d Cir. 2009) (court found no evidence that the adverse action against the plaintiff was based upon his race because the decision was made by a high level decision maker who had never met the plaintiff and was unaware of his race); *Woodman v. WWOR-TV, Inc.*, 411 F.3d 69, 90 (2d Cir. 2005) ("ADEA plaintiff who is replaced by a significantly younger worker must offer some evidence of a defendant's knowledge as to the significant age discrepancy to support a prima facie inference of discriminatory intent."). The *Raytheon* litmus test can also apply to areas of Title VII such as discrimination on account of religion, see Section 5D, p. 421, and perhaps even national origin.

D. Reconciling the Tension Between Disparate Treatment and Disparate Impact

Page 316.   Add new principal case before Problem 4.2:

Ricci v. DeStefano
129 S. Ct. 2658 (2009)

Justice KENNEDY delivered the opinion of the Court.

In the fire department of New Haven, Connecticut — as in emergency-service agencies throughout the Nation — firefighters prize their promotion to and within the officer ranks. An agency's officers command respect within the department and in the whole community; and, of course, added responsibilities command increased salary and benefits. Aware of the intense competition for promotions, New Haven, like many cities, relies on objective examinations to identify the best qualified candidates.

In 2003, 118 New Haven firefighters took examinations to qualify for promotion to the rank of lieutenant or captain. Promotion examinations in New Haven (or City) were infrequent, so the stakes were high. The results would determine which firefighters would be considered for promotions during the next two years, and the order in which they would be considered. Many firefighters studied for months, at considerable personal and financial cost.

When the examination results showed that white candidates had outperformed minority candidates, the mayor and other local politicians opened a public debate that turned rancorous. Some firefighters argued the tests should be discarded because the results showed the tests to be discriminatory. They threatened a discrimination lawsuit if the City made promotions based on the tests. Other firefighters said the exams were neutral and fair. And they, in turn, threatened a discrimination lawsuit if the City, relying on the statistical racial disparity, ignored the test results and denied promotions to the candidates who had performed well. In the end the City took the side of those who protested the test results. It threw out the examinations.

Certain white and Hispanic firefighters who likely would have been promoted based on their good test performance sued the City and some of its officials. . . .

The District Court granted summary judgment for the defendants, and the Court of Appeals affirmed.

We conclude that race-based action like the City's in this case is impermissible under Title VII unless the employer can demonstrate a strong basis in evidence that, had it not taken the action, it would have been liable under the disparate-impact statute. The respondents, we further determine, cannot meet that threshold standard. As a result, the City's action in discarding the tests was a violation of Title VII. In light of our ruling under the statutes, we need not reach the question whether respondents' actions may have violated the Equal Protection Clause.

I . . .

A . . .

[The promotion process was governed by the city charter, which included a civil service merit system as determined by job-related tests and a collective bargaining agreement with the firefighters' union. The CBA required that any written promotion examination would account for 60 percent and an oral examination 40 percent of each applicant's total score. To sit for the examinations, the collective bargaining agreement set certain experience and education requirements. For promotion, test-takers were ranked by score, and the city charter imposed a "rule of three"—whoever was promoted had to be among the top three scorers.]

After reviewing bids from various consultants, the City hired Industrial/Organizational Solutions, Inc. (IOS) to develop and administer the examinations, at a cost to the City of $100,000. IOS is an Illinois company that specializes in designing entry-level and promotional examinations for fire and police departments. In order to fit the examinations to the New Haven Department, IOS began the test-design process by performing job analyses to identify the tasks, knowledge, skills, and abilities that are essential for the lieutenant and captain positions. IOS representatives interviewed incumbent captains and lieutenants and their supervisors. They rode with and observed other on-duty officers. Using information from those interviews and ride-alongs, IOS wrote job-analysis questionnaires and administered them to most of the incumbent battalion chiefs, captains, and lieutenants in the Department. At every stage of the job analyses, IOS, by deliberate choice, oversampled minority firefighters to ensure that the results—which IOS would use to develop the examinations—would not unintentionally favor white candidates.

With the job-analysis information in hand, IOS developed the written examinations to measure the candidates' job-related knowledge. For each test, IOS compiled a list of training manuals, Department procedures, and other materials to use as sources for the test questions. IOS presented the proposed sources to the New Haven fire chief and assistant fire chief for their approval. Then, using the approved sources, IOS drafted a multiple-choice test for each position. Each test had 100 questions, as required by CSB rules, and was written below a 10th-grade reading level. After IOS prepared the tests, the City opened a 3-month study period. It gave candidates a list that identified the source material for the questions, including the specific chapters from which the questions were taken.

IOS developed the oral examinations as well. These concentrated on job skills and abilities. Using the job-analysis information, IOS wrote hypothetical situations to test incident-command skills, firefighting tactics, interpersonal skills, leadership, and management ability, among other things. Candidates would be presented with these hypotheticals and asked to respond before a panel of three assessors.

IOS assembled a pool of 30 assessors who were superior in rank to the positions being tested. At the City's insistence (because of controversy surrounding previous examinations), all the assessors came from outside Connecticut. IOS submitted the assessors' resumes to City officials for approval. They were battalion chiefs, assistant chiefs, and chiefs from departments of similar sizes to New Haven's throughout the country. Sixty-six percent of the panelists were minorities, and each of the nine three-member assessment panels contained two minority members. IOS trained the panelists for several hours on the day before it administered the examinations, teaching them how to score the candidates' responses consistently using checklists of desired criteria.

Candidates took the examinations in November and December 2003. Seventy-seven candidates completed the lieutenant examination—43 whites, 19 blacks, and 15 Hispanics. Of those, 34 candidates passed—25 whites, 6 blacks, and 3 Hispanics. Eight lieutenant positions were vacant at the time of the examination. As the rule of three operated, this meant that the top 10 candidates were eligible for an immediate promotion to lieutenant. All 10 were white. Subsequent vacancies would have allowed at least 3 black candidates to be considered for promotion to lieutenant.

Forty-one candidates completed the captain examination—25 whites, 8 blacks, and 8 Hispanics. Of those, 22 candidates passed—16 whites, 3 blacks, and 3 Hispanics. Seven captain positions were vacant at the time of the examination. Under the rule of three, 9 candidates were eligible for an immediate promotion to captain—7 whites and 2 Hispanics.

B

[Although the City's contract with IOS contemplated "a technical report" by IOS after the examinations, no such report was ever issued. Instead, in January 2004, City officials, including its counsel, Thomas Ude, met with IOS Vice President Chad Legel, who had led the IOS team that developed and administered the tests. The] City officials expressed concern that the tests had discriminated against minority candidates. Legel defended the examinations' validity, stating that any numerical disparity between white and minority candidates was likely due to various external factors and was in line with results of the Department's previous promotional examinations.

Several days after the meeting, Ude sent a letter to the CSB [New Haven Civil Service Board] purporting to outline its duties with respect to the examination results. Ude stated that under federal law, "a statistical demonstration of disparate impact," standing alone, "constitutes a sufficiently serious claim of racial discrimination to serve as a predicate for employer-initiated, voluntar[y] remedies — even . . . race-conscious remedies."

1

The CSB first met to consider certifying the results on January 22, 2004. Tina Burgett, director of the City's Department of Human Resources, opened the meeting by telling the CSB that "there is a significant disparate impact on these two exams." She distributed lists showing the candidates' races and scores (written, oral, and composite) but not their names. Ude also described the test results as reflecting "a very significant disparate impact," and he outlined possible grounds for the CSB's refusing to certify the results.

Although they did not know whether they had passed or failed, some firefighter-candidates spoke at the first CSB meeting in favor of certifying the test results. Michael Blatchley stated that "[e]very one" of the questions on the written examination "came from the [study] material. . . . [I]f you read the materials and you studied the material, you would have done well on the test." Frank Ricci stated that the test questions were based on the Department's own rules and procedures and on "nationally recognized" materials that represented the "accepted standard[s]" for firefighting. Ricci stated that he had "several learning disabilities," including dyslexia; that he had spent more than $1,000 to purchase the materials and pay his neighbor to read them on tape so he could "give it [his] best shot"; and that he had studied "8 to 13 hours a day to prepare" for the test. "I don't even know if I made it," Ricci told the CSB, "[b]ut the people who passed should be promoted. When your life's on the line, second best may not be good enough."

Other firefighters spoke against certifying the test results. They described the test questions as outdated or not relevant to firefighting practices in New Haven. Gary Tinney stated that source materials "came out of New York. . . . Their makeup of their city and everything is totally different than ours." And they criticized the test materials, a full set of which cost about $500, for being too expensive and too long.

2

[There was a second CSB meeting on February 5, at which both proponents and opponents of the test appeared. Some asked for a validation study to determine whether the tests were job-related, while others suggested that "the City could 'adjust' the test results to 'meet the criteria of having a certain amount of minorities get elevated to the rank of Lieutenant and Captain.'"]

3

At a third meeting, on February 11, Legel addressed the CSB on behalf of IOS. Legel stated that IOS had previously prepared entry-level firefighter examinations for the City but not a promotional examination. He explained that IOS had developed examinations for departments in communities with demographics similar to New Haven's, including Orange County, Florida; Lansing, Michigan; and San Jose, California.

Legel explained the exam-development process to the CSB. . . . Near the end of his remarks, Legel "implor[ed] anyone that had . . . concerns to review the content of the exam. In my professional opinion, it's facially neutral. There's nothing in those examinations . . . that should cause somebody to think that one group would perform differently than another group."

4

At the next meeting, on March 11, the CSB heard from three witnesses it had selected to "tell us a little bit about their views of the testing, the process, [and] the methodology." The first, Christopher Hornick, spoke to the CSB by telephone. Hornick is an industrial/organizational psychologist from Texas who operates a consulting business that "direct[ly]" competes with IOS. Hornick, who had not "stud[ied] the test at length or in detail" and had not "seen the job analysis data," told the CSB that the scores indicated a "relatively high adverse impact." He stated that "[n]ormally, whites outperform ethnic minorities on the majority of standardized testing procedures," but that he was "a little surprised" by the disparity in the candidates' scores — although "[s]ome of it is fairly typical of what we've seen in other areas of the countr[y] and other tests." Hornick stated that the "adverse impact on the written exam was somewhat higher but generally in the range that we've seen professionally."

When asked to explain the New Haven test results, Hornick opined in the telephone conversation that the collective-bargaining agreement's requirement of using written and oral examinations with a 60/40 composite score might account for the statistical disparity. He also stated that "[b]y not having anyone from within the [D]epartment review" the tests before they were administered — a limitation the City had imposed to protect the security of the exam questions — "you inevitably get things in there" that are based on the source materials but are not relevant to New Haven. Hornick suggested that testing candidates at an "assessment center" rather than using written and oral examinations "might serve [the City's] needs better." Hornick stated that assessment centers, where candidates face real-world situations and respond just as they would in the field, allow candidates "to demonstrate how they would address a particular problem as opposed to just verbally saying it or identifying the correct option on a written test."

Hornick made clear that he was "not suggesting that [IOS] somehow created a test that had adverse impacts that it should not have had." He described the IOS examinations as "reasonably good test[s]." He stated that the CSB's best option might be to "certify the list as it exists" and work to change the process for future tests, including by "[r]ewriting the Civil Service Rules." Hornick concluded his telephonic remarks by telling the CSB that "for the future," his company "certainly would like to help you if we can."

[The Court then described at length further proceedings, including (1) statements by a Homeland Security fire program specialist who viewed the questions as job-relevant, and (2) statements by a Boston College professor specializing in "race and culture as they influence performance on tests," who had not reviewed the test themselves but viewed the racial impact as consistent with results across the country. The City's counsel argued against the tests, claiming that they "had one of the most severe adverse impacts that he had seen" and that "there are much better alternatives to identifying [firefighting] skills." He offered his "opinion that promotions . . . as a result of these tests would not be consistent with federal law." The mayor's representative took a similar tack. Ultimately, the CSB voted 2 to 2 on the use of the test results, which meant that the results would not be certified.]

C

The CSB's decision not to certify the examination results led to this lawsuit. The plaintiffs—who are the petitioners here—are 17 white firefighters and 1 Hispanic firefighter who passed the examinations but were denied a chance at promotions when the CSB refused to certify the test results. They include the named plaintiff, Frank Ricci, who addressed the CSB at multiple meetings. . . .

[The District Court granted summary judgment for respondents, and the Second Circuit affirmed.] We now reverse.

II . . .

A

Title VII prohibits employment discrimination on the basis of race, color, religion, sex, or national origin. Title VII prohibits both intentional discrimination (known as "disparate treatment") as well as, in some cases, practices that are not intended to discriminate but in fact have a disproportionately adverse effect on minorities (known as "disparate impact").

As enacted in 1964, Title VII's principal nondiscrimination provision held employers liable only for disparate treatment. That section retains its original wording today. It makes it unlawful for an employer "to fail or refuse to hire or to discharge any individual, or otherwise to discriminate against any individual with respect to his compensation, terms, conditions, or privileges of employment, because of such individual's race, color, religion, sex, or national origin." §2000e-2(a)(1). Disparate-treatment cases present "the most easily understood type of discrimination," *Teamsters v. United States,* and occur where an employer has "treated [a] particular person less favorably than others because of" a protected trait. *Watson v. Fort Worth Bank & Trust.* A disparate-treatment plaintiff must establish "that the defendant had a discriminatory intent or motive" for taking a job-related action.

The Civil Rights Act of 1964 did not include an express prohibition on policies or practices that produce a disparate impact. But in *Griggs v. Duke Power Co.,* the Court interpreted the Act to prohibit, in some cases, employers' facially neutral practices that, in fact, are "discriminatory in operation." The *Griggs* Court stated that the "touchstone" for disparate-impact liability is the lack of "business necessity": "If an employment practice which operates to exclude [minorities] cannot be shown to be related to job performance, the practice is prohibited." Under those precedents, if an employer met its burden by showing that its practice was job-related, the plaintiff was required to show a legitimate alternative that would have resulted in less discrimination.

Twenty years after *Griggs,* the Civil Rights Act of 1991 was enacted. The Act included a provision codifying the prohibition on disparate-impact discrimination. That provision is now in force along with the disparate-treatment section already noted. Under the disparate-impact statute, a plaintiff establishes a prima facie violation by showing that an employer uses "a particular employment practice that causes a disparate impact on the basis of race, color, religion, sex, or national origin." An employer may defend against liability by demonstrating that the practice is "job related for the position in question and consistent with business necessity." Even if the employer meets that burden, however, a plaintiff may still succeed by showing that the employer refuses to adopt an available alternative employment practice that has less disparate impact and serves the employer's legitimate needs.

B

Petitioners allege that when the CSB refused to certify the captain and lieutenant exam results based on the race of the successful candidates, it discriminated against them in violation of Title VII's disparate-treatment provision. The City counters that its decision was permissible because the tests "appear[ed] to violate Title VII's disparate-impact provisions."

Our analysis begins with this premise: The City's actions would violate the disparate-treatment prohibition of Title VII absent some valid defense. All the evidence demonstrates that the City chose not to certify the examination results because of the statistical disparity based on race—*i.e.*, how minority candidates had performed when compared to white candidates. As the District Court put it, the City rejected the test results because "too many whites and not enough minorities would be promoted were the lists to be certified." Without some other justification, this express, race-based decisionmaking violates Title VII's command that employers cannot take adverse employment actions because of an individual's race.

The District Court did not adhere to this principle, however. It held that respondents' "motivation to avoid making promotions based on a test with a racially disparate impact . . . does not, as a matter of law, constitute discriminatory intent." And the Government makes a similar argument in this Court. It contends that the "structure of Title VII belies any claim that an employer's intent to comply with Title VII's disparate-impact provisions constitutes prohibited discrimination on the basis of race." But both of those statements turn upon the City's objective — avoiding disparate-impact liability — while ignoring the City's conduct in the name of reaching that objective. Whatever the City's ultimate aim — however well intentioned or benevolent it might have seemed — the City made its employment decision because of race. The City rejected the test results solely because the higher scoring candidates were white. The question is not whether that conduct was discriminatory but whether the City had a lawful justification for its race-based action.

We consider, therefore, whether the purpose to avoid disparate-impact liability excuses what otherwise would be prohibited disparate-treatment discrimination. Courts often confront cases in which statutes and principles point in different directions. Our task is to provide guidance to employers and courts for situations when these two prohibitions could be in conflict absent a rule to reconcile them. In providing this guidance our decision must be consistent with the important purpose of Title VII — that the workplace be an environment free of discrimination, where race is not a barrier to opportunity.

With these principles in mind, we turn to the parties' proposed means of reconciling the statutory provisions. . . . Petitioners would have us hold that, under Title VII, avoiding unintentional discrimination cannot justify intentional discrimination. That assertion, however, ignores the fact that, by codifying the disparate-impact provision in 1991, Congress has expressly prohibited both types of discrimination. We must interpret the statute to give effect to both provisions where possible. We cannot accept petitioners' broad and inflexible formulation.

Petitioners next suggest that an employer in fact must be in violation of the disparate-impact provision before it can use compliance as a defense in a disparate-treatment suit. Again, this is overly simplistic and too restrictive of Title VII's purpose. The rule petitioners offer would run counter to what we have recognized as Congress's intent that "voluntary compliance" be "the preferred means of achieving the objectives of Title VII." *Firefighters v. Cleveland*, 478 U.S. 501, 515 (1986); see also *Wygant v. Jackson Bd. of Ed.*, 476 U.S. 267, 290 (1986) (O'Connor, J., concurring in part and concurring in judgment). Forbidding employers to act unless they know, with certainty, that a practice violates the disparate-impact provision would bring compliance efforts to a near standstill. Even in the limited situations when this restricted standard could be met, employers likely would hesitate before taking voluntary action for fear of later being proven wrong in the course of litigation and then held to account for disparate treatment.

At the opposite end of the spectrum, respondents and the Government assert that an employer's good-faith belief that its actions are necessary to comply with Title VII's disparate-impact provision should be enough to justify race-conscious conduct. But the original, foundational prohibition of Title VII bars employers from taking adverse action "because of . . . race." §2000e-2(a)(1). And when Congress codified the disparate-impact provision in 1991, it made no exception to disparate-treatment liability for actions taken in a good-faith effort to comply with the new, disparate-impact provision in subsection (k). Allowing employers to violate the disparate-treatment prohibition based on a mere good-faith fear of disparate-impact liability would encourage race-based action at the slightest hint of disparate impact. A minimal standard could cause employers to discard the results of lawful and beneficial promotional examinations even where there is little if any evidence of disparate-impact discrimination. That would amount to a *de facto* quota system, in which a "focus on statistics . . . could put undue pressure on employers to adopt inappropriate prophylactic measures." *Watson.* Even worse, an employer could discard test results (or other employment practices) with the intent of obtaining the employer's preferred racial balance. That operational principle could not be justified, for Title VII is express in disclaiming any interpretation of its requirements as calling for outright racial balancing. §2000e-2(j). The purpose of Title VII "is to promote hiring on the basis of job qualifications, rather than on the basis of race or color." *Griggs.*

In searching for a standard that strikes a more appropriate balance, we note that this Court has considered cases similar to this one, albeit in the context of the Equal Protection Clause of the Fourteenth Amendment. The Court has held that certain government actions to remedy past racial discrimination — actions that are themselves based on race — are constitutional only where there is a "'strong basis in evidence'" that the remedial actions were necessary. *Richmond* v. *J. A. Croson Co.,* 488 U.S. 469, 500 (1989). This suit does not call on us to consider whether the statutory constraints under Title VII must be parallel in all respects to those under the Constitution. That does not mean the constitutional authorities are irrelevant, however. Our cases discussing constitutional principles can provide helpful guidance in this statutory context. . . .

The same interests [as operated in *Wygant* and *Croson*] are at work in the interplay between the disparate-treatment and disparate-impact provisions of Title VII. Congress has imposed liability on employers for unintentional discrimination in order to rid the workplace of "practices that are fair in form, but discriminatory in operation." *Griggs.* But it has also prohibited employers from taking adverse employment actions "because of" race. Applying the strong-basis-in-evidence standard to Title VII gives effect to both the disparate-treatment and disparate-impact provisions, allowing violations of one in the name of compliance with the other only in certain, narrow circumstances. The standard leaves ample room for employers' voluntary compliance efforts, which are essential to the statutory scheme and to Congress's efforts to eradicate workplace discrimination. And the standard appropriately constrains employers' discretion in making race-based decisions: It limits that discretion to cases in which there is a strong basis in evidence of disparate-impact liability, but it is not so restrictive that it allows employers to act only when there is a provable, actual violation.

Resolving the statutory conflict in this way allows the disparate-impact prohibition to work in a manner that is consistent with other provisions of Title VII, including the prohibition on adjusting employment-related test scores on the basis of race. See §2000e-2(*l*). Examinations like those administered by the City create legitimate expectations on the part of those who took the tests. As is the case with any promotion exam, some of the firefighters here invested substantial time, money, and personal commitment in preparing for the tests. Employment tests can be an important part of a neutral selection system that safeguards against the very racial animosities Title VII was intended to prevent. Here, however, the firefighters saw their efforts invalidated by the City in sole reliance upon race-based statistics.

If an employer cannot rescore a test based on the candidates' race, §2000e-2(*l*), then it follows *a fortiori* that it may not take the greater step of discarding the test altogether to achieve a more desirable racial distribution of promotion-eligible candidates — absent a strong basis in evidence that the test was deficient and that discarding the results is necessary to avoid violating the disparate-impact provision. Restricting an employer's ability to discard test results (and thereby discriminate against qualified candidates on the basis of their race) also is in keeping with Title VII's express protection of bona fide promotional examinations. See §2000e-2(h) ("[N]or shall it be an unlawful employment practice for an employer to give and to act upon the results of any professionally developed ability test provided that such test, its administration or action upon the results is not designed, intended or used to discriminate because of race"); cf. *AT&T Corp. v. Hulteen*, 556 U.S., (2009).

For the foregoing reasons, we adopt the strong-basis-in-evidence standard as a matter of statutory construction to resolve any conflict between the disparate-treatment and disparate-impact provisions of Title VII.

Our statutory holding does not address the constitutionality of the measures taken here in purported compliance with Title VII. We also do not hold that meeting the strong-basis-in-evidence standard would satisfy the Equal Protection Clause in a future case. As we explain below, because respondents have not met their burden under Title VII, we need not decide whether a legitimate fear of disparate impact is ever sufficient to justify discriminatory treatment under the Constitution.

Nor do we question an employer's affirmative efforts to ensure that all groups have a fair opportunity to apply for promotions and to participate in the process by which promotions will be made. But once that process has been established and employers have made clear their selection criteria, they may not then invalidate the test results, thus upsetting an employee's legitimate expectation not to be judged on the basis of race. Doing so, absent a strong basis in evidence of an impermissible disparate impact, amounts to the sort of racial preference that Congress has disclaimed, §2000e-2(j), and is antithetical to the notion of a workplace where individuals are guaranteed equal opportunity regardless of race.

Title VII does not prohibit an employer from considering, before administering a test or practice, how to design that test or practice in order to provide a fair opportunity for all individuals, regardless of their race. And when, during the test-design stage, an employer invites comments to ensure the test is fair, that process can provide a common ground for open discussions toward that end.

We hold only that, under Title VII, before an employer can engage in intentional discrimination for the asserted purpose of avoiding or remedying an unintentional disparate impact, the employer must have a strong basis in evidence to believe it will be subject to disparate-impact liability if it fails to take the race-conscious, discriminatory action.

C

The City argues that, even under the strong-basis-in-evidence standard, its decision to discard the examination results was permissible under Title VII. That is incorrect. Even if respondents were motivated as a subjective matter by a desire to avoid committing disparate-impact discrimination, the record makes clear there is no support for the conclusion that respondents had an objective, strong basis in evidence to find the tests inadequate, with some consequent disparate-impact liability in violation of Title VII.

On this basis, we conclude that petitioners have met their obligation to demonstrate that there is "no genuine issue as to any material fact" and that they are "entitled to judgment as a matter of law." Fed. Rule Civ. Proc. 56(c). . . .

The racial adverse impact here was significant, and petitioners do not dispute that the City was faced with a prima facie case of disparate-impact liability. On the captain exam, the pass rate for white candidates was 64 percent but was 37.5 percent for both black and Hispanic candidates. On the lieutenant exam, the pass rate for white candidates was 58.1 percent; for black candidates, 31.6 percent; and for Hispanic candidates, 20 percent. The pass rates of minorities, which were approximately one-half the pass rates for white candidates, fall well below the 80-percent standard set by the EEOC to implement the disparate-impact provision of Title VII. See 29 CFR §1607.4(D) (2008) (selection rate that is less than 80 percent "of the rate for the group with the highest rate will generally be regarded by the Federal enforcement agencies as evidence of adverse impact"); *Watson* (EEOC's 80-percent standard is "a rule of thumb for the courts"). Based on how the passing candidates ranked and an application of the "rule of three," certifying the examinations would have meant that the City could not have considered black candidates for any of the then-vacant lieutenant or captain positions.

Based on the degree of adverse impact reflected in the results, respondents were compelled to take a hard look at the examinations to determine whether certifying the results would have had an impermissible disparate impact. The problem for respondents is that a prima facie case of disparate-impact liability — essentially, a threshold showing of a significant statistical disparity, *Connecticut* v. *Teal*, and nothing more — is far from a strong basis in evidence that the City would have been liable under Title VII had it certified the results. That is because the City could be liable for disparate-impact discrimination only if the examinations were not job related and consistent with business necessity, or if there existed an equally valid, less-discriminatory alternative that served the City's needs but that the City refused to adopt. We conclude there is no strong basis in evidence to establish that the test was deficient in either of these respects. We address each of the two points in turn, based on the record developed by the parties through discovery — a record that concentrates in substantial part on the statements various witnesses made to the CSB.

1

There is no genuine dispute that the examinations were job-related and consistent with business necessity. The City's assertions to the contrary are "blatantly contradicted by the record" [including the statements of Chad Legel and city officials outlining the detailed steps taken to develop and administer the examinations. The only outside witness who reviewed the examinations in any detail was the only one with any firefighting experience, and he stated that the "questions were relevant for both exams."]

The City, moreover, turned a blind eye to evidence that supported the exams' validity. Although the City's contract with IOS contemplated that IOS would prepare a technical report consistent with EEOC guidelines for examination-validity studies, the City made no request for its report. After the January 2004 meeting between Legel and some of the city-official respondents, in which Legel defended the examinations, the City sought no further information from IOS, save its appearance at a CSB meeting to explain how it developed and administered the examinations. IOS stood ready to provide respondents with detailed information to establish the validity of the exams, but respondents did not accept that offer.

2

Respondents also lacked a strong basis in evidence of an equally valid, less-discriminatory testing alternative that the City, by certifying the examination results, would necessarily have refused to adopt. Respondents raise three arguments to the contrary, but each argument fails. First, respondents refer to testimony before the CSB that a different composite-score calculation—weighting the written and oral examination scores 30/70—would have allowed the City to consider two black candidates for then-open lieutenant positions and one black candidate for then-open captain positions. (The City used a 60/40 weighting as required by its contract with the New Haven firefighters' union.) But respondents have produced no evidence to show that the 60/40 weighting was indeed arbitrary. In fact, because that formula was the result of a union-negotiated collective-bargaining agreement, we presume the parties negotiated that weighting for a rational reason. Nor does the record contain any evidence that the 30/70 weighting would be an equally valid way to determine whether candidates possess the proper mix of job knowledge and situational skills to earn promotions. Changing the weighting formula, moreover, could well have violated Title VII's prohibition of altering test scores on the basis of race. See §2000e-2(*l*). On this record, there is no basis to conclude that a 30/70 weighting was an equally valid alternative the City could have adopted.

Second, respondents argue that the City could have adopted a different interpretation of the "rule of three" [in the city charter to produce less discriminatory results. But the charter was interpreted by a state court to prohibit "banding" — "rounding scores to the nearest whole number and considering all candidates with the same whole-number score as being of one rank."] . . . A state court's prohibition of banding, as a matter of municipal law under the charter, may not eliminate banding as a valid alternative under Title VII. See 42 U.S.C. §2000e-7. We need not resolve that point, however. Here, banding was not a valid alternative for this reason: Had the City reviewed the exam results and then adopted banding to make the minority test scores appear higher, it would have violated Title VII's prohibition of adjusting test results on the basis of race. §2000e-2(*l*); see also *Chicago Firefighters Local 2 v. Chicago*, 249 F. 3d 649, 656 (CA7 2001) (Posner, J.) ("We have no doubt that if banding were adopted in order to make lower black scores seem higher, it would indeed be . . . forbidden"). As a matter of law, banding was not an alternative available to the City when it was considering whether to certify the examination results.

Third, and finally, respondents refer to statements by Hornick in his telephone interview with the CSB regarding alternatives to the written examinations. Hornick stated his "belie[f]" that an "assessment center process," which would have evaluated candidates' behavior in typical job tasks, "would have demonstrated less adverse impact." But Hornick's brief mention of alternative testing methods, standing alone, does not raise a genuine issue of material fact that assessment centers were available to the City at the time of the examinations and that they would have produced less adverse impact. . . .

3

On the record before us, there is no genuine dispute that the City lacked a strong basis in evidence to believe it would face disparate-impact liability if it certified the examination results. In other words, there is no evidence — let alone the required strong basis in evidence — that the tests were flawed because they were not job-related or because other, equally valid and less discriminatory tests were available to the City. Fear of litigation alone cannot justify an employer's reliance on race to the detriment of individuals who passed the examinations and qualified for promotions. The City's discarding the test results was impermissible under Title VII, and summary judgment is appropriate for petitioners on their disparate-treatment claim.

* * *

The record in this litigation documents a process that, at the outset, had the potential to produce a testing procedure that was true to the promise of Title VII: No individual should face workplace discrimination based on race. Respondents thought about promotion qualifications and relevant experience in neutral ways. They were careful to ensure broad racial participation in the design of the test itself and its administration. As we have discussed at length, the process was open and fair.

The problem, of course, is that after the tests were completed, the raw racial results became the predominant rationale for the City's refusal to certify the results. The injury arises in part from the high, and justified, expectations of the candidates who had participated in the testing process on the terms the City had established for the promotional process. Many of the candidates had studied for months, at considerable personal and financial expense, and thus the injury caused by the City's reliance on raw racial statistics at the end of the process was all the more severe. Confronted with arguments both for and against certifying the test results — and threats of a lawsuit either way — the City was required to make a difficult inquiry. But its hearings produced no strong evidence of a disparate-impact violation, and the City was not entitled to disregard the tests based solely on the racial disparity in the results.

Our holding today clarifies how Title VII applies to resolve competing expectations under the disparate-treatment and disparate-impact provisions. If, after it certifies the test results, the City faces a disparate-impact suit, then in light of our holding today it should be clear that the City would avoid disparate-impact liability based on the strong basis in evidence that, had it not certified the results, it would have been subject to disparate-treatment liability. . . .

Justice SCALIA, concurring.

I join the Court's opinion in full, but write separately to observe that its resolution of this dispute merely postpones the evil day on which the Court will have to confront the question: Whether, or to what extent, are the disparate-impact provisions of Title VII of the Civil Rights Act of 1964 consistent with the Constitution's guarantee of equal protection? The question is not an easy one. See generally Primus, Equal Protection and Disparate Impact: Round Three, 117 Harv. L. Rev. 493 (2003).

The difficulty is this: Whether or not Title VII's disparate-treatment provisions forbid "remedial" race-based actions when a disparate-impact violation would *not* otherwise result — the question resolved by the Court today — it is clear that Title VII not only permits but affirmatively *requires* such actions when a disparate-impact violation *would* otherwise result. But if the Federal Government is prohibited from discriminating on the basis of race, *Bolling v. Sharpe*, 347 U.S. 497, 500 (1954), then surely it is also prohibited from enacting laws mandating that third parties — *e.g.*, employers, whether private, State, or municipal — discriminate on the basis of race. As the facts of these cases illustrate, Title VII's disparate-impact provisions place a racial thumb on the scales, often requiring employers to evaluate the racial outcomes of their policies, and to make decisions based on (because of) those racial outcomes. That type of racial decisionmaking is, as the Court explains, discriminatory.

To be sure, the disparate-impact laws do not mandate imposition of quotas, but it is not clear why that should provide a safe harbor. Would a private employer not be guilty of unlawful discrimination if he refrained from establishing a racial hiring quota but intentionally designed his hiring practices to achieve the same end? Surely he would. Intentional discrimination is still occurring, just one step up the chain. Government compulsion of such design would therefore seemingly violate equal protection principles. Nor would it matter that Title VII requires consideration of race on a wholesale, rather than retail, level. "[T]he Government must treat citizens as individuals, not as simply components of a racial, religious, sexual or national class." *Miller v. Johnson*, 515 U.S. 900, 911 (1995) (internal quotation marks omitted). And of course the purportedly benign motive for the disparate-impact provisions cannot save the statute. See *Adarand Constructors, Inc. v. Peña*, 515 U.S. 200, 227 (1995).

It might be possible to defend the law by framing it as simply an evidentiary tool used to identify genuine, intentional discrimination — to "smoke out," as it were, disparate treatment. Disparate impact is sometimes a signal of something illicit, so a regulator might allow statistical disparities to play some role in the evidentiary process. But arguably the disparate-impact provisions sweep too broadly to be fairly characterized in such a fashion — since they fail to provide an affirmative defense for good-faith (*i.e.*, nonracially motivated) conduct, or perhaps even for good faith plus hiring standards that are entirely reasonable. This is a question that this Court will have to consider in due course. It is one thing to free plaintiffs from proving an employer's illicit intent, but quite another to preclude the employer from proving that its motives were pure and its actions reasonable.

The Court's resolution of these cases makes it unnecessary to resolve these matters today. But the war between disparate impact and equal protection will be waged sooner or later, and it behooves us to begin thinking about how — and on what terms — to make peace between them.

Justice ALITO, with whom Justice SCALIA and Justice THOMAS join, concurring.

[The concurrence "join[ed] the Court's opinion in full" but wrote separately to correct what he said were important omissions in Justice Ginsberg's dissent.] [W]hen all of the evidence in the record is taken into account, it is clear that, even if the legal analysis in Parts II and III-A of the dissent were accepted, affirmance of the decision below is untenable.

I . . .

The question on which the opinion of the Court and the dissenting opinion disagree concerns the objective component of the determination that must be made when an employer justifies an employment decision, like the one made in this litigation, on the ground that a contrary decision would have created a risk of disparate-impact liability. The Court holds — and I entirely agree — that concern about disparate-impact liability is a legitimate reason for a decision of the type involved here only if there was a "substantial basis in evidence to find the tests inadequate." The Court ably demonstrates that in this litigation no reasonable jury could find that the city of New Haven (City) possessed such evidence and therefore summary judgment for petitioners is required. Because the Court correctly holds that respondents cannot satisfy this objective component, the Court has no need to discuss the question of the respondents' actual intent. As the Court puts it, "[e]ven if respondents were motivated as a subjective matter by a desire to avoid committing disparate-impact discrimination, the record makes clear there is no support for the conclusion that respondents had an objective, substantial basis in evidence to find the tests inadequate."

The dissent advocates a different objective component of the governing standard. According to the dissent, the objective component should be whether the evidence provided "good cause" for the decision, and the dissent argues — incorrectly, in my view — that no reasonable juror could fail to find that such evidence was present here. But even if the dissent were correct on this point, I assume that the dissent would not countenance summary judgment for respondents if respondents' professed concern about disparate-impact litigation was simply a pretext. Therefore, the decision below, which sustained the entry of summary judgment for respondents, cannot be affirmed unless no reasonable jury could find that the City's asserted reason for scrapping its test — concern about disparate-impact liability — was a pretext and that the City's real reason was illegitimate, namely, the desire to placate a politically important racial constituency.

II

A

As initially described by the dissent, the process by which the City reached the decision not to accept the test results was open, honest, serious, and deliberative. But even the District Court admitted that "a jury could rationally infer that city officials worked behind the scenes to sabotage the promotional examinations because they knew that, were the exams certified, the Mayor would incur the wrath of [Rev. Boise] Kimber and other influential leaders of New Haven's African-American community."

This admission finds ample support in the record. [There follows an extensive recitation of Reverend Kimber's influence in New Haven politics, his close connection to Mayor DeStefano, and the behind-the-scenes efforts of the city administration to get the test results rejected.]

C

Taking into account all the evidence in the summary judgment record, a reasonable jury could find the following. Almost as soon as the City disclosed the racial makeup of the list of firefighters who scored the highest on the exam, the City administration was lobbied by an influential community leader to scrap the test results, and the City administration decided on that course of action before making any real assessment of the possibility of a disparate-impact violation. To achieve that end, the City administration concealed its internal decision but worked — as things turned out, successfully — to persuade the CSB that acceptance of the test results would be illegal and would expose the City to disparate-impact liability. But in the event that the CSB was not persuaded, the Mayor, wielding ultimate decisionmaking authority, was prepared to overrule the CSB immediately. Taking this view of the evidence, a reasonable jury could easily find that the City's real reason for scrapping the test results was not a concern about violating the disparate-impact provision of Title VII but a simple desire to please a politically important racial constituency. It is noteworthy that the Solicitor General—whose position on the principal legal issue in this case is largely aligned with the dissent—concludes that "[n]either the district court nor the court of appeals . . . adequately considered whether, viewing the evidence in the light most favorable to petitioners, a genuine issue of material fact remained whether respondents' claimed purpose to comply with Title VII was a pretext for intentional racial discrimination. . . . "

III

I will not comment at length on the dissent's criticism of my analysis, but two points require a response.

The first concerns the dissent's statement that I "equat[e] political considerations with unlawful discrimination." The dissent misrepresents my position: I draw no such equation. Of course "there are many ways in which a politician can attempt to win over a constituency — including a racial constituency — without engaging in unlawful discrimination." But—as I assume the dissent would agree—there are some things that a public official cannot do, and one of those is engaging in intentional racial discrimination when making employment decisions. [Justice Alito's second point related to cat's paw liability and the opinion in this regard superseded by *Staub v. Proctor Hospital*, p. 9 of this Supplement.]

* * *

. . . Petitioners were denied promotions for which they qualified because of the race and ethnicity of the firefighters who achieved the highest scores on the City's exam. The District Court threw out their case on summary judgment, even though that court all but conceded that a jury could find that the City's asserted justification was pretextual. The Court of Appeals then summarily affirmed that decision.

The dissent grants that petitioners' situation is "unfortunate" and that they "understandably attract this Court's sympathy." But "sympathy" is not what petitioners have a right to demand. What they have a right to demand is evenhanded enforcement of the law — of Title VII's prohibition against discrimination based on race. And that is what, until today's decision, has been denied them.

Justice GINSBURG, with whom Justice STEVENS, Justice SOUTER, and Justice BREYER join, dissenting.

In assessing claims of race discrimination, "[c]ontext matters." *Grutter v. Bollinger*, 539 U.S. 306, 327 (2003). In 1972, Congress extended Title VII of the Civil Rights Act of 1964 to cover public employment. At that time, municipal fire departments across the country, including New Haven's, pervasively discriminated against minorities. The extension of Title VII to cover jobs in firefighting effected no overnight change. It took decades of persistent effort, advanced by Title VII litigation, to open firefighting posts to members of racial minorities.

The white firefighters who scored high on New Haven's promotional exams understandably attract this Court's sympathy. But they had no vested right to promotion. Nor have other persons received promotions in preference to them. New Haven maintains that it refused to certify the test results because it believed, for good cause, that it would be vulnerable to a Title VII disparate-impact suit if it relied on those results. The Court today holds that New Haven has not demonstrated "a strong basis in evidence" for its plea. In so holding, the Court pretends that "[t]he City rejected the test results solely because the higher scoring candidates were white." That pretension, essential to the Court's disposition, ignores substantial evidence of multiple flaws in the tests New Haven used. The Court similarly fails to acknowledge the better tests used in other cities, which have yielded less racially skewed outcomes.[1]

By order of this Court, New Haven, a city in which African-Americans and Hispanics account for nearly 60 percent of the population, must today be served — as it was in the days of undisguised discrimination — by a fire department in which members of racial and ethnic minorities are rarely seen in command positions. In arriving at its order, the Court barely acknowledges the pathmarking decision in *Griggs v. Duke Power Co.*, which explained the centrality of the disparate-impact concept to effective enforcement of Title VII. The Court's order and opinion, I anticipate, will not have staying power.

I

A

[The dissent traced a history of racial discrimination in firefighting in the nation as documented by the U.S. Commission on Civil Rights.]

The city of New Haven (City) was no exception. In the early 1970's, African-Americans and Hispanics composed 30 percent of New Haven's population, but only 3.6 percent of the City's 502 firefighters. The racial disparity in the officer ranks was even more pronounced: "[O]f the 107 officers in the Department only one was black, and he held the lowest rank above private." *Firebird Soc. of New Haven, Inc. v. New Haven Bd. of Fire Comm'rs*, 66 F. R. D. 457, 460 (Conn. 1975).

---

1. Never mind the flawed tests New Haven used and the better selection methods used elsewhere, Justice Alito's concurring opinion urges. Overriding all else, racial politics, fired up by a strident African-American pastor, were at work in New Haven. Even a detached and disinterested observer, however, would have every reason to ask: Why did such racially skewed results occur in New Haven, when better tests likely would have produced less disproportionate results?

4. *The Interrelation of the Three Theories of Discrimination*

Following a lawsuit and settlement agreement, the City initiated efforts to increase minority representation in the New Haven Fire Department (Department). Those litigation-induced efforts produced some positive change. New Haven's population includes a greater proportion of minorities today than it did in the 1970's: Nearly 40 percent of the City's residents are African-American and more than 20 percent are Hispanic. Among entry-level firefighters, minorities are still underrepresented, but not starkly so. As of 2003, African-Americans and Hispanics constituted 30 percent and 16 percent of the City's firefighters, respectively. In supervisory positions, however, significant disparities remain. Overall, the senior officer ranks (captain and higher) are nine percent African-American and nine percent Hispanic. Only one of the Department's 21 fire captains is African-American. It is against this backdrop of entrenched inequality that the promotion process at issue in this litigation should be assessed.

B

By order of its charter, New Haven must use competitive examinations to fill vacancies in fire officer and other civil-service positions. Such examinations, the City's civil service rules specify, "shall be practical in nature, shall relate to matters which fairly measure the relative fitness and capacity of the applicants to discharge the duties of the position which they seek, and shall take into account character, training, experience, physical and mental fitness." The City may choose among a variety of testing methods, including written and oral exams and "[p]erformance tests to demonstrate skill and ability in performing actual work."

New Haven, the record indicates, did not closely consider what sort of "practical" examination would "fairly measure the relative fitness and capacity of the applicants to discharge the duties" of a fire officer. Instead, the City simply adhered to the testing regime outlined in its two-decades-old contract with the local firefighters' union: a written exam, which would account for 60 percent of an applicant's total score, and an oral exam, which would account for the remaining 40 percent. . . .

Pursuant to New Haven's specifications [for a 60-40 split between the two portions], IOS developed and administered the oral and written exams. The results showed significant racial disparities. . . . More striking still, although nearly half of the 77 lieutenant candidates were African-American or Hispanic, none would have been eligible for promotion to the eight positions then vacant. The highest scoring African-American candidate ranked 13th; the top Hispanic candidate was 26th. As for the seven then-vacant captain positions, two Hispanic candidates would have been eligible, but no African-Americans. The highest scoring African-American candidate ranked 15th.

These stark disparities, the Court acknowledges, sufficed to state a prima facie case under Title VII's disparate-impact provision. New Haven thus had cause for concern about the prospect of Title VII litigation and liability. City officials referred the matter to the New Haven Civil Service Board (CSB), the entity responsible for certifying the results of employment exams. . . .

[Justice Ginsburg describes additional facts about the testimony taken at the five public meetings on all sides of the issue. She noted that Mr. Ude correctly recognized that statistical imbalance alone did not trigger liability. Some opposed to the certification of the test noted unequal access to study materials, claiming some candidates had the necessary books even before the syllabus was issued, while others had to wait to receive books on back order. Further, they argued that minority applicants were "first generation firefighters" who lacked the support network that others had from relatives who were firefighters.]

A representative of the Northeast Region of the International Association of Black Professional Firefighters, Donald Day, spoke at the second meeting. Statistical disparities, he told the CSB, had been present in the Department's previous promotional exams. On earlier tests, however, a few minority candidates had fared well enough to earn promotions. Day contrasted New Haven's experience with that of nearby Bridgeport, where minority firefighters held one-third of lieutenant and captain positions. Bridgeport, Day observed, had once used a testing process similar to New Haven's, with a written exam accounting for 70 percent of an applicant's score, an oral exam for 25 percent, and seniority for the remaining five percent. Bridgeport recognized, however, that the oral component, more so than the written component, addressed the sort of "real-life scenarios" fire officers encounter on the job. Accordingly, that city "changed the relative weights" to give primacy to the oral exam. Since that time, Day reported, Bridgeport had seen minorities "fairly represented" in its exam results.

[As for IOS representative Legel, he recounted that the City] had set the "parameters" for the exams, specifically, the requirement of written and oral components with a 60/40 weighting. For security reasons, Department officials had not been permitted to check the content of the questions prior to their administration. Instead, IOS retained a senior fire officer from Georgia to review the exams "for content and fidelity to the source material." . . .

[Dr. Hornick testified that] "an assessment center process, which is essentially an opportunity for candidates . . . to demonstrate how they would address a particular problem as opposed to just verbally saying it or identifying the correct option on a written test." Such selection processes, Hornick said, better "identif[y] the best possible people" and "demonstrate dramatically less adverse impacts." Hornick added:

> "I've spoken to at least 10,000, maybe 15,000 firefighters in group settings in my consulting practice and I have never one time ever had anyone in the fire service say to me, 'Well, the person who answers—gets the highest score on a written job knowledge, multiple-guess test makes the best company officer.' We know that it's not as valid as other procedures that exist."

[Hornick also said,] "I think a person's leadership skills, their command presence, their interpersonal skills, their management skills, their tactical skills could have been identified and evaluated in a much more appropriate way."

Hornick described the written test itself as "reasonably good," but he criticized the decision not to allow Department officials to check the content. According to Hornick, this "inevitably" led to "test[ing] for processes and procedures that don't necessarily match up into the department." He preferred "experts from within the department who have signed confidentiality agreements . . . to make sure that the terminology and equipment that's being identified from standardized reading sources apply to the department."

Asked whether he thought the City should certify the results, Hornick hedged: "There is adverse impact in the test. That will be identified in any proceeding that you have. You will have industrial psychology experts, if it goes to court, on both sides. And it will not be a pretty or comfortable position for anyone to be in." Perhaps, he suggested, New Haven might certify the results but immediately begin exploring "alternative ways to deal with these issues" in the future. . . .

C . . .

[The district court granted summary judgment against the plaintiffs.] Under Second Circuit precedent, the District Court explained, "the intent to remedy the disparate impact" of a promotional exam "is not equivalent to an intent to discriminate against non-minority applicants." Rejecting petitioners' pretext argument, the court observed that the exam results were sufficiently skewed "to make out a prima facie case of discrimination" under Title VII's disparate-impact provision. Had New Haven gone forward with certification and been sued by aggrieved minority test takers, the City would have been forced to defend tests that were presumptively invalid. And, as the CSB testimony of Hornick and others indicated, overcoming that presumption would have been no easy task. Given Title VII's preference for voluntary compliance, the court held, New Haven could lawfully discard the disputed exams even if the City had not definitively "pinpoint[ed]" the source of the disparity and "ha[d] not yet formulated a better selection method."

Respondents were no doubt conscious of race during their decisionmaking process, the court acknowledged, but this did not mean they had engaged in racially disparate treatment. The conclusion they had reached and the action thereupon taken were race-neutral in this sense: "[A]ll the test results were discarded, no one was promoted, and firefighters of every race will have to participate in another selection process to be considered for promotion." New Haven's action, which gave no individual a preference, "was 'simply not analogous to a quota system or a minority set-aside where candidates, on the basis of their race, are not treated uniformly.'" For these and other reasons, the court also rejected petitioners' equal protection claim.

II

A

[The dissent began this portion of the opinion by arguing that *Griggs* had correctly interpreted Title VII as it was originally enacted. "Only by ignoring

Griggs could one maintain that intentionally disparate treatment alone was Title VII's 'original, foundational prohibition,' and disparate impact a mere afterthought." It then recounted the facts and holding of *Griggs* in some detail, and then went on to describe subsequent cases, including *Albemarle Paper Co. v. Moody,* reproduced at p. 276, and circuit court authority that had applied the disparate impact principle.]

. . . Among selection methods cast aside for lack of a "manifest relationship" to job performance were a number of written hiring and promotional examinations for firefighters.[4]

Moving in a different direction, in *Wards Cove Packing Co. v. Atonio,* a bare majority of this Court significantly modified the *Griggs-Albemarle* delineation of Title VII's disparate-impact proscription. As to business necessity for a practice that disproportionately excludes members of minority groups, *Wards Cove* held, the employer bears only the burden of production, not the burden of persuasion. And in place of the instruction that the challenged practice "must have a manifest relationship to the employment in question," *Wards Cove* said that the practice would be permissible as long as it "serve[d], in a significant way, the legitimate employment goals of the employer."

In response to *Wards Cove* and "a number of [other] recent decisions by the United States Supreme Court that sharply cut back on the scope and effectiveness of [civil rights] laws," Congress enacted the Civil Rights Act of 1991. H. R. Rep. No. 102-40, pt. 2, p. 2 (1991). Among the 1991 alterations, Congress formally codified the disparate-impact component of Title VII. In so amending the statute, Congress made plain its intention to restore "the concepts of 'business necessity' and 'job related' enunciated by the Supreme Court in Griggs v. Duke Power Co. . . . and in other Supreme Court decisions prior to Wards Cove Packing Co. v. Atonio." §3(2), 105 Stat. 1071. Once a complaining party demonstrates that an employment practice causes a disparate impact, amended Title VII states, the burden is on the employer "to demonstrate that the challenged practice is job related for the position in question and consistent with business necessity." If the employer carries that substantial burden, the complainant may respond by identifying "an alternative employment practice" which the employer "refuses to adopt."

B

Neither Congress' enactments nor this Court's Title VII precedents (including the now-discredited decision in *Wards Cove*) offer even a hint of "conflict" between an employer's obligations under the statute's disparate-treatment and disparate-impact provisions. Standing on an equal footing, these twin pillars of

---

4. *See, e.g., Nash v. Jacksonville,* 837 F. 2d 1534 (CA11 1988), vacated, 490 U. S. 1103 (1989), opinion reinstated, 905 F. 2d 355 (CA11 1990); *Vulcan Pioneers, Inc. v. New Jersey Dept. of Civil Serv.,* 832 F. 2d 811 (CA3 (1987); *Guardians Assn. of N. Y. City Police Dept. v. Civil Serv. Comm'n,* 630 F. 2d 79 (CA2 1980); *Ensley Branch of NAACP v. Seibels,* 616 F. 2d 812 (CA5 1980); *Firefighters Inst. for Racial Equality v. St. Louis,* 616 F. 2d 350 (CA8 1980); *Boston Chapter, NAACP v. Beecher,* 504 F. 2d 1017 (CA1 1974).

Title VII advance the same objectives: ending workplace discrimination and promoting genuinely equal opportunity. See *McDonnell Douglas Corp. v. Green.*

Yet the Court today sets at odds the statute's core directives. When an employer changes an employment practice in an effort to comply with Title VII's disparate-impact provision, the Court reasons, it acts "because of race" — something Title VII's disparate-treatment provision generally forbids. This characterization of an employer's compliance-directed action shows little attention to Congress' design or to the *Griggs* line of cases Congress recognized as pathmarking. . . . [Because a court is bound to read the provisions of any statute as harmonious] Title VII's disparate-treatment and disparate-impact proscriptions must be read as complementary.

In codifying the *Griggs* and *Albemarle* instructions, Congress declared unambiguously that selection criteria operating to the disadvantage of minority group members can be retained only if justified by business necessity.[5] In keeping with Congress' design, employers who reject such criteria due to reasonable doubts about their reliability can hardly be held to have engaged in discrimination "because of" race. A reasonable endeavor to comply with the law and to ensure that qualified candidates of all races have a fair opportunity to compete is simply not what Congress meant to interdict. I would therefore hold that an employer who jettisons a selection device when its disproportionate racial impact becomes apparent does not violate Title VII's disparate-treatment bar automatically or at all, subject to this key condition: The employer must have good cause to believe the device would not withstand examination for business necessity. Cf. *Faragher* v. *Boca Raton*, 524 U.S. 775, 806 (1998) (observing that it accords with "clear statutory policy" for employers "to prevent violations" and "make reasonable efforts to discharge their duty" under Title VII).

EEOC's interpretative guidelines are corroborative. "[B]y the enactment of title VII," the guidelines state, "Congress did not intend to expose those who comply with the Act to charges that they are violating the very statute they are seeking to implement." 29 CFR §1608.1(a) (2008). Recognizing EEOC's "enforcement responsibility" under Title VII, we have previously accorded the Commission's position respectful consideration. Yet the Court today does not so much as mention EEOC's counsel. . . .

This litigation does not involve affirmative action. But if the voluntary affirmative action at issue in *Johnson* [*v. Transportation Agency, Santa Clara Cty.*, reproduced at p. 184] does not discriminate within the meaning of Title VII, neither does an employer's reasonable effort to comply with Title VII's disparate-impact provision by refraining from action of doubtful consistency with business necessity.

C

To "reconcile" the supposed "conflict" between disparate treatment and disparate impact, the Court offers an enigmatic standard. Employers may attempt to comply with Title VII's disparate-impact provision, the Court declares, only where

---

5. What was the "business necessity" for the tests New Haven used? How could one justify, *e.g.*, the 60/40 written/oral ratio under that standard? Neither the Court nor the concurring opinions attempt to defend the ratio.

there is a "strong basis in evidence" documenting the necessity of their action. The Court's standard, drawn from inapposite equal protection precedents, is not elaborated. One is left to wonder what cases would meet the standard and why the Court is so sure this case does not.

1

In construing Title VII, I note preliminarily, equal protection doctrine is of limited utility. The Equal Protection Clause, this Court has held, prohibits only intentional discrimination; it does not have a disparate-impact component. See *Personnel Administrator of Mass. v. Feeney,* [reproduced at p. 155]; *Washington v. Davis,* 426 U.S. 229, 239 (1976). Title VII, in contrast, aims to eliminate all forms of employment discrimination, unintentional as well as deliberate. Until today, (Scalia, J., concurring), this Court has never questioned the constitutionality of the disparate-impact component of Title VII, and for good reason. By instructing employers to avoid needlessly exclusionary selection processes, Title VII's disparate-impact provision calls for a "race-neutral means to increase minority . . . participation" — something this Court's equal protection precedents also encourage. See *Adarand Constructors, Inc. v. Peña* 515 U.S. 200, 238 (1995) (quoting *Richmond v. J. A. Croson Co*)., 488 U.S. 469, 507 (1989)). "The very radicalism of holding disparate impact doctrine unconstitutional as a matter of equal protection," moreover, "suggests that only a very uncompromising court would issue such a decision." Primus, Equal Protection and Disparate Impact: Round Three, 117 Harv. L. Rev. 493, 585 (2003).

The cases from which the Court draws its strong-basis-in-evidence standard are particularly inapt; they concern the constitutionality of absolute racial preferences. See *Wygant Jackson Bd. of Ed.,* 476 U.S. 267, 277 (1986) (plurality opinion) (invalidating a school district's plan to lay off nonminority teachers while retaining minority teachers with less seniority); *Croson* (rejecting a set-aside program for minority contractors that operated as "an unyielding racial quota"). An employer's effort to avoid Title VII liability by repudiating a suspect selection method scarcely resembles those cases. Race was not merely a relevant consideration in *Wygant* and *Croson;* it was the decisive factor. Observance of Title VII's disparate-impact provision, in contrast, calls for no racial preference, absolute or otherwise. The very purpose of the provision is to ensure that individuals are hired and promoted based on qualifications manifestly necessary to successful performance of the job in question, qualifications that do not screen out members of any race.[6]

---

6. Even in Title VII cases involving race-conscious (or gender-conscious) affirmative-action plans, the Court has never proposed a strong-basis-in-evidence standard. In *Johnson v. Transportation Agency, Santa Clara Cty.,* the Court simply examined the municipal employer's action for reasonableness: "Given the obvious imbalance in the Skilled Craft category, and given the Agency's commitment to eliminating such imbalances, it was plainly not unreasonable for the Agency . . . to consider as one factor the sex of [applicants] in making its decision." See also *Firefighters v. Cleveland,* 478 U.S. 501, 516 (1986) ("Title VII permits employers and unions voluntarily to make use of reasonable race-conscious affirmative action.").

2

The Court's decision in this litigation underplays a dominant Title VII theme. This Court has repeatedly emphasized that the statute "should not be read to thwart" efforts at voluntary compliance. *Johnson*. Such compliance, we have explained, is "the preferred means of achieving [Title VII's] objectives." *Firefighters v. Cleveland*, 478 U.S. 501, 515 (1986). See also *Kolstad v. American Dental Assn.*, 527 U.S. 526, 545 (1999) ("Dissuading employers from [taking voluntary action] to prevent discrimination in the workplace is directly contrary to the purposes underlying Title VII."). The strong-basis-in-evidence standard, however, as barely described in general, and cavalierly applied in this case, makes voluntary compliance a hazardous venture.

As a result of today's decision, an employer who discards a dubious selection process can anticipate costly disparate-treatment litigation in which its chances for success — even for surviving a summary-judgment motion — are highly problematic. Concern about exposure to disparate-impact liability, however well grounded, is insufficient to insulate an employer from attack. Instead, the employer must make a "strong" showing that (1) its selection method was "not job related and consistent with business necessity," or (2) that it refused to adopt "an equally valid, less-discriminatory alternative." It is hard to see how these requirements differ from demanding that an employer establish "a provable, actual violation" *against itself*. There is indeed a sharp conflict here, but it is not the false one the Court describes between Title VII's core provisions. It is, instead, the discordance of the Court's opinion with the voluntary compliance ideal. Cf. *Wygant* (O'Connor, J., concurring in part and concurring in judgment) ("The imposition of a requirement that public employers make findings that they have engaged in illegal discrimination before they [act] would severely undermine public employers' incentive to meet voluntarily their civil rights obligations.").[7]

3

The Court's additional justifications for announcing a strong-basis-in-evidence standard are unimpressive. First, discarding the results of tests, the Court suggests, calls for a heightened standard because it "upset[s] an employee's legitimate expectation." This rationale puts the cart before the horse. The legitimacy of an employee's expectation depends on the legitimacy of the selection method. If an employer reasonably concludes that an exam fails to identify the

---

7. Notably, prior decisions applying a strong-basis-in-evidence standard have not imposed a burden as heavy as the one the Court imposes today. In *Croson*, the Court found no strong basis in evidence because the City had offered "nothing approaching a prima facie case." *Richmond v. J. A. Croson Co.*, 488 U.S. 469, 500 (1989). The Court did not suggest that anything beyond a prima facie case would have been required. In the context of race-based electoral districting, the Court has indicated that a "strong basis" exists when the "threshold conditions" for liability are present. *Bush v. Vera*, 517 U.S. 952, 978 (1996) (plurality opinion).

most qualified individuals and needlessly shuts out a segment of the applicant pool, Title VII surely does not compel the employer to hire or promote based on the test, however unreliable it may be. Indeed, the statute's prime objective is to prevent exclusionary practices from "operat[ing] to 'freeze' the status quo." *Griggs.*

Second, the Court suggests, anything less than a strong-basis-in-evidence standard risks creating "a *de facto* quota system, in which . . . an employer could discard test results . . . with the intent of obtaining the employer's preferred racial balance." Under a reasonableness standard, however, an employer could not cast aside a selection method based on a statistical disparity alone.[8] The employer must have good cause to believe that the method screens out qualified applicants and would be difficult to justify as grounded in business necessity. Should an employer repeatedly reject test results, it would be fair, I agree, to infer that the employer is simply seeking a racially balanced outcome and is not genuinely endeavoring to comply with Title VII.

D

The Court stacks the deck further by denying respondents any chance to satisfy the newly announced strong-basis-in-evidence standard. When this Court formulates a new legal rule, the ordinary course is to remand and allow the lower courts to apply the rule in the first instance. I see no good reason why the Court fails to follow that course in this case. Indeed, the sole basis for the Court's peremptory ruling is the demonstrably false pretension that respondents showed "nothing more" than "a significant statistical disparity."[9]

---

8. Infecting the Court's entire analysis is its insistence that the City rejected the test results "in sole reliance upon race-based statistics." But as the part of the story the Court leaves out plainly shows — the long history of rank discrimination against African-Americans in the firefighting profession, the multiple flaws in New Haven's test for promotions — "sole reliance" on statistics certainly is not descriptive of the CSB's decision.

9. The Court's refusal to remand for further proceedings also deprives respondents of an opportunity to invoke 42 U.S.C. §2000e-12(b) as a shield to liability. Section 2000e-12(b) provides: "In any action or proceeding based on any alleged unlawful employment practice, no person shall be subject to any liability or punishment for or on account of (1) the commission by such person of an unlawful employment practice if he pleads and proves that the act or omission complained of was in good faith, in conformity with, and in reliance on any written interpretation or opinion of the [EEOC]. . . . Such a defense, if established, shall be a bar to the action or proceeding, notwithstanding that (A) after such act or omission, such interpretation or opinion is modified or rescinded or is determined by judicial authority to be invalid or of no legal effect. . . . "Specifically, given the chance, respondents might have called attention to the EEOC guidelines set out in 29 CFR §§1608.3 and 1608.4 (2008). The guidelines recognize that employers may "take affirmative action based on an analysis which reveals facts constituting actual or potential adverse impact." §1608.3(a). If "affirmative action" is in order, so is the lesser step of discarding a dubious selection device.

III

A

Applying what I view as the proper standard to the record thus far made, I would hold that New Haven had ample cause to believe its selection process was flawed and not justified by business necessity. Judged by that standard, petitioners have not shown that New Haven's failure to certify the exam results violated Title VII's disparate-treatment provision.[10]

The City, all agree, "was faced with a prima facie case of disparate-impact liability": The pass rate for minority candidates was half the rate for nonminority candidates, and virtually no minority candidates would have been eligible for promotion had the exam results been certified. Alerted to this stark disparity, the CSB heard expert and lay testimony, presented at public hearings, in an endeavor to ascertain whether the exams were fair and consistent with business necessity. Its investigation revealed grave cause for concern about the exam process itself and the City's failure to consider alternative selection devices.

Chief among the City's problems was the very nature of the tests for promotion. In choosing to use written and oral exams with a 60/40 weighting, the City simply adhered to the union's preference and apparently gave no consideration to whether the weighting was likely to identify the most qualified fire-officer candidates.[11] There is strong reason to think it was not.

Relying heavily on written tests to select fire officers is a questionable practice, to say the least. Successful fire officers, the City's description of the position makes clear, must have the "[a]bility to lead personnel effectively, maintain discipline, promote harmony, exercise sound judgment, and cooperate with other officials."

---

10. The lower courts focused on respondents' "intent" rather than on whether respondents in fact had good cause to act. Ordinarily, a remand for fresh consideration would be in order. But the Court has seen fit to preclude further proceedings. I therefore explain why, if final adjudication by this Court is indeed appropriate, New Haven should be the prevailing party.

11. This alone would have posed a substantial problem for New Haven in a disparate-impact suit, particularly in light of the disparate results the City's scheme had produced in the past. Under the Uniform Guidelines on Employee Selection Procedures (Uniform Guidelines), employers must conduct "an investigation of suitable alternative selection procedures." See also *Officers for Justice v. Civil Serv. Comm'n*, 979 F. 2d 721, 728 (CA9 1992) ("before utilizing a procedure that has an adverse impact on minorities, the City has an *obligation* pursuant to the *Uniform Guidelines* to explore alternative procedures and to implement them if they have less adverse impact and are substantially equally valid"). It is no answer to "presume" that the two-decades-old 60/40 formula was adopted for a "rational reason" because it "was the result of a union-negotiated collective bargaining agreement." That the parties may have been "rational" says nothing about whether their agreed-upon selection process was consistent with business necessity. It is not at all unusual for agreements negotiated between employers and unions to run afoul of Title VII. *See, e.g., Peters v. Missouri-Pacific R. Co.*, 483 F. 2d 490, 497 (CA5 1973) (an employment practice "is not shielded [from the requirements of Title VII] by the facts that it is the product of collective bargaining and meets the standards of fair representation").

These qualities are not well measured by written tests. Testifying before the CSB, Christopher Hornick, an exam-design expert with more than two decades of relevant experience, was emphatic on this point: Leadership skills, command presence, and the like "could have been identified and evaluated in a much more appropriate way."

Hornick's commonsense observation is mirrored in case law and in Title VII's administrative guidelines. Courts have long criticized written firefighter promotion exams for being "more probative of the test-taker's ability to recall what a particular text stated on a given topic than of his firefighting or supervisory knowledge and abilities." . . .

Given these unfavorable appraisals, it is unsurprising that most municipal employers do not evaluate their fire-officer candidates as New Haven does. Although comprehensive statistics are scarce, a 1996 study found that nearly two-thirds of surveyed municipalities used assessment centers ("simulations of the real world of work") as part of their promotion processes. P. Lowry, A Survey of the Assessment Center Process in the Public Sector, 25 Public Personnel Management 307, 315 (1996). That figure represented a marked increase over the previous decade, so the percentage today may well be even higher. Among municipalities still relying in part on written exams, the median weight assigned to them was 30 percent — half the weight given to New Haven's written exam.

Testimony before the CSB indicated that these alternative methods were both more reliable and notably less discriminatory in operation. According to Donald Day of the International Association of Black Professional Firefighters, nearby Bridgeport saw less skewed results after switching to a selection process that placed primary weight on an oral exam. And Hornick described assessment centers as "demonstrat[ing] dramatically less adverse impacts" than written exams. Considering the prevalence of these proven alternatives, New Haven was poorly positioned to argue that promotions based on its outmoded and exclusionary selection process qualified as a business necessity. Cf. *Robinson v. Lorillard Corp.*, 444 F. 2d 791, 798, n. 7 (CA4 1971) ("It should go without saying that a practice is hardly 'necessary' if an alternative practice better effectuates its intended purpose or is equally effective but less discriminatory.").[15]

---

15. Finding the evidence concerning these alternatives insufficiently developed to "create a genuine issue of fact," the Court effectively confirms that an employer cannot prevail under its strong-basis-in-evidence standard unless the employer decisively proves a disparate-impact violation against itself. The Court's specific arguments are unavailing. First, the Court suggests, changing the oral/written weighting may have violated Title VII's prohibition on altering test scores. No one is arguing, however, that the results of the exams given should have been altered. Rather, the argument is that the City could have availed itself of a better option when it initially decided what selection process to use. Second, with respect to assessment centers, the Court identifies "statements to the CSB indicat[ing] that the Department could not have used [them] for the 2003 examinations." The Court comes up with only a single statement on this subject — an offhand remark made by petitioner Ricci, who hardly qualifies as an expert in testing methods. Given the large number of municipalities that regularly use assessment centers, it is impossible to fathom why the City, with proper planning, could not have done so as well.

Ignoring the conceptual and other defects in New Haven's selection process, the Court describes the exams as "painstaking[ly]" developed to test "relevant" material and on that basis finds no substantial risk of disparate-impact liability. Perhaps such reasoning would have sufficed under *Wards Cove*, which permitted exclusionary practices as long as they advanced an employer's "legitimate" goals. But Congress repudiated *Wards Cove* and reinstated the "business necessity" rule attended by a "manifest relationship" requirement. Like the chess player who tries to win by sweeping the opponent's pieces off the table, the Court simply shuts from its sight the formidable obstacles New Haven would have faced in defending against a disparate-impact suit. See *Lanning v. Southeastern Pa. Transp. Auth.*, 181 F. 3d 478, 489 (CA3 1999) ("Judicial application of a standard focusing solely on whether the qualities measured by an . . . exam bear some relationship to the job in question would impermissibly write out the business necessity prong of the Act's chosen standard.").

That IOS representative Chad Legel and his team may have been diligent in designing the exams says little about the exams' suitability for selecting fire officers. IOS worked within the City's constraints. Legel never discussed with the City the propriety of the 60/40 weighting and "was not asked to consider the possibility of an assessment center." The IOS exams, Legel admitted, had not even attempted to assess "command presence": "[Y]ou would probably be better off with an assessment center if you cared to measure that." Cf. *Boston Chapter, NAACP v. Beecher*, 504 F. 2d 1017, 1021-1022 (CA1 1974) ("A test fashioned from materials pertaining to the job . . . superficially may seem job-related. But what is at issue is whether it demonstrably selects people who will perform better the required on-the-job behaviors.").

In addition to the highly questionable character of the exams and the neglect of available alternatives, the City had other reasons to worry about its vulnerability to disparate-impact liability. Under the City's ground rules, IOS was not allowed to show the exams to anyone in the New Haven Fire Department prior to their administration. This "precluded [IOS] from being able to engage in [its] normal subject matter expert review process" — something Legel described as "very critical." As a result, some of the exam questions were confusing or irrelevant, and the exams may have over-tested some subject-matter areas while missing others. Testimony before the CSB also raised questions concerning unequal access to study materials and the potential bias introduced by relying principally on job analyses from nonminority fire officers to develop the exams.[16] . . .

---

16. The I-O Psychologists Brief identifies still other, more technical flaws in the exams that may well have precluded the City from prevailing in a disparate-impact suit. Notably, the exams were never shown to be suitably precise to allow strict rank ordering of candidates. A difference of one or two points on a multiple-choice exam should not be decisive of an applicant's promotion chances if that difference bears little relationship to the applicant's qualifications for the job. Relatedly, it appears that the line between a passing and failing score did not accurately differentiate between qualified and unqualified candidates. A number of fire-officer promotional exams have been invalidated on these bases. *See, e.g., Guardians Assn.*, 630 F. 2d, at 105 ("When a cutoff score unrelated to job performance produces disparate racial results, Title VII is violated."); *Vulcan Pioneers, Inc. v. New Jersey Dept. of Civil Serv.*, 625 F. Supp. 527, 538 (NJ 1985) ("[T]he tests here at issue are not appropriate for ranking candidates.").

In sum, the record solidly establishes that the City had good cause to fear disparate-impact liability. Moreover, the Court supplies no tenable explanation why the evidence of the tests' multiple deficiencies does not create at least a triable issue under a strong-basis-in-evidence standard.

B

Concurring in the Court's opinion, Justice Alito asserts that summary judgment for respondents would be improper even if the City had good cause for its noncertification decision. A reasonable jury, he maintains, could have found that respondents were not actually motivated by concern about disparate-impact litigation, but instead sought only "to placate a politically important [African-American] constituency." As earlier noted, I would not oppose a remand for further proceedings fair to both sides. It is the Court that has chosen to short-circuit this litigation based on its pretension that the City has shown, and can show, nothing more than a statistical disparity. Justice Alito compounds the Court's error.

Offering a truncated synopsis of the many hours of deliberations undertaken by the CSB, Justice Alito finds evidence suggesting that respondents' stated desire to comply with Title VII was insincere, a mere "pretext" for discrimination against white firefighters. In support of his assertion, Justice Alito recounts at length the alleged machinations of Rev. Boise Kimber (a local political activist), Mayor John DeStefano, and certain members of the mayor's staff.

Most of the allegations Justice Alito repeats are drawn from petitioners' statement of facts they deem undisputed, a statement displaying an adversarial zeal not uncommonly found in such presentations. What cannot credibly be denied, however, is that the decision against certification of the exams was made neither by Kimber nor by the mayor and his staff. The relevant decision was made by the CSB, an unelected, politically insulated body. It is striking that Justice Alito's concurrence says hardly a word about the CSB itself, perhaps because there is scant evidence that its motivation was anything other than to comply with Title VII's disparate-impact provision. Notably, petitioners did not even seek to take depositions of the two commissioners who voted against certification. Both submitted uncontested affidavits declaring unequivocally that their votes were "based solely on [their] good faith belief that certification" would have discriminated against minority candidates in violation of federal law.

Justice Alito discounts these sworn statements, suggesting that the CSB's deliberations were tainted by the preferences of Kimber and City officials, whether or not the CSB itself was aware of the taint. Kimber and City officials, Justice Alito speculates, decided early on to oppose certification and then "engineered" a skewed presentation to the CSB to achieve their preferred outcome.

As an initial matter, Justice Alito exaggerates the influence of these actors. The CSB, the record reveals, designed and conducted an inclusive decisionmaking process, in which it heard from numerous individuals on both sides of the certification question. Kimber and others no doubt used strong words to urge the CSB not to certify the exam results, but the CSB received "pressure" from supporters of certification as well as opponents. Petitioners, for example, engaged counsel to speak on their behalf before the CSB. Their counsel did not mince words: "[I]f you discard these results," she warned, "you will get sued. You will force the taxpayers of the city of New Haven into protracted litigation." The local firefighters union — an organization required by law to represent all the City's firefighters — was similarly outspoken in favor of certification. Discarding the test results, the union's president told the CSB, would be "totally ridiculous." He insisted, inaccurately, that the City was not at risk of disparate-impact liability because the exams were administered pursuant to "a collective bargaining agreement." Never mentioned by Justice Alito in his attempt to show testing expert Christopher Hornick's alliance with the City, the CSB solicited Hornick's testimony at the union's suggestion, not the City's. Hornick's cogent testimony raised substantial doubts about the exams' reliability.

There is scant cause to suspect that maneuvering or overheated rhetoric, from either side, prevented the CSB from evenhandedly assessing the reliability of the exams and rendering an independent, good-faith decision on certification. Justice Alito acknowledges that the CSB had little patience for Kimber's antics. As to petitioners, Chairman Segaloff — who voted to certify the exam results — dismissed the threats made by their counsel as unhelpful and needlessly "inflammatory." Regarding the views expressed by City officials, the CSB made clear that they were entitled to no special weight.[20]

In any event, Justice Alito's analysis contains a more fundamental flaw: It equates political considerations with unlawful discrimination. As Justice Alito sees it, if the mayor and his staff were motivated by their desire "to placate a . . . racial constituency," then they engaged in unlawful discrimination against petitioners. But Justice Alito fails to ask a vital question: "[P]lacate" how? That political officials would have politics in mind is hardly extraordinary, and there are many ways in which a politician can attempt to win over a constituency — including a racial constituency — without engaging in unlawful discrimination. As courts have recognized, "[p]oliticians routinely respond to bad press . . . , but it is not a violation of Title VII to take advantage of a situation to gain political favor." *Henry v. Jones*, 507 F. 3d 558, 567 (CA7 2007).

The real issue, then, is not whether the mayor and his staff were politically motivated; it is whether their attempt to score political points was legitimate (*i.e.*, nondiscriminatory). Were they seeking to exclude white firefighters from promotion (unlikely, as a fair test would undoubtedly result in the addition of white firefighters to the officer ranks), or did they realize, at least belatedly, that their tests could be toppled in a disparate-impact suit? In the latter case, there is no

---

20. Justice Alito points to evidence that the mayor had decided not to make promotions based on the exams even if the CSB voted to certify the results, going so far as to prepare a press release to that effect. If anything, this evidence reinforces the conclusion that the CSB — which made the noncertification decision — remained independent and above the political fray. The mayor and his staff needed a contingency plan precisely because they did not control the CSB.

disparate-treatment violation. Justice Alito, I recognize, would disagree. In his view, an employer's action to avoid Title VII disparate-impact liability qualifies as a presumptively improper race-based employment decision. I reject that construction of Title VII. As I see it, when employers endeavor to avoid exposure to disparate-impact liability, they do not thereby encounter liability for disparate treatment.

Applying this understanding of Title VII, supported by *Griggs* and the long line of decisions following *Griggs*, the District Court found no genuine dispute of material fact. That court noted, particularly, the guidance furnished by Second Circuit precedent. Petitioners' allegations that City officials took account of politics, the District Court determined, simply "d[id] not suffice" to create an inference of unlawful discrimination. The noncertification decision, even if undertaken "in a political context," reflected a legitimate "intent not to implement a promotional process based on testing results that had an adverse impact." Indeed, the District Court perceived "a total absence of any evidence of discriminatory animus towards [petitioners]." ("Nothing in the record in this case suggests that the City defendants or CSB acted 'because of' discriminatory animus toward [petitioners] or other non-minority applicants for promotion."). Perhaps the District Court could have been more expansive in its discussion of these issues, but its conclusions appear entirely consistent with the record before it.

It is indeed regrettable that the City's noncertification decision would have required all candidates to go through another selection process. But it would have been more regrettable to rely on flawed exams to shut out candidates who may well have the command presence and other qualities needed to excel as fire officers. Yet that is the choice the Court makes today. It is a choice that breaks the promise of *Griggs* that groups long denied equal opportunity would not be held back by tests "fair in form, but discriminatory in operation."

* * *

This case presents an unfortunate situation, one New Haven might well have avoided had it utilized a better selection process in the first place. But what this case does not present is race-based discrimination in violation of Title VII. I dissent from the Court's judgment, which rests on the false premise that respondents showed "a significant statistical disparity," but "nothing more."

NOTES

1. *Putting It All Together or Tearing It All Apart?* If you want an opportunity to think about big concepts spread across the entire course, *Ricci* has it all: systemic disparate treatment (Chapter 2), disparate impact (Chapter 3), testing (Chapter 3), affirmative action from a statutory or constitutional perspective (Chapter 2), the cat's paw doctrine (Chapter 1), and pretext (again, mostly from Chapter 1). What more could a professor (or student) ask for? The other perspective on *Ricci*, however, is that it tears apart quite a lot of what you've learned to this point. Indeed, there are those who think that it is the end of disparate impact liability.

That may be an overstatement, but *Ricci* is at least a sea change that will reverberate in a variety of ways.

2. *Procedural Oddities.* The district court had granted summary judgment for the defendants. A panel of the Second Circuit, including then-Judge Sonia Sotomayor, affirmed in a short, unsigned opinion; the en banc Circuit had also affirmed on rehearing, seven to six. Prior to the decision, but after the Court had granted certiorari, President Obama nominated Judge Sotomayor to replace outgoing Justice Souter. Before *Ricci* was handed down by the Supreme Court, Sotomayor's role in the case had become a major focus of opposition to her nomination. *E.g.*, Suzanne Sataline, *A Sotomayor Ruling Gets Scrutiny*, WALL ST. J., May 29, 2009, at A3. Thus, as the *Ricci* opinions were being written, many wondered how the Court would handle a case that might be critical (in both sense of the word) for someone who was nominated to join it. You be the judge — but keep in mind how unusual was the majority's result: not only did the Supreme Court reject summary judgment in favor of the defendants but it also found that plaintiffs were entitled to summary judgment. That means that the Court found that no material facts existed that would justify a trial

3. *The Holding.* The majority was clear: defendants' decision not to use test results because that would have meant no promotions for African Americans and only two for Hispanics, who together made up over half of the test takers, was intentional disparate treatment discrimination against the white test takers who would have been promoted had the test been certified. Further, the fact that granting promotions on the basis of the test results amounted to a prima facie case of disparate impact discrimination was not a defense to a disparate treatment case – unless the employer also has a strong basis in evidence to believe that it will be liable under the disparate impact theory, which means that it has no business necessity/job relation defense and there is no viable alternative employment practice.

4. *Relation to Affirmative Action.* Only Justice Ginsburg in dissent puts *Ricci* in context with the Court's Title VII affirmative action decisions. Recall that under *Weber/Johnson*, see p. 183, a prima facie case of disparate treatment is not required in order to justify an affirmative action plan; all that is necessary is a manifest imbalance in a traditionally segregated job category and no unnecessary trammeling of majority rights. In *Ricci*, however, even an uncontested prima facie case of disparate impact is not enough to permit the employer to take steps to reduce or eliminate the impact.

The parallels between affirmative action analysis under Title VII and *Ricci*'s approach to the intersection of disparate treatment and disparate impact are obvious. In both, race is allowed to influence an employer's decision, but only under certain circumstances. For a valid affirmative action plan, there must be a manifest imbalance and majority interests must not be unduly trammeled. For tests with a disparate impact, the test may be thrown out because of that impact, but only under a strong basis in evidence test. So both doctrines allow disparate treatment under more-or-less tight constraints.

Prior to *Ricci*, some wondered if the Roberts Court would overrule *Weber/Johnson*'s approval of voluntary affirmative action. Does *Ricci* suggest that the answer is no because it allows some systemic disparate treatment? On the other hand, *Ricci* was not an affirmative action case, at least as that term is normally used. No one was preferred over anyone else, although white firefighters lost promotions they would otherwise have gotten. Since the majority condemned actions taken for racial reasons absent a strong basis in evidence for disparate impact liability, *Ricci* can be viewed as harsher than the affirmative action cases. And the "strong basis in evidence test" clearly requires more in the way of proof than "manifest imbalance" does in the affirmative action context. *See generally* George Rutherglen, Ricci v. DeStefano: *Affirmative Action and the Lessons of Adversity*, 2009 SUP. CT. REV. 83, 85 ("*Ricci* might be doctrinally intricate, as many earlier decisions on affirmative action have been, but it boils down to a simple cautionary tale. Affirmative action plans never will escape scrutiny. The only question is how much they receive.")

In *United States v. Brennan*, 2011 U.S. App. LEXIS 9455, 120-122 (2d Cir. May 5, 2011), the court tried to explicate the meaning of *Ricci:* "we hold that, under *Ricci*, a "strong basis in evidence" of non-job-relatedness or of a less discriminatory alternative requires more than speculation, more than a few scattered statements in the record, and more than a mere fear of litigation, but less than the preponderance of the evidence that would be necessary for actual liability. This is what it means when courts say that the employer must have an objectively reasonable fear of disparate-impact liability." But, perhaps more meaningfully, the *Brennan* court went further to apply the strong basis in evidence test not only to the employer's general reaction to possible disparate impact liability but to the subsidiary questions of who might sue and what relief they might be entitled to.

5. *Does Knowledge Equal Intentional Discrimination?* The key factual finding of the Court was that "the City chose not to certify the examination results because of the statistical disparity based on race—*i.e.,* how minority candidates had performed compared to white candidates. . . . " But does this fact necessarily lead to the majority's conclusion—"[T]he city made its employment decision because of race. The City rejected the test results solely because the higher scoring candidates were white"? Is there a difference between intending not to disadvantage African-American and Hispanic candidates and intending to discriminate against white candidates?

This take us back to *Personnel Administrator v. Feeney*, p. 155, where the Court held, admittedly in the equal protection context, that acting with knowledge of a certain result (in that case, that a veteran's preference would disadvantage women) did not mean that the decision maker acted intentionally to achieve that result. " 'Discriminatory purpose,' however, implies more than intent as volition or intent as awareness of consequences. It implies that the decisionmaker . . . selected or reaffirmed a particular course of action at least in part 'because of,' not merely 'in spite of,' its adverse effects upon an identifiable group." Did New Haven invalidate the test in order to deprive whites of promotions? Or was that merely a foreseeable consequence? In *United States v. Brennan*, 2011 U.S. App. LEXIS 9455, 69-70 (2d Cir. May 5, 2011), the Second Circuit attempted to square *Ricci* with more traditional Title VII analysis:

Because the Supreme Court's majority opinion in *Ricci* does not explicitly cite *McDonnell Douglas* or any other case in that line, one might reasonably ask whether some other framework ought to apply in reverse-discrimination cases of this sort. In our view, however, *Ricci* fits well within the *McDonnell Douglas* framework. As the *Ricci* Court explained, New Haven "rejected the test results solely because the higher scoring candidates were white. The question is . . . whether the City had a lawful justification for its race-based action. " In other words, because the City's decision to reject the test results was explicitly based on a statistical racial disparity, it was beyond dispute that the plaintiffs had made out a prima facie case, so the burden shifted to the defendants to give a legitimate justification for the adverse employment action. The Court then held that, on summary judgment, the defendants had failed to provide a legitimate justification; and so the "pretext"" step of the inquiry was not reached.

See Michael J. Zimmer, Ricci's *Color-Blind Standard in a Race Conscious Society: A Case of Unintended Consequences?*, 2010 B.Y.U. L. REV. 1257, 1301 (prior to *Ricci*, "an employer acting with knowledge of the racial consequences of that action has not faced much risk of liability based on that knowledge alone; much more was needed to prove an action was 'because of' the race of the plaintiff. *Ricci* changes that. Knowing the racial consequences of an action now violates this 'color-blind' approach and anyone adversely affected by that action could bring a challenge."). *See also* Kerri Stone, *The Unexpected Appearance of Transferred Intent in Title VII*, 55 LOYOLA L. REV. 752 (2010), (finding "because of race" to be satisfied by action not directed at the particular plaintiffs adversely affected could be viewed as expanding the doctrines of "transferred intent" or "third party standing"). Helen Norton, *The Supreme Court's Post-Racial Turn Towards a Zero-Sum Understanding of Equality*, 52 WM. & MARY L. REV. 197, 200 (2010) ("*Ricci's* redefinition of culpable mental state for antidiscrimination purposes thus destabilizes the longstanding premise that the Court does not view decisionmakers attention to race to address patterns of racial hierarchy as itself suspicious.")

Justice Alito took a different tack. He concluded that, because an important participant in the political process was an African-American preacher who strongly resisted certifying the test, the decision of the CSB was "because of race." Does that follow? Justice Ginsburg argues that the decision may have been made "because of politics" and not race. But the term "racial politics" is pretty common, and both might have entered into the CSB's decision.

While the Court doesn't mention *Desert Palace*, is the majority applying a kind of motivating factor analysis? Of course, even if race is a motivating factor sufficient for liability, *Ricci* creates an additional defense beyond the usual "same decision anyway," and that is the "strong basis in evidence" of disparate impact liability.

6. *A Hierarchy of Theories?* The majority thinks that disparate treatment is the main evil that Congress proscribed; disparate impact is a late addition to the statute, and must be tailored to minimize any conflict with the disparate treatment bar. Justice Ginsberg, of course, takes an opposite view — *Griggs* made clear that disparate impact was implicit in Title VII from the beginning. This difference influences the approach of each side: disparate treatment can be sacrificed to

disparate impact, for the majority, only if the "strong basis in evidence" test is met, thus ensuring that disparate treatment is generally avoided. (You might also wonder, from a legislative intent perspective, why it matters to the majority that disparate impact was added only in the 1991 Civil Rights Act. Doesn't the application of the theory, no matter when, require trying to reconcile both in a nongrudging manner?) We leave it to you to decide whether the majority or the dissent has a more accurate view of history.

But let's probe Justice Ginsburg's view a bit more. She sees no conflict between disparate treatment and disparate impact claims. Disparate treatment prohibits intentional discrimination but, even if the employer's practices were not intentionally discriminatory, there is a duty to not use practices with a disparate impact unless the practices were justified as job-related and consistent with business necessity. By enacting both theories, Congress thus intended to allow race consciousness to avoid an unjustified racial impact. To put it another way, such race consciousness could not be the kind of disparate treatment Title VII meant to proscribe. For the dissent, the *Ricci* Court's equation of consciousness of race with intent to discriminate creates the tension that it then resolves with its new hierarchy of theories.

7. What's the Disagreement on the Standard? The various opinions disagree about a lot, especially about the application of the appropriate standard to the facts of the case. But Supreme Court decisions are usually more about law than facts, and is there much difference between the majority and the Ginsberg dissent? The majority articulates the "strong basis in evidence" standard. Justice Ginsberg would "hold that an employer who jettisons a selection device when its disproportionate racial impact becomes apparent does not violate Title VII's disparate-treatment bar automatically or at all, subject to this key condition: The employer must have good cause to believe the device would not withstand examination for business necessity." So the difference is "strong basis" vs. "good cause." A tempest in a teapot? *See generally* Herman N. Johnson, Jr., *The Evolving Strong-Basis-In-Evidence Standard*, ___ Berkeley J. Emp. & Lab. L. ___ (forthcoming) (analyzing the *Ricci* defense and arguing that, while the standard imposes a burden of persuasion on defendants, satisfying it requires something less than a preponderance of the evidence standard because the employer does not have to prove disparate impact discrimination).

At one point, Justice Ginsberg argues against the majority's standard because "[i]t is hard to see how these requirements differ from demanding that an employer establish" a provable, actual violation *against itself.*" (emphasis in original). In the affirmative action cases, we saw that some Justices sought to avoid requiring an employer, in defending an affirmative action plan favoring minorities, having to adduce proof that would make it liable to minorities. This would, obviously, discourage the adoption of such plans. But how does this argument apply here? By definition, if there is such a "strong basis," the employer can scrub the test. There will then be no disparate impact liability because the test is never used, and there will be no disparate treatment liability because of the strong basis for disparate impact liability.

8. *Isn't There Strong Basis for Disparate Impact Liability?* The Court conceded that, "[t]he racial adverse impact here was significant, and . . . the City was faced with a prima facie case of disparate-impact liability." The Court, however, minimizes the significance of such a conclusion — such a prima facie case "is far from a strong basis in evidence that the City would have been liable under Title VII had it certified the results." Can that be true in light of §703(k), which shifts the burden of persuasion to the defendant upon the showing of disparate impact? In other words, if black firefighters were to mount a disparate impact attack, they would win upon showing the fact of impact — unless the employer carried its burden of showing business necessity/job relation defense. *Ricci*, however, requires the employer seeking to avoid disparate impact liability in the first place to show that it has no business necessity, or at least show that it has a strong basis in evidence that it has no business necessity. *Wards Cove* shifted the burden of proving no business necessity to black plaintiffs. Is *Ricci* a very convoluted way of doing a version of the same thing, with the employer acting as a kind of proxy for potential black plaintiffs?

9. *Was the Test Job-Related and Consistent with Business Necessity as a Matter of Law?* Given (1) the majority's strong basis in evidence test, (2) its acknowledgment of the existence of a prima facie case, and (3) its grant of summary judgment to the white firefighters, it must follow that the test was valid as a matter of law. The process of test construction and administration in *Ricci* should be familiar to you from Chapter 3, p. 275. Under the Uniform Guidelines, IOS constructed a test that was supposedly content validated, i.e., that it was a sample of the job. Even though taking written or oral exams was not a part of the jobs in question, we've seen that content validation has been stretched pretty far. Do you think the exam was content valid under the precedents we've studied — or at least valid enough that the CSB had no strong basis in evidence to doubt its validity? Was there not even a question of material fact whether criterion or construct validation should have been required here? If so, the Court's disposition was wrong. "Assessment centers," where test takers perform tasks that replicate the actual job, can be content validated as job samples, but that approach was not used by the City of New Haven. Isn't there at least a question of fact whether the test that was used was not job-related and not consistent with business necessity? But the *Ricci* majority does not address the jurisprudence associated with the test exception in original §703(h). Why? *See generally* Mark S. Brodin, Ricci v. DeStefano: *The New Haven Firefighters Case and the Triumph of White Privilege*, ____ S. CAL. REV. L. & SOC. JUSTICE ____ (forthcoming 2011), *available at* http://papers.ssrn.com/sol3/papers.cfm?abstract_id=1691083; exploring society's "obsession with testing and its stubborn equation of merit with exam success, regardless of whether the exam actually predicts job performance."); Melissa Hart, *From* Wards Cove *to* Ricci: *Struggling Against the "Built-in-Headwinds" of a Skeptical Court* (Univ. of Colo. Law School, Working Paper No. 11-07, 2011) (despite the contrary evidence, the Court believed the tests to be valid because the results mirrored the racially-correlated expectations our culture had taught the Justices to equate with merit.); Cheryl I. Harris & Kimberly West-Faulcon, *Reading* Ricci: *White(ning) Discrimination, Race-ing Test Fairness*, 58 UCLA L. REV. 73, 73 (2010) ("New Haven's exams did not identify

the most qualified candidates but instead unfairly and unnecessarily reproduced the fire department's racially skewed status quo.").

10. *Alternative Employment Practices.* We've seen that even a valid test can't be used if there's an alternative employment practice that achieves the same purposes with lesser racial impact. The record before the CSB showed alternatives that were less discriminatory — simply altering the ratio of written to oral scores (as did Bridgeport, a city just down the interstate from New Haven), using "assessment centers," or altering the "rule of three" to a banding approach — all were alternatives that may have had less impact and that may have equally served the employer's needs. So why not remand on this question?

11. *Should the Minority Test Takers Claim Disparate Impact Discrimination?* Pursuant to the *Ricci* decision, the City will certify the test results. Suppose the African-American and Hispanic test takers now bring a disparate impact claim. Remember, they weren't parties to the litigation, which means that under normal principles of res judicata, they are not technically bound by the result (admittedly there is a possibility that they may be bound by virtue of a special provision inserted in Title VII by the Civil Rights Act of 1991, see p. 731, ironically, one designed to assist minority plaintiffs). *See* Charles A. Sullivan, Ricci v. DeStefano: *End of the Line or Just Another Turn on the Disparate Impact Road?,* 104 Nw. U. L. Rev. Colloquy 201 (2009). But, civil procedure principles aside, Justice Kennedy concluded the opinion for the Court with a rather enigmatic statement about a subsequent disparate impact suit:

> If, after it certifies the test results, the City faces a disparate-impact suit, then in light of our holding today it should be clear that the City would avoid disparate-impact liability based on the strong basis in evidence that, had it not certified the results, it would have been subject to disparate-treatment liability.

In other words, no disparate impact liability when an employer's fear of disparate treatment liability leads it to use a practice with a disparate impact.

In fact, a black firefighter did sue, and the district court rejected the claim, relying heavily on Justice Kennedy's sentence without coming to grips with the complicated preclusion questions just noted. *Briscoe v. City of New Haven,* 2010 U.S. Dist. LEXIS 69018, *22 (D. Conn. July 12, 2010) ("If, as he contends, Briscoe is denied his day in court or is bound by a decision in a case to which he was not a party, it is because the Supreme Court decided as much, and this court is bound by the decisions of the high court.").

12. *A New Defense to Impact Claims?* Looking at the same convoluted sentence in Justice Kennedy's majority opinion, Joseph Seiner & Benjamin Gutman, *Does* Ricci *Herald a New Disparate Impact?* 90 B.U. L. Rev. 2181, 2185 (2010), argue that *Ricci* creates of yet another affirmative defense to disparate impact discrimination: "the Supreme Court's concluding language could instead be read more broadly to suggest a new affirmative defense to disparate-impact claims [that] would protect an employer that, before using a workplace test, (1) reasonably examined the test for potential disparate impact; (2) uncovered evidence that the test results might disproportionately affect a minority protected group; and yet (3) did not uncover

evidence calling into question the test's validity." Does this make sense to you? Does it matter how rigorous the employer's search for evidence of invalidity? Accepting this argument does come close to making the fox the keeper of the chicken coop.

Let's probe this a bit more. While the *Ricci* majority *allows* an employer to take race into account when it has the requisite strong basis, does Kennedy's sentence suggest that the employer can *choose* never to apply disparate impact because doing so will always be disparate treatment? Under this view, avoidance of disparate treatment is always a complete defense to disparate impact. Or does the sentence make sense only when the employer does not (as New Haven didn't) have a strong basis to believe that it was subject to disparate impact liability? Under this view, an employer *must* avoid a practice with a disparate impact, even if it results in disparate treatment, so long as it has the requisite strong basis in evidence. But hold it—that can't be right. Before *Ricci*, an employer could prevail in a suit by black firefighters only by proving that it had a business necessity for its practice, not by showing that it had a strong basis in evidence that it had a business necessity.

The problem is a kind of infinite regression with Justice Kennedy's sentence: there's no disparate treatment liability when avoidance of disparate impact is sufficiently shown, but avoidance of disparate impact liability seems to turn on whether the employer can avoid disparate treatment liability. Is your head hurting yet?

13. *Or Maybe It Matters When?* The *Ricci* opinions focus on the decision whether or not to certify the test. At that point, the CSB had to favor either those who were successful or those who were not, with obvious racial consequences. But the majority also recognized that, in deciding whether or what to test, and before the competing expectations crystallized, potential racial effects can be taken into account:

> Nor do we question an employer's affirmative efforts to ensure that all groups have a fair opportunity to apply for promotions and to participate in the process by which promotions will be made. . . . Title VII does not prohibit an employer from considering, before administering a test or practice, how to design that test or practice in order to provide a fair opportunity for all individuals, regardless of their race. And when, during the test-design stage, an employer invites comments to ensure the test is fair, that process can provide a common ground for open discussions toward that end.

This strongly suggests, consistent with Justice Kennedy's stance in *Parents Involved in Community Schools v. Seattle School District No. 1*, 551 U.S. 701 (2007), see p. 201, that an employer need not be color-blind in its approach to test design. *See* Reva B. Siegel, *From Colorblindness to Antibalkanization: An Emerging Ground of Decision in Race Equality cases*, 120 YALE L. J. 1278, 1285-86 (2011) (throwing out a test once administered for reasons to be race has the potential to estrange and balkanize communities, which provides a principled basis for limiting *Ricci* to cases of retesting while preserving disparate impact for other situations); Nancy L. Zisk,

Failing the Test: How Ricci v. DeStefano *Failed to Clarify Disparate Impact and Disparate Treatment Law* 34 HAMLINE L. REV. 27, 28-29 (2011).

14. *Is This 1989 Redux?* It has been 20 years, but has a new conservative majority in the Roberts Court been able to undermine Title VII just as the Rehnquist Court majority did in 1989? Is the fear that employers would have an incentive to use racial quotas what drives the *Ricci* decision, just as it drove the decision in *Wards Cove*? Will Justice Ginsburg's prediction that this decision will not last prove true? If Congress were to act to create a statutory defense less stringent than strong basis in evidence, would this new majority take the step suggested by Justice Scalia to embed *Ricci* in the Constitution by striking down disparate impact analysis as unconstitutional? Politically, how likely is a legislative response now comparable to the Civil Rights Act of 1991?

5 Special Problems in Applying Title VII, Section 1981, and the ADEA

B. Coverage of Title VII, Section 1981, and the ADEA

Page 323. Delete present Note 2; replace with new Notes:

2. *Independent Contractors.* The Supreme Court has recognized that the definitional terms in most employment-related statutes are "completely circular and explain[] nothing,", *e.g., Clackamas Gastroenterology Assocs., P.C. v. Wells*, 538 U.S. 440, 444 (2003) (ADA); *Nationwide Mut. Ins. Co. v. Darden*, 503 U.S. 318, 322 (1992) (ERISA). As a result, the Court viewed Congress as having meant by "employment" what it described in *Community for Creative Non-Violence v. Reid*, 490 U.S. 730, 740 (1989), as "the conventional master-servant relationship as understood by common-law agency doctrine." Master-servant law, however, was designed largely to determine when a master would be liable to a third party for the torts of his servants; it is not surprising that it focuses on the right of a master to "control" the actions of his servant, which would thereby justify holding the master responsible since he could have avoided the tort by virtue of better supervision. Nevertheless, *Reid's* statement of the common law principles has come to dominate all subsequent discussions of the issue of when an individual is an employee as opposed to an independent contractor. The passage *Lerohl* quoted from *Reid* begins by saying "In determining whether a hired party is an employee under the general common law of agency, we consider the hiring party's right to control the manner and means by which the product is accomplished." The remaining twelve "factors" seem to be ways, among others, to ascertain "control."

Under this reading, the two plaintiffs in *Lerohl* were clearly employees because their work was very closely controlled—a conductor not only dictates when and where an orchestra member plays, but also how she plays, what she wears, and even her facial expressions. The alternative approach, the one used by the *Lerohl* court, is to assess the factors and, using some undefined weighting scheme, conclude whether or not the individual is an employee. Under this view, which seems to be the more common, the question is less "control" in the abstract than adding and subtracting factors. *E.g., Brown v. J. Kaz, Inc.*, 581 F.3d 175 (3d Cir. 2009) (sales representatives were independent contractors not employees when representatives could schedule their own appointments; the firm made only general suggestions as to sales pitches and barred false or misleading statements; representatives had to provide most of their own equipment, their own office supplies, and their her own transportation to appointments; and representatives were provided no office space and paid on a commission basis only); *Alberty-Velez v. Corporacion de P.R. para la Difusion Publica*, 361 F.3d 1, 7-9 (1st Cir. 2004) (female co-host of a television show was an independent contractor); *Weary v. Cochran*, 377 F.3d 522, 526 (6th Cir. 2004) (2-1) (plaintiff insurance agent was an independent contractor); Does either approach make sense in terms of the aims of the antidiscrimination laws? Remember, the Court views these laws as simply adopting common law concepts, concepts developed mostly for purposes of liability to third parties.

2A. *Avoiding Liability by Using Independent Contractors*. Did Sinfonia structure its relationships with its musicians to avoid being covered by antidiscrimination and other laws? The "independent contractor" category offers an escape hatch from laws regulating employment, and some companies have radically restructured their operations by converting "employees" to "independent contractors." See Joseph B. Treaster, *Federal Agency Sues Allstate, Claiming Age Discrimination*, N.Y. TIMES, Oct. 8, 2004, at C5. There have been challenges to such conversions as disparate treatment. *See Isbell v. Allstate Ins. Co.*, 418 F.3d 788, 795 (7th Cir. 2005) (Allstate did not violate the ADEA when it eliminated employee-agent positions; "every employee in that position lost his job, *regardless* of age," and every employee was offered a new position, although not necessarily as an employee) (emphasis in original). However, some efforts to outsource employment pose their own problems. *See Halpert v. Manhattan Apts., Inc.*, 580 F.3d 86, 88 (2d Cir. 2009) (while a firm is not liable for hiring decisions made by independent contractors hiring on their own behalf, a firm that "gives an individual authority to interview job applicants and make hiring decisions on the company's behalf . . . may be held liable if that individual improperly discriminates against applicants on the basis of age."). *See generally* Richard R. Carlson, *Why The Law Still Can't Tell An Employee When It Sees One and How It Ought to Stop Trying*, 22 BERKELEY J. EMP. & LAB. L. 295 (2001); Lewis L. Maltby & David C. Yamada, *Beyond "Economic Realities": The Case for Amending Federal Employment Discrimination Laws to Include Independent Contractors*, 38 B.C. L. REV. 239 (1997).

Page 325. Add in carryover Note 3, *Owners as Employees*, following *Id.* at 449 cite immediately after extract:

See Fichman v. Media Ctr., 512 F.3d 1157, 1161 (9th Cir. 2008) (applying the six *Clackamas* factors to find the members of the board of directors were not Media Center employees in large part because they received no compensation).

5. Special Problems in Applying Title VII, Section 1981, and the ADEA

Page 325.   Add at end of carryover Note 3, *Owners as Employees*:

But see Frank J. Menetrez, *Employee Status and the Concept of Control in Federal Employment Discrimination Law* 63 SMU L. REV. 137 (2010) (given the Supreme Court's holding that whether an individual is an employee for purposes of federal antidiscrimination law is to be governed by the common law of agency, the entire body of case law regarding whether owners can also be employees must be rethought since the common law often viewed employers also as employees).

Page 326.   Delete Note 7 and replace with the following:

7. *Integrated Enterprises and Joint Employers.* It is sometimes possible to aggregate two or more entities into a statutory employer. The "integrated enterprise" or "single employer" doctrine views two or more formally distinct legal entities as being in reality a single employer, thus allowing the employees of all to be aggregated to reach the required minimum number. *See Arculeo v. On-Site Sales & Mktg., L.L.C.*, 425 F.3d 193, 199 (2d Cir. 2005) ("although nominally and technically distinct, several entities [may] properly seen as a single integrated entity."). One court suggested three situations in which a company and its affiliates are a single employer:

(1) a company splits itself into entities with less than fifteen employees intending to evade Title VII's reach;

(2) a parent company has directed the subsidiary's discriminatory act of which the plaintiff is complaining;

(3) as in bankruptcy law, when "two or more entities' affairs are so interconnected that they collectively caused the alleged discriminatory employment practice. More colloquially, the question is whether the 'eggs'—consisting of the ostensibly separate companies—are so scrambled that we decline to unscramble them. We note, however, that substantive consolidation is an equitable remedy and is difficult to achieve."

Nesbit v. Gears Unlimited, Inc., 347 F.3d 72, 85-86 (3d Cir. 2003). *But see Garrett-Woodberry v. Miss. Bd. of Pharm.*, 300 F. App'x 289 (5th Cir. 2008) ("single employer" test should not be applied to a state agency; even were it applied, the Board of Pharmacy could not be properly aggregated with other state agencies when there was no centralized control of labor relations). *See generally* Richard R. Carlson, *The Small Firm Exemption and the Single Employer Doctrine in Employment Discrimination Law*, 80 ST. JOHN'S L. REV. 1197 (2006).

Distinct from the single employer/integrated enterprise doctrine is the "joint employment" doctrine under which an employee of one entity may hold another entity liable; the premise is not that two entities are one but rather that "they co-determine the essential terms and conditions of employment." *Bristol v. Bd. of County Comm'rs*, 312 F.3d 1213, 1218 (10th Cir. 2002). One of the entities may be too small to be a statutory employer, which may make joint employment critical to liability for anyone. *See Sanford v. Main St. Baptist Church Manor, Inc.*, 327 F. App'x 587, 594 (6th Cir. 2009) ("aggregation of joint employees for the purposes of establishing the Title VII numerosity requirement is permissible when one joint employer exercises control over the employees of the other joint employer"). But joint employment also expands the number of entities that may be held liable for a particular violation, which can be critical should one of the entities be in financial difficulty.

Page 327.   Add in Note 8, *Interns and Volunteers*, before *York* cite:

Fichman v. Media Ctr., 512 F.3d 1157, 1160 (9th Cir. 2008) (members of a board of directors were not employees when they were not compensated for their service beyond travel reimbursement and food supplied at Board meetings;

Page 328.   Add at end of carryover Note 10, *Federal Government*:

Walch v. Adjutant General's Dep't of Texas, 533 F.3d 289 (5th Cir. 2008) (when military and civilian duties are entangled, a plaintiff may not raise Title VII claims even as to otherwise actionable civilian employment);

Page 328.   In Note 12, *Creative Applications*, delete *from Shah* citation; replace with the following:

Lopez v. Massachusetts, 588 F.3d 69 (1st Cir. 2009) (state agency that administered promotional exams for local police officers under state civil service system was not a Title VII "employer" when acting in that capacity).

The expanding control hospitals exercise over physicians with admitting privileges may mean that such persons are employees. Traditionally, physicians with clinical privileges were found not to be employees. *E.g.*, *Shah v. Deaconess Hosp.*, 355 F.3d 496, 500 (6th Cir. 2004), but changes in the way health care is delivered may alter that. *See Salamon v. Our Lady of Victory Hosp.*, 514 F.3d 217 (2d Cir. 2008) (hospital exercised substantial control not only over the treatment outcomes of a physician with clinical privileges but also of the details and methods of her work, timing of procedures, and her choices about which medications to prescribe, which created a fact question as to whether an employee- employer relationship existed).

Page 328.   Delete Note 13, and replace with new Note 13:

13. *Exemptions*. There are several explicit exemptions in the antidiscrimination statutes. Title VII, for example, exempts a "bona fide private membership club." §701(b)(2), 42 U.S.C. §2000e(b)(2), and also exempts Indian tribes. §701(b),

5. Special Problems in Applying Title VII, Section 1981, and the ADEA

42 U.S.C. §2000e(b) (2007). *E.g., Thomas v. Choctaw Management/Services Enter.*, 313 F.3d 910 (5th Cir. 2002) (business owned entirely by the Choctaw Nation did not constitute an "employer" under Title VII). *See also Nanomantube v. Kickapoo Tribe*, 631 F.3d 1150 (10th Cir. 2011) (tribal sovereign immunity deprived federal court of jurisdiction where Congress specifically exempted Indian tribes from Title VII' and agreement to comply with Title VII contained in tribe's employee handbook was not unequivocal waiver of immunity). While this exception is not expressly included in the ADEA, it has been read into the statute.

While not a formal exemption, the denial of a security clearance may also effectively preclude Title VII suit, even if the plaintiff claims that this is merely a pretext for a decision taken for discriminatory reasons. *See Makky v. Chertoff*, 541 F.3d 205 (3d Cir. 2008) (a mixed-motive plaintiff fails to establish a prima facie case if there is unchallenged objective evidence that he did not possess the bare minimum qualifications for the position he sought to obtain or retain; like a license, a security clearance is a basic qualification for some jobs). *But see Bennett v. Chertoff*, 425 F.3d 999, 1003-04 (D.C. Cir. 2005) (court cannot adjudicate whether revocation of clearance is pretextual since that would require the trier of fact to evaluate the validity of the agency's security determination.).

Other exceptions from the antidiscrimination statutes may be found in other federal laws or treaties. For example, in *Sumitomo Shoji, America, Inc. v. Avagliano*, 457 U.S. 176 (1982), the Supreme Court considered a claim that, by virtue of the Friendship, Commerce, and Navigation Treaty between the United States and Japan, the defendant was immune for discrimination against non-Japanese in filling certain positions. The Court rejected the defense on the ground that the defendant, a New York-incorporated subsidiary of a Japanese corporation, did not qualify as a "company of Japan," but it indicated that a true "company of Japan" can invoke this defense. *See also Papaila v. Uniden Am. Corp.*, 51 F.3d 54 (5th Cir. 1995) (U.S. subsidiary can invoke treaty where discrimination dictated by parent); *MacNamara v. Korean Air Lines*, 863 F.2d 1135 (3d Cir. 1988) (reading the treaty to allow citizenship discrimination but to prohibit a beneficiary of the treaty from intentionally discriminating, even in its executive positions, on the basis of age, sex, religion, or race); *Brzak v. U.N.*, 597 F.3d 107, 111 (2d Cir. 2010) (the U.N. and its officers immune from Title VII suit).

Page 329.   Delete Note on Coverage of §1981; replace with the following:

Note on Coverage of §1981

Questions of "employment" as such do not arise under §1981 since that statute reaches all "contract" relations, not merely employment. *See Runyon v. McCrary*, 427 U.S. 160 (1976). Thus, §1981 embraces relationships that do not constitute "employment" under Title VII, such as partnership or independent contractor status. *E.g., Brown v. J. Kaz, Inc.*, 581 F.3d 175 (3d Cir. 2009) (independent contractor may sue for race discrimination); *Wortham v. Am. Family Ins. Group*, 385 F.3d 1139 (8th Cir. 2004) (while Title VII suit was barred because plaintiff was an independent "contractor," he was protected by §1981). The statute has been held applicable to at-will employment, despite that argument that, in some states, such employment is not contractual under state law. *Walker v. Abbott Labs.*, 340 F.3d 471 (7th Cir. 2003). *But see Jimenez v. Wellstar Health Sys.*, 596 F.3d 1304 (11th Cir. 2010) (because a doctor's hospital privileges were not contractual in nature under Georgia law, §1981 offered no relief from a discriminatory suspension of them).

Further, §1981 reaches all employers, except the federal government, *Brown v. General Serv. Admin.*, 425 U.S. 820, 825 (1976) (Title VII exclusive discrimination remedy for federal employment within its scope), thus covering employers exempt from Title VII. As for the contractual relationships of state and local governmental employers, any doubt as to this was resolved by the 1991 Civil Rights Act adding paragraph (c), providing that "[t]he rights protected by this section are protected against impairment by nongovernmental discrimination and impairment under color of State law." One circuit has held this language reaches local governments, *Federation of African Am. Contractors v. City of Oakland*, 96 F.3d 1204 (9th Cir. 1996) (concluding 1991 amendments to §1981 imply a cause of action against state actors), but most circuit courts have held to the contrary. *McGovern v. City of Phila.*, 554 F.3d 114 (3d Cir. 2009); *Bolden v. City of Topeka*, 441 F.3d 1129 (10th Cir. 2006).

The courts holding against application of §1981 to state and local governments follow a complicated path to avoid what seems to be the plain language of the provision. They rely on *Jett v. Dallas Independent Sch. Dist.*, 491 U.S. 701 (1989), in which the Supreme Court held a plaintiff must use the remedial provisions of 42 U.S.C. §1983 to enforce §1981. In turn, §1983 does not authorize suit against the states at all, *Will v. Michigan Dep't of State Police*, 491 U.S. 58, 63 (1989), and §1983 suits against local governments are circumscribed by a web of immunities. *Jett* predated the Civil Rights Act of 1991 and, therefore, arguably was legislatively overruled by that statute's addition of paragraph (c) to §1981. However, the courts holding against §1981 as an independent source of rights against state and local government discrimination have found paragraph (c) to be insufficiently clear to overrule *Jett*.

C. Sex Discrimination

1. Discrimination "Because of Sex"

Page 335. Add at the end of Note 2, *Harassment Need Not Be "Sexual" to Be Actionable*:

Even where conduct occurs in an open area where men and women work together, profanity and other "sex-specific" language and conduct may be deemed harassment "based on sex." In *Gallagher v. C.H. Robinson Worldwide, Inc.*, 567 F.3d 263, 273 (6th Cir. 2009), the Sixth Circuit reasoned that:

The natural effect of exposure to such offensive conduct is embarrassment, humiliation and degradation, irrespective of the harasser's motivation—especially and all the more so if the captive recipient of the harassment is a woman. . . . Hence, even though members of both sexes were exposed to the offensive conduct in the Cleveland office, considering the nature of the patently degrading and anti-female nature of the harassment, it stands to reason that women would suffer, as a result of the exposure, greater disadvantage in the terms and conditions of employment than men.

Id. at 272.

Page 336.   Add at end of Note 4, The "Equal Opportunity" Harasser:

See also Smith v. Hy-Vee, Inc., 622 F.3d 904, 908 (8th Cir. 2010) (despite evidence that harasser touched plaintiff and made sexual references, there was not sufficient basis to infer that she was motivated by sexual desire because she subjected both men and women to the same behavior); *Love v. Motiva Enters. LLC*, 349 F. App'x 900, 903 (5th Cir. 2009) (although harassment was framed in sexual terms, the conduct did not amount to implicit proposals for sex, where the conduct was generally accompanied by derogatory comments about employee's appearance and character and harasser had a history of treating others rudely and disrespectfully).

Page 336.   Add at beginning of Note 6, *Academic Commentary*:

Ann C. McGinley, *Creating Masculine Identities: Bullying and Harassment "Because of Sex,"* 79 U. COLO. L. REV. 1151, 1154-55 (2008) (many group behaviors, such as bullying "occur with the conscious or unconscious motivation of reinforcing gender norms in the workplace or punishing those who do not conform to those norms");

a.   Discrimination Because of Sexual Orientation

Page 343.   Add at end of carryover Note 1, *Sexual Orientation ≠ Sex Under Title VII*:

See Love v. Motiva Enters. LLC, 349 F. App'x 900 (5th Cir. 2009) (even though a female co-worker's rude and obnoxious actions often, but not always, took a sexual form, the failure of plaintiff to show that her harasser was lesbian meant that the plaintiff could not show they were because of sex). *But see* Ann McGinley, *Erasing Boundaries: Masculinities, Sexual Minorities and Employment Discrimination*, 43 U. MICH. J.L. REFORM 713 (2010) (Title VII's sex discrimination prohibition should protect sexual minorities from discrimination and should provide reasonable accommodation to allow sexual minorities to live and work with dignity and security); L. Camille Hébert, *Transforming Transsexual and Transgender Rights*, 15

Wm. & Mary J. Women & L. 535, 989-90 (2009) ("the term 'sex" should be defined more broadly than courts have seen fit to do with respect to sexual minorities" to extend protection not only on biological status but gender-linked traits, including gender identity).

Page 343.   Delete Note 2; replace:

2. *Distinguishing Sexual Orientation from Sex Stereotyping.* Although the lower courts have rejected claims based on sexual orientation per se, claims based on a failure to conform to sex stereotypes have been upheld, with courts relying on *Price Waterhouse. See Prowel v. Wise Bus. Forms, Inc.*, 579 F.3d 285, 291 (3d Cir. 2009) (while "the line between sexual orientation discrimination and discrimination 'because of sex' can be difficult to draw," harassment based on a male plaintiff's effeminacy and lack of conformity to male gender stereotype precluded summary judgment); *Lewis v. Heartland Inns of Am., L.L.C.*, 591 F.3d 1033, 1039 (8th Cir. 2010) (discrimination based on sex stereotyping, in this case criticisms of the plaintiff for being tomboyish rather than a having a "Midwestern girl look," could be actionable); *Nichols v. Azteca Restaurant Enterprises, Inc.*, 256 F.3d 864 (9th Cir. 2001) ("because of sex" element was established where a male employee was subject to verbal abuse because of his "feminine mannerisms");

Even though the *Vickers* court rejected plaintiff's discrimination claim, it agreed that a sex stereotyping claim could be actionable. Do you find convincing the majority's explanation for why Vickers had no claim for sex stereotyping? Was Vickers the victim of the egregious harassment he suffered because he was believed to be homosexual? And if so, was he so viewed because he failed to conform to masculine stereotypes? The *Vickers* majority observed that recognizing Vickers' sex stereotyping claim would make any discrimination based on sexual orientation actionable. Do you agree? And if so, was that a legitimate basis for denying the claim? Does the principle cut both ways? *See Medina v. Income Support Division*, 413 F.3d 1131 (10th Cir. 2005) (woman claiming harassment for failure to conform to what she termed "lesbian stereotypes" had no claim because heterosexuality is not protected by Title VII). *See also* Zachary A. Kramer, *Heterosexuality and Title VII*, 103 NW. U. L. Rev. 205, 227-30 (2009) (since society tends not to think of heterosexuals as having a sexual orientation, courts are unable to see when an employee's sex discrimination claim implicates her heterosexuality. As a result, heterosexual employees are simply not at risk of losing their sex discrimination claims because of their sexual orientation.).

Page 345.   Add before Secunda citation after extract:

See also Witt v. Dep't of the Air Force, 527 F.3d 806, 819 (9th Cir. 2008) ("when the government attempts to intrude upon the personal and private lives of homosexuals, in a manner that implicates the rights identified in *Lawrence* [such as the military's Don't Ask, Don't Tell policy], the government must advance an important governmental interest, the intrusion must significantly further that interest, and the intrusion must be necessary to further that interest. In other words, for the third factor, a less intrusive means must be unlikely to achieve substantially the government's interest.").

b. "Reverse Discrimination" and "Personal Relationships"

Page 347. Add in first full paragraph before *Pipkins* cite:

See also Forrest v. Brinker Int'l Payroll Co., LP, 511 F.3d 225, 229 (1st Cir. 2007) ("In cases involving a prior failed relationship between an accused harasser and alleged victim, reasoning that the harassment could not have been motivated by the victim's sex because it was instead motivated by a romantic relationship gone sour establishes a false dichotomy. Presumably the prior relationship would never have occurred if the victim were not a member of the sex preferred by the harasser, and thus the victim's sex is inextricably linked to the harasser's decision to harass.").

c. Grooming and Dress Codes

Page 353. Add before *Carbado* cite in Note 3, *Grooming Codes as "Sex Stereotyping"*:

Meredith M. Render, *Gender Rules*, 22 YALE J.L. & FEMINISM 133 (2010) (arguing that sex-based employer rules, like the one at issue in *Jespersen*, entrench gender generalizations; Angela Onwauchi-Willig, *Another Hair Piece, Exploring New Strands of Analysis*, 2010, 98 GEO. L.J. 1079, 1087 (2010) ("braids, locks, and twists are the functional equivalents of Afros and should be viewed "in the same light as other phenotypical and racial characteristics, such as skin color and nose width."); D. Wendy Greene, Black Women Can't Have Blonde Hair . . . in the Workplace, 14 GENDER, RACE & JUST. 405 (2011).

d. Discrimination Because of Pregnancy

Page 355. Insert before the asterisks in middle of the page:

Although the PDA was enacted over 30 years ago, the impact of the Supreme Court's *Gilbert* decision lingers. In *AT&T Corp. v. Hulteen*, 129 S. Ct. 1962 (2009), the Court held that a company benefits policy providing less retirement credit for pre-PDA pregnancy leave than for other medical leave was not a violation of Title VII. Prior to the PDA, AT&T treated pregnancy leave less favorably than other temporary disability leaves when calculating length of service. After the PDA, pregnancy and other temporary disability leaves were treated the same. Upon retirement, however, women who had taken pre-PDA pregnancy leave received less service credit than workers who had taken other forms of leave, thereby reducing their pension benefits. Plaintiffs challenged this failure to provide full service credit for pre-PDA pregnancy leaves, claiming it constituted a present act of discrimination, actionable under Title VII.

The Court disagreed. The original denial of seniority credit was not discriminatory within the meaning of Title VII because of *Gilbert*: pregnancy discrimination did not constitute sex discrimination at that time. While the PDA did equate pregnancy discrimination with sex discrimination, it was not retroactive, and, after the PDA was passed in 1978, AT&T did treat women disabled by pregnancy the same as similarly disabled males. As for the fact that the company was perpetuating the pre-PDA discrimination after the effective date of the PDA by continuing to deny seniority credit, the Court said that there was no present act of intentional discrimination because the company was simply applying its seniority system's service credit rules. The rules themselves were facially neutral; the only intentional adverse treatment of pregnancy engaged in by AT&T occurred at a time when discrimination against pregnancy was not unlawful. Moreover, the effect or impact of that intentional adverse treatment, although continuing into the present through the seniority system's rules for calculating length of service, could not be challenged due to the shield for seniority systems provided by §703(h).

Justice Ginsburg, joined by Justice Breyer, dissented. The PDA made clear, said Ginsburg, Congress's complete rejection of *Gilbert*'s reasoning, and thus permitting *Gilbert*'s rationale to insulate AT&T from liability in the present was at odds with the wording and purpose of the PDA.

Page 359.   Add at end of first paragraph of Note 1, Is the PDA's Protection Only Status Protection?:

See also Kucharski v. Cort Furniture Rental, 342 F. App'x 712 (2d Cir. 2009) (failure to return to work after four weeks' paid medical leave provided by employer's policy was legitimate reason to discharge pregnant employee, even though her inability to return was due to medical complications, where the policy was applied uniformly regardless of sex or medical condition).

Page 360.   Add at the end of carryover Note 2, *The Two Clauses of the PDA*:

See also Spees v. James Marine, Inc., 617 F.3d 380 (6th Cir. 2010) (employer's decision to terminate employee because she was unable to work pursuant to a doctor's note prescribing bed rest and lacked any available medical leave did not establish pregnancy discrimination). While this suggests the limitations of the PDA, one writer stresses that the statute has nevertheless had very important implications. Michelle A. Travis, *The PDA's Causation Effect: Observations of an Unreasonable Woman*, YALE J.L. & FEMINISM 51 (2009).

Page 360.   Add in Note 3, *Proving Discrimination* after *Fjelsta* cite:

Elam v. Regions Fin. Corp., 601 F.3d 873 (8th Cir. 2010) (references to plaintiff's pregnancy prior to her discharge for excessive absences did not constitute evidence of discrimination and to her morning sickness when they merely reflected her condition without further indication of bias);).

Page 361.   Add before *Martinez* **cite in Note 5,** *The Question of Accommodation*:

Puente v. Ridge, 324 F. App'x 423 (5th Cir. 2009) ("Assuming without deciding that [plaintiff seeking breastfeeding accommodation] would fall within the class of persons protected by the PDA, 'the PDA does not impose an affirmative obligation on employers to grant preferential treatment . . . ' ");

Page 361.   Add at end of Note 5, *The Question of Accommodation:*

The Patient Protection and Affordable Care Act, better known as the Healthcare Reform Act, amends the Fair Labor Standards Act to provide for break times for nursing mothers. 29 U.S.C. §207(r) (2011). The act requires "reasonable break time" and a place other than a bathroom which is "shielded from view and free from intrusion" each time an employee needs to express breast milk for her nursing child for a year after the child's birth. §207(r)(1). However, an employer is not required to compensate employees during these breaks beyond any compensation ordinarily provided for break time. Further, employers with fewer than 50 employees may be exempt from this requirement if it would impose an undue hardship. §207(r)(2)-(3).

Page 361.   Delete Note 6; replace with:

6. *Contraception and Other Health Plan Coverage Issues*. The PDA protects against discrimination not only on account of pregnancy but also on account of "childbirth and related medical conditions." As a result, Title VII bars discrimination based on a woman having an in vitro procedure, *Hall v. Nalco Co.*, 534 F.3d 644, 645 (7th Cir. 2008) ("Although infertility affects both men and women, Hall claims she was terminated for undergoing a medical procedure — a particular form of surgical impregnation — performed only on women on account of their childbearing capacity. Because adverse employment actions taken on account of childbearing capacity affect only women, Hall has stated a cognizable sex-discrimination claim . . . "), or an abortion, *Doe v. C.A.R.S. Prot. Plus*, 527 F.3d 358 (3d Cir. 2008) (Title VII protects a woman from discrimination because she had had an abortion).

Is it sex discrimination for an employer's prescription drug plan to exclude coverage for contraceptives? One circuit has held no. *See Standridge v. Union Pac. R.R. Co.*, 479 F.3d 936 (8th Cir. 2007) (holding that the PDA does not apply to contraception and it is not gender discrimination for health plan to exclude coverage of prescription contraceptive). Addressing a related benefits issue, *Saks v. Franklin Covey Co.*, 316 F.3d 337 (2d Cir. 2003), rejected a claim that denial of coverage for fertility treatments violated Title VII. The court viewed the proper test for reviewing a sex discrimination challenge to a health benefits plan as "whether sex-specific conditions exist, and if so, whether exclusion of benefits for those conditions results in a plan that provides inferior coverage to one sex." *Id.* at 344. "[B]ecause the exclusion of surgical impregnation procedures disadvantages infertile male and female employees equally, Saks's claim does not fall within the purview of the PDA." *Id.* at 346. Further, while the particular procedure plaintiff sought was performed on women, there was no sex discrimination in denying coverage since "the need for the procedures may be traced to male, female, or couple infertility with equal frequency. Thus, surgical impregnation procedures may be recommended regardless of the gender of the ill patient." Id. at 347. *But see Erickson v. Bartell Drug Co.*, 141 F. Supp. 2d 1266 (W.D. Wash. 2001) (exclusion of contraceptive coverage violates Title VII); Stephen F. Befort & Elizabeth Canney Borer, *Equitable Prescription Drug Coverage: Preventing Sex Discrimination in Employer-Provided Health Plans,* 70 LA. L. REV. 205, 207 (2009) (arguing that employers that exclude prescription contraceptives from employee health insurance plans violate the PDA because the failure to provide such insurance coverage "necessarily affects a sex-related medical condition since only women can become pregnant"). What if a plan excludes coverage for Viagra? Is that sex discrimination? *See generally* Brietta R. Clark, Erickson v. Bartell Drug Co.: *A Roadmap for Gender Equality in Reproductive Health Care or an Empty Promise?*, 23 J. L. & INEQUALITY 299 (2005) (Title VII challenges to prescription contraception are more likely to be successful than challenges to infertility benefits even though both exclusions reflect gender stereotyping based on pervasive notions of motherhood and sexual freedom and both exclusions have significant adverse health effects on women); Ernest F. Lidge III , *An Employer's Exclusion of Coverage for Contraceptive Drugs Is Not Per Se Sex Discrimination,* 76 TEMPLE L. REV. 533 (2003). *See also* Melissa Cole, *Beyond Sex Discrimination: Why Employers Discriminate Against Women with Disabilities When Their Employee Health Plans Exclude Contraceptives from Prescription Coverage,* 43 ARIZ. L. REV. 501 (2001) (exclusion of contraceptives from prescription coverage may violate the ADA).

Page 362.   Add a new Note 7:

7. *Using Title VII to Break Down the "Maternal Wall."* Professor Joan Williams has used the term "maternal wall" to refer to barriers that impede the workplace advancement of women with childcare responsibilities, including differential accommodation, hostility, and stereotyping. *See* Joan C. Williams & Nancy Segal, *Beyond the Maternal Wall: Relief for Family Caregivers Who Are Discriminated Against on the Job,* 26 HARV. WOMEN'S L.J. 77 (2003). She argues that Title VII has been more effective in dealing with "maternal wall" cases than is often realized, *e.g., Walsh v. National Computer Systems,* 332 F.3d 1150 (8th Cir. 2003) (upholding verdict in favor of a plaintiff who had been discriminated against because she had been pregnant, had taken a maternity leave, and might become pregnant again). Williams also details a number of other legal theories under existing

discrimination law that may be brought to bear in workplaces that do not accommodate mothers. *Id.* at 124, 151-60; *see also* Joan C. Williams & Stephanie Bornstein, *The Evolution of "FReD": Family Responsibilities Discrimination and Developments in the Law of Stereotyping and Implicit Bias*, 59 HASTINGS L.J. 1311 (2008); Joan C. Williams, *Using Social Science to Litigate Gender Discrimination Cases and Defang the "Cluelessness" Defense*, 7 EMPL. RTS. & EMPLOY. POL'Y J. 401 (2003). The EEOC has also addressed the question of how Title VII prohibits discrimination against caregivers. *See* EEOC, *Enforcement Guidance: Unlawful Disparate Treatment of Workers with Caregiving Responsibilities* (2007); http://archive.eeoc.gov/policy/docs/caregiving.html; EEOC, *Employer Best Practices for Workers with Caregiving Responsibilities* (2009), http://www.eeoc.gov/policy/docs/caregiver-best-practices.html.

Page 369. Add at end of Note on the Family and Medical Leave Act:

While Title VII, unlike the FMLA, does not require maternity leave, maternity leave may not be treated less favorably than other forms of leave In *Orr v. City of Albuquerque*, 531 F.3d 1210 (10th Cir. 2008), the two female plaintiffs were required to use their sick leave before taking FMLA leave. They claimed that other workers were allowed to use FMLA leave without exhausting their sick leave, and the court agreed that a showing that "other employees seeking FMLA leave for purposes unrelated to a pregnancy were routinely allowed to use vacation or compensatory time" would establish a Title VII violation. *Id.* at 1216.

Grouping family and medical leave into a single legal regime may foreclose the possibility of generous pregnancy leave for many women. Should pregnancy leave be separated from other medical leave and should pregnant women and new mothers be given more generous leave opportunities? Some commentators have suggested that separating leave in this way conflicts with antidiscrimination law which is designed to combat paternalism and gender stereotypes, *See* Julie C. Suk, *Are Gender Stereotypes Bad for Women? Rethinking Antidiscrimination Law and Work-Family Conflict*, 110 COLUM. L. REV. 1, 5 (2010) (significant features of European efforts to reconcile work and family would be rejected as "stereotypes" from an American perspective; these include the separation of maternity and parental leave regimes from other forms of family and medical leave, gender-differentiated entitlements, and paternalism).

2. Sexual and Other Discriminatory Harassment

Page 375. Add before *El-Hakeem* cite in last paragraph:

Watson v. CEVA Logistics U.S., Inc., 619 F.3d 936 (8th Cir. 2010) (racially hostile comments made directly to plaintiffs coupled with racist graffiti, the display of the Confederate flag by co-workers, and instances of disparate treatment sufficed); *Fuller v. Fiber Glass Sys., LP*, 618 F.3d 858 (8th Cir. 2010) (evidence that a co-worker/trainer told plaintiff that she did not like black people on plaintiff's first day on the job, continuously demeaned her, and instructed her to stay off the phones because customers weren't used to hearing a black voice, and that her manager made "monkey or gorilla gestures" behind her back for co-worker's amusement justified jury verdict on severity and pervasiveness); *Tademy v. Union Pac. Corp.*, 520 F.3d 1149 (10th Cir. 2008) (a life-size noose hung prominently coupled with racist graffiti on plaintiff's locker and on restroom walls and racist cartoons posted on company billboards may be sufficiently pervasive to violate Title VII).

Page 376. Add after Chew cite in third line after extract:

Pat K. Chew, *Seeing Subtle Racism*, 6 STANFORD J. C.R. & C.L. 183 (2011) (arguing for a more expansive view of racism in racial harassment cases than some courts have adopted).

Page 376. Add before Bourini cite in carryover *Note on Other Discriminatory Harassment*:

Colenburg v. Starcon Int'l, Inc., 619 F.3d 986 (8th Cir. 2010) (racial harassment not severe or pervasive even though it included supervisor's comments to plaintiff analogizing pace of his work to speed at which black man in Texas had been dragged to death behind truck).

a. Severe or Pervasive Harassment

Page 379. Delete Note 1; replace with:

1. *How Bad Is Bad Enough?* *Harris* reaffirms the *Meritor* standard: "For sexual harassment to be actionable, it must be sufficiently severe or pervasive 'to alter the conditions of [the victim's] employment and create an abusive working environment.'" What does this standard reveal about drawing the line between acceptable social behavior and actionable sexual harassment? Does *Harris* make the standard *any cl*earer than it was after *Meritor*? Justice Scalia's concurrence stressed the vagueness of the standard, leaving "virtually unguided juries [to] decide whether sex-related conduct engaged in (or permitted by) an employer is egregious enough to warrant an award of damages." However, because "I know of no test more faithful to the inherently vague statutory language than the one the Court today adopts," he joined the Court's opinion. What should the district court find on remand? Was Hardy's conduct "severe" or "pervasive" or both? If none of the acts of harassment in this case was severe, did when did they become pervasive enough to be actionable?

Almost two decades after *Harris*, courts are struggling to apply its standard. Many have found the at-issue conduct actionable, usually because it was "pervasive." *See Hoyle v. Freightliner, LLC*, 2011 U.S. App. LEXIS 6628, 24-26 (4th Cir. Apr. 1, 2011) (various incidents that were "far from "mildly inappropriate," including an incident where co-workers left a tampon tied to a key ring on a truck in her work area, and displays "that consistently painted women in a sexually subservient and demeaning light" created a jury question on the "severe and pervasive" element); *Mosby-Grant v. City of Hagerstown*, 630 F.3d 326 (4th Cir. 2010) (finding a triable claim of sexual harassment when police academy recruit produced evidence that she was targeted because of her sex; consistently made to feel like an outsider by her classmates and some instructors; sexist comments were frequently made to her or in her presence; and she was consistently subjected to taunting); *Vera v. McHugh*, 622 F.3d 17, 28 (1st Cir. 2010) (male supervisor's staring at plaintiff in a sexual way, repeatedly invading her personal space by standing too close to her, and once calling her "babe" could support a reasonable jury finding of sexual harassment); *Billings v. Town of Grafton*, 515 F.3d 39 (1st Cir. 2008) (even absent touching, sexual advances, or overtly sexual comments, a manager's repeatedly staring at his subordinate's breasts could constitute actionable harassment); *Schiano v. Quality Payroll Sys. Inc.*, 445 F.3d 597, 608 (2d Cir. 2006) (given the frequency of the conduct, "the nature of the words exchanged, the context in which they were uttered, the physical nature of some of acts complained of, the response of the harasser to the steps Schiano took to repel the unwanted advances, and the effect of it all on Schiano's ability to do her job," a reasonable jury could find a violation); *Harvill v. Westward Communs., L.L.C.*, 433 F.3d 428 (5th Cir. 2005) (reaffirming that harassment can result from conduct that is either severe *or* pervasive, the court held that fondling by a male co-worker, numerous times, over seven-month period sufficed).

However, some decisions find very questionable conduct not to be actionable. In *Henthorn v. Capitol Communs., Inc.*, 359 F.3d 1021, 1027-28 (8th Cir. 2004), the court found the harasser's behavior "inappropriate, immature, and unprofessional," but it did not cross "the high threshold" for sexual harassment:

> Parker's requests that Henthorn go out with him were repetitive and annoying, but they were not lewd or threatening. Parker did not touch Henthorn inappropriately, nor did he make sexual comments about her in her presence. His two late-night/early morning calls urged her to accept his social invitations and expressed his interest in her, but they did not contain sexual propositions. Although Henthorn was made uncomfortable by Parker's conduct, she was able to continue to perform her assignments, and Parker's actions did not result in a change of her probationary status.

See also Scruggs v. Garst Seed Co., 587 F.3d 832 (7th Cir. 2009) (environment not objectively severe or pervasive, where plaintiff's supervisor made occasional inappropriate comments — including that she was "made for the back seat of a car" and looked like a "dyke" — when most negative comments related to plaintiff's work habits or alleged lack of sophistication, which were the kinds of comments he made to both male and female employees); *Ladd v. Grand Trunk Western R.R.*, 552 F.3d 495, 501 (6th Cir. 2009) (where no actual touching took place and plaintiff testified to only one specific incident of a sex- or race-based epithet directed at her, a "total lack of specificity" as to other verbal abuse directed at her justified summary judgment for the employer despite evidence of other epithets — "lesbian," "dyke," and "gay" — that were not directed at her); *LeGrand v. Area*

Res. for Cmty. & Human Servs., 394 F.3d 1098 (8th Cir. 2005) (viewing LeGrand's claim in light of the "demanding standard" required, "Father Nutt's behavior did not rise to the level of actionable hostile work environment sexual harassment. None of the incidents was physically violent or overtly threatening. [T]hree isolated incidents, which occurred over a nine-month period, were not so severe or pervasive as to poison LeGrand's work environment.").

A recent article argues for a renewed focus on context in terms of the harasser's role in the employer's hierarchy in determining whether the conduct was severe and pervasive. Susan Grover & Kimberley Piro, *Consider the Source: When the Harasser Is the Boss*, 79 FORDHAM L. REV. 499 (2010) (the analytic framework for workplace harassment incorrectly fails to require courts to consider whether the harasser is the target's supervisor in assessing whether harassment is severe or pervasive, thus skewing results in favor of the employer).

Page 379.   Add before *Little* cite in Note 2, *Severe or Pervasive*:

Berry v. Chi. Transit Auth., 618 F.3d 688 (7th Cir. 2010) (noting that a single act can create a hostile environment if it is severe enough, the Seventh Circuit found that plaintiff had provided enough evidence to allow her hostile work environment claim to go forward where supervisor grabbed plaintiff's breasts, lifted her, and rubbed her body against his);

Page 380.   Add at end of carryover Note 2, *Severe or Pervasive*:

But see Paul v. Northrop Grumman Ship Systems, 309 F. App'x 825 (5th Cir. 2009) (single incident of "chesting up" to plaintiff and rubbing pelvic region across her hips and buttocks in confrontation lasting approximately 90 seconds is not sufficiently severe or pervasive to constitute actionable Title VII claim).

Page 380.   Add at end of Note 4, *Non-Targeted Harassment*:

The cases have generally not found the absence of targeting to be fatal to a claim. *See Gallagher v. C.H. Robinson Worldwide, Inc.*, 567 F.3d 263, 273 (6th Cir. 2009) ("Whether the offensive conduct was intentionally directed specifically at Gallagher or not, the fact remains that she had no means of escaping her co-workers' loud insulting language and degrading conversations; she was unavoidably exposed to it."); *Patane v. Clark*, 508 F.3d 106 (2d Cir. 2007) (sexual harassment claim stated as to professor's watching of pornographic video tapes even though plaintiff; while his secretary did not see them she alleged she regularly observed the professor viewing them and handled such videos while opening his mail; the mere presence of pornography in the workplace can alter the status of women). In *Reeves v. C.H. Robinson Worldwide, Inc.*, 594 F.3d 798 (11th Cir. 2010), the vulgar language used in the workplace was not generally targeted at plaintiff, and much was not gender-specific (including words such as "fuck," "fucker," and "asshole"), but there was "a substantial corpus of gender-derogatory language addressed specifically to women as a group in the workplace," including referred to other women as "bitch," "fucking bitch," "fucking whore," "crack whore," and "cunt." The court held that "words and conduct that are sufficiently gender-specific and either severe or pervasive may state a claim of a hostile work environment, even if the words are not directed specifically at the plaintiff," and that the plaintiff's claim satisfied that standard. Like *Reeves*, other cases have combined non-targeted sexualized conduct with more targeted actions in order to find the "because of sex" criterion satisfied. *E.g., Hoyle v. Freightliner, LLC*, 2011 U.S. App. LEXIS 6628, 19-22 (4th Cir. Apr. 1, 2011) (photos of women nude or in sexually provocative poses in common areas could be found detrimental to female employees since such action was particularly offensive to women and could signal hostility to women in the workplace, as could placing a tampon on plaintiff's truck). *See also Kaytor v. Elec. Boat Corp.*, 609 F.3d 537 (2d Cir. 2010) (rational juror could infer from supervisor's overtly sexual comments that the facially gender-neutral threats he directed at plaintiff were, in fact, "because of" her sex).

Further, when harassment is targeted at the plaintiff, harassment of other women may be relevant to establishing that the conduct was actionable. After recognizing that its precedents permitted the factfinder to "consider similar acts of harassment of which a plaintiff becomes aware during the course of his or her employment, even if the harassing acts were directed at others or occurred outside of the plaintiff's presence," *Hawkins v. Anheuser-Busch, Inc.*, 517 F.3d 321, 336 (6th Cir. 2008), went on to state:

> The degree to which a past act of harassment is relevant to the determination of whether a plaintiff's work environment is hostile is a fact-specific inquiry that requires courts to determine the relevancy of past acts on a case-by-case basis. . . . [M]ore weight should be given to acts committed by a serial harasser if the plaintiff knows that the same individual committed offending acts in the past. This is because a serial harasser left free to harass again leaves the impression that acts of harassment are tolerated at the workplace and supports a plaintiff's claim that the workplace is both objectively and subjectively hostile.

Id. at 336-37. *See also Ziskie v. Mineta*, 547 F.3d 220 (4th Cir. 2008) (district court erred in not considering affidavits of plaintiff's female co-workers regarding harassment not experienced firsthand by plaintiff; such evidence could lend credence to her mistreatment claims, show the harassment was pervasive, or support a finding that she was treated poorly by co-workers because of her sex, and not some other reason).

Page 380. Add at end of Note 5, Pervasiveness and Timeliness:

But see Wilkie v. Dep't of Health and Human Servs., 638 F.3d 944 (8th Cir. 2011) (misconduct occurring outside of the statutory filing period, including "sexual advances" and the harasser coming to plaintiff's home while intoxicated and passing out naked in her bed was substantially different than the misconduct occurring within the statutory time period and therefore not "so similar in nature, frequency, and severity" that the tolling exception to the filing period applied).

Page 383.   Add at end of second sentence in last full paragraph:

See EEOC v. Prospect Airport Servs., 621 F.3d 991, 997-98 (9th Cir. 2010) (the fact that most men might welcome sexual advances from a woman does not establish that the plaintiff did since "welcomeness is inherently subjective"; nevertheless, "for the conduct to be unwelcome for purposes of employer's liability, unwelcomeness has to be communicated).

d.   Vicarious Liability

Page 391.   Add at end of Note 1, *Employer Liability and Harassment Claims*:

Scholars have proposed alternative approaches to the theory of employer liability put forward in *Meritor, See generally* Sandra F. Sperino, *A Modern Theory of Direct Corporate Liability for Title VII*, 61 Ala. L. Rev. 773, 774-75 (2010) ("the corporation has a life and intent of its own, separate from the individual actions of its agents," which would permit borrowing from criminal law and corporate law scholarship to develop a fuller conception of direct liability).

Page 392.   delete Note 3; replace with:

3. *Who Is a Supervisor?* In the more usual situation, the threshold question will be whether the harasser is a supervisor or not. Supervisors are capable of taking "tangible employment actions" and thus incurring employer liability automatically. They are also capable of other kinds of harassment for which the employer is presumptively liable, although the employer is able to assert the affirmative defense.   Is any individual with supervisory status necessarily a supervisor for purposes of imposing vicarious liability under *Ellerth* and *Faragher?* The cases suggest the answer is no. *See Swinton v. Potomac Corp.*, 270 F.3d 794 (9th Cir. 2001) (actions of supervisor who had no authority over the plaintiff could not subject employer to vicarious liability); *Neely v. McDonald's Corp.*, 340 F. App'x 83 (3d Cir. 2009) ("assistant manager" did not have authority to hire, fire, discipline, or schedule staff was therefore not a supervisor for Title VII purposes). *But see Whitten v. Fred's, Inc.*, 601 F.3d 231, 245 (4th Cir. 2010) ("the absence of authority to take tangible employment action does not establish that the harasser is merely a coworker; other factors include the harasser's title as store manager, the fact that he was the highest ranking employee in the store, and he directed plaintiff's activities and assignments).

5. Special Problems in Applying Title VII, Section 1981, and the ADEA

Some cases have been grudging over who counts as a "supervisor" even when the harasser supervises the plaintiff's work. *E.g., Rhodes v. Ill. Dep't of Transp.*, 359 F.3d 498, 506 (7th Cir. 2004) (although harassers "managed plaintiff's work assignments, investigated complaints and disputes, and made recommendations concerning sanctions for rule violations," neither had authority to affect the terms and conditions of her employment)*; Weyers v. Lear Operations Corp.*, 359 F.3d 1049, 1057-58 (8th Cir. 2004) (harasser was not plaintiff's supervisor even though he had authority as team leader to assign employees to particular tasks when he could not reassign them to significantly different duties; nor did the fact that he signed at least three of plaintiff's performance evaluations, which were one of the bases for her termination, mean that he supervised her). *Cf. Valentine v. City of Chi.*, 452 F.3d 670, 678 (7th Cir. 2006) (question of fact as to whether an individual was plaintiff's supervisor since a supervisor is one who has "the power to hire, fire, demote, promote, transfer, or discipline an employee," and the alleged harasser had at least the power to transfer employees between lots).

Page 393. **Add at end of carryover paragraph of Note 4,** *Tangible Employment Actions***:**

See also Whitten v. Fred's, Inc., 601 F.3d 231, 247-28 (4th Cir. 2010) (changes in work schedule and verbal and physical abuse were not tangible employment actions when there was no economic harm to plaintiff nor a change in her employment status"); *Lucero v. Nettle Creek School Corp.*, 566 F.3d 720 (7th Cir. 2009) (reassigning 12th grade Honors teacher to position as "floater teacher" is not a materially adverse employment action, even if reassignment might damage her career prospects and make her more vulnerable to reductions in force); *Anderson v. Wintco, Inc.*, 314 F. App'x 135 (10th Cir. 2009) (requiring carhop to work fountain position where employees do not earn tips is not a tangible employment action where typical job duties of carhop include some fountain work). *But see Agusty-Reyes v. Dep't of Educ.*, 601 F.3d 45 (1st Cir. 2010) ("failure to grant tenure could also lead to a meaningful change in an employee's benefits in an up-or-out situation at a time when budgetary constraints loomed.").

Page 393. **Add at end of last full paragraph of Note 4,** *Tangible Employment Actions***:**

Kerri Lynn Stone, *Consenting Adults?: Why Women Who Submit to Supervisory Sexual Harassment Are Faring Better in Court Than Those Who Say No . . . and Why They Shouldn't*, 20 YALE J.L. & FEMINISM 25 (2008) (exploring the tension between holding women responsible for their choice to delay reporting and not holding them responsible for their choice to submit to sexual advances).

Page 408.   Add at end of first paragraph in Note 2, *Prong 1(a): Reasonable Care to Prevent Harassment*:

See also Berry v. Chi. Transit Auth., 618 F.3d 688, 692 (7th Cir. 2010) (employer could be found negligent in investigating plaintiff's complaint when investigating supervisor said that he didn't care what happened because plaintiff was "a pain in the butt," predicted that she would lose her job if she filed charges, and threatened to do "whatever it takes" to protect the employer); *Bruno v. Monroe County*, 383 F. App'x 845, 849-50 (11th Cir. 2010) ("Although the express terms of Monroe County's sexual harassment policy clearly made it applicable to the county's "agents," such as elected commissioners, the evidence at trial showed that the policy could be considered largely ineffective as to them."); *Agusty-Reyes v. Dep't of Educ.*, 601 F.3d 45 (1st Cir. 2010) (fact questions as to the affirmative defense because there was no showing that the defendant communicated its antiharassment policy to employees or supervisors and the absence of an opportunity for the complaining party to be present at a hearing, while according the alleged harasser that right, could be found by a jury as inherently unreasonable). *See also* Kerri Lynn Stone, *License to Harass: Holding Defendants Accountable for Retaining Recidivist Harassers*, 41 AKRON L. REV. 1059, 1062 (2008) (the affirmative defense should not be established where the plaintiff has sustained otherwise actionable harm without the opportunity to report it before it occurred and where the employer situated a known harasser as that victim's supervisor).

Page 409.   Add at end of Note 4, *Bullet-Proofing or Real Structural Change?*:

See also Jason R. Brent, *Systemic Harassment*, 77 TENN. L. REV. 151 (2009) (exploring litigating systemic harassment claims, whether by the EEOC or private class actions).

Page 409.   Delete Note 5; replace with:

5. *Prong 1(b): Reasonable Steps to Correct Harassment.* In addition to taking reasonable care to prevent harassment, the employer also must establish that it took reasonable steps to *correct* harassment when it is reported. Matvia's employer suspended Terbush and then terminated him following the investigation. But the court finds the company's response to the "ostracism and vilification of Matvia" irrelevant to this prong of the affirmative defense because the conduct lacked a sexual component. Is this correct? Can an employer that tolerates misconduct directed toward an employee because she has complained of sexual harassment be acting reasonably to correct the harassment?

An employer may learn of harassment by means other than the victim's complaint, which would seem to trigger the duty to promptly correct harassment. Not all courts agree. *See Chaloult v. Interstate Brands Corp.*, 540 F.3d 64 (1st Cir. 2008) (the fact that many acts of harassment occurred in front of a second supervisor, and the employer's policy required all supervisors to report harassment, did not mean the employer had notice of the conduct as a matter of law since to so hold would discourage employers from adopting such policies).

An employer may act reasonably if it takes no action against the accused when a reasonable investigation is unable to corroborate a woman's complaint of harassment. *See Sutherland v. Wal-Mart Stores, Inc.*, 632 F.3d 990, 994 (7th Cir. 2011) (employer was not required to take drastic remedial measures following an initial complaint when the misconduct at issue did not suggest that the harasser was likely to engage in sexual assault); *Thornton v. Fed. Express Corp.*, 530 F.3d 451, 457 (6th Cir. 2008) (when employer's investigation did not corroborate harassment, the employer's offer to transfer plaintiff to a different supervisor satisfied its responsibility to take reasonable steps to correct any harassment that may have occurred); *Baldwin v. Blue Cross/Blue Shield of Ala.*, 480 F.3d 1287, 1303 (11th Cir. 2007 ("The requirement of a reasonable investigation does not include a requirement that the employer credit uncorroborated statements the complainant makes if they are disputed by the alleged harasser."). *See also Adams v. O'Reilly Auto., Inc.*, 538 F.3d 926 (8th Cir. 2008) (employer's requirement of a witness to corroborate the harassment did not bar the affirmative defense)

However, delay in responding to complaints, even if the ultimate response is adequate, can be fatal to the affirmative defense. *See EEOC v. Cent. Wholesalers, Inc.*, 573 F.3d 167 (4th Cir. 2009) (a reasonable jury could find that the employer either failed to respond in a timely manner or failed to respond to at all, even though its anti-harassment policy required the company to promptly investigate all such complaints and to take appropriate action, and therefore that the affirmative defense was unavailable); *Aryain v. Wal-Mart Stores Tex. LP*, 534 F.3d 473, 483 (5th Cir. 2008) (evidence indicating that the employer had notice of the harassment as much as two or three months before commencing its investigation required denial of summary judgment). In addition to being prompt, an employer's response must be sufficiently aggressive and professional. *See West v. Tyson Foods*, 374 F. App'x 624 (6th Cir. 2010) (failure to initially respond to complaint and then merely offering to move plaintiff and watch her occasionally for the next few days was "woefully insufficient," especially given the supervisors' directive to plaintiff to not report the matter to HR). *See also Williams v. Waste Mgmt. of Ill., Inc.*, 361 F.3d 1021, 1030 (7th Cir. 2004) (remedial actions had the purpose and effect of eliminating further race-based harassment even though "the investigation was by no means textbook in its execution");

Promptly firing the harasser will certainly suffice as reasonable corrective action. *Green v. Franklin Nat'l Bank*, 459 F.3d 903, 912 (8th Cir. 2006) (firing harasser within a month was sufficiently prompt remedial action to avoid liability). But employers who discipline harassers in order to avoid liability under Title VII must be careful to avoid liability to the harassing employee. Employees who have individual employment contracts, civil service rights, or academic tenure, or who work under the protection of a policy manual or a collective bargaining agreement may be protected against discharge without just cause.

Moreover, employers who have disciplined harassers have been sued for discrimination by the *harassing* employees, although usually unsuccessfully. *See, e.g., Hawn v. Exec. Jet Mgmt.*, 615 F.3d 1151 (9th Cir. 2010) (three male pilots fired after a female flight attendant accused them of sexual harassment could not establish sex discrimination because no similarly situated woman were treated more favorably: the woman who participated in sexual conduct and banter without discipline had never been the subject of a complaint); *Farr v. St. Francis Hosp. & Health Ctrs.*, 570 F.3d 829 (7th Cir. 2009) (plaintiff, who was the only male in his department and was the first in his department to be investigated for accessing pornography sites on his work computer, could not establish that he was targeted because of his sex when there were other bases for selecting him to be investigated); *Wright v. Murray Guard, Inc.*, 455 F.3d 702 (6th Cir. 2006) (where black male's alleged sexual harassment was substantially greater than female co-worker's alleged misconduct, there was no showing of discrimination in his discharge despite failure of decisionmaker to independently investigate). *But see Sassaman v. Gamache*, 566 F.3d 307 (2d Cir. 2009) (while an employer is required to take charges of harassment seriously, it is sex discrimination to conclude that an accused male is a harasser because "you probably did what she said you did because you're male and nobody would believe you anyway"); *Russell v. City of Kansas City*, 414 F.3d 863, 868 (8th Cir. 2005) (white female supervisor demoted for allegedly fostering racially harassing workplace may have been the victim of discrimination when black and white males were given only a "slap on the wrist");

Page 411. Add in carryover Note 6, *Requests for Confidentiality* after *Nurse "Be"* cite:

Porter v. Erie Foods Int'l, 576 F.3d 629 (7th Cir. 2009) (negligence could not be found in employer's response to harassment complaint when the plaintiff repeatedly declined to name coworkers who harassed him).

Page 411. Delete Note 7; replace with:

7. *Prong 2, Did the Employee Act Unreasonably?* Even if the employer took reasonable preventive and corrective action, the affirmative defense will still fail unless the employer also proves that the employee unreasonably failed to take advantage of preventive or corrective opportunities. *See, e.g., Chapman v. Carmike Cinemas*, 307 F. App'x 164, 170 (10th Cir. 2009) (the employer failed to establish the second element of the *Ellerth/Faragher* affirmative defense for respondeat superior liability where plaintiff presented evidence that she immediately reported a sexual assault by her supervisor and no evidence of other preventative measures that employee failed to take). Matvia waited until the final incident to complain, arguing it was sufficiently severe that that should be the focus of her "duty" to complain. The court disagrees, reasoning that her actions throughout the period

of harassment must be assessed. Is this correct? Must a victim complain at the earliest opportunity to preserve her claim? Was Matvia acting reasonably when she waited to determine whether Terbush was an interested man or a predator?

In *Watts v. Kroger Co.*, 170 F.3d 505, 510 (5th Cir. 1999), the Fifth Circuit reversed summary judgment on the ground that the employer could not, as a matter of law, establish that Watts "unreasonably failed to take advantage of any preventive or corrective opportunities provided by the employer." Although Watts alleged that her supervisor had harassed her for nearly a year, she did not complain until the harassment intensified. The court believed that a jury might find it "not unreasonable" to hold off complaining under these circumstances. *See also Monteagudo v. Asociacion de Empleados del Estado Libre Asociado*, 554 F.3d 164 (1st Cir. 2009) (a jury could find plaintiff's failure to report harassment reasonable when the harasser was close friends with the director of human resources to whom she should have reported under the employer's policy). However, when an employee takes action, some courts have required that it conform to the employer's policy. *See Taylor v. Solis*, 571 F.3d 1313 (D.C. Cir. 2009) (not reasonable for plaintiff to notify her team leader when the employer's policy required her to contact an EEO counselor or manager; the failure of the team leader to take action did not render the employer liable). *See also Wyatt v. Hunt Plywood Co.*, 297 F.3d 405 (5th Cir. 2002) (plaintiff was barred from recovering for a four-month period of harassment by her failure to report harassment by her boss and his supervisor during that time when, when she did report both were fired). Is there an absolute rule that a victim must report the first act of harassment, or is the test whether a reasonable person would report at a particular point in time? *See generally* Margaret E. Johnson, *"Avoiding Harm Otherwise": Reframing Women Employees' Responses to the Harms of Sexual Harassment*, 80 TEMP. L. REV. 743 (2007) (explaining the difficulties of proving that the employee reported the harassment in a timely manner and attempting to resuscitate the "avoid harm otherwise" component of the affirmative defense).

Suppose the employee does complain to a supervisor. If nothing is done, is her failure to then complain to others also identified in the employer's policy unreasonable? *See Gorzynski v. JetBlue Airways Corp.*, 596 F.3d 93, 104-05 (2d Cir. 2010) (rejecting the argument that, when plaintiff complained to her manager pursuant to the employer's policy allowed without response, it was unreasonable for her not to pursue alternate avenues that the defendant provided); *but see Lauderdale v. Tex. Dep't of Crim. Justice*, 512 F.3d 157 (5th Cir. 2007) (in §1983 suit, a correctional officer's failure to make second complaint about sexual harassment by warden after her immediate supervisor refused to act on her first complaint established that prong of the affirmative defense). *See also Brenneman v. Famous Dave's of Am., Inc.*, 507 F.3d 1139, 1145-46 (8th Cir. 2007) (plaintiff failed to take advantage of preventive opportunities by not cooperating with the Human Resources person who offered to transfer her to a nearby restaurant while he dealt with her allegations).

Page 412. Add at end of first paragraph of carryover Note 9, *Law Changing Norms:*

Cf. David J. Walsh, Small Change: *An Empirical Analysis of the Effect of Supreme Court Precedents on Federal Appellate Court Decisions in Sexual Harassment Cases, 1993-2005,* 30 BERKELEY J. EMP. & LAB. L. 461, 523 (2010) (the changes in the law wrought by *Faragher* and *Oncale* were relatively small as reflected in plaintiff success rates in the circuit courts).

Page 413. Delete Note 10; replace with:

10. *Both Prongs of the Affirmative Defense Must Be Satisfied.* What happens if a supervisor commits a severe act of harassment, such as a rape or attempted rape, and the employee immediately reports the harassment to her employer? If the employer has a strong antiharassment policy in place and engages in prompt and effective corrective action, can the employer still be vicariously liable for the hostile work environment? Since it is the employer's burden to establish *both* prongs of the affirmative defense, the answer should be yes. The employer would be unable to establish the second prong of the defense because the employee has acted reasonably. See *Frederick v. Sprint/United Mgt. Co.,* 246 F.3d 1305 (11th Cir. 2001); *Harrison v. Eddy Potash Inc.,* 248 F.3d 1014 (10th Cir. 2001); *Johnson v. West,* 218 F.3d 725 (7th Cir. 2000). However, one circuit has answered the question in the negative. *See McCurdy v. Arkansas State Police,* 375 F.3d 762, 771 (8th Cir. 2004) (Title VII does not "envision[s] strict employer liability for a supervisor's single incident of sexual harassment when the employer takes swift and effective action to insulate the complaining employee from further harassment the moment the employer learns about the harassing conduct"). *See generally* Kerri Lynn Stone, *License to Harass,* 41 AKRON L. REV. 1059 (2008) (examining whether an employer may avoid liability for a single incident of rape even though it is reported immediately by the victim).

In light of *Ellerth* and the availability of damages under the 1991 Act, how would you advise employers? Is there any way for an employer to avoid liability short of taking aggressive and serious steps to ensure that no supervisory harassment occurs? How should an employer respond if it has reason to believe that a supervisor has been harassing employees, but the victims are unwilling to make a formal complaint? Are restrictions of socio-sexual activity among employees an appropriate response? What about "dating waivers," i.e., documents executed by employees "desiring to undertake and pursue a mutually consensual social and/or amorous relationship"?

Page 415. Add after *Id.* cite in first line after extract:

See also Aguiar v. Bartlesville Care Ctr., 2011 U.S. App. LEXIS 1804, 5 (10th Cir. Jan. 28, 2011) (a jury could find that employer's efforts to deal with harassment of nurse by resident of a home were inadequate when harassment continued even though employer talked to resident and ordered two nurses to be present when caring for him; an employer can be liable for harassing conduct "regardless of whether the environment is created by a fellow employee or nonemployee, such as a customer, because the employer ultimately controls the conditions of the work environment").

Page 415.   Add at end of paragraph continuing after extract:

See generally Noah Zatz, *Managing the Macaw: Third-Party Harassers, Accommodation, and the Disaggregation of Discriminatory Intent*, 109 COLUM. L. REV. 1357 (2009) (employers' liability for not protecting employees from harassment by customers or other third parties does not flow from either disparate treatment or disparate impact theories; instead, these cases essentially assert denial of reasonable accommodations, notwithstanding the consensus that Title VII disallows such claims).

Page 415.   Add before Note on the First Amendment Implications of Sexual Harassment Liability:

Can a school system be held liable for acts of sexual harassment against its teachers by students? The Seventh Circuit has suggested that such claims might be actionable under Title VII in the appropriate circumstances. *See Lucero v. Nettle Creek School Corp.*, 566 F.3d 720 (7th Cir. 2009) (reasoning that although students' conduct — including leaving 20 copies of *Playboy* magazine on teacher's desk — was inappropriate behavior, the isolated incidents were neither sufficiently severe nor pervasive to rise to level of actionable harassing conduct); *Schroeder v. Hamilton School Dist.*, 282 F.3d 946, 951 (7th Cir. 2002) (recognizing cause of action for student-on-teacher harassment under Equal Protection Clause and suggesting that school system could also be held liable under Title VII if plaintiff "demonstrated that [the school system] knew he was being harassed and failed to take reasonable measures to try to prevent it"). *See generally* Richard D. Shane, Note, *Teachers as Sexual Harassment Victims: The Inequitable Protections of Title VII in Public Schools*, 61 FLA. L. REV. 355 (2009).

Page 417.   Add at end of last full paragraph:

See generally Lawrence Rosenthal, *The Emerging First Amendment Law of Managerial Prerogative*, 77 FORDHAM L. REV. 33 (2008) (arguing, inter alia, that *Garcetti* reduces the First Amendment questions otherwise posed by speech restrictions in public employment). *Cf. DeJohn v. Temple Univ.*, 537 F.3d 301 (3d Cir. 2008) (striking down university's harassment policy as facially invalid because it prohibited expression by students even in the absence of a hostile environment).

D. *Discrimination on Account of Religion*

Page 418.   Add in second full paragraph, before *Mandell* cite:

Dixon v. Hallmark Cos., 627 F.3d 849 (11th Cir. 2010) ("You're fired, too. You're too religious," constitutes direct evidence of discrimination sufficient to survive summary judgment, where supervisor uttered remark to Christian employee right after terminating his wife for hanging religious picture in violation of employer's policies); *Fischer v. Forestwood Co.*, 525 F.3d 972 (10th Cir. 2008) (secret tape recordings of plaintiff's conversation with his father, who refused to rehire him unless he rejoined the Church, were admissible direct evidence of discrimination);

Page 422.   Add at end of carryover paragraph:

See also Dixon v. Hallmark Cos., 627 F.3d 849 (11th Cir. 2010) (defendant's awareness that plaintiffs were sincere, committed Christians who opposed efforts to remove God from public places satisfied the knowledge requirement for accommodation). *But see Xodus v. Wackenhut Corp.*, 619 F.3d 683 (7th Cir. 2010) (upholding a finding that wearing dreadlocks and referring to unspecified "beliefs" was insufficient to apprise the potential employer of the religious nature of the plaintiff's beliefs in order to trigger a duty to accommodate).

Page 422.   Delete Note 3; replace with the following:

3. *"Knowledge Plus" for the Prima Facie Case?* Judge Posner cites approvingly *Shapolia v. Los Alamos National Laboratory*, 992 F.2d 1033, 1033 (10th Cir. 1993), which focused on tension between the employer's religion and that of the employee, suggesting that perhaps knowledge, while necessary, is not sufficient for a prima facie case. Another requirement may be proof that the employee "fail[ed] to hold or follow his or her employer's religious beliefs." Perhaps the point is that, given the pervasiveness of religion in the United States, there has to be some basis beyond a disparity of formal religious affiliation for the court to conclude that religion is the basis of the discrimination. But that doesn't mean that, say, a Baptist can't discriminate against another Baptist. Given the recurrent history of theological disputes, not only between religions but within what is otherwise viewed as a single religion, this is certainly possible. Where plaintiffs claimed to have been fired because of their employer's belief that homosexual conduct was sinful, the Seventh Circuit made clear that "a plaintiff may proceed on a claim that 'her supervisors, though also Christian, did not like her brand of Christianity' because '[t]he issue is whether the plaintiff's specific religious beliefs were a ground for' an adverse employment action." *Patterson v. Ind. Newspapers, Inc.*, 589 F.3d 357 (7th Cir. 2009) (quoting *Grossman v. S. Shore Pub. Sch. Dist.*, 507 F.3d 1097, 1098 (7th Cir. 2007).

The point can be generalized to ask how likely it is that an adherent of Faith X would discriminate against an adherent of Faith Y on the basis of religion. So framed, the question is not susceptible of an answer. Americans practice hundreds of different religions, (see the Religious Movements Homepage at the University of Virginia, www.religiousmovements.org), and they take them more or less seriously. Some religions are inclusive and some exclusive. Some are viewed sympathetically by most Americans while some are viewed with suspicion by many Americans. In this setting, something akin to the "background circumstances" or "additional evidence" tests for reverse discrimination claims, see p. 76, may be required for a prima facie case. That is, plaintiff might have to adduce evidence why this employer would be hostile to a person of plaintiff's religion. Another way to say this is that perhaps it is more likely that an individual will be fired for being a Wiccan than, say, for being a Methodist, *see Van Koten v. Family Health Mgmt.*, 955 F. Supp. 898 (N.D. Ill. 1997), or for being a Muslim than a Catholic. Indeed, even where there is knowledge of the employee's religion, courts have been reluctant to infer discrimination on the basis of religion, *DeFreitas v. Horizon Inv. Mgmt. Corp.*, 577 F.3d 1151 (10th Cir. 2009) (although plaintiff presented evidence that the employer's supposed reasons for firing her were pretextual, she did not present evidence that would allow the inference that her predominantly Mormon employer fired her because she was a Catholic when her religion was known through her tenure and she was given promotions and raises). In *Reed* itself, and supposing Reed were Jewish, would a showing that the Gideons stressed the New Testament and Jesus as God be sufficient evidence to infer discrimination?

Perhaps for this reason, most successful religion cases turn on some statements by the employer implicating religious bias, even if circumstantial evidence also played a role. *E.g., Hasan v. Foley & Lardner LLP*, 552 F.3d 520 (7th Cir. 2009) (a reasonable jury could find discrimination based on religion and national origin where a partner, who participated in the termination decision, made an extreme anti-Muslim comment and other partners made anti-Muslim comments simultaneously with the associate's department beginning to steer work away from him); *Campos v. City of Blue Springs, Mo.*, 289 F.3d 546 (8th Cir. 2002) (city youth outreach counselor who observed tenets of Native American spirituality was constructively discharged because she was not Christian); *EEOC v. Univ. of Chi. Hosps.*, 276 F.3d 326 (7th Cir. 2002) (hospital recruiter's constructive discharge could be found to be religious discrimination when her supervisor repeatedly asked her to tone down her religious expression).

Page 425. Add before *Berry* cite in Note 7(c), *Justifying Religious Discrimination*:

Grossman v. S. Shore Pub. Sch. Dist., 507 F.3d 1097 (7th Cir. 2007) (when a Lutheran guidance counselor's contract was not renewed because she threw out literature on condom use, taught abstinence, and prayed with students, there was no reason to find discrimination because of her Christian *beliefs*, and Establishment Clause concerns justified limitations on belief-inspired *conduct*);

Page 427.   Add before *Morrisette-Brown* cite:

EEOC v. Firestone Fibers & Textiles Co., 515 F.3d 307 (4th Cir. 2008) (Congress required only reasonable accommodation, not total accommodation, and thus there was no violation when the employer had many mechanisms to allow plaintiff to avoid working on his holy days other than allowing him unpaid leave, which would burden his co-workers and risk violating the collective bargaining agreement); *Bush v. Regis Corp.*, 257 F. App'x 219 (11th Cir. 2007) (employer reasonably accommodated plaintiff when it scheduled her Sunday work after her services ended and allowed her to swap shifts to attend religious conventions; while her religion also required "field service," it did not require it to be performed on Sundays);

Page 427.   Add before *Baker* cite:

Sturgill v. UPS, 512 F.3d 1024 (8th Cir. 2008) (although it was harmless error, the jury should not have been instructed that to be reasonable an accommodation needs to eliminate conflict between an employee's religious beliefs and the employer's work requirements: "in many circumstances that the employee must either compromise a religious observance or practice, or accept a less desirable job or less favorable working conditions.");

Page 428.   Delete rest of paragraph after extract; replace with:

Perhaps the most obvious reasons that an accommodation may be unreasonable or constitute an undue hardship are safety or security concerns. *See EEOC v. Geo Group, Inc.*, 616 F.3d 265 (3d Cir. 2010) (a prison need not accommodate female Muslim guards' religious-based desire to wear khimars when the policy against headgear was justified by security concerns, including the risk that they could be used to smuggle contraband and conceal the identity of the wearer); *EEOC v. Kelly Servs.*, 598 F.3d 1022 (8th Cir. 2010) (employment agency's refusal to refer a Muslim worker who refused to remove her khimar for work in an industrial printing plant did not violate Title VII when the plant's neutral policy against loose-fitting clothing was justified by safety concerns about such apparel getting caught in the machinery's moving parts*). See also Burdette v. Fed. Express Corp.*, 367 F. App'x 628 (6th Cir. 2010) (no failure to accommodate claims where accommodating plaintiff's demands would have created an undue hardship due to safety risks in loading and unloading planes without all workers available).

But beyond safety cases, "de miminis cost" has been found to include not only monetary costs, as in *Hardison,* but a wide range of other costs, often intangible ones rendering the proposed accommodation an undue hardship. *E.g., Webb v. City of Philadelphia*, 562 F.3d 256 (3d Cir. 2009) (police department's need to appear religiously neutral in dealing with the public and working cooperatively satisfied the more than de minimis cost test when the department refused to accommodate plaintiff's request to wear a headscarf); *Harrell v. Donahue*, 2011 U.S. App. LEXIS 6621, 11-13 (8th Cir. Mar. 31, 2011) (it would have been an undue hardship for the employer to accommodate a Seventh Day Adventist by either altering its seniority system or excusing him from Saturday work every sixth week because granting plaintiff leave would have been a substantially imposition on his co-workers).

Nonetheless, the mere existence of a seniority system does not necessarily preclude reasonable accommodation since some practices may be accommodated without violating the system, *see Balint v. Carson City, Nev.*, 180 F.3d 1047 (9th Cir. 1999). Nevertheless, violation of a collective bargaining agreement has been frequently held to be an undue hardship. *E.g., Virts v. Consolidated Freightways Corp. of Del.*, 285 F.3d 508 (6th Cir. 2002) (undue hardship for trucking company to accommodate a Christian truck driver who refused to make overnight runs with female drivers because it would require violating a collective bargaining agreement under which drivers are dispatched in the order of seniority). Even where a CBA does not control, courts have been reluctant to require accommodations that burden co-workers. *E.g., Aron v. Quest Diagnostics Inc.*, 174 F. App'x 82, 84 (3d Cir. 2006) (undue hardship established by showing that accommodating plaintiff's religious need not to work on Saturday "would result in unequal treatment of the other employees and negatively affect employee morale."); *but see Phillips v. Collings*, 256 F.3d 843 (8th Cir. 2001) (not undue hardship to excuse social worker from placing foster children in homosexual parents' homes when few homosexual couples applied). *See generally* Rachel M. Birnbach, Note, *Love Thy Neighbor: Should Religious Accommodations that Negatively Affect Coworkers' Shift Preferences Constitute an Undue Hardship on the Employer Under Title VII?*, 78 FORDHAM L. REV. 1331, 1350 (2009)

Page 433. Delete Notes 4 and 5 and replace with the following:

4. *Accommodation or Discrimination?* Why is *Wilson* an accommodation case as opposed to an affirmative discrimination case? *See EEOC v. Thompson Contr., Grading, Paving, & Utils., Inc.*, 333 F. App'x 768 (4th Cir. 2009) (reversing summary judgment for employer on discrimination claim while noting that summary judgment might still be appropriate for failure to accommodate); *Wilkerson v. New Media Tech. Charter Sch., Inc.*, 522 F.3d 315 (3d Cir. 2008) (plaintiff could not assert a failure to accommodate claim when she failed to alert her employer that she could not participate in a "libations ceremony" at a staff banquet for religious reasons, but she could proceed on her discrimination case claiming she was discharged for her Christian beliefs). Would plaintiff have been better off eschewing any accommodation claim and arguing instead that she was discharged simply because of her religion? Reread the statute. While "undue hardship" is a defense to a reasonable accommodation claim, it is not a defense to a charge of disparate treatment religious discrimination. It is true that BFOQ might be a defense in theory, but did U.S. West establish the elements of a BFOQ?

Or is the employer entitled to raise the accommodation issue — that it could not reasonably accommodate plaintiff's religious beliefs without undue hardship — as a defense to an individual disparate treatment case? In *Brown v. Polk County, Iowa*, 61 F.3d 650 (8th Cir. 1995) (en banc) the plaintiff made a straightforward claim that he was terminated because of his religion. The employer then raised accommodation as a defense: it argued that, because plaintiff never explicitly asked for accommodation of his religious activities, he could not claim the protections of Title VII. The court seemed to accept this approach. While it held against the defendant on the facts, it did suggest that the employer could prevail if it could show that any accommodation of the plaintiff's religious expression was an undue hardship. *Id.* at 655. How could that be? Is "undue hardship" another name for BFOQ in this setting?

5. *Religious Harassment.* Was Wilson "harassed" because of her religious beliefs or merely because she wore something, admittedly for religious reasons, that offended others for reasons having nothing to do with religion? Religious harassment is certainly actionable. *See EEOC v. Sunbelt Rentals, Inc.*, 521 F.3d 306, 311 (4th Cir. 2008) (severe or pervasive harassment of plaintiff, a Muslim, which included "a steady stream of demeaning comments and degrading actions," including "religiously-charged epithets" such as "Taliban" and "towel head," was actionable religious harassment); *Winspear v. Cmty. Dev., Inc.*, 574 F.3d 604 (8th Cir. 2009) (finding claim of religious harassment when coworker, who knew that plaintiff was still distraught by suicide of his brother, repeatedly told him that she could speak with the dead and that his late brother was in hell and was trying to tell him that he also would go to hell if he did not "find God"). However, courts have been careful to distinguish situations where observant individuals were offended by conduct that was not motivated by religion. *See Rivera v. P.R. Aqueduct & Sewers Auth.*, 331 F.3d 183, 190 (1st Cir. 2003) (there "is a conceptual gap between an environment that is offensive to a person of strong religious sensibilities and an environment that is offensive because of hostility to the religion guiding those sensibilities"). Maybe that describes Wilson situation.

Could it be that Wilson was "harassing" others because of her religious beliefs? *See Powell v. Yellow Book USA, Inc.*, 445 F.3d 1074, 1078 (8th Cir. 2006) (employers have no obligation to suppress religious expression merely because it annoys a single employee). We examined sexual and other kinds of harassment in the preceding section, but religious harassment raises some distinctive issues. Indeed, the EEOC has attempted to formulate guidelines for such harassment without success. *See generally* Nantiya Ruan, *Accommodating Respectful Religious Expression in the Workplace*, 92 MARQ. L. REV. 1, 31-32 (2008); Kent Greenawalt, *Title VII and Religious Liberty*, 33 LOY. U. CHI. L.J. 1 (2001); Eugene Volokh, *Freedom of Speech, Religious Harassment Law, and Religious Accommodation Law*, 33 LOY. U. CHI. L.J. 57 (2001); David L. Gregory, *Religious Harassment in the Workplace: An Analysis of the EEOC's Proposed Guidelines*, 56 MONT. L. REV. 119 (1995).

The problem, of course, is that one person's harassment is another person's free exercise of religion. In this regard, Title VII poses a problem within itself: both the person expressing herself religiously and the person who is offended by that expression may seek the protection of the statute. Further, the Constitution can come into play. To the extent that the statute curbs religious expression, it implicates free exercise notions. *Cf.* Note on the First Amendment Implications of Sexual Harassment Liability, p. 415

Page 436.   Add at end of carryover paragraph in *Note on Religious Institutions' Exemption from the Prohibition of Religious Discrimination*:

The courts are divided as to the precise test for the exemption. *Compare LeBoon v. Lancaster Jewish Cmty. Ctr. Ass'n*, 503 F.3d 217 (3d Cir. 2007) (finding nonprofit community center within the exception after applying multi-factor test), *with Spencer v. World Vision Inc.*, 633 F.3d 723 (9th Cir. 2011) (panel divided three ways the appropriate test for the exemption but nevertheless deciding 2-1 that a nonprofit humanitarian aid organization was with the statute's exemptions even though it was not a church or church-affiliated organization).

Page 438.   Change title of Note to:

Note on the Free Exercise Clause and the Religious Freedom Restoration Act

Page 439.   Add before *Francis* cite near the end of the fourth full paragraph:

See Potter v. District of Columbia, 558 F.3d 542, 547 (D.C. Cir. 2009) (summary judgment against the District was appropriate; while firefighter safety was a compelling state interest, the District failed to show why safety would be threatened by using the breathing equipment sought by plaintiffs as an accommodation).

Page 440.   Delete second-to-last paragraph through second full paragraph on page 441; replace with:

But see EEOC v. Hosanna-Tabor Evangelical Lutheran Church & Sch., 597 F.3d 769 (6th Cir. 2010), *cert granted*, 2011 U.S. LEXIS 2445 (2011) (ministerial exception does not bar religious elementary school teacher's ADA claim where the vast bulk of her teaching was of secular subjects and teachers need not be of same religion to lead religious activities). Further, despite the exception, the antidiscrimination statutes may apply to some church actions where religion is not implicated. *See Elvig v. Calvin Presbyterian Church*, 375 F.3d 951, 964 (9th Cir. 2004) (inquiry into a church's decision to terminate plaintiff's ministry foreclosed, but plaintiff's hostile environment claims may be pursued since this inquiry "does not require interpretations of religious doctrine or scrutiny of the Defendants' ministerial choices.").

While *Hosanna-Tabor* suggested the limits some courts have imposed on the exception, particularly with respect to teachers of secular subjects in religious schools, there is no doubt that the exception is broader than its title might suggest. While ministers and priests have been barred from suing, *see Alcazar v. Corp. of the Catholic Archbishop of Seattle*, 627 F.3d 1288 (9th Cir. 2010) (finding a seminarian to be within the ministerial exception for purposes of dismissing a state minimum wage claim), other individuals whose jobs are less clearly ministerial have also been precluded. For example, *Alicea-Hernandez v. Catholic Bishop*, 320 F.3d 698, 704 (7th Cir. 2003), held that plaintiff's duties as press secretary for the diocese, "responsible for conveying the message of an organization to the public as a whole," fell within the ministerial exception). *Accord Skrzypczak v. Roman Catholic Diocese*, 611 F.3d 1238 (10th Cir. 2010) (a lay director of a diocese's Department of Religious Formation fell within the ministerial exception when the position's responsibilities furthered the core of the diocese's spiritual mission and she taught multiple religious courses); *Starkman v. Evans*, 198 F.3d 173 (5th Cir. 1999) (choir director qualifies as "minister" for purposes of the ministerial exception because she "participated in religious rituals and had numerous religious duties"). *See also Curay-Cramer v. Ursuline Acad. of Wilmington, Del., Inc.*, 450 F.3d 130 (3d Cir. 2006) (Congress had not spoken clearly enough to justify applying Title VII to a decision by a religious school to dismiss teacher for pro-choice actions when assessment of whether her conduct was comparable to that of a male would require assessment of the degree to which Catholic teachings were implicated by their respective actions).

While the exemption seems to be predicated at least in part on a judicial desire to avoid passing on theological questions, some courts have explicitly rejected any such limitation. As *Combs*, phrased it:

> [T]he First Amendment concerns are two-fold. The first concern is that secular authorities would be involved in evaluating or interpreting religious doctrine. The second quite independent concern is that in investigating employment discrimination claims by ministers against their church, secular authorities would necessarily intrude into church governance in a manner that would be inherently coercive, even if the alleged discrimination were purely nondoctrinal.

173 F.3d. at 350. *See generally* Caroline Mala Corbin, *Above The Law? The Constitutionality of the Ministerial Exemption from Antidiscrimination Law*, 75 FORDHAM L. REV. 1965 (2007). John H. Mansfield, *A Tale of Two Organists: Suits Against Churches for Employment Discrimination and Sexual Abuse by Ministers*, 7 GEO. J.L. & PUB. POL'Y 237 (2009).

The interaction of RFRA with the ministerial exception is unclear. One argument is that RFRA in effect amended Title VII pro tanto to incorporate some version of the ministerial exception. At least one court, however, views RFRA as completely displacing the exception. *Hankins v. Lyght*, 441 F.3d 96, 102 (2d Cir. 2006), held that, rather than employing the judicially-created ministerial exception, "RFRA must be deemed the full expression of Congress's intent with regard to the religion-related issues . . . and displace earlier judge-made doctrines that might have been used to ameliorate the ADEA's impact on religious organizations and activities." *Contra Tomic v. Catholic Diocese of Peoria*, 442 F.3d 1036 (7th Cir. 2006) (rejecting *Hankins* as "unsound" to the extent that decision would "invalidate the many decisions in this and other circuits recognizing the ministerial exception to federal employment discrimination law"). *See also Rweyemamu v. Cote*, 520 F.3d 198 (2d Cir. 2008) (ministerial exception barred suit by black Catholic priest when the defendants expressly waived any RFRA defense). Still other judges seem to believe that RFRA bars suits by the EEOC but not by private plaintiffs. *Hankins*, 441 F.3d at 114-15 (Sotomayor dissenting. Might RFRA in fact operate to expand the exception beyond the scope accorded it by the earlier cases? Or might Title VII be nevertheless applied as written — there is a compelling governmental interest in eliminating discrimination? Does *Boy Scouts of Am. v. Dale*, see page 330, help answer the question?

E. National Origin and Alienage Discrimination

Page 453. Delete Note 7; replace with:

7. *Did Elite Get It Right?* The fact that Elite was walking a legal tightrope doesn't mean it got it right. The dramatic split in the en banc court revealed serious divisions about when compliance with IRCA turns into national origin discrimination. A bright line would find a violation of Title VII when an employer did anything more than IRCA requires employers to do. Under that view, cases such as *New El Rey Sausage Co. v. INS*, 925 F.2d 1153, 1157-58 (9th Cir. 1991), would be wrong. The downside of this approach is obvious — by refusing to allow employers to question documents or discrepancies, IRCA's mandate to stop employment of unauthorized immigrants would be undercut. But isn't the converse also true? That is, by encouraging employers to act when discrepancies arise, such as in *Zamora* itself, doesn't IRCA create a perverse incentive for employers to discriminate on the basis of national origin? Is there much question that Elite pressed the issue with Mr. Zamora at least in part because his name and lack of English language skills, both tied to his Mexican national origin, suggested he was an alien? Why did a majority of the court privilege IRCA over Title VII?

Although *El Rey* is out of the Ninth Circuit, another Ninth Circuit case decided that same year recognized the problem of competing incentives. *Collins Foods Intl., Inc. v. INS*, 948 F.2d 549 (9th Cir. 1991), reversed a finding that the employer had constructive knowledge of a person's status as an unauthorized alien from facts such as the employer's failing to compare the employee's Social Security card with the sample in the INS Service Manual. *Collins* stressed that not only did Congress not intend the statute to force employers to become experts in employment authorization documents, but also that expanding liability by the constructive knowledge doctrine would cause employers to discriminate against people on national origin or citizenship grounds. *See also Aramark Facility Servs. v. SEIU, Local 1877*, 530 F.3d 817 (9th Cir. 2008) (arbitrator's ruling ordering reinstatement of workers who were discharged after being given only three days to produce adequate documentation after the employer received "no match" letters from the Social Security Administration did not violate public policy since no match letters are not sufficiently probative to put the employer on constructive notice that the workers were undocumented).

7A. *State Laws Deterring Employing Undocumented Aliens.* The last few years have seen a rash of state laws (and local ordinances) seeking to deal with undocumented aliens by a variety of employer-directed sanctions. Although the laws take varying approaches, they often try to minimize the possibility of being preempted by the federal immigration statutes by closely tracking federal provisions. For example, Arizona's law imposes penalties on employers who hired undocumented aliens, as the federal law defines them, including loss of the right to do business in the state. It also requires employers to use the federal E-Verify system, which is an option, not a command, under federal law.

In *Chamber of Commerce of the United States v. Whiting,* 131 S. Ct. 642 (2010), the Supreme Court upheld the law against a preemption challenge. Although Justice Thomas concurred in the result, he did not join all of Chief Justice Roberts's opinion for three other justices, resulting in a plurality on several points even though a majority upheld the Arizona law.

The plurality's analysis focused on three separate points. The first was express pre-emption. Although IRCA has an express preemption provision, 8 U.S.C.A. §1324a(a)(1)(A), that section saves from preemption state "licensing and similar laws." The majority found that articles of incorporation and grants of authority to out of state companies to do business in the state qualified under the savings clause; thus, Arizona was free to grant or withhold them despite IRCA. The second point was implied preemption, with a majority also agreeing that the statute was not impliedly preempted to the extent it imposed sanctions beyond those found in IRCA itself; however, Justice Thomas did not join in this part of the plurality's opinion. The third point was the Arizona law's requirement that employers use the federal E-Verify system to determine whether employees are authorized to work. Again four justices held in favor of this requirement, with Justice Thomas concurring in the result but not in the plurality opinion.

In short, while *Whiting* opens the door for other states to act, the preemption question remains a complicated one to the extent the law in question does not track the Arizona statute. *See generally* Kati L. Griffith, *Discovering "Immployment" Law: The Constitutionality of Subfederal Immigration Regulation at Work,* 29 YALE L. & POL'Y REV. 389 (2011).

Page 456. Add at end of last full paragraph:

James Leonard, *Title VII and the Protection of Minority Languages in the American Workplace: The Search for a Justification,* 72 MO. L. REV. 745 (2007).

Page 457. Add at end of last full paragraph:

Cf. D. Wendy Greene, *Title VII: What's Hair (and Other Race-Based Characteristics) Got to Do With It?,* 79 U. COLO. L. REV. 1355, 1393 (2008) (courts should expand the definition of "race" to include historical and contemporary understandings of race, which would require employers "to assert a more substantial reason for implementing grooming and appearance policies than that they seek to present a 'conservative' or 'business-like image.' ").

Page 459.   Add at end of section:

Craig Robert Senn, *Proposing a Uniform Remedial Approach for Undocumented Workers Under Federal Employment Discrimination Law,* 77 FORDHAM L. REV. 113 (2008) (proposing that undocumented workers be disqualified from backpay and front pay only when they violate provisions prohibiting fraudulent conduct); Jarod S. Gonzalez, *Employment Law Remedies for Illegal Immigrants,* 40 TEX. TECH. L. REV. 987, 999 (2008) ("Employers should pay the same price when they violate the standards, regardless of the aggrieved victim's immigration status."). Keith Cunningham-Parmeter, *Redefining the Rights of Undocumented Workers,* 58 AM. U. L. REV. 1361 (2009).

F.   Union Liability

Page 460.   Delete NLRA in ninth line; replace with:

Railway Labor Act

G.   Retaliation

Page 461.   Insert after Title VII excerpt:

In 2011, the EEOC announced that for the first time the number of complaints filed for discriminatory retaliation surpassed the number filed for race discrimination, making it the most frequently filed charge with the EEOC. EEOC Reports Job Bias Charges Hit Record High of Nearly 100,000 in Fiscal Year 2010 (January 1, 2011) (available at http://www.eeoc.gov/eeoc/newsroom/release/1-11-11.cfm*).

Page 461.   Delete second full paragraph; replace with:

Although §1981 does not expressly prohibit retaliation, the Supreme Court recently held that it encompasses retaliation claims. In *CBOS West, Inc. v Humphries,* 553 U.S. 442 (2008), the Court held that principles of *stare decisis* strongly indicated that §1981 should be interpreted to include a prohibition against retaliation. Section 1981 had long been interpreted similarly to §1982, a post–Civil War statute enacted to protect property rights of black citizens, and §1982 has been held to include retaliation claims. Further, the Court noted that its interpretation was bolstered by the actions of Congress in overriding *Patterson v. McLean Credit Union*, 491 U.S. 164 (1988), to the extent it restricted the coverage of §1981.

By a parity of reasoning, federal employees are also protected from retaliation even though they are covered under separate provisions of Title VII and the ADEA that do not expressly reach such conduct. *Bonds v. Leavitt*, 629 F.3d 369, 384-385 (4th Cir. 2011) (Title VII's protection against retaliation based on employee's opposition to unlawful employment practice extends to federal employees.). State laws may also provide such protection. *See* Alex B. Long, *Viva State Employment Law! State Law Retaliation Claims in a Post*-Crawford/Burlington Northern *World*, 77 TENN. L. REV. 253, 257 (2010) (the Supreme Court decisions leave sufficient room for complementary state statutes "to serve as a safety net to protect employees who are unfairly left without protection from retaliation under federal law.")

Page 464. Delete Note 1; replace with the following:

1. *Broader Protection Under the Opposition Clause.* Shirley Breeden presented two distinct claims of retaliation. One was for opposition conduct (her internal complaints), while the other was for participation conduct (her filing of charges with the state agency and the EEOC). Many courts and commentators have perceived a sharp distinction between the protections of the "opposition" clause and the "participation" clause. While a plaintiff invoking the opposition clause must demonstrate a reasonable, good faith belief that the conduct complained of is unlawful, the protections of the participation clause have been almost absolute. One of the first "participation" cases, *Pettway v. American Cast Iron Pipe Co.*, 411 F.2d 998 (5th Cir. 1969), set the tone for these decisions by finding actionable retaliation when a worker was fired for filing an allegedly false and malicious charge with the EEOC — namely, that the employer had bought off an EEOC investigator. The court wrote:

> There can be no doubt about the purpose of §704(a). In unmistakable language it is to protect the employee who utilizes the tools provided by Congress to protect his rights. The Act will be frustrated if the employer may unilaterally determine the truth or falsity of charges and take independent action.

Id. at 1004-05. *See also Glover v. S.C. Law Enf.*, 170 F.3d 411 (4th Cir. 1999) (unreasonable deposition testimony protected by participation clause); *Clover v. Total Sys. Serv., Inc.*, 176 F.3d 1346 (11th Cir. 1999) (reasonable belief not needed for participation clause protections to be triggered). Recently, however, some courts have been more willing to find certain participation conduct unprotected. *See Hatmaker v. Mem'l Med. Ctr.*, 619 F.3d 741, 745 (7th Cir. 2010) (participation in an investigation of employment discrimination "doesn't insulate an employee from being discharged for conduct that, if it occurred outside an investigation, would warrant termination. This includes making frivolous accusations, or accusations grounded in prejudice."); *Niswander v. Cincinnati Ins. Co.*, 529 F.3d 714, 722 (6th Cir. 2008) (plaintiff's intentional conduct in turning over confidential employment documents to her attorney in response to a discovery request was not protected under the participation clause when the documents were irrelevant to her claim); *Mattson v. Caterpillar, Inc.*, 359 F.3d 885, 889-90 (7th Cir. 2004) (plaintiff was not sexually harassed when his supervisor's breast allegedly brushed against his arm on a single occasion; the state and federal sexual harassment charges Mattson filed were unprotected because it was "both objectively and subjectively unreasonable, as well as made with the bad faith purpose of retaliating against his female supervisor...": "this Court has consistently stated that utterly baseless claims do not receive protection under Title VII.").

After the *Breeden* Court disposed of the plaintiff's "opposition clause" claim by deciding that no reasonable person could believe that she had been sexually harassed, it went on to consider the causation issue on her "participation" clause claim. Doesn't *Breeden* thus establish that the participation clause prohibits retaliation even where the underlying discrimination claim lacks a reasonable basis? Why should that be so? Bad faith lawsuits can be sanctioned by attorney's fees. What if the plaintiff's charge and suit had been filed in bad faith? *Cf. Christiansburg Garment Co. v. EEOC* (reproduced at page 703) (employer can be awarded attorneys' fees for Title VII action that was "frivolous, unreasonable, or groundless" or in bad faith). Is there a reason to allow courts to decide the bad faith of claims while precluding employers from doing so by taking adverse employment actions? *See generally* Lawrence D. Rosenthal, *Reading Too Much into What the Court Doesn't Write: How Some Federal Courts Have Limited Title VII's Participation Clause's Protections After* Clark County School District v. Breeden, 83 WASH. L. REV. 345 (2008) (some courts after *Breeden* are requiring plaintiff to prove a good faith, objectively reasonable belief of an unlawful employment practice in claims under both the opposition and participation clauses; this requirement contradicts the plain language of the participation clause as well as the position of the EEOC on this issue).

Page 465. Add at end of fourth line in Note 2, *Distinguishing Participation Conduct from Opposition Conduct:*

Opposition need not be verbal; non-verbal communications may also suffice. *See Collazo v. Bristol-Myers Squibb Mfg.*, 617 F.3d 39 (1st Cir. 2010) (a supervisor's accompanying a subordinate to file a sexual harassment complaint several times constituted protected "opposition" conduct even though he did not utter any words of support).

Page 465. Delete in Note 3, *Retaliation and the* Ellerth *Affirmative Defense*, from *Crawford* cite to the end of Note; replace with:

In *Crawford v. Metro Gov't of Nashville & Davidson Counties*, 555 U.S. 271 (2009), the Supreme Court held that participation in employer internal investigations could be protected opposition conduct. *See* p. 148 of this Supplement.

Page 466.   Add before *Russell Robinson* citation in first full paragraph of carryover Note 4, *Reasonable Good Faith Belief*:

But see Butler v. Ala. DOT, 536 F.3d 1209, 1213 (11th Cir. 2008) ("not every uncalled for, ugly, racist statement by a co-worker is an unlawful employment practice," particularly when the incident occurred away from work, out of the presence of supervisors, and the racial remarks were not directed at the plaintiff); *Barker v. Mo. Dep't of Corr.*, 513 F.3d 831 (8th Cir. 2008) (a single, isolated statement that women were more nurturing and better suited for the job in question could not be the basis of an objectively reasonable belief that the employer had engaged in sexual harassment under Title VII).

Page 466.   Add at end of carryover paragraph in carryover Note 4, *Reasonable, Good Faith Belief*:

B. Glenn George, *Revenge*, 83 Tul. L. Rev. 439 (2008) (in hostile environment sexual harassment cases, the reasonable belief doctrine should not be applied strictly; instead, the employee should be protected from retaliation as long as she reasonably believes the employer's sexual harassment policy has been violated); Deborah L. Brake & Joanna L. Grossman, *The Failure of Title VII as a Rights Claiming System*, 86 N.C. L. Rev. 859, 619 (2008) (the reasoning behind the "reasonable belief" doctrine is sound, but courts apply it too strictly, "grossly oversimplify [ing] complex legal and social questions about what 'discrimination' the law does and should encompass"); Brianne J. Gorod, *"Rejecting Reasonableness": A New Look at Title VII's Anti-Retaliation Provision*, 56 Am. u. l. rev. 1469 (2007) (reasonable belief doctrine should be rejected altogether and the conduct of the plaintiffs should be protected under the opposition clause unless the employer could show the complaint was made in bad faith).

Courts, however, have not always been clear about what makes a belief reasonable. *See e.g., Dixon v. Hallmark Cos.*, 627 F.3d 849, 855 (11th Cir. 2010) (where plaintiffs were terminated because of their resistance to removing religious artwork from the workplace, the court found that plaintiffs stated a claim for failure to reasonably accommodate, but it nevertheless rejected a retaliation claim because plaintiffs failed to call attention to any statutory or case law that can reasonably be believed to prohibit a private employer from keeping its own workplace free of religious references).

Page 466.   Replace incomplete *Russell Robinson* citation in carryover Note 4, *Reasonable, Bad Faith Belief* with:

Russell Robinson, *Perceptual Segregation*, 108 Colum. L. Rev. 1093 (2008).

Page 466.   Delete Note 5; replace with the following:

5. *Determining Causation.* In analyzing the participation claim, the *Breeden* Court thought it "immaterial" that the transfer was finalized a month after suit

was filed, reasoning that the transfer was contemplated earlier. Should the trier of fact have been allowed to determine the decisionmaker's motivation in "finalizing" a transfer? Would a contrary ruling in practice have required employers to "suspend previously planned transfers upon discovering that a Title VII suit has been filed"? Must a plaintiff now present evidence regarding the proximity between the decisionmaker's knowledge of the protected activity and its initial contemplation of the adverse employment action?

Breeden might be read to hold that the plaintiff always loses on a summary judgment motion where the employer has denied retaliation and the plaintiff's only evidence of causation is that the adverse employment action occurred three months or more after the decision-maker learned of the protected activity. *See Tyler v. Univ. of Ark. Bd. of Trs.*, 628 F.3d 980, 986-87 (8th Cir. 2011) ("Generally, 'more than a temporal connection is required to present a genuine factual issue on retaliation,' and only in cases where the temporary proximity is very close can the plaintiff rest on it exclusively. As more time passes between the protected conduct and the retaliatory act, the inference of retaliation becomes weaker and requires stronger alternate evidence of causation.") (citations omitted); *El Sayed v. Hilton Hotels Corp.*, 627 F.3d 931, 933 (2d Cir. 2010) ("The temporal proximity of events may give rise to an inference of retaliation for the purposes of establishing a prima facie case of retaliation under Title VII, but without more, such temporal proximity is insufficient to satisfy appellant's burden to bring forward some evidence of pretext."); *Hall v. Forest River, Inc.*, 536 F.3d 615 (7th Cir. 2008) (plaintiff must point to more than temporal proximity to establish causation, particularly where the claimed incident is the failure to promote, which may depend on factors outside the employer's control). *But see Pinkerton v. Colorado Dept. of Transp.*, 563 F.3d 1052 (10th Cir. 2009) (termination within a few days of verification of the complaint plaintiff filed with employer, together with evidence that employer's reasons for firing plaintiff may not have been credible, held sufficient); *Mickey v. Zeidler Tool & Die Co.*, 516 F.3d 516 (6th Cir. 2008) (termination the day employer received notice of EEOC charge sufficed). *EEOC v. Kohler, Inc.*, 335 F.3d 766 (8th Cir. 2003) (termination less than one month after employee complained of racial discrimination, together with evidence of supervisor's reaction to complaint and inconsistent enforcement of attendance policy, sufficed); *Lampley v. Onyx Acceptance Corp.*, 340 F.3d 478 (7th Cir. 2003) (employee was terminated three days after going to EEOC; evidence that the company covered up the retaliatory reason for the termination supported award of compensatory and punitive damages). *See generally* Troy B. Daniels & Richard A. Bales, *Plus at Pretext: Resolving the Split Regarding the Sufficiency of Temporal Proximity Evidence in Title VII Retaliation Cases*, 44 GONZ. L. REV. 493 (2008/2009). Turning the reasoning of *Breeden* on its head, what if the decision-maker began "contemplating" such action within three months of learning of the protected activity?

The fact that an adverse employment action was motivated by retaliatory intent may, however, be proven by evidence other than temporal proximity. *See Buckley v. Mukasey*, 538 F.3d 306 (4th Cir. 2008) (district court's refusal to admit evidence of plaintiff's involvement in prior successful discrimination suit in order to establish retaliatory intent was an abuse of discretion that necessitated a new trial); *Templeton v. First Tenn. Bank*, 2011 WL 1525559, 2 (4th Cir. Apr. 22, 2011) (even though two years had elapsed since plaintiff's harassment complaint, the employer's refusal to rehire her was its first opportunity to retaliate; its stated reason that she had "issues with management" created an issue of fact as to whether employer's refusal to rehire was causally-related to the previous harassment complaint).

Page 467. Add at end of carryover Note 6, *Retaliation Claims and Mixed Motive Analysis*:

Fye v. Oklahoma Corp. Comm'n, 516 F.3d 1217 (10th Cir. 2008). It is not clear the effect, if any, of *Gross v. FBL Financial Services*, 129 S. Ct. 2343 (2009), reproduced on p. 26 of this Supplement, on this question.

1. Protected Conduct

Page 467. Add after *Bd. of Governors* cite in second full paragraph:

But see Richardson v. Comm'n on Human Rights & Opportunities, 532 F.3d 114 (2d Cir. 2008) (election-of-remedies provision in a collective bargaining agreement, which provided that employee alleging discrimination may not arbitrate a grievance if she filed a charge with the state agency, did not violate Title VII when the employee remained free to file a charge with the EEOC and pursue an action in federal court); *Vaughn v. Epworth Villa*, 537 F.3d 1147 (10th Cir. 2008) (plaintiff engaged in protected conduct when she submitted unredacted medical records to the EEOC to support her charge, but employer could terminate her for this conduct when other employees engaging in similar conduct unrelated to a charge of discrimination would also have been terminated).

Page 467. Add at end of last full paragraph:

See also Kelley v. City of Albuquerque, 542 F.3d 802 (10th Cir. 2008) (attorney discharged by new mayor because of her representation of the city in EEOC mediation with mayor's then-client had a retaliation claim).

page 471. Add at end of Note 2, *The Prima Facie Case*:

In some retaliation cases, the knowledge requirement might be satisfied by the principles announced in *Staub v. Proctor Hospital*, reproduced at p. 9 of this Supplement. *See Gollas v. Univ. of Tex. Health Sci. Ctr. at Houston*, 2011 WL 1834248 (5th Cir. May 12, 2011) (no causal link between protected activity and plaintiff's termination from residency because final decisionmakers did not know of that activity, and there was not enough evidence to support plaintiff's "cat's-paw" theory.)

Page 472. Delete Note 3; replace with:

3. *"Prima Facie Unprotected."* The Fourth Circuit found in *Laughin* that plaintiff had no prima facie case because the conduct was unprotected under the opposition clause. In so doing, the court acknowledges the broader protection Laughlin would have received had she been able to convince the court she was engaged in participation clause activities. Had the investigation of her co-worker's claim been ongoing, presumably this court would have found that Laughlin's copying the documents and sending them to her co-worker was protected activity.

But, as we've seen earlier and as *Laughlin* confirms, the protections of the opposition clause are far less sweeping. *McDonnell Douglas,* reproduced at page 50, establishes that some conduct is too unreasonable to be protected. And in a footnote omitted from your text, *Laughlin* asserts it is "black letter law" that illegal actions are not protected by Title VII. As is clear from the case, even legal actions that are deemed sufficiently unreasonable can be unprotected as well. At the same time, the mere fact that the employer perceives the conduct to be disloyal does not, of itself, deprive the conduct of protection. *Magyar v. St. Joseph Reg'l Med. Ctr.,* 544 F.3d 766 (7th Cir. 2008) (plaintiff engaged in protected opposition conduct when she complained that her harassment charge was not being handled properly). *Laughlin* uses a balancing test to determine, at the prima facie case stage, whether the opposition conduct is protected. Essentially, this approach concludes that some *forms* of opposition are so beyond the pale as to prevent plaintiff from establishing a prima facie case.

Page 472. Add at end of Note 4, *Or Legitimate Nondiscriminatory Reason?*:

See also Pye v. Nu Aire, Inc., 641 F.3d 1011 (8th Cir. 2011) ("a jury could believe Pye's version of what transpired at the November 15, 2007 meeting, and could further believe that Nu Aire's assertions of intimidation, coercion, and threatening behavior were pretext for, if not further evidence of, Nu Aire's true prohibited reason for Pye's termination which was that Pye was trying to extort a monetary settlement of his claim"); *Alvarez v. Royal Atl. Developers, Inc.,* 610 F.3d 1253 (11th Cir. 2010) (an employer violated Title VII's retaliation provision by accelerating plaintiff's pending discharge when she engaged in protected conduct; while an employer might be permitted to do so when it had reasonable fears that the employee might sabotage its operations, no such fears were present when the employee made no threats); *Franklin v. Local 2 of the Sheet Metal Workers Ass'n,* 565 F.3d 508 (8th Cir. 2009) (fact question as to whether union's actions were pretextual when it claimed it was necessary to post and read out loud plaintiffs' names after they filed charges with the EEOC as part of its requirement to post all legal bills).

Page 472.   Add before *Cruz* cite in Note 5, *Applying the Balancing Test*:

Argyropoulos v. City of Alton, 539 F.3d 724 (7th Cir. 2008) (secretly recording plaintiff's meeting with supervisors not protected).

Page 473.   Add after second full paragraph in carryover Note 5, *Applying the Balancing Test*:

See also McCollugh v. Univ. of Arkansas for Med. Serv., 559 F.3d 855 (8th Cir. 2009) (belief that plaintiff was untruthful in filing sexual harassment claims against his co-workers entitled employer to terminate plaintiff); *Vaughn v. Epworth Villa*, 537 F.3d 1147 (10th Cir. 2008) (although plaintiff engaged in prima facie protected conduct under participation clause when she submitted unredacted medical records to the EEOC to support her charge, employer could terminate her for this conduct when other employees engaging in similar conduct would have been terminated). An employee may also be terminated for misconduct related to the complaint or investigation of the complaint. *See Formella v. U.S. Dep't of Labor*, 628 F.3d 381, 393 (7th Cir. 2010) (termination of whistleblower was not retaliatory where the employee was disruptive in making his complaint: "although some allowance must be made for impulsive and emotional behavior [the complaining employee] can nonetheless be expected to demonstrate civility and respect for his superiors in voicing those concerns."); *Gant v. Kash'n Karry Food Stores, Inc.*, 390 F. App'x 943 (11th Cir. 2010) (discharge of plaintiff for revealing to other managers her pending internal complaint about race discrimination in violation of employer's confidentiality policy was not prohibited retaliation unless it could be shown to be a pretext for retaliating for the initial complaint).

Page 473.   Delete Note 6; replace with:

6. *Who Is Protected?* In *Crawford v. Metropolitan Government of Nashville and Davidson County*, 129 S. Ct. 846 (2009), the Court held that an employee who speaks out about discrimination in response to inquiries made during an employer's internal investigation is protected by the opposition clause. In so doing, it rejected the lower court's conclusion that, because the plaintiff had merely answered questions rather than initiating a complaint, she lacked protection against retaliation. As the Court stated, "nothing in the statute requires a freakish rule protecting an employee who reports discrimination on her own initiative but not one who reports the same discrimination in the same words when her boss asks a question." *Id.* at 852. The Court noted that protecting the employee who speaks up when questioned by the employer was in keeping with the *Ellerth-Faragher* affirmative defense:

> The appeals court's rule would thus create a real dilemma for any knowledgeable employee in a hostile work environment if the boss took steps to assure a defense under our cases. If the employee reported discrimination in response to the enquiries, the employer might well be free to penalize her for speaking up. But if she kept quiet

about the discrimination and later filed a Title VII claim, the employer might well escape liability, arguing that it "exercised reasonable care to prevent and correct [any discrimination] promptly" but "the plaintiff employee unreasonably failed to take advantage of . . . preventive or corrective opportunities provided by the employer." *Ellerth*. Nothing in the statute's text or our precedent supports this catch-22.

Id. at 852-53. The Court did not decide whether the conduct also would be protected under the participation clause.

In a subsequent case, also from the Sixth Circuit, the Supreme Court was called upon to decide whether an employee who was fired after his fiancé had filed a discrimination charge was protected by Title VII's anti-retaliation provision. The Sixth Circuit had said he was not, and the Court reversed in the following opinion.

Thompson v. North American Stainless, LP
131 S. Ct. 863 (2011)

Justice SCALIA delivered the opinion of the Court.

Until 2003, both petitioner Eric Thompson and his fiancee, Miriam Regalado, were employees of respondent North American Stainless (NAS). In February 2003, the Equal Employment Opportunity Commission (EEOC) notified NAS that Regalado had filed a charge alleging sex discrimination. Three weeks later, NAS fired Thompson. [Thompson then filed a charge with the EEOC and ultimately sued "claiming that NAS had fired him in order to retaliate against Regalado for filing her charge with the EEOC."]

I

Title VII provides that "[i]t shall be an unlawful employment practice for an employer to discriminate against any of his employees . . . because he has made a charge" under Title VII. 42 U.S.C. §2000e-3(a). The statute permits "a person claiming to be aggrieved" to file a charge with the EEOC alleging that the employer committed an unlawful employment practice, and, if the EEOC declines to sue the employer, it permits a civil action to "be brought . . . by the person claiming to be aggrieved . . . by the alleged unlawful employment practice." §2000e-5(b), (f)(1).

It is undisputed that Regalado's filing of a charge with the EEOC was protected conduct under Title VII. In the procedural posture of this case, we are also required to assume that NAS fired Thompson in order to retaliate against Regalado for filing a charge of discrimination. This case therefore presents two questions: First, did NAS's firing of Thompson constitute unlawful retaliation? And second, if it did, does Title VII grant Thompson a cause of action?

II

With regard to the first question, we have little difficulty concluding that if the facts alleged by Thompson are true, then NAS's firing of Thompson violated Title

VII. In *Burlington N. & S. F. R. Co.* v. *White* we held that Title VII's antiretaliation provision must be construed to cover a broad range of employer conduct. We reached that conclusion by contrasting the text of Title VII's antiretaliation provision with its substantive antidiscrimination provision. Title VII prohibits discrimination on the basis of race, color, religion, sex, and national origin " 'with respect to . . . compensation, terms, conditions, or privileges of employment,' " and discriminatory practices that would " 'deprive any individual of employment opportunities or otherwise adversely affect his status as an employee.' " In contrast, Title VII's antiretaliation provision prohibits an employer from " 'discriminat[ing] against any of his employees' " for engaging in protected conduct, without specifying the employer acts that are prohibited. Based on this textual distinction and our understanding of the antiretaliation provision's purpose, we held that "the antiretaliation provision, unlike the substantive provision, is not limited to discriminatory actions that affect the terms and conditions of employment." Rather, Title VII's antiretaliation provision prohibits any employer action that "well might have dissuaded a reasonable worker from making or supporting a charge of discrimination."

We think it obvious that a reasonable worker might be dissuaded from engaging in protected activity if she knew that her fiancé would be fired. Indeed, NAS does not dispute that Thompson's firing meets the standard set forth in *Burlington*. NAS raises the concern, however, that prohibiting reprisals against third parties will lead to difficult line-drawing problems concerning the types of relationships entitled to protection. Perhaps retaliating against an employee by firing his fiancee would dissuade the employee from engaging in protected activity, but what about firing an employee's girlfriend, close friend, or trusted co-worker? Applying the *Burlington* standard to third-party reprisals, NAS argues, will place the employer at risk any time it fires any employee who happens to have a connection to a different employee who filed a charge with the EEOC.

Although we acknowledge the force of this point, we do not think it justifies a categorical rule that third-party reprisals do not violate Title VII. As explained above, we adopted a broad standard in *Burlington* because Title VII's antiretaliation provision is worded broadly. We think there is no textual basis for making an exception to it for third-party reprisals, and a preference for clear rules cannot justify departing from statutory text.

We must also decline to identify a fixed class of relationships for which third-party reprisals are unlawful. We expect that firing a close family member will almost always meet the *Burlington* standard, and inflicting a milder reprisal on a mere acquaintance will almost never do so, but beyond that we are reluctant to generalize. As we explained in *Burlington*, "the significance of any given act of retaliation will often depend upon the particular circumstances." Given the broad statutory text and the variety of workplace contexts in which retaliation may occur, Title VII's antiretaliation provision is simply not reducible to a comprehensive set of clear rules. We emphasize, however, that "the provision's standard for judging harm must be objective," so as to "avoi[d] the uncertainties and unfair discrepancies that can plague a judicial effort to determine a plaintiff's unusual subjective feelings."

III

The more difficult question in this case is whether Thompson may sue NAS for its alleged violation of Title VII. The statute provides that "a civil action may be brought . . . by the person claiming to be aggrieved." 42 U.S.C. §2000e-5(f)(1). The Sixth Circuit concluded that this provision was merely a reiteration of the requirement that the plaintiff have Article III standing. We do not understand how that can be. The provision unquestionably permits a person "claiming to be aggrieved" to bring "a civil action." It is arguable that the aggrievement referred to is nothing more than the minimal Article III standing, which consists of injury in fact caused by the defendant and remediable by the court. See *Lujan* v. *Defenders of Wildlife*, 504 U.S. 555, 560-561 (1992). But Thompson's claim undoubtedly meets those requirements, so if that is indeed all that aggrievement consists of, he may sue.

We have suggested in dictum that the Title VII aggrievement requirement conferred a right to sue on all who satisfied Article III standing. *Trafficante* v. *Metropolitan Life Ins. Co.*, 409 U.S. 205 (1972), involved the "person aggrieved" provision of Title VIII (the Fair Housing Act) rather than Title VII. In deciding the case, however, we relied upon, and cited with approval, a Third Circuit opinion involving Title VII, which, we said, "concluded that the words used showed 'a congressional intention to define standing as broadly as is permitted by Article III of the Constitution.'" We think that dictum regarding Title VII was too expansive. Indeed, the *Trafficante* opinion did not adhere to it in expressing its Title VIII holding that residents of an apartment complex could sue the owner for his racial discrimination against prospective tenants. The opinion said that the "person aggrieved" of Title VIII was coextensive with Article III *insofar as tenants of the same housing unit that is charged with discrimination are concerned*." (emphasis added). Later opinions, we must acknowledge, reiterate that the term "aggrieved" in Title VIII reaches as far as Article III permits, see *Bennett* v. *Spear*, 520 U.S. 154, 165-166 (1997); *Gladstone, Realtors* v. *Village of Bellwood*, 441 U.S. 91 (1979), though the holdings of those cases are compatible with the "zone of interests" limitation that we discuss below. In any event, it is Title VII rather than Title VIII that is before us here, and as to that we are surely not bound by the *Trafficante* dictum.

We now find that this dictum was ill-considered, and we decline to follow it. If any person injured in the Article III sense by a Title VII violation could sue, absurd consequences would follow. For example, a shareholder would be able to sue a company for firing a valuable employee for racially discriminatory reasons, so long as he could show that the value of his stock decreased as a consequence. At oral argument Thompson acknowledged that such a suit would not lie. We agree, and therefore conclude that the term "aggrieved" must be construed more narrowly than the outer boundaries of Article III.

At the other extreme from the position that "person aggrieved" means anyone with Article III standing, NAS argues that it is a term of art that refers only to the employee who engaged in the protected activity. We know of no other context in which the words carry this artificially narrow meaning, and if that is what

Congress intended it would more naturally have said "person claiming to have been discriminated against" rather than "person claiming to be aggrieved." We see no basis in text or prior practice for limiting the latter phrase to the person who was the subject of unlawful retaliation. Moreover, such a reading contradicts the very holding of *Trafficante*, which was that residents of an apartment complex were "person[s] aggrieved" by discrimination against prospective tenants. We see no reason why the same phrase in Title VII should be given a narrower meaning.

In our view there is a common usage of the term "person aggrieved" that avoids the extremity of equating it with Article III and yet is fully consistent with our application of the term in *Trafficante*. The Administrative Procedure Act, 5 U.S.C. §551 *et seq.*, authorizes suit to challenge a federal agency by any "person . . . adversely affected or aggrieved . . . within the meaning of a relevant statute." §702. We have held that this language establishes a regime under which a plaintiff may not sue unless he "falls within the 'zone of interests' sought to be protected by the statutory provision whose violation forms the legal basis for his complaint." *Lujan* v. *National Wildlife Federation*, 497 U.S. 871, 883 (1990). We have described the "zone of interests" test as denying a right of review "if the plaintiff's interests are so marginally related to or inconsistent with the purposes implicit in the statute that it cannot reasonably be assumed that Congress intended to permit the suit." *Clarke* v. *Securities Industry Assn.*, 479 U.S. 388, 399-400 (1987). We hold that the term "aggrieved" in Title VII incorporates this test, enabling suit by any plaintiff with an interest "arguably [sought] to be protected by the statutes," *National Credit Union Admin.* v. *First Nat. Bank & Trust Co.*, 522 U.S. 479, 495 (1998), while excluding plaintiffs who might technically be injured in an Article III sense but whose interests are unrelated to the statutory prohibitions in Title VII.

Applying that test here, we conclude that Thompson falls within the zone of interests protected by Title VII. Thompson was an employee of NAS, and the purpose of Title VII is to protect employees from their employers' unlawful actions. Moreover, accepting the facts as alleged, Thompson is not an accidental victim of the retaliation—collateral damage, so to speak, of the employer's unlawful act. To the contrary, injuring him was the employer's intended means of harming Regalado. Hurting him was the unlawful act by which the employer punished her. In those circumstances, we think Thompson well within the zone of interests sought to be protected by Title VII. He is a person aggrieved with standing to sue.

[Justices GINSBURG and BREYER concurred, essentially on the grounds that the EEOC's Compliance Manual reached the same result and its "statements in the Manual merit deference under *Skidmore* v. *Swift & Co.*, 323 U.S. 134 (1944). Justice KAGAN took no part in the case.]

NOTES

1. *Why Double-Clutch?* To reach its result, the Court framed the issues as two-fold: whether Thompson's firing constituted retaliation against Regalado in violation of Title VII and whether the statute granted Thompson a cause of action.

Dividing the inquiry into two separate questions was scarcely inevitable, but it may have been necessary in order to avoid frustrating the purpose of the antiretaliation provision. If the court found that the firing violated Title VII but Thompson did *not* have a claim, it is not clear whether Regalado would have an adequate remedy. The core backpay remedy would be inapplicable. She might be able to get an injunction requiring the employer to rehire Thompson, but that under the circumstances, would that be a logical remedy? She might also be able to recover for her emotional distress in causing her fiancé to be fired, but that is not the most likely of remedies. In the meantime, under this view, Thompson would suffer loss of backpay and possible other damages but recover nothing. Do you think this was a potential driving force behind the Court's decision?

2. *Restricting Standing to Those Within the "Zone of Interests."* The Court's somewhat labored analysis regarding standing in *North American Stainless* suggests that the Court was concerned with a potentially overly broad application of "dicta" in earlier Fair Housing Act cases that suggested that Title VII "person aggrieved" standing reached as far as Article III would permit. Like Goldilocks, Scalia found Article III standing too broad but limiting standing to the employee who engaged in the protected conduct too narrow. Instead, the "just right" standard was drawn from the Administrative Procedure Act, permitting suit by those within the "zone of interests" the statute was designed to protect.

The "zone of interests" test is malleable, allowing the courts leeway to deny a right of review to any plaintiff with interests that are "so marginally related to or inconsistent with the purposes implicit in the statute that it cannot reasonably be assumed that Congress intended to permit the suit." Under this standard, in *North American Stainless* itself, the Court stated that a corporate shareholder whose stock has decreased in value after the company fired a valuable employee for racially discriminatory reasons is outside Title VII's zone of interests. On the other hand, Thompson did fall within the zone of interests because he was not "collateral damage" of the employer's discriminatory act.

3. *Applications of the "Zone of Interests" Test.* In *North American Stainless*, the Court did not expressly overturn the cases that accorded standing for those denied the benefits of interracial association. The interest of groups protected by Title VII associating with other groups may continue to be within Title VII's zone of interests. *See generally* Camille Gear Rich, *Marginal Whiteness*, 98 CALIF. L. REV. 1497, 1499 (2010) (under Title VII"s "interracial solidarity doctrine" plaintiff may claim frustration of his associational interests on the basis that whites are entitled to the economic, cultural, and educational relationships they can form by associating with minorities or they can claim violation of his right to a "colorblind" or nondiscriminatory workplace).

4. *How Close Is Close Enough?* The zone of interests test might suggest that whenever X is fired to punish Y for protected conduct, Title VII is violated and the discharged person has standing to bring suit. But not so fast. The *North American Stainless* Court avoided decision on which third parties are protected by its rule—probably "firing a close family member" and probably not "milder reprisal against a mere acquaintance," but "beyond that we are reluctant to generalize." Context is apparently all. Presumably, then, some retaliatory action is not a violation — even

if the employer's purpose is to retaliate. For an excellent pre-*North American Stainless* discussion of the entire question of third-party retaliation, *see* Alex. B. Long, *The Troublemaker's Friend: Retaliation Against Third Parties and the Right of Association in the Workplace*, 59 FLA. L. REV. 931 (2007).

5. *A Pro-Plaintiff Pattern?* Plaintiffs have recently done very well before the Supreme Court in retaliation cases. Obvious examples besides *Crawford* and *North American Stainless* are *Burlington Northern,* reproduced at p. 473, and *CBOCS West, Inc. v. Humphries*, 553 U.S. 442 (2008). In addition, *Gomez-Perez v. Potter*, 553 U.S. 474 (2008), decided the same day as *CBOCS*, was also a win for the plaintiff; it held that the section of the ADEA barring discrimination by federal employers also bars retaliation for opposing age discrimination. And in *Kasten v. Saint-Gobain Performance Plastics Corp.*, 131 S. Ct. 1325 (2011), the Court held that oral, not just written, complaints are protected by the FLSA's anti-retaliation provision. *See Generally* Michael J. Zimmer, *A Pro-Employee Supreme Court?: The Retaliation Decisions*, 60 S.C. L. REV. 917 (2009). (arguing the recent pro-employee decisions are a result of a "pragmatic approach to judicial decision making.").

2.   Adverse Action

Page 480.   Add at end of first paragraph of Note 1, *Section 703 vs. Section 704*:

See Lisa Durham Taylor, *Parsing Supreme Court Dicta and the Example of Non-Work-place Harms*, 57 DRAKE L. REV. 75 (2008) (since *Burlington Northern*'s discussion of non-workplace harms was dictum, blind adherence by the lower courts is inadvisable).

Page 480.   Add at end of Note 4, *Employer Liability*:

See generally B. Glenn George, *Revenge*, 83 TUL. L. REV. 439, 493 (2008) (arguing that "[s]ystematic 'shunning' or 'snubbing' orchestrated by management" should be treated as an adverse employment action, while unfriendliness as a result of dislike or resentment of the complaining employee should not be); Sandra Sperino, *The "Disappearing" Dilemma: Why Agency Principles Should Now Take Center Stage in Retaliation Cases*, 57 U. Kan. L. REV. 157 (2008) (arguing that in order for retaliation law to be consistent with discrimination principles, courts must employ the concept of a tangible employment action in deciding whether an employer is vicariously liable for actions committed by supervisors).

Page 480.   Delete Note 5; replace with the following:

5. *What Counts as Materially Adverse?* Would denying an employee the opportunity to have her work reviewed by a different supervisor with more authority be viewed by a reasonable employee as materially adverse? In a decision preceding *White*, the D.C. Circuit said no. *Broderick v. Donaldson*, 437 F.3d 1226 (D.C. Cir.

2006). Could ignoring the complaint completely suffice to meet the materially adverse standard? *Fincher v. Depository Trust and Clearing Corp.*, 604 F.3d 712, 721 (2d Cir. 2010), found that an employer's failure to investigate a complaint of discrimination is not an adverse employment action taken in retaliation for the filing of the same discrimination complaint. *Id.* It reasoned that affirmative efforts to punish a complaining employee are at the heart of any retaliation claim and an employee whose complaint is not investigated cannot be said to have thereby suffered a punishment. *Id.* Do you agree?

More generally, what would deter a reasonable employee from opposing discrimination or participating in proceedings? Some post-*Burlington* cases have viewed employees as being made of pretty stern stuff. *See E.g., Dehart v. Baker Hughes Oilfield Operations, Inc.*, 214 F. App'x 437 (5th Cir. 2007) (written disciplinary warning not an adverse action); *Carpenter v. Con-Way Cent. Express, Inc.*, 481 F.3d 611 (8th Cir. 2007) (failure to stop co-worker's slurs and placement of garbage in plaintiff's truck not materially adverse). *But see Young-Losee v. Graphic Packaging Int'l, Inc.*, 631 F.3d 909 (8th Cir. 2011) (plaintiff suffered "materially adverse" employment action when, at a meeting with her supervisor to discuss her formal complaint of harassment, he wadded up her complaint, called it "total bullshit," threw it in the garbage can, told her to leave, and said he never wanted to see her again); *Donaldson v. CDB, Inc.*, 335 F. App'x 494 (5th Cir. 2009) (fact question existed whether a meeting among female employees held in response to plaintiff's complain of sexual harassment was retaliatory when plaintiff felt "attacked and humiliated" and meeting could be interpreted as an attempt to intimidate potential witnesses); *Ridley v. Costco Wholesale Corp.*, 217 F .App'x 130 (3d Cir. 2007) (transfer that required several hours of commuting each day could have been found likely to deter*); Kessler v. Westchester County Dep't of Soc. Servs.*, 461 F.3d 199 (2d Cir. 2006) (transfer to an outlying office, resulting in plaintiff's going from supervising 100 employees to none with other reductions in responsibilities created an issue of fact whether an adverse action had occurred). *Cf. Vance v. Ball State Univ.*, 2011 U.S. LEXIS 11195 (7th Cir. June 3, 2011) (a promotion with a modest pay raise could not be materially adverse despite plaintiff being assigned to more menial tasks when plaintiff sought out the promotion.) *See generally* Ernest F. Lidge III, *What Types of Employer Actions Are Cognizable Under Title VII?: The Ramifications of* Burlington Northern & Santa Fe Railroad Co. v. White, 59 RUTGERS L. REV. 497, 531 (2007) (*White*'s contextual approach will require courts to consider a number of indeterminate factors); Lisa Durham Taylor, *Adding Subjective Fuel to the Vague-Standard Fire: A Proposal for Congressional Intervention after* Burlington Northern & Santa Fe Railway Co. v. White, 9 U. PA. J. LAB. & EMP. L. 533 (2007) (critiquing *Burlington Northern's* "vague and subjective standard").

Page 481. Delete Note 6; replace with the following:

6. *Threats Just Fine?* One consequence of the Court's definition of actionable retaliation in *White* is that threats to retaliate are not necessarily actionable. Suppose White's boss threatened to fire her, but didn't; or suppose he just threatened to "get even," without being more specific? In two recent cases the Seventh Circuit

seems to hold that an unfulfilled threat cannot violate the antiretaliation provisions of the federal statutes. *Chapin v. Fort-Rohr Motors, Inc.*, 621 F.3d 673 (7th Cir. 2010) (no adverse action where employer threatened to discharge plaintiff if he did not withdraw his EEOC charges when there was no other basis to indicate imminent firing and employer asked him to return to work); *Goodman v. NSA, Inc.*, 621 F.3d 651, 656 (7th Cir. 2010) (unfulfilled threats that result in no material harm cannot be considered an adverse employment action under Title VII). *See also Ahern v. Shinseki*, 629 F.3d 49, 56 (1st Cir. 2010) ("Merely proposing a change in an employee's schedule does not, in and of itself, constitute a materially adverse action. To qualify, the proposal must be brought to fruition."). Similarly, in *EEOC v. Sundance Rehab. Corp.*, 466 F.3d 490 (6th Cir. 2006), the court found no facial violation of anti-retaliation provisions in severance pay agreement conditioned on not filing charges with the EEOC. Although the threat was implicit that suit might be brought to recover the payments, that wasn't enough for the court. The agreement might have been unenforceable, which would have made the threat not meaningful. But is that true? Might a reasonable employee, who didn't want to risk her severance or retain an attorney to defend a suit, forbear from filing a charge?

6A. *Persistence in Protected Conduct.* Some courts seem to believe that the employee's persistence in opposition conduct is at least a factor, and perhaps a weighty one, in determining that the claimed action was not likely to deter a reasonable employee from engaging in protected conduct. *Somoza v. Univ. of Denver*, 513 F.3d 1206, 1214 (10th Cir. 2008) ("[T]he fact that an employee continues to be undeterred in his or her pursuit of a remedy, as here was the case, may shed light as to whether the actions are sufficiently material and adverse to be actionable."). Does this impermissibly shift the focus from the reasonable employee to the actual employee?

H. Age Discrimination

Page 481. In sixth line of first paragraph in section H, delete rest of sentence from "but the courts . . . "; replace with:

but in *Gross v. FBL Financial Services*, 129 S. Ct. 2343 (2009), the Supreme Court not only rejected the application of Title VII's motivating factor analysis under §703(m) to cases under the ADEA, but also refused to apply *Price Waterhouse* analysis to ADEA cases, reaffirming that a plaintiff claiming age discrimination must prove that discrimination was a determinative factor in a challenged decision. See p. 26 of this Supplement.

Page 482.   Insert at end of carryover paragraph:

See also Meacham v. Knolls Atomic Power Laboratory, 554 U.S. 84 (2008), reproduced at p. 53 of this Supplement, which held the business necessity/job relation defense inapplicable to the ADEA in light of the ADEA's reasonable factor other than age affirmative defense.

A final difference between the ADEA and Title VII is with respect to facial discrimination. Although we saw in both *Los Angeles Department of Water & Power v. Manhart*, reproduced at p. 116, and *International Union, UAW v. Johnson Controls*, reproduced at p. 173, that facial discrimination is always illegal under Title VII, except when within a statutory exception, the Court refused to so hold with respect to the ADEA. Over a strong dissent, a five-Justice majority in *Kentucky Retirement Systems v. EEOC*, 554 U.S. 135 (2008), upheld the use of age as a criterion for pension eligibility even when it resulted in some older workers losing pension benefits.

At issue in *Kentucky Retirement Systems* was a provision of a state retirement plan for police and firefighters that allowed an employee who became disabled after five years of service to obtain "normal retirement benefits"; otherwise, such benefits were earned only after 20 years of service. While this did not per se raise any discrimination questions, the mechanism by which the benefits were calculated did: the plan provided "imputed years of service" to bring the disabled employee up to the required 20 years' service, but differentiated on the basis of age in determining how many years were imputed. If a worker was already eligible for retirement at age 55, no imputed years were imputed.

The majority's reason for finding this scheme not discriminatory seems to be that it did not reflect age-based animus, and much of the opinion is devoted to establishing that it is not "actually motivated by bias," 554 U.S. at 135, that it could work to the advantage as well as the disadvantage of older workers, *id.* at 146 , and that it "does not rely on any of the sorts of stereotypical assumptions that the ADEA sought to eradicate." *Id.* But the Court was firm that "our opinion in no way unsettles the rule that a statute or policy that facially discriminates on the basis of age suffices to show disparate treatment under the ADEA." *Id.* For the majority, this case was different because it dealt with "the quite special case of different treatment based on *pension status*, where pension status — with the explicit blessing of the ADEA itself turns, in part, on age." *Id.* at 148 (emphasis in original). The Court wrote:

> The ADEA permits an employer to condition pension eligibility upon age. Thus, we must decide whether a plan that (1) lawfully makes age in part a condition of pension eligibility, and (2) treats workers differently in light of their pension status, (3) *automatically* discriminates *because of* age.

Id. at 143 (emphasis in original). As explored later in this section, age qualifications under the ADEA are permissible in pension plans.

In short, *Kentucky Retirement Systems*, while in tension with the rule that a facial differentiation on prohibited grounds is discrimination, is limited to the ADEA and, even within the ADEA, to differentiations that flow from pension plans. Even in this context, the Court devoted some effort to ascertaining that the facial discrimination was not the result of the kinds of biases against which the statute was directed.

Page 482.   Add at end of page:

Kannady v. City of Kiowa, 590 F.3d 1161, 1173 (10th Cir. 2010) (merely showing that the legislature took financial considerations into account when adopting the pension system's hiring-age ceiling did not demonstrate that the system was a subterfuge to frustrate another, "a non-hiring substantive provision of the ADEA").

4.   Early Retirement Incentive Plans

Page 485.   Add at end of carryover sentence:

E.g., Adams v. Lucent Techs., Inc., 284 F. App'x 296, 301-02 (6th Cir. 2008) (plaintiffs, who accepted an early retirement offer in the light of a pending merger, could not show an adverse employment action through constructive discharge when the employer did not inform them that the merger talks had collapsed; plaintiffs were not certain to lose their jobs in any event).

6 | *Disability Discrimination*

Page 487. Replace pages 487 to 532 with the following:

A. Introduction

The Americans with Disabilities Act of 1990 (ADA) prohibits employment discrimination against persons with disabilities. Title I, 42 U.S.C. §§12111-12117 (2009), covers most employment agencies, labor organizations, and employers, including state and local governments. Title II, 42 U.S.C. §§12131-12134, which generally prohibits disability discrimination by state and local governments, may also prohibit such entities from discriminating in employment. Thus, private employers are subject only to Title I, but state and local public employers *may* be subject to both Title I and Title II. The circuits are split, however, on whether Title II encompasses employment discrimination claims by government employees. *See generally* Jamie L. Ireland & Richard Bales, *Employment Discrimination Under Title II of the Americans with Disabilities Act*, 28 N. ILL. U. L. REV. 183 (2008). Before Congress enacted the ADA, the most comprehensive federal legislation prohibiting disability discrimination was the Rehabilitation Act of 1973, 29 U.S.C. §§701-795(I) (2009), which barred disability discrimination in most federal employment and by those doing business with the federal government or receiving federal financial assistance from it.

The ADA was amended in 2008 by the ADA Amendments Act of 2008 (ADAAA), Pub. L. No. 110-325, 122 Stat. 3553. Those amendments make significant changes to the ADA, particularly in defining who is an individual with a disability. The ADAAA was enacted primarily in response to decisions of the Supreme Court that had narrowly defined those who could claim the protections of the Act. *See generally* Jeannette Cox, *Crossroads and Signposts: The ADA Amendments Act of 2008*, 85 IND. L. J. 187 (2010); Jeff Jones, *Enfeebling the ADA: The ADA Amendment Act of 2008*, 62 OKLA. L. REV. 667 (2010). This chapter will discuss the ADA as originally enacted by Congress, along with the changes to the Act brought about by the ADAAA.

The ADAAA has been held not to apply retroactively. Accordingly, claims that accrued prior to January 1, 2009 are governed by the ADA as originally enacted, while claims that accrue on or after that date will be governed by the amended statute. *Lytes v. DC Water & Sewer Auth.,* 572 F.3d 936, 940 (D.C. Cir. 2009) However, a request for reasonable accommodation that is renewed after the effective date of the amended statute will be resolved under the amended statute, according to the EEOC. http://www.eeoc.gov/laws/regulations/ada_qa_final_rule.cfm.

The statutory scheme for protecting individuals with disabilities from discrimination in employment is somewhat more complicated than the other antidiscrimination statutes. Prohibiting discrimination because of disability poses difficult practical and legal problems. The legal problems associated with ending disability discrimination result primarily from the fact that disabilities are sometimes relevant to an individual's ability to work. Some disabilities deprive people of the physical and/or mental prerequisites to perform essential job functions. Prohibiting disability-based "discrimination" against such individuals would unduly interfere with employers' ability to select a qualified workforce. Other disabled individuals may be qualified to work but only if employers accommodate their disability in some way. These individuals, unlike most other statutorily protected groups, require some form of accommodation or different treatment in order to enjoy equal access to employment opportunities and benefits. Guaranteeing equal treatment for similarly situated individuals is an inadequate legal response to the problem of promoting employment for individuals who may require different treatment or accommodation.

The ADA, as amended, seeks to deal with these problems in two separate ways. First, the statute protects only an individual with a disability who is qualified, which means that employers are permitted to engage in disparate treatment when the disabled employee is unable to perform the essential functions of the job with or without reasonable accommodation. In addition, employers are free to use qualification standards that screen out disabled individuals if those qualifications are job related and consistent with business necessity.

Counterbalancing this, disabled individuals have rights beyond those guaranteed to most other groups protected by antidiscrimination legislation. The centerpiece of disability discrimination law is the employer's affirmative duty to provide reasonable accommodation to ensure that individuals with disabilities secure equal employment opportunities and benefits. The focus of the duty to accommodate is on equal employment opportunity, rather than on equal treatment.

As a result, employers are legally obligated to treat covered employees equally or differently depending on the circumstances — employers *must treat individuals with disabilities equally* if they are qualified and their disabilities do not require accommodation; employers are *permitted to treat such individuals differently* if their disabilities cannot be accommodated; and employers *are required to treat such individuals differently* if reasonable accommodations are necessary to ensure equal employment opportunity and benefits.

Further, accommodation providing equal opportunity for individuals with disabilities can sometimes be costly for employers. The ADA, therefore, includes an "undue hardship" defense, which makes cost, usually irrelevant under other anti-discrimination statutes, an expressly enumerated statutory defense to discrimination based on the duty to accommodate.

Restrictive interpretations of the ADA by the Supreme Court, particularly decisions interpreting who is an "individual with a disability" within the meaning of the statute, led Congress to amend the ADA. Under the original statute as interpreted by the Court, conditions such as epilepsy, breast cancer, diabetes, and intellectual disabilities, just to name a few, were often found by lower courts not to constitute disabilities. Moreover, the Court's interpretation of the ADA had too frequently led to a Catch-22 — individuals disabled enough to meet the Court's narrow interpretation of an "individual with a disability" were often too disabled to be deemed qualified individuals with a disability. As Congress noted in its findings under the ADAAA, "as a result of these Supreme Court cases, lower courts have incorrectly found in individual cases that people with a range of substantially limiting impairments are not people with disabilities." §2(a)(6). Accordingly, it amended the statute.

A general overview of those amendments is provided by the EEOC in its Notice Concerning the ADAAA:

> On September 25, 2008, the President signed the Americans with Disabilities Act Amendments Act of 2008 ("ADA Amendments Act" or "Act"). The Act emphasizes that the definition of disability should be construed in favor of broad coverage of individuals to the maximum extent permitted by the terms of the ADA and generally shall not require extensive analysis.
>
> The Act makes important changes to the definition of the term "disability" by rejecting the holdings in several Supreme Court decisions and portions of EEOC's ADA regulations. The effect of these changes is to make it easier for an individual seeking protection under the ADA to establish that he or she has a disability within the meaning of the ADA.
>
> The Act retains the ADA's basic definition of "disability" as an impairment that substantially limits one or more major life activities, a record of such an impairment, or being regarded as having such an impairment. However, it changes the way that these statutory terms should be interpreted in several ways. Most significantly, the Act:
>
> - directs EEOC to revise that portion of its regulations defining the term "substantially limits";
> - expands the definition of "major life activities" by including two non-exhaustive lists:
>   - the first list includes many activities that the EEOC has recognized (e.g., walking) as well as activities that EEOC has not specifically recognized (e.g., reading, bending, and communicating);
>   - the second list includes major bodily functions (e.g., "functions of the immune system, normal cell growth, digestive, bowel, bladder, neurological, brain, respiratory, circulatory, endocrine, and reproductive functions");
> - states that mitigating measures other than "ordinary eyeglasses or contact lenses" shall not be considered in assessing whether an individual has a disability;
> - clarifies that an impairment that is episodic or in remission is a disability if it would substantially limit a major life activity when active;

Definition

- changes the definition of "regarded as" so that it no longer requires a showing that the employer perceived the individual to be substantially limited in a major life activity; instead, an applicant or employee is "regarded as" disabled if he or she is subject to an action prohibited by the ADA (e.g., failure to hire or termination) based on an impairment that is not transitory and minor;
- provides that individuals covered only under the "regarded as" prong are not entitled to reasonable accommodation.

The EEOC's regulations interpreting the amended act became effective May 24, 2011. In construing the amendments, the regulations emphasize that the primary purpose of the ADAAA is to make it easier for people with disabilities to obtain ADA protection, and the regulations interpret the statute accordingly.

The focus of this chapter will be Title I of the ADA, originally and as amended. This chapter will proceed as follows: Section B focuses on what constitutes a "disability" under the ADA, a threshold question that has generated considerable litigation; Section C then turns to what makes a disabled individual "qualified," in the process exploring the concepts of "essential function," "reasonable accommodation," and "undue hardship"; Section D examines discriminatory qualification standards, including the provision that employers may discriminate against employees who pose a "direct threat" to health or safety; and Section E addresses special problems under the ADA, including coverage for individuals addicted to drugs or alcohol, medical examinations and inquiries, retaliation, harassment, relationships with covered individuals, health and disability insurance plans, and rights under the Family and Medical Leave Act. Changes to the statute as a result of the ADAAA will be noted where applicable.

B. The Meaning of "Disability"

In contrast to other statutes prohibiting discrimination in employment, establishing membership in the ADA's protected classification was often not intuitive under the original ADA and still requires attention under the ADAAA. Generally speaking, to claim protection under the ADA, a plaintiff must be "a qualified individual" — that is, the plaintiff must be able to perform essential job functions with or without reasonable accommodation — who has been discriminated against on the basis of the disability.

Section 3(2), as originally promulgated, defined "disability" as

(A) a physical or mental impairment that substantially limits one or more of the major life activities of . . . [an] individual;

(B) a record of such an impairment; or

(C) being regarded as having such an impairment.

However, §§508 and 511 expressly exclude certain practices or conditions from this definition. Many of these are sex-related, such as homosexuality, bisexuality, transvestism, pedophilia, transexualism, and exhibitionism. Also excluded are compulsive gambling, kleptomania, pyromania, and disorders resulting from the current illegal use of psychoactive drugs.

As the above definition makes clear, ADA coverage did (and does) not depend on establishing an actual, present disability. An individual who has a "record" of a physical or mental impairment that substantially limits a major life activity is within the definition of disability. Even if a person does not currently have such an impairment or was previously misclassified as having such an impairment, he is within the definition if he has a record of such an impairment.

A final method of establishing a "disability" is to show that an employer regarded the individual as having a disability. The ADA regulations, promulgated pre-ADAAA, defined "regarded as having such an impairment" to mean:

(1) Has a physical or mental impairment that does not substantially limit major life activities but is treated by a covered entity as constituting such limitation;

(2) Has a physical or mental impairment that substantially limits major life activities only as a result of the attitudes of others toward such impairment; or

(3) Has none of the impairments [discussed above] but is treated by a covered entity as having a substantially limiting impairment.

29 C.F.R. §1630.2(*l*).

The ADAAA, however, amended the "regarded as" prong. Under the amended statute, an "individual meets the requirement of 'being regarded as having such an impairment' if the individual establishes that he or she has been subjected to an action prohibited under this Act because of an actual or perceived physical or mental impairment whether or not the impairment limits or is perceived to limit a major life activity." This change is significant: if an employee was discriminated against because of an impairment, real or perceived, the protections of the Act are triggered so long as the impairment is not transitory and minor. She need not show the impairment substantially limited a major life activity. All she need show is that her employer took a prohibited action because of the impairment, actual or perceived. However, the ADAAA also provides that "regarded as" plaintiffs are not entitled to reasonable accommodations. The amendments, therefore, create for the first time a two-tier structure under which rights vary depending on whether a person is actually disabled or has a record of disability, on the one hand, or is merely regarded as disabled, on the other. Both kinds of individuals are protected from discrimination, but only the former group must be accommodated. *See generally* Kemi Lynn Stone, *Substantial Limitation: Reflections on the ADAAA,* 14 N.Y.U. J. Leg. & Pub. ____ (2011).

In its regulations implementing the ADAAA, the EEOC makes clear that it expects all claims where reasonable accommodation is not at issue to proceed under the "regarded as" prong. Doing so eliminates the need for analyzing whether the impairment substantially limits one or more major life activities. Rather, all plaintiff must show is that an employer took a prohibited action because of the real or perceived impairment. The regulations also make clear the agency's position that proving the impairment was transitory and minor is the defendant's burden, once the plaintiff has established an action was based on the impairment.

However, if reasonable accommodation is sought, then disability must be established using the actual disability or record of disability routes. Reasonable accommodation is available for either actual disability or record of disability claimants but not for "regarded as" claimants.

In sum, a person can be disabled within the meaning of the statute not only if he has an "actual disability" but also if he is "regarded as" disabled or has a "record" of a disability. Employers are among the ADA's "covered entities" and the focus of Title I.

1. Actual Disability

The Supreme Court considered the meaning of the three-pronged definition of disability for the first time in *School Board of Nassau County v. Arline*, 480 U.S. 273 (1987). Although *Arline* was a Rehabilitation Act case, the definition of "handicapped" individual (the term used at the time in the Rehabilitation Act) was identical to the definition of individual with a disability under the original ADA. In *Arline,* the school board had fired plaintiff, an elementary school teacher, because it believed her active tuberculosis posed a threat to the health of others. Essentially, the school board contended that a person with a contagious disease was not within the protections of the Rehabilitation Act if the adverse employment action was based on the employee's contagiousness and not on the condition itself. In finding Arline to be a handicapped individual, the Supreme Court refused to allow the school board to disassociate the contagious effects of the teacher's impairment from the impairment itself. As the Court stated, "Arline's contagiousness and her physical impairment each resulted from the same underlying condition, tuberculosis. It would be unfair to allow an employer to seize upon the distinction between the effects of a disease on others and the effects of a disease on a patient and use that distinction to justify discriminatory intent." *Id.* at 282.

In light of *Arline*'s holding that a contagious disease can be a "disability," a person who has developed acquired immune deficiency syndrome (AIDS) is undoubtedly an "individual with a disability" under both the Rehabilitation Act and the ADA. Active AIDS clearly qualifies as a physical impairment and also substantially limits major life activities. But *Arline* left open the question of whether a person can be considered "handicapped" purely on the basis of contagiousness alone. Is a person who tests positively for the antibodies produced in reaction to HIV, the virus that causes AIDS, an "individual with a disability"? The Supreme Court addressed this issue in its first ADA case confronting the definition of disability. Although *Bragdon v. Abbott* was a Title III case involving public accommodation discrimination, the at-issue definition of disability applies to Titles I and II as well.

Bragdon v. Abbott
524 U.S. 624 (1998)

Justice KENNEDY delivered the opinion of the Court, in which Justices STEVENS, SOUTER, GINSBURG, and BREYER, joined.

6. Disability Discrimination

We address in this case the application of the Americans with Disabilities Act of 1990 (ADA) to persons infected with the human immunodeficiency virus (HIV). We granted certiorari to review, first, whether HIV infection is a disability under the ADA when the infection has not yet progressed to the so-called symptomatic phase. . . .

I

Respondent Sidney Abbott has been infected with HIV since 1986. When the incidents we recite occurred, her infection had not manifested its most serious symptoms. On September 16, 1994, she went to the office of petitioner Randon Bragdon in Bangor, Maine, for a dental appointment. She disclosed her HIV infection on the patient registration form. Petitioner completed a dental examination, discovered a cavity, and informed respondent of his policy against filling cavities of HIV-infected patients. He offered to perform the work at a hospital with no added fee for his services, though respondent would be responsible for the cost of using the hospital's facilities. Respondent declined.

Respondent sued petitioner under . . . §302 of the ADA, alleging discrimination on the basis of her disability. . . . [Section 302 of Title III of the ADA prohibits discrimination on the basis of disability "by any person who . . . operates a place of public accommodation." The term "public accommodation" is defined to include the "professional office of a health care provider." §12181(7)(F).]

II

We first review the ruling that respondent's HIV infection constituted a disability under the ADA. The statute defines disability as:

(A) a physical or mental impairment that substantially limits one or more of the major life activities of such individual;
(B) a record of such an impairment; or
(C) being regarded as having such impairment.

§12102(2). We hold respondent's HIV infection was a disability under subsection (A) of the definitional section of the statute. In light of this conclusion, we need not consider the applicability of subsections (B) or (C).

Our consideration of subsection (A) of the definition proceeds in three steps. First, we consider whether respondent's HIV infection was a physical impairment. Second, we identify the life activity upon which respondent relies (reproduction and child bearing) and determine whether it constitutes a major life activity under the ADA. Third, tying the two statutory phrases together, we ask whether the impairment substantially limited the major life activity. In construing the statute, we are informed by interpretations of parallel definitions in previous statutes and the views of various administrative agencies which have faced this interpretive question.

165

A

The ADA's definition of disability is drawn almost verbatim from the definition of "handicapped individual" included in the Rehabilitation Act of 1973. . . . Congress' repetition of a well-established term carries the implication that Congress intended the term to be construed in accordance with pre-existing regulatory interpretations. In this case, Congress did more than suggest this construction; it adopted a specific statutory provision in the ADA directing as follows:

> Except as otherwise provided in this chapter, nothing in this chapter shall be construed to apply a lesser standard than the standards applied under title V of the Rehabilitation Act of 1973 or the regulations issued by Federal agencies pursuant to such title.

42 U.S.C. §12201(a). The directive requires us to construe the ADA to grant at least as much protection as provided by the regulations implementing the Rehabilitation Act.

1

The first step in the inquiry under subsection (A) requires us to determine whether respondent's condition constituted a physical impairment. [The governing regulations were first issued by the Department of Health, Education and Welfare (HEW) under the Rehabilitation Act in 1977. They continue to govern without change although enforcement responsibility for §504 has been transferred to the Department of Justice. They define] "physical or mental impairment" to mean:

(A) any physiological disorder or condition, cosmetic disfigurement, or anatomical loss affecting one or more of the following body systems: neurological; musculoskeletal; special sense organs; respiratory, including speech organs; cardiovascular; reproductive, digestive, genito-urinary; hemic and lymphatic; skin; and endocrine; or

(B) any mental or psychological disorder, such as mental retardation, organic brain syndrome, emotional or mental illness, and specific learning disabilities.

45 CFR §84.3(j)(2)(i) (1997). In issuing these regulations, HEW decided against including a list of disorders constituting physical or mental impairments, out of concern that any specific enumeration might not be comprehensive. 42 Fed. Reg. 22685 (1977), reprinted in 45 CFR pt. 84, App. A, p. 334 (1997). The commentary accompanying the regulations, however, contains a representative list of disorders and conditions constituting physical impairments, including "such diseases and conditions as orthopedic, visual, speech, and hearing impairments, cerebral palsy, epilepsy, muscular dystrophy, multiple sclerosis, cancer, heart disease, diabetes,

mental retardation, emotional illness, and . . . drug addiction and alcoholism." Id. . . .

HIV infection is not included in the list of specific disorders constituting physical impairments, in part because HIV was not identified as the cause of AIDS until 1983. HIV infection does fall well within the general definition set forth by the regulations, however.

The disease follows a predictable and, as of today, an unalterable course. Once a person is infected with HIV, the virus invades different cells in the blood and in body tissues. Certain white blood cells, known as helper T-lymphocytes or CD4+ cells, are particularly vulnerable to HIV. The virus attaches to the CD4 receptor site of the target cell and fuses its membrane to the cell's membrane. HIV is a retrovirus, which means it uses an enzyme to convert its own genetic material into a form indistinguishable from the genetic material of the target cell. The virus' genetic material migrates to the cell's nucleus and becomes integrated with the cell's chromosomes. Once integrated, the virus can use the cell's own genetic machinery to replicate itself. Additional copies of the virus are released into the body and infect other cells in turn.

The virus eventually kills the infected host cell. CD4+ cells play a critical role in coordinating the body's immune response system, and the decline in their number causes corresponding deterioration of the body's ability to fight infections from many sources. Tracking the infected individual's CD4+ cell count is one of the most accurate measures of the course of the disease.

The initial stage of HIV infection is known as acute or primary HIV infection. In a typical case, this stage lasts three months. The virus concentrates in the blood. The assault on the immune system is immediate. The victim suffers from a sudden and serious decline in the number of white blood cells. There is no latency period. Mononucleosis-like symptoms often emerge between six days and six weeks after infection, at times accompanied by fever, headache, enlargement of the lymph nodes (lymphadenopathy), muscle pain (myalgia), rash, lethargy, gastrointestinal disorders, and neurological disorders. Usually these symptoms abate within 14 to 21 days. HIV antibodies appear in the bloodstream within 3 weeks; circulating HIV can be detected within 10 weeks.

After the symptoms associated with the initial stage subside, the disease enters what is referred to sometimes as its asymptomatic phase. The term is a misnomer, in some respects, for clinical features persist throughout, including lymphadeno-pathy, dermatological disorders, oral lesions, and bacterial infections. Although it varies with each individual, in most instances this stage lasts from 7 to 11 years. The virus now tends to concentrate in the lymph nodes, though low levels of the virus continue to appear in the blood. It was once thought the virus became inactive during this period, but it is now known that the relative lack of symptoms is attributable to the virus' migration from the circulatory system into the lymph nodes. The migration reduces the viral presence in other parts of the body, with a corresponding diminution in physical manifestations of the disease. The virus, however, thrives in the lymph nodes, which, as a vital point of the body's immune response system, represents an ideal environment for the infection of other CD4+ cells.

A person is regarded as having AIDS when his or her CD4+ count drops below 200 cells/mm3 of blood or when CD4+ cells comprise less than 14% of his or her total lymphocytes. During this stage, the clinical conditions most often associated with HIV, such as pneumocystis carninii pneumonia, Kaposi's sarcoma, and non-Hodgkin's lymphoma, tend to appear. In addition, the general systemic disorders present during all stages of the disease, such as fever, weight loss, fatigue, lesions, nausea, and diarrhea, tend to worsen. In most cases, once the patient's CD4+ count drops below 10 cells/mm3, death soon follows.

In light of the immediacy with which the virus begins to damage the infected person's white blood cells and the severity of the disease, we hold it is an impairment from the moment of infection. As noted earlier, infection with HIV causes immediate abnormalities in a person's blood, and the infected person's white cell count continues to drop throughout the course of the disease, even when the attack is concentrated in the lymph nodes. In light of these facts, HIV infection must be regarded as a physiological disorder with a constant and detrimental effect on the infected person's hemic and lymphatic systems from the moment of infection. HIV infection satisfies the statutory and regulatory definition of a physical impairment during every stage of the disease.

2

The statute is not operative, and the definition not satisfied, unless the impairment affects a major life activity. Respondent's claim throughout this case has been that the HIV infection placed a substantial limitation on her ability to reproduce and to bear children. Given the pervasive, and invariably fatal, course of the disease, its effect on major life activities of many sorts might have been relevant to our inquiry. Respondent and a number of amici make arguments about HIV's profound impact on almost every phase of the infected person's life. In light of these submissions, it may seem legalistic to circumscribe our discussion to the activity of reproduction. We have little doubt that had different parties brought the suit they would have maintained that an HIV infection imposes substantial limitations on other major life activities. . . .

We have little difficulty concluding that [reproduction is a major life activity]. As the Court of Appeals held, "the plain meaning of the word 'major' denotes comparative importance" and "suggests that the touchstone for determining an activity's inclusion under the statutory rubric is its significance." Reproduction falls well within the phrase "major life activity." Reproduction and the sexual dynamics surrounding it are central to the life process itself.

While petitioner concedes the importance of reproduction, he claims that Congress intended the ADA only to cover those aspects of a person's life which have a public, economic, or daily character. The argument flounders on the statutory language. Nothing in the definition suggests that activities without a public, economic, or daily dimension may somehow be regarded as so unimportant or insignificant as to fall outside the meaning of the word "major." The breadth of the term confounds the attempt to limit its construction in this manner.

6. Disability Discrimination

As we have noted, the ADA must be construed to be consistent with regulations issued to implement the Rehabilitation Act. Rather than enunciating a general principle for determining what is and is not a major life activity, the Rehabilitation Act regulations instead provide a representative list, defining the term to include "functions such as caring for one's self, performing manual tasks, walking, seeing, hearing, speaking, breathing, learning, and working." 45 CFR §84.3(j)(2)(ii) (1997); 28 CFR §41.31(b)(2) (1997). As the use of the term "such as" confirms, the list is illustrative, not exhaustive.

These regulations are contrary to petitioner's attempt to limit the meaning of the term "major" to public activities. The inclusion of activities such as caring for one's self and performing manual tasks belies the suggestion that a task must have a public or economic character in order to be a major life activity for purposes of the ADA. On the contrary, the Rehabilitation Act regulations support the inclusion of reproduction as a major life activity, since reproduction could not be regarded as any less important than working and learning. Petitioner advances no credible basis for confining major life activities to those with a public, economic, or daily aspect. . . . [R]eproduction is a major life activity for the purposes of the ADA.

3

The final element of the disability definition in subsection (A) is whether respondent's physical impairment was a substantial limit on the major life activity she asserts. The Rehabilitation Act regulations provide no additional guidance.

Our evaluation of the medical evidence leads us to conclude that respondent's infection substantially limited her ability to reproduce in two independent ways. First, a woman infected with HIV who tries to conceive a child imposes on the man a significant risk of becoming infected. The cumulative results of 13 studies collected in a 1994 textbook on AIDS indicates that 20% of male partners of women with HIV became HIV-positive themselves, with a majority of the studies finding a statistically significant risk of infection.

Second, an infected woman risks infecting her child during gestation and childbirth, i.e., perinatal transmission. Petitioner concedes that women infected with HIV face about a 25% risk of transmitting the virus to their children. Published reports available in 1994 confirm the accuracy of this statistic.

Petitioner points to evidence in the record suggesting that antiretroviral therapy can lower the risk of perinatal transmission to about 8%. . . . It cannot be said as a matter of law that an 8% risk of transmitting a dread and fatal disease to one's child does not represent a substantial limitation on reproduction.

The Act addresses substantial limitations on major life activities, not utter inabilities. Conception and childbirth are not impossible for an HIV victim but, without doubt, are dangerous to the public health. This meets the definition of a substantial limitation. The decision to reproduce carries economic and legal consequences as well. There are added costs for antiretroviral therapy, supplemental insurance, and long-term health care for the child who must be examined and, tragic to think, treated for the infection. The laws of some States, moreover, forbid persons infected with HIV from having sex with others, regardless of consent.

In the end, the disability definition does not turn on personal choice. When significant limitations result from the impairment, the definition is met even if the difficulties are not insurmountable. For the statistical and other reasons we have cited, of course, the limitations on reproduction may be insurmountable here. . . . Respondent's HIV infection is a physical impairment which substantially limits a major life activity, as the ADA defines it. In view of our holding, we need not address the second question presented, i.e., whether HIV infection is a per se disability under the ADA. . . .

NOTES

1. *A Three-Step Inquiry.* As *Bragdon* makes clear, determining whether an actual disability exists requires examination of three separate elements: whether there is a (1) physical or mental impairment that (2) substantially limits (3) one or more major life activities. Moreover, under the original ADA, analysis of each of these elements must occur regardless of which of the three routes to disability status is at issue — actual, "record of," or "regarded as." As noted previously, however, the ADAAA changes this for "regarded as" claims. There need be no finding that the impairment was regarded as substantially limiting a major life activity; all that need be shown for "regarded as" claims is that the employer took the prohibited act because of the impairment.

2. *Is There an Impairment?* As in *Bragdon,* whether an impairment exists is often not difficult to determine. But sometimes it is. The EEOC has stated that the term "physical or mental impairment" does not include physical characteristics, such as weight, height, and eye color that are in the "normal range" and are not the result of a physiological disorder. The Interpretive Guidance also excludes common personality traits, illiteracy, economic disadvantages, and temporary physical conditions. Advanced age also is excluded, although physical and mental impairments associated with aging are not. *See* 29 C.F.R. pt. 1630, app. §1630.2(h), (j). This approach continues under the newly issued regulations. *See* 76 F.R. 16978, 17007. Is any physical characteristic outside the normal range an "impairment"? Consider unusual strength or high intelligence. Are these impairments (because they are out of the normal range), but not disabilities (because they do not substantially impair life activities)? Or are they not impairments at all because they are out of the normal range on the "positive," rather than the "negative," side?

(a) *Pregnancy.* Pregnancy shares many of the characteristics of a disability as defined by the ADA. Nonetheless, the EEOC takes the position that pregnancy is not a disability covered by the statute because pregnancy is not an impairment. *See* 29 C.F.R pt. 1630, app. §1630.2(h). However, impairments resulting from pregnancy, such as gestational diabetes, can trigger the ADA's protections. *See* 29 C.F. R. pt. 1630, app. §1630.2(h). *But see* Melissa Cole, *Beyond Sex Discrimination: Why Employers Discriminate Against Women with Disabilities When Their Employee Health Plans Exclude Contraceptives from Prescription Coverage*, 42 ARIZ. L. REV. 501 (2001).

6. Disability Discrimination

(b) *Voluntary Conditions.* Can a physical condition that is caused at least in part by voluntary conduct constitute an impairment? In *Cook v. Rhode Island Dep't of Mental Health*, 10 F.3d 17 (1st Cir. 1993), the First Circuit held, in a claim under the Rehabilitation Act, that morbid obesity could be an impairment, rejecting the defendant's argument that "mutable" conditions or those "caused, or at least exacerbated, by voluntary conduct," were not impairments. As the court stated,

> [t]he Rehabilitation Act contains no language suggesting that its protection is linked to how an individual became impaired, or whether an individual contributed to his or her impairment. On the contrary, the Act indisputably applies to numerous conditions that may be caused or exacerbated by voluntary conduct, such as alcoholism, AIDS, diabetes, cancer resulting from cigarette smoking, heart disease resulting from excesses of various types, and the like. Consequently, voluntariness, like mutability, is relevant only in determining whether a condition has a substantially limiting effect.

Id. at 24. *Cf. EEOC v. Watkins Motor Lines, Inc.*, 463 F.3d 436 (6th Cir. 2006) (morbid obesity, not related to any physiological cause, was not an impairment). Under the original ADA, the EEOC took the position that "common obesity" was not an impairment. Would that still hold true under the ADA as amended? *See* Jane Byeff Korn, *Too Fat*, 17 VA. J. SOC. POL'Y & L. 209, 211-12 (2010) (the ADAAA will not extend statutory protection to the obese who are unable to show their condition is caused by a physiological disorder unless the courts either ignore the cause of a person's physical condition or start to view obesity as a cosmetic disfigurement, which the statute does reach).

(c) *Temporary Impairments.* Another question is whether temporary impairments are covered by the Rehabilitation Act or the ADA. In *Toyota Motor Mfg. Co. v. Williams*, reproduced at p. 174 of this Supplement, the Supreme Court stated that to substantially limit performance of manual tasks, "the impairment's impact must also be permanent or long-term." Subsequent to *Toyota,* the Fourth Circuit concluded that a medical condition necessitating surgery and a recovery period requiring a nine-month leave of absence was temporary and thus not substantially limiting. *See Pollard v. High's of Baltimore, Inc.*, 281 F.3d 462 (4th Cir. 2002).

The ADAAA addresses a piece of this question: it provides that the "regarded as" prong does not apply to transitory and minor impairments and defines "transitory" as an actual or expected duration of less than six months. But what about under the other two prongs? Is there a durational requirement there, too? Or is that problem to be resolved for "actual" disability and "record of" claims by determining whether the impairment is substantially limiting, an inquiry that is now not required under prong 3? The EEOC takes the position that the six month durational requirement does *not* apply under the "actual" or "regarded as" prongs, reasoning that if an impairment substantially limits a major life activity, the definition is met, even if the duration is less than six months. *See* 29 C.F.R. Part 1630, app. Section 1630.2(j)(1)(ix).

In *Vande Zande v. Wisconsin Dep't of Admin.*, 44 F.3d 538 (7th Cir. 1995), reproduced at p. 552, Vande Zande, who is paralyzed from the waist down, sought ADA accommodations relating to pressure ulcers caused by her paralysis. Her employer argued that, because her ulcers were intermittent and episodic impairments, they did not fit the definition of a disability. The Seventh Circuit disagreed:

> [A]n intermittent impairment that is a characteristic manifestation of an admitted disability is, we believe, a part of the underlying disability. . . . Often the disabling aspect of a disability is, precisely, an intermittent manifestation of the disability, rather than the underlying impairment. The AIDS virus progressively destroys the infected person's immune system. The consequence is a series of opportunistic diseases which . . . often prevent the individual from working. If they are not part of the disability, then people with AIDS do not have a disability which seems to us a very odd interpretation of the law, and one expressly rejected by the regulations. We hold that Vande Zande's pressure ulcers are a part of her disability.

Id. at 544. *Vande Zande*'s treatment of the symptom of a disability is consistent with the Supreme Court's treatment of contagiousness in *Arline*. Moreover, it has been endorsed by Congress in the ADAAA. The amendments provide that "an impairment that is episodic or in remission is a disability if it would substantially limit a major life activity when active." 42 U.S.C §12102(4)(D) (2009). *See also EEOC v. Chevron Phillips Chem. Co.,* 570 F.3d 606 (5th Cir. 2009) (district court erred in finding that discharged employee was not disabled under ADA; experiencing symptoms for over six months was not intermittent, and employee remained substantially limited in major life activities, such as caring for herself, sleeping, and thinking).

(d) *Genetic Conditions as Impairments.* Is an individual with a genetic propensity to disease impaired within the meaning of the ADA? If so, does this impairment substantially limit any major life activity? A few diseases, like Huntington's disease, are inevitable for those with the allele, although they may not manifest the symptoms until late in life. Most "genetic diseases," however, simply make individuals more susceptible to the condition (although sometimes increasing the risk factor enormously). Is someone with the Huntington's allele but no symptoms impaired? If so, does this impairment substantially limit any major life activity? Even if the answer is yes, what about those genetic diseases whose appearance is not inevitable? *See* John V. Jacobi, *Genetic Discrimination in a Time of False Hopes* 30 Fla. St. U. L. Rev. 363, 362 (2003).

3. *Meet GINA.* The Genetic Information Non-Discrimination Act (GINA), Pub. L. No. 110-233, 122 Stat. 881, codified at 42 U.S.C. §2000ff, was enacted in May 2008, and its employment provisions took effect on Nov. 21, 2009. GINA prohibits discrimination by employers and health insurers based on genetic information. The EEOC is charged with enforcing the Act's employment provisions and has promulgated regulations to carry out Title II (the employment chapter). 29 C.F.R. Part 1635 (2011). In a nutshell, Title II of GINA prohibits the use of genetic information in employment, generally prohibits the intentional acquisition of genetic information about applicants and employees, and imposes strict confidentiality requirements. It applies to employers, public and private, with 15 or more employees. The EEOC regards the protections of GINA as absolute when it comes to an employer's *use* of genetic information; any use is strictly prohibited.

Moreover, acquisition of genetic information by employers is restricted. The EEOC has stated that "although the ADA currently permits a covered entity to obtain family medical history or conduct genetic tests of job applicants once an offer of employment has been made, provided this is done for all entering employees in the same job category, such action will be prohibited upon the effective date of GINA." Background Information for EEOC Notice of Proposed Rulemaking On Title II of the Genetic Information Nondiscrimination Act of 2008 (May 12, 2009) http://www.eeoc.gov/policy/docs/qanda_geneticinfo.html. This is discussed further in the section on Medical Examinations and Inquiries.

4. *Major Life Activities.* The Court's holding in *Bragdon* that reproduction is a major life activity has significance beyond the question of whether HIV infection is a disability within the meaning of the ADA, given that *Bragdon* acknowledges that the §1630.2(i) list of major life activities is not exclusive. After *Bragdon,* what other activities are major life activities under the original ADA? In *Toyota Motor Mfg. Co. v. Williams*, reproduced at p. 174 of this Supplement, the Supreme Court held that performing manual tasks is a major life activity. What about the ability to eat, drink, sleep, drive a car, think, or get along with people? Are these major life activities under the original ADA? *See Adams v. Rice*, 531 F.3d 936 (D.C. Cir. 2008) (2-1) (engaging in sexual relations is a major life activity under both the Rehabilitation Act and the ADA, and plaintiff produced sufficient evidence that her cancer and treatment substantially limited her in that activity both because of her surgery and its psychological effects); *Desmond v. Mukasey*, 530 F.3d 944 (D.C. Cir. 2008) (sleeping is a major life activity under the Rehabilitation Act); *Kellogg v. Energy Safety Services, Inc.*, 544 F.3d 1121, 1126 (10th Cir. 2008) (driving is not a major life activity under the ADA); *Carlson v. Liberty Mut. Ins. Co.*, 237 F. App'x 446 (11th Cir. 2007) (same); *Winsley v. Cook County*, 563 F.3d 598, 610 (7th Cir. 2009) (holding that, while driving is in itself not a major life activity, the inability to drive could nevertheless create a disability if it impaired a separate major life activity, such as working); *Eshelman v. Agere Sys., Inc.*, 554 F.3d 426, 434 (3d Cir. 2009) ("thinking" is a major life activity under the ADA); *Littleton v. Wal-Mart*, 231 F. App'x 874 (11th Cir. 2007) (learning is a major life activity; unclear whether thinking, communicating, or social interaction are major life activities); *Head v. Glacier Nw., Inc.*, 413 F.3d 1053, 1058 (9th Cir. 2005) (thinking, reading, interacting with others, sleeping were all major life activities); *Rohan v. Networks Presentation LLC*, 375 F.3d 266 (4th Cir. 2004) (questioning whether interacting with others is a major life activity and collecting cases); *Fraser v. Goodale*, 342 F.3d 1032 (9th Cir. 2003) (eating is a major life activity); *Heiko v. Colombo Sav. Bank*, 434 F.3d 249, 255 (4th Cir. 2006) (waste elimination is a major life activity); *Fiscus v. Wal-Mart Stores, Inc.*, 385 F.3d 378 (3d Cir. 2004) (same); *Jacques v. DiMarzio, Inc.*, 386 F.3d 192, 203-04 (2d Cir. 2004) (interacting with others is a major life activity, but to be substantially limited in this respect, "the impairment [must] severely limit the plaintiff's ability to connect with others, i.e., to initiate contact with other people and respond to them, or to go among other people — at the most basic level of these activities"). For a discussion of cases before and after *Bragdon* confronting the question of what constitutes a major life activity, see Curtis D. Edmonds, S*nakes and Ladders: Expanding the Definition of "Major Life Activity" in*

the Americans with Disabilities Act, 33 TEX. TECH. L. REV. 321 (2002); Wendy F. Hensel, *Interacting with Others: A Major Life Activity Under the Americans with Disabilities Act?*, WIS. L. REV. 1139 (2002); Ann Hubbard, *Meaningful Lives and Major Life Activities*, 55 ALA. L. REV. 997 (2004); Ann Hubbard, *The Major Life Activity of Belonging*, 39 WAKE FOREST L. REV. 217 (2004); Ann Hubbard, *The Myth of Independence and the Major Life Activity of Caring*, 8 J. GENDER, RACE & JUST. 327 (2004).

Whereas the ADA, as originally enacted, did not define "major life activities," the amended ADAAA does. And that definition is sweeping. Major life activities "include but are not limited to, caring for oneself, performing manual tasks, seeing, hearing, eating, sleeping, walking, lifting, bending, speaking, breathing, reading, concentrating, thinking, communicating and working." 42 U.S.C.S. §12102(2)(A). Also, the term includes "the operation of a major bodily function, including, but not limited to, functions of the immune system, normal cell growth, digestive, bowel, bladder, neurological, brain, respiratory, circulatory, endocrine, and reproductive functions." *Id.* at §12102(2)(B). Accordingly, many of the interpretive questions the courts struggled with in the cases listed above have now been answered by the statutory amendments. For claims that accrued prior to the ADAAA's effective date, will courts look to the amended statute for guidance in determining what Congress originally meant by the term "major life activities"? *See Rohr v. Salt River Project Agric. Improvement & Power Dist.*, 555 F.3d 850, 861 (9th Cir. 2009) (suggesting courts should).

5. *Substantially Limits. Bragdon* resolves the issue of ADA coverage for *most* individuals who are infected with HIV. Does the decision provide any assistance to HIV-infected plaintiffs who are unable to bear children for reasons other than their HIV infection? What about an HIV-infected woman who had her fallopian tubes tied prior to her infection? Is such an individual "substantially limited" for other reasons? In *Blanks v. Southwestern Bell Corp.*, 310 F.3d 398 (5th Cir. 2002), the court held that an HIV-positive worker who did not intend to have more children failed to establish a disability under the ADA. But doesn't the *Bragdon* opinion support an argument that HIV infection is substantially limiting because it restricts an individual's freedom to engage in sexual intercourse? In its regulations implementing the amended act, the EEOC makes clear that HIV infection will substantially limit immune function, thus making HIV an actual disability. *See* 29 C.F.R. §1630.3(iii).

The Court further explored what it means for an impairment to substantially limit a major life activity in the following case.

Toyota Motor Manufacturing, Kentucky, Inc. v. Williams
534 U.S. 184 (2002)

Justice O'CONNOR delivered the opinion of the Court.

Under the Americans with Disabilities Act of 1990 (ADA or Act), a physical impairment that "substantially limits one or more . . . major life activities" is a "disability." 42 U.S.C. §12102(2)(A). Respondent, claiming to be disabled because of her carpal tunnel syndrome and other related impairments, sued petitioner, her former employer, for failing to provide her with a reasonable accommodation as required by the ADA. See §12112(b) (5)(A). The District Court granted summary judgment to petitioner, finding that respondent's impairments did not substantially limit any of her major life activities. The Court of Appeals for the Sixth Circuit reversed, finding that the impairments substantially limited respondent in the major life activity of performing manual tasks, and therefore granting partial summary judgment to respondent on the issue of whether she was disabled under the ADA. We conclude that the Court of Appeals did not apply the proper standard in making this determination because it analyzed only a limited class of manual tasks and failed to ask whether respondent's impairments prevented or restricted her from performing tasks that are of central importance to most people's daily lives.

I

Respondent began working at petitioner's automobile manufacturing plant in Georgetown, Kentucky, in August 1990. She was soon placed on an engine fabrication assembly line, where her duties included work with pneumatic tools. Use of these tools eventually caused pain in respondent's hands, wrists, and arms. . . . Respondent consulted a personal physician who placed her on permanent work restrictions that precluded her from lifting more than 20 pounds or from "frequently lifting or carrying of objects weighing up to 10 pounds," engaging in "constant repetitive . . . flexion or extension of [her] wrists or elbows," performing "overhead work," or using "vibratory or pneumatic tools."

In light of these restrictions, for the next two years petitioner assigned respondent to various modified duty jobs. . . . [P]etitioner placed respondent on a team in Quality Control Inspection Operations (QCIO). QCIO is responsible for four tasks: (1) "assembly paint"; (2) "paint second inspection"; (3) "shell body audit"; and (4) "ED surface repair." Respondent was initially placed on a team that performed only the first two of these tasks, and for a couple of years, she rotated on a weekly basis between them. . . . The parties agree that respondent was physically capable of performing both of these jobs and that her performance was satisfactory.

During the fall of 1996, petitioner announced that it wanted QCIO employees to be able to rotate through all four of the QCIO processes. . . . A short while after the shell body audit job was added to respondent's rotations, she began to experience pain in her neck and shoulders. . . . Respondent requested that petitioner accommodate her medical conditions by allowing her to return to doing only her original two jobs in QCIO, which respondent claimed she could still perform without difficulty.

The parties disagree about what happened next. According to respondent, petitioner refused her request and forced her to continue working in the shell body audit job, which caused her even greater physical injury. According to petitioner, respondent simply began missing work on a regular basis. Regardless, it is clear that on December 6, 1996, the last day respondent worked at petitioner's plant, she was placed under a no-work-of-any-kind restriction by her treating physicians. On January 27, 1997, respondent received a letter from petitioner that terminated her employment, citing her poor attendance record. . . .

[The District Court granted summary judgment for defendant, finding that at the time respondent requested accommodation, she was not disabled within the meaning of the statute because her impairment did not substantially limit any major life activity. It further found that at the time of her termination she was not a qualified individual with a disability because her doctor had precluded her from performing any work whatsoever.]

The Court of Appeals for the Sixth Circuit reversed the District Court's ruling on whether respondent was disabled at the time she sought an accommodation. . . . The Court of Appeals held that in order for respondent to demonstrate that she was disabled due to a substantial limitation in the ability to perform manual tasks at the time of her accommodation request, she had to "show that her manual disability involved a 'class' of manual activities affecting the ability to perform tasks at work." Respondent satisfied this test, according to the Court of Appeals, because her ailments "prevented her from doing the tasks associated with certain types of manual assembly line jobs, manual product handling jobs and manual building trade jobs (painting, plumbing, roofing, etc.) that require the gripping of tools and repetitive work with hands and arms extended at or above shoulder levels for extended periods of time." In reaching this conclusion, the court disregarded evidence that respondent could "tend to her personal hygiene [and] carry out personal or household chores," finding that such evidence "does not affect a determination that her impairment substantially limited her ability to perform the range of manual tasks associated with an assembly line job." Because the Court of Appeals concluded that respondent had been substantially limited in performing manual tasks and, for that reason, was entitled to partial summary judgment on the issue of whether she was disabled under the Act, it found that it did not need to determine whether respondent had been substantially limited in the major life activities of lifting or working, or whether she had had a "record of" a disability or had been "regarded as" disabled. . . .

III

The question presented by this case is whether the Sixth Circuit properly determined that respondent was disabled under subsection (A) of the ADA's disability definition [an actual disability, that is, "a physical or mental impairment that substantially limits one or more of the major life activities of such individual"] at the time that she sought an accommodation from petitioner. 42 U.S.C. §12102(2)(A). The parties do not dispute that respondent's medical conditions, which include carpal tunnel syndrome, myotendinitis, and thoracic outlet compression, amount to physical impairments. The relevant question, therefore, is whether the Sixth Circuit correctly analyzed whether these impairments substantially limited respondent in the major life activity of performing manual tasks.

Answering this requires us to address an issue about which the EEOC regulations are silent: what a plaintiff must demonstrate to establish a substantial limitation in the specific major life activity of performing manual tasks.

Our consideration of this issue is guided first and foremost by the words of the disability definition itself. "Substantially" in the phrase "substantially limits" suggests "considerable" or "to a large degree." See Webster's Third New International Dictionary 2280 (1976) (defining "substantially" as "in a substantial manner" and "substantial" as "considerable in amount, value, or worth" and "being that specified to a large degree or in the main"); see also 17 Oxford English Dictionary 66-67 (2d ed. 1989) ("substantial": "relating to or proceeding from the essence of a thing; essential"; "of ample or considerable amount, quantity, or dimensions"). The word "substantial" thus clearly precludes impairments that interfere in only a minor way with the performance of manual tasks from qualifying as disabilities. Cf. *Albertson's, Inc. v. Kirkingburg* 527 U.S. 555 (1999) [reproduced at p. 576] (explaining that a "mere difference" does not amount to a "significant restriction" and therefore does not satisfy the EEOC's interpretation of "substantially limits").

"Major" in the phrase "major life activities" means important. See Webster's, supra, at 1363 (defining "major" as "greater in dignity, rank, importance, or interest"). "Major life activities" thus refers to those activities that are of central importance to daily life. In order for performing manual tasks to fit into this category — a category that includes such basic abilities as walking, seeing, and hearing — the manual tasks in question must be central to daily life. If each of the tasks included in the major life activity of performing manual tasks does not independently qualify as a major life activity, then together they must do so.

That these terms need to be interpreted strictly to create a demanding standard for qualifying as disabled is confirmed by the first section of the ADA, which lays out the legislative findings and purposes that motivate the Act. See 42 U.S.C. §12101. When it enacted the ADA in 1990, Congress found that "some 43,000,000 Americans have one or more physical or mental disabilities." §12101(a)(1). If Congress intended everyone with a physical impairment that precluded the performance of some isolated, unimportant, or particularly difficult manual task to qualify as disabled, the number of disabled Americans would surely have been much higher. Cf. *Sutton v. United Air Lines, Inc.*, 527 U.S. 471 (1999) [reproduced at p. 191 of this Supplement] (finding that because more than 100 million people need corrective lenses to see properly, "had Congress intended to include all persons with corrected physical limitations among those covered by the Act, it undoubtedly would have cited a much higher number [than 43 million disabled persons] in the findings").

We therefore hold that to be substantially limited in performing manual tasks, an individual must have an impairment that prevents or severely restricts the individual from doing activities that are of central importance to most people's daily lives. The impairment's impact must also be permanent or long-term. See 29 CFR §§1630.2(j)(2)(ii)-(iii) (2001).

It is insufficient for individuals attempting to prove disability status under this test to merely submit evidence of a medical diagnosis of an impairment. Instead, the ADA requires those "claiming the Act's protection . . . to prove a disability by

[handwritten margin note: Major life activity]

offering evidence that the extent of the limitation [caused by their impairment] in terms of their own experience . . . is substantial." *Albertson's, Inc. v. Kirkingburg* (holding that monocular vision is not invariably a disability, but must be analyzed on an individual basis, taking into account the individual's ability to compensate for the impairment). That the Act defines "disability" "with respect to an individual," 42 U.S.C. §12102(2), makes clear that Congress intended the existence of a disability to be determined in such a case-by-case manner. See *Sutton v. United Air Lines, Inc.*; *Albertson's, Inc. v. Kirkingburg*; cf. *Bragdon v. Abbott* (relying on unchallenged testimony that the respondent's HIV infection controlled her decision not to have a child, and declining to consider whether HIV infection is a *per se* disability under the ADA); 29 CFR pt. 1630, App. §1630.2(j) (2001).

An individualized assessment of the effect of an impairment is particularly necessary when the impairment is one whose symptoms vary widely from person to person. Carpal tunnel syndrome, one of respondent's impairments, is just such a condition. While cases of severe carpal tunnel syndrome are characterized by muscle atrophy and <u>extreme sensory deficits</u>, mild cases generally do not have either of these effects and create only intermittent symptoms of numbness and tingling. Carniero, Carpal Tunnel Syndrome: The Cause Dictates the Treatment, 66 Cleveland Clinic J. Medicine 159, 161-162 (1999). Studies have further shown that, even without surgical treatment, one quarter of carpal tunnel cases resolve in one month, but that in 22 percent of cases, symptoms last for eight years or longer. See DeStefano, Nordstrom, & Uierkant, Long-term Symptom Outcomes of Carpal Tunnel Syndrome and its Treatment, 22A J. Hand Surgery 200, 204-205 (1997). When pregnancy is the cause of carpal tunnel syndrome, in contrast, the symptoms normally resolve within two weeks of delivery. See Ouellette, Nerve Compression Syndromes of the Upper Extremity in Women, 17 Journal of Musculoskeletal Medicine 536 (2000). Given these large potential differences in the severity and duration of the effects of carpal tunnel syndrome, an individual's carpal tunnel syndrome diagnosis, on its own, does not indicate whether the individual has a disability within the meaning of the ADA.

IV

The Court of Appeals' analysis of respondent's claimed disability suggested that in order to prove a substantial limitation in the major life activity of performing manual tasks, a "plaintiff must show that her manual disability involves a 'class' of manual activities," and that those activities "affect the ability to perform tasks at work." Both of these ideas lack support.

The Court of Appeals relied on our opinion in *Sutton v. United Air Lines, Inc.*, for the idea that a "class" of manual activities must be implicated for an impairment to substantially limit the major life activity of performing manual tasks. But *Sutton* said only that "*when the major life activity under consideration is that of working,* the statutory phrase 'substantially limits' requires . . . that plaintiffs allege that they are unable to work in a broad class of jobs." (emphasis added). Because of the conceptual difficulties inherent in the argument that working could be a major life activity, we have been hesitant to hold as much, and we need not decide this difficult question today. In *Sutton,* we noted that even assuming that working is a major life activity, a claimant would be required to show an inability to work in a "broad range of jobs," rather than a specific job. But *Sutton* did not suggest that a class-based analysis should be applied to any major life activity other than working. Nor do the EEOC regulations. In defining "substantially limits," the EEOC regulations only mention the "class" concept in the context of the major life activity of working. 29 CFR §1630.2(j)(3) (2001) ("With respect to the major life activity of *working*[,] the term *substantially limits* means significantly restricted in the ability to perform either a class of jobs or a broad range of jobs in various classes as compared to the average person having comparable training, skills and abilities"). Nothing in the text of the Act, our previous opinions, or the regulations suggests that a class-based framework should apply outside the context of the major life activity of working.

While the Court of Appeals in this case addressed the different major life activity of performing manual tasks, its analysis circumvented *Sutton* by focusing on respondent's inability to perform manual tasks associated only with her job. This was error. When addressing the major life activity of performing manual tasks, the central inquiry must be whether the claimant is unable to perform the variety of tasks central to most people's daily lives, not whether the claimant is unable to perform the tasks associated with her specific job. Otherwise, *Sutton*'s restriction on claims of disability based on a substantial limitation in working will be rendered meaningless because an inability to perform a specific job always can be recast as an inability to perform a "class" of tasks associated with that specific job.

There is also no support in the Act, our previous opinions, or the regulations for the Court of Appeals' idea that the question of whether an impairment constitutes a disability is to be answered only by analyzing the effect of the impairment in the workplace. Indeed, the fact that the Act's definition of "disability" applies not only to Title I of the Act, 42 U.S.C. §§12111-12117, which deals with employment, but also to the other portions of the Act, which deal with subjects such as public transportation, §§12141-12150, 42 U.S.C. §§12161-12165, and privately provided public accommodations, §§12181-12189, demonstrates that the definition is intended to cover individuals with disabling impairments regardless of whether the individuals have any connection to a workplace.

Even more critically, the manual tasks unique to any particular job are not necessarily important parts of most people's lives. As a result, occupation-specific tasks may have only limited relevance to the manual task inquiry. In this case, "repetitive work with hands and arms extended at or above shoulder levels for extended periods of time," the manual task on which the Court of Appeals relied, is not an important part of most people's daily lives. The court, therefore, should not have considered respondent's inability to do such manual work in her specialized assembly line job as sufficient proof that she was substantially limited in performing manual tasks.

At the same time, the Court of Appeals appears to have disregarded the very type of evidence that it should have focused upon. It treated as irrelevant "the fact that [respondent] can . . . tend to her personal hygiene [and] carry out personal or household chores." Yet household chores, bathing, and brushing one's teeth are among the types of manual tasks of central importance to people's daily lives, and should have been part of the assessment of whether respondent was substantially limited in performing manual tasks.

The District Court noted that at the time respondent sought an accommodation from petitioner, she admitted that she was able to do the manual tasks required by her original two jobs in QCIO. In addition, according to respondent's deposition testimony, even after her condition worsened, she could still brush her teeth, wash her face, bathe, tend her flower garden, fix breakfast, do laundry, and pick up around the house. The record also indicates that her medical conditions caused her to avoid sweeping, to quit dancing, to occasionally seek help dressing, and to reduce how often she plays with her children, gardens, and drives long distances. But these changes in her life did not amount to such severe restrictions in the activities that are of central importance to most people's daily lives that they establish a manual-task disability as a matter of law. On this record, it was therefore inappropriate for the Court of Appeals to grant partial summary judgment to respondent on the issue whether she was substantially limited in performing manual tasks, and its decision to do so must be reversed. . . .

NOTES

1. *A Narrow Holding.* The decision in *Toyota* was unanimous, presumably because of the very narrow holding of the case. The Court did not determine whether Williams's impairment substantially limited her ability to perform manual tasks. Nor did it determine whether Williams's impairment substantially limited her ability to perform any other major life activity. Williams also had contended that lifting and working were major life activities and that her impairment substantially limited those activities as well. The appeals court did not rule on those contentions, and neither did the Supreme Court. The ADAAA, however, includes both lifting and working as major life activities.

Although the *Toyota* holding is narrow, its language is very broad, insisting that the definition of disability be "interpreted strictly to create a demanding standard for qualifying as disabled." Why? Given that disability status is but a threshold step toward protected status under Title I, did the Court's interpretation of "disability" raise the bar too high? Congress clearly thought so. The *Toyota* decision was a major impetus for the statutory amendments, and Congress listed as a purpose for the ADAAA its intent to reject specifically the language from *Toyota* quoted above.

Understand the Catch-22 the *Toyota* Court's construction of "disability" posed for persons such as Williams. One who can perform basic life functions despite her impairment would have a difficult time establishing she is disabled. However, once Williams's condition worsened to the point where she was placed on a "no work of any kind" restriction, her termination was held by both lower courts to be lawful.

She was no longer a "qualified" individual, whether or not she had a disability. The ADAAA was intended to reduce or even eliminate this Catch-22.

2. *Performing Manual Tasks as a Major Life Activity.* Importantly, the Court agreed with the Sixth Circuit that performing manual tasks *is* a major life activity, and the ADAAA includes performing manual tasks within the statutory definition. But the *Toyota* Court held that the manual tasks, either singly or together, must be "central to daily life." If a particular manual task is central to daily life, is it a major life activity, standing alone? When would one need a combination of tasks central to daily life for her performance to be a major life activity, particularly under the amended statute? What are the manual tasks "central to daily life"? Is using one's arms and hands to communicate with others a manual task? *See Thornton v. McClatchy Newspapers, Inc.*, 292 F.3d 1045, 1046 (9th Cir. 2002) ("While most lawyers or law office personnel would undoubtedly consider continuous keyboarding and handwriting to be activities of central importance to their lives, we cannot say that is so for 'most people's daily lives,' as *Williams* requires.").

The Sixth Circuit had focused only on a "class" of manual tasks that were work related. The appeals court had not determined that Williams was substantially limited in her ability to work, and yet the only limitations it had considered were those that were work related. Was the Court concerned that the Sixth Circuit may have been trying to circumvent the rigors of establishing that an individual is substantially limited in her ability to work? *See Sutton,* reproduced at p. 191 of this Supplement. Would Williams have been served by relying on working as a major life activity and focusing on the impairment's impact on her ability to work? *See McKay v. Toyota Motor Mfg., U.S.A., Inc.*, 110 F.3d 369 (6th Cir. 1997) (plaintiff whose carpal tunnel syndrome precluded repetitive factory work not substantially limited in the major life activity of working). *But see EEOC v. AutoZone, Inc.*, 630 F.3d 635, 640 (7th Cir. 2010) (deposition testimony from plaintiff and his wife that his back condition prevented him from bathing, grooming, or dressing himself without assistance raised a fact issue as to whether he was substantially limited in the major life activity of self-care; medical testimony was not required).

3. *Substantially Limits.* The primary question before the *Toyota* Court was whether Williams's impairment *substantially limited* her major life activity of performing manual tasks. The Court answered that question by stating that only if the impairment "prevents or severely restricts the individual from doing activities that are of central importance to most people's daily lives" will it be substantially limiting. Moreover, the impairment's impact must also be permanent or long-term. Congress emphatically rejected this interpretation of the statute. Its findings and purposes in the ADAAA so state. But Congress did not define "substantially limited" in the ADAAA. Instead, it directed the EEOC to revise its regulations in a manner consistent with the purposes of the ADAAA.

The EEOC's regulations in place at the time *Toyota* was decided had defined "substantially limited" to mean "unable to perform a major life activity that the average person in the general population can perform" or "significantly restricted as to the condition, manner or duration under which an individual can perform a particular major life activity as compared to the condition, manner, or duration under which the average person in the general population can perform that same major life activity." 29 C.F.R. §1630.2(j). Congress in the ADAAA found the EEOC's regulation "to require a greater degree of limitation than was intended by Congress" and directed the agency to revise its regulations in a manner that would "be consistent with" the ADAAA, which purpose was to "reinstate[e] a broad scope of protection to be available under the ADA."

In its amended regulations, the EEOC opted not to define "substantially limits" but instead issued nine Rules of Construction to be used in construing the term. These include:

- the term "substantially limits" requires a lower degree of functional limitation than that previously used by the courts
- the term "substantially limits" is to be construed broadly
- an individualized assessment is required to determine if an impairment is substantially limiting
- other than for eyeglasses or contacts, the assessment is to be made without regard to mitigating measures
- the determination of disability should not require extensive analysis

29 C.FR. 1630.2(j). The thrust of the statute and the regulations is clear — Congress has flatly rejected the *Toyota* Court's view that the path to disability status be a demanding one.

4. *Is Comparative Evidence Needed?* One of the rules of construction for "substantially limits," while retaining comparison of the individual's performance of a major life activity to that of most people in the general population, makes clear that no scientific, medical or statistical evidence will usually be needed. This approach is in keeping with the decision in the *Hayes v. United Parcel Serv., Inc.,* 17 F. App'x 317, 321 (6th Cir. 2001), where the court found that when plaintiff could sit only 20 to 25 minutes. "[c]ommon sense and life experiences will permit finders of fact to determine whether someone who cannot sit for more than this period of time is significantly restricted as compared to the average person." *Id.* at 321. *Accord Gribben v. UPS,* 528 F.3d 1166 (9th Cir. 2008) (no comparator evidence on an "average person in the general population" required; plaintiff's testimony of his limitations sufficient for jury to determine whether he was disabled).

However, when the major life activity is working, some courts applying the original ADA required plaintiffs to present specific evidence about the relevant labor market and the jobs the impairments preclude them from performing. *See, e.g., Gelabert-Ladenheim v. Am. Airlines, Inc.,* 252 F.3d 54 (1st Cir. 2001). *See generally* Cheryl L. Anderson, *Comparative Evidence or Common Experience: When Does "Substantial Limitation" Require Substantial Proof Under the Americans with Disabilities Act?,* 57 Am. U. L. Rev. 409 (2007).

5. *A Question of Fact or a Question of Law? Bristol v. Bd. of County Comm'rs of Clear Creek,* 281 F.3d 1148, 1156, *vacated in part on other grounds,* 312 F.3d 1213 (10th Cir. 2002), stated that determining whether a condition constitutes an impairment or a major life activity is a question for the court, but whether the impairment *substantially limits* the major life activity is a question of fact for the jury. Would the *Toyota* Court agree?

6. *Applying the Substantially Limits Test.* In *Muller v. Costello*, 187 F.3d 298 (2d Cir. 1999), a corrections officer suffered from bronchitis and asthma that made it difficult for him to breathe in smoky environments. Exposure to smoke at work caused him to suffer sufficiently serious breathing problems that he was required to leave work for one to ten days at a time, visit his doctor, and on some occasions report to a hospital emergency room. Muller's medical evidence indicated that his lung function diminished 45 percent when exposed to irritants. Nevertheless, the court found that Muller was not substantially limited with respect to breathing: "Other than Muller's difficulties while at work at Midstate, what we are left with is testimony that Muller was physically active outside of work, that he could potentially have severe reactions to environmental irritants, and that, on one occasion, he did have such a reaction." *Id.* at 314. *See also Williams v. Excel Foundry & Machine, Inc.*, 489 F.3d 227 (7th Cir. 2007) (foundry worker with fractured spine unable to stand for more than 30-40 minutes not substantially limited in major life activity of standing); *McWilliams v. Jefferson County*, 463 F.3d 1113, 1117 (10th Cir. 2006) (although intermittent depressive episodes caused plaintiff difficulty in sleeping and getting along with co-workers, "she has not shown how these limitations prevented her from performing her job 'or that she is unable to perform any of the life activities completely'"); *Holt v. Grand Lake Mental Health Ctr., Inc.*, 443 F.3d 762 (10th Cir. 2006) (plaintiff with cerebral palsy, who could not cut her own nails, slice food, and button her clothes without assistance, not substantially limited in performing manual tasks). Aren't these cases consistent with *Toyota*? Do they help you understand why Congress amended the ADA?

7. *Differently Abled?* In *Albertson's v. Kirkingburg*, 527 U.S. 555 (1999), reproduced at p. 576, the Supreme Court held that the fact that an impairment requires an individual to perform a major life activity differently does not mean it is substantially limiting. As the Court stated,

> [T]he Ninth Circuit . . . conclud[ed] that because Kirkingburg had presented "uncontroverted evidence" that his vision was effectively monocular, he had demonstrated that "the manner in which he sees differs significantly from the manner in which most people see." That difference in manner, the court held, was sufficient to establish disability. . . . But in several respects the Ninth Circuit was too quick to find a disability. First, although the EEOC definition of "substantially limits" cited by the Ninth Circuit requires a "significant restriction" in an individual's manner of performing a major life activity, the court appeared willing to settle for a mere difference. By transforming "significant restriction" into "difference," the court undercut the fundamental statutory requirement that only impairments causing "substantial limitations" in individuals' ability to perform major life activities constitute disabilities. While the Act "addresses substantial limitations on major life activities, not utter inabilities," *Bragdon v. Abbott*, it concerns itself only with limitations that are in fact substantial.

527 U.S. at 461. This does not mean, however, that just because someone with a disability has been able to overcome that disability in many aspects of his life that he is no longer disabled. *See Emory v. AstraZeneca Pharms. LP*, 401 F.3d 174, 181 (3d Cir. 2005) ("'That [a plaintiff], through sheer force of will, learned

accommodations, and careful planning, is able to perform a wide variety of activities despite his physical impairments does not mean that those activities are not substantially more difficult for him than they would be for an unimpaired individual.' . . . What a plaintiff confronts, not overcomes, is the measure of substantial limitation under the ADA."). See also 29 C.F.R. §1630.2(j)(4).

NOTE ON MITIGATING MEASURES

One issue concerning "substantial limitation" arose in many disability cases and had divided the lower courts. Were impairments that were controlled or corrected by medication or other mitigating measures to be assessed in their mitigated or unmitigated states in determining whether the impairment was substantially limiting? In *Sutton v. United Air Lines, Inc.*, 527 U.S. 471 (1999), along with two companion cases, *Murphy v. United Parcel Service, Inc.*, 527 U.S. 516 (1999); *Albertson's, Inc. v. Kirkingburg*, 527 U.S. 535 (1999), the Supreme Court confronted this issue.

Karen Sutton and Kimberly Hinton were twins who sought employment as commercial airline pilots. Each had severe myopia; without eyeglasses they were legally blind, but their vision was at least 20/20 when wearing their glasses. United Air Lines rejected their applications because the twins could not meet United's requirement that its pilots have at least 20/100 uncorrected vision. The twins had sued under the ADA, and the Tenth Circuit had held the women were not within the ADA's protected class.

The Supreme Court agreed. It concluded that the EEOC's position that individuals should be assessed in their "hypothetical uncorrected state" was an impermissible interpretation of the ADA. The Court reached its conclusion by looking to three provisions of the ADA. First, the phrase "substantially limits" is in the "present indicative verb form," which the Court viewed as requiring assessment of the individual in his present, i.e., mitigated, state. Second, the Court found the statute's focus on the "individual" was at odds with a hypothetical inquiry on an impairment's unmitigated effect. And, third, the Court said the ADA's findings referenced "some 43,000,000 Americans" with disabilities, a number that would be significantly higher were impairments to be assessed without regard to mitigating measures. Because Sutton and Hinton could see just fine while wearing corrective lenses, their impairment, assessed in its mitigated state, did not substantially limit any major life activity. They thus lacked any actual disability within the meaning of the ADA.

The impact of *Sutton* and its companion cases was huge. Under *Sutton*, an employer was free to discriminate against someone who had a corrected physical or mental impairment, even when the employer was taking action based on the impairment's unmitigated effects. As Justice Stevens pointed out in dissent, "the Court's approach would seem to allow an employer to refuse to hire every person who has epilepsy or diabetes that is controlled by medication, or every person who functions effectively with a prosthetic limb." 527 U.S. at 509. The Court's decision was particularly troubling when one recalls that the ADA's employment provisions generally protect only *qualified* individuals with disabilities — those who can perform the essential job functions. And often it is the mitigating measure that allows the individual to do the job; after all, the twins were not contending they were qualified to fly commercial airliners in their unmitigated state. Rather, they contended they were qualified to fly airplanes despite their disability. The question in *Sutton* was not whether the petitioners were qualified to fly airplanes but whether they had a disability within the meaning of the ADA. By holding there was no actual disability, the case ended there, whether or not the twins were qualified to do the job.

Murphy v. United Parcel Serv., 527 U.S. 516 (1999), decided the same day as *Sutton*, considered the claim of a mechanic dismissed from his job because of high blood pressure. The plaintiff asserted that the disability determination should be made without reference to the medication he took to control his blood pressure; the Court rejected this argument in light of its resolution of this issue in *Sutton*. And in *Albertson's, Inc. v. Kirkingburg*, reproduced at p. 576, also decided the same day as *Sutton*, the plaintiff had monocular vision, but his brain had subconsciously adjusted to the impairment. Although the Ninth Circuit had ignored the impact of those adjustments, the Supreme Court held that a body's coping mechanisms that mitigate an impairment must be considered in assessing disability status. "We see no principled basis for distinguishing between measures undertaken with artificial aids, like medications and devices, and measures undertaken, whether consciously or not, with the body's own systems." 527 U.S. at 565. The *Kirkingburg* Court also criticized the Ninth Circuit's determination that monocular vision was a per se disability, emphasizing, as it had in *Sutton*, the need for a case-by-case determination of whether a disability exists.

Again a Catch-22, after *Sutton*, *Murphy*, and *Kirkingburg*, individuals would not be considered "disabled" in their mitigated state but would often not be "qualified" in their unmitigated state. In the wake of *Sutton*, numerous individuals with serious but correctable conditions were found outside the protections of the statute.

In these cases, the Court rejected the EEOC's contrary interpretation of the ADA. It did so by finding that no agency had been given authority to promulgate regulations fleshing out the definition of disability. While the agency had been given rule-making authority with respect to Title I, the employment section of the ADA, the definition of disability was found in the "definitions" section of the statute, which precedes the various Titles committed to the EEOC and other agencies. This left considerable uncertainty over whether the EEOC's regulations and interpretive guidance interpreting "disability" were entitled to any deference from the courts.

Congress responded to the *Sutton* trilogy in the ADAAA. The amendments provide that "the determination of whether an impairment substantially limits a major life activity shall be made *without regard* to the ameliorative effects of mitigating measures . . . " and lists a number of mitigating measures such as medication, prosthetics, and hearing aids. However, the amended statute goes on to provide that "the ameliorative effects of the mitigating measures of ordinary eyeglasses or contact lenses shall be considered in determining whether an impairment substantially limits a major life activity." Accordingly, while Congress amended the statute in direct response to the result in *Sutton*, it essentially agreed that Sutton and Hinton were not to be considered persons with *actual* disabilities within the meaning of the ADA. Oddly enough, however, the ADAAA also requires any vision standard to be job related. 42 USC §12113(c).

The twins, however, had also contended that even if they lacked an actual disability under the ADA, they were regarded as having a disability. This portion of *Sutton* and Congress's response to it in the ADAAA, is set forth at p. 191 of this Supplement.

While the ADAAA ensures that individuals using mitigating measures will not thereby be excluded from the statute's protected class, there remains a problem regarding those who do not use measures when they are available. Such individuals will be disabled (a matter which divided the courts prior to the ADAAA), but the failure to mitigate may sometimes make them unqualified. As we will see, a disabled person is otherwise qualified if she can perform the essential functions of the position with or without reasonable accommodation. The obvious question that will arise is the extent to which an employer must accommodate an individual who does not use mitigating measures to enable her to do the job at issue. *See generally* Jeannette Cox, *"Corrective" Surgery and the Americans with Disabilities Act*, 46 SAN DIEGO L. REV. 113, 130 (2009) ("By making used medical technology that removes an individual's substantial limitation no longer relevant to the individual's membership in the ADA's protected class, the [ADAAA] appear[s] to make the availability of unused medical technology irrelevant as well."; Reagan S. Bissonnette, Note, *Reasonably Accommodating Nonmitigating Plaintiffs after the ADA Amendments Act of 2008*, 50 B.C. L. REV. 859, 859 (2009) (proposing that a plaintiff who chooses not to mitigate must establish that "the burdens imposed on the plaintiff to mitigate the effects of his disability are not substantially less than the burdens imposed on the employer to accommodate the plaintiff's disability in order to show that an accommodation is reasonable").

Finally, there is the question of whether the use of a mitigating measure might itself create a disability where none previously existed. *Sulima v. Tobyhanna Army Depot*, 602 F.3d 177, 187 (3d Cir. 2010), held that the side effects from medical treatment may themselves constitute an impairment under the ADA even if the condition treated is not itself disabling; however, since " 'disability' " connotes an involuntary condition," a plaintiff seeking protection on this theory must show both that the treatment was required in the "prudent judgment" of the medical profession and there is not an available alternative that is equally efficacious but lacks similarly disabling side effects.

NOTE ON DEFERENCE TO THE EEOC

The EEOC is a federal administrative agency charged with the administration and enforcement of Title VII, the ADEA, and the ADA. Importantly, each of these statutes requires a complaining party to file charges with the EEOC prior to filing suit. The EEOC enforcement process is explored in Chapter 7. Additionally, we have seen in a number of cases that the EEOC may be a plaintiff in Title VII litigation, bringing suit on behalf of workers it contends are victims of discrimination.

To what extent, however, is the EEOC entitled to meaningful deference from the courts in its *interpretation* of the statutes it administers? As we have seen in earlier chapters, the Court's willingness to defer to EEOC interpretations of Title VII's substantive provisions has been limited. Although Congress gave the EEOC the power to issue procedural regulations under Title VII, it withheld from the agency the power to issue substantive regulations under that statute. *See Gen. Elec. Co. v. Gilbert*, 429 U.S. 125, 140-42 (1976) (because "Congress . . . did not confer upon the EEOC authority to promulgate rules or regulations," the level of deference afforded depends on "the thoroughness evident in its consideration, the validity of its reasoning, its consistency with earlier and later pronouncements, and all those factors which give it power to persuade, if lacking power to control.").

But there is good reason to believe that deference to the EEOC should be greater under the Americans with Disabilities Act. This question was presented to, but not answered by, the Court in *Sutton*. The question is complicated by the fact that the EEOC has issued not only regulations but also Interpretive Guidances, and other materials, and that, as we saw in *Bragdon*, other agencies are also charged with administration and enforcement of the ADA. Congress was aware when it enacted the ADA that considerable uncertainty over the rights and obligations conferred by the statute would exist, and it charged various agencies with authority to promulgate regulations to carry out particular subchapters.

Title I of the ADA confers substantive rule-making authority on the EEOC. The statute directs that "Not later than one year after July 26, 1990, the Commission shall issue regulations in an accessible format to carry out this subchapter in accordance with [the Administrative Procedure Act.]" 42 U.S.C. §12116 (2009). The EEOC carried out that mandate, issuing regulations promulgated after notice and comment. The regulations contained as an appendix an Interpretive Guidance.

The Supreme Court's decision in *Bragdon v. Abbott*, reproduced at p. 164 of this Supplement, suggested the Court not only was willing to adopt an expansive approach to the definition of disability but also was willing to allow agencies a leading role in interpreting the statute. However, the Court's deference to the HEW regulations in *Bragdon* was a product of Congress's directive that the ADA be interpreted in accordance with those regulations.

Sutton v. United Air Lines, Inc., presented the question of what deference was due the EEOC's Interpretive Guidance, arguably agency action that was entitled to less deference than its regulations. The Interpretive Guidance provided that an impairment was to be assessed in its unmitigated state in determining whether a disability was present. The EEOC, backed by the Justice Department, urged the Court to defer to its interpretation.

The basis of that argument was *Chevron U.S.A., Inc. v. Natural Res. Def. Council, Inc.*, 467 U.S. 837 (1984), in which the Supreme Court recognized that agency interpretations of silent or ambiguous statutes are due deference from the courts when Congress has delegated law-interpreting power to the agency. More recently, in *United States v. Mead Corp.*, 533 U.S. 218 (2001), the Court explained when such an implied delegation would be found. A delegation of rule-making or adjudicative authority to an agency will support an implied delegation of interpretive authority. Other comparable indicia may also support an implied delegation of interpretive authority. *Chevron* review will attach to such an agency's statutory interpretations, if the agency was exercising that authority when it promulgated the interpretation for which deference is claimed. Even when an agency has not been delegated interpretive authority, however, its interpretations of the statutes it administers still will merit attention from the courts. Such interpretations may be persuasive, depending on "the thoroughness evident in its consideration, the validity of its reasoning, its consistency with earlier and later pronouncements, and all [other] factors which give it power to persuade, if lacking power to control." *Skidmore v. Swift & Co.*, 323 U.S. 134 (1944). This level of deference is referred to as *Skidmore* deference.

In *Sutton,* the EEOC contended its position on the mitigating measures question was deserving of heightened deference under *Chevron.* But the Supreme Court refused to defer to the agency's view as expressed in its Interpretive Guidance. It found the EEOC's reading was an impermissible interpretation of the statute because it was inconsistent with the statutory text. Under *Chevron*, a reviewing court will *not* defer to an agency's construction of a statute if it finds that Congress itself has spoken to the precise question at issue. In such cases, no implied delegation has occurred since Congress itself has made the policy choice. The *Sutton* Court, through its textualist approach, appeared to find that Congress had determined impairments are to be assessed in their mitigated state.

In rejecting the EEOC's Interpretive Guidance as an impermissible interpretation of the ADA, the Court was able to sidestep difficult, but important, questions concerning the EEOC's role in interpreting the ADA. However, even if the *Sutton* Court had conceded ambiguity in the statutory definition, it is not clear it would have deferred to the EEOC's interpretation. That is because the Court noted that the definition of disability is not contained within Title I but instead is in the generally applicable provisions of the Act. Although the EEOC was given authority to issue regulations carrying out Title I, "no agency has been delegated authority to interpret the term 'disability,'" said the Court in *Sutton.* 527 U.S. at 479. Thus, the Court questioned, although it did not decide, whether the EEOC's extensive regulations and Interpretive Guidance addressing what constitutes a disability were entitled to any deference at all. Justice Breyer's suggestion in a dissent in *Sutton* that the EEOC's authority to interpret the term "qualified individual with a disability" necessarily carried with it the authority to determine what constitutes a disability was dismissed as "an imaginative interpretation of the Act's delegation provisions."

Congress, in enacting the ADAAA, responded to this aspect of *Sutton* as well. The amendments expressly give the EEOC (and other agencies charged with administering other Titles of the ADA) the authority to issue regulations implementing the definition of disability in Section 3 of the Act, as well as the definitions in Section 4 of the Act. Thus, the EEOC now has the expressly delegated authority to interpret "disability," something the Court had found lacking in *Sutton,* along with the substantive rule-making authority it has had from the outset under Title I of the ADA. Issues concerning what constitutes an essential job function, a reasonable accommodation, an undue hardship, or a direct threat, for example, would implicate the terms of Title I, where Congress had clearly delegated interpretive authority to the EEOC. Accordingly, its regulations, and perhaps the appendix to those regulations, interpreting that subchapter are entitled to analysis under *Chevron*. Recognizing this point, the Supreme Court deferred, under *Chevron*, to an EEOC regulation interpreting "direct threat" in *Chevron U.S.A., Inc. v. Echazabal*, 536 U.S. 73 (2002), reproduced at p. 568.

Another complicating factor in *Sutton*, however, was that the EEOC's position on mitigating measures was found not in the text of the regulation itself but in the Interpretive Guidance, which was issued as an appendix accompanying the regulations. That appendix, however, had also been subject to notice and comment proceedings. The Court noted, but did not resolve, the format issue. *See Christensen v. Harris County*, 529 U.S. 576 (2000) (*Chevron* deference not due Labor Department opinion letter). *But see Chase Bank USA, N.A. v. McCoy*, 131 S. Ct. 871, 882 (2011) (deferring to an agency interpretation advanced by the Federal Reserve Board in an amicus brief as long as it is not inconsistent with the agency's regulation). In other words, the Court may extend *Chevron* deference to the EEOC's disability regulations but not to its Interpretive Guidance.

The EEOC also has issued various other interpretations in even more informal forms. Its Compliance Manual sets forth Enforcement Guidances, and it also has promulgated a Technical Assistance Manual. Although the failure to follow notice and comment procedures presumably deprives these interpretations of deference under *Chevron*, they still are entitled to deference under a *Skidmore* review standard. *See Nat'l R.R. Passenger Corp. v. Morgan*, 536 U.S. 101 (2002). *See generally* Rebecca Hanner White, *Deference and Disability Discrimination*, 99 Mich. L. Rev. 532 (2000); Lisa Eichhorn, *The* Chevron *Two-Step and the* Toyota *Sidestep: Dancing Around the EEOC's "Disability" Regulations Under the ADA*, 39 Wake Forest L. Rev. 177, 202-03 (2004); Melissa Hart, *Skepticism and Expertise: The Supreme Court and the EEOC*, 74 Fordham L. Rev. 1937, 1938 (2006); Rebecca Hanner White, *The EEOC, the Courts, and Employment Discrimination Policy: Recognizing the Agency's Leading Role in Statutory Interpretation*, 1995 Utah L. Rev. 51.

PROBLEM 6.1

Sarah Smith is an assembly-line worker who is diabetic and dependent on insulin injections to maintain her glucose level. She must inject up to four times a day to maintain ideal glucose levels. If her glucose level drops too low, she will become hypoglycemic and go into a coma. If her glucose level is too high, it will cause long-term physical deterioration of numerous body systems. Eating increases glucose levels, so Sarah needs to inject one half-hour before eating larger meals. Her doctor has recommended that she eat smaller and more frequent meals to help her modulate variations in her glucose levels. Outside of work, Sarah leads an active life and exercises regularly. She must be careful to time her injections depending on her exercise and eating patterns. Exercise reduces glucose levels on a short-term basis and can upset the balance of insulin and glucose in the body, possibly resulting in a hypoglycemic reaction. Because

Sarah is careful about her eating, exercise, and treatment regimen, her diabetes is reasonably well controlled. She does not yet exhibit any physical damage related to excess glucose levels. She carries small amounts of sugar with her to minimize the incidence of hypoglycemic reactions. Assembly-line workers operate on a very rigid schedule. Sarah wants to seek accommodations from her employer to make it easier for her to maintain her glucose levels while at work. Is Sarah an individual with a disability under the original ADA? Under the ADA as amended? *See, e.g., Nawrot v. CPC Int'l*, 277 F.3d 896 (7th Cir. 2002) (finding diabetic plaintiff to be a qualified individual with a disability where even with medication his ability to think and to care for himself was substantially limited and raising but not resolving whether permitting plaintiff to take short breaks to monitor and adjust his blood sugar violated the duty of reasonable accommodation); *Rohr v. Salt River Project Agric. Improvement & Power Dist.*, 555 F.3d 850, 859 (9th Cir. 2009) (plaintiff raised a genuine issue of material fact as to whether his diabetes substantially limits his life activity of eating given the strict monitoring of each day's blood tests, medications, and food intake).

PROBLEM 6.2

Serum alpha-1 antitrypsin (SAT) is a serum protein that protects the lungs from proteolytic enzymes. Approximately 80 percent of individuals who inherit an SAT deficiency from both parents develop chronic obstructive pulmonary disease (COPD). Individuals who inherit the deficiency from only one parent have a much lower risk, but nevertheless have a higher risk than the general population of developing COPD (one in ten), especially if they smoke or work in dusty environments. Tuan, who inherited SAT deficiency from both of his parents, does not yet suffer from any symptoms of COPD. Is Tuan impaired? Is he substantially limited with respect to a major life activity and, therefore, disabled under the ADA, either as originally enacted or as amended? Whether or not he is an individual with a disability within the meaning of the ADA, would he be entitled to the protections of GINA?

2. Record of Such an Impairment

Section 3(2) of the ADA defines disability to include having a "record" of an impairment that substantially limits a major life activity. A variety of records contain such information, including employment records, medical records, and education records. Individuals with impairments that, as a result of successful treatment, are not currently substantially limiting may seek to establish that they are protected by the ADA based on a "record" of an impairment. However, "[t]he impairment indicated in the record must be an impairment that would substantially limit one or more of the individual's major life activities." 29 C.F.R. pt. 1630, app. §1630.2(k).

What evidence is necessary to meet this requirement? Numerous courts have held that impairments resulting in hospitalization and subsequent extended recuperation do not constitute substantially limiting impairments (or records of such impairments) in the absence of some chronic long-term impact. Under the amended ADA, however, would such interpretations be consistent with Congress's direction to construe the Act in favor of broad coverage? Moreover, the amendments provide that "an impairment that is episodic or in remission is a disability if it would substantially limit a major life activity when active."

The EEOC has taken the position that the ADA "protects former cancer patients from discrimination on the basis of their prior medical history." 29 C. F.R. pt. 1630, app. §1630.2(k). For a discussion of how the ADA's definition of "disability" treats cancer survivors, with a particular focus on breast cancer survivors, see Jane Byeff Korn, *Cancer and the ADA: Rethinking Disability*, 74 S. CAL. L. REV. 399 (2001).

Are individuals who establish coverage under the ADA by demonstrating a record of a substantially limiting impairment entitled to reasonable accommodations relating to continuing nonsubstantial limitations associated with their impairment? *See* 76 FR 17014. The EEOC's position is yes; an employer, for example, may need to accommodate an employee's need for periodic checkups related to the currently in remission disability. And, for liability to exist, must the employer discriminate based on the record of disability rather than on the basis of continuing nonsubstantial limitations? In thinking about how best to answer these questions, reconsider *Arline. See generally* Alex B. Long, *(Whatever Happened to) The ADA's "Record of" Prong(?)*, 81 WASH. L. REV. 669 (2006) (analyzing the puzzling disappearance of the record of disability prong).

PROBLEM 6.3

Reconsider Problems 6.1 and 6.2. Could you make a "record of impairment" argument on behalf of Sarah or Tuan?

3. Regarded as Having Such an Impairment

Sutton v. United Air Lines, Inc.
527 U.S. 471 (1999)

O'CONNOR, J. delivered the opinion of the Court.
[The facts of this case are included in the Note on Mitigating Measures.]

IV

Our conclusion that petitioners have failed to state a claim that they are actually disabled under subsection (A) of the disability definition does not end our inquiry. Under subsection (C), individuals who are "regarded as" having a disability are disabled within the meaning of the ADA. See §12102(2)(C). Subsection (C) provides that having a disability includes "being regarded as having," §12102(2)(C), "a physical or mental impairment that substantially limits one or more of the major life activities of such individual," §12102(2)(A). There are two apparent ways in which individuals may fall within this statutory definition: (1) a covered entity mistakenly believes that a person has a physical impairment that substantially limits one or more major life activities, or (2) a covered entity mistakenly believes that an actual, nonlimiting impairment substantially limits one or more major life activities. In both cases, it is necessary that a covered entity entertain misperceptions about the individual—it must believe either that one has a substantially limiting impairment that one does not have or that one has a substantially limiting impairment when, in fact, the impairment is not so limiting. These misperceptions often "result from stereotypic assumptions not truly indicative of . . . individual ability." See 42 U.S.C. §12101(7).

There is no dispute that petitioners are physically impaired. Petitioners do not make the obvious argument that they are regarded due to their impairments as substantially limited in the major life activity of seeing. They contend only that respondent mistakenly believes their physical impairments substantially limit them in the major life activity of working. To support this claim, petitioners allege that respondent has a vision requirement, which is allegedly based on myth and stereotype. Further, this requirement substantially limits their ability to engage in the major life activity of working by precluding them from obtaining the job of global airline pilot, which they argue is a "class of employment." In reply, respondent argues that the position of global airline pilot is not a class of jobs and therefore petitioners have not stated a claim that they are regarded as substantially limited in the major life activity of working.

Standing alone, the allegation that respondent has a vision requirement in place does not establish a claim that respondent regards petitioners as substantially limited in the major life activity of working. By its terms, the ADA allows employers to prefer some physical attributes over others and to establish physical criteria. An employer runs afoul of the ADA when it makes an employment decision based on a physical or mental impairment, real or imagined, that is regarded as substantially limiting a major life activity. Accordingly, an employer is free to decide that physical characteristics or medical conditions that do not rise to the level of an impairment—such as one's height, build, or singing voice—are preferable to others, just as it is free to decide that some limiting, but not substantially limiting, impairments make individuals less than ideally suited for a job.

Considering the allegations of the amended complaint in tandem, petitioners have not stated a claim that respondent regards their impairment as substantially limiting their ability to work. The ADA does not define "substantially limits," but "substantially" suggests "considerable" or "specified to a large degree." See Webster's Third New International Dictionary 2280 (1976) (defining "substantially" as "in a substantial manner" and "substantial" as "considerable in amount, value, or worth" and "being that specified to a large degree or in the main"). The EEOC has codified regulations interpreting the term "substantially limits" in this manner, defining the term to mean "unable to perform" or "significantly restricted." See 29 CFR §§1630.2(j)(1)(i),(ii) (1998).

When the major life activity under consideration is that of working, the statutory phrase "substantially limits" requires, at a minimum, that plaintiffs allege they are unable to work in a broad class of jobs. Reflecting this requirement, the EEOC uses a specialized definition of the term "substantially limits" when referring to the major life activity of working:

> significantly restricted in the ability to perform either a class of jobs or a broad range of jobs in various classes as compared to the average person having comparable training, skills and abilities. The inability to perform a single, particular job does not constitute a substantial limitation in the major life activity of working.

§1630.2(j)(3)(i). The EEOC further identifies several factors that courts should consider when determining whether an individual is substantially limited in the major life activity of working, including the geographical area to which the individual has reasonable access, and "the number and types of jobs utilizing similar training, knowledge, skills or abilities, within the geographical area, from which the individual is also disqualified." §§1630.2(j)(3)(ii)(A), (B). To be substantially limited in the major life activity of working, then, one must be precluded from more than one type of job, a specialized job, or a particular job of choice. If jobs utilizing an individual's skills (but perhaps not his or her unique talents) are available, one is not precluded from a substantial class of jobs. Similarly, if a host of different types of jobs are available, one is not precluded from a broad range of jobs.

Because the parties accept that the term "major life activities" includes working, we do not determine the validity of the cited regulations. We note, however, that there may be some conceptual difficulty in defining "major life activities" to include work, for it seems "to argue in a circle to say that if one is excluded, for instance, by reason of [an impairment, from working with others] . . . then that exclusion constitutes an impairment, when the question you're asking is, whether the exclusion itself is by reason of handicap." Tr. of Oral Argument in [*Arline*] (argument of Solicitor General). Indeed, even the EEOC has expressed reluctance to define "major life activities" to include working and has suggested that working be viewed as a residual life activity, considered, as a last resort, *only* "if an individual is not substantially limited with respect to *any other* major life activity." 29 CFR pt. 1630, App. §1630.2(j) (1998) (emphasis added).

Assuming without deciding that working is a major life activity and that the EEOC regulations interpreting the term "substantially limits" are reasonable, petitioners have failed to allege adequately that their poor eyesight is regarded as an impairment that substantially limits them in the major life activity of working. They allege only that respondent regards their poor vision as precluding them from holding positions as a "global airline pilot." Because the position of global airline pilot is a single job, this allegation does not support the claim that respondent regards petitioners as having a substantially limiting impairment. See 29 CFR §1630.2(j)(3)(i) ("The inability to perform a single, particular job does not constitute a substantial limitation in the major life activity of working"). Indeed, there are a number of other positions utilizing petitioners' skills, such as regional pilot and pilot instructor to name a few, that are available to them. Even under the EEOC's Interpretative Guidance, to which petitioners ask us to defer, "an individual who cannot be a commercial airline pilot because of a minor vision impairment, but who can be a commercial airline co-pilot or a pilot for a courier service, would not be substantially limited in the major life activity of working." 29 CFR pt. 1630, App. §1630.2.

Petitioners also argue that if one were to assume that a substantial number of airline carriers have similar vision requirements, they would be substantially limited in the major life activity of working. Even assuming for the sake of argument that the adoption of similar vision requirements by other carriers would represent a substantial limitation on the major life activity of working, the argument is nevertheless flawed. It is not enough to say that if the physical criteria of a single employer were *imputed* to all similar employers one would be regarded as substantially limited in the major life activity of working *only as a result of this imputation*. An otherwise valid job requirement, such as a height requirement, does not become invalid simply because it would limit a person's employment opportunities in a substantial way if it were adopted by a substantial number of employers. Because petitioners have not alleged, and cannot demonstrate, that respondent's vision requirement reflects a belief that petitioners' vision substantially limits them, we agree with the decision of the Court of Appeals affirming the dismissal of petitioners' claim that they are regarded as disabled.

NOTES

1. *Working as a Major Life Activity.* The analysis of how broad a class of jobs needs to be arises only if "working" is a major life activity under the ADA. Note that the *Sutton* Court reserved the question, and *Toyota* did as well. Congress answered the question in the ADAAA; working is listed as a major life activity. However, given the expansive definition of major life activity in the amended statute, it should now be the unusual case where a plaintiff relies on working as the major life activity substantially limited by his impairment.

2. *Substantially Limited in Ability to Work.* The *Sutton* Court's analysis of the plaintiffs' claim that they were regarded as substantially limited with respect to working is consistent with the EEOC regulations insofar as the Court requires the plaintiffs to establish that they were regarded as excluded from "either a class of jobs or a broad range of jobs" as compared to persons with "comparable training, skills and abilities." The opinion also rests comfortably within the EEOC's then-existing Interpretive Guidance in concluding that the plaintiffs were not substantially limited with respect to working because other airline positions were open to them.

What is a broad class or range of jobs? As we shall see below, this question is no longer important for "regarded as" claims covered by the ADAAA. But it remains important for those (presumably now rare cases) claiming an actual disability or a record of such a disability when the major life activity in question is "working." In *Murphy v. United Parcel Serv.*, 527 U.S. 516 (1999), the plaintiff was denied DOT certification to drive a commercial truck because of his high blood pressure. UPS dismissed Murphy from his job because he could not obtain the certification. The Court held that the defendant did not regard Murphy as substantially limited in the activity of working but only regarded Murphy as unable to perform mechanics' jobs that required driving a commercial motor vehicle (defined as a vehicle weighing over 10,000 pounds, designed to carry 16 or more passengers, or used in the transportation of hazardous materials).

In *Giordano v. City of New York*, 274 F.3d 740 (2d Cir. 2001), the court held plaintiff had not shown he was regarded as being substantially limited in his ability to work. His employer regarded him as unable to perform police or other investigative work that involved a risk of physical confrontation, and he thus had no evidence he was regarded as being unable to work in a broad class of jobs. Do you agree? Is firefighting a class of jobs? *See Bridges v. City of Bossier*, 92 F.3d 329 (5th Cir. 1996) (no). Is law enforcement generally? *See McKenzie v. Dovola*, 242 F.3d 967 (10th Cir. 2001) (yes). *But see Rossbach v. City of Miami*, 371 F.3d 1354 (11th Cir. 2004) (even assuming the city perceived officers as being precluded by their impairments from working as police officers, "police officer" was not a "class of jobs" or "broad range of jobs" for ADA purposes). In *Gasser v. District of Columbia*, 442 F.3d 758 (D.C. Cir. 2006), a jury verdict in plaintiff's favor was reversed where plaintiff failed to introduce evidence of the jobs he was regarded as unable to perform because of the risk of bleeding. *See also Nealey v. Water District No. 1*, 324 F. App'x 744 (10th Cir. 2009) (granting summary judgment for defendant on plaintiff's "regarded as" claim despite evidence that, while plaintiff was recovering from lung cancer surgery, defendant inquired specifically into her compliance with the company's drug and alcohol use, granted FMLA leave, suggested that plaintiff acquire disability insurance, and transferred plaintiff to multiple full-time positions with the same pay and benefits before ultimately terminating her; the record did not support inference plaintiff was regarded as unable to perform a broad class or range of jobs); *Faiola v. APCO Graphics, Inc.*, 629 F.3d 43, 48 (1st Cir. 2010) ("Faiola's alleged inability to attend the APCO sales conference does not constitute a substantial limitation as to work. It was not a restriction relating to the performance of a class of jobs or broad range of jobs, nor was it even a 'single, particular job' that she was restricted in performing."). *But see Justice v. Crown Cork & Seal Co.*, 527 F.3d 1080 (10th Cir. 2008) (employer apparently believed plaintiff's balance and vertigo problems disqualified him from working as electrician; its offer of only a janitor's job supported the inference that he was regarded as unable to perform broad range of jobs).

3. *Must There Be an Impairment?* Is ADA coverage dependent on the perceived disability at least meeting the statutory definition of impairment? The First Circuit in *Cook v. Rhode Island Dep't of Mental Health*, 10 F.3d 17, 25 (1st Cir. 1993), suggested that an individual with turquoise eyes would be covered under the "regarded as" provision if an employer regarded people with blue eyes as incapable of lifting heavy weights. Is this correct? Addressing allegations of discrimination on the basis of weight, both the Second and the Sixth Circuits have held that

plaintiffs claiming perceived disability must establish that the defendant perceived an impairment as defined by the statute. *See Andrews v. Ohio*, 104 F.3d 803 (6th Cir. 1997); *Francis v. City of Meriden*, 129 F.3d 281 (2d Cir. 1997). *See also Keeler v. Fla. Dep't of Health*, 324 F. App'x 850 (11th Cir. 2009) (former employee's failure to accommodate claim failed because she had not disclosed her disability to her employer. The fact that she cried and complained that her job was too stressful when asking for a transfer was not sufficient to put her employer on notice that she suffered from attention deficit disorder and obsessive compulsive disorder or to suggest that she was substantially limited in any major life activity).

4. *Genetic Information.* Reconsider ADA coverage for individuals with a genetic propensity for disease. The EEOC's Compliance Manual, §902: Definition of the Term "Disability," states:

> Covered entities that discriminate against individuals on the basis of . . . genetic information are regarding the individuals as having impairments that substantially limit a major life activity. Those individuals, therefore, are covered by the third part of the definition of "disability." See 136 Cong. Rec. H4623 (daily ed. July 12, 1990) (statement of Rep. Owens); *id.* at H4624-25 (statement of Rep. Edwards); *id.* at H4627 (statement of Rep. Waxman).

Recall, too, that GINA protects individuals from an employer's use of genetic information.

5. *Applying the "Regarded as" Test.* Lower courts have varied in their approaches to the ADA's "regarded as" provision. For example, *Stewart v. County of Brown*, 86 F.3d 107 (7th Cir. 1996), declined to find that a deputy sheriff was regarded as having a substantially limiting mental illness despite evidence that the deputy sheriff's employer referred to him as "excitable," ordered psychological evaluations for him, and told third parties that he considered him to be emotionally or psychologically imbalanced. How would you prove that an employer regarded an employee as psychologically disabled? *See also Cassimy v. Bd. of Educ.*, 461 F.3d 932, 937 (7th Cir. 2006) (while plaintiff told members of the board of education that he was being treated for depression and anxiety, and the board received medical records so indicating, the record "does not show . . . that the Board held exaggerated views about the seriousness of his illness"); *Tockes v. Air-Land Transp. Serv. Inc.*, 343 F.3d 895 (7th Cir. 2003) (plaintiff failed to establish regarded as status even though he was told by his manager, when he was fired, that it had been a "mistake" to hire someone who was "handicapped" and manager called him crippled and disabled; while plaintiff had established his employer regarded him as disabled, he did not establish the employer regarded him as disabled within the meaning of the ADA). On the other hand, in *Levelle v. Penske Logistics*, 197 F. App'x 729 (10th Cir. 2006), the court found a delivery driver with lifting restrictions to have been regarded as unable to perform a broad range of jobs where he was not considered for other positions and a clerk job was filled shortly after his discharge and he was not hired for other delivery positions.

6. *"Regarded as" Claims and Stereotyping.* When plaintiffs have prevailed in "regarded as" claims, it is usually when there is evidence that an employer is acting

on the basis of bias, prejudice, or stereotypes. For example, in *Josephs v. Pacific Bell*, 443 F.3d 1050 (9th Cir. 2006), the Ninth Circuit upheld a jury verdict in favor of a service technician. Years before being hired by PacBell, plaintiff had been found not guilty of attempted murder by reason of insanity and had been institutionalized. There was evidence PacBell employees had considered Josephs unemployable because he had spent time in a "mental ward" and might "go off" on a customer. Since PacBell considered Josephs unfit for any job with the company, the jury could find that it viewed him as having a mental disability that "substantially limited" him in the "major life activity" of working. And in *EEOC v. Heartway Corp.*, 466 F.3d 1156 (10th Cir. 2006), a nursing home cook with hepatitis C was regarded as disabled in the major life activity of working where an administrator's remarks indicated that he did not believe that she could work in any food-related position. *See also Wilson v. Phoenix Specialty Mfg. Co.*, 513 F.3d 378, 385 (4th Cir. 2008) (finding plaintiff regarded as disabled in part because employer had such a firm perception that he was disabled as to discount a specialist's medical opinion that he was capable of returning to work and in part because of plaintiff's testimony that senior management treated him "like [he] was a handicapped person" after his panic attack); *Eshelman v. Agere*, 554 F.3d 426 (3d Cir. 2009) (finding that the jury reasonably concluded that plaintiff's admission that her chemotherapy-related memory problems impaired her ability to drive led her employer to regard her as substantially limited in her ability to work and think where, following this admission, employer drastically reduced plaintiff's score on an objective skills evaluation test and ultimately terminated her based on the results of this test); *Finan v. Good Earth Tools, Inc.*, 565 F.3d 1076 (8th Cir. 2009) (evidence was sufficient to support a jury award for backpay and damages to an epileptic traveling sales representative, discharged because he was regarded as disabled when he was fit to drive and perform the essential functions of the job without accommodation). *See generally* Dale Larson, Comment, *Unconsciously Regarded as Disabled: Implicit Bias and the Regarded-As Prong of the Americans With Disabilities Act*, 56 UCLA L. REV. 451, 477 (2008) (noting that studies find substantial implicit bias against the disabled coupled with a great discrepancy between express and implicit bias).

However, animus, in the sense of bad faith or ill will, is not necessary for a violation. A good faith, or "innocent misperception," can still result in liability under the regarded as prong. *See Taylor v. Pathmark Stores, Inc.*, 177 F.3d 180 (3d Cir. 1999) ("the law in this circuit is that a 'regarded as' plaintiff can make out a case if the employer is innocently wrong about the extent of his or her impairment"); *see also Arline v. School Bd. of Nassau County*, 480 U.S. 273 (1987). *See generally* Michelle A. Travis, *Perceived Disabilities, Social Cognition, and "Innocent Mistakes,"* 55 VAND. L. REV. 481 (2002).

7. *"Regarded as" Plaintiffs and Reasonable Accommodation Under the Original ADA.* Is an employee who is "regarded as" disabled entitled to reasonable accommodation? In *D'Angelo v. Conagra Foods*, 422 F.3d 1220, 1235 (11th Cir. 2005), the Eleventh Circuit said yes, reasoning that "the plain language of the ADA yields no statutory basis for distinguishing among individuals who are disabled in the actual-impairment sense and those who are disabled only in the regarded-as sense; both are entitled to reasonable accommodations." The courts that went the other

way view the plain meaning as insufficient to overcome the oddity of accommodating individuals who do not require an accommodation. *Weber v. Strippirt, Inc.*, 186 F.3d 907 (8th Cir. 1999); *See generally* Michelle A. Travis, *Leveling the Playing Field or Stacking the Deck? The "Unfair Advantage" Critique of Perceived Disability Claims*, 78 N.C. L. REV. 901 (2000); Lawrence D. Rosenthal, *Reasonable Accommodations for Individuals Regarded as Having Disabilities Under the Americans with Disabilities Act? Why "No" Should Not Be the Answer*, 36 SETON HALL L. REV. 895 (2006).

NOTE ON "REGARDED AS" CLAIMS UNDER THE ADAAA

One of the most significant changes the ADAAA makes to the ADA is in the definition of "regarded as" claims. The amendments provide as follows:

(A) An individual meets the requirement of "being regarded as having such an impairment" if the individual establishes that he or she has been subjected to an action prohibited under this Act because of an actual or perceived physical or mental impairment whether or not the impairment limits or is perceived to limit a major life activity.

(B) Paragraph 1(C) [the regarded as prong] shall not apply to impairments that are transitory and minor. A transitory impairment is an impairment with an actual or expected duration of 6 months or less.

42 U.S.C. §12102(3)(A)-(B). The "regarded as" prong in many ways now provides the broadest protection under the statute. There need be no finding that the impairment, real or perceived, was regarded as substantially limiting a major life activity. Rather, all plaintiff need show is that the employer took a prohibited action because of the impairment, which in turn can be either real or perceived. Take, for example, Karen Sutton. She presumably has no actual disability under the ADA, originally or as amended. Under both, her corrective lenses may be taken into account in determining whether her impairment substantially limits one or more major life activities. But, corrected or not, she does have myopia, an impairment. And her prospective employer denied her employment because of her myopia. She thus would be an individual with a disability under the "regarded as" prong under the amended statute.

But would she be a "qualified individual with a disability"? The ADAAA also provides that an employer shall not use a qualification standard based on uncorrected vision unless that standard was job related for the position in question and consistent with business necessity. 42 U.S.C. §12112(b)(6)-(7). Under the amended ADA, Sutton's and Hinton's claims would have turned on this provision, that is, whether United's insistence that its pilots have uncorrected vision of at least 20/100 is job related for the position in question and consistent with business necessity.

Although the ADA amendments dramatically widen the class of protected persons by requiring only that the employer act on the basis of an impairment rather than a disability, the ADAAA simultaneously cut back on the protection accorded. The amendments provide that "regarded as" plaintiffs are not entitled to reasonable accommodation. Thus, such persons may not be discriminated against, but their impairments need not be accommodated. *See generally* Stephen F. Befort, *Let's Try This Again: The ADA Amendments Act of 2008 Attempts to Reinvigorate the "Regarded As" Prong of the Statutory Definition of Disability,* 2010 UTAH L. REV. 993 (ADAAA "expands the class of individuals protected against disability discrimination and employment decisions premised on stereotypical preconceptions. The 'regarded as' compromise, however, also comes with a series of lingering questions that have the potential to hinder the ultimate goals of the new legislation and perhaps even unleash a new judicial backlash)."

The Definition of Disability Under the ADAAA

As anticipated, the ADA Amendments Act is resulting in substantially easier access to "disability" status under the statute. Individuals who would have been unlikely to have been deemed disabled under the original ADA are finding a very different reception from the courts under the amended statute The overwhelming trend in the cases interpreting the ADAAA has been to find a disability.

For example, in *Hoffman v. Carefirst of Fort Wayne, Inc.*, 737 F. Supp. 2d 976 (N.D. Ind. 2010), a plaintiff with renal cancer in remission brought suit under the ADA alleging that his employer discriminated against him when it failed to accommodate his request for a work schedule and work location that would allow him to work a 40 hour work week. The employer argued that the plaintiff did not have a physical impairment that substantially limited any major life activity because plaintiff's cancer was in remission, he had returned to work without restrictions, he carried out his regular job duties of 40 hours a week as a service technician for a full year, and he did not miss any significant time off work. *Id.* at 986. Despite these contentions, the court still found that "under the clear language of the ADAAA" which provides that "an impairment that is episodic or in remission is a disability if it would substantially limit a major life activity when active" 42 U.S.C. §12102(4)(D), the plaintiff was indeed "disabled" under the ADA. *Id.* at 985-86. *See also Horgan v. Simmons*, 704 F.Supp.2d 814, 817 (N.D. Ill. 2010) (Even if plaintiff's HIV-positive status did not substantially limit a major life activity, allegations that company president asked plaintiff "how [he] could ever perform his job with his HIV positive condition and how he could continue to work with a terminal illness" and also allegedly told plaintiff that "a General Manager needs to be respected by the employees and have the ability to lead" and that he "did not know how [Plaintiff] could lead if the employees knew about his condition" were sufficient to support a "regarded as" claim); *Markham v. Salina Concrete Products, Inc.*, 2010 WL 5093769, 3 (D. Kan. Dec 8, 2010) ("While the allegations in the Complaint are brief, they do allege plausible discrimination in violation of the ADA: Plaintiff was told to lift concrete blocks; he could not lift the blocks because of an injury that caused pain when lifting heavy objects, so he was fired. At this stage in the litigation, those facts are enough to survive a motion to dismiss"); *Naber v. Dover Healthcare Associates, Inc.*, 2011 WL 657336, 14 (D. Del. February 24, 2011) (the court found that there was a question of fact as to whether plaintiff's "previously-diagnosed depression [was] the cause of her inability to sleep one or two nights a week and whether that sleeplessness [was] substantially limiting as compared to the average person in the general population"); *Feldman v. Law Enforcement Associates Corp.*, 2011 WL 891447, 7 (E.D.N.C. March 10, 2011) (citing *Hoffman*, the court found that plaintiff who suffered from episodic MS flare ups stated a question of fact as to whether he had a physical impairment that constitutes a disability; "the ADAAA 'make[s] it easier for a plaintiff with an episodic condition . . . to establish that he is an 'individual with a disability' ").

While it is indeed too early to make sweeping generalizations, the results from those cases litigated under the ADAAA suggest the courts have gotten Congress's message. Accordingly, disability status will be less likely to take center stage in the litigation, and instead focus will be on whether the individual with a disability is qualified for the job at issue, with or without reasonable accommodation.

C. The Meaning of "Qualified Individual with a Disability"

Page 533. Add after 42 U.S.C. §12112(a) after first extract:

The ADAAA amends this section by "striking 'with a disability because of the disability of such individual' and inserting 'on the basis of disability.' "

Page 533. Add after cite to 42 U.S.C. §12111(8) after second extract:

See Jakubowski v. Christ Hosp., Inc., 627 F.3d 195, 201-202 (6th Cir. 2010) (while staff education about his Asperger's condition might have improved the ability of plaintiff, a medical resident, to communicate with professional colleagues, he did not propose an accommodation that would have improved his patient communications skills and thus rendered him otherwise qualified); *Kinneary v. City of New York*, 601 F.3d 151 (2d Cir. 2010) (plaintiff was not qualified when, despite his employer providing a reasonable accommodation to deal with his shy bladder syndrome which prevented his participation in random drug screenings, he failed to take advantage of the opportunity and thus lost his captain's license).

1. Essential Job Functions

Page 536. Add at end of Note 1, *The Employer's Judgment:*

Gratzl v. Office of the Chief Judges of the 12th, 18th, 19th & 22nd Judicial Circuits, 601 F.3d 674, 679-80 (7th Cir. 2010) (employer considered in-court reporting an essential function of the "Official Court Reporter" job and plaintiff cited no evidence to that could effectively rebut employer's claim; "We presume that an employer's understanding of the essential functions of the job is correct, unless the plaintiff offers sufficient evidence to the contrary"). In other cases, what is important is not necessarily what the employer claims to be an essential function but rather whether the employer treats a function as essential. *See Carmona v. Sw. Airlines Co.*, 604 F.3d 848 (5th Cir. 2010) ("Even if we assume that attendance was an essential function of Carmona's job, Southwest's own measure of whether or not a flight attendant's attendance was adequate was its attendance policy, which was extremely lenient." Therefore, notwithstanding plaintiff's poor attendance as a result of psoriatic arthritis, he was able to perform the essential functions of his job); Miller v. Illinois Dept. of Transp. 2011 WL 1756119 (7th Cir. May 10, 2011) (maintainer on a bridge crew with fear of heights might nevertheless be able to perform essential functions of his job when it was normal for individual members of bridge crew to substitute and reassign tasks among themselves according to individual preferences).

Page 537.   Add at end of Note 2, *Burden of Proof*:

Cf. Bates v. UPS, 511 F.3d 974 (9th Cir. 2007) (en banc) ("Although the plaintiff bears the ultimate burden of persuading the fact finder that he can perform the job's essential functions, we agree with the Eighth Circuit's approach that 'an employer who disputes the plaintiff's claim that he can perform the essential functions must put forth evidence establishing those functions.'") (quoting a pre-*Rehrs* case, *EEOC v. Wal-Mart*, 477 F.3d 561, 568 (8th Cir. 2007)).

Page 537.   Add before *Cf. Turner* in Note 3, *Defining the Term*:

See also Richardson v. Friendly Ice Cream Corp., 594 F.3d 69, 78 (1st Cir. 2010) (where an assistant manager's disability prevented her from performing a substantial number of the manual tasks that were part of the daily operations of the restaurant and where there were a limited number of employees among whom those tasks could be distributed, the assistant manager was not able to fulfill one of her fundamental job duties); *Dargis v. Sheahan*, 526 F.3d 981 (7th Cir. 2008) (corrections officer was not qualified because of his inability to rotate through positions requiring inmate contact, despite claim that some co-workers were assigned to no-contact positions).

Page 537.   Add before *Mulloy* cite in Note 4, *Attendance as an Essential Job Function*:

Vandenbroek v. PSEG Power Conn. LLC, 356 F. App'x 457, 460 (2d Cir. 2009) (an alcoholic whose resultant absenteeism caused his discharge was not within the statute's protection, even if the discharge could have been viewed as caused by his disability, since he was not otherwise qualified; reliable attendance at scheduled shifts was an essential function of a boiler utility operator at the power plant); *Theilig v. United Tech Corp.* 2011 WL 1054027 (2d Cir. March 24, 2011) (plaintiff's accommodation request of working at home, unsupervised, with no contact with any co-workers, and in particular, his two supervisors, based on psychiatrist's evaluation that plaintiff posed a risk of harm to himself and others, was unreasonable as a matter of law);

Page 538. Add at end of Note 5, *Essential Job Functions and the Duty of Reasonable Accommodation*:

Some courts have stressed that there is no ADA duty of accommodation (as opposed to the prohibition of discrimination) when the employer has a policy of excusing workers from all or some of their duties when they are temporarily incapacitated. In such cases, failure to treat a disabled worker equally is impermissible. *See Duello v. Buchanan County Bd. of Supervisors*, 628 F.3d 968, 974 (8th Cir. 2010) (holding that "an employer may run afoul of the ADA by terminating a "regarded as" disabled employee, instead of providing him with a routine benefit" but finding that the plaintiff, who was unable to drive and work around machinery after a seizure, failed to adduce evidence that the employer regularly excused other workers from those tasks).

Page 538. Add a new Note 6:

6. *Essential Even if Infrequent.* While the frequency with which a job function is performed may be relevant to whether it is "essential," even rarely performed functions may be essential. In *Hennagir v. Utah Dep't of Corr.*, 587 F.3d 1255 (10th Cir. 2009), the court held that a physician's assistant who could not perform activities necessary for a prison's emergency-response training program was unable to perform an essential job function. Because the PAs had daily contact with inmates, the training was an essential, if rarely performed, function.

2. The Duty of Reasonable Accommodation

Page 539. Add at end of first full paragraph:

See also DeRosa v. Nat'l Envelope Corp., 595 F.3d 99 (2d Cir. 2010) (employee's statements on his SSDI application, that he did not speak on the phone or use the computer due to pain, related to his social interactions, not his capability to perform the essential functions of his job as a customer service representative, and therefore did not judicially estop his reasonable accommodation claim; employee stated that the work effect of his disabilities was that he "could no longer commute" to work, and did not indicate an inability, or an unwillingness, to work from home despite some pain);.*Bisker v. GGS Info. Servs.*, 342 F. App'x 791, 795 (3d Cir. 2009) ("the proper focus of the judicial estoppel analysis is not on [plaintiff's] general contention that she is unable to work, but rather on the specific factual representations she made in support of that contention. . . . [T]he picture [plaintiff] painted of her condition in her SSDI submissions is not any different from the one she painted in her accommodation request"). *But see Butler v. Round Lake Police Dep't*, 585 F.3d 1020 (7th Cir. 2009) (a police officer's testimony at disability pension hearing that he was unable to perform the essential functions of his position judicially estopped his subsequent ADA claim).

Page 548.   Add a new Note 4 after first paragraph of Note 3, *Reasonable Accommodation as Special Treatment*:

4. *Benefits to the Non-disabled?* The special treatment critique of the duty of reasonable accommodation often, as in *Barnett*, focuses on the costs that accommodation imposes on other workers. Left out of the equation, however, are the benefits that the ADA creates for non-disabled co-workers. *See generally* Michelle A. Travis, *Lashing Back at the ADA Backlash: How the Americans With Disabilities Act Benefits Americans Without Disabilities*, 76 TENN. L. REV. 311 (2009) (exploring the variety of ways in which the ADA aligns the interests of workers with and without disabilities, rather than pitting them against each other in a zero-sum game, thereby giving all workers a stake in the ADA's future); Elizabeth F. Emens, *Integrating Accommodation*, 156 U. PA. L. REV. 839, 921 (2008) (while courts have recognized that accommodations may create third-party costs, they have overlooked the potential for third-party benefits; recognition of such benefits "can lead to a form of contact between accommodations and coworkers that improves attitudes toward disability and the ADA.") *cf.*, Cass R. Sunstein, Response, *Caste and Disability: The Moral Foundations of the ADA*, 156 U. PA. L. REV. PENNUMBRA 165, 21 (2008), http://www.pennumbra.com/responses/ 10-2008/Sunstein.pdf (endorsing Emens's emphasis on reasonable accommodations that benefit a wide variety of individuals, disabled and able-bodied alike, as a means of furthering the integrationist objectives of the ADA); *but see* Martha Minow, Response, *Accommodating Integration* 156 U. PA. L. REV. PENNUMBRA 165 (2008), http://www.pennumbra. com/responses/10-2008/Minow.pdf (critiquing Emens's focus on the individual-based model of disability accommodation and advocating "conceptualizing inclusive human settings in ways that benefit everyone" as preferential method for the advancement and integration of persons with disabilities).

Page 551.   Add at end of first paragraph of Note 1, *Special Treatment and Affirmative Action*:

To begin with, it seems clear that whatever the reassignment obligations of an employer might be to a disabled employee, they do not require creating a new job. *See Toronka v. Cont'l Airlines, Inc.*, 2011 U.S. App. LEXIS 2883, 17-18 (5th Cir. Feb.

14, 2011) ("For reassignment to be a reasonable accommodation, a position 'must first exist and be vacant.' Therefore, if [plaintiff] was not qualified for any of the existing, vacant positions at Continental, then Continental did all it could. . . . ").

Page 552.   Add at end of carryover Note 2:

See also Nicole B. Porter, *Reasonable Burdens: Resolving the Conflict Between Disabled Employees and Their Coworkers*, 34 FLA. ST. U. L. REV. 313 (2007) (proposing amending the ADA so that most accommodations would be reasonable even if they affect other employees, unless the accommodation results in the termination of another employee); Nicholas A. Dorsey, Note, *Mandatory Reassignment Under the ADA: The Circuit Split and Need for a Socio-Political Understanding of Disability* 94 CORNELL L. REV. 443 (2009); Carrie L. Flores, *A Disability Is Not a Trump Card: The Americans With Disabilities Act Does Not Entitle Disabled Employees to Automatic Reassignment*, 43 VAL. U. L. REV. 195 (2008); Stacey M. Hickox, *Transfer as an Accommodation: Standards from Discrimination Cases and Theory*, 62 ARK. L. REV. 195 (2009).

Page 552.   Insert new note 3

3. *When Is a Position Vacant?* Whatever the parameters of the duty of reasonable accommodation when an employer has a vacant position, any such obligation depends on the position in fact being available. The courts have tended to view positions as not vacant for purposes of accommodation if any other worker might have a claim on them. *E.g., Duvall v. Georgia-Pacific Consumer Prods., L.P.*, 607 F.3d 1255, 1262 (10th Cir. 2010) ("we hold that a position is 'vacant' with respect to a disabled employee for the purposes of the ADA if it would be available for a similarly-situated non-disabled employee"; thus, positions filled by "temporary" workers were not vacant within the meaning of the ADA where other employees could not seek them); *McFadden v. Ballard Spahr Andrews & Ingersoll, LLP*, 611 F.3d 1 (D.C. Cir. 2010) (failure to reassign plaintiff to a receptionist position was not violation of the duty to accommodate even though the position was temporarily open since it was occupied by a long-term permanent receptionist on disability leave and there was no reason to believe the employer did not expect her to return).

Page 556.   Add at the first paragraph in Note 3, Forms of Reasonable Accommodation:

See, e.g,. Ekstrand v. Sch. Dist. of Somerset, 583 F.3d 972 (7th Cir. 2009) (transfer of an elementary school teacher with seasonal affective disorder to a classroom with natural light was a reasonable accommodation that could have been provided with little hardship).

Page 556.   Add new Note 4A:

4A. *Conflicting Duties?* Suppose accommodating one disabled worker causes problems for another. What about the unique situation where an accommodation for one disabled employee triggers a disability of another? *See* Steven Greenhouse, *When Treating One Worker's Allergy Sets Off Another's*, NY TIMES, May 10, 2010, A-10, recounting how a service dog used by one employee to warn of the presence of paprika, to which she had a rare and potentially fatal allergy, triggered another employee's asthma attack as the result of an allergic reaction. "Legal experts say her case raises tough questions about how to balance the sometimes clashing interests of co-workers with disabilities and how far employers need to go to make reasonable accommodations for workers under the Americans with Disabilities Act." How would you resolve this conflict? Is there a way to reach an equitable result in this case?

Page 560.   Delete Note 1; replace with:

1. *Facially Discriminatory?* The Ninth Circuit holds that taking action based on misconduct that is a product of the underlying disability is the same as acting on the basis of the disability itself. Remember the Seventh Circuit's treatment of symptoms of a disability in *Vande Zande,* reproduced at page 552, and the Supreme Court's treatment of the same issue in *Arline,* discussed in this Supplement at p. 164. Is the Ninth Circuit correct in viewing misconduct as comparable to the contagiousness in *Arline* or the pressure ulcers in *Vande Zande?* In cases with similar facts, other circuits have reached a different result from the Ninth. For example, in *Macy v. Hopkins County*, 484 F.3d 357 (6th Cir. 2007), the court upheld summary judgment for the employer who fired a teacher for making threats and inappropriate remarks, even though the conduct was a product of a head injury: "this court has repeatedly stated that an employer may legitimately fire an employee for conduct, even conduct that occurs as a result of a disability, if that conduct disqualifies the employee from his or her job." *See also Budde v. Kane County Forest Pres.*, 597 F.3d 860, 862 (7th Cir. 2010) (rejecting a police chief's ADA claim for being fired after having his license suspended for causing an accident by driving while intoxicated, the court held that "[v]iolation of a workplace rule, even if it is caused by a disability [here alcoholism], is no defense to discipline up to and including termination."); *Sista v. CDC Ixis North America, Inc.*, 445 F. 3d 161 (2d Cir. 2006) (making threats is a legitimate, nondiscriminatory reason for termination, even if the threats were caused by disability). Which is the better view of the statute? *Cf. McNary v. Schreiber Foods, Inc.*, 535 F.3d 765 (8th Cir. 2008) (affirming grant of summary judgment for the defendant because its proffered explanation for plaintiff's termination—his violation of a workplace policy prohibiting sleeping while at work—constituted a legitimate nondiscriminatory reason and was not shown to be pretextual, even though plaintiff contended he was only resting his eyes due to eye pain caused by Graves disease); *Dovenmuehler v. St. Cloud Hosp.*, 509

F.3d 435 (8th Cir. 2007) (there was no duty to accommodate a nurse's state-imposed work restrictions when those restrictions followed from drug-related misconduct, not from her addictionperse).

Page 561.   Add a new Note 4:

4. *Failure of Accommodation and Constructive Discharge.* We explore constructive discharge in Chapter 7. A variation on this theme occurs when an employer fails to provide a required accommodation, resulting in the employee resigning her position. While the denial of some accommodations may not satisfy the requirements for a constructive discharge, other denials will leave the employee no reasonable choice. *See Talley v. Family Dollar Stores of Ohio, Inc.*, 542 F.3d 1099 (6th Cir. 2008) (failure to accommodate plaintiff's osteoarthritis by allowing her to sit while working could constitute a constructive discharge); *cf., Benaugh v. Ohio Civil Rights Comm'n*, 278 F. App'x 501 (6th Cir. 2008) (finding genuine issue of fact on plaintiff's constructive discharge claim brought under the Rehabilitation Act where defendant repeatedly failed to accommodate plaintiff's asthma and sarcoidosis by refusing to provide her with an office with a separate climate control unit); *Lafata v. Church of Christ Home for the Aged*, 325 F. App'x 416 (6th Cir. 2009) (finding genuine issue of material fact as to whether the employer participated in good faith in the mandatory interactive process under the ADA in order to accommodate the employee's disability when employer offered employee only one position after her return from FMLA leave, which she could not perform due to previous injury).

Page 561.   Add at end of first paragraph in *Note on Accommodations Necessary to Enjoy Benefits and Privileges of Employment*:

See EEOC v. UPS Supply Chain Solutions, 620 F.3d 1103, 1111-12 (9th Cir. 2010) (fact question as to whether employer-provided agendas, contemporaneous notes, and written summaries of oral communications were sufficient to enable a hearing-impaired person reading those documents to enjoy the same benefits and privileges of attending and participating in the weekly meetings as other employees).

Page 562.   Add before *Wood* cite in first full paragraph:

Colwell v. Rite Aid Corp., 602 F.3d 495, 505-06 (3d Cir. 2010) ("under certain circumstances the ADA can obligate an employer to accommodate an employee's disability-related difficulties in getting to work, if reasonable;" here, by accommodating a shift change when the employee's vision disability prevents her from driving to work at night);

Page 563.   Add before *Lucas* cite in first full paragraph:

McBride v. BIC Consumer Prods. Mfg. Co., 583 F.3d 92, 97 (2d Cir. 2009) (where "plaintiff provided no evidence that there existed any potential accommodation that would have allowed her to continue to work," failure to engage in interactive process not a violation);

Page 563.   Add after *Hennenfent* cite at the end of the last paragraph:

Likewise, an employee who fails to inform the employer that an accommodation is needed may forfeit his right to that accommodation. See *Kobus v. College of St. Scholastica, Inc.*, 608 F.3d 1034 (8th Cir. 2010) (employee who failed to reveal that he was under treatment for depression and whose limitations were not apparent at work had no claim for failure to accommodate when he was fired for excessive absenteeism which resulted from the depression).

3.   *Undue Hardship*

Page 565.   Add in fifth paragraph after *Kiel* citation:

But see Jeannette Cox, *Disability Stigma and Intraclass Discrimination*, 62 FLA. L. REV. 429, 432-33 (2010) ("although many courts have wholly or partially abandoned the requirement that ADA plaintiffs identify a comparator outside the ADA's protected class, many courts continue to limit intraclass disability discrimination claims by requiring plaintiffs to demonstrate that their disabilities are more biologically severe than the disabilities of persons who received more favorable treatment.").

D.   *Discriminatory Qualification Standards*

Page 573.   Add at end of Note 1, *Individual Medical Inquiry*:

Nor did the *Echazabel* Court indicate whether the plaintiff or defendant had the burden of proof as to whether an employee posed a direct threat. Circuits have been split on this issue. *See Branham v. Snow*, 392 F.3d 896, 906 n.5 (7th Cir. 2004) (recognizing a split in the circuits). *See generally* Rene L. Duncan, Note, *The "Direct Threat" Defense Under the ADA: Posing a Threat to the Protection of Disabled Employees*, 73 MO. L. REV. 1303 (2008) (arguing that the legislative history of the ADA indicates that the employer has the burden of proof on this defense).

2. Job Related and Consistent with Business Necessity

Page 580. In Note 3, *Job Related to the Position in Question and Consistent with Business Necessity*, delete Morton citation; replace with:

In *Bates v. UPS*, 511 F.3d 974 (9th Cir. 2007) (en banc), the court rejected its prior adoption of BFOQ analysis for safety standards under the ADA:

> To show "job-relatedness," an employer must demonstrate that the qualification standard fairly and accurately measures the individual's actual ability to perform the essential functions of the job. When every person excluded by the qualification standard is a member of a protected class — that is, disabled persons — an employer must demonstrate a predictive or significant correlation between the qualification and performance of the job's essential functions.
>
> To show that the disputed qualification standard is "consistent with business necessity" the employer must show that it "substantially promote[s]" the business's needs. "The 'business necessity' standard is quite high, and is not to be confused with mere expediency." For a safety-based qualification standard, "[i]n evaluating whether the risks addressed by . . . [the] qualification standard constitute a business necessity, the court should take into account the magnitude of possible harm as well as the probability of occurrence."
>
> Finally, to show that "performance cannot be accomplished by reasonable accommodation," the employer must demonstrate either that no reasonable accommodation currently available would cure the performance deficiency or that such reasonable accommodation poses an "undue hardship" on the employer.

Id. at 996 (citations and footnotes omitted). The court then turned to the qualification standard allocation of burdens of proof, which it viewed as parallel to those for the direct threat defense. It explained:

> Because UPS has linked hearing with safe driving, UPS bears the burden to prove that nexus as part of its defense to use of the hearing qualification standard. The employees, however, bear the ultimate burden to show that they are qualified to perform the essential function of safely driving a package car. . . .
>
> By requiring UPS to justify the hearing test under the business necessity defense, but also requiring plaintiffs to show that they can perform the essential functions of the job, we are not saying, nor does the ADA require, that employers must hire employees who cannot safely perform the job, particularly where safety itself is an essential function. Nor are we saying that an employer can never impose a safety standard that exceeds minimum requirements imposed by law. However, when an employer asserts a blanket safety-based qualification standard — beyond the essential job function — that is not mandated by law and that qualification standard screens out or tends to screen out an individual with a disability, the employer — not the employee — bears the burden of showing that the higher qualification standard is job-related and consistent with business necessity, and that performance cannot be achieved through reasonable accommodation.

6. Disability Discrimination

Id. at 992. *But see Allmond v. Akal Sec. Inc.*, 558 F.3d 1312 (11th Cir. 2009) (hearing aid ban for federal marshals was job related and consistent with business necessity when it was developed after a detailed analysis of the security officer position to identify the essential functions of the job and the medical qualifications necessary to perform it given the tremendous harm that could result if a security officer could not perform the essential hearing functions of his job at a given moment).

3. Disparate Impact

Page 581. Add at the end of the page:

The burden of proof required under the ADA for disparate impact claims will often make bringing these claims very difficult. For example, in *Lopez v. Pacific Maritime Ass'n*, 636 F.3d 1197 (9th Cir. 2011), the Ninth Circuit found that the plaintiff must demonstrate some statistically significant evidence in support of his claim that the employer's "one-strike" rule, permanently eliminating from consideration for employment any applicant who tested positive for drug or alcohol use during pre-employment screening process, discriminated against recovering addicts. In making the determination, the court recognized the plaintiff's concerns that the standard placed an unfair burden on him because "he has no way to know how many recovering or recovered drug addicts Defendant has disqualified. Neither can he determine the proportion of recovering or recovered drug addicts in the relevant labor market because, he argues, state law prevents him from inquiring into a person's history of drug abuse." *Id.* at 1201. The court noted the challenges involved for the plaintiff in bringing a disparate impact claim in these cases, but nevertheless found that statistical evidence was required "under both logic and precedent." *Id.*

E. Special Problems of Disability Discrimination

1. Drug or Alcohol users

Page 582. Add at end of the page:

See also Mauerhan v. Wagner Corp., 2011 WL 1467571, *6 (10th Cir. April 19, 2011) (employee was not qualified for the safe harbor after a 30-day inpatient drug rehabilitation program where an addiction specialist testified that approximately three months of treatment would be necessary for an addict like plaintiff to reach a "threshold of significant improvement" in his addiction).

Special issues may also arise in the context of drug and alcohol abuse as to whether an individual was "disabled" within the meaning of the ADA. *See Ames v. Home Depot U.S.A., Inc.*, 629 F.3d 665 (11th Cir. 2011) (plaintiff could not show that her alcoholism was a disability because she presented no evidence that her alcohol problem substantially limited her activities at home and she testified that her alcohol problem did not affect her work performance). After the ADAAA Act, however, this problem should rarely arise.

2. Medical Examinations and Inquiries

a. Pre-employment Medical Examinations and Inquiries

Page 583. Add at end of first full paragraph:

However, the Genetic Information Non-Discrimination Act of 2008, 42 U.S.C. §2000ff, does restrict the scope of such post-offer medical inquiries and examinations. GINA, with very limited exceptions, prohibits employers from requiring disclosure of genetic information, including family medical history. Nor may employers acquire genetic information in determining continuing fitness for duty.

b. Medical Examinations and Inquiries of Current Employees

Page 584. Add after "permitted" in second line:

but see Indergard v. Georgia-Pacific Corp., 582 F.3d 1049 (9th Cir. 2009) ("physical capacity evaluation" of paper mill employee with knee injuries who sought to return to work after disability leave was medical examination under ADA; it included range of motion, muscle strength, and treadmill tests with recorded heart rate and breathing data and the evaluation results were submitted to physician; the broad range of tests allowed discovery of impairments beyond physical agility);

Page 584, change "Ninth and Tenth Circuits" in last full paragraph to "Eighth, Ninth, Tenth, and Eleventh Circuits," and add before *Fredenburg* cite:

Harrison v. Benchmark Elecs. Huntsville, Inc., 593 F.3d 1206, 1214 (11th Cir. 2010) ("we now explicitly recognize that a plaintiff has a private right of action [for an improper medical inquiry] irrespective of his disability status"); *Cossette v. Minn. Power & Light*, 188 F.3d 964, 969 (8th Cir. 1999) ("we are persuaded by the holdings of the Ninth and Tenth Circuits that a plaintiff need not be disabled to state a claim for the unauthorized gathering or disclosure of confidential medical information.").

Page 584. Delete subsection b; replace with

b. Medical Examinations and Inquiries

Employers are prohibited from requiring medical examinations and inquiries of current employees, unless such examination or inquiry is job related and consistent with a business necessity. *See Denman v. Davey Tree Expert Co.*, 266 F. App'x 377 (6th Cir. 2007) (permissible for an employer to request that plaintiff submit to an independent medical examination when the employee requested an accommodation and the employer had a reasonable belief that his performance as foreman might have been impaired by his medical condition); *Ward v. Merck & Co., Inc.*, 226 F. App'x 131 (3d Cir. 2007) (finding employer request that employee complete a fitness-for-duty evaluation was job related and consistent with business necessity after the employee's work- place conduct and performance deteriorated as a result of his anxiety disorder); *Coffman v. Indianapolis Fire Dep't*, 578 F.3d 559 (7th Cir. 2009) (referral of plaintiff for fitness for duty examination was permissible as job-related and consistent with business necessity when the department had recently had two deaths by suicide and there were multiple reports that employee seemed withdrawn and uncommunicative with symptoms of depression, and her supervisors showed genuine concern that her behavior was uncharacteristic and adversely impacting her job performance); *Brownfield v. City of Yakima*, 612 F.3d 1140, 1146 (9th Cir. 2010) ("the business necessity standard may be met even before an employee's work performance declines if the employer is faced with significant evidence that could cause a reasonable person to inquire as to whether an employee is still capable of performing his job. An employee's behavior cannot be merely annoying or inefficient to justify an examination; rather, there must be genuine reason to doubt whether that employee can perform job-related functions."); *Wisbey v. City of Lincoln*, 612 F.3d 667, 674 *abrogated on other grounds* (8th Cir. 2010) (the nature of position in question supported finding a fitness-for-duty to be a business necessity: "As [an emergency] dispatcher, [plaintiff] played an essential role in emergency functions and her position required her to be present to answer calls and alert at all times. In this position, people's lives are often at risk and a dispatcher's ability to focus and concentrate at all times is essential to adequate job performance; *Thomas v. Corwin*, 483 F.3d 516 (8th Cir. 2007) (employer's request that employee submit to fitness for duty examination was job-related and consistent with business necessity when employer had reason to doubt employee's ability to perform duties due to stress and anxiety); *Gajda v. Manhattan & Bronx Surface Transit Operating Auth.*, 396 F.3d 187, 189 (2d Cir. 2005) (requiring an employee to disclose the results of HIV tests was permissible in order for the employer to determine whether plaintiff could safely perform his duties in light of representations by plaintiff and his doctor that he was unable to perform his job and needed "intermittent leave at undetermined times for lifetime"). *But see Brown v. City of Long Branch*, 380 F. App'x 235 (3d Cir. 2010) (discrimination claim challenging discharge of police office after fitness-for-duty examination found that he was danger to himself and others was viable where plaintiff alleged that he previously had been permitted to serve in unarmed desk duty); *Duncan v. Fleetwood Motor Homes of Ind.*, 518 F.3d 486 (7th Cir. 2008) (overturning dismissal of plaintiff's ADA claim even though he failed a functional capacity evaluation to gauge his fitness for duty after a back injury; the evaluation was based on a job description that did not match the duties of the actual position and entailed far greater heavier lifting than the job in fact demanded *See* Enforcement Guidance on Disability-Related Inquiries and Medical

Examinations of Employees under the Americans with Disabilities Act No. 915.002 (July 26, 2000), ("Enforcement Guidance on Employees.").

The ADA permits *voluntary* medical exams and inquiries of current employees as part of an employee health program. HIPAA and the Patient Protection and Affordability Act encourage "wellness" programs, permitting employers to offer incentives to employees to complete health risk assessments or to demonstrate healthy behaviors. At what point, however, does an incentive become great enough to render an employee's participation in the wellness program involuntary? In an informal guidance, the EEOC has stated that requiring employees to participate in a health risk assessment as a condition for participating in an employer's health insurance plan is not voluntary within the meaning of the ADA. Letter from *EEOC Office of Legal Counsel staff members to respond to a request for public comment from a federal agency or department* (Aug. 10, 2009) (available at http://www.eeoc.gov/eeoc/foia/letters/2009/ada_health_risk_assessment.html).

Nor, to date, has the EEOC been willing to endorse HIPAA or the PPAA's incentive structure as necessarily consistent with the ADA's "voluntariness" requirement. Presently, the EEOC is examining what level of financial inducement, if any, to participate in a wellness program would be permissible under the ADA, but at some point, a financial inducement would render the employee's participation "involuntary" and thus impermissible under the ADA.

Recently, however, a district court held that the ADA was not violated by an employer's $20 bi-weekly penalty on employees who refused to complete a health risk assessment and undergo a biometric screening did not violate the ADA. Rather than determining whether the program was "voluntary," the court instead determined that the prohibition on involuntary medical exams and inquiries does not apply to a wellness program offered by an employer health plan where the program meets the ADA's safe harbor for bona fide benefit plans. *Seff v. Broward County*, 2011 U.S. Dist. LEXIS 44807 (S.D. Fla. April 11, 2011). It found the program was a term of the health care plan and the program was based on underwriting, classifying, and administering risks, thus bringing it within the safe harbor.

Wellness programs also implicate GINA. GINA specifically permits an employer to request genetic information as part of a wellness program if the employee provides prior, knowing, *voluntary* and written authorization. 29 C.F.R. §1635.8(b)(2). In its final regulations interpreting GINA, the EEOC provided that if a financial inducement is offered to participate in a wellness program, the employer must make clear that the inducement will be made available whether or not the participant answers questions concerning genetic information. And the EEOC makes it clear that compliance with GINA does not necessarily satisfy the ADA.

Page 585. Add at end of first paragraph of Retaliation and Interference:

While the other antidiscrimination statutes do not explicitly reach third party retaliation claims, they have recently been held actionable under Title VII. See *Thompson v. North American Stainless, LP*, 131 S. Ct. 863 (2011), reproduced at p. 149 of this Supplement.

5. Protected Relationships

Page 587. Add in second full paragraph after discussion of *Ennis*:

In contrast, in *Dewitt v. Proctor Hosp.*, 517 F.3d 944 (7th Cir. 2008), a claim of discrimination on account of the plaintiff's association with her disabled husband was allowed to proceed where there was evidence that her discharge was an effort to avoid the high costs of her husband's cancer treatment; her supervisor's comments about "creative" cost-cutting and her suggestion that less expensive hospice care be considered, coupled with plaintiff's discharge shortly after review of medical claims, allowed inference that employer was concerned that husband might require treatment indefinitely. In *Dewitt*, Judge Posner concurred, suggesting, however, that, if the employer would have discriminated against anyone who ran up such high medical bills, there would have been no discrimination on the basis of disability. What do you think of that argument? *See also Trujillo v. PacifiCorp*, 524 F.3d 1149 (10th Cir. 2008) (married employees raised factual issue as to whether the alleged reason for their discharges was a pretext for avoiding the high costs of their son's medical expenses).

6. Health and Disability Insurance

Page 591. Add a new Note 2A:

2A. *Worker's Compensation.* An employer is also required to provide equal access to worker's compensation benefits. See *Baker v. Windsor Republic Doors,* 2011 WL 805768, 8 (6th Cir. May 8, 2011) ("to continue to condition employment of a qualified individual with a pacemaker on the relinquishment of that employee's workers' compensation rights is repugnant to the ideals expressed in the broad, remedial provisions of the ADA").

Page 591. Add new Notes 4 and 5:

4. *Standing.* Beyond the complicated question of whether particular insurance schemes are discriminatory, there have been legal impediments to challenging particular policies. One recurrent problem is the standing of former employees to sue. For example, in *McKnight v. GMC*, 550 F.3d 519 (6th Cir. 2008), *cert. denied,* 129 S. Ct. 2862 (2009), disabled former employees challenged their prior employer's offsetting of pension benefits by the amounts they received for social security disability. The court held that the plaintiffs were not qualified individuals with a disability under Title I of the ADA and therefore had no standing to sue for pension benefits, although it also indicated that their challenge would fail on the merits.

5. In a March 6, 2009, opinion letter, the EEOC stated that an employer's requirement that all employees take a health risk assessment that includes

disability-related inquiries and medical examinations as a prerequisite for obtaining health insurance coverage likely violates the ADA. Peggy R. Mastroianni, EEOC Informal Opinion Letter, *ADA: Disability-Related Inquiries and Medical Examinations; Health Risk Assessment*, http://www.eeoc.gov/foia/letters/2009/ada_disability_medexam_healthrisk.html. The letter concerned a county employer's requirement that its employees participate in a clinical health risk assessment in order to be eligible for its healthcare plan. The assessment included answering a short questionnaire, a blood pressure test, and a blood analysis. Individual results were kept confidential.

In its letter, the EEOC warned that such assessments do not appear to be job related and consistent with business necessity, and do not fall within the limited exceptions for disability-related inquiries — such as those following a request for accommodation or where periodic exams are required for public safety purposes. In addition, the program in question was not voluntary, and thus, not part of a voluntary wellness program.

7 Procedures for Enforcing Antidiscrimination Laws

B. The Administrative Phase: Charge Filing

Page 596. Add in eighth line after "private plaintiff":

See EEOC v. Philip Servs. Corp., 635 F.3d 164 (5th Cir. 2011) (refusing to enforce an oral conciliation agreement the EEOC reached with the defendant because of the statutory limitations on disclosure the consequent risk "less open communication necessary to reach voluntary settlements during the conciliation process.").

Page 597. Delete all text from 597 through the end of page 616, including the principal *Ledbetter* case; replace with the following:

2. Filing a Timely Charge

Every private Title VII suit and ADEA suit must begin with a charge under oath filed with the Equal Employment Opportunity Commission. §706(b), 42 U.S.C. §20003-5(b).

a. What Constitutes a Charge?

The statutes, however, do not define what constitutes a "charge"; EEOC regulations attempt to fill that gap, *see* 29 C.F.R. §1601.12(b) (2008), but in its most detailed encounter with the question, the Supreme Court declared in *Federal Express Corp. v. Holowecki* that those regulations "fall short of a comprehensive definition." 552 U.S. 389, 395 (2008). According to the Court, the regulations define a charge as "a statement filed with the Commission" alleging discrimination; the pertinent regulation "identifies five pieces of information a "charge should contain," *id.* at 396, but the Court further noted that the regulations seem to make these elements only hortatory since a charge is "sufficient" if it is "in writing and . . . name[s] the prospective respondent and . . . generally allege[s] the discriminatory act[s]." *Id.* at 396.

Since the regulations apparently allow a charge to be very informal, issues often arise as to whether a particular document is a charge. In fact, the *Holowecki* Court reported that the EEOC receives some 175,000 "inquiries" each year, but only 76,000 of these are docketed as charges. *Id.* at 401. It is the docketing by the agency that triggers the EEOC's notification to the employer and its subsequent investigation. If, however, some of the other 100,000 inquiries are, in the eyes of the law, "charges," then the employee had done whatever he or she is required to do as a condition of suit, even though no agency action follows. This was the problem the Court confronted in *Holowecki*, where the plaintiff had filled out an EEOC Intake Questionnaire and submitted an affidavit to the Commission but the EEOC never docketed the charge and so never notified the defendant or began processing the dispute.

Although much of *Holowecki* is an exercise in administrative law, the resulting rule is clear: the charge must have the minimal information required by the regulations, "an allegation and the name of the charged party," and "it must be reasonably construed as a request for the agency to take remedial action to protect the employee's rights or otherwise settle a dispute between the employer and the employee." *Id.* at 402. It is not enough for the employee to subjectively intend to activate the agency's charge-processing machinery; rather, the question is whether it objectively appears that such an intent exists. *Id.* In the case before it, the Court found that an Intake Questionnaire is insufficient by itself, but that the plaintiff's affidavit expressed a request that the agency take action to protect her rights. The fact that the defendant was not notified, and that the statutory scheme of EEOC investigation was frustrated by the Commission's failure to proceed, was irrelevant to the plaintiff's rights (although the Court suggested that the EEOC reconsider its procedures to avoid this problem, *id.* at 403, which it has yet to do). *See also Holender v. Mut. Indus. N., Inc.*, 527 F.3d 352 (3d Cir. 2008) (an EEOC Form 5, entitled Charge of Discrimination, to be a charge even though the box for filing with the EEOC and a state agency wasn't checked and the form was not notarized).

Since a charge can be relatively minimal, another EEOC regulation comes into play allowing amendment of the first filing and providing that such amendments, including verification of the charge and "amendment alleging additional acts which constitute unlawful employment practices related to or growing out of the subject matter of the original charge will relate back to the date the charge was first received." §1601.12(b). *Edelman v. Lynchburg College*, 535 U.S. 106, 114 (2002), upheld this regulation. *See also McWilliams v. Latah Sanitation, Inc.*, 149 F. App'x 588, 590 (9th Cir. 2005) (charge may be verified after the time for filing had expired; since the original charge put the employer on notice of the claims and allowed the agency to investigate the charges, the initial failure to verify did not prejudice the employer).

b.   When Does the Violation "Occur"?

The first step in applying any period of limitation is to determine when the statute begins to run. Since Title VII requires filing a charge within 180/300 days "after the alleged unlawful employment practice occurred," 42 U.S.C. §2000e-5(e), §706(e), the question has been framed in terms of when an act of discrimination "occurs." In some cases, such as when a worker is discharged effective immediately, the "occurrence" is easily identified: the act and its consequences occur simultaneously. In the employment context, however, decisions by the employer may not be transparent to an employee; for example, she may know that she received a 3 percent raise but not know that her male co-workers received a 5 percent increase. Further, employment decisions often have downstream consequences that may not emerge for a long time.

Notice of Adverse Action Rule

In a number of cases, culminating with *Ledbetter v. Goodyear Tire & Rubber Co.*, 550 U.S. 618 (2007), the Supreme Court applied a one-size-fits-all rule to most "occurred" questions, holding that discrimination occurs for purposes of the filing requirement when the employee is notified of an adverse employment decision. Thus, Ms. Ledbetter, who had won a jury verdict finding that Goodyear had discriminated against her in a series of compensation decisions, lost her judgment because the decisions she challenged were too far in the past: she "should have filed an EEOC charge within 180 days after each allegedly discriminatory pay decision was made and communicated to her." *Id.* at 628. A major exception to this "notice of decision" rule is for contaminated work environment harassment, which may be charged to the EEOC within 180/300 days of any act constituting the same course of harassment. *Amtrak v. Morgan*, 536 U.S. 101 (2002). Two other exceptions have been recognized, but are rarely applicable. Thus, facially discriminatory practices can be challenged at any time, e.g., *Lorance v. AT&T Technologies*, 490 U.S. 900 (1989); *Ledbetter*, 550 U.S. at 634, and pursuant to the 1991 Civil Rights Act, which overrode *Lorance v. AT&T Technologies*, 490 U.S. 900 (1989), discriminatory seniority systems can be challenged whenever they affect individuals. *Ledbetter*, 550 U.S. at 627 n. 2.

None of these exceptions, however, applied to the case before it, and the *Ledbetter* opinion applied the notice of decision rule to dismiss Ms. Ledbetter's claims. The decision itself was not a significant departure from most of the earlier precedents but it flew in the face of the language of *Bazemore v. Friday*, 478 U.S. 385 (1986), which had stated that:

> when an employer adopts a facially discriminatory pay structure that puts some employees on a lower scale because of race, the employer engages in intentional discrimination whenever it issues a check to one of these disfavored employees. An employer that adopts and intentionally retains such a pay structure can surely be regarded as intending to discriminate on the basis of race as long as the structure is used.

Id. at 395-96. Accordingly, "[e]ach week's paycheck that delivered less to a black than to a similarly situated white is a wrong actionable under Title VII, regardless of the fact that this pattern was begun prior to the effective date of Title VII." *Id.* at 395-96. Although one could question whether the discrimination in *Bazemore* was "facial" (the case turned on the use of multiple regression analysis to show that an older, de jure policy of pay discrimination continued past the effective date of Title VII), the *Ledbetter* majority clearly limited any paycheck rule to facial discrimination.

Whether it was this reinterpretation of *Bazemore* or some deeper outrage with the grudging approach of the Court to antidiscrimination time limits, *Ledbetter* struck a nerve both on the Court and in Congress. Justice Ginsberg read a strong dissent from the bench in which she called on Congress to override the majority. She argued that it was unrealistic to expect employees to challenge each pay decision, in part because they would often have no reason to even know that they were receiving less than fellow workers and in part because individual decisions might be too insignificant to challenge until they accumulated and were magnified by percentage raises into large discrepancies.

The Lilly Ledbetter Fair Pay Act of 2009

The Ginsberg dissent triggered the congressional response she had called for, culminating in President Obama signing the Lilly Ledbetter Fair Pay Act (FPA) of 2009, Pub. L. No. 111-2, §3, 123 Stat. 5, 5-6 (2009), codified at 42 U.S.C. §2000e-5(e)(3)(A), as one of the first acts of his presidency. That statute amends Title VII to provide:

> an unlawful employment practice occurs, with respect to discrimination in compensation in violation of this title, when a discriminatory compensation decision or other practice is adopted, when an individual becomes subject to a discriminatory compensation decision or other practice, or when an individual is affected by application of a discriminatory compensation decision or other practice, including each time wages, benefits, or other compensation is paid, resulting in whole or in part from such a decision or other practice.

The FPA similarly amended the other antidiscrimination laws, including the ADEA and ADA. For all these statutes, it thus codified a "paycheck" rule — a plaintiff who suffered discrimination in compensation can file a timely charge, *inter alia*, within 180/300 days of receiving a paycheck that is lower than it would have been but for the discrimination. *See also Groesch v. City of Springfield*, 635 F.3d 1020 (7th Cir. 2011) (applying the FPA's "paycheck accrual rule" to claims under §1983 equal protection claims).

What's more, the Fair Pay Act is explicitly retroactive since it "take[s] effect as if enacted on May 28, 2007," which is the day *before* the Supreme Court handed down *Ledbetter*. There seems little doubt that Congress has the constitutional power to, in effect, revive claims that would have been barred by the *Ledbetter* decision. Charles A. Sullivan, *Raising the Dead: The Lilly Ledbetter Fair Pay Act*, 84 Tul. L. Rev. 499 (2010). The result is that potential plaintiffs can file timely charges as to any discriminatory decision that affects their compensation, even decisions made years or decades earlier. It is true that the FPA limits backpay recovery to no more than two years prior to the filing of a charge, §3 (codified at 42 U.S.C. §2000e-5(e)(3)(B)), but the conduct itself is actionable.

An Overview of the Fair Pay Act's Reach

At first glance, the Lilly Ledbetter Fair Pay Act seems to consign to the scrap heap the Supreme Court's prior timeliness jurisprudence. Clearly, "compensation decisions" with present consequences on pay are actionable — no matter how far in the past they were made. Some have suggested that the amendment reaches beyond compensation decisions because of the references to "other practices." However, a careful reading of the language suggests a more limited view: the actionable discrimination must be "with respect to discrimination in compensation in violation of this title," although such discrimination may be "a discriminatory compensation decision or other practice." Under this reading, any employer action — regardless of whether it is a "compensation decision" per se — that affects compensation is within the expanded FPA notion of "occurrence." A less expansive reading would argue that "discriminatory compensation" modifies not just "decision" but also "other practices," which would mean that no action that is not a "compensation" action is within the FPA's expanded notion of "occurrence." However, this reading has its own problems (including making "decision or" irrelevant), and the legislative history generally supports the broader, causation-focused view. *See* Sullivan, *Raising the Dead*, 84 Tul. L. Rev. 520-36. In any event, even under the more restrictive view, it would still be necessary to define a "compensation" action, and many decisions, e.g., a failure to promote, seem to be best viewed as compensation decisions. *Contra Shuler v. PricewaterhouseCoopers, LLP*, 595 F.3d 370 (D.C. Cir. 2010) (denial of a promotion with continuing effects on plaintiff's compensation not actionable more than 180/300 days after notice of the denial; "discrimination in compensation" means "paying different wages or providing different benefits to similarly situated employees, not promoting one employee but not another to a more remunerative position."); *Noel v. Boeing Co.*, 622 F.3d 266 (3d Cir. 2010) (failure to promote claim not saved by Fair Pay Act, at least where plaintiff had not characterized it as a failure to give a raise until late in the proceedings).

Even under the broadest view, however, the Fair Pay Act does not reach all acts of discrimination. While it is meaningfully limited, its limitations may not be as significant as it first appears for two reasons. First, some of the practices that do not affect compensation will not be actionable at all under current doctrine, thus reducing the extent to which procedural limitations (as opposed to a substantive rule) pose a problem. For example, you might recall from Chapter 1 that it is not clear that the blue and pink offices constitute an adverse employment practice to begin with. Second, perhaps the Supreme Court's jurisprudence ought to be reconsidered in light of the FPA, even where the amendment does not textually require a change. The argument is, essentially, that statutory overrides at least sometimes imply that the courts' entire approach to the whole question is mistaken. *See generally* Deborah A. Widiss, *Shadow Precedents and the Separation of Powers: Statutory Interpretation of Congressional Overrides*, 84 Notre Dame L. Rev. 511 (2009).

effect

On the other hand, history suggests that earlier precedents will not go quietly into the good night, and the courts are likely to read the amendment as limited to what it said, without regard to broader congressional disapproval. Widiss, at 514-15. Further, some conduct that is indisputably an adverse employment action — such as a discharge or failure to hire — and has continuing effects on compensation (or the lack thereof) is not likely to be found to fall within the FPA's expansion of Title VII time limits. Although the language of the amendment could be read to allow these individuals to sue (plaintiffs' failure as nonemployees to get a check is the result of a prior discriminatory firing), this interpretation will almost certainly be rejected. From a textual perspective, the language "each time wages, benefits, or other compensation is paid" (although only an illustration) suggests that continued employment is the sine qua non of a later charge. From a more purposive perspective, one of the rationales underlying the FPA is that employees should not be prejudiced by decisions of which they were not aware (say, that they were paid less than a male for similar work) or for which they had no reason to suspect discrimination. In contrast, when a plaintiff is fired, she might well be required to explore all of her potential claims on pain of forfeiting them.

Reconsidering the Vitality of Pre-FPA Precedents

In any event, to understand the law in the wake of the Fair Pay Act, it is useful to analyze some of the prior precedents to see what, if any, vitality they retain. Some of the Court's prior holdings seem to be undercut but not overridden. For example, in *Delaware State College v. Ricks*, 449 U.S. 250 (1980), the Court held both that the filing period ran from the point where the employee was notified of the adverse action and that the period would not be tolled by pursuit of internal remedies or grievance procedures. In the wake of the Fair Pay Act, the tolling question would not, per se, be affected, but Mr. Ricks's filing would be timely. The alleged discriminatory act — the notice of termination — would permit him to file a charge measured from that point. But that act would be a practice that resulted in ending his compensation (along with his employment) a year later. Measured from the point where his paycheck stopped, Ricks would have 180/300 days to file a charge. In fact, he had filed before his employment ended, so he would have satisfied the LLFPA had it been operative.

United Air Lines, Inc. v. Evans is more complicated. There, the plaintiff had been forced from her position as a flight attendant in 1968 because of United Airlines' sex-discriminatory "no marriage" policy for flight attendants, a policy that was later held illegal. In 1972 Evans was rehired by United but was treated as a new employee in accordance with the controlling collective bargaining agreement. Evans filed a charge of discrimination with the EEOC in 1973. Under pre-FPA precedents, Ms. Evans's original discharge would trigger the requirement that she file a charge. However, the policy was also facially discriminatory, which would, under *Lorance/Bazemore,* allow her to file a charge within 180/300 days after its discontinuance. But Ms. Evans did not file with the EEOC until more than 180/300 days of the discontinuance of the policy; indeed, she did not file a timely charge as measured from United's initial refusal to credit her prior seniority upon her rehire when she was treated as a new employee in accordance with the controlling collective bargaining agreement.

Under the *Lorance*-inspired amendment to Title VII, the seniority system could be timely charged at any time it adversely affected plaintiff, and, if seniority affected compensation, under the LLFPA, a charge would be filed timely within 180/300 days of any lower paycheck. But *Evans* had held that the seniority system was not itself discriminatory. While the system had the effect of perpetuating the consequences of the discriminatory discharge in 1968, a mere disparate impact from a seniority system is not illegal. Thus, under the *Lorance* amendment, there would be no timeliness problem but the suit would be dismissed because there was no actionable discrimination.

This view of *Evans* was confirmed by *AT&T Corp v. Hulteen*, 129 S. Ct. 1962 (2009), which was decided after the passage of the Fair Pay Act. At issue was whether the employer's calculation of service time for retirement purposes was discriminatory when it did not credit pregnancy leave but did credit other short-term leaves. The leave for which credit had been denied was taken prior to the passage of the Pregnancy Discrimination Act (PDA), when, as we saw in Chapter 5, disfavoring pregnancy was not sex discrimination within the meaning of Title VII. For the *Hulteen* majority, this meant that there was no violation when AT&T's policy first denied credit for pregnancy leave. 129 S. Ct. at 910. The PDA reversed this interpretation prospectively, but the majority found that statute not retroactive. Thus, the original denial of leave was not actionable. *Id.* at 909. As for the fact that the employer's seniority system carried forward the effects of this denial of credit past the PDA's effective date, the *Hulteen* majority held these consequences not actionable because of Title VII's exemption of seniority systems. While we saw in Chapter 3 that such systems can be attacked to the extent that they are the result of intentional discrimination, AT&T's seniority system was not intentionally discriminatory merely because it perpetuated the consequences of an act that was nondiscriminatory when taken.

This analysis allowed the majority to skirt the Fair Pay Act, which it cited but found inapposite: "AT&T's pre-PDA decision not to award Hulteen service credit for pregnancy leave was not discriminatory, with the consequence that Hulteen has not been 'affected by application of a discriminatory compensation decision or other practice.'" *Id.* at 911. Presumably, while a charge would have been timely under the FPA as to the effects of the seniority system since that system affected compensation, there was no violation. *Hulteen*, however, suggests that *Evans* itself would come out differently, at least assuming an effect on her compensation: given the illegality of the original discharge, the decision not to credit Evans's past seniority would allow a timely charge to be filed measured from any paycheck, and, unlike *Hulteen* itself, that action would perpetuate the effects of a past act of discrimination—unless, of course, the courts were to find that the LLFPA is trumped by Title VII's immunization of seniority systems. We have seen that the Court has often viewed seniority systems as almost sacrosanct.

Contaminated Environment Harassment

Prior to *Ledbetter, Amtrak v. Morgan,* 536 U.S. 101 (2002), had carved out an important exception to the notice of decision doctrine. Consistent with its earlier precedents, *Morgan* reaffirmed that " '[d]iscrete acts' such as termination, failure to promote, denial of transfer, or refusal to hire are easy to identify" and each constitutes a "separate actionable 'unlawful employment practice' " that must be timely charged. *Id.* at 114. However, the Court recognized that hostile environment sexual harassment claims "are different in kind from discrete acts. Their very nature involves repeated conduct." *Id.* at 103. It elaborated: "The 'unlawful employment practice' therefore cannot be said to occur on any particular day. It occurs over a series of days or perhaps years and, in direct contrast to discrete acts, a single act of harassment may not be actionable on its own. Such claims are based on the cumulative effect of individual acts." *Id.* at 115 (citations omitted). For that reason,

> a hostile environment claim is comprised of a series of separate acts that collectively constitute one "unlawful employment practice." The timely filing provision only requires that a Title VII plaintiff file a charge within a certain number of days after the unlawful practice happened. It does not matter, for purposes of the statute, that some of the component acts of the hostile work environment fall outside the statutory time period. Provided that an act contributing to the claim occurs within the filing period, the entire time period of the hostile environment may be considered by a court for the purposes of determining liability.

536 U.S. at 117. The only limitation on this principle is that, for there to be "one" employment practice, there must be a sufficient relationship between the various acts that comprise the putative violation. *Compare Rowe v. Hussmann Corp.,* 381 F.3d 775, 781 (8th Cir. 2004) (the same harasser, committing the same harassing acts, and the absence of any intervening action meant as a matter of law that the acts "must be considered to be part and parcel of the hostile work environment that constituted the unlawful employment practice that gave rise to this action"), with *Holmes v. State of Utah,* 483 F.3d 1057 (10th Cir. 2007) (acts within charge-filing period were insufficient alone to support a hostile environment claim, nor could they be linked to prior acts outside the filing limitation). *See also Stewart v. Miss. Transp. Comm'n,* 586 F.3d 321 (5th Cir. 2009) (assigning an employee away from a harassing supervisor for 16 months constituted an "intervening action" which barred linked the pre- and post-assignment harassment as one continuing act).

Summary of the Current Law

To summarize: a hostile environment can be timely charged within 180/300 days of any act that contributes to the same contaminated environment. The same may be true of any action taken pursuant to a facially discriminatory policy, compensation, seniority, or otherwise. However, all other discrete acts must be charged within 180/300 days of the time they occur, unless they fall within the FPA. Acts that fall within the Fair Pay Act are limited to those affecting the compensation of continuing employees (or, at least, those with a continuing connection to the employer, such as the retirees in *Hulteen*). These acts may be challenged from as late as 180/300 days from the last time "wages, benefits, or other compensation is paid, resulting in whole or in part from such a decision."

Even the complicated scheme we have sketched here may not resolve all questions. One issue is the intersection of the adverse employment action doctrine we met in Chapter 1 with the "occurrence" question. For example, most circuits would find a lateral transfer, by definition involving no significant change in pay or status, not to be actionable in the first place — even if motivated by discrimination. But assume that the transfer results a year later in the employee's discharge for nondiscriminatory reasons (perhaps because the new office is closed). Does *Hulteen* suggest any claim is time-barred? Would that make sense?

"Old" Evidence

Although the filing limitations will bar a cause of action based on incidents prior to the filing period, this does not mean that such incidents never occurred. Rather, to the extent that they are relevant to showing intent to discriminate, the Supreme Court indicated in *Evans* that such events can be "relevant background evidence in a proceeding in which the status of a current practice is at issue." 431 U.S. 558. It repeated the same point in *Morgan*, 536 U.S. at 113 ("Nor does the statute bar an employee from using the prior acts as background evidence in support of a timely claim."). *See also Wedow v. City of Kansas*, 442 F.3d 661, 671 (8th Cir. 2006) ("The district court correctly permitted acts occurring outside the 300-day window to be admitted as relevant to discriminatory intent and correctly limited recovery to acts occurring within the limitations period."); *Bright v. Hill's Pet Nutrition, Inc.*, 510 F.3d 766 (7th Cir. 2007) (error for trial court to instruct jury not to consider evidence of harassment that occurred more than 300 days before the charge filing whether or not employer had disciplined the harassers);

Page 617. Delete from last paragraph in Note on Timeliness in Pattern and Practice Cases to end of Note; replace with:

Another possible way to explain *Bazemore* was that it was a disparate impact case. While the original low salaries for blacks were intentional, the continuing discrepancy was the result of a facially neutral policy that built on prior salaries. In such cases does the violation occur whenever the effects are felt (which seems contrary to *Evans*) or perhaps when the policy is used? In *Lewis v. City of Chicago*, 130 S. Ct. 2191, 2199 (2010), the Supreme Court addressed whether a plaintiff who does not file a timely charge challenging the adoption of a practice by an employer may nevertheless assert a disparate-impact claim in a timely charge challenging the employer's later *application* of the adopted process. The Seventh Circuit had held that the suit was untimely because the EEOC charges were filed more than 300 days after the occurrence of what it viewed as the only discriminatory act—the publication of a list sorting the scores into three categories, with only those in the topmost "well-qualified" category being relatively sure of being hired in subsequent rounds of selections from the list over a period of years. The Supreme Court unanimously disagreed, holding that the applicants could bring a disparate impact suit as to any of the ten rounds of selection from the list that occurred within the 300-day charging period.

For the Court, the critical passage was found in §2000e-2(k)(i), which provides:

> a complaining party demonstrates that a respondent uses a particular employment practice that causes a disparate impact on the basis of race, color, religion, sex, or national origin and the respondent fails to demonstrate that the challenged practice is job related for the position in question and consistent with business necessity.

Despite the City argument that the only unlawful employment practice here occurred in 1996 when it created the hiring hierarchy, the Court held that new violations occurred each time City "used" the results of the test by hiring from the lists it established: "Although the City had adopted the eligibility list (embodying the score cutoffs) earlier and announced its intention to draw from that list, it made use of the practice of excluding those who scored 88 or below each time it filled a new class of firefighters." 130 S. Ct. at 2198. Therefore, if the plaintiffs could successfully show that the City's repeatedly used the test as a selection criterion with a disparate impact, the plaintiffs could prevail for any filing within 300 days of such use.

While *Lewis* resolves the continuing violation question for may systemic disparate impact, cases, it is not clear if it has significance for systemic disparate treatment suits. *See generally* Jason R. Bent, *What the Lilly Ledbetter Fair Pay Act Doesn't Do: "Discrete Acts" and the Future of Pattern or Practice Litigation*, 33 RUTGERS L. REC. 31 (2009). Take the easiest case: an employer has a policy of not hiring women for certain positions (perhaps a prison limits positions to preserve male inmate privacy). *See Henry v. Milwaukee County*, 539 F.3d 573 (7th Cir. 2008). The policy may have been initiated for discriminatory reasons many years before plaintiff applied and perhaps before she was even born, While it hardly seems fair to deny her a chance to challenge it measured from the point when she's denied a job based on the policy, §703(a)(1) does not speak of "use" but rather of discrimination against any individual. Isn't she discriminated against at that point? And subparagraph (2) prohibits an employer from "limit[ing], segregat[ing], or classify[ing] his employees or applicants for employment in any way which would deprive or tend to deprive" then of opportunities. A policy such as the one posited might well tend to deprive female applicants of opportunities.

With respect to systemic disparate treatment, we have seen that the Court's precedents make it clear that a facially discriminatory policy can be challenged any time it affects an individual, That itself might allow an attack on same sex policies regarding inmate privacy. Further, presumably, the Fair Pay Act also makes systemic disparate treatment chargeable within 180/300 days of any effect on compensation, regardless of whether the discrimination is facial. Further, some pre-*Morgan/Ledbetter* lower courts allowed such claims even when the discrimination was not facial. The continued vitality of such authority is unclear outside of the compensation context, and the impact of *Lewis* is also unclear.

At one point, the Court drew a sharp line between disparate treatment and disparate impact claims. Reviewing its prior precedents, it wrote:

> As relevant here, those cases establish only that a Title VII plaintiff must show a "present violation" within the limitations period. What that requires depends on the claim asserted. For disparate-treatment claims — and others for which discriminatory intent is required — that means the plaintiff must demonstrate deliberate discrimination within the limitations period. But for claims that do not require discriminatory intent, no such demonstration is needed. Our opinions, it is true, described the harms of which the unsuccessful plaintiffs in those cases complained as "present effect[s]" of past discrimination. But the reason they could not be the present effects of present discrimination was that the charged discrimination required proof of discriminatory intent, which had not even been alleged. That reasoning has no application when, as here, the charge is disparate impact, which does not require discriminatory intent.

130 S. Ct. at 2199. This passage does not differentiate between individual and systemic disparate treatment claims. This demarcation is reinforced by the statutory language. *Lewis*, in effect, turns on the statute's use of the word "use" in describing disparate impact discrimination in §703(m). This takes us back to the question of whether the continued use of a facially neutral policy adopted for discriminatory reasons violates §703(a). The answer might turn on whether a systemic disparate treatment case is viewed as an attack on a covert "policy" of discrimination (analogous to a facially discriminatory policy) or on a pattern of individual cases. Lower court decisions have not been receptive to arguments that would push the filing period further back than the adverse employment action being challenged. *See* Davis v. Coca-Cola Bottling Co. Consol. 516 F.3d 955, 970 (11th Cir. 2008) (employer's hiring decisions, light work assignments, and alleged retaliation treated as discrete acts and could not avoid the Title VII and §1981 time-bars); Williams v. Giant Food, Inc., 370 F.3d 423, 429 (4th Cir. 2004) ("even if Williams is correct that Giant Food's failures to promote her during the applicable limitations period were part of a broader pattern or practice of discrimination, those failures to promote remain discrete acts of discrimination."); Davidson v. Am. Online, Inc., 337 F.3d 1179, 1185-86 (10th Cir. 2003) (allegations that failure to hire occurred as a result of employer's company-wide systemic policy do not extend the statutory limitations period). *But see* Croy v. COBE Labs., Inc., 345 F.3d 1199 (10th Cir. 2003) (continuing-violations doctrine should apply to a "glass ceiling" claim regarding the advancement of female employees as akin to a hostile environment claim, but still required a specific act within the limitations period).

Page 618. Add new text before Note on Waiver, Tolling, and Estoppel:

NOTE ON STATE DEFERRAL REQUIREMENTS

We've repeatedly referred to the filing period as 180/300 days, which may be confusing. *Ledbetter* referred to the filing period as 180 days, which is the operative period in states without a state (or local) fair employment practices agency (like Alabama, where *Ledbetter* arose). But most states now have their own fair employment practices agencies, and in those states the filing period is extended to "ensure[] that employees are neither time barred from later filing their charges with the EEOC nor dissuaded from first filing with a state agency." *Morgan*, 536 U. S. at 120. In these "deferral states" (so called because the EEOC must defer to the state agency), a plaintiff has 300 days to file with the EEOC, although there is also a requirement of filing with the relevant state agency.

In brief, Title VII and the ADA (which incorporates Title VII procedures by reference) require a filing with the state agency prior to filing with the EEOC, 42 U.S.C. §2000e-5(c), §706(c). Further, the state agency must be accorded 60 days to act before the EEOC can commence its processes. This scheme creates complications. While a charge lodged with the EEOC may be held by it in "suspended animation" during the required period of state deferral, *Love v. Pullman*, 404 U.S. 522 (1972), the EEOC filing becomes effective only when the required period for state deferral has expired. *Mohasco Corp. v. Silver*, 447 U.S. 807 (1980). This means that charges must normally be filed with both the EEOC and the state agency within 240 days of the violation (in order to ensure compliance with the 60-day period for state deferral and the 300-day period for EEOC filing). A possible escape hatch from this requirement exists if the agency completes its processes (or can be induced to terminate its proceedings) in fewer than 60 days. The ADEA is more relaxed than Title VII since a charge of age discrimination may be filed simultaneously with the state and the federal agencies. *See Oscar Mayer & Co. v. Evans*, 441 U.S. 750, 765 (1979).

The difficulties these rules have generated are often ameliorated by "worksharing" agreements between the EEOC and state agencies, which typically divide charge-processing responsibility between the federal and state agencies, as by providing that the agency with which the charge was first filed will process it. The agreements often speak in terms of each agency "waiving" its right to process a charge, or authorize each agency to process a charge on behalf of the other. *See EEOC v. Commercial Office Products Co.*, 486 U.S. 107 (1988) (state waiver of its exclusive period of charge processing in worksharing agreement terminated the deferral period, thereby allowing the EEOC to begin its processes immediately). *See also Schuler v. Pricewaterhousecoopers, LLP*, 514 F.3d 1365 (D.C. Cir.

2008) (charge filed with the EEOC satisfied state deferral requirement both by virtue of the worksharing agreement with the D.C. fair employment practices agency and by the EEOC's cross-filing with the NY agency). A filing need not be timely under state law to satisfy the federal statute. *Commercial Office Products; Oscar Mayer.*

Page 618.   Add before first paragraph of *Note on Waiver, Tolling, and Estoppel*:

One of the most remarkable aspects of the whole "occurrence" saga is the failure of the Court in that case or in prior decisions to address a doctrine with the potential to ameliorate at least the more severe aspects of the notice of decision rule. Although as we will see, the Court recognized that the strict time limits can be influenced by waiver, tolling, and estoppel, the Court never recognized a "discovery" rule, which would have tolled the charge-filing period until the employee knew (or reasonably should have known) that an adverse action was discriminatory. In a footnote, the *Ledbetter* majority noted, "We have previously declined to address whether Title VII suits are amenable to a discovery rule [citing *Morgan*]. Because Ledbetter does not argue that such a rule would change the outcome in her case, we have no occasion to address this issue." While Justices O'Connor, Rehnquist, and Breyer stated in a separate opinion in *Morgan* that "some version of the discovery rule applies to discrete-act claims," two of those Justices are no longer on the Court.

The enactment of the Lilly Ledbetter Fair Pay Act obviously largely moots the question of a discovery rule, although the complications of the limitations scheme we have explored might suggest that a limited role could remain for such an exception. Two issues would have to be addressed in developing "some version" of such a rule. First, does the plaintiff know (or should she have known) that she has been treated differently than other employees? Second, even if the plaintiff knows about a disparity, does she know have reason to know any difference is the result of discrimination? *See Beamon v. Marshall & Ilsley Trust Co.*, 411 F.3d 854 (7th Cir. 2005) (no equitable tolling for black employee since a reasonable person would have been aware that discrimination could be one possible basis for the employer's actions when, without any explanation from his employer, he was replaced by a white employee); *Wastak v. Lehigh Valley Health Network*, 342 F.3d 281 (3d Cir. 2003) (age discrimination claim accrued on date employee was fired although he had little reason to believe he had been the victim of age discrimination until he learned that he had been replaced by a younger employee nine months later).

A discovery rule aside,

Page 619.   Add after *Yang* cite in carryover paragraph:

Taylor v. UPS, 554 F.3d 510 (5th Cir. 2008) (a certified class action tolled the relevant statutes of limitations for §1981 claims that arose from 1993 until 2004, when the class claims were finally dismissed).

C.   Filing Suit

Page 621.   Add Delete fourth full paragraph; replace with:

Filing suit with 90 days is, however, not always required. *Zipes v. Trans World Airlines*, 455 U.S. 385 (1984), held the time limit for filing a charge with the EEOC not to be "jurisdictional," but "a requirement that, like a statute of limitations, is subject to waiver, estoppel, and equitable tolling." 455 U.S. at 393. *See also Allen v. Highlands Hosp. Corp.*, 545 F.3d 387, 402 (6th Cir. 2008) (holding that the ADEA's administrative-exhaustion requirement in 29 U.S.C. §626(d) for filing a charge with the EEOC "is not jurisdictional in nature, but is instead best understood as a prudential prerequisite to filing a claim in federal court"). *Zipes* has been carried over by several lower courts to the 90-day suit-filing provision, and the Supreme Court strongly suggested in *Baldwin County* that this was correct. In *Baldwin County*, however, the Court held that the mere filing of the right-to-sue letter did not constitute timely filing of suit and listed a number of possible bases for tolling the suit-filing period, including the pendency of a motion for court appointment of counsel. *See also Gordon v. England*, 354 F. App'x 975, 980-81 (6th Cir. 2009) (finding tolling possible when the attorney's conduct went far beyond "garden variety" neglect, including avoiding an EEOC investigation by falsely stating that a Title VII case was proceeding and thenfiling a voluntary non-suit, effectively aborting his client's claim.). *But see Harris v. Boyd Tunica, Inc.*, 628 F.3d 237 (5th Cir. 2010) (no tolling for ordinary neglect when plaintiff failed to file within 90 day period due to clerical error in her attorney's office).

Page 623.   Add at end of second full paragraph:

The continued vitality of some of this authority has been cast into question by the Supreme Court's recent decision in *Thompson v. North American Stainless*, reproduced at page 149 of this Supplement. Although leaving the holding of *Trafficante* intact, the Court curbed its broadest applications which would have found standing whenever the Constitution permitted. According Title VII standing to anyone suffering a injury within the meaning of Article III would result in "absurd consequences," such as allowing a stockholder to sue for firing a valuable employee. 131 S. Ct. at 839. However, limiting standing to merely "the person claiming to be discriminated against" was narrower than the statute's language of "person aggrieved" justified, and it would result in overruling *Trafficante*. *Id.* Instead, the Court looked to from the Administrative Procedure Act, 5 U.S.C. §702, which authorizes suit to challenge a federal agency by any "person . . . adversely affected or aggrieved . . . within the meaning of a relevant statute." The Court viewed this "zone of interests" test as the appropriate one for Title VII standing. The actual holding of *Thompson* – that a person fired in retaliation for his fiance's protected conduct – is of little use in the present context, leaving it unclear whether plaintiffs such as those in *Anjelino* and *Childress* have standing.

D. Relationship of the EEOC Charge to Private Suit

Page 625. Add before *Duncan* cite in carryover paragraph:

Younis v. Pinnacle Airlines, Inc., 610 F.3d 359 (6th Cir. 2010) (plaintiff's EEOC charge did not adequately raise claim of a hostile work environment harassment when it cited only three or four isolated comments by his peers that occurred over a three-year period).")

Page 626. Add at end of carryover paragraph:

While the statute of limitations may be longer for a filing under §1981 than for Title VII, the courts have tried to conform the accrual of the cause of action to Title VII principles. *Lukovsky v. City & County of San Francisco*, 535 F.3d 1044, 1049 (9th Cir. 2008) (a claim under §1981 accrued upon plaintiff's "awareness of the actual injury, i.e., the adverse employment action, and not when the plaintiff suspects a legal wrong"). *Accord Amini v. Oberlin College*, 259 F.3d 493 (6th Cir. 2001). *Lukovsky* concluded that, even though state limitations law is borrowed (at least for claims that would have been viable under §1981 as originally enacted), federal law determines when an action accrues. Despite this, however, it would seem a state law question as to whether the borrowed statute would be tolled by a discovery rule or whether defendant's misconduct would estop it from pleading the statute.

Page 626. Add at the end of first sentence of second full paragraph:

E.g., *Elkadrawy v. Vanguard Group, Inc.*, 584 F.3d 169, 173 (3d Cir. 2009) (dismissal of a prior Title VII claim barred a subsequent §1981 suit because the dismissal constituted a "final judgment on the merits" and arose from the "same material facts" as his Title VII claims, since both arose out of the same employment relationship and involved some form of race or national origin bias).

E. The Interrelationship of Various Rights and Remedies

Page 627. Add at end of sentence beginning with *Kremer*:

If the state in question would accord the state court decision preclusive effects in state court.

Page 627. Add at end of second full paragraph:

See generally Lisa M. Durham Taylor, *Untangling the Web Spun by Title VII's Referral & Deferral Scheme*, 59 CATH. U. L. REV. 427 (2010).

F. Class Actions

2. Requirements of Rule 23(a)

Page 630. Delete last sentence of carryover paragraph and replace with:

Finally, Rule 23(a)(4) considers adequacy of representation in terms of the qualifications of the class representative and possible conflicts of interest with other class members. The adequacy of class counsel was originally also considered under this prong, but is now analyzed under new Rule 23(g) which codifies the various requirements regarding attorneys that are applicable to class actions.

Page 631. Add at end of carryover paragraph:

See also Randall v. Rolls-Royce Corp., 637 F.3d 818 (7th Cir. 2011) (representation of class members by named plaintiffs was inadequate both because they had weaker claims than some of the unnamed members and because they had authority over compensation; "[a]lthough we doubt that the plaintiffs would deliberately depress the salary of female employees whom they supervise, or increase the salary of male employees whom they supervise, in order to create evidence of discrimination, the possibility of such strategic conduct (which might be unconscious) creates a conflict of interest between the plaintiffs and unnamed members of the class.").

Page 632. Delete last full paragraph and entire Ninth Circuit decision in *Dukes v. Wal-Mart, Inc.* and accompanying notes; replace with:

Wal-Mart Stores, Inc. v. Dukes
131 S. Ct. 2541 (2011)

Justice SCALIA delivered the opinion of the Court.

We are presented with one of the most expansive class actions ever. The District Court and the Court of Appeals approved the certification of a class comprising about one and a half million plaintiffs, current and former female employees of petitioner Wal-Mart who allege that the discretion exercised by their local supervisors over pay and promotion matters violates Title VII by discriminating against women. In addition to injunctive and declaratory relief, the plaintiffs seek an award of backpay. We consider whether the certification of the plaintiff class was consistent with Federal Rules of Civil Procedure 23(a) and (b)(2).

I

A

Petitioner Wal-Mart is the Nation's largest private employer. It operates four types of retail stores throughout the country: Discount Stores, Supercenters, Neighborhood Markets, and Sam's Clubs. Those stores are divided into seven nationwide divisions, which in turn comprise 41 regions of 80 to 85 stores apiece. Each store has between 40 and 53 separate departments and 80 to 500 staff positions. In all, Wal-Mart operates approximately 3,400 stores and employs more than one million people.

Pay and promotion decisions at Wal-Mart are generally committed to local managers' broad discretion, which is exercised "in a largely subjective manner." Local store managers may increase the wages of hourly employees (within limits) with only limited corporate oversight. As for salaried employees, such as store managers and their deputies, higher corporate authorities have discretion to set their pay within preestablished ranges.

Promotions work in a similar fashion. Wal-Mart permits store managers to apply their own subjective criteria when selecting candidates as "support managers," which is the first step on the path to management. Admission to Wal-Mart's management training program, however, does require that a candidate meet certain objective criteria, including an above-average performance rating, at least one year's tenure in the applicant's current position, and a willingness to relocate. But except for those requirements, regional and district managers have discretion to use their own judgment when selecting candidates for management training. Promotion to higher office — e.g., assistant manager, co-manager, or store manager — is similarly at the discretion of the employee's superiors after prescribed objective factors are satisfied.

B

The named plaintiffs in this lawsuit, representing the 1.5 million members of the certified class, are three current or former Wal-Mart employees who allege that the company discriminated against them on the basis of their sex by denying them equal pay or promotions, in violation of Title VII. . . .

These plaintiffs, respondents here, do not allege that Wal-Mart has any express corporate policy against the advancement of women. Rather, they claim that their local managers' discretion over pay and promotions is exercised disproportionately in favor of men, leading to an unlawful disparate impact on female employees, see 42 U.S.C. §2000e-2(k). And, respondents say, because Wal-Mart is aware of this effect, its refusal to cabin its managers' authority amounts to disparate treatment, see §2000e-2(a). Their complaint seeks injunctive and declaratory relief, punitive damages, and backpay. It does not ask for compensatory damages.

Importantly for our purposes, respondents claim that the discrimination to which they have been subjected is common to *all* Wal-Mart's female employees. The basic theory of their case is that a strong and uniform "corporate culture" permits bias against women to infect, perhaps subconsciously, the discretionary decisionmaking of each one of Wal-Mart's thousands of managers—thereby making every woman at the company the victim of one common discriminatory practice. Respondents therefore wish to litigate the Title VII claims of all female employees at Wal-Mart's stores in a nationwide class action.

C

[The party seeking certification must demonstrate that the class meets the requirements of Rule 23(a), and, for the category of certification sought here, the requirements of Rule 23(b)(2), which applies when "the party opposing the class has acted or refused to act on grounds that apply generally to the class, so that final injunctive relief or corresponding declaratory relief is appropriate respecting the class as a whole."]

Invoking these provisions, respondents moved the District Court to certify a plaintiff class consisting of " '[a]ll women employed at any Wal-Mart domestic retail store at any time since December 26, 1998, who have been or may be subjected to Wal-Mart's challenged pay and management track promotions policies and practices.'" As evidence that there were indeed "questions of law or fact common to" all the women of Wal-Mart, as Rule 23(a)(2) requires, respondents relied chiefly on three forms of proof: statistical evidence about pay and promotion disparities between men and women at the company, anecdotal reports of discrimination from about 120 of Wal-Mart's female employees, and the testimony of a sociologist, Dr. William Bielby, who conducted a "social framework analysis" of Wal-Mart's "culture" and personnel practices, and concluded that the company was "vulnerable" to gender discrimination.

Wal-Mart unsuccessfully moved to strike much of this evidence. It also offered its own countervailing statistical and other proof in an effort to defeat Rule 23(a)'s requirements of commonality, typicality, and adequate representation. Wal-Mart further contended that respondents' monetary claims for backpay could not be certified under Rule 23(b)(2), first because that Rule refers only to injunctive and declaratory relief, and second because the backpay claims could not be manageably tried as a class without depriving Wal-Mart of its right to present certain statutory defenses. [The District Court granted certification, and the Ninth Circuit, sitting en banc, substantially affirmed.]

I

The class action is "an exception to the usual rule that litigation is conducted by and on behalf of the individual named parties only." Califano v. Yamasaki, 442 U.S. 682, 700-701 (1979). In order to justify a departure from that rule, "a class representative must be part of the class and 'possess the same interest and suffer the same injury' as the class members." East Tex. Motor Freight System, Inc. v. Rodriguez, 431 U.S. 395, 403 (1977). Rule 23(a) ensures that the named plaintiffs are appropriate representatives of the class whose claims they wish to litigate. The Rule's four requirements — numerosity, commonality, typicality, and adequate representation — "effectively 'limit the class claims to those fairly encompassed by the named plaintiff's claims.'" General Telephone Co. of Southwest v. Falcon, 457 U.S. 147, 156 (1982).

The crux of this case is commonality — the rule requiring a plaintiff to show that "there are questions of law or fact common to the class." Rule 23(a)(2). That language is easy to misread, since "[a]ny compententently crafted class complaint literally raises common 'questions.'" Nagareda, Class Certification in the Age of Aggregate Proof, 84 N.Y.U. L. Rev. 97, 131-132 (2009). For example: Do all of us plaintiffs indeed work for Wal-Mart? Do our managers have discretion over pay? Is that an unlawful employment practice? What remedies should we get? Reciting these questions is not sufficient to obtain class certification. Commonality requires the plaintiff to demonstrate that the class members "have suffered the same injury," *Falcon*. This does not mean merely that they have all suffered a violation of the same provision of law. Title VII, for example, can be violated in many ways — by intentional discrimination, or by hiring and promotion criteria that result in disparate impact, and by the use of these practices on the part of many different superiors in a single company. Quite obviously, the mere claim by employees of the same company that they have suffered a Title VII injury, or even a disparate-impact Title VII injury, gives no cause to believe that all their claims can productively be litigated at once. Their claims must depend upon a common contention — for example, the assertion of discriminatory bias on the part of the same supervisor. That common contention, moreover, must be of such a nature that it is capable of classwide resolution — which means that determination of its truth or falsity will resolve an issue that is central to the validity of each one of the claims in one stroke.

> What matters to class certification . . . is not the raising of common 'questions' — even in droves — but, rather the capacity of a classwide proceeding to generate common answers apt to drive the resolution of the litigation. Dissimilarities within the proposed class are what have the potential to impede the generation of common answers.

Nagareda.

Rule 23 does not set forth a mere pleading standard. A party seeking class certification must affirmatively demonstrate his compliance with the Rule — that is, he must be prepared to prove that there are *in fact* sufficiently numerous parties, common questions of law or fact, etc. We recognized in *Falcon* that "sometimes it may be necessary for the court to probe behind the pleadings before coming to rest on the certification question," and that certification is proper only if "the trial court is satisfied, after a rigorous analysis, that the prerequisites of Rule 23(a) have been satisfied." Frequently that "rigorous analysis" will entail some overlap with the merits of the plaintiff's underlying claim. That cannot be helped. "'[T]he class determination generally involves considerations that are enmeshed in the factual and legal issues comprising the plaintiff's cause of action.'" *Falcon*.[6] Nor is there anything unusual about that consequence: The necessity of touching aspects of the merits in order to resolve preliminary matters, e.g., jurisdiction and venue, is a familiar feature of litigation. See Szabo v. Bridgeport Machines, Inc., 249 F.3d 672, 676-677 (CA7 2001) (Easterbrook, J.).

In this case, proof of commonality necessarily overlaps with respondents' merits contention that Wal-Mart engages in *a pattern or practice* of discrimination.[7] That is so because, in resolving an individual's Title VII claim, the crux of the inquiry is "the reason for a particular employment decision," Cooper v. Federal Reserve Bank of Richmond, 467 U.S. 867, 876 (1984). Here respondents wish to sue about literally millions of employment decisions at once. Without some glue holding the alleged *reasons* for all those decisions together, it will be impossible to say that examination of all the class members' claims for relief will produce a common answer to the crucial question *why was I disfavored*.

B

This Court's opinion in *Falcon* describes how the commonality issue must be approached. There an employee who claimed that he was deliberately denied a

---

6. A statement in one of our prior cases, Eisen v. Carlisle & Jacquelin, 417 U.S. 156, 177 (1974), is sometimes mistakenly cited to the contrary: "We find nothing in either the language or history of Rule 23 that gives a court any authority to conduct a preliminary inquiry into the merits of a suit in order to determine whether it may be maintained as a class action." But in that case, the judge had conducted a preliminary inquiry into the merits of a suit, not in order to determine the propriety of certification under Rules 23(a) and (b) (he had already done that), but in order to shift the cost of notice required by Rule 23(c)(2) from the plaintiff to the defendants. To the extent the quoted statement goes beyond the permissibility of a merits inquiry for any other pretrial purpose, it is the purest dictum and is contradicted by our other cases.

Perhaps the most common example of considering a merits question at the Rule 23 stage arises in class-action suits for securities fraud. Rule 23(b)(3)'s requirement that "questions of law or fact common to class members predominate over any questions affecting only individual members" would often be an insuperable barrier to class certification, since each of the individual investors would have to prove reliance on the alleged misrepresentation. But the problem dissipates if the plaintiffs can establish the applicability of the so-called "fraud on the market" presumption, which says that all traders who purchase stock in an efficient market are presumed to have relied on the accuracy of a company's public statements. To invoke this presumption, the plaintiffs seeking 23(b)(3) certification must prove that their shares were traded on an efficient market, an issue they will surely have to prove again at trial in order to make out their case on the merits.

7. In a pattern-or-practice case, the plaintiff tries to "establish by a preponderance of the evidence that . . . discrimination was the company's standard operating procedure[,] the regular rather than the unusual practice." Teamsters v. United States [reproduced at p. 123]; see also Franks v. Bowman Transp. Co., [reproduced at p. 656]. If he succeeds, that showing will support a rebuttable inference that all class members were victims of the discriminatory practice, and will justify "an award of prospective relief," such as "an injunctive order against the continuation of the discriminatory practice." *Teamsters*.

promotion on account of race obtained certification of a class comprising all employees wrongfully denied promotions and all applicants wrongfully denied jobs. We rejected that composite class for lack of commonality and typicality, explaining:

> Conceptually, there is a wide gap between (a) an individual's claim that he has been denied a promotion [or higher pay] on discriminatory grounds, and his otherwise unsupported allegation that the company has a policy of discrimination, and (b) the existence of a class of persons who have suffered the same injury as that individual, such that the individual's claim and the class claim will share common questions of law or fact and that the individual's claim will be typical of the class claims."

Falcon suggested two ways in which that conceptual gap might be bridged. First, if the employer "used a biased testing procedure to evaluate both applicants for employment and incumbent employees, a class action on behalf of every applicant or employee who might have been prejudiced by the test clearly would satisfy the commonality and typicality requirements of Rule 23(a)." Second, "[s]ignificant proof that an employer operated under a general policy of discrimination conceivably could justify a class of both applicants and employees if the discrimination manifested itself in hiring and promotion practices in the same general fashion, such as through entirely subjective decisionmaking processes." We think that statement precisely describes respondents' burden in this case. The first manner of bridging the gap obviously has no application here; Wal-Mart has no testing procedure or other company-wide evaluation method that can be charged with bias. The whole point of permitting discretionary decisionmaking is to avoid evaluating employees under a common standard.

The second manner of bridging the gap requires "significant proof" that Wal-Mart "operated under a general policy of discrimination." That is entirely absent here. Wal-Mart's announced policy forbids sex discrimination, and as the District Court recognized the company imposes penalties for denials of equal employment opportunity. The only evidence of a "general policy of discrimination" respondents produced was the testimony of Dr. William Bielby, their sociological expert. Relying on "social framework" analysis, Bielby testified that Wal-Mart has a "strong corporate culture," that makes it " 'vulnerable' " to "gender bias." He could not, however, "determine with any specificity how regularly stereotypes play a meaningful role in employment decisions at Wal-Mart. At his deposition . . . Dr. Bielby conceded that he could not calculate whether 0.5 percent or 95 percent of the employment decisions at Wal-Mart might be determined by stereotyped thinking." The parties dispute whether Bielby's testimony even met the standards for the admission of expert testimony under Federal Rule of Evidence 702 and our *Daubert* case, see *Daubert v. Merrell Dow Pharmaceuticals, Inc.*, 509 U.S. 579 (1993).[8] The

---

8. Bielby's conclusions in this case have elicited criticism from the very scholars on whose conclusions he relies for his social-framework analysis. See Monahan, Walker, & Mitchell, Contextual Evidence of Gender Discrimination: The Ascendance of "Social Frameworks," 94 Va. L. Rev. 1715, 1747 (2008) [arguing that Bielby's research did not satisfy professional standards since Bielby testified about facts specific to Wal-Mart and "social framework necessarily contains only general statements about reliable patterns of relations among variables . . . and goes no further. . . . "]

District Court concluded that *Daubert* did not apply to expert testimony at the certification stage of class-action proceedings. We doubt that is so, but even if properly considered, Bielby's testimony does nothing to advance respondents' case. "[W]hether 0.5 percent or 95 percent of the employment decisions at Wal-Mart might be determined by stereotyped thinking" is the essential question on which respondents' theory of commonality depends. If Bielby admittedly has no answer to that question, we can safely disregard what he has to say. It is worlds away from "significant proof" that Wal-Mart "operated under a general policy of discrimination."

C

The only corporate policy that the plaintiffs' evidence convincingly establishes is Wal-Mart's "policy" of *allowing discretion* by local supervisors over employment matters. On its face, of course, that is just the opposite of a uniform employment practice that would provide the commonality needed for a class action; it is a policy *against having* uniform employment practices. It is also a very common and presumptively reasonable way of doing business — one that we have said "should itself raise no inference of discriminatory conduct," *Watson v. Fort Worth Bank & Trust*, 487 U.S. 977, 990 (1988).

To be sure, we have recognized that, "in appropriate cases," giving discretion to lower-level supervisors can be the basis of Title VII liability under a disparate-impact theory — since "an employer's undisciplined system of subjective decisionmaking [can have] precisely the same effects as a system pervaded by impermissible intentional discrimination." But the recognition that this type of Title VII claim "can" exist does not lead to the conclusion that every employee in a company using a system of discretion has such a claim in common. To the contrary, left to their own devices most managers in any corporation — and surely most managers in a corporation that forbids sex discrimination — would select sex-neutral, performance-based criteria for hiring and promotion that produce no actionable disparity at all. Others may choose to reward various attributes that produce disparate impact — such as scores on general aptitude tests or educational achievements, see *Griggs v. Duke Power Co.* And still other managers may be guilty of intentional discrimination that produces a sex-based disparity. In such a company, demonstrating the invalidity of one manager's use of discretion will do nothing to demonstrate the invalidity of another's. A party seeking to certify a nationwide class will be unable to show that all the employees' Title VII claims will in fact depend on the answers to common questions.

Respondents have not identified a common mode of exercising discretion that pervades the entire company — aside from their reliance on Dr. Bielby's social frameworks analysis that we have rejected. In a company of Wal-Mart's size and geographical scope, it is quite unbelievable that all managers would exercise their discretion in a common way without some common direction. Respondents attempt to make that showing by means of statistical and anecdotal evidence, but their evidence falls well short.

The statistical evidence consists primarily of regression analyses performed by Dr. Richard Drogin, a statistician, and Dr. Marc Bendick, a labor economist.

Drogin conducted his analysis region-by-region, comparing the number of women promoted into management positions with the percentage of women in the available pool of hourly workers. After considering regional and national data, Drogin concluded that "there are statistically significant disparities between men and women at Wal-Mart . . . [and] these disparities . . . can be explained only by gender discrimination." Bendick compared work-force data from Wal-Mart and competitive retailers and concluded that Wal-Mart "promotes a lower percentage of women than its competitors."

Even if they are taken at face value, these studies are insufficient to establish that respondents' theory can be proved on a classwide basis. In *Falcon*, we held that one named plaintiff's experience of discrimination was insufficient to infer that "discriminatory treatment is typical of [the employer's employment] practices." A similar failure of inference arises here. As Judge Ikuta observed in her dissent [below], "[i]nformation about disparities at the regional and national level does not establish the existence of disparities at individual stores, let alone raise the inference that a company-wide policy of discrimination is implemented by discretionary decisions at the store and district level." A regional pay disparity, for example, may be attributable to only a small set of Wal-Mart stores, and cannot by itself establish the uniform, store-by-store disparity upon which the plaintiffs' theory of commonality depends.

There is another, more fundamental, respect in which respondents' statistical proof fails. Even if it established (as it does not) a pay or promotion pattern that differs from the nationwide figures or the regional figures in all of Wal-Mart's 3,400 stores, that would still not demonstrate that commonality of issue exists. Some managers will claim that the availability of women, or qualified women, or interested women, in their stores' area does not mirror the national or regional statistics. And almost all of them will claim to have been applying some sex-neutral, performance-based criteria — whose nature and effects will differ from store to store. In the landmark case of ours which held that giving discretion to lower-level supervisors can be the basis of Title VII liability under a disparate-impact theory, the plurality opinion conditioned that holding on the corollary that merely proving that the discretionary system has produced a racial or sexual disparity *is not enough*. "[T]he plaintiff must begin by identifying the specific employment practice that is challenged." *Watson*; accord, *Wards Cove Packing Co. v. Atonio* (approving that statement), superseded by statute on other grounds, 42 U.S.C. §2000e-2(k). That is all the more necessary when a class of plaintiffs is sought to be certified. Other than the bare existence of delegated discretion, respondents have identified no "specific employment practice" — much less one that ties all their 1.5 million claims together. Merely showing that Wal-Mart's policy of discretion has produced an overall sex-based disparity does not suffice.

Respondents' anecdotal evidence suffers from the same defects, and in addition is too weak to raise any inference that all the individual, discretionary personnel decisions are discriminatory. In *Teamsters v. United States*, in addition to substantial statistical evidence of company-wide discrimination, the Government (as plaintiff) produced about 40 specific accounts of racial discrimination from particular individuals. That number was significant because the company involved had only 6,472 employees, of whom 571 were minorities, and the class itself consisted of around 334. The 40 anecdotes thus represented roughly one account for every eight members of the class. Moreover, the Court of Appeals noted that the anecdotes came from individuals "spread throughout" the company who "for the most part" worked at the company's operational centers that employed the largest numbers of the class members. Here, by contrast, respondents filed some 120 affidavits reporting experiences of discrimination—aabout 1 for every 12,500 class members—relating to only some 235 out of Wal-Mart's 3,400 stores. More than half of these reports are concentrated in only six States (Alabama, California, Florida, Missouri, Texas, and Wisconsin); half of all States have only one or two anecdotes; and 14 States have no anecdotes about Wal-Mart's operations at all. Even if every single one of these accounts is true, that would not demonstrate that the entire company "operate[s] under a general policy of discrimination," *Falcon*, which is what respondents must show to certify a company-wide class.[9]

The dissent misunderstands the nature of the foregoing analysis. It criticizes our focus on the dissimilarities between the putative class members on the ground that we have "blend[ed]" Rule 23(a)(2)'s commonality requirement with Rule 23(b)(3)'s inquiry into whether common questions "predominate" over individual ones. That is not so. We quite agree that for purposes of Rule 23(a)(2) " '[e]ven a single [common] question' " will do, (quoting Nagareda, The Preexistence Principle and the Structure of the Class Action, 103 Colum. L. Rev. 149, 176, n. 110 (2003)). We consider dissimilarities not in order to determine (as Rule 23(b)(3) requires) whether common questions *predominate*, but in order to determine (as Rule 23(a)(2) requires) whether there is "[e]ven a single [common] question." And there is not here. Because respondents provide no convincing proof of a company-wide discriminatory pay and promotion policy, we have concluded that they have not established the existence of any common question.[10]

In sum, we agree with Chief Judge Kozinski['s dissent below] that the members of the class:

> held a multitude of different jobs, at different levels of Wal-Mart's hierarchy, for variable lengths of time, in 3,400 stores, sprinkled across 50 states, with a kaleidoscope of supervisors (male and female), subject to a variety of regional policies that all differed] . . . . Some thrived while others did poorly. They have little in common but their sex and this lawsuit.

---

9. The dissent says that we have adopted "a rule that a discrimination claim, if accompanied by anecdotes, must supply them in numbers proportionate to the size of the class." (Ginsburg , J., concurring in part and dissenting in part). That is not quite accurate. A discrimination claimant is free to supply as few anecdotes as he wishes. But when the claim is that a company operates under a general policy of discrimination, a few anecdotes selected from literally millions of employment decisions prove nothing at all.

10. For this reason, there is no force to the dissent's attempt to distinguish *Falcon* on the ground that in that case there were " 'no common questions of law or fact' between the claims of the lead plaintiff and the applicant class" Here also there is nothing to unite all of the plaintiffs' claims, since (contrary to the dissent's contention, the same employment practices do not "touch and concern all members of the class."

III

We also conclude that respondents' claims for backpay were improperly certified under Federal Rule of Civil Procedure 23(b)(2). Our opinion in *Ticor Title Ins. Co. v. Brown*, 511 U.S. 117, 121 (1994) (*per curiam*) expressed serious doubt about whether claims for monetary relief may be certified under that provision. We now hold that they may not, at least where (as here) the monetary relief is not incidental to the injunctive or declaratory relief.

A

Rule 23(b)(2) allows class treatment when "the party opposing the class has acted or refused to act on grounds that apply generally to the class, so that final injunctive relief or corresponding declaratory relief is appropriate respecting the class as a whole." One possible reading of this provision is that it applies *only* to requests for such injunctive or declaratory relief and does not authorize the class certification of monetary claims at all. We need not reach that broader question in this case, because we think that, at a minimum, claims for *individualized* relief (like the backpay at issue here) do not satisfy the Rule. The key to the (b)(2) class is "the indivisible nature of the injunctive or declaratory remedy warranted—the notion that the conduct is such that it can be enjoined or declared unlawful only as to all of the class members or as to none of them." Nagareda. In other words, Rule 23(b)(2) applies only when a single injunction or declaratory judgment would provide relief to each member of the class. It does not authorize class certification when each individual class member would be entitled to a different injunction or declaratory judgment against the defendant. Similarly, it does not authorize class certification when each class member would be entitled to an individualized award of monetary damages.

That interpretation accords with the history of the Rule [which] reflects a series of decisions involving challenges to racial segregation—conduct that was remedied by a single classwide order. In none of the cases cited by the Advisory Committee as examples of (b)(2)'s antecedents did the plaintiffs combine any claim for individualized relief with their classwide injunction. See Advisory Committee's Note, 39 F.R.D. 69, 102 (1966) (citing cases).

Permitting the combination of individualized and classwide relief in a (b)(2) class is also inconsistent with the structure of Rule 23(b). Classes certified under (b)(1) and (b)(2) share the most traditional justifications for class treatment—that individual adjudications would be impossible or unworkable, as in a (b)(1) class,[11]

---

11. Rule 23(b)(1) applies where separate actions by or against individual class members would create a risk of "establish[ing] incompatible standards of conduct for the party opposing the class," Rule 23(b)(1)(A), such as "where the party is obliged by law to treat the members of the class alike," *Amchem Products, Inc. v. Windsor*, 521 U.S. 591, 614 (1997), or where individual adjudications "as a practical matter, would be dispositive of the interests of the other members not parties to the individual adjudications or would substantially impair or impede their ability to protect their interests," Rule 23(b)(1)(B), such as in "'limited fund' cases, . . . in which numerous persons make claims against a fund insufficient to satisfy all claims."

or that the relief sought must perforce affect the entire class at once, as in a (b)(2) class. For that reason these are also mandatory classes: The Rule provides no opportunity for (b)(1) or (b)(2) class members to opt out, and does not even oblige the District Court to afford them notice of the action. Rule 23(b)(3), by contrast, is an "adventuresome innovation" of the 1966 amendments, framed for situations "in which 'class-action treatment is not as clearly called for.' " It allows class certification in a much wider set of circumstances but with greater procedural protections. Its only prerequisites are that "the questions of law or fact common to class members predominate over any questions affecting only individual members, and that a class action is superior to other available methods for fairly and efficiently adjudicating the controversy." Rule 23(b)(3). And unlike (b)(1) and (b)(2) classes, the (b)(3) class is not mandatory; class members are entitled to receive "the best notice that is practicable under the circumstances" and to withdraw from the class at their option. See Rule 23(c)(2)(B).

Given that structure, we think it clear that individualized monetary claims belong in Rule 23(b)(3). The procedural protections attending the (b)(3) class — predominance, superiority, mandatory notice, and the right to opt out — are missing from (b)(2) not because the Rule considers them unnecessary, but because it considers them unnecessary *to a (b)(2) class*. When a class seeks an indivisible injunction benefitting all its members at once, there is no reason to undertake a case-specific inquiry into whether class issues predominate or whether class action is a superior method of adjudicating the dispute. Predominance and superiority are self-evident. But with respect to each class member's individualized claim for money, that is not so — which is precisely why (b)(3) requires the judge to make findings about predominance and superiority before allowing the class. Similarly, (b)(2) does not require that class members be given notice and opt-out rights, presumably because it is thought (rightly or wrongly) that notice has no purpose when the class is mandatory, and that depriving people of their right to sue in this manner complies with the Due Process Clause. In the context of a class action predominantly for money damages we have held that absence of notice and opt-out violates due process. See *Phillips Petroleum Co. v. Shutts*, 472 U.S. 797, 812 (1985). While we have never held that to be so where the monetary claims do not predominate, the serious possibility that it may be so provides an additional reason not to read Rule 23(b)(2) to include the monetary claims here.

B

Against that conclusion, respondents argue that their claims for backpay were appropriately certified as part of a class under Rule 23(b)(2) because those claims do not "predominate" over their requests for injunctive and declaratory relief. They rely upon the Advisory Committee's statement that Rule 23(b)(2) "does not extend to cases in which the appropriate final relief relates *exclusively* or *predominantly* to money damages." 39 F.R.D., at 102 (emphasis added). The negative implication, they argue, is that it *does* extend to cases in which the appropriate final relief relates only partially and nonpredominantly to money damages. Of course it is the Rule itself, not the Advisory Committee's description of it, that governs. And a mere negative inference does not in our view suffice to establish a disposition that has no basis in the Rule's text, and that does obvious violence to the Rule's structural features. The mere "predominance" of a proper (b)(2) injunctive claim does nothing to justify elimination of Rule 23(b)(3)'s procedural protections: It neither establishes the superiority of *class* adjudication over *individual* adjudication nor cures the notice and opt-out problems. We fail to see why the Rule should be read to nullify these protections whenever a plaintiff class, at its option, combines its monetary claims with a request — even a "predominating request" — for an injunction.

Respondents' predominance test, moreover, creates perverse incentives for class representatives to place at risk potentially valid claims for monetary relief. In this case, for example, the named plaintiffs declined to include employees' claims for compensatory damages in their complaint. That strategy of including only backpay claims made it more likely that monetary relief would not "predominate." But it also created the possibility (if the predominance test were correct) that individual class members' compensatory-damages claims would be *precluded* by litigation they had no power to hold themselves apart from. If it were determined, for example, that a particular class member is not entitled to backpay because her denial of increased pay or a promotion was *not* the product of discrimination, that employee might be collaterally estopped from independently seeking compensatory damages based on that same denial. That possibility underscores the need for plaintiffs with individual monetary claims to decide *for themselves* whether to tie their fates to the class representatives' or go it alone — a choice Rule 23(b)(2) does not ensure that they have.

The predominance test would also require the District Court to reevaluate the roster of class members continually. . . .

Finally, respondents argue that their backpay claims are appropriate for a (b)(2) class action because a backpay award is equitable in nature. The latter may be true, but it is irrelevant. The Rule does not speak of "equitable" remedies generally but of injunctions and declaratory judgments. As Title VII itself makes pellucidly clear, backpay is neither. See 42 U.S.C. §2000e-5(g)(2)(B)(i) and (ii) (distinguishing between declaratory and injunctive relief and the payment of "backpay," see §2000e-5(g)(2)(A)).

C

[Even assuming that monetary relief "incidental to requested injunctive or declaratory relief," might be permissible under the Rule and consistent with the Due Process Clause, the plaintiffs do not satisfy this standard because] Wal-Mart is entitled to individualized determinations of each employee's eligibility for backpay. Title VII includes a detailed remedial scheme. If a plaintiff prevails in showing that an employer has discriminated against him in violation of the statute, the court "may enjoin the respondent from engaging in such unlawful employment practice, and order such affirmative action as may be appropriate, [including] reinstatement or hiring of employees, with or without backpay . . . or any other equitable relief as the court deems appropriate." §2000e-5(g)(1). But if the employer can show that it took an adverse employment action against an employee for any reason other than discrimination, the court cannot order the "hiring, reinstatement, or promotion of an individual as an employee, or the payment to him of any backpay." §2000e-5(g)(2)(A).

We have established a procedure for trying pattern-or-practice cases that gives effect to these statutory requirements. When the plaintiff seeks individual relief such as reinstatement or backpay after establishing a pattern or practice of discrimination, "a district court must usually conduct additional proceedings . . . to determine the scope of individual relief." *Teamsters*. At this phase, the burden of proof will shift to the company, but it will have the right to raise any individual affirmative defenses it may have, and to "demonstrate that the individual applicant was denied an employment opportunity for lawful reasons."

[The Court of Appeals had suggested what Justice Scalia called "Trial by Formula." which involved hearings for a sample drawn from the class members, with the results being extrapolated across the class.] We disapprove that novel project. Because the Rules Enabling Act forbids interpreting Rule 23 to "abridge, enlarge or modify any substantive right," 28 U.S.C. §2072(b), a class cannot be certified on the premise that Wal-Mart will not be entitled to litigate its statutory defenses to individual claims. And because the necessity of that litigation will prevent backpay from being "incidental" to the classwide injunction, respondents' class could not be certified even assuming, *arguendo*, that "incidental" monetary relief can be awarded to a 23(b)(2) class. . . .

Justice GINSBURG, with whom Justice BREYER , Justice SOTOMAYOR , and Justice KAGAN join, concurring in part and dissenting in part.

The class in this case, I agree with the Court, should not have been certified under Federal Rule of Civil Procedure 23(b)(2). The plaintiffs, alleging discrimination in violation of Title VII, 42 U.S.C. §2000e et seq., seek monetary relief that is not merely incidental to any injunctive or declaratory relief that might be available. A putative class of this type may be certifiable under Rule 23(b)(3), if the plaintiffs show that common class questions "predominate" over issues affecting individuals — e.g., qualification for, and the amount of, backpay or compensatory damages — and that a class action is "superior" to other modes of adjudication.

Whether the class the plaintiffs describe meets the specific requirements of Rule 23(b)(3) is not before the Court, and I would reserve that matter for consideration and decision on remand. The Court, however, disqualifies the class at the starting gate, holding that the plaintiffs cannot cross the "commonality" line set by Rule 23(a)(2). In so ruling, the Court imports into the Rule 23(a) determination concerns properly addressed in a Rule 23(b)(3) assessment.

I. . . .

B

Even a single question of law or fact common to the members of the class is sufficient for Rule 23(a) purposes. The District Court, recognizing that "one significant issue common to the class may be sufficient to warrant certification" found that the plaintiffs easily met that test. Absent an error of law or an abuse of discretion, an appellate tribunal has no warrant to upset the District Court's finding of commonality.

The District Court certified a class of "[a]ll women employed at any Wal-Mart domestic retail store at any time since December 26, 1998." The named plaintiffs, led by Betty Dukes, propose to litigate, on behalf of the class, allegations that Wal-Mart discriminates on the basis of gender in pay and promotions. They allege that the company "[r]eli[es] on gender stereotypes in making employment decisions such as . . . promotion[s] [and] pay." Wal-Mart permits those prejudices to infect personnel decisions, the plaintiffs contend, by leaving pay and promotions in the hands of "a nearly all male managerial workforce" using "arbitrary and subjective criteria." Further alleged barriers to the advancement of female employees include the company's requirement, "as a condition of promotion to management jobs, that employees be willing to relocate." Absent instruction otherwise, there is a risk that managers will act on the familiar assumption that women, because of their services to husband and children, are less mobile than men. See Dept. of Labor, Federal Glass Ceiling Commission, Good for Business: Making Full Use of the Nation's Human Capital 151 (1995).

Women fill 70 percent of the hourly jobs in the retailer's stores but make up only "33 percent of management employees." "[T]he higher one looks in the organization the lower the percentage of women." The plaintiffs' "largely uncontested descriptive statistics" also show that women working in the company's stores "are paid less than men in every region" and "that the salary gap widens over time even for men and women hired into the same jobs at the same time."

The District Court identified "systems for . . . promoting in-store employees" that were "sufficiently similar across regions and stores" to conclude that "the manner in which these systems affect the class raises issues that are common to all class members. The selection of employees for promotion to in-store management" is fairly characterized as a 'tap on the shoulder' process," in which managers have discretion about whose shoulders to tap. Vacancies are not regularly posted; from among those employees satisfying minimum qualifications, managers choose whom to promote on the basis of their own subjective impressions.

Wal-Mart's compensation policies also operate uniformly across stores, the District Court found. The retailer leaves open a $2 band for every position's hourly pay rate. Wal-Mart provides no standards or criteria for setting wages within that band, and thus does nothing to counter unconscious bias on the part of supervisors.

Wal-Mart's supervisors do not make their discretionary decisions in a vacuum. The District Court reviewed means Wal-Mart used to maintain a "carefully constructed . . . corporate culture," such as frequent meetings to reinforce the common way of thinking, regular transfers of managers between stores to ensure uniformity throughout the company, monitoring of stores "on a close and constant basis," and "Wal-Mart TV," "broadcas[t] . . . into all stores."

The plaintiffs' evidence, including class members' tales of their own experiences,[4] suggests that gender bias suffused Wal-Mart's company culture. Among illustrations, senior management often refer to female associates as "little Janie Qs." One manager told an employee that "[m]en are here to make a career and women aren't." A committee of female Wal-Mart executives concluded that "[s] tereotypes limit the opportunities offered to women."

Finally, the plaintiffs presented an expert's appraisal to show that the pay and promotions disparities at Wal-Mart "can be explained only by gender discrimination and not by . . . neutral variables. . . . Using regression analyses, their expert, Richard Drogin, controlled for factors including, inter alia, job performance, length of time with the company, and the store where an employee worked.[5] The results, the District Court found, were sufficient to raise an" inference of discrimination.?"

C

The District Court's identification of a common question, whether pay and promotions policies gave rise to unlawful discrimination, was hardly infirm. The practice of delegating to supervisors large discretion to make personnel decisions, uncontrolled by formal standards, has long been known to have the potential to produce disparate effects. Managers, like all humankind, may be prey to biases of which they are unaware.[6] The risk of discrimination is heightened when those managers are predominantly of one sex, and are steeped in a corporate culture that perpetuates gender stereotypes.

We have held that "discretionary employment practices" can give rise to Title VII claims, not only when such practices are motivated by discriminatory intent but also when they produce discriminatory results. See *Watson v. Fort Worth Bank & Trust* [reproduced at p. 232]. [The dissent "but see" cited the majority that

---

4. The majority purports to derive from *Teamsters v. United States* a rule that a discrimination claim, if accompanied by anecdotes, must supply them in numbers proportionate to the size of the class. *Teamsters*, the Court acknowledges, instructs that statistical evidence alone may suffice; that decision can hardly be said to establish a numerical floor before anecdotal evidence can be taken into account.

5. The Court asserts that Drogin showed only average differences at the "regional and national level" between male and female employees. In fact, his regression analyses showed there were disparities within stores. The majority's contention to the contrary reflects only an arcane disagreement about statistical method—which the District Court resolved in the plaintiffs' favor. Appellate review is no occasion to disturb a trial court's handling of factual disputes of this order.

6. An example vividly illustrates how subjective decisionmaking can be a vehicle for discrimination. Performing in symphony orchestras was long a male preserve. Goldin and Rouse, Orchestrating Impartiality: The Impact of "Blind" Auditions on Female Musicians, 90 Am. Econ. Rev. 715, 715-716 (2000). In the 1970's orchestras began hiring musicians through auditions open to all comers. Reviewers were to judge applicants solely on their musical abilities, yet subconscious bias led some reviewers to disfavor women. Orchestras that permitted reviewers to see the applicants hired far fewer female musicians than orchestras that conducted blind auditions, in which candidates played behind opaque screens.

"[P]roving that [a] discretionary system has produced a . . . disparity is *not enough*."
]. In *Watson*, as here, an employer had given its managers large authority over promotions. An employee sued the bank under Title VII, alleging that the "discretionary promotion system" caused a discriminatory effect based on race. Four different supervisors had declined, on separate occasions, to promote the employee. Their reasons were subjective and unknown. The employer, we noted " not developed precise and formal criteria for evaluating candidates"; "[i]t relied instead on the subjective judgment of supervisors."

Aware of "the problem of subconscious stereotypes and prejudices," we held that the employer's "undisciplined system of subjective decisionmaking" was an "employment practic[e]" that may be analyzed under the disparate impact approach. *See also* Wards *Cove Packing Co. v. Atonio* [reproduced at p. 213] (recognizing "the use of 'subjective decision making' " as an "employment practic[e]" subject to disparate-impact attack).

The plaintiffs' allegations state claims of gender discrimination in the form of biased decisionmaking in both pay and promotions. The evidence reviewed by the District Court adequately demonstrated that resolving those claims would necessitate examination of particular policies and practices alleged to affect, adversely and globally, women employed at Wal-Mart's stores. Rule 23(a)(2), setting a necessary but not a sufficient criterion for class-action certification, demands nothing further.

II

A

The Court gives no credence to the key dispute common to the class: whether Wal-Mart's discretionary pay and promotion policies are discriminatory. "What matters," the Court asserts, "is not the raising of common 'questions,' " but whether there are "[d]issimilarities within the proposed class" that "have the potential to impede the generation of common answers."

The Court blends Rule 23(a)(2)'s threshold criterion with the more demanding criteria of Rule 23(b)(3), and thereby elevates the (a)(2) inquiry so that it is no longer "easily satisfied," 5 J. Moore et al., Moore's Federal Practice §23.23[2], p. 23-72 (3d ed. 2011).[7] Rule 23(b)(3) certification requires, in addition to the four

---

7. The Court places considerable weight on *General Telephone Co. of Southwest v. Falcon*. That case has little relevance to the question before the Court today. The lead plaintiff in *Falcon* alleged discrimination evidenced by the company's failure to promote him and other Mexican-American employees and failure to hire Mexican-American applicants. There were "no common questions of law or fact" between the claims of the lead plaintiff and the applicant class. The plaintiff-employee alleged that the defendant-employer had discriminated against him intentionally. The applicant class claims, by contrast, were "advanced under the 'adverse impact' theory," appropriate for facially neutral practices. "[T]he only commonality [wa]s that respondent is a Mexican-American and he seeks to represent a class of Mexican-Americans." Here the same practices touch and concern all members of the class.

23(a) findings, determinations that "questions of law or fact common to class members predominate over any questions affecting only individual members" and that "a class action is superior to other available methods for . . . adjudicating the controversy."

The Court's emphasis on differences between class members mimics the Rule 23(b)(3) inquiry into whether common questions "predominate" over individual issues. And by asking whether the individual differences "impede" common adjudication, the Court duplicates 23(b)(3)'s question whether "a class action is superior" to other modes of adjudication. Indeed, Professor Nagareda, whose "dissimilarities" inquiry the Court endorses, developed his position in the context of Rule 23(b)(3). "The Rule 23(b)(3) predominance inquiry" is meant to "tes[t] whether proposed classes are sufficiently cohesive to warrant adjudication by representation." *Amchem Products, Inc. v. Windsor,* 521 U.S. 591, 623 (1997). If courts must conduct a "dissimilarities" analysis at the Rule 23(a)(2) stage, no mission remains for Rule 23(b)(3).

Because Rule 23(a) is also a prerequisite for Rule 23(b)(1) and Rule 23(b)(2) classes, the Court's "dissimilarities" position is far reaching. Individual differences should not bar a Rule 23(b)(1) or Rule 23(b)(2) class, so long as the Rule 23(a) threshold is met. For example, in *Franks v. Bowman Transp. Co.,* [reproduced at p. 658], a Rule 23(b)(2) class of African-American truck drivers complained that the defendant had discriminatorily refused to hire black applicants. We recognized that the "qualification[s] and performance" of individual class members might vary. "Generalizations concerning such individually applicable evidence," we cautioned, "cannot serve as a justification for the denial of [injunctive] relief to the entire class."

B

The "dissimilarities" approach leads the Court to train its attention on what distinguishes individual class members, rather than on what unites them. Given the lack of standards for pay and promotions, the majority says, "demonstrating the invalidity of one manager's use of discretion will do nothing to demonstrate the invalidity of another's."

Wal-Mart's delegation of discretion over pay and promotions is a policy uniform throughout all stores. The very nature of discretion is that people will exercise it in various ways. A system of delegated discretion, *Watson* held, is a practice actionable under Title VII when it produces discriminatory outcomes. A finding that Wal-Mart's pay and promotions practices in fact violate the law would be the first step in the usual order of proof for plaintiffs seeking individual remedies for company-wide discrimination. *Teamsters v. United States;* see *Albemarle Paper Co. v. Moody* [reproduced at p. 276]. That each individual employee's unique circumstances will ultimately determine whether she is entitled to backpay or damages, §2000e-5(g)(2)(A) (barring backpay if a plaintiff "was refused . . . advancement . . . for any reason other than discrimination"), should not factor into the Rule 23(a)(2) determination.

* * *

The Court errs in importing a "dissimilarities" notion suited to Rule 23(b)(3) into the Rule 23(a) commonality inquiry. I therefore cannot join Part II of the Court's opinion.

NOTES

1. *Procedure and Substance*. As Justice Scalia makes clear, the class action certification question is intimately bound up with the merits determination, which is apparently not a problem. While, as the majority opinion states, courts frequently decide preliminary questions that are also relevant to the merits of a claim, this means that *Wal-Mart* is not merely a "procedural" case: the answer to the procedural question of whether there is a class sufficiently homogeneous to challenge a pattern of discrimination, in effect, requires answering the substantive question of whether, under either systemic disparate treatment or systemic disparate impact theories, there exists the requisite policy or practice of discrimination. The Court reaches its certification decision by clarifying (many would say changing) substantive theories. Ultimately, the majority rejects the two systemic theories on the facts before it and sees the named plaintiffs as asserting cases of individual disparate treatment, essentially unconnected to other class members' claims. See further discussion in Chapters 2 and 3, *supra*. Is *Wal-Mart* the *Iqbal* and *Twombly* of class actions?

2. *Bad Stats*. As the case reached the Court, there wasn't much dispute that the district court could have properly found that Wal-Mart's gender profile of pay and promotions very unfavorable to women. Although Wal-Mart had proffered its own statistical studies to the contrary, the lower court had accepted the plaintiffs' evidence in this regard, the testimony of Drs. Drogin and Benedick. Dr. Drogin found statistical evidence of discrimination at the regional level by comparing male and female employees within Wal-Mart. Dr. Marc Bendick's conducted a "benchmarking" study comparing Wal-Mart with its big box competitors, with women faring worse at Wal-Mart in pay and promotions. Given the EEOC's failure in *EEOC* v. *Sears*, reproduced at p. 157, it's easy to see how important it was for the plaintiffs to rule out the lack of interest defense through Bendick's work. Thus, there was substantial statistical evidence that something was rotten in Wal-Mart. Indeed, it's not only plaintiffs' experts who see a problem with Wal-Mart's gender profile. *See* Steven Greenhouse, *Lawyers Alerted Wal-Mart to Risks Years Before a Bias Suit*, N.Y. TIMES, June 3, 2010, at D1 (Wal-Mart retained Akin Gump Strauss Hauer & Feld to examine its exposure, and the firm "found widespread gender disparities in pay and promotion at Wal-Mart and Sam's Club stores and urged the company to take basic steps — like posting every job opening and creating specific goals to promote women and minorities — to avoid liability.").

But, these statistical showings weren't enough to certify a class that included every woman at every Wal-Mart store. The Court saw two problems. First, even taking these studies at face value, "[a] regional pay disparity, for example, may be attributable to only a small set of Wal-Mart stores, and cannot by itself establish the uniform, store-by-store disparity upon which the plaintiffs' theory of commonality depends." Second, and more fundamentally, even if this proof

> established (as it does not) a pay or promotion pattern that differs from the nationwide figures or the regional figures in *all* of Wal-Mart's 3,400 stores, that would still not demonstrate that commonality of issue exists. Some managers will claim that the availability of women, or qualified women, or interested women, in their stores' area does not mirror the national or regional statistics. And almost all of them will claim to have been applying some sex-neutral, performance-based criteria—whose nature and effects will differ from store to store.

In short, even if each store reflected a gender disparity in its stats, there might be varying explanations for those results, not all of which are discrimination. The point seems to be that such proof wouldn't establish nation-wide systemic disparate treatment.

3. Decentralized Decisions as a Central Policy. What plaintiffs needed was some centralized, corporate-wide policy that would implicate Wal-Mart as a whole and thus justify a firm-wide class action. And they had to link that policy to the gender disparities the other experts had uncovered. Without some unifying policy, the statistical showing of female underrepresentation in higher level positions and lower salaries would allow only a class action against individual stores or regions since it seemed undisputed that the differentials were due to store-level decisions. Plaintiffs thought that the glue that tied the underrepresentation to the policy of giving store managers unstructured and unreviewed discretion in pay and promotions was that all the women faced the same risk that their managers would individually discriminate against them because the Wal-Mart policy enable them to do so. *Wal-Mart*, however, is consistent with prior cases that had narrowed class actions when it became clear that challenged practices were established locally and not centrally, e.g., *Cooper v. S. Co.*, 390 F.3d 695, 714-715 (11th Cir. 2004) (no commonality, since "the hiring, compensation, and promotion decisions at issue were made by different managers in different companies implementing different policies"). *But see Brown v. Nucor Corp.*, 576 F.3d 149 (4th Cir. 2009) (district court erred in finding insufficient commonality due to the plant's departmental structure with respect to their hostile work environment claims given proof of plant-wide racist acts, including the broadcasting of racial slurs and monkey noises over the plantwide speaker system and plant-wide displays of the confederate flag.). Even within a single store, a class might be narrowed if some policies or practices applied to some kinds of employees and not others, limiting the certification. *Cooper v. Fed. Reserve Bank of Richmond*, 467 U.S. 867 (1984) (named plaintiffs did not have claims typical of members of the putative class who were denied senior management positions).

Plaintiffs' strategy was clever, if ultimately unsuccessful. They claimed that Wal-Mart's centralized policy of delegating relatively unfettered discretion to individual store managers in making pay and promotion decisions was the question common to all members of the putative class because it allowed their discriminatory decisions to go unchecked, even though Wal-Mart received data concerning all pay and promotion decisions. Plaintiffs used the multiple regression studies that rejected the null hypothesis that such asymmetrical outcomes in pay and promotion were unrelated to sex. That was strong evidence that these outcomes were because of sex.

To further support the inference of Wal-Mart's intent to discriminate, the plaintiff turned to a social framework expert, Dr. Bielby. While he did not view the centralized polices as discriminatory per se, Bielby testified that, precisely by virtue of decentralizing decisionmaking, these policies facilitated discrimination at the store level. This raised two questions. First, whether Dr. Bielby's testimony was admissible? Second, if so, did it support the class certification?

4. *Speaking of Experts*. The majority was quite disdainful of Bielby and, likely, his entire area of expertise. But a rich body of social science literature documents discrimination from a social framework perspective; indeed, you have encountered these studies repeatedly in this book. Nor is there much doubt that Dr. Bielby was qualified to speak to that literature, at least in a general way. But the academic debate referred to in the majority's footnote 8 questioned whether an expert should be permitted to testify as to the applicability of social framework literature to the facts at Wal-Mart. The essential argument is that, before a social scientist can opine on such matters, he or she should conduct a detailed study of the institution in question, not merely rely on information obtained in discovery by attorneys who obviously have a predisposition to seek damaging data. John Monahan, Laurens Walker & Gregory Mitchell *Contextual Evidence of Gender Discrimination: The Ascendance of "Social Frameworks*, 94 VA. L. REV. 1715 (2008). *See also* Gregory Mitchell, *Good Causes and Bad Science*, 63 VANDERBILT L. REV. EN BANC 133 (2010); David L. Faigman, Nilanjana Dasgupta & Cecilia L. Ridgeway, *A Matter of Fit: The Law of Discrimination and the Science of Implicit Bias*, 59 HASTINGS L.J. 1389, 1431 (2008). There is, however, another side to the debate. *See* Melissa Hart & Paul M. Secunda, *A Matter of Context: Social Framework Evidence in Employment Discrimination Class Actions*, 78 FORDHAM L. REV. 37, (2009). The *Wal-Mart* majority merely notes the expertise question and does not resolve it since it found that, even accepting Bielby's testimony at face value, it did not justify certification.

5. *Retreating from* Watson. Whatever the merits of "battle of the experts," the Court wasn't buying the argument that a policy of delegating authority was actionable: "It is also a very common and presumptively reasonable way of doing business—one that we have said 'should itself raise no inference of discriminatory conduct,'" citing *Watson*. But *Watson* had held that subjective employment practices can be attacked if they result in disparate impact. Didn't Bielby's testimony, coupled with the statistical evidence, create a common question of whether Wal-Mart had a central policy with a disparate impact?

Plaintiffs argued that their cases fit exactly *Watson v. Fort Worth Bank & Trust*, reproduced at p. 232, which had recognized that subjective policies with a disproportionate impact could be attacked by the disparate impact theory, at least in part because of the possibility that lower-level managers might be acting on the basis of stereotypical views. The Court acknowledged *Watson* to be a "landmark case," but then proceeded to gut it. Justice Scalia noted that the *Watson* "plurality opinion *conditioned* that holding on the corollary that merely proving that the discretionary system has produced a racial or sexual disparity *is not enough.*'[T]he plaintiff must begin by identifying the specific employment practice that is challenged.'" The Court cited *Wards Cove Packing Co.* v. *Atonio.* Thus, Dr. Bielby may have a identified a general policy of "delegated discretion, [but] respondents have identified no "specific employment practice" — much less one that ties all their 1.5 million claims together. Merely showing that Wal-Mart's policy of discretion has produced an overall sex-based disparity does not suffice."

What's left of *Watson?* The Court writes that plaintiffs "have not identified a common mode of exercising discretion that pervades the entire company." Can you imagine what that "mode" might be? Suppose plaintiffs had claimed that the policy of requiring employees seeking promotion to be willing to relocate. Would that suffice to create common question if plaintiffs could adduce evidence of disparate impact?

6. *Bye-bye (b)(2).* Although the majority's resolution of the commonality question was enough to require reversal, it went further to resolve a dispute that had been simmering in the lower courts for decades: assuming commonality, can a Title VII class action be certified under Rule 23(b)(2)? As we have seen, the distinction is of great significance in large part because notice to class members, and the concomitant right to opt out, is required under (b)(3) but not under (b)(2).

Because of its language focusing on injunctive and declaratory relief, there was a long-running dispute in the circuits as to whether class actions seeking monetary relief could ever be certified under (b)(2). Those who favored such certification argued that Title VII suits, being essentially equitable, could fall within the paragraph, at least if the monetary relief sought did not "predominate." *See generally* Suzette Malveaux, *Class Actions at the Crossroads: An Answer to* Wal-Mart v. Dukes, 5 HARV. L. & POL'Y REV. ___ (2011); Suzette M. Malveaux, *Fighting to Keep Employment Discrimination Class Actions Alive: How* Allison v. Citgo's *Predomination Requirement Threatens to Undermine Title VII Enforcement,* 26 BERKELEY J. EMP. & LAB. L. 405, 408 (2005).

That dispute came to an abrupt end with *Wal-Mart.* Although there was a dissent on the issue of commonality, the justices were unanimous that (b)(2) was inapplicable when monetary relief was more than incidental to equitable relief, regardless of whether the monetary relief was framed as legal (damages) or equitable (backpay). The majority even questioned whether "incidental" monetary relief would be appropriate when a class is certified under (b)(2). This means that, for all practical purposes, employment discrimination suits will have to be brought under Rule 23(b)(3), which requires initial notice to class members and the right to opt out of the suit. From a plaintiff's perspective, notice is typically prohibitively expensive for very large class actions.

7. *Due Process and Rules Enabling Act.* Because it found no commonality, the majority did not focus on precisely how this case might have been tried, given its size and variety. The question is not likely to arise in the future in employment discrimination actions since *Wal-Mart's* combined of tightening the commonality requirement and eliminating Rule 23(b)(2) certification means that any classes that can be certified are likely to be relatively small and therefore much more manageable. But it's worth noting the Court's slap-down of cases like *Hilao v. Estate of Marcos.* And whether or not the Court's rejection of "Trial by Formula" governs other areas, it's pretty clear that no such approach can be taken with Title VII cases

in light of the majority's invocation of the Rules Enabling Act as a limitation on reading Rule 23 to trump substantive rights: even if a plaintiff class succeeds on a systemic theory, defendants have the right to show that each woman, although having in some sense been a victim of discrimination, was not actually harmed by the challenged decision.

8. *The Policy Debates.* While *Wal-Mart* clearly resolves many class action questions as a matter of doctrine, in the process probably ending sprawling employment discrimination class actions, it's worth a moment to consider the underlying policy concerns of the class action debate. Reservations about the general desirability of class actions can be traced to three themes: unfairness to class members; unfairness to defendants; and distortion of the attorney-client relationship.

As the *Wal-Mart* majority notes, class actions may be unfair to class members, who may find their claims lost by virtue of preclusion if they are not adequately represented in the litigation. To a large extent, however, these concerns are ameliorated for 23(b)(3) certifications with their concomitant notice and opt-out rights. Further, the Supreme Court has held that preclusive effects on class members are much more limited than might first appear. In *Cooper v. Fed. Reserve Bank of Richmond*, 467 U.S. 867, 869 (1984), the Court held "a judgment in a class action determining that an employer did not engage in a general pattern or practice of racial discrimination against the certified class of employees [does not preclude] a class member from maintaining a subsequent civil action alleging an individual claim of racial discrimination against the employer."

A second concern is that class actions are unfair to defendants, who may be forced to settle regardless of the merits by the sheer magnitude of potential liability and costs of defense. This because of a straightforward economic calculation: as exposure rises, even a very small risk of liability will push an economically rational defendant to settle. But given Wal-Mart's notorious success in obtaining price concessions from its vendors because of its huge buying power, do you find it odd to be concerned that the potential liability generated by its very size is problematic? And is there something wrong with a system that finds some defendants "too big to sue"?

The third set of concerns arises from fears that class actions may be inimical because they effectively divorce the attorney from her client. This is a standard objection to class actions, and there are certainly many instances where the major beneficiaries of a class action are not the class members but rather the attorneys. *See generally* Charlotte S. Alexander, *Would an Opt In Requirement Fix the Class Action Settlement? Evidence from the Fair Labor Standards Act* 80 Miss. L.J. 443 (2010).

9. *What's Left of Antidiscrimination Class Action?* The clearest message of *Wal-Mart* is a practical one: plaintiffs need to first address the size of the class in terms of having the resources to provide notice. It's not impossible that the outer limits of classes will be defined by plaintiffs' attorneys' budgets. Secondly, plaintiffs must identify a class-wide issue, and *Wal-Mart* makes it harder. It seems likely that traditional disparate impact attacks on objective measures such as tests can continue to be mounted. *See Parra v. Bashas', Inc.*, 536 F.3d 975, 979 (9th Cir. 2008) (permitting attack on pay scales that were common for all employees). The same would be true of systemic disparate treatment cases focused on bias of the same

decisionmaker (although these might run afoul of the numerosity requirement). However, the extent to which plaintiffs can identify subjective policies that are nevertheless sufficiently specific under the *Wal-Mart* analysis to be subject to disparate impact analysis remains unclear.

Further, ADA suits would seem to pose particularly difficult questions. Although ADA claims have been certified as class actions in the past, a pre-*Wal-Mart* recent decision suggests that they are not appropriate for class certification. *Hohider v. UPS*, 574 F.3d 169 (3d Cir. 2009), involved an ADA challenge to the employer's "100 percent healed" policy, which barred employees from returning to work under any medical restrictions. Although the court assumed that a pattern and practice case could be brought under the ADA, it found that plaintiffs' claims "cannot be adjudicated within the parameters of Rule 23" since "establishing the unlawful discrimination alleged by plaintiffs would require determining whether class members are 'qualified' under the ADA," which is too individualized a question for certification under Rule 23(a) and (b)(2). *Id.* at 186. This was true even if the policy were per se discriminatory since such a finding "cannot give rise to a finding of liability and relief under the ADA without the statutorily required inquiry into whether those affected by the policy are disabled and able to perform the essential functions of the jobs they seek or desire with or without reasonable accommodation." *Id.* at 195. Does this reflect the same mistake that the dissent accused the majority of making — confusing the common question with the predominance inquiry?

4. Settling Class Actions

Page 646. In carryover paragraph delete sentence beginning "Judge Kleinfeld" and add at end:

See also Nantiya Ruan, *Bringing Sense to Incentives: An Examination of Incentive Payments to Named Plaintiffs in Employment Discrimination Class Actions*, 10 EMP. RTS. & EMP. POL'Y J. 395, 426 (2006) (examining when settlements involving incentive payments to class representatives should be permissible and arguing that, because of the risks and costs to such persons, precedents limiting such awards in the securities and consumer contexts should not control).

G. Federal Government Enforcement

Page 646. Delete last full paragraph; replace with:

The enforcement scheme we have examined means that the EEOC is the recipient of a huge number of charges of discrimination, recently exceeding 75,000. The ability of the Commission to effectively process these charges has been a subject of continued concern. *See generally* Nancy M. Modesitt, *Reinventing the EEOC*, 63 SMU L. REV.1237 (2010); Marcia L. McCormick, *The Truth Is Out There: Revamping Federal Antidiscrimination Enforcement for the Twenty-First Century*, 30 BERKLEY J. EMP. & LAB. L. 193 (2009); Julie Chi-hye Suk, *Antidiscrimination Law in the Administrative State*, 2006 U. ILL. L. REV. 405, 467-73 (2006); Michael Selmi, *The Value of the EEOC: The Agency's Role in Employment Discrimination Law*, 57 OHIO ST. L.J. 1 (1996).

Page 647.   Add after *Shell Oil* cite in first full paragraph:

EEOC v. Fed. Express Corp., 543 F.3d 531 (9th Cir. 2008) (EEOC may issue administrative subpoena against employer even after charging party has been issued right-to-sue letter and files suit);

Page 647.   Add at end of second full paragraph:

EEOC v. UPS, 587 F.3d 136 (2d Cir. 2009) (at the investigatory stage, the EEOC is not required to show probable cause that discrimination occurred or to produce evidence to establish a prima facie case of discrimination); *EEOC v. Watkins Motor Lines, Inc.*, 553 F.3d 593 (7th Cir. 2009) (once a valid charge is filed, the EEOC may determine how to investigate regardless of the attempted withdrawal of the charge by the filing party).

H.   Suit Against Governmental Employers

1.   State and Local Government Employment

a.   Tenth and Eleventh Amendment Challenges

Page 648.   Add before *State Police* cite in last full paragraph:

EEOC v. Bd. of Supervisors for Univ. of La. Sys., 539 F.3d 270 (5th Cir. 2009) (EEOC could sue a state to enforce the ADEA, without regard to Eleventh Amendment immunity, and could seek make-whole relief in that suit on behalf of individuals who would be barred by the Eleventh Amendment from suing the state themselves);

Page 648.   Add at end of last full paragraph:

Burrus v. State Lottery Comm'n of Ind., 546 F.3d 417 (7th Cir. 2008) (Indiana state lottery was not arm of the state because it raised its own revenue and judgments against it would not be paid out of state coffers, even though such judgments might reduce the proceeds the lottery paid to the state).

Page 648.   Add after *Lapides* cite in last paragraph:

But see Lombardo v. Commonwealth, 540 F.3d 190 (3d Cir. 2008) (even though the state waived its Eleventh Amendment immunity to suit by removal to federal court, it did not waive its immunity from liability).

Page 649.   Add at end of carryover paragraph:

Some of the circuit court spending clause authority may be cast into doubt by *Sossamon v. Texas*, 131 S. Ct. 1651 (2011), a case decided under the Religious Land Use and Institutionalized Persons Act. While the Court did not question the authority of Congress to condition receipt of federal funds on susceptibility to private suit, it did not find RLUIPA language to be sufficiently clear: "RLUIPA's authorization of 'appropriate relief against a government,' §2000cc-2(a), is not the unequivocal expression of state consent that our precedents require. 'Appropriate relief' does not so clearly and unambiguously waive sovereign immunity to private suits for damages that we can 'be certain that the State in fact consents to such a suit.'" 131 S. Ct. at 1658-59.

Page 649.   Add in second full paragraph before *Kovacevich* cite:

Alaska v. EEOC, 564 F.3d 1062 (9th Cir. 2009) (since plaintiff's Title VII claims alleged actual violations of the Fourteenth Amendment in terms of sex discrimination (as opposed to conduct that could be proscribed only prophylactically under §5), the Government Employee Rights Act validly abrogated Alaska's Eleventh Amendment immunity were that otherwise to apply in EEOC administrative proceedings);

Page 650.   Add at the end of carryover section:

While §1981(c) explicitly authorizes private suits against state and local governments, there is a question as to whether suits against such entities are subject to the constraints applicable to §1983. See pp. 111 of this Supplement.

Page 650.   Add at end of first full paragraph:

"b. Exemptions"

For example, the exemption has been applied to bar sexual harassment claims against a sheriff by his female chief deputy. *Townsend v. Shook*, 323 F. App'x 245 (4th Cir. 2009), and to assistant prosecutors. *Opp v. Office of the State's Atty.*, 630 F.3d

616, 621 (7th Cir. 2010) (all assistant states attorneys were "appointees on the policymaking level" under the ADEA because the position categorically "authorizes, either directly or indirectly, meaningful input into governmental decision-making on issues where there is room for principled disagreement on goals or their implementation." (internal quotations omitted).

Page 650.   Add in last full paragraph before *Bd. of County Com'rs* cite:

Marion County Coroner's Office v. EEOC, 612 F.3d 924 (7th Cir. 2010) (EEOC findings of discrimination under GERA should be upheld unless they are "(1) arbitrary, capricious, an abuse of discretion, or otherwise not consistent with law; (2) not made consistent with required procedures; or (3) unsupported by substantial evidence.");

2.   *Federal Employment*

Page 651.   Add in fifth line after "to the ADEA":

Although these provisions do not speak expressly of retaliation, there is no doubt that they bar both discrimination on the prohibited grounds and retaliation against federal employees. *Gomez-Perez v. Potter*, 128 S. Ct. 1931 (2008).

Page 651.   In first paragraph, delete sentence beginning with "While the substantive coverage," including citation.

Page 651.   Add at end of page:

See also Nancy M. Modesitt, *The Hundred-Years War: The Ongoing Battle Between Courts and Agencies over the Right to Interpret Federal Law*, 74 Mo. L. Rev. 949 (2009) (critiquing the EEOC's policy of nonacquiescence in federal circuit decisions in administrative resolution of federal employee discrimination complaints).

8   *Judicial Relief*

A. Introduction

Page 658.   **Add at end of Note 4,** *Equitable vs. Legal Remedies*:

See Tyler J. Bowles, *Employment Discrimination: Distinguishing Between Equitable Remedies and Compensatory Damages,* 15 J. LEGAL ECON. 11 (2008).

B. Equitable Relief to the Victims of Discrimination

3. Limits on Backpay

a. The Backpay Period

Page 669.   **In Note 6,** *Is Each Victim Entitled to Full Relief,* **Delete citation to** *Wal-Mart*; **replace with:**

But see Wal-Mart Stores, Inc. v. Dukes, 131 S. Ct. 2541 (2011) reproduced at p. 230 of this supplement (in the class action certification context, holding that "Trial by Forumula" not appropriate because the defendant was entitled to show that it had not discriminated against every member of the putative class).

Page 675.   **Add at end of Note 2,** *Probing* **Ford** *More Deeply*:

See Mary Price Birk & Roger G. Trim, *Strategic Use of an Offer of Reinstatement to Cut Off Damages,* 34 EMP. REL. L.J. 58 (2008).

8. Judicial Relief

Page 679. In Note 4, *Chilling Effects?*, replace Melissa Hart cite with:

Melissa Hart, *Retaliatory Litigation Tactics: The Chilling Effects of "After-Acquired Evidence,"* 40 Ariz. St. L.J. 401, 451-52 (2008) (urging the abandonment of the after-acquired evidence rule because it risks filtering out serious instances of discrimination by putting the plaintiff on trial or, as importantly, by raising that risk in the mind of the potential plaintiff and her lawyer, but urging at least recognition that raising that defense be considered retaliatory when doing so is designed to discourage discrimination claims).

b. The Duty to Mitigate Damages

Page 680. Add at end of carryover paragraph:

See also Stremple v. Nicholson, 289 F. App'x 571 (3d Cir. 2008) (plaintiff made reasonable attempts to mitigate in light of (a) the highly specialized nature of his former position, (b) his unsuccessful applications for chief of surgery in the few suitable hospitals in the area, and (c) the prohibitive costs of malpractice insurance given his financial position; plaintiff's ceasing to maintain his license was a financial necessity, and not a disqualifying factor with respect to the award).

4. Front Pay

Page 680. Add at end of third sentence of Front Pay section:

See Lulaj v. Wackenhut Corp., 512 F.3d 760, 767 (6th Cir. 2008) ("the period of liability will end if plaintiff voluntarily quits his employment with the defendant absent a constructive discharge. Furthermore, front pay is analogous to back pay in that it imagines the situation that gives rise to back pay continuing to some future date. Thus it is equivalent to suing for back pay at that future date. '[I]n order for an employee to recover back pay for lost wages beyond the date of his retirement or resignation, the evidence must establish that the employer constructively discharged the employee.'") (citations and internal quotations omitted).

Page 683. Add at end of first paragraph of Note 5, *Experts*:

See Donlin v. Philips Lighting N. Am. Corp., 564 F.3d 207, 216-17 (3d Cir. 2009) (while plaintiff could testify as to facts within her personal knowledge (such as her current and past earnings), she was not permitted to testify as to portions of the damage requiring technical or specialized knowledge, such as the probability of annual pay raises and present-value discounting).

C. Legal Remedies to Victims of Discrimination

Page 684.   Add after extract in paragraph 4:

See generally Scott A. Moss & Peter H. Huang, *How the New Economics Can Improve Discrimination Law, and How Economics Can Survive the Demise of the "Rational Actor,"* 51 WM. & MARY L. REV. 183 (2009) (while the limitations on recovery for emotional distress and punitive damages mean that the basic Title VII damages are lost income, the endowment effect and happiness research indicate that discharged long-term employees typically suffer great psychic loss);

Page 685.   Add near end of carryover paragraph after "for age discrimination":

Collazo v. Nicholson, 535 F.3d 41 (1st Cir. 2008)

Page 686.   Add at end of Note 1, *Proving Mental Distress***:**

Any privacy interests in a patient's treatment for mental distress will be waived should the plaintiff put her psychological state in issue by seeking damages for such harm. *Fisher v. Sw. Bell Tel. Co.*, 361 F. App'x 974 (10th Cir. 2010).

2. Punitive Damages

Page 695.   Delete Note 5(b); replace with the following:

5(b). *Employer's Good Faith Compliance*. Even if a manager acting within the scope of his employment discriminates maliciously, the employer is still not liable for punitive damages if it made a good faith effort to prevent discrimination. *See Sturgill v. UPS*, 512 F.3d 1024, 1035 (8th Cir. 2008) (no punitive damages in failure to accommodate religion case where UPS followed a nationwide, multi-step protocol for considering employee requests for religious accommodations and no agent acted with malice or reckless indifference to the accommodation request); *Romano v. U-Haul Int'l*, 233 F.3d 655 (1st Cir. 2000), held this to be an affirmative defense on which the employer had the burden of proof.

Note the Supreme Court's reference in *Kolstad* to "good faith efforts to *enforce* an antidiscrimination policy" (emphasis added). Thus, a nondiscrimination policy is not by itself sufficient. *Romano*, 233 F. 3d at 670 ("A defendant must also show that efforts have been made to implement its anti-discrimination policy, through education of its employees and actual enforcement of its mandate."). *See Parker v. Gen. Extrusions, Inc.*, 491 F.3d 596, 604 (6th Cir. 2007) ("a rational fact-finder could plausibly [find that] any investigation into those complaints was, at best, half-hearted and, at worst, a sham"); *Heaton v. Weitz Co.*, 534 F.3d 882 (8th Cir. 2008) (punitive damages award appropriate when a reasonable jury could find that, despite initially handling a complaint appropriately, the employer placed a "biased or perceived partial person" in charge of investigations that were cursory and indifferent); *EEOC v. Fed. Express Corp.*, 513 F.3d 360, 373-74 (4th Cir. 2008) (despite appropriate employer policy, a jury could award punitive damages when a manager perceived the risk of an ADA violation but nevertheless failed to respond to a deaf employee's request for complete notes of daily meetings or ASL/close-captioning assistance). *See also McInnis v. Fairfield Cmtys., Inc.*, 458 F.3d 1129 (10th Cir. 2006) (upholding punitive damages despite contention that employer made good-faith efforts to educate its employees about its written policies against discrimination and retaliation.

Nevertheless, a number of employers have successfully invoked the defense despite deficiencies in their enforcement efforts. *See Hatley v. Hilton Hotels Corp.*, 308 F.3d 473 (5th Cir. 2002) (employer who had a policy forbidding sexual harassment, trained new employees on sexual harassment, had grievance procedure for complaints, and initiated investigation of complaints had a good faith defense to punitive damages although its agent failed to respond to employee's complaints and acted with reckless indifference); *Bryant v. Aiken Reg'l Med. Ctrs., Inc.*, 333 F.3d 536, 548-49 (4th Cir. 2003) (equal employment opportunity policy, grievance policy, assurance that employees would not be retaliated against, diversity training program, and voluntary monitoring of departmental demographics "to keep the employee base reflective of the pool of potential employees in the area" were "widespread anti-discrimination efforts" that barred the award of punitive damages).

Page 696. Add new Note 7A:

7A. *The Prevalence of Punitive Damages.* The effect of these rules on the ground is discussed in Joseph Seiner, *The Failure of Punitive Damages in Employment Discrimination Cases: A Call for Change*, 50 WM. & MARY L. REV. 735 (2008) (an analysis of all federal district court decisions during 2004 and 2005 revealed that, of more than 600 relevant opinions, only 24 either awarded punitive damages under Title VII or upheld a jury's award of such relief; slightly over 17 percent of those Title VII cases that went to a jury resulted in a punitive damage award by the jury, with 29 percent of the juries that found in favor of the plaintiff also awarding punitive damages).

Page 696. In Note 10, *Are Compensatory and Punitive Damages Linked?* Add before *Tisdale* cite:

Abner v. Kan. City S. R.R. Co., 513 F.3d 154, 160 (5th Cir. 2008) ("a punitive damages award under Title VII and §1981 need not be accompanied by compensatory damages. We base our holding on the language of the statute, its provision of a cap, and the purpose of punitive damages under Title VII.").

Page 697. Add after *see generally* cite at end of first paragraph of Note 11, *Substantive Due Process Limits on Punitive Damages*:

Sandra Sperino, *Judicial Preemption of Punitive Damages*, 78 U. CIN. L. REV. 227 (2009) (judges are too assertive in defining excessive in punitive damages, including focusing on statutory caps and ignoring combination uncapped causes of action when drawing comparisons).

Page 697. Add before *Lust* cite in last paragraph of Note 11, *Substantive Due Process Limits on Punitive Damages*:

EEOC v. Fed. Express Corp., 513 F.3d 360, 378 (4th Cir. 2008) ("the fact that the punitive damages award, when aggregated with the compensatory damages award, was substantially below the $300,000 statutory cap on such damages, as provided for by 42 U.S.C. §1981a, provides additional support for the reasonableness and constitutionality of the punitive damages award. The statutory cap of $300,000 provided FedEx with fair notice of the range of available civil penalties for acts of discrimination that contravened the ADA.").

Page 698. Add after *Kramer* cite in carryover Note 12, *Compensatory and Punitive Damages*:

Alvarado v. Cajun Operating Co., 588 F.3d 1261 (9th Cir. 2009) (same).

Page 699. Add in last full paragraph of Note on Personal Liability of Employees before *Dearth* cite:

Fantini v. Salem State Coll., 557 F.3d 22 (1st Cir. 2009) (no individual employee liability under Title VII).

D. Attorneys' Fees

Page 707. In carryover Note 2, *When Is a Prevailing Defendant Entitled to Attorneys' Fees?* delete *Balmer* cite and add':

See also Stover v. Hattiesburg Pub. Sch. Dist., 549 F.3d 985 (5th Cir. 2008) (no fees award to prevailing defendant despite unanimous verdict for defendant when the trial court had denied employer's motions for summary judgment and judgment as matter of law); *Cf. Harris v. Maricopa County Superior Court*, 631 F.3d 963, 973 (9th Cir. 2011) (a prevailing employer could be awarded attorneys' fees only for claims falling within Title VII's scope, and it was therefore impermissible to award pro-rata share of "general fees" incurred defending both frivolous and nonfrivolous claims).

Even when a defendant establishes that some of the plaintiff's claims are frivolous and the defendant is therefore entitled to attorneys' fees, it does not follow that the defendant is compensated for all the work entailed in the case when the plaintiff has asserted nonfrivolous claims. It can recover only for fees related to the frivolous claims, and only "rough justice" is required in sorting out the compensable work from that would have been entailed in the absence of the frivolous claims. *Fox v. Vice*, 131 S. Ct. _____ (2011) ("But trial courts need not, and indeed should not, become green-eyeshade accountants. The essential goal in shifting fees (to either party) is to do rough justice, not to achieve auditing perfection. So trial courts may take into account their overall sense of a suit, and may use estimates in calculating and allocating an attorney's time. . . . That means the trial court must determine whether the fees requested would not have accrued but for the frivolous claim.").

Page 707.   Delete Note 3; replace with:

3. *When Does a Party Prevail?* Under the fee provisions, only a "prevailing party" is eligible for a fee award. After the meaning of this term had produced conflicting views, the Supreme Court attempted to clarify the matter in *Farrar v. Hobby*, 506 U.S. 103 (1992). The precise issue was whether a plaintiff who had recovered only nominal damages in a §1983 action was the "prevailing party." After reviewing its previous decisions, the Court said:

> [T]o qualify as a prevailing party, a civil rights plaintiff must obtain at least some relief on the merits of his claim. The plaintiff must obtain an enforceable judgment against the defendant from whom fees are sought, or comparable relief through a consent decree or settlement. Whatever relief the plaintiff secures must directly benefit him at the time of the judgment or settlement. . . . Only under these circumstances can civil rights litigation effect "the material alteration of the legal relationship of the parties" and thereby transform the plaintiff into a prevailing party. In short, a plaintiff "prevails" when actual relief on the merits of his claim materially alters the legal relationship between the parties by modifying the defendant's behavior in a way that directly benefits the plaintiff.

Id. at 111. Later in the opinion, the Court commented, "No material alteration of the legal relationship . . . occurs until the plaintiff becomes entitled to enforce a judgment, consent decree, or settlement against the defendant." *Id.* at 114. The Court then held that the instant plaintiff was the "prevailing party" because he could enforce the nominal damages award. *See generally* Lawrence D. Rosenthal, *Adding Insult to No Injury: The Denial of Attorney's Fees to "Victorious" Employment Discrimination and Other Civil Rights Plaintiffs*, 37 FLA. ST. U.L. REV. 49 (2009) (critiquing the failure of courts to generally award attorney's fees in cases in which only nominal damages are recovered). In a recent case, the Seventh Circuit held that a court order requiring defendant to destroy the test results of an illegally administered test made plaintiff a prevailing party: "It is a close question, but we are convinced that the value of the destruction of the test results is at least as great as the $1 in nominal damages which made the plaintiff in *Farrar* a prevailing party." *Karraker v. Rent-A-Center, Inc.*, 492 F.3d 896, 898 (7th Cir. 2007). *See also Flitton v. Primary Residential Mortg., Inc.*, 614 F.3d 1173 (10th Cir. 2010) (the district court properly concluded that plaintiff's successful retaliation claim and her unsuccessful discrimination claims were interrelated, thus permitting a fee award for both, and it was not an abuse of discretion to not reduce the award based on degree of success).

Page 707.   Add in Note 4, *Rule 68* after *See generally*:

Harold S. Lewis & Thomas A. Eaton, *The Contours of a New FRCP, Rule 68.1: A Proposed Two-Way Offer of Settlement Provision for Federal Fee-Shifting Cases* (2008), *available at* http://papers.ssrn.com/sol3/papers.cfm?abstract_id=1318251 (Rule 68 should be amended in several ways to make it a more effective tool for stimulating the prompt and fair resolution of civil rights and employment discrimination actions; the amendments should include allowing plaintiffs, not just defendants, to initiate offers; devising incentives and sanctions calculated to promote the resolution of disputes without unduly threatening either party; and incorporating time frames for making and responding to offers).

Page 715.   Delete Note 1; replace with:

1. *The Reasonable Client Standard.* The *Arbor Hills* court does an excellent job of reviewing the somewhat tangled history of methodologies of calculating attorneys' fees in civil rights cases, which include the employment discrimination laws. But its ultimate synthesis is a dramatic departure from prior methods, at least in theory. For *Arbor Hills*, the critical factor is what a paying client would pay, and the other methods were merely different ways of coming at that ultimate issue. *See also Simmons v. N.Y. City Transit Auth.*, 575 F.3d 170, 172 (2d Cir. 2009) ("in order to receive an attorney's fee award based on higher out-of-district rates, a litigant must overcome a presumption in favor of the forum rule [calculating fees based on the rates where the litigation was brought] by persuasively establishing that a reasonable client would have selected out-of-district counsel because doing so would likely (not just possibly) produce a substantially better net result.").

Recently, however, in *Perdue v. Kenny A.*, 130 S. Ct. 1662 (2010), the Supreme Court reaffirmed the centrality of the lodestar calculation, although the case involved a fee enhancement, not the question of the relationship between the lodestar and what a reasonable client would pay. The Court, while noting the possibility of appropriate enhancements, recognized a strong presumption that the lodestar figure is reasonable. This presumption can be overcome only in rare circumstances where the lodestar does not adequately result in a reasonable fee, such as when the lodestar hourly rate does not reflect the attorney's true market value. Although *Kenny A.* did not cite *Arbor Hills*, the primacy of the lodestar is in some tension with a "reasonable client" standard.

In any event, the reasonable client principle has a deceptive appeal, but there is a fundamental flaw. Certainly when discounted by the possibility of losing, the monetary claims of employment discrimination plaintiffs — backpay, front pay, compensatory and punitive damages — are often too low to induce an attorney to take a case on a contingency fee arrangement. That can't mean that attorneys' fees are not available if a reasonable client would forego the claim absent the prospect of an attorneys' fees award.

But if it doesn't mean that, does the *Arbor Hills* touchstone make any sense? One possibility is that the court was trying to focus on what a cost-conscious client would do if she had decided to bring suit. But even that formulation is problematic. After all, even a cost-conscious client might spend more to enhance her chances of winning. Isn't that what Gibson Dunn's "muscle" meant? *See generally* Seth Hanft, Comment, *Questioning the "Presumptively Reasonable Fee" as a Substitute for the Lodestar Method*, 76 U. CIN. L. REV. 1371 (2008).

Page 718.   In second full paragraph after *Comm'r v. Banks* cite add:

See also Green v. Comm'r, 312 F. App'x 929 (9th Cir. 2009) (successful discrimination plaintiff must pay federal income tax on statutory attorneys' fees awarded to her under state law even though that law treats fees as belonging to attorney who earned them since the employer's payment of fees to her attorney reduced her own payment obligation and was thus constructively received by her).

Page 718.   Add at end of Taxation section:

Even after the new statute, the award of a lump sum in backpay will result in greater tax liability than the plaintiff would have incurred had the compensation been paid nondiscriminatorily, for example, when the award pushes the employee into a higher tax bracket. *Eshelman v. Agere Sys., Inc.*, 554 F.3d 426 (3d Cir. 2009) (not an abuse of discretion for the district court to "gross up" a backpay award to compensate plaintiff for the negative tax consequences of receiving lump sum backpay). *See generally* Tim Canney, Note, *Tax Gross-Ups: A Practical Guide to Arguing and Calculating Awards for Negative Tax Consequences in Discrimination Suits*, 59 CATH. U. L. REV. 1111 (2010) (arguing that courts have authority to gross-up awards where there is unfair tax treatment).

Page 719.   Add at end of first full paragraph:

See Cornett Mgmt. Co., LLC v. Fireman's Fund Ins. Co., 332 F. App'x 146 (4th Cir. 2009) (no personal injury coverage for sexual harassment and false-imprisonment claims by female employees who were required to strip in the investigation of a theft in light of exclusion for "employment-related practices, policies, acts or omissions").

Page 719.   Add at end of first sentence in *Bankruptcy* subsection:

See Rederford v. US Airways, Inc., 589 F.3d 30 (1st Cir. 2009) (an employment discrimination claim is discharged if the employee is notified of the bankruptcy and fails to submit proof of her claim even though the plaintiff sought reinstatement).

Page 720.   Add before *Barger* cite in last paragraph:

White v. Wyndham Vacation Ownership, Inc., 617 F.3d 472 (6th Cir. 2010) (incomplete disclosure of harassment claim in bankruptcy filings was inconsistent with plaintiff's later suit justified stopping her from proceeding with that claim); *Robinson v. Tyson Foods, Inc.,* 595 F.3d 1269 (11th Cir. 2010) (bankrupt employee estopped from pursuing race discrimination suit because of her failure to disclose that claim as one of her assets even though she paid all of her debts in full under her Chapter 13 plan);

9 Managing Risks in Employment Discrimination Disputes

A. Settlements and Releases

Page 723.   Add after *Dillard* cite in carryover paragraph:

But see Magallanes v. Ill. Bell Tel. Co., 535 F.3d 582 (7th Cir. 2008) (error to enforce settlement agreement when the employer failed to prove that plaintiff's attorney had authority to settle the case).

Page 728.   Delete Note 2, replace with:

2. *Releases Under Other Discrimination Statutes.* OWBPA on its face reaches only ADEA claims, not claims under other antidiscrimination statutes. Yet, since releases that satisfy OWBPA are the "gold standard," employers are likely to structure their forms to ensure that they meet the OWBPA and to use them for their releases for all kinds of discrimination claims. *See Neely v. Good Samaritan Hosp.*, 345 F. App'x 39 (6th Cir. 2009) (race discrimination claimant properly revoked settlement agreement invoking language in it required for effective OWBPA releases even though plaintiff never made an ADEA claim). However, when employers fail to do so, the law governing releases under other federal laws is less clear. Some courts have applied the policies underlying OWBPA to statutes such as Title VII, the ADA, or §1981. *See Richardson v. Sugg*, 448 F.3d 1046, 1054 (8th Cir. 2006) (the policy concerns that led *Oubre* to reject the tender back requirement for the ADEA also apply to Title VII).

The dominant approach, however, is more amorphous: The courts look to the "totality of the circumstances" to determine whether the release was "knowing and voluntary." *E.g., Hampton v. Ford Motor Co.*, 561 F.3d 709 (7th Cir. 2009) (plaintiff barred from suit by knowingly and voluntarily signing a waiver of a pending charge of discrimination in return for $100,000: she had full capacity; the language was clear; Ford provided her six weeks to agree, and a month to rescind; and she could have consulted her attorney); *Melanson v. Browning-Ferris Indus.*, 281 F.3d 272 (1st Cir. 2002); *See generally* Daniel P. O'Gorman, *Show Me the Money: The Applicability of Contract Law's Ratification and Tender-Back Doctrines to Title VII Releases*, 84 TUL. L. REV. 675, 728 (2010); Daniel Gorman, *A State of Disarray: The "Knowing and Voluntary" Standard for Releasing Claims Under Title VII of the Civil Rights Act of 1964*, 8 U. PA. J. LAB. & EMP. L. 73 (2005); Craig Robert Senn, *Knowing and Voluntary Waivers of Federal Employment Claims: Replacing the Totality of Circumstances Test With a "Waiver Certainty" Test*, 58 FLA. L. REV. 305 (2006). At the very least, this approach allows courts to enforce releases that would not be valid under OWBPA. However, it is a somewhat more demanding standard than would govern under normal contract law.

Page 730. Add at end of in Note 8, *Gag Clauses*:

See also Jon Bauer, *Buying Witness Silence: Evidence-Suppressing Settlements and Lawyers' Ethics*, 87 OR. L. REV. 481, 486-87 (2008) (Model Rule 3.4(f) "prohibits a lawyer from requesting any person, other than the lawyer's client or the client's relatives or employees, to refrain from voluntarily providing relevant information to another party. Lawyers who make settlement offers conditioned on noncooperation are doing precisely what the rule prohibits . . . ").

Page 730. Add in Note 9, *Enforcing Settlements* after *Kokkonen* parenthetical:

Cf. Palmer v. Salazar, 324 F. App'x 729 (10th Cir. 2009) (district court had jurisdiction to determine the validity of a waiver of ADEA rights under the Older Workers Benefit Protection Act but no jurisdiction with regard to the validity of the waiver for Title VII or ADA rights).

Page 732. Correct cite at end of first paragraph as follows:

11 EMP. RTS. & EMP. POL'Y J. 405 (2007).

B. Arbitrating Discrimination Claims

Page 740. Delete current Note 1, replace with the following:

1. Gilmer *Trumps* Gardner-Denver. Because *Gardner-Denver* arose in the context of a collective bargaining agreement, almost all circuits held that it remained the governing law in that context even after *Gilmer*. Under this view, *Gilmer* would govern all arbitration except that which occurred under the aegis of a collective

bargaining agreement. The rationale was in part the recognition that the union controls the individual employee's claim when arbitration is conducted under a collective bargaining agreement, and *Gardner-Denver* was obviously unwilling to trust individual antidiscrimination rights to a union. Further, *Gilmer* arose under the Federal Arbitration Act, not the National Labor Relations Act, which could justify a difference in approach in the two contexts.

This distinction was extinguished by *14 Penn Plaza LLC v. Pyett*, 129 S. Ct. 1456, 1461 (2009), which held that "a collective-bargaining agreement that clearly and unmistakably requires union members to arbitrate ADEA claims is enforceable as a matter of federal law." *Pyett* found the arbitration clause well within the authority granted to labor unions by the NLRA to contract concerning the rights of their members. While unions could not waive their members' rights to be free of discrimination, "[t]he right to a judicial forum is not the nonwaivable 'substantive' right protected by the ADEA. Thus, although Title VII and ADEA rights may well stand on 'different ground' than statutory rights that protect 'majoritarian processes,' the voluntary decision to collectively bargain for arbitration does not deny those statutory antidiscrimination rights the full protection they are due." 129 S. Ct. at 1464 n.5.

In fact, the majority read arbitration as enforceable under *Gardner-Denver* itself since it limited that case to its precise holding—that arbitration of a collective bargaining agreement-based discrimination claim did not bar later suit on a statute-based discrimination claim. While the *Pyett* majority recognized *Gardner-Denver*'s "broad dicta that was highly critical of the use of arbitration for the vindication of statutory rights," *id.* at 1469, it stressed that this skepticism had been abandoned by the Court in a number of cases, including *Gilmer*. As for the possibility that the union would not vigorously pursue its members' rights, which in fact happened in the case before it, the *Pyett* majority noted that members could sue the union for breach of its duty of fair representation should the union not prosecute a grievance to arbitration. *Id.* at 1473. *See generally* Alan Hyde, *Labor Arbitration of Discrimination Claims After* 14 Penn Plaza v. Pyett: *Letting Discrimination Defendants Decide Whether Plaintiffs May Sue Them*, 25 OHIO ST. J. DISP. RESOL. 975, 976 (2010); Sarah Rudolph Cole, *Let the Grand Experiment Begin:* Pyett *Authorizes Arbitration of Unionized Employees' Statutory Discrimination Claims*, 14 LEWIS & CLARK L. REV. 861 (2010); Margaret L. Moses, *The Pretext of Textualism: Disregarding Stare Decisis in* 14 Penn Plaza v. Pyett, 14 LEWIS & CLARK L. REV. 825 (2010); David L. Gregory & Edward McNamara, *Mandatory Labor Arbitration of Statutory Claims, and the Future of Fair Employment:* 14 Penn Plaza v. Pyett, 19 CORNELL J. L. & PUB. POL'Y 429 (2010).

Page 743. At end of Note 8, *Antiretaliation*:

However, discharge for failure to sign a compulsory arbitration agreement that would cover a pending charge has been held retaliatory. *Goldsmith v. Bagby Elevator Co.*, 513 F.3d 1261 (11th Cir. 2008).

Page 743.   Delete Note 10, replace with:

10. *Who Decides Whether an Agreement Is Valid?* In its two most recent encounters with that question of who decides whether an agreement to arbitrate is valid, the Supreme Court provided some guidance. *Granite Rock Co. v. International Brotherhood of Teamsters,* 130 S. Ct. 2847 (2010), viewed as "well settled that where the dispute at issue concerns contract formation, the dispute is generally for the court to decide." As the majority described the "proper framework" for deciding who decides arbitrability, "a court may order arbitration of a particular dispute only where the court is satisfied that the parties intended to arbitrate *that dispute.*" 130 S. Ct at 2856 (emphasis in original). Indeed, at one point the Court wrote:

> Arbitration is strictly "a matter of consent," and thus "is a way to resolve those disputes — *but only those disputes* — that the parties have agreed to submit to arbitration." Applying this principle, our precedents hold that courts should order arbitration of a dispute only where the court is satisfied that neither the formation of the parties' arbitration agreement nor (absent a valid provision specifically committing such disputes to an arbitrator) its enforceability or applicability to the dispute is in issue. Where a party contests either or both matters, "the court" must resolve the disagreement.

Id. at 2857-58 (citations omitted) (emphasis in original). This would seem to include questions not only of formation (in the sense of offer/acceptance) but also questions as to enforceability, such as consideration, and perhaps satisfaction of any formalities, such as an adequate writing. *See also Mathews v. Denver Newspaper Agency LLP,* 2011 U.S. App. LEXIS 5142, 16-18 (10th Cir. Mar. 16, 2011) (because the arbitration agreement empowered the arbitrator to resolve only the dispute submitted, and because the dispute submitted made no mention of statutory claims, the arbitral decision could in no way determine the question of Mathews's statutory rights.).

However, the same week that *Granite Rock,* was decided, the Court handed down *Rent-A-Center West, Inc. v. Jackson,* 130 S. Ct. 2772 (2010), which held that unconscionability could be decided in arbitration. There is obviously a tension here, but, as rationalized by the *Granite Rock* Court, *Rent-A-Center West* fell within the exception stated by its formulation: "A valid provision specifically committ[ed] such disputes to an arbitrator." *Id.* at 2858. This approach was possible due to the long-standing principle that an arbitration clause is severable from the rest of the agreement as a matter of federal law. Thus, an attack (whether for fraud, illegality, or unconscionability) on the contract in which the clause is embedded is not necessarily an attack on the arbitration clause.

In sum, reading the two opinions together, the rule is that courts decide questions of arbitrability that go to whether the contract providing for arbitration is valid, but the parties can agree that such questions are to be decided by an arbitrator. The obvious likelihood is that arbitration clauses in the future will be drawn to try to make the exception into the rule. It remains to be seen whether courts will honor such clauses when it comes to the question of whether an agreement was reached to arbitrate in the first place.

Page 744.   Add a new Note 12.

12. *Waiver.* Even if there is a valid arbitration agreement, the parties may waive the right to arbitrate and litigate the claim in court. The most common waiver is the defendant's failure to move to stay the court proceedings pending arbitration. However, a failure to invoke arbitration during an EEOC investigation does not amount to a waiver. *McNamara v. Yellow Transp., Inc.*, 570 F.3d 950 (8th Cir. 2009).

Page 745.   After David S. Schwartz citation, add:

8 NEV. L.J. 400 (2007). *Cf.* Suzette M. Malveaux, *Is It the "Real Thing:' How Coke's One-Way Binding Arbitration May Bridge the Divide Between Litigation and Arbitration*, 2009 J. DISP. RES. 77.

Page 750.   Add at end of last full paragraph:

See also Alonso v. Huron Valley Ambulance Inc., 375 F. App'x 487 (6th Cir. 2010) (no knowing and voluntary waiver of a judicial forum when plaintiffs had no idea at the time of execution of the documents what the relevant process entailed or of their right to revoke).

Page 753.   Add at end of carryover Note 6, *Invalidating Doctrines*:

Martin H. Malin, *Due Process in Employment Arbitration: The State of the Law and the Need for Self-Regulation,* 11 EMP. RTS. & EMP. POL'Y J. 363, 403 (2007) ("Although not a substitute for strict judicial policing, vigorous self-regulation by the neutral community can go a long way to ensuring that employment arbitration functions as a fair, even-handed forum whose efficiency and cost advantages over litigation can work to the advantage of employees as well as employers.").

Page 754.   Add at end of carryover Note 7, *Fixing Overreaching*?:

See also Ragone v. Atl. Video, 595 F.3d 115 (2d Cir. 2010) (when employer agrees to waive potentially unconscionable provisions regarding a shortened statute of limitations and attorneys' fees, the court should enforce the arbitration agreement after severing such terms; the result might have been different if the employer tried to enforce the objectionable clauses).

Page 754.   Delete Note 9, replace with:

9. *Class Actions and Arbitration.* One potentially critical advantage of arbitration for employers is avoiding class actions. Class arbitrations are permissible, but only if the parties in fact so agree. *See Stolt-Nielsen S. A. v. AnimalFeeds Int'l Corp.*, 130 S. Ct. 1758, 1770 (2010) ("In sum, instead of identifying and applying a rule of decision derived from the FAA or either maritime or New York law, the arbitration panel imposed its own policy choice and thus exceeded its powers."). But employers would generally prefer to bar any kind of aggregate procedure which might increase exposure while reducing the litigation costs of individuals. As a result, provisions barring arbitrations and class actions are common in the consumer context. Although a number of decisions, especially in California, struck down such class action waivers, the Supreme Court upheld them in *AT&T Mobility LLC v. Concepcion*, 131 S. Ct. 1740 (2011), finding that the Federal Arbitration Act prohibits states from conditioning the enforceability of certain arbitration agreements on the availability of classwide arbitration procedures. The plaintiffs, AT&T customers, brought a class action against the telephone company claiming that AT&T's offer of a free phone to anyone who signed up for cell service with the company was fraudulent because the company charged the customers sales tax on the retail value of the supposedly "free" device. *Id.* at 1744. However, AT&T's standard form contract, while providing for arbitration for all disputes between the parties, required that such claims be brought individually, not as a class. *Id.*

The Ninth Circuit found both the provision unconscionable under California law and held that that law was not preempted by the FAA. Section 2 of the FAA holds arbitration agreements "valid, irrevocable, and enforceable, save upon such grounds as exist at law or in equity for the revocation of any contract." According to this line of analysis, California's unconscionability analysis was applicable to all contracts (or at least all dispute-resolution contracts) within the state, and therefore did not differentiate arbitration agreements from "any [other] contract." Justice Scalia's majority opinion disagreed. While §2 of the FAA preserved generally applicable contract defenses, it did not intend to preserve state-law rules impeding the accomplishment of the FAA's objectives. The Court noted that a "federal statute's saving clause" cannot in reason be construed as [allowing] a common law right, the continued existence of which would be absolutely inconsistent with the provisions of the act. In other words, the act cannot be held to destroy itself." 131 S. Ct. 1748 (quoting American Telephone & Telegraph Co. v. Central Office Telephone, Inc., 524 U.S. 214 (1998) (internal quotation marks omitted).

The Court then held that the FAA preempted the California holding because prohibiting class arbitration by state law, as opposed to by the choice of the parties involved, was inconsistent with the FAA for three reasons. First, shifting from bilateral arbitration to class arbitration destroys informality, a principal advantage of arbitration, and ultimately makes the process slower and more costly. 131 S. Ct. at 1751. Second, it is unlikely that Congress would have wanted to leave the necessary procedural requirements for a binding class arbitration award to an arbitrator, especially since class arbitration was not even considered during the passage of the FAA in 1925. Finally, class arbitration increases risks for defendants because informal procedures increase the likelihood that errors go uncorrected. While tolerable as the cost of process savings in individual cases, such risks are a much more serious concern in class arbitrations where potential damages can be so large that defendants will be forced to settle rather than run even a small risk of huge recoveries. 131 S. Ct. at 1752.

Concepcion will likely result in the disappearance of class litigation—either in court or before arbitrators—in consumer contracts. Given the threat class actions pose to employers in the discrimination context, it seems likely that most employers will add class waiver such provisions to standard documents, which already tend to require arbitration. As a result, it seems likely that employment discrimination class actions will tend to disappear in the future, entirely aside from the results in *Wal-Mart Stores Inc. v. Dukes*. See p. . . . of this Supplement.

Page 755.   Add after Christopher R. Drahozal cite in second full paragraph:

David S. Schwartz, *Mandatory Arbitration and Fairness*, 84 NOTRE DAME L. REV. 1247 (2009).

Page 756.   Add at end of first full paragraph before *Estlund* cite:

See also Mazera v. Varsity Ford Mgmt. Servs., LLC, 565 F.3d 997 (6th Cir. 2009) (an employee could not avoid arbitration by showing that it was functionally unavailable because of costs unless he first sought and was denied a waiver of the fee he had to pay).

Page 757.   Add at end of carryover sentence:

But see Hall St. Assocs. v. Mattel, Inc., 552 U.S. 576, 585 (2008) ("Maybe the term 'manifest disregard' was meant to name a new ground for review, but maybe it merely referred to the §10 grounds collectively, rather than adding to them. Or, as some courts have thought, 'manifest disregard' may have been shorthand for §10(a)(3) or §10(a)(4), the subsections authorizing vacatur when the arbitrators were 'guilty of misconduct' or 'exceeded their powers.'"); *Grain v. Trinity Health*, 551 F.3d 374 (6th Cir. 2008) ("manifest disregard" of law, even if still valid after *Hall Street*, can be invoked only to vacate arbitration awards, not to modify them by increasing the amount awarded).

Page 757. In the second full paragraph, delete *Hall St.* cite and the remainder of the paragraph and replace with:

Although some arbitration agreements have attempted to expand the FAA's narrow scope of review, the Supreme Court firmly rejected such efforts in *Hall St. Assocs. v. Mattel, Inc.*, 552 U.S. 576, 590 (2008)(2008) (FAA "§§10 and 11 provide exclusive regimes for the review provided by the statute" although review outside the FAA may be possible). *See generally* Margaret L. Moses, *Arbitration Law: Who's in Charge*, 40 SETON HALL L. REV. 147, 152 (2010) (critiquing *Hall Street* for not seriously engaging the text or the legislative history of the statute and calling for Congress to take back control of arbitration law by either limiting mandatory arbitration, or providing for heightened judicial scrutiny).

Statutes

Age Discrimination in Employment Act*

29 U.S.C. §§621–633a

§621 [§2]. Statement of Findings and Purpose

(a) The Congress hereby finds and declares that—

(1) in the face of rising productivity and affluence, older workers find themselves disadvantaged in their efforts to retain employment, and especially to regain employment when displaced from jobs;

(2) the setting of arbitrary age limits regardless of potential for job performance has become a common practice, and certain otherwise desirable practices may work to the disadvantage of older persons;

(3) the incidence of unemployment, especially long-term unemployment with resultant deterioration of skill, morale, and employer acceptability is, relative to the younger ages, high among older workers; their numbers are great and growing; and their employment problems grave;

(4) the existence in industries affecting commerce, of arbitrary discrimination in employment because of age, burdens commerce and the free flow of goods in commerce.

(b) It is therefore the purpose of this chapter to promote employment of older persons based on their ability rather than age; to prohibit arbitrary age discrimination in employment; to help employers and workers find ways of meeting problems arising from the impact of age on employment.

§622 [§3]. Education and Research Program

(a) The Secretary of Labor shall undertake studies and provide information to labor unions, management, and the general public concerning the needs and abilities of older workers, and their potentials for continued employment and contribution to the economy. In order to achieve the purposes of this chapter, the

---

* The functions of the Secretary of Labor and the Civil Service Commission, referred to in this Act, were transferred to the Equal Employment Opportunity Commission by Reorg. Plan No. 1, Feb. 23, 1978, 44 Fed. Reg. 1053.

Secretary of Labor shall carry on a continuing program of education and information, under which he may, among other measures—

(1) undertake research, and promote research, with a view to reducing barriers to the employment of older persons, and the promotion of measures for utilizing their skills;

(2) publish and otherwise make available to employers, professional societies, the various media of communication, and other interested persons the findings of studies and other materials for the promotion of employment;

(3) foster through the public employment service system and through cooperative effort the development of facilities of public and private agencies for expanding the opportunities and potentials of older persons;

(4) sponsor and assist State and community informational and educational programs.

(b) Not later than six months after the effective date of this chapter, the Secretary shall recommend to the Congress any measures he may deem desirable to change the lower or upper age limits set forth in section 631 of this title.

§623 [§4]. Prohibition of Age Discrimination

(a) Employment practices. It shall be unlawful for an employer—

(1) to fail or refuse to hire or to discharge any individual or otherwise discriminate against any individual with respect to his compensation, terms, conditions, or privileges of employment, because of such individual's age;

(2) to limit, segregate, or classify his employees in any way which would deprive or tend to deprive any individual of employment opportunities or otherwise adversely affect his status as an employee, because of such individual's age; or

(3) to reduce the wage rate of any employee in order to comply with this chapter.

(b) Employment agency practices. It shall be unlawful for an employment agency to fail or refuse to refer for employment, or otherwise to discriminate against, any individual because of such individual's age, or to classify or refer for employment any individual on the basis of such individual's age.

(c) Labor organization practices. It shall be unlawful for a labor organization—

(1) to exclude or to expel from its membership, or otherwise to discriminate against, any individual because of his age;

(2) to limit, segregate, or classify its membership, or to classify or fail to refuse to refer for employment any individual, in any way which would deprive or tend to deprive any individual of employment opportunities, or would limit such employment opportunities or otherwise adversely affect his status as an employee or as an applicant for employment, because of such individual's age;

(3) to cause or attempt to cause an employer to discriminate against an individual in violation of this section.

(d) Opposition to unlawful practices; participation in investigations, proceedings, or litigation. It shall be unlawful for any employer to discriminate against any of his employees or applicants for employment, for an employment agency to discriminate against any individual, or for a labor organization to discriminate against any member thereof or applicant for membership, because such individual, member, or applicant for membership, has opposed any practice made unlawful by this section, or because such individual, member, or applicant for membership has made a charge, testified, assisted, or participated in any manner in an investigation, proceeding, or litigation under this Act.

(e) Printing or publication of notice or advertisement indicating preference, limitation, etc. It shall be unlawful for an employer, labor organization, or employment agency to print or publish, or cause to be printed or published, any notice or advertisement relating to employment by such an employer or membership in or any classification or referral for employment by such a labor organization, or relating to any classification or referral for employment by such an employment agency, indicating any preference, limitation, specification, or discrimination, based on age.

(f) Lawful practices; age an occupational qualification; other reasonable factors; seniority system; employee benefit plan; discharge or discipline for good cause. It shall not be unlawful for an employer, employment agency, or labor organization —

(1) to take any action otherwise prohibited under subsection (a), (b), (c), or (e) of this section where age is a bona fide occupational qualification reasonably necessary to the normal operation of the particular business, or where the differentiation is based on reasonable factors other than age or where such practices involve an employee in a workplace in a foreign country, and compliance with such subsections would cause such employer, or a corporation controlled by such employer, to violate the laws of the country in which such workplace is located;

(2) to take any action otherwise prohibited under subsection (a), (b), (c), or (e) of this section —

(A) to observe the terms of a bona fide seniority system that is not intended to evade the purposes of this Act, except that no such seniority system shall require or permit the involuntary retirement of any individual specified by section 12(a) because of the age of such individual; or

(B) to observe the terms of a bona fide employee benefit plan —

(i) where, for each benefit or benefit package, the actual amount of payment made or cost incurred on behalf of an older worker is no less than that made or incurred on behalf of a younger worker, as permissible under section 1625.10, title 29, Code of Federal Regulations; or

(ii) that is a voluntary early retirement incentive plan consistent with the relevant purpose or purposes of this Act.

Notwithstanding clause (i) or (ii) of subparagraph (B), no such employee benefit plan or voluntary early retirement incentive plan shall excuse the failure to hire any individual, and no such employee benefit plan shall require or permit the involuntary retirement of any individual specified by section 12(a), because of the age of such individual. An employer, employment agency, or labor organization acting under subparagraph (A), or under clause (i) or (ii) of subparagraph (B), shall have the burden of proving that such actions are lawful in any civil enforcement proceeding brought under this Act; or

(3) to discharge or otherwise discipline an individual for good cause.

(g) [Deleted]

(h) Foreign practices.

(1) If an employer controls a corporation whose place of incorporation is in a foreign country, any practice by such corporation prohibited under this section shall be presumed to be such practice by such employer.

(2) The prohibitions of this section shall not apply where the employer is a foreign person not controlled by an American employer.

(3) For the purpose of this subsection the determination of whether an employer controls a corporation shall be based upon the—

   (A) interrelation of operations,

   (B) common management,

   (C) centralized control of labor relations, and

   (D) common ownership or financial control, of the employer and the corporation.

(i) Employee pension benefit plans; cessation or reduction of benefit accrual or of allocation to employee account; distribution of benefits after attainment of normal retirement age; compliance; highly compensated employees.

(1) Except as otherwise provided in this subsection, it shall be unlawful for an employer, an employment agency, a labor organization, or any combination thereof to establish or maintain an employee pension benefit plan which requires or permits—

   (A) in the case of a defined benefit plan, the cessation of an employee's benefit accrual, or the reduction of the rate of an employee's benefit accrual, because of age, or

   (B) in the case of a defined contribution plan, the cessation of allocations to an employee's account, or the reduction of the rate at which amounts are allocated to an employee's account, because of age.

(2) Nothing in this section shall be construed to prohibit an employer, employment agency, or labor organization from observing any provision of an employee pension benefit plan to the extent that such provision imposes (without regard to age) a limitation on the amount of benefits that the plan provides or a limitation on the number of years of service or years of participation which are taken into account for purposes of determining benefit accrual under the plan.

(3) In the case of an employee who, as of the end of any plan year under a defined benefit plan, has attained normal retirement age under such plan—

   (A) if distribution of benefits under such plan with respect to such employee has commenced as of the end of such plan year, then any requirement of this subsection for continued accrual of benefits under such plan with respect to such employee during such plan year shall be treated as satisfied to the extent of the actuarial equivalent of inservice distribution of benefits, and

(B) if distribution of benefits under such plan with respect to such employee has not commenced as of the end of such year in accordance with section 1056(a)(3) of this title [Employee Retirement Income Security Act of 1974] and section 401(a)(14)(C) of title 26 [Internal Revenue Code of 1986], and the payment of benefits under such plan with respect to such employee is not suspended during such plan year pursuant to section 1053(a)(3)(B) of this title [Employee Retirement Income Security Act of 1974] or section 411(a)(3)(B) of title 26 [Internal Revenue Code of 1986], then any requirement of this subsection for continued accrual of benefits under such plan with respect to such employee during such plan year shall be treated as satisfied to the extent of any adjustment in the benefit payable under the plan during such plan year attributable to the delay in the distribution of benefits after the attainment of normal retirement age. The provisions of this paragraph (3) shall apply in accordance with regulations of the Secretary of the Treasury. Such regulations shall provide for the application of the preceding provisions of this paragraph to all employee pension benefit plans subject to this subsection and may provide for the application of such provisions in the case of any such employee, with respect to any period of time within a plan year.

(4) Compliance with the requirements of this subsection with respect to an employee pension benefit plan shall constitute compliance with the requirements of this section relating to benefit accrual under such plan.

(5) Paragraph (1) shall not apply with respect to any employee who is a highly compensated employee (within the meaning of section 414(q) of title 26 [Internal Revenue Code of 1986]) to the extent provided in regulations prescribed by the Secretary of Treasury for the purposes of precluding discrimination in favor of highly compensated employees within the meaning of subchapter D of chapter I of title 26.

(6) A plan shall not be treated as failing to meet the requirements of paragraph (1) solely because the subsidized portion of any early retirement benefit is disregarded in determining benefit accruals.

(7) Any regulations prescribed by the Secretary of the Treasury pursuant to clause (v) of section 411(b)(1)(H) of title 26 and subparagraphs (C) and (D) of section 411(b)(2) of such title 26 shall apply with respect to the requirements of this subsection in the same manner and to the same extent as such regulations apply with respect to the requirements of such section 411(b)(1)(H) and 411(b)(2) of title 26.

(8) A plan shall not be treated as failing to meet the requirements of this section solely because such plan provides a normal retirement age described in section 1002(24)(B) of this title [Employee Retirement Income Security Act of 1974] and section 411(a)(8)(B) of title 26. [Internal Revenue Code of 1986.]

(9) For purposes of this subsection—

(A) The terms "employee pension benefit plan," "defined benefit plan," "defined contribution plan," and "normal retirement age" have the meanings provided such terms in section 1002 of this title. [Employee Retirement Income Security Act of 1974.]

(B) The term "compensation" has the meaning provided by section 414(s) of title 26. [Internal Revenue Code of 1986.]

(j) Employment as firefighter or law enforcement officer. It shall not be unlawful for an employer which is a State, a political subdivision of a State, an agency or instrumentality of a State or a political subdivision of a State, or an interstate agency to fail or refuse to hire or to discharge any individual because of such individual's age if such action is taken —

(1) with respect to the employment of an individual as a firefighter or as a law enforcement officer, the employer has complied with section 3(d)(2) of the Age Discrimination in Employment Amendments of 1996 if the individual was discharged after the date described in such section, and the individual has attained —

(A) the age of hiring or retirement, respectively, in effect under applicable State or local law on March 3, 1983; or

(B)(i) if the individual was not hired, the age of hiring in effect on the date of such failure or refusal to hire under applicable State or local law enacted after September 30, 1996; or

(ii) if applicable State or local law was enacted after September 30, 1996, and the individual was discharged, the higher of —

(I) the age of retirement in effect on the date of such discharge under such law; and

(II) age 55; and

(2) pursuant to a bona fide hiring or retirement plan that is not a subterfuge to evade the purposes of this chapter.

(k) Seniority system or employee benefit plan; compliance. A seniority system of employee benefit plan shall comply with this Act regardless of the date of adoption of such system or plan.

(*l*) Lawful practices; minimum age as condition of eligibility for retirement benefits; deduction from severance pay; reduction of long term disability benefits. Notwithstanding clause (i) or (ii) of subsection (f)(2)(B) —

(1)(A) It shall not be a violation of subsection (a), (b), (c), or (e) solely because —

(i) an employee pension benefit plan (as defined in section 3(2) of the Employee Retirement Income Security Act of 1974) provides for the attainment of a minimum age as a condition of eligibility for normal or early retirement benefits; or

(ii) a defined benefit plan (as defined in section 3(35) of such Act) provides for —

(I) payments that constitute the subsidized portion of an early retirement benefit; or

(II) social security supplements for plan participants that commence before the age and terminate at the age (specified by the plan) when participants are eligible to receive reduced or unreduced old-age insurance benefits under title II of the Social

Security Act and that do not exceed such old-age insurance benefits.

(B) A voluntary early retirement incentive plan that—

(i) is maintained by—

(I) a local educational agency (as defined in section 7801 of Title 20), or

(II) an education association which principally represents employees of 1 or more agencies described in subclause (I) and which is described in section 501(c)(5) or (6) of Title 26 and exempt from taxation under section 501(a) of Title 26, and

(ii) makes payments or supplements described in subclauses (I) and (II) of subparagraph (A)(ii) in coordination with a defined benefit plan (as so defined) maintained by an eligible employer described in section 457(e)(1)(A) of Title 26 or by an education association described in clause (i)(II),

shall be treated solely for purposes of subparagraph (A)(ii) as if it were a part of the defined benefit plan with respect to such payments or supplements. Payments or supplements under such a voluntary early retirement incentive plan shall not constitute severance pay for purposes of paragraph (2).

(2)(A) It shall not be a violation of subsection (a), (b), (c), or (e) solely because following a contingent event unrelated to age—

(i) the value of any retiree health benefits received by an individual eligible for an immediate pension;

(ii) the value of any additional pension benefits that are made available solely as a result of the contingent event unrelated to age and following which the individual is eligible for not less than an immediate and unreduced pension, are deducted from severance pay made available as a result of the contingent event unrelated to age; or

(iii) the values described in both clauses (i) and (ii).

(B) For an individual who receives immediate pension benefits that are actuarially reduced under subparagraph (A)(i), the amount of the deduction available pursuant to subparagraph (A)(i) shall be reduced by the same percentage as the reduction in the pension benefits.

(C) For purposes of this paragraph, severance pay shall include that portion of supplemental unemployment compensation benefits that—

(i) constitutes additional benefits of up to 52 weeks;

(ii) has the primary purpose and effect of continuing benefits until an individual becomes eligible for an immediate and unreduced pension; and

(iii) is discontinued once the individual becomes eligible for an immediate and unreduced pension.

(D) For purposes of this paragraph and solely in order to make the deduction authorized under this paragraph, the term "retiree health benefits" means benefits provided pursuant to a group health plan covering retirees, for which (determined as of the contingent event un-related to age)—

(i) the package of benefits provided by the employer for the retirees who are below age 65 is at least comparable to benefits provided under title XVIII of the Social Security Act;

(ii) the package of benefits provided by the employer for the retirees who are age 65 and above is at least comparable to that offered under a plan that provides a benefit package with one-fourth the value of benefits provided under title XVIII of such Act; or

(iii) the package of benefits provided by the employer is as described in clauses (i) and (ii).

(E)(i) If the obligation of the employer to provide retiree health benefits is of limited duration, the value for each individual shall be calculated as a rate of $3,000 per year for benefit years before age 65, and $750 per year for benefit years beginning at age 65 and above.

(ii) If the obligation of the employer to provide retiree health benefits is of unlimited duration, the value for each individual shall be calculated at a rate of $48,000 for individuals below age 65, and $24,000 for individuals age 65 and above.

(iii) The values described in clauses (i) and (ii) shall be calculated based on the age of the individual as of the date of the contingent event unrelated to age. The values are effective on the date of enactment of this subsection, and shall be adjusted on an annual basis, with respect to a contingent event that occurs subsequent to the first year after the date of enactment of this subsection, based on the medical component of the Consumer Price Index for all urban consumers published by the Department of Labor.

(iv) If an individual is required to pay a premium for retiree health benefits, the value calculated pursuant to this subparagraph shall be reduced by whatever percentage of the overall premium the individual is required to pay.

(F) If an employer that has implemented a deduction pursuant to subparagraph (A) fails to fulfill the obligation described in subparagraph (E), any aggrieved individual may bring an action for specific performance of the obligation described in subparagraph (E). The relief shall be in addition to any other remedies provided under Federal or State law.

(3) It shall not be a violation of subsection (a), (b), (c) or (e) solely because an employer provides a bona fide employee benefit plan or plans under which long-term disability benefits received by an individual are reduced by any pension benefits (other than those attributable to employee contributions)—

(A) paid to the individual that the individual voluntarily elects to receive; or

(B) for which an individual who has attained the later of age 62 or normal retirement age is eligible.

(m) Voluntary retirement incentive plans
Notwithstanding subsection (f)(2)(b), it shall not be a violation of subsection (a), (b), (c) or (e) solely because a plan of an institution of higher education (as defined in section 1001 of title 20) offers employees who are serving under a contract of unlimited tenure (or similar arrangement providing for unlimited tenure) supplemental benefits upon voluntary retirement that are reduced or eliminated on the basis of age, if—

(1) such institution does not implement with respect to such employees any age-based reduction or cessation of benefits that are not such supplemental benefits, except as permitted by other provisions of this chapter;

(2) such supplemental benefits are in addition to any retirement or severance benefits which have been offered generally to employees serving under a contract of unlimited tenure (or similar arrangement providing for unlimited tenure), independent of any early retirement or exit-incentive plan, within the preceding 365 days; and

(3) any employee who attains the minimum age and satisfies all non-age-based conditions for receiving a benefit under the plan has an opportunity lasting not less than 180 days to elect to retire and to receive the maximum benefit that could then be elected by a younger but otherwise similarly situated employee, and the plan does not require retirement to occur sooner than 180 days after such election.

§624 [§5]. Study by Secretary of Labor; Reports to President and Congress; Scope of Study; Implementation of Study; Transmittal Date of Reports

(a)(1) The Secretary of Labor is directed to undertake an appropriate study of institutional and other arrangements giving rise to involuntary retirement, and report his findings and any appropriate legislative recommendations to the President and to the Congress. Such study shall include—

(A) an examination of the effect of the amendment made by section 3(a) of the Age Discrimination in Employment Act Amendments of 1978 [amending 29 USCS §631] in raising the upper age limitation established by section 12(a) of this Act [29 USCS §631(a)] to 70 years of age;

(B) a determination of the feasibility of eliminating such limitation;

(C) a determination of the feasibility of raising such limitation above 70 years of age; and

(D) an examination of the effect of the exemption contained in section 12(c) [29 USCS §631(c)], relating to certain executive employees, and the exemption contained in section 12(d) [29 USCS §631(d)], relating to tenured teaching personnel.

(2) The Secretary may undertake the study required by paragraph (1) of this subsection directly or by contract or other arrangement.

(b) The report required by subsection (a) of this section shall be transmitted to the President and to the Congress as an interim report not later than January 1, 1981, and in final form not later than January 1, 1982.

§625 [§6]. Administration

The Secretary shall have the power —

(a) to make delegations, to appoint such agents and employers, and to pay for technical assistance on a fee-for-service basis, as he deems necessary to assist him in the performance of his functions under this chapter;

(b) to cooperate with regional, State, local, and other agencies, and to co-operate with and furnish technical assistance to employers, labor organizations, and employment agencies to aid in effectuating the purposes of this chapter.

§626. Recordkeeping, Investigation, and Enforcement

(a) Attendance of witnesses; investigations, inspections, records, and home-work regulations. The Secretary shall have the power to make investigations and require the keeping of records necessary or appropriate for the administration of this Act in accordance with the powers and procedures provided in sections 9 and 11 of the Fair Labor Standards Act of 1938, as amended (29 U.S.C. 209 and 211).

(b) Enforcement; prohibition of age discrimination under fair labor standards; unpaid minimum wages and unpaid overtime compensation; liquidated damages; judicial relief; conciliation, conference, and persuasion. The provisions of this Act shall be enforced in accordance with the powers, remedies, and procedures provided in sections 11(b), 16 (except for subsection (a) thereof), and 17 of the Fair Labor Standards Act of 1938, as amended (29 U.S.C. 211(b), 216, 217), and subsection (c) of this section. Any act prohibited under section 4 of this Act [29 USCS §623] shall be deemed to be a prohibited act under section 15 of the Fair Labor Standards Act of 1938, as amended (29 U.S.C. 215). Amounts owing to a person as a result of a violation of this Act shall be deemed to be unpaid minimum wages or unpaid over-time compensation for purposes of sections 16 and 17 of the Fair Labor Standards Act of 1938, as amended (29 U.S.C. 216, 217): *Provided,* That liquidated damages shall be payable only in cases of willful violations of this Act. In any action brought to enforce this Act the court shall have jurisdiction to grant such legal or equitable relief as may be appropriate to effectuate the purposes of this Act, including without limitation judgments compelling employment, reinstatement or promotion, or enforcing the liability for amounts deemed to be unpaid minimum wages or unpaid overtime compensation under this section. Before instituting any action under this section, the Secretary shall attempt to eliminate the discriminatory practice or practices alleged, and to effect voluntary compliance with the requirements of this Act through informal methods of conciliation, conference, and persuasion.

(c) Civil actions; persons aggrieved; jurisdiction; judicial relief; termination of individual action upon commencement of action by Secretary; jury trial.

(1) Any person aggrieved may bring a civil action in any court of competent jurisdiction for such legal or equitable relief as will effectuate the purposes of this Act: *Provided,* That the right of any person to bring such action shall terminate upon the commencement of an action by the Secretary to enforce the right of such employee under this Act.

(2) In an action brought under paragraph (1), a person shall be entitled to a trial by jury of any issue of fact in any such action for recovery of amounts

owing as a result of a violation of this Act, regardless of whether equitable relief is sought by any party in such action.

(d)(1) Filing of charge with Secretary; timeliness; conciliation, conference, and persuasion. No civil action may be commenced by an individual under this section until 60 days after a charge alleging unlawful discrimination has been filed with the Secretary. Such a charge shall be filed—

(A) within 180 days after the alleged unlawful practice occurred; or

(B) in a case to which section 14(b) [29 USCS §633(b)] applies, within 300 days after the alleged unlawful practice occurred, or within 30 days after receipt by the individual of notice of termination of proceedings under State law, whichever is earlier.

(2) Upon receiving such a charge, the Secretary shall promptly notify all persons named in such charge as prospective defendants in the action and shall promptly seek to eliminate any alleged unlawful practice by informal methods of conciliation, conference, and persuasion; and

(3) For purposes of this section, an unlawful practice occurs, with respect to discrimination in compensation in violation of this Act, when a discriminatory compensation decision or other practice is adopted, when a person becomes subject to a discriminatory compensation decision or other practice, or when a person is affected by application of a discriminatory compensation decision or other practice, including each time wages, benefits, or other compensation is paid, resulting in whole or in part from such a decision or other practice.

(e) Reliance on administrative rulings; notice of dismissal or termination; civil action after receipt of notice. Section 10 of the Portal-to-Portal Act of 1947 [29 USCS §259] shall apply to actions under this Act. If a charge filed with the Commission under this Act is dismissed or the proceedings of the Commission are otherwise terminated by the Commission, the Commission shall notify the person aggrieved. A civil action may be brought under this section by a person defined in section 11(a) [29 USCS §630(a)] against the respondent named in the charge within 90 days after the date of the receipt of such notice.

(f) Waiver.

(1) An individual may not waive any right or claim under this Act unless the waiver is knowing and voluntary. Except as provided in paragraph (2), a waiver may not be considered knowing and voluntary unless at a minimum—

(A) the waiver is part of an agreement between the individual and the employer that is written in a manner calculated to be understood by such individual, or by the average individual eligible to participate;

(B) the waiver specifically refers to rights or claims arising under this Act;

(C) the individual does not waive rights or claims that may arise after the date the waiver is executed;

(D) the individual waives rights or claims only in exchange for consideration in addition to anything of value to which the individual already is entitled;

(E) the individual is advised in writing to consult with an attorney prior to executing the agreement;

(F)(i) the individual is given a period of at least 21 days within which to consider the agreement; or

(ii) if a waiver is requested in connection with an exit incentive or other employment termination program offered to a group or class of employees, the individual is given a period of at least 45 days within which to consider the agreement;

(G) the agreement provides that for a period of at least 7 days following the execution of such agreement, the individual may revoke the agreement, and the agreement shall not become effective or enforceable until the revocation period has expired;

(H) if a waiver is requested in connection with an exit incentive or other employment termination program offered to a group or class of employees, the employer (at the commencement of the period specified in subparagraph (F)) informs the individual in writing in a manner calculated to be understood by the average individual eligible to participate, as to—

(i) any class, unit, or group of individuals covered by such program, any eligibility factors for such program, and any time limits applicable to such program; and

(ii) the job titles and ages of all individuals eligible or selected for the program, and the ages of all individuals in the same job classification or organizational unit who are not eligible or selected for the program.

(2) A waiver in settlement of a charge filed with the Equal Employment Opportunity Commission, or an action filed in court by the individual or the individual's representative, alleging age discrimination of a kind prohibited under section 4 or 15 [29 USCS §623 or 633a] may not be considered knowing and voluntary unless at a minimum—

(A) subparagraphs (A) through (E) of paragraph (1) have been met; and

(B) the individual is given a reasonable period of time within which to consider the settlement agreement.

(3) In any dispute that may arise over whether any of the requirements, conditions, and circumstances set forth in subparagraph (A), (B), (C), (D), (E), (F), (G), or (H) of paragraph (1), or subparagraph (A) or (B) of paragraph (2), have been met, the party asserting the validity of a waiver shall have the burden of proving in a court of competent jurisdiction that a waiver was knowing and voluntary pursuant to paragraph (1) or (2).

(4) No waiver agreement may affect the Commission's rights and responsibilities to enforce this Act. No waiver may be used to justify interfering with the protected right of an employee to file a charge or participate in an investigation or proceeding conducted by the Commission.

§627 [§8]. Notices to Be Posted

Every employer, employment agency, and labor organization shall post and keep posted in conspicuous places upon its premises a notice to be prepared or approved by the Secretary setting forth information as he deems appropriate to effectuate the purposes of this chapter.

§628 [§9]. Rules and Regulations; Exemptions

In accordance with the provisions of subchapter II of chapter 5 of title 5, United States Code, the Secretary may issue such rules and regulations as he may consider necessary or appropriate for carrying out this chapter, and may establish such reasonable exemptions to and from any or all provisions of this chapter as it may find necessary and proper in the public interest.

§629 [§10]. Criminal Penalties

Whoever shall forcibly resist, oppose, impede, intimidate, or interfere with a duly authorized representative of the Secretary while he is engaged in the performance of duties under this Act shall be punished by a fine of not more than $500 or by imprisonment for not more than one year, or by both: *Provided, however,* That no person shall be imprisoned under this section except when there has been a prior conviction hereunder.

§630 [§11]. Definitions

For the purposes of this Act—

(a) The term "person" means one or more individuals, partnerships, associations, labor organizations, corporations, business trusts, legal representatives, or any organized groups of persons.

(b) The term "employer" means a person engaged in an industry affecting commerce who has twenty or more employees for each working day in each of twenty or more calendar weeks in the current or preceding calendar year: Provided, that prior to June 30, 1968, employers having fewer than fifty employees shall not be considered employers. The term also means (1) any agent of such a person, and (2) a State or political subdivision of a State and any agency or instrumentality of a State or a political subdivision of a State, and any interstate agency but such term does not include the United States, or a corporation wholly owned by the Government of the United States.

(c) The term "employment agency" means any person regularly undertaking with or without compensation to procure employees for an employer and includes an agent of such a person; but shall not include an agency of the United States.

(d) The term "labor organization" means a labor organization engaged in an industry affecting commerce, and any agent of such an organization, and includes any organization of any kind, any agency, or employee representation committee, group, association, or plan so engaged in which employees participate and which exists for the purpose, in whole or in part, of dealing with employers concerning grievances, labor disputes, wages, rates of pay, hours, or other terms or conditions of employment, and any conference, general committee, joint or system board, or joint council so engaged which is subordinate to a national or international labor organization.

(e) A labor organization shall be deemed to be engaged in an industry affecting commerce if (1) it maintains or operates a hiring hall or hiring office which procures employees for an employer or procures for employees opportunities to work for an employer, or (2) the number of its members (or, where it is a labor organization composed of other labor organizations or their representatives, if the aggregate number of the members of such other labor organization) is fifty or more prior to July 1, 1968, or twenty-five or more on or after July 1, 1968, and such labor organization —

(1) is the certified representative of employees under the provisions of the National Labor Relations Act, as amended, or the Railway Labor Act, as amended; or

(2) although not certified, is a national or international labor organization or a local labor organization recognized or acting as the representative of employees of an employer or employers engaged in an industry affecting commerce; or

(3) has chartered a local labor organization or subsidiary body which is representing or actively seeking to represent employees of employers within the meaning of paragraph (1) or (2); or

(4) has been chartered by a labor organization representing or actively seeking to represent employees within the meaning of paragraph (1) or (2) as to local or subordinate body through which such employees may enjoy membership or become affiliated with such labor organization; or

(5) is a conference, general committee, joint or system board or joint council subordinate to a national or international labor organization, which includes a labor organization engaged in an industry affecting commerce within the meaning of any of the preceding paragraphs of this subsection.

(f) The term "employee" means any individual employed by an employer except that the term "employee" shall not include any person elected to public office in any State or political subdivision of any State by the qualified voters thereof, or any person chosen by such officer to be on such officer's personal staff, or an appointee on the policy-making level or an immediate adviser with respect to the exercise of the constitutional or legal powers of the office. The exemption set forth in the preceding sentence shall not include employees subject to the civil service laws of a State government, governmental agency, or political subdivision. The term "employee" includes any individual who is a citizen of the United States employed by an employer in a workplace in a foreign country.

(g) The term "commerce" means trade, traffic, commerce, transportation, transmission, or communication among the several States, or between a State and any place outside thereof; or within the District of Columbia, or a possession of the United States, or between points in the same State but through a point outside thereof.

(h) The term "industry affecting commerce" means any activity, business, or industry in commerce or in which a labor dispute would hinder or obstruct commerce or the free flow of commerce and includes any activity or industry "affecting commerce" within the meaning of the Labor-Management Reporting and Disclosure Act of 1959.

(i) The term "State" includes a State of the United States, the District of Columbia, Puerto Rico, the Virgin Islands, American Samoa, Guam, Wake Island, the Canal Zone, and Outer Continental Shelf Lands defined in the Outer Continental Shelf Lands Act.

(j) The term "firefighter" means an employee, the duties of whose position are primarily to perform work directly connected with the control and extinguishment of fires or the maintenance and use of firefighting apparatus and equipment, including an employee engaged in this activity who is transferred to a supervisory or administrative position.

(k) The term "law enforcement officer" means an employee, the duties of whose position are primarily the investigation, apprehension, or detention of individuals suspected or convicted of offenses against the criminal laws of a State, including an employee engaged in this activity who is transferred to a supervisory or administration position. For the purpose of this subsection, "detention" includes the duties of employees assigned to individuals incarcerated in any penal institution.

(*l*) The term "compensation, terms, conditions, or privileges of employment" encompasses all employee benefits, including such benefits provided pursuant to a bona fide employee benefit plan.

§631 [§12]. Age Limits

(a) Individuals at least 40 years of age. The prohibitions in this Act shall be limited to individuals who are at least 40 years of age.

(b) Employees or applicants for employment in Federal Government. In the case of any personnel action affecting employers or applicants for employment which is subject to the provisions of section 633a of this title, the prohibitions established in section 633a of this title shall be limited to individuals who are at least 40 years of age.

(c) Bona fide executives or high policymakers. (1) Nothing in this chapter shall be construed to prohibit compulsory retirement of any employee who has attained 65 years of age, and who, for the two-year period immediately before retirement, is employed in a bona fide executive or a high policymaking position, if such employee is entitled to an immediate nonforfeitable annual retirement benefit from a pension, profit-sharing, savings, or deferred compensation plan, or any combination of such plans, of the employer of such employee, which equals, in aggregate, at least $44,000.

(2) In applying the retirement benefit test of paragraph (1) of this subsection, if any such retirement benefits is in a form other than a straight life annuity (with no ancillary benefits), or if employees contribute to any such plan or make rollover contributions, such benefit shall be adjusted in accordance with regulations prescribed by the Equal Employment Opportunity Commission, after consultation with the Secretary of the Treasury, so that the benefit is the equivalent of a straight life annuity (with no ancillary benefits) under a plan to which employees do not contribute and under which no rollover contributions are made.

§633 [§14]. Federal-State Relationship

(a) Federal action superseding State action. Nothing in this chapter shall affect the jurisdiction of any agency of any State performing like functions with regard to discriminatory employment practices on account of age except that upon commencement of an action under this Act such action shall supersede any State action.

(b) Limitation of Federal Action upon commencement of State proceedings. In the case of an alleged unlawful practice occurring in a State which has a law prohibiting discrimination in employment because of age and establishing or authorizing a State authority to grant or seek relief from such discriminatory practice, no suit may be brought under section 626 of this title before the expiration of sixty days after proceedings have been commenced under the State law, unless such proceedings have been earlier terminated: *Provided*, That such sixty-day period shall be extended to one hundred and twenty days during the first year after the effective date of such State law. If any requirement for the commencement of such proceedings is imposed by a State authority other than a requirement of the filing of a written and signed statement of the facts upon which the proceedings is based, the proceeding shall be deemed to have been commenced for the purposes of this subsection at the time such statement is sent by registered mail to the appropriate State authority.

§633a [§14a]. *Nondiscrimination on Account of Age in Federal Government Employment*

(a) Federal agencies affected. All personnel actions affecting employees or applicants for employment who are at least 40 years of age (except personnel actions with regard to aliens employed outside the limits of the United States) in military departments as defined in section 102 of title 5, in executive agencies as defined in section 105 of title 5, (including employees and applicants for employment who are paid from non-appropriated funds), in the United States Postal Service and the Postal Rate Commission, in those units in the government of the District of Columbia having positions in the competitive service, and in those units of the legislative and judicial branches of the Federal Government having positions in the competitive service, and in the Library of Congress shall be made free from any discrimination based on age.

(b) Enforcement by Civil Service Commission and by Librarian of Congress in the Library of Congress; remedies; rules, regulations, orders, and instructions of Commission: compliance by Federal agencies; powers and duties of Commission; notification of final action on complaint of discrimination; exemptions: bona fide occupational qualification. Except as otherwise provided in this subsection, the Civil Service Commission is authorized to enforce the provisions of subsection (a) of this section through appropriate remedies, including reinstatement of hiring of employees with or without backpay, as will effectuate the policies of this section. The Civil Service Commission shall issue such rules, regulations, orders, and instructions as it deems necessary and appropriate to carry out its responsibilities under this section. The Civil Service Commission shall—

(1) be responsible for the review and evaluation of the operation of all agency programs designed to carry out the policy of this section, periodically obtaining and publishing (on at least a semiannual basis) progress reports from each department, agency, or unit referred to in subsection (a) of this section;

(2) consult with and solicit the recommendations of interested individuals, groups, and organizations relating to non-discrimination in employment on account of age; and

(3) provide for the acceptance and processing of complaints of discrimination in Federal employment on account of age.

The head of each such department, agency, or unit shall comply with such rules, regulations, orders, and instructions of the Civil Service Commission which shall include a provision that an employee or applicant for employment shall be notified of any final action taken on any complaint or discrimination filed by him thereunder. Reasonable exemptions to the provisions of this section may be established by the Commission but only when the Commission has established a maximum age requirement on the basis of a determination that age is a bona fide occupational qualification necessary to the performance of the duties of the position. With respect to employment in the Library of Congress, authorities granted in this subsection to the Equal Employment Opportunity Commission shall be exercised by the Librarian of Congress.

(c) Civil actions; jurisdiction; relief. Any person aggrieved may bring a civil action in any Federal district court of competent jurisdiction for such legal or equitable relief as will effectuate the purposes of this chapter.

(d) Notice to Commission; time of notice; Commission notification of prospective defendants; Commission elimination of unlawful practices. When the individual has not filed a complaint concerning age discrimination with the Commission, no civil action may be commenced by any individual under this section until the individual has given the Commission not less than thirty days' notice of an intent to file such action. Such notice shall be filed within one hundred and eighty days after the alleged unlawful practice occurred. Upon receiving a notice of intent to sue, the Commission shall promptly notify all persons named therein as prospective defendants in the action and take any appropriate action to assure the elimination of any unlawful practice.

(e) Duty of Government agency or official. Nothing contained in this section shall relieve any Government agency or official of the responsibility to assure nondiscrimination on account of age in employment as required under any provision of Federal law.

(f) Applicability of Statutory provisions to personnel action of Federal departments, etc. Any personnel action of any department, agency, or other entity referred to in subsection (a) of this section shall not be subject to, or affected by, any provision of this chapter, other than the provisions of sections 626(d)(3) and 631(b) of this title and the provisions of this section.

(g) Study and report to President and Congress by Civil Service Commission; scope. (1) The Civil Service Commission shall undertake a study relating to the effects of the amendments made to this section by the Age Discrimination in Employment Act Amendments of 1978, and the effects of section 631(b) of this title.

(2) The Civil Service Commission shall transmit a report to the President and to the Congress containing the findings of the Commission resulting from the study of the Commission under paragraph (1) of this subsection. Such report shall be transmitted no later than January 1, 1980.

Americans with Disabilities Act

Table of Contents, Title I, Title II, and Title V
42 U.S.C. §§12101–12102, 12111–12117, 12131–12134,
12201–12213 [Pub. L. No. 101–336, 104 Stat. 327 (1990),
as amended by the Civil Rights Act of 1991, Pub. L. No.
102–166, 105 Stat. 1071 (1991)]

TABLE OF CONTENTS

§12101. Findings and purposes.
§12102. Definition of disability.
§12103. Additional definitions.

TITLE I—EMPLOYMENT

§12111. Definitions.
§12112. Discrimination.
§12113. Defenses.
§12114. Illegal use of drugs and alcohol.
§12115. Posting notices.
§12116. Regulations.
§12117. Enforcement.

TITLE II—PUBLIC SERVICES

Subtitle A—Prohibition Against Discrimination and Other Generally
Applicable Provisions

§12131. Definition.
§12132. Discrimination.
§12133. Enforcement.
§12134. Regulations.

Subtitle B—Actions Applicable to Public Transportation Provided by Public
Entities Considered Discriminatory

Part I—Public Transportation Other Than by Aircraft or Certain
Rail Operations

§12141. Definitions.
§12142. Public entities operating fixed route systems.
§12143. Paratransit as a complement to fixed route service.
§12144. Public entity operating a demand responsive system.
§12145. Temporary relief where lifts are unavailable.
§12146. New facilities.
§12147. Alterations of existing facilities.
§12148. Public transportation programs and activities in existing facilities and
one car per train rule.
§12149. Regulations.
§12150. Interim accessibility requirements.

Part III—Public Transportation by Intercity and Commuter Rail

§12161. Definition.
§12162. Intercity and commuter rail actions considered discriminatory.
§12163. Conformance of accessibility standards.
§12164. Regulations.
§12165. Interim accessibility requirements.

TITLE III—PUBLIC ACCOMMODATIONS AND SERVICES
OPERATED BY PRIVATE ENTITIES [omitted]

§12181. Definitions.
§12182. Prohibition of discrimination by public accommodations.
§12183. New construction and alterations in public accommodations and
commercial facilities.
§12184. Prohibition of discrimination in public transportation services provided
by private entities.
§12185. Study.
§12186. Regulations.
§12187. Exemptions for private clubs and religious organizations.
§12188. Enforcement.
§12189. Examinations and courses.

TITLE V—MISCELLANEOUS PROVISIONS

§12201. Construction.
§12202. State immunity.
§12203. Prohibition against retaliation and coercion.
§12204. Regulations by the Architectural and Transportation Barriers
Compliance Board.

§12205. Attorney's fees.

§12205a. Rule of construction regarding regulatory authority.

§12206. Technical assistance.

§12207. Federal wilderness areas.

§12208. Transvestites.

§12209. Instrumentalities of the Congress.

§12210. Illegal use of drugs.

§12211. Definitions.

§12212. Alternative means of dispute resolution.

§12213. Severability.

§12101 [§2]. Findings and Purposes

(a) Findings. — The Congress finds that —

(1) physical or mental disabilities in no way diminish a person's right to fully participate in all aspects of society, yet many people with physical or mental disabilities have been precluded from doing so because of discrimination; others who have a record of a disability or are regarded as having a disability also have been subjected to discrimination;

(2) historically, society has tended to isolate and segregate individuals with disabilities, and, despite some improvements, such forms of discrimination against individuals with disabilities continue to be a serious and pervasive social problem;

(3) discrimination against individuals with disabilities persists in such critical areas as employment, housing, public accommodations, education, transportation, communication, recreation, institutionalization, health services, voting, and access to public services;

(4) unlike individuals who have experienced discrimination on the basis of race, color, sex, national origin, religion, or age, individuals who have experienced discrimination on the basis of disability have often had no legal recourse to redress such discrimination;

(5) individuals with disabilities continually encounter various forms of discrimination, including outright intentional exclusion, the discriminatory effects of architectural, transportation, and communication barriers, overprotective rules and policies, failure to make modifications to existing facilities and practices, exclusionary qualification standards and criteria, segregation, and relegation to lesser services, programs, activities, benefits, jobs, or other opportunities;

(6) census data, national polls, and other studies have documented that people with disabilities, as a group, occupy an inferior status in our society, and are severely disadvantaged socially, vocationally, economically, and educationally;

(7) the Nation's proper goals regarding individuals with disabilities are to assure equality of opportunity, full participation, independent living, and economic self-sufficiency for such individuals; and

(8) the continuing existence of unfair and unnecessary discrimination and prejudice denies people with disabilities the opportunity to compete on an equal basis and to pursue those opportunities for which our free society is justifiably famous, and costs the United States billions of dollars in unnecessary expenses resulting from dependency and nonproductivity.

(b) Purpose. — It is the purpose of this Act —

(1) to provide a clear and comprehensive national mandate for the elimination of discrimination against individuals with disabilities;

(2) to provide clear, strong, consistent, enforceable standards addressing discrimination against individuals with disabilities;

(3) to ensure that the Federal Government plays a central role in enforcing the standards established in this Act on behalf of individuals with disabilities; and

(4) to invoke the sweep of congressional authority, including the power to enforce the fourteenth amendment and to regulate commerce, in order to address the major areas of discrimination faced day-to-day by people with disabilities.

§12102 [§3]. *Definition of Disability*

As used in this Act:

(1) Disability. — The term "disability" means, with respect to an individual —

(A) a physical or mental impairment that substantially limits one or more of the major life activities of such individual;

(B) a record of such an impairment; or

(C) being regarded as having such an impairment (as described in paragraph (3)).

(2) Major life activities. —

(A) In general. — For purposes of paragraph (1), major life activities include, but are not limited to, caring for oneself, performing manual tasks, seeing, hearing, eating, sleeping, walking, standing, lifting, bending, speaking, breathing, learning, reading, concentrating, thinking, communicating, and working.

(B) Major bodily functions. — For purposes of paragraph (1), a major life activity also includes the operation of a major bodily function, including but not limited to, functions of the immune system, normal cell growth, digestive, bowel, bladder, neurological, brain, respiratory, circulatory, endocrine, and reproductive functions.

(3) Regarded as having such an impairment. — For purposes of paragraph (1)(C):

(A) An individual meets the requirement of "being regarded as having such an impairment" if the individual establishes that he or she has been subjected to an action prohibited under this Act because of an actual or perceived physical or mental impairment whether or not the impairment limits or is perceived to limit a major life activity.

(B) Paragraph (1)(C) shall not apply to impairments that are transitory and minor. A transitory impairment is an impairment with an actual or expected duration of 6 months or less.

(4) Rules of construction regarding the definition of disability. — The definition of "disability" in paragraph (1) shall be construed in accordance with the following:

(A) The definition of disability in this Act shall be construed in favor of broad coverage of individuals under this Act, to the maximum extent permitted by the terms of this Act.

(B) The term "substantially limits" shall be interpreted consistently with the findings and purposes of the ADA Amendments Act of 2008.

(C) An impairment that substantially limits one major life activity need not limit other major life activities in order to be considered a disability.

(D) An impairment that is episodic or in remission is a disability if it would substantially limit a major life activity when active.

(E)(i) The determination of whether an impairment substantially limits a major life activity shall be made without regard to the ameliorative effects of mitigating measures such as —

(I) medication, medical supplies, equipment, or appliances, low-vision devices (which do not include ordinary eyeglasses or contact lenses), prosthetics including limbs and devices, hearing aids and cochlear implants or other implantable hearing devices, mobility devices, or oxygen therapy equipment and supplies;

(II) use of assistive technology;

(III) reasonable accommodations or auxiliary aids or services; or

(IV) learned behavioral or adaptive neurological modifications.

(ii) The ameliorative effects of the mitigating measures of ordinary eyeglasses or contact lenses shall be considered in determining whether an impairment substantially limits a major life activity.

(iii) As used in this subparagraph —

(I) the term "ordinary eyeglasses or contact lenses" means lenses that are intended to fully correct visual acuity or eliminate refractive error; and

(II) the term "low-vision devices" means devices that magnify, enhance, or otherwise augment a visual image.

§12103 [§4]. Additional Definitions

As used in this Act:

(1) Auxiliary aids and services. — The term "auxiliary aids and services" includes —

(A) qualified interpreters or other effective methods of making aurally delivered materials available to individuals with hearing impairments;

(B) qualified readers, taped texts, or other effective methods of making visually delivered materials available to individuals with visual impairments;

(C) acquisition or modification of equipment or devices; and

(D) other similar services and actions.

(2) State. — The term "State" means each of the several States, the District of Columbia, the Commonwealth of Puerto Rico, Guam, American Samoa, the Virgin Islands of the United States, the Trust Territory of the Pacific Islands, and the Commonwealth of the Northern Mariana Islands.

TITLE I — EMPLOYMENT

§12111 [§101]. Definitions

As used in this title:

(1) Commission. — The term "Commission" means the Equal Employment Opportunity Commission established by section 705 of the Civil Rights Act of 1964 (42 U.S.C. 2000e-4).

(2) Covered Entity. — The term "covered entity" means an employer, employment agency, labor organization, or joint labor-management committee.

(3) Direct Threat. — The term "direct threat" means a significant risk to the health or safety of others that cannot be eliminated by reasonable accommodation.

(4) Employee. — The term "employee" means an individual employed by an employer. With respect to employment in a foreign country, such term includes an individual who is a citizen of the United States.

(5) Employer. —

(A) In general. — The term "employer" means a person engaged in an industry affecting commerce who has 15 or more employees for each working day in each of 20 or more calendar weeks in the current or preceding calendar years, and any agent of such person, except that, for two years following the effective date of this title, an employer means a person engaged in an industry affecting commerce who has 25 or more employees for each working day in each of 20 or more calendar weeks in the current or preceding year, and any agent of such person.

(B) Exceptions. — The term "employer" does not include —

(i) the United States, a corporation wholly owned by the government of the United States, or an Indian tribe; or

(ii) a bona fide private membership club (other than a labor organization) that is exempt from taxation under section 501(c) of the Internal Revenue Code of 1986.

(6) Illegal Use of Drugs. —

(A) In general. — The term "illegal use of drugs" means the use of drugs, the possession or distribution of which is unlawful under the

Controlled Substances Act (21 U.S.C. 812). Such term does not include the use of a drug taken under supervision by a licensed health care professional, or other uses authorized by the Controlled Substances Act or other provisions of Federal law.

(B) Drugs. — The term "drug" means a controlled substance, as defined in schedules I through V of section 202 of the Controlled Substances Act.

(7) Person, etc. — The terms "person," "labor organization," "employment agency," "commerce," and "industry affecting commerce," shall have the same meaning given such terms in section 701 of the Civil Rights Act of 1964 (42 U.S.C. 2000e).

(8) Qualified individual. The term "qualified individual" means an individual who, with or without reasonable accommodation, can perform the essential functions of the employment position that such individual holds or desires. For the purposes of this title, consideration shall be given to the employer's judgment as to what functions of a job are essential, and if an employer has prepared a written description before advertising or interviewing applicants for the job, this description shall be considered evidence of the essential functions of the job.

(9) Reasonable accommodation. The term "reasonable accommodation" may include

(A) making existing facilities used by employees readily accessible to and usable by individuals with disabilities; and

(B) job restructuring, part-time or modified work schedule, reassignment to a vacant position, acquisition or modification of equipment or devices, appropriate adjustment or modifications of examinations, training materials or policies, the provision of qualified readers or interpreters, and other similar accommodations for individuals with disabilities.

(10) Undue hardship. —

(A) In general. — The term "undue hardship" means an action requiring significant difficulty or expense, when considered in light of the factors set forth in subparagraph (B).

(B) Factors to be considered. — In determining whether an accommodation would impose an undue hardship on a covered entity, factors to be considered include —

(i) the nature and cost of the accommodation needed under this Act;

(ii) the overall financial resources of the facility or facilities involved in the provision of the reasonable accommodation; the number of persons employed at such facility; the effect on expenses and resources, or the impact otherwise of such accommodation upon the operation of the facility;

(iii) the overall financial resources of the covered entity; the overall size of the business of a covered entity with respect to the number of its employees; the number, type, and location of its facilities; and

(iv) the type of operation or operations of the covered entity, including the composition, structure, and functions of the workforce of such entity; the geographic separateness, administrative, or fiscal relationship of the facility or facilities in question to the covered entity.

§12112 [§102]. Discrimination

(a) General rule. — No covered entity shall discriminate against a qualified individual on the basis of disability in regard to job application procedures, the hiring, advancement, or discharge of employees, employee compensation, job training and other terms, conditions, and privileges of employment.

(b) Construction. — As used in subsection (a), the term "discriminate against a qualified individual on the basis of disability" includes —

(1) limiting, segregating, or classifying a job applicant or employee in a way that adversely affects the opportunities or status of such applicant or employee because of the disability of such applicant or employee;

(2) participating in a contractual or other arrangement or relationship that has the effect of subjecting a covered entity's qualified applicant or employee with a disability to the discrimination prohibited by this title (such relationship includes a relationship with an employment or referral agency, labor union, an organization providing fringe benefits to an employee of the covered entity, or an organization providing training and apprenticeship programs);

(3) utilizing standards, criteria, or methods of administration —

(A) that have the effect of discrimination on the basis of disability; or

(B) that perpetuate the discrimination of others who are subject to common administrative control;

(4) excluding or otherwise denying equal jobs or benefits to a qualified individual because of the known disability of an individual with whom the qualified individual is known to have a relationship or association;

(5)(A) not making reasonable accommodations to the known physical or mental limitations of an otherwise qualified individual with a disability who is an applicant or employee, unless such covered entity can demonstrate that the accommodation would impose an undue hardship on the operation of the business of such covered entity; or

(B) denying employment opportunities to a job applicant or employee who is an otherwise qualified individual with a disability, if such denial is based on the need of such covered entity to make reasonable accommodation to the physical or mental impairments of the employee or applicant;

(6) using qualification standards, employment tests or other selection criteria that screen out or tend to screen out an individual with a disability or a class of individuals with disabilities unless the standard, test or other selection criteria, as used by the covered entity, is shown to be job-related for the position in question and is consistent with business necessity; and

(7) failing to select and administer tests concerning employment in the most effective manner to ensure that, when such test is administered to a job applicant or employee who has a disability that impairs sensory, manual, or

speaking skills, such test results accurately reflect the skills, aptitude, or whatever other factor of such applicant or employee that such test purports to measure, rather than reflecting the impaired sensory, manual, or speaking skills of such employee or applicant (except where such skills are the factors that the test purports to measure).

(c) Covered entities in foreign countries. —

(1) In general. — It shall not be unlawful under this section for a covered entity to take any action that constitutes discrimination under this section with respect to an employee in a workplace in a foreign country if compliance with this section would cause such covered entity to violate the law of the foreign country in which such workplace is located.

(2) Control of corporation. —

(A) Presumption. — If an employer controls a corporation whose place of incorporation is a foreign country, any practice that constitutes discrimination under this section and is engaged in by such corporation shall be presumed to be engaged in by such employer.

(B) Exception. — This section shall not apply with respect to the foreign operations of an employer that is a foreign person not controlled by an American employer.

(C) Determination. — For purposes of this paragraph, the determination of whether an employer controls a corporation shall be based on —

(i) the interrelation of operations;

(ii) the common management;

(iii) the centralized control of labor relations; and

(iv) the common ownership or financial control, of the employer and the corporation.

(d) Medical examinations and inquiries. —

(1) In general. — The prohibition against discrimination as referred to in subsection (a) shall include medical examinations and inquiries.

(2) Preemployment. —

(A) Prohibited examination or inquiry. — Except as provided in paragraph (3), a covered entity shall not conduct a medical examination or make inquiries of a job applicant as to whether such applicant is an individual with a disability or as to the nature or severity of such disability.

(B) Acceptable inquiry. — A covered entity may make preemployment inquiries into the ability of an applicant to perform job-related functions.

(3) Employment entrance examination. — A covered entity may require a medical examination after an offer of employment has been made to a job applicant and prior to the commencement of the employment duties of such applicant, and may condition an offer of employment on the results of such examination, if —

(A) all entering employees are subjected to such an examination regardless of disability;

(B) information obtained regarding the medical condition or history of the applicant is collected and maintained on separate forms and in separate medical files and is treated as a confidential medical record, except that—

(i) supervisors and managers may be informed regarding necessary restrictions on the work or duties of the employee and necessary accommodations;

(ii) first aid and safety personnel may be informed, when appropriate, if the disability might require emergency treatment; and

(iii) government officials investigating compliance with this Act shall be provided relevant information on request; and

(C) the results of such examination are used only in accordance with this title.

(4) Examination and inquiry.—

(A) Prohibited examinations and inquiries.—A covered entity shall not require a medical examination and shall not make inquiries of an employee as to whether such employee is an individual with a disability or as to the nature or severity of the disability, unless such examination or inquiry is shown to be job-related and consistent with business necessity.

(B) Acceptable examinations and inquiries.—A covered entity may conduct voluntary medical examinations, including voluntary medical histories, which are part of an employee health program available to employees at that work site. A covered entity may make inquiries into the ability of an employee to perform job-related functions.

(C) Requirement.—Information obtained under subparagraph (B) regarding the medical condition or history of any employee are subject to the requirements of subparagraphs (B) and (C) of paragraph (3).

§12113 [§103]. Defenses

(a) In General.—It may be a defense to a charge of discrimination under this Act that an alleged application of qualification standards, tests, or selection criteria that screen out or tend to screen out or otherwise deny a job or benefit to an individual with a disability has been shown to be job-related and consistent with business necessity, and such performance cannot be accomplished by reasonable accommodation, as required under this title.

(b) Qualification Standards. The term "qualification standards" may include a requirement that an individual shall not pose a direct threat to the health or safety of other individuals in the workplace.

(c) Qualification Standards and Tests Related to Uncorrected Vision.— Notwithstanding section 3(4)(E)(ii), a covered entity shall not use qualification standards, employment tests, or other selection criteria based on an individual's uncorrected vision unless the standard, test, or other selection criteria, as used by the covered entity, is shown to be job-related for the position in question and consistent with business necessity.

(d) Religious Entities.

(1) In general. This title shall not prohibit a religious corporation, association, educational institution, or society from giving preference in

employment to individuals of a particular religion to perform work connected with the carrying on by such corporation, association, educational institution, or society of its activities.

(2) Religious tenets requirements. Under this title, a religious organization may require that all applicants and employees conform to the religious tenets of such organization.

(e) List of Infectious and Communicable Diseases.

(1) In general. The Secretary of Health and Human Services, not later than 6 months after the date of enactment of this Act [enacted July 26, 1990], shall

    (A) review all infectious and communicable diseases which may be transmitted through handling the food supply;

    (B) publish a list of infectious and communicable diseases which are transmitted through handling the food supply;

    (C) publish the methods by which such diseases are transmitted; and

    (D) widely disseminate such information regarding the list of diseases and their modes of transmissability [transmissibility] to the general public. Such list shall be updated annually.

(2) Applications. — In any case in which an individual has an infectious or communicable disease that is transmitted to others through the handling of food, that is included on the list developed by the Secretary of Health and Human Services under paragraph (1), and which cannot be eliminated by reasonable accommodation, a covered entity may refuse to assign or continue to assign such individual to a job involving food handling.

(3) Construction. — Nothing in this Act shall be construed to preempt, modify, or amend any State, county, or local law, ordinance, or regulation applicable to food handling which is designed to protect the public health from individuals who pose a significant risk to the health or safety of others, which cannot be eliminated by reasonable accommodation, pursuant to the list of infectious or communicable diseases and the modes of transmissability [transmissibility] published by the Secretary of Health and Human Services.

§12114 [§104]. Illegal Use of Drugs and Alcohol

(a) Qualified Individual With a Disability. For purposes of this title, a qualified individual with a disability shall not include any employee or applicant who is currently engaging in the illegal use of drugs, when the covered entity acts on the basis of such use.

(b) Rules of Construction. Nothing in subsection (a) shall be construed to exclude as a qualified individual with a disability an individual who

    (1) has successfully completed a supervised drug rehabilitation program and is no longer engaging in the illegal use of drugs, or has otherwise been rehabilitated successfully and is no longer engaging in such use;

    (2) is participating in a supervised rehabilitation program and is no longer engaging in such use; or

    (3) is erroneously regarded as engaging in such use, but is not engaging in such use; except that it shall not be a violation of this Act for a covered

entity to adopt or administer reasonable policies or procedures, including but not limited to drug testing, designed to ensure that an individual described in paragraph (1) or (2) is no longer engaging in the illegal use of drugs.

(c) Authority of Covered Entity. A covered entity

(1) may prohibit the illegal use of drugs and the use of alcohol at the workplace by all employees;

(2) may require that employees shall not be under the influence of alcohol or be engaging in the illegal use of drugs at the workplace;

(3) may require that employees behave in conformance with the requirements established under the Drug-Free Workplace Act of 1988 (41 U.S.C. 701 et seq.);

(4) may hold an employee who engages in the illegal use of drugs or who is an alcoholic to the same qualification standards for employment or job performance and behavior that such entity holds other employees, even if any unsatisfactory performance or behavior is related to the drug use or alcoholism of such employee; and

(5) may, with respect to Federal regulations regarding alcohol and the illegal use of drugs, require that

(A) employees comply with the standards established in such regulations of the Department of Defense, if the employees of the covered entity are employed in an industry subject to such regulations, including complying with regulations (if any) that apply to employment in sensitive positions in such an industry, in the case of employees of the covered entity who are employed in such positions (as defined in the regulations of the Department of Defense);

(B) employees comply with the standards established in such regulations of the Nuclear Regulatory Commission, if the employees of the covered entity are employed in an industry subject to such regulations, including complying with such regulations (if any) that apply to employment in sensitive positions in such an industry, in the case of employees of the covered entity who are employed in such positions (as defined in the regulations of the Nuclear Regulatory Commission); and

(C) employees comply with the standards established in such regulations of the Department of Transportation, if the employees of the covered entity are employed in a transportation industry subject to such regulations, including complying with such regulations (if any) that apply to employment in sensitive positions in such an industry, in the case of employees of the covered entity who are employed in such positions (as defined in the regulations of the Department of Transportation).

(d) Drug Testing.

(1) In general. For purposes of this title, a test to determine the illegal use of drugs shall not be considered a medical examination.

(2) Construction. Nothing in this title shall be constructed to encourage, prohibit, or authorize the conducting of drug testing for the illegal use of drugs by job applicants or employees or making employment decisions based on such test results.

(e) Transportation Employees. Nothing in this title shall be construed to encourage, prohibit, restrict, or authorize the otherwise lawful exercise by entities subject to the jurisdiction of the Department of Transportation of authority to —

   (1) test employees of such entities in, and applicants for, positions involving safety-sensitive duties for the illegal use of drugs and for on-duty impairment by alcohol; and

   (2) remove such persons who test positive for illegal use of drugs and on-duty impairment by alcohol pursuant to paragraph (1) from safety-sensitive duties in implementing subsection (c).

§12115 [§105]. Posting Notices

Every employer, employment agency, labor organization, or joint labor-management committee covered under this title shall post notices in an accessible format to applicants, employees, and members describing the applicable provisions of this Act, in the manner prescribed by section 711 of the Civil Rights Act of 1964 (42 U.S.C. 2000e-10).

§12116 [§106]. Regulations

Not later than 1 year after the date of enactment of this Act, the Commission shall issue regulations in an accessible format to carry out this title in accordance with subchapter II of chapters of title 5, United States Code.

§12117 [§107]. Enforcement

(a) Powers, Remedies, and Procedures. — The powers, remedies, and procedures set forth in sections 705, 706, 707, 709, and 710 of the Civil Rights Act of 1964 (42 U.S.C. 2000e-4, 2000e-5, 2000e-6, 2000e-8, and 2000e-9) shall be the powers, remedies, and procedures this title provides to the Commission, to the Attorney General, or to any person alleging discrimination on the basis of disability in violation of any provision of this Act, or regulations promulgated under section 106, concerning employment.

(b) Coordination. — The agencies with enforcement authority for actions which allege employment discrimination under this title and under the Rehabilitation Act of 1973 shall develop procedures to ensure that administrative complaints filed under this title and under the Regulations Act of 1973 are dealt with in a manner that avoids duplication of effort and prevents imposition of inconsistent or conflicting standards for the same requirements under this title and the Rehabilitation Act of 1973. The Commission, the Attorney General, and the Office of Federal Contract Compliance Programs shall establish such coordinating mechanisms (similar to provisions contained in the joint regulations promulgated by the Commission and the Attorney General at part 42 of title 28 and part 1691 of title 29, Code of Federal Regulations, and the Memorandum of Understanding between the Commission and the Office of Federal Contact Compliance Programs dated January 16, 1981 (46 Fed. Reg. 7435, January 23, 1981)) in regulations implementing this title and Rehabilitation Act of 1973 not later than 18 months after the date of enactment of this Act.

TITLE II — PUBLIC SERVICE

§12131 [§201]. Definitions

As used in this title:

(1) Public entity. The term "public entity" means

(A) any State or local government;

(B) any department, agency, special purpose district, or other instrumentality of a State or States or local government; and

(C) the National Railroad Passenger Corporation, and any commuter authority (as defined in section 502(8) of Title 45).

(2) Qualified individual with a disability. The term "qualified individual with a disability" means an individual with a disability who, with or without reasonable modifications to rules, policies, or practices, the removal of architectural, communication, or transportation barriers, or the provision of auxiliary aids and services, meets the essential eligibility requirements for the receipt of services or the participation in programs or activities provided by a public entity.

§12132 [§202]. Discrimination

Subject to the provisions of this subchapter, no qualified individual with a disability shall, by reason of such disability, be excluded from participation in or be denied the benefits of the services, programs, or activities of a public entity, or be subjected to discrimination by any such entity.

§12133 [§203]. Enforcement

The remedies, procedures, and rights set forth in section 794a of Title 29 shall be the remedies, procedures, and rights this subchapter provides to any person alleging discrimination on the basis of disability in violation of section 12132 of this title.

§12134 [§204]. Regulations

(a) In General. Not later than 1 year after July 26, 1990, the Attorney General shall promulgate regulations in an accessible format that implement this part. Such regulations shall not include any matter within the scope of the authority of the Secretary of Transportation under section 12143, 12149, or 12164 of this title.

(b) Relationship to Other Regulations. Except for "program accessibility, existing facilities," and "communications," regulations under subsection (a) of this section shall be consistent with this chapter and with the coordination regulations under part 41 of title 28, Code of Federal Regulations (as promulgated by the Department of Health, Education, and Welfare on January 13, 1978), applicable to recipients of Federal financial assistance under section 794 of Title 29. With respect to "program accessibility, existing facilities," and "communications," such regulations shall be consistent with regulations and analysis as in part 39 of title 28 of the Code of Federal Regulations, applicable to federally conducted activities under such section 794 of Title 29.

(c) Standards. Regulations under subsection (a) of this section shall include standards applicable to facilities and vehicles covered by this part, other than facilities, stations, rail passenger cars, and vehicles covered by part B of this subchapter. Such standards shall be consistent with the minimum guidelines and requirements issued by the Architectural and Transportation Barriers Compliance Board in accordance with section 12204(a) of this title.

TITLE V — MISCELLANEOUS PROVISIONS

§12201 [§501]. Construction

(a) In General. Except as otherwise provided in this Act, nothing in this Act shall be construed to apply a lesser standard than the standards applied under title V of the Rehabilitation Act of 1973; (29 U.S.C. 790 et seq.) or the regulations issued by Federal agencies pursuant to such title.

(b) Relationship to Other Laws. Nothing in this Act shall be construed to invalidate or limit the remedies, rights, and procedures of any Federal law or law of any State or political subdivision of any State or jurisdiction that provides greater or equal protection for the rights of individuals with disabilities than are afforded by this Act. Nothing in this Act shall be construed to preclude the prohibition of, or the imposition of restrictions on, smoking in places of employment covered by title I, in transportation covered by title II or III, or in places of public accommodation covered by title III.

(c) Insurance. Titles I through IV of this Act shall not be construed to prohibit or restrict

(1) an insurer, hospital or medical service company, health maintenance organization, or any agent, or entity that administers benefit plans, or similar organizations from underwriting risks, classifying risks, or administering such risks that are based on or not inconsistent with State law; or

(2) a person or organization covered by this Act from establishing, sponsoring, observing or administering the terms of a bona fide benefit plan that are based on underwriting risks, classifying risks, or administering such risks that are based on or not inconsistent with State law; or

(3) a person or organization covered by this Act from establishing, sponsoring, observing or administering the terms of a bona fide benefit plan that is not subject to State laws that regulate insurance.

Paragraphs (1), (2), and (3) shall not be used as a subterfuge to evade the purposes of titles I and III.

(d) Accommodations and Services. Nothing in this Act shall be construed to require an individual with a disability to accept an accommodation, aid, service, opportunity, or benefit which such individual chooses not to accept.

(e) Benefits Under State Worker's Compensation Laws. — Nothing in this Act alters the standards for determining eligibility for benefits under State worker's compensation laws or under State and Federal disability benefit programs.

(f) Fundamental Alteration. — Nothing in this Act alters the provision of section 302(b)(2)(A)(ii) [*42 U.S.C. 12182(b)(2)(A)(ii)*], specifying that reasonable modifications in policies, practices, or procedures shall be required, unless an entity can demonstrate that making such modifications in policies, practices, or procedures, including academic requirements in postsecondary education, would fundamentally alter the nature of the goods, services, facilities, privileges, advantages, or accommodations involved.

(g) Claims of No Disability. — Nothing in this Act shall provide the basis for a claim by an individual without a disability that the individual was subject to discrimination because of the individual's lack of disability.

(h) Reasonable accommodations and modifications. A covered entity under title I [*42 U.S.C. 12111* et seq.], a public entity under title II [*42 U.S.C. 12131* et seq.], and any person who owns, leases (or leases to), or operates a place of public accommodation under title III [*42 U.S.C. 12181* et seq.], need not provide a reasonable accommodation or a reasonable modification to policies, practices, or procedures to an individual who meets the definition of disability in section 3(1) [*42 U.S.C. 12102(1)*] solely under subparagraph (C) of such section.

§12202 [§502]. *State Immunity*

A State shall not be immune under the eleventh amendment to the Constitution of the United States from an action in Federal or State court of competent jurisdiction for a violation of this Act. In any action against a State for a violation of the requirements of this Act, remedies (including remedies both at law and in equity) are available for such a violation to the same extent as such remedies are available for such a violation in an action against any public or private entity other than a State.

§12203 [§503]. *Prohibition against Retaliation and Coercion*

(a) Retaliation. No person shall discriminate against any individual because such individual has opposed any act or practice made unlawful by this Act or because such individual made a charge, testified, assisted, or participated in any manner in an investigation, proceeding, or hearing under this Act.

(b) Interference, Coercion, or Intimidation. It shall be unlawful to coerce, intimidate, threaten, or interfere with any individual in the exercise or enjoyment of, or on account of his or her having exercised or enjoyed, or on account of his or her having aided or encouraged any other individual in the exercise or enjoyment of, any right granted or protected by this Act.

(c) Remedies and Procedures. The remedies and procedures available under sections 107, 203, and 308 of this Act shall be available to aggrieved persons for violations of subsections (a) and (b), with respect to title I, title II and title III, respectively.

§12204 [§504]. *Regulations by the Architectural and Transportation Barriers Compliance Board*

(a) Issuance of Guidelines. Not later than 9 months after the date of enactment of this Act, the Architectural and Transportation Barriers Compliance Board shall issue minimum guidelines that shall supplement the existing Minimum

Guidelines and Requirements for Accessible Design for purposes of titles II and III of this Act.

(b) Contents of Guidelines. The supplemental guidelines issued under subsection (a) shall establish additional requirements, consistent with this Act, to ensure that buildings, facilities, rail passenger cars, and vehicles are accessible, in terms of architecture and design, transportation, and communication, to individuals with disabilities.

(c) Qualified Historic Properties.

(1) In general.—The supplemental guidelines issued under subsection (a) shall include procedures and requirements for alterations that will threaten or destroy the historic significance of qualified historic buildings and faculties as defined in 4.17(1)(a) of the Uniform Federal Accessibility Standards.

(2) Sites eligible for listing in national register.—With respect to alterations of buildings, or facilities that are eligible for listing in the National Register of Historic Places under the National Historic Preservation Act (16 U.S.C. 470 et seq.), the guidelines described in paragraph (1) shall, at a minimum, maintain the procedures and requirements established in 4.17(1) and (2) of the Uniform Federal Accessibility Standards.

(3) Other sites.—With respect to alterations of buildings or facilities designated as historic under State or local law, the guidelines described in paragraph (1) shall establish procedures equivalent to those established by 4.17(1)(b) and (c) of the Uniform Federal Accessibility Standards, and shall require, at a minimum, compliance with the requirements established in 4.17(2) of such standards.

§12205 [§505]. Attorney's Fees

In any action or administrative proceeding commenced pursuant to this Act, the court or agency, in its discretion, may allow the prevailing party, other than the United States, a reasonable attorney's fee, including litigation expenses, and costs, and the United States shall be liable for the foregoing the same as a private individual.

§12205a [§506]. Rule of Construction Regarding Regulatory Authority

The authority to issue regulations granted to the Equal Employment Opportunity Commission, the Attorney General, and the Secretary of Transportation under this chapter includes the authority to issue regulations implementing the definitions of disability in section 12102 [§3] of this title (including rules of construction) and the definitions in section 12103 [§4] of this title, consistent with the ADA Amendments Act of 2008.

§12206 [§507]. Technical Assistance

(a) Plan for Assistance.

(1) In general. Not later than 180 days after the date of enactment of this Act, the Attorney General, in consultation with the Chair of the Equal Employment Opportunity Commission, the Secretary of Transportation, the

Chair of the Architectural and Transportation Barriers Compliance Board, and the Chairman of the Federal Communications Commission, shall develop a plan to assist entities covered under this Act, and other Federal agencies, in understanding the responsibility of such entities and agencies under this Act.

(2) Publication of plan. The Attorney General shall publish the plan referred to in paragraph (1) for public comment in accordance with subchapter II of chapter 5 of title 5, United States Code (commonly known as the Administrative Procedure Act).

(b) Agency and Public Assistance. The Attorney General may obtain the assistance of other Federal agencies in carrying out subsection (a), including the National Council on Disability, the President's Committee on Employment of People with Disabilities, the Small Business Administration, and the Department of Commerce.

(c) Implementation.

(1) Rendering assistance. Each federal agency that has responsibility under paragraph (2) for implementing this Act may render technical assistance to individuals and institutions that have rights or duties under the respective title or titles for which such agency has responsibility.

(2) Implementation of titles.

(A) Title I. The Equal Employment Opportunity Commission and the Attorney General shall implement the plan for assistance developed under subsection (a), for title I.

(B) Title II.

(i) Subtitle A. The Attorney General shall implement such plan for assistance for subtitle A of title II.

(ii) Subtitle B. The Secretary of Transportation shall implement such plan for assistance for subtitle B of title II.

(C) Title III. The Attorney General, in coordination with the Secretary of Transportation and the Chair of the Architectural Transportation Barriers Compliance Board, shall implement such plan for assistance for title III, except for section 304, the plan for assistance for which shall be implemented by the Secretary of Transportation.

(D) Title IV. The Chairman of the Federal Communications Commission, in coordination with the Attorney General, shall implement such plan for assistance for title IV.

(3) Technical assistance manuals. Each Federal agency that has responsibility under paragraph (2) for implementing this Act shall, as part of its implementation responsibilities, ensure the availability and provision of appropriate technical assistance manuals to individuals or entities with rights or duties under this Act no later than six months after applicable final regulations are published under titles I, II, III, and IV.

(d) Grants and Contracts.

(1) In general. Each Federal agency that has responsibility under subsection (c)(2) for implementing this Act may make grants or award contracts to effectuate the purposes of this section. Such grants and contracts may be awarded to individuals, institutions not organized for profit and no part of

the net earnings of which inures to the benefit of any private shareholder or individual (including educational institutions), and associations representing individuals who have rights or duties under this Act. Contracts may be awarded to entities organized for profit, but such entities may not be the recipients of grants described in this paragraph.

(2) Dissemination of information. Such grants and contracts, among other uses, may be designed to ensure wide dissemination of information about the rights and duties established by this Act and to provide information and technical assistance about techniques for effective compliance with this Act.

(e) Failure to Receive Assistance. An employer, public accommodation, or other entity covered under this Act shall not be excused from compliance with the requirements of this Act because of any failure to receive technical assistance under this section, including any failure in the development or dissemination of any technical assistance manual authorized by this section.

§12207 [§508]. Federal Wilderness Areas

(a) Study. The National Council on Disability shall conduct a study and report on the effect that wilderness designations and wilderness land management practices have on the ability of individuals with disabilities to use and enjoy the National Wilderness Preservation System as established under the Wilderness Act (16 U.S.C. 1131 et seq.).

(b) Submission of Report. Not later than 1 year after the enactment of this Act, the National Council on Disability shall submit the report required under subsection (a) to Congress.

(c) Specific Wilderness Access.

(1) In general. Congress reaffirms that nothing in the Wilderness Act is to be construed as prohibiting the use of a wheelchair in a wilderness area by an individual whose disability requires use of a wheelchair, and consistent with the Wilderness Act no agency is required to provide any form of special treatment or accommodation, or to construct any facilities or modify any conditions of lands within a wilderness area in order to facilitate such use.

(2) Definition. For purposes of paragraph (1), the term "wheelchair" means a device designated solely for use by a mobility-impaired person for locomotion, that is suitable for use in an indoor pedestrian area.

§12208 [§509]. Transvestites

For the purposes of this Act, term "disabled" or "disability" shall not apply to an individual solely because that individual is a transvestite.

§12209 [§510]. Instrumentalities of the Congress

The General Accounting Office [Government Accountability Office], the Government Printing Office, and the Library of Congress shall be covered as follows:

(1) In general. The rights and protections under this Act shall, subject to paragraph (2), apply with respect to the conduct of each instrumentality of the Congress.

(2) Establishment of remedies and procedures by instrumentalities. The chief official of each instrumentality of the Congress shall establish remedies and procedures to be utilized with respect to the rights and protections provided pursuant to paragraph (1).

(3) Report to Congress. The chief official of each instrumentality of the Congress shall, after establishing remedies and procedures for purposes of paragraph (2), submit to the Congress a report describing the remedies and procedures.

(4) Definition of instrumentalities. For purposes of this section, the term "instrumentality of the Congress" means the following: the General Accounting Office [Government Accountability Office], the Government Printing Office, and the Library of Congress.

(5) Enforcement of employment rights. The remedies and procedures set forth in section 717 of the Civil Rights Act of 1964 (42 U.S.C. 2000e-16) shall be available to any employee of an instrumentality of the Congress who alleges a violation of the rights and protections under sections 102 through 104 of this Act [42 USCS §§12112-12114] that are made applicable by this section, except that the authorities of the Equal Employment Opportunity Commission shall be exercised by the chief official of the instrumentality of the Congress.

(6) Enforcement of rights to public services and accommodations. The remedies and procedures set forth in section 717 of the Civil Rights Act of 1964 (42 U.S.C. 2000e-16) shall be available to any qualified person with a disability who is a visitor, guest, or patron of an instrumentality of Congress and who alleges a violation of the rights and protections under sections 201 through 230 or section 302 or 303 of this Act [42 USCS §§12131-12150 or §12182 or §12183] that are made applicable by this section, except that the authorities of the Equal Employment Opportunity Commission shall be exercised by the chief official of the instrumentality of the Congress.

(7) Construction. Nothing in this section shall alter the enforcement procedures for individuals with disabilities provided in the General Accounting Office Personnel Act of 1980 and regulations promulgated pursuant to that Act.

§12210 [§511]. Illegal Use of Drugs

(a) In General. For purposes of this Act, the term "individual with a disability" does not include an individual who is currently engaging in the illegal use of drugs, when the covered entity acts on the basis of such use.

(b) Rules of Construction. Nothing in subsection (a) shall be construed to exclude as an individual with a disability an individual who

(1) has successfully completed a supervised drug rehabilitation program and is no longer engaging in the illegal use of drugs, or has otherwise been rehabilitated successfully and is no longer engaging in such use;

(2) is participating in a supervised rehabilitation program and is no longer engaging in such use; or

(3) is erroneously regarded as engaging in such use, but is not engaging in such use; except that it shall not be a violation of this Act for a covered entity to adopt or administer reasonable policies or procedures, including but not limited to drug testing, designed to ensure that an individual described in paragraph (1) or (2) is no longer engaging in the illegal use of drugs; however, nothing in this section shall be construed to encourage, prohibit, restrict, or authorize the conducting of testing for illegal use of drugs.

(c) Health and Other Services. Notwithstanding subsection (a) and section 512(b)(3), an individual shall not be denied health services, or services provided in connection with drug rehabilitation, on the basis of the current illegal use of drugs if the individual is otherwise entitled to such services.

(d) Definition of Illegal Use of Drugs.

(1) In general. The term "illegal use of drugs" means the use of drugs, the possession or distribution of which is unlawful under the Controlled Substances Act (21 U.S.C. 812). Such term does not include the use of a drug taken under supervision by a licensed health care professional, or other uses authorized by the Controlled Substances Act or other provisions of Federal law.

(2) Drugs. The term "drug" means a controlled substance, as defined in schedules I through IV of section 202 of the Controlled Substances Act.

§12211 [§512]. Definitions

(a) Homosexuality and Bisexuality. For purposes of the definition of "disability" in section 3(2), homosexuality and bisexuality are not impairments and as such are not disabilities under this Act.

(b) Certain Conditions. Under this Act, the term "disability" shall not include

(1) transvestism, transsexualism, pedophilia, exhibitionism, voyeurism, gender identity disorders not resulting from physical impairments, or other sexual behavior disorders;

(2) compulsive gambling, kleptomania, or pyromania; or

(3) psychoactive substance use disorders resulting from current illegal use of drugs.

§12212 [§514]. Alternative Means of Dispute Resolution

Where appropriate and to the extent authorized by law, the use of alternative means of dispute resolution, including settlement negotiations, conciliation, facilitation, mediation, factfinding, minitrials, and arbitration, is encouraged to resolve disputes arising under this Act.

§12213 [§515]. Severability

Should any provision in this Act be found to be unconstitutional by a court of law, such provision shall be severed from the remainder of the Act, and such action shall not affect the enforceability of the remaining provisions of the Act.

ADA Amendments Act of 2008

Pub. L. No. 110-325; 122 Stat. 3553

[Editors' Note: The ADA Amendments Act of 2008, as its title suggests, amended the American with Disabilities Act. The amendments have been incorporated in the ADA. The ADAAA, however, is reproduced for convenience of reference.]

Be it enacted by the Senate and House of Representatives of the United States of America in Congress assembled,

Sec. 1. Short Title

This Act may be cited as the "ADA Amendments Act of 2008".

Sec. 2. Findings and Purposes

(a) Findings. — Congress finds that —

    (1) in enacting the Americans with Disabilities Act of 1990 (ADA), Congress intended that the Act "provide a clear and comprehensive national mandate for the elimination of discrimination against individuals with disabilities" and provide broad coverage;

    (2) in enacting the ADA, Congress recognized that physical and mental disabilities in no way diminish a person's right to fully participate in all aspects of society, but that people with physical or mental disabilities are frequently precluded from doing so because of prejudice, antiquated attitudes, or the failure to remove societal and institutional barriers;

    (3) while Congress expected that the definition of disability under the ADA would be interpreted consistently with how courts had applied the definition of a handicapped individual under the Rehabilitation Act of 1973, that expectation has not been fulfilled;

    (4) the holdings of the Supreme Court in *Sutton v. United Air Lines, Inc., 527 U.S. 471 (1999)* and its companion cases have narrowed the broad scope of protection intended to be afforded by the ADA, thus eliminating protection for many individuals whom Congress intended to protect;

    (5) the holding of the Supreme Court in *Toyota Motor Manufacturing, Kentucky, Inc. v. Williams, 534 U.S. 184 (2002)* further narrowed the broad scope of protection intended to be afforded by the ADA;

313

(6) as a result of these Supreme Court cases, lower courts have incorrectly found in individual cases that people with a range of substantially limiting impairments are not people with disabilities;

(7) in particular, the Supreme Court, in the case of *Toyota Motor Manufacturing, Kentucky, Inc. v. Williams, 534 U.S. 184 (2002)*, interpreted the term "substantially limits" to require a greater degree of limitation than was intended by Congress; and

(8) Congress finds that the current Equal Employment Opportunity Commission ADA regulations defining the term "substantially limits" as "significantly restricted" are inconsistent with congressional intent, by expressing too high a standard.

(b) Purposes. — The purposes of this Act are —

(1) to carry out the ADA's objectives of providing "a clear and comprehensive national mandate for the elimination of discrimination" and "clear, strong, consistent, enforceable standards addressing discrimination" by reinstating a broad scope of protection to be available under the ADA;

(2) to reject the requirement enunciated by the Supreme Court in *Sutton v. United Air Lines, Inc., 527 U.S. 471 (1999)* and its companion cases that whether an impairment substantially limits a major life activity is to be determined with reference to the ameliorative effects of mitigating measures;

(3) to reject the Supreme Court's reasoning in *Sutton v. United Air Lines, Inc., 527 U.S. 471 (1999)* with regard to coverage under the third prong of the definition of disability and to reinstate the reasoning of the Supreme Court in *School Board of Nassau County v. Arline, 480 U.S. 273 (1987)* which set forth a broad view of the third prong of the definition of handicap under the Rehabilitation Act of 1973;

(4) to reject the standards enunciated by the Supreme Court in *Toyota Motor Manufacturing, Kentucky, Inc. v. Williams, 534 U.S. 184 (2002)*, that the terms "substantially" and "major" in the definition of disability under the ADA "need to be interpreted strictly to create a demanding standard for qualifying as disabled," and that to be substantially limited in performing a major life activity under the ADA "an individual must have an impairment that prevents or severely restricts the individual from doing activities that are of central importance to most people's daily lives";

(5) to convey congressional intent that the standard created by the Supreme Court in the case of *Toyota Motor Manufacturing, Kentucky, Inc. v. Williams, 534 U.S. 184 (2002)* for "substantially limits", and applied by lower courts in numerous decisions, has created an inappropriately high level of limitation necessary to obtain coverage under the ADA, to convey that it is the intent of Congress that the primary object of attention in cases brought under the ADA should be whether entities covered under the ADA have complied with their obligations, and to convey that the question of whether an individual's impairment is a disability under the ADA should not demand extensive analysis; and

(6) to express Congress' expectation that the Equal Employment Opportunity Commission will revise that portion of its current regulations that

defines the term "substantially limits" as "significantly restricted" to be consistent with this Act, including the amendments made by this Act.

Sec. 3. Codified Findings

Section 2(a) of the Americans with Disabilities Act of 1990 (*42 U.S.C. 12101*) is amended—
    (1) by amending paragraph (1) to read as follows:

"(1) physical or mental disabilities in no way diminish a person's right to fully participate in all aspects of society, yet many people with physical or mental disabilities have been precluded from doing so because of discrimination; others who have a record of a disability or are regarded as having a disability also have been subjected to discrimination;";
    (2) by striking paragraph (7); and
    (3) by redesignating paragraphs (8) and (9) as paragraphs (7) and (8), respectively.

Sec. 4. Disability Defined and Rules of Construction

(a) Definition of Disability.—Section 3 of the Americans with Disabilities Act of 1990 (*42 U.S.C. 12102*) is amended to read as follows:

"Sec. 3. DEFINITION OF DISABILITY.
"As used in this Act:
"(1) Disability.—The term 'disability' means, with respect to an individual—
    "(A) a physical or mental impairment that substantially limits one or more major life activities of such individual;
    "(B) a record of such an impairment; or
    "(C) being regarded as having such an impairment (as described in paragraph (3)).
"(2) Major life activities.—
    "(A) In general.—For purposes of paragraph (1), major life activities include, but are not limited to, caring for oneself, performing manual tasks, seeing, hearing, eating, sleeping, walking, standing, lifting, bending, speaking, breathing, learning, reading, concentrating, thinking, communicating, and working.
    "(B) Major bodily functions.—For purposes of paragraph (1), a major life activity also includes the operation of a major bodily function, including but not limited to, functions of the immune system, normal cell growth, digestive, bowel, bladder, neurological, brain, respiratory, circulatory, endocrine, and reproductive functions.
"(3) Regarded as having such an impairment.—For purposes of paragraph (1)(C):
    "(A) An individual meets the requirement of 'being regarded as having such an impairment' if the individual establishes that he or she has been subjected to an action prohibited under this Act because of an actual or perceived physical or mental impairment whether or not the impairment limits or is perceived to limit a major life activity.

"(B) Paragraph (1)(C) shall not apply to impairments that are transitory and minor. A transitory impairment is an impairment with an actual or expected duration of 6 months or less.

"(4) Rules of construction regarding the definition of disability. — The definition of 'disability' in paragraph (1) shall be construed in accordance with the following:

"(A) The definition of disability in this Act shall be construed in favor of broad coverage of individuals under this Act, to the maximum extent permitted by the terms of this Act.

"(B) The term 'substantially limits' shall be interpreted consistently with the findings and purposes of the ADA Amendments Act of 2008.

"(C) An impairment that substantially limits one major life activity need not limit other major life activities in order to be considered a disability.

"(D) An impairment that is episodic or in remission is a disability if it would substantially limit a major life activity when active."

"(E)(i) The determination of whether an impairment substantially limits a major life activity shall be made without regard to the ameliorative effects of mitigating measures such as —

"(I) medication, medical supplies, equipment, or appliances, low-vision devices (which do not include ordinary eyeglasses or contact lenses), prosthetics including limbs and devices, hearing aids and cochlear implants or other implantable hearing devices, mobility devices, or oxygen therapy equipment and supplies;

"(II) use of assistive technology;

"(III) reasonable accommodations or auxiliary aids or services; or

"(IV) learned behavioral or adaptive neurological modifications.

"(ii) The ameliorative effects of the mitigating measures of ordinary eyeglasses or contact lenses shall be considered in determining whether an impairment substantially limits a major life activity.

"(iii) As used in this subparagraph —

"(I) the term 'ordinary eyeglasses or contact lenses' means lenses that are intended to fully correct visual acuity or eliminate refractive error; and

"(II) the term 'low-vision devices' means devices that magnify, enhance, or otherwise augment a visual image.".

(b) Conforming Amendment. — The Americans with Disabilities Act of 1990 (*42 U.S.C. 12101* et seq.) is further amended by adding after section 3 the following:

"Sec. 4. ADDITIONAL DEFINITIONS.

"As used in this Act:

"(1) Auxiliary aids and services. — The term 'auxiliary aids and services' includes —

"(A) qualified interpreters or other effective methods of making aurally delivered materials available to individuals with hearing impairments;

"(B) qualified readers, taped texts, or other effective methods of making visually delivered materials available to individuals with visual impairments;

"(C) acquisition or modification of equipment or devices; and

"(D) other similar services and actions.

"(2) State. — The term 'State' means each of the several States, the District of Columbia, the Commonwealth of Puerto Rico, Guam, American Samoa, the Virgin Islands of the United States, the Trust Territory of the Pacific Islands, and the Commonwealth of the Northern Mariana Islands.".

(c) Amendment to the Table of Contents. — The table of contents contained in section 1(b) of the Americans with Disabilities Act of 1990 is amended by striking the item relating to section 3 and inserting the following items:

"Sec. 3. Definition of disability.
"Sec. 4. Additional definitions.".

Sec. 5. Discrimination on the Basis of Disability

(a) On the Basis of Disability. — Section 102 of the Americans with Disabilities Act of 1990 (*42 U.S.C. 12112*) is amended —

(1) in subsection (a), by striking "with a disability because of the disability of such individual" and inserting "on the basis of disability"; and

(2) in subsection (b) in the matter preceding paragraph (1), by striking "discriminate" and inserting "discriminate against a qualified individual on the basis of disability".

(b) Qualification Standards and Tests Related to Uncorrected Vision. — Section 103 of the Americans with Disabilities Act of 1990 (*42 U.S.C. 12113*) is amended by redesignating subsections (c) and (d) as subsections (d) and (e), respectively, and inserting after subsection (b) the following new subsection:

"(c) Qualification Standards and Tests Related to Uncorrected Vision. — Notwithstanding section 3(4)(E)(ii), a covered entity shall not use qualification standards, employment tests, or other selection criteria based on an individual's uncorrected vision unless the standard, test, or other selection criteria, as used by the covered entity, is shown to be job-related for the position in question and consistent with business necessity.".

(c) Conforming Amendments. —

(1) Section 101(8) of the Americans with Disabilities Act of 1990 (*42 U.S.C. 12111(8)*) is amended —

(A) in the paragraph heading, by striking "with a disability"; and

(B) by striking "with a disability" after "individual" both places it appears.

(2) Section 104(a) of the Americans with Disabilities Act of 1990 (*42 U.S.C. 12114(a)*) is amended by striking "the term 'qualified individual with a disability' shall" and inserting "a qualified individual with a disability shall".

Sec. 6. Rules of Construction

(a) Title V of the Americans with Disabilities Act of 1990 (*42 U.S.C. 12201 et seq.*) is amended —

(1) by adding at the end of section 501 the following:

"(e) Benefits Under State Worker's Compensation Laws.—Nothing in this Act alters the standards for determining eligibility for benefits under State worker's compensation laws or under State and Federal disability benefit programs.

"(f) Fundamental Alteration.—Nothing in this Act alters the provision of section 302(b)(2)(A)(ii), specifying that reasonable modifications in policies, practices, or procedures shall be required, unless an entity can demonstrate that making such modifications in policies, practices, or procedures, including academic requirements in postsecondary education, would fundamentally alter the nature of the goods, services, facilities, privileges, advantages, or accommodations involved.

"(g) Claims of No Disability.—Nothing in this Act shall provide the basis for a claim by an individual without a disability that the individual was subject to discrimination because of the individual's lack of disability.

"(h) Reasonable Accommodations and Modifications.—A covered entity under title I, a public entity under title II, and any person who owns, leases (or leases to), or operates a place of public accommodation under title III, need not provide a reasonable accommodation or a reasonable modification to policies, practices, or procedures to an individual who meets the definition of disability in section 3(1) solely under subparagraph (C) of such section.";

(2) by redesignating section 506 through 514 as sections 507 through 515, respectively, and adding after section 505 the following:

"Sec. 506. RULE OF CONSTRUCTION REGARDING REGULATORY AUTHORITY.

"The authority to issue regulations granted to the Equal Employment Opportunity Commission, the Attorney General, and the Secretary of Transportation under this Act includes the authority to issue regulations implementing the definitions of disability in section 3 (including rules of construction) and the definitions in section 4, consistent with the ADA Amendments Act of 2008."; and

(3) in section 511 (as redesignated by paragraph (2)) (*42 U.S.C. 12211*), in subsection (c), by striking "511(b)(3)" and inserting "512(b)(3)".

(b) The table of contents contained in section 1(b) of the Americans with Disabilities Act of 1990 is amended by redesignating the items relating to sections 506 through 514 as the items relating to sections 507 through 515, respectively, and by inserting after the item relating to section 505 the following new item:

"Sec. 506. Rule of construction regarding regulatory authority.".

Sec. 7. Conforming Amendments

Section 7 of the Rehabilitation Act of 1973 (*29 U.S.C. 705*) is amended—

(1) in paragraph (9)(B), by striking "a physical" and all that follows through "major life activities", and inserting "the meaning given it in section 3 of the Americans with Disabilities Act of 1990 (*42 U.S.C. 12102*)"; and

(2) in paragraph (20)(B), by striking "any person who" and all that follows through the period at the end, and inserting "any person who has a disability as defined in section 3 of the Americans with Disabilities Act of 1990 (*42 U.S.C. 12102*).".

Sec. 8. Effective Date

This Act and the amendments made by this Act shall become effective on January 1, 2009.

Civil Rights Act of 1991

Pub. L. No. 102–166, 105 Stat. 1071

[Editors' Note: The Civil Rights Act of 1991 amended a variety of other statutes, most notably Title VII and 42 U.S.C. §1981. These amendments have been incorporated in the relevant statutes as they are reproduced elsewhere in this Supplement. The core provisions of the 1991 Act, however, are reproduced here for convenience of reference. Where the text of the statute does not so indicate, brackets after the title specify where the sections are codified or noted in the U.S.C.]

Be it enacted by the Senate and House of Representatives of the United States of America in Congress assembled,

Sec. 1. Short Title [42 U.S.C. 1981 note]

This Act may be cited as the "Civil Rights Act of 1991."

Sec. 2. Findings [42 U.S.C. 1981 note]

The Congress finds that—
(1) additional remedies under Federal law are needed to deter unlawful harassment and intentional discrimination in the workplace;
(2) the decision of the Supreme Court in *Wards Cove Packing Co. v. Atonio*, 490 U.S. 642 (1989) has weakened the scope and effectiveness of Federal civil rights protections; and
(3) legislation is necessary to provide additional protections against unlawful discrimination in employment.

Sec. 3. Purposes [42 U.S.C. 1981 note]

The purposes of this Act are—
(1) to provide appropriate remedies for intentional discrimination and unlawful harassment in the workplace;
(2) to codify the concepts of "business necessity" and "job related" enunciated by the Supreme Court in *Griggs v. Duke Power Co.*, 401 U.S. 424 (1971),

and in the other Supreme Court decisions prior to *Wards Cove Packing Co. v. Atonio*, 490 U.S. 642 (1989);

(3) to confirm statutory authority and provide statutory guidelines for the adjudication of disparate impact suits under title VII of the Civil Rights Act of 1964 (42 U.S.C. 2000e et seq.); and

(4) to respond to recent decisions of the Supreme Court by expanding the scope of relevant civil rights statutes in order to provide adequate protection to victims of discrimination.

TITLE I — FEDERAL CIVIL RIGHTS REMEDIES

Sec. 101. *Prohibition Against All Racial Discrimination in the Making and Enforcement of Contracts*

Section 1977 of the Revised Statutes (42 U.S.C. 1981) is amended —

(1) by inserting "(a)" before "All persons within"; and

(2) by adding at the end the following new subsections:

(b) For purposes of this section, the term "make and enforce contracts" includes the making, performance, modification, and termination of contracts, and the enjoyment of all benefits, privileges, terms, and conditions of the contractual relationship.

(c) The rights protected by this section are protected against impairment by nongovernmental discrimination and impairment under color of State law.

Sec. 102. *Damages in Cases of Intentional Discrimination*

The Revised Statutes are amended by inserting after section 1977 (42 U.S.C. 1981) the following new section:

Sec.1977A [42 U.S.C. 1981a]. Damages in Cases of Intentional Discrimination in Employment

(a) Right of Recovery —

(1) Civil rights. — In an action brought by a complaining party under section 706 or 717 of the Civil Rights Act of 1964 (42 U.S.C. 2000e-5) against a respondent who engaged in unlawful intentional discrimination (not an employment practice that is unlawful because of its disparate impact) prohibited under section 703, 704, or 717 of the Act (42 U.S.C. 2000e-2 or 2000e-3), and provided that the complaining party cannot recover under section 1977 of the Revised Statutes (42 U.S.C. 1981), the complaining party may recover compensatory and punitive damages as allowed in subsection (b), in addition to any relief authorized by section 706(g) of the Civil Rights Act of 1964, from the respondent.

(2) Disability. — In an action brought by a complaining party under the powers, remedies, and procedures set forth in section 706 or 717 of the Civil Rights Act of 1964 (as provided in section 107(a) of the Americans with

Disabilities Act of 1990 (42 U.S.C. 12117(a)), and section 505(a)(1) of the Rehabilitation Act of 1973 (29 U.S.C. 794a(a)(1)), respectively) against a respondent who engaged in unlawful intentional discrimination (not an employment practice that is unlawful because of its disparate impact) under section 501 of the Rehabilitation Act of 1973 (29 U.S.C. 791) and the regulations implementing section 501, or who violated the requirements of section 501 of the Act or the regulations implementing section 501 concerning the provision of a reasonable accommodation, or section 102 of the Americans with Disabilities Act of 1990 (42 U.S.C. 12112), or committed a violation of section 102(b)(5) of the Act, against an individual, the complaining party may recover compensatory and punitive damages as allowed in subsection (b), in addition to any relief authorized by section 706(g) of the Civil Rights Act of 1964, from the respondent.

(3) Reasonable accommodation and good faith effort. — In cases where a discriminatory practice involves the provision of a reasonable accommodation pursuant to section 102(b)(5) of the Americans with Disabilities Act of 1990 or regulations implementing section 501 of the Rehabilitation Act of 1973, damages may not be awarded under this section where the covered entity demonstrates good faith efforts, in consultation with the person with the disability who has informed the covered entity that accommodation is needed, to identify and make a reasonable accommodation that would provide such individual with an equally effective opportunity and would not cause an undue hardship on the operation of the business.

(b) Compensatory and Punitive Damages. —

(1) Determination of punitive damages. A complaining party may recover punitive damages under this section against a respondent (other than a government, government agency or political subdivision) if the complaining party demonstrates that the respondent engaged in a discriminatory practice or discriminatory practices with malice or with reckless indifference to the federally protected rights of an aggrieved individual.

(2) Exclusions from compensatory damages. — Compensatory damages awarded under this section shall not include backpay, interest on backpay, or any other type of relief authorized under section 706(g) of the Civil Rights Act of 1964.

(3) Limitations. — The sum of the amount of compensatory damages awarded under this section for future pecuniary losses, emotional pain, suffering, inconvenience, mental anguish, loss of enjoyment of life, and other non-pecuniary losses, and the amount of punitive damages awarded under this section, shall not exceed, for each complaining party —

(A) in the case of a respondent who has more than 14 and fewer than 101 employees in each of 20 or more calendar weeks in the current or preceding calendar year, $50,000;

(B) in the case of a respondent who has more than 100 and fewer than 201 employees in each of 20 or more calendar weeks in the current or preceding calendar year, $100,000; and

(C) in the case of a respondent who has more than 200 and fewer than 501 employees in each of 20 or more calendar weeks in the current or preceding calendar year, $200,000; and

(D) in the case of a respondent who has more than 500 employees in each of 20 or more calendar weeks in the current or preceding calendar year, $300,000.

(4) Construction. Nothing in this section shall be construed to limit the scope of, or the relief available under, section 1977 of the Revised Statutes (42 U.S.C. 1981).

(c) Jury Trial. — If a complaining party seeks compensatory or punitive damages under this section —

(1) any party may demand a trial by jury; and

(2) the court shall not inform the jury of the limitations described in subsection (b)(3).

(d) Definitions. — As used in this section:

(1) Complaining party. — The term "complaining party" means —

(A) in the case of a person seeking to bring an action under subsection (a)(1), the Equal Employment Opportunity Commission, the Attorney General, or a person who may bring an action or proceeding under title VII of the Civil Rights Act of 1964 (42 U.S.C. 2000e et seq.); or

(B) in the case of a person seeking to bring an action under subsection (a)(2), the Equal Employment Opportunity Commission, the Attorney General, a person who may bring an action or proceeding under section 505(a)(1) of the Rehabilitation Act of 1973 (29 U.S.C. 794a (a)(1)), or a person who may bring an action or proceeding under title I of the Americans with Disabilities Act of 1990 (42 U.S.C. 12010 et seq.).

(2) Discriminatory practice. — The term "discriminatory practice" means the discrimination described in paragraph (1), or the discrimination or the violation described in paragraph (2), of subsection (a).

Sec. 103. Attorney's Fees

The last sentence of section 722 of the Revised Statutes (42 U.S.C. 1988) is amended by inserting, "1977A" after "1977." [42 U.S.C. 1981a]

Sec. 104. Definitions

Section 701 of the Civil Rights Act of 1964 (42 U.S.C. 2000e) is amended by adding at the end the following new subsections:

(*l*) The term "complaining party" means the Commission, the Attorney General, or a person who may bring an action or proceeding under this title.

(m) The term "demonstrates" means meets the burdens of production and persuasion.

(n) The term "respondent" means an employer, employment agency, labor organization, joint labor-management committee controlling apprenticeship or other training or retraining program, including an on-the-job training program, or Federal entity subject to section 717.

Sec. 105. *Burden of Proof in Disparate Impact Cases*

(a) Section 703 of the Civil Rights Act of 1964 (42 U.S.C. 2000e-2) is amended by adding at the end the following new subsection:

(k)(1)(A) An unlawful employment practice based on disparate impact is established under this title only if—

> (i) a complaining party demonstrates that a respondent uses a particular employment practice that causes a disparate impact on the basis of race, color, religion, sex, or national origin and the respondent fails to demonstrate that the challenged practice is job related for the position in question and consistent with business necessity; or

> (ii) the complaining party makes the demonstration described in subparagraph (C) with respect to an alternative employment practice and the respondent refuses to adopt such alternative employment practices.

(B)(i) With respect to demonstrating that a particular employment practice causes a disparate impact as described in subparagraph (A)(i), the complaining party shall demonstrate that each particular challenged employment practice causes a disparate impact, except that if the complaining party can demonstrate to the court that the elements of a respondent's decisionmaking process are not capable of separation for analysis, the decisionmaking process may be analyzed as one employment practice.

> (ii) If the respondent demonstrates that a specific employment practice does not cause the disparate impact, the respondent shall not be required to demonstrate that such practice is required by business necessity.

(C) The demonstration referred to by subparagraph (A)(ii) shall be in accordance with the law as it existed on June 4, 1989, with respect to the concept of "alternative employment practice."

(2) A demonstration that an employment practice is required by business necessity may not be used as a defense against a claim of intentional discrimination under this title.

(3) Notwithstanding any other provision of this title, a rule barring the employment of an individual who currently and knowingly uses or possesses a controlled substance, as defined in schedules I and II of section 102(6) of the Controlled Substances Act (21 U.S.C. 802(6)), other than the use or possession of a drug taken under the supervision of a licensed health care professional, or any other use or possession authorized by the Controlled Substances Act or any other provision of Federal law, shall be considered an unlawful employment practice under this title only if such rule is adopted or applied with an intent to discriminate because of race, color, religion, sex, or national origin.

(b) No statements other than the interpretive memorandum appearing at Vol. 137 Congressional Record S 15276 (daily ed. Oct. 25, 1991) shall be considered legislative history of, or relied upon in any way as legislative history in construing or applying, any provision of this Act that relates to *Wards Cove* — Business necessity/cumulation/alternative business practice.

Sec. 106. *Prohibition Against Discriminatory Use of Test Scores*

Section 703 of the Civil Rights Act of 1964 (42 U.S.C. 2000e-2) (as amended by section 105) is further amended by adding at the end the following new subsection:

(1) It shall be an unlawful employment practice for a respondent, in connection with the selection or referral of applicants or candidates for employment or promotion, to adjust the scores of, use different cutoff scores for, or otherwise alter the results of, employment related tests on the basis of race, color, religion, sex, or national origin.

Sec. 107. *Clarifying Prohibition Against Impermissible Consideration of Race, Color, Religion, Sex, or National Origin in Employment Practices*

(a) In General. — Section 703 of the Civil Rights Act of 1964 (42 U.S.C. 2000e-2) (as amended by sections 105 and 106) is further amended by adding at the end the following new subsection:

(m) Except as otherwise provided in this title, an unlawful employment practice is established when the complaining party demonstrates that race, color, religion, sex, or national origin was a motivating factor for any employment practice, even though other factors also motivated the practice.

(b) Enforcement Provisions. — Section 706(g) of such Act (42 U.S.C. 2000e-5(g)) is amended —

(1) by designating the first through third sentences as paragraph (1);

(2) by designating the fourth sentence as paragraph (2)(A) and indenting accordingly; and

(3) by adding at the end the following new subparagraph:

(B) On a claim in which an individual proves a violation under section 703(m) and a respondent demonstrates that the respondent would have taken the same action in the absence of the impermissible motivating factor, the court —

(i) may grant declaratory relief, injunctive relief (except as provided in clause (ii)), and attorney's fees and costs demonstrated to be directly attributable only to the pursuit of a claim under section 703(m); and

(ii) shall not award damages or issue an order requiring any admission, reinstatement, hiring, promotion, or payment, described in subparagraph (A).

Sec. 108. *Facilitating Prompt and Orderly Resolution of Challenges to Employment Practices Implementing Litigated or Consent Judgments or Orders*

Section 703 of the Civil Rights Act of 1964 (42 U.S.C. 2000e-2) (as amended by sections 105, 106, and 107 of this title) is further amended by adding at the end the following new subsection:

(n)(1)(A) Notwithstanding any other provision of law, and except as provided in paragraph (2), an employment practice that implements and is within the scope of a litigated or consent judgment or order that resolves a claim of employment discrimination under the Constitution or Federal civil rights laws may not be challenged under the circumstances described in subparagraph (B).

 (B) A practice described in subparagraph (A) may not be challenged in a claim under the Constitution or Federal civil rights laws —

  (i) by a person who, prior to the entry of the judgment or order described in subparagraph (A), had —

   (I) actual notice of the proposed judgment or order sufficient to apprise such person that such judgment or order might adversely affect the interests and legal rights of such person and that an opportunity was available to present objections to such judgment or order by a future date certain; and

   (II) a reasonable opportunity to present objections to such judgment or order; or

  (ii) by a person whose interests were adequately represented by another person who had previously challenged the judgment or order on the same legal grounds and with a similar factual situation, unless there has been an intervening change in law or fact.

(2) Nothing in this subsection shall be construed to —

 (A) alter the standards for intervention under rule 24 of the Federal Rules of Civil Procedure or apply to the rights of parties who have successfully intervened pursuant to such rule in the proceeding in which the parties intervened;

 (B) apply to the rights of parties to the action in which a litigated or consent judgment or order was entered, or of members of a class represented or sought to be represented in such action, or of members of a group on whose behalf relief was sought in such action by the Federal Government;

 (C) prevent challenges to a litigated or consent judgment or order on the ground that such judgment or order was obtained through collusion or fraud, or is transparently invalid or was entered by a court lacking subject matter jurisdiction; or

 (D) authorize or permit the denial to any person of the due process of law required by the Constitution.

(3) Any action not precluded under this subsection that challenges an employment consent judgment or order described in paragraph (1) shall be brought in the court, and if possible before the judge, that entered such judgment or order. Nothing in this subsection shall preclude a transfer of such action pursuant to section 1404 of title 28, United States Code.

Sec. 109. *Protection of Extraterritorial Employment*

(a) Definition of Employee. — Section 701(f) of the Civil Rights Act of 1964 (42 U.S.C. 2000e(f)) and section 101(4) of the Americans with Disabilities Act of

1990 (42 U.S.C. 12111(4)) are each amended by adding at the end the following: "With respect to employment in a foreign country, such term includes an individual who is a citizen of the United States."

(b) Exemption. —

(1) Civil Rights Act of 1964. — Section 702 of the Civil Rights Act of 1964 (42 U.S.C. 2000e-1) is amended —

(A) by inserting "(a)" after "Sec. 702."; and

(B) by adding at the end the following:

(b) It shall not be unlawful under section 703 or 704 for an employer (or a corporation controlled by an employer), labor organization, employment agency, or joint labor-management committee controlling apprenticeship or other training or retraining (including on-the-job training programs) to take any action otherwise prohibited by such section, with respect to an employee in a workplace in a foreign country if compliance with such section would cause such employer (or such corporation), such organization, such agency, or such committee to violate the law of the foreign country in which such workplace is located.

(c)(1) If an employer controls a corporation whose place of incorporation is a foreign country, any practice prohibited by section 703 or 704 engaged in by such corporation shall be presumed to be engaged in by such employer.

(2) Sections 703 and 704 shall not apply with respect to the foreign operations of an employer that is a foreign person not controlled by an American employer.

(3) For purposes of this subsection, the determination of whether an employer controls a corporation shall be based on —

(A) the interrelation of operations;

(B) the common management;

(C) the centralized control of labour relations; and

(D) the common ownership or financial control, of the employer and the corporation.

(2) Americans with Disabilities Act of 1990. — Section 102 of the Americans with Disabilities Act of 1990 (42 U.S.C. 12112) is amended —

(A) by redesignating subsection (c) as subsection (d); and

(B) by inserting after subsection (b) the following new subsection:

(c) Covered Entities in Foreign Countries. —

(1) In general. — It shall not be unlawful under this section for a covered entity to take any action that constitutes discrimination under this section with respect to an employee in a workplace in a foreign country if compliance with this section would cause such covered entity to violate the law of the foreign country in which such workplace is located.

(2) Control of corporation. —

(A) Presumption. — If an employer controls a corporation whose place of incorporation is a foreign country, any practice that constitutes discrimination under this section and is engaged in by such corporation shall be presumed to be engaged in by such employer.

(B) Exception. — This section shall not apply with respect to the foreign operations of an employer that is a foreign person not controlled by an American employer.

(C) Determination. — For purposes of this paragraph, the determination of whether an employer controls a corporation shall be based on —

(i) the interrelation of operations;

(ii) the common management;

(iii) the centralized control of labor relations; and

(iv) the common ownership or financial control, of the employer and the corporation.

(c) Application of Amendments. — The amendments made by this section shall not apply with respect to conduct occurring before the date of the enactment of this Act.

Sec. 110. *Technical Assistance Training Institute*

(a) Technical Assistance. — Section 705 of the Civil Rights Act of 1964 (42 U.S.C. 2000e-4) is amended by adding at the end the following new subsection:

(j)(1) The Commission shall establish a Technical Assistance Training Institute, through which the Commission shall provide technical assistance and training regarding the laws and regulations enforced by the Commission.

(2) An employer or other entity covered under this title shall not be excused from compliance with the requirements of this title because of any failure to receive technical assistance under this subsection.

(3) There are authorized to be appropriated to carry out this subsection such sums as may be necessary for fiscal year 1992.

(b) Effective Date. — The amendment made by this section shall take effect on the date of the enactment of this Act.

Sec. 111. *Education and Outreach*

Section 705(h) of the Civil Rights Act of 1964 (42 U.S.C. 2000e-4(h)) is amended —

(1) by inserting "(1)" after "(h)"; and

(2) by adding at the end the following new paragraph:

(2) In exercising its powers under this title, the Commission shall carry out educational and outreach activities (including dissemination of information in languages other than English) targeted to —

(A) individuals who historically have been victims of employment discrimination and have not been equitably served by the Commission; and

(B) individuals on whose behalf the Commission has authority to enforce any other law prohibiting employment discrimination, concerning rights and obligations under this title or such law, as the case may be.

Sec. 112. Expansion of Right to Challenge Discriminatory Seniority Systems

Section 706(e) of the Civil Rights Act of 1964 (42 U.S.C. 2000e-5(e)) is amended —

(1) by inserting "(1)" before "A charge under this section"; and

(2) by adding at the end the following new paragraph:

(2) For purposes of this section, an unlawful employment practice occurs, with respect to a seniority system that has been adopted for an intentionally discriminatory purpose in violation of this title (whether or not the discriminatory purpose is apparent on the face of the seniority provision), when the seniority system is adopted, when an individual becomes subject to the seniority system, or when a person aggrieved is injured by the application of the seniority system or provision of the system.

Sec. 113. Authorizing Award of Expert Fees

(a) Revised Statutes. — Section 722 of the Revised Statutes [42 U.S.C. 1988] is amended —

(1) by designating the first and second sentences as subsections (a) and (b), respectively, and indenting accordingly; and

(2) by adding at the end the following new subsection:

(c) In awarding an attorney's fee under subsection (b) in any action or proceeding to enforce a provision of sections 1977 or 1977A of the Revised Statutes, the court, in its discretion, may include expert fees as part of the attorney's fee.

(b) Civil Rights Act of 1964. — Section 706(k) of the Civil Rights Act of 1964 (42 U.S.C. 2000e-5(k)) is amended by inserting "(including expert fees)" after "attorney's fee."

Sec. 114. Providing for Interest and Extending the Statute of Limitations in Actions Against the Federal Government

Section 717 of the Civil Rights Act of 1964 (42 U.S.C. 2000e-16) is amended —

(1) in subsection (c), by striking "thirty days" and inserting "90 days"; and

(2) in subsection (d), by inserting before the period, "and the same interest to compensate for delay in payment shall be available as in cases involving nonpublic parties."

Sec. 115. Notice or Limitations Period Under the Age Discrimination in Employment Act of 1967

Section 7(e) of the Age Discrimination in Employment Act of 1967 (29 U.S.C. 626(e)) is amended —

(1) by striking paragraph (2);

(2) by striking the paragraph designation in paragraph (1);

(3) by striking "Sections 6 and" and inserting "Section"; and

(4) by adding at the end the following: If a charge filed with the Commission under this Act is dismissed or the proceedings of the Commission are

otherwise terminated by the Commission, the Commission shall notify the person aggrieved. A civil action may be brought under this section by a person defined in section 11(a) against the respondent named in the charge within 90 days after the date of the receipt of such notice.

Sec. 116. Lawful Court-Ordered Remedies, Affirmative Action, and Conciliation Agreements Not Affected

Nothing in the amendments made by this title shall be construed to affect court-ordered remedies, affirmative action, or conciliation agreements, that are in accordance with the law.

Sec. 117. Coverage of House of Representatives and the Agencies of the Legislative Branch [2 U.S.C. 601]

(a) Coverage of the House of Representatives. —

(1) In general. — Notwithstanding any provision of title VII of the Civil Rights Act of 1964 (42 U.S.C. 2000e et seq.) or of other law, the purposes of such title shall, subject to paragraph (2), apply in their entirety to the House of Representatives.

(2) Employment in the House. —

(A) Application. — The rights and protections under title VII of the Civil Rights Act of 1964 (42 U.S.C. 2000e et seq.) shall, subject to paragraph (B), apply with respect to any employee in an employment position in the House of Representatives and any employing authority of the House of Representatives.

(B) Administration. —

(i) In general. — In the administration of this paragraph, the remedies and procedures made applicable pursuant to the resolution described in clause (ii) shall apply exclusively.

(ii) Resolution. — The resolution referred to in clause (i) is the Fair Employment Practices Resolution (House Resolution 558 of the One Hundredth Congress, as agreed to October 4, 1988), as incorporated into the Rules of the House of Representatives of the One Hundred Second Congress as Rule LI, or any other provision that continues in effect the provisions of such resolution.

(C) Exercise of rulemaking power. — The provisions of subparagraph (B) are enacted by the House of Representatives as an exercise of the rulemaking power of the House of Representatives, with full recognition of the right of the House to change its rules, in the same manner, and to the same extent as in the case of any other rule of the House.

(b) Instrumentalities of Congress. —

(1) In general. — The rights and protections under this title and title VII of the Civil Rights Act of 1964 (42 U.S.C. 2000e et seq.) shall, subject to paragraph (2), apply with respect to the conduct of each instrumentality of the Congress.

(2) Establishment of remedies and procedures by instrumentalities. — The chief official of each instrumentality of the Congress shall establish remedies and procedures to be utilized with respect to the rights and protections provided pursuant to paragraph (1). Such remedies and procedures shall apply exclusively, except for the employees who are defined as Senate employees, in section 301(c)(1).

(3) Report to Congress. — The chief official of each instrumentality of the Congress shall, after establishing remedies and procedures for purposes of paragraph (2), submit to the Congress a report describing the remedies and procedures.

(4) Definition of instrumentalities. — For purposes of this section, instrumentalities of the Congress include the following: the Architect of the Capitol, the Congressional Budget Office, the General Accounting Office, the Government Printing Office, the Office of Technology Assessment, and the United States Botanic Garden.

(5) Construction. — Nothing in this section shall alter the enforcement procedures for individuals protected under section 71 of title VII for the Civil Rights Act of 1964 (42 U.S.C. 2000e-16).

Sec. 118. *Alternative Means of Dispute Resolution* *[42 U.S.C. 1981 note]*

Where appropriate and to the extent authorized by law, the use of alternative means of dispute resolution, including settlement negotiations, conciliation, facilitation, mediation, factfinding, minitrials, and arbitration, is encouraged to resolve disputes arising under the Acts or provisions of Federal law amended by this title.

... TITLE IV — GENERAL PROVISIONS

Sec. 401. *Severability [42 U.S.C. 1981 note]*

If any provision of this Act, or an amendment made by this Act, or the application of such provision to any person or circumstances is held to be invalid, the remainder of this Act and the amendments made by this Act, and the application of such provision to other persons and circumstances, shall not be affected.

Sec. 402. *Effective Date [42 V.S.C. 1981 note]*

(a) General. — Except as otherwise specifically provided, this Act and the amendments made by this Act shall take effect upon enactment.

(b) Certain Disparate Impact Cases. — Notwithstanding any other provision of this Act, nothing in this Act shall apply to any disparate impact cases for which a complaint was filed before March 1, 1975, and for which an initial decision was rendered after October 30, 1983.

Congressional Accountability Act

2 U.S.C. §§1301–1302, 1311–1313, 1317, 1361

Sec. 1301. Definitions

Except as otherwise specifically provided in this chapter, as used in this chapter.

    (1) Board. The term "Board" means the Board of Directors of the Office of Compliance.

    (2) Chair. The term "Chair" means the Chair of the Board of Directors of the Office of Compliance.

    (3) Covered employee. The term "covered employee" means any employee of

        (A) the House of Representatives;

        (B) the Senate;

        (C) the Capitol Guide Service;

        (D) the Capitol Police;

        (E) the Congressional Budget Office;

        (F) the Office of the Architect of the Capitol;

        (G) the Office of the Attending Physician;

        (H) the Office of Compliance; or

        (I) the Office of Technology Assessment.

    (4) Employee. The term "employee" includes an applicant for employment and a former employee.

    (5) Employee of the Office of the Architect of the Capitol. The term "employee of the Office of the Architect of the Capitol" includes any employee of the Office of the Architect of the Capitol, the Botanic Garden.

    (6) Employee of the Capitol Police. The term "employee of the Capitol Police" includes any member or officer of the Capitol Police.

    (7) Employee of the House of Representatives. The term "employee of the House of Representatives" includes an individual occupying a position the pay for which is disbursed by the Clerk of the House of Representatives, or another official designated by the House of Representatives, or any employment position in an entity that is paid with funds derived from the clerk-hire

allowance of the House of Representatives but not any such individual employed by any entity listed in subparagraphs (C) through (I) of paragraph (3).

(8) Employee of the Senate. The term "employee of the Senate" includes any employee whose pay is disbursed by the Secretary of the Senate, but not any such individual employed by any entity listed in subparagraphs (C) through (I) of paragraph (3).

(9) Employing office. The term "employing office" means

(A) the personal office of a Member of the House of Representatives or of a Senator;

(B) a committee of the House of Representatives or the Senate or a joint committee;

(C) any other office headed by a person with the final authority to appoint, hire, discharge, and set the terms, conditions, or privileges of the employment of an employee of the House of Representatives or the Senate; or

(D) the Office of Congressional Accessibility Services, the United States Capitol Police, the Congressional Budget Office, the Office of the Architect of the Capitol, the Office of Attending Physician, the Office of Compliance, and the Office of Technology Assessment.

(10) Executive Director. The term "Executive Director" means the Executive Director of the Office of Compliance.

(11) General Counsel. The term "General Counsel" means the General Counsel of the Office of Compliance.

(12) Office. The term "Office" means the Office of Compliance.

Sec. 1302. *Application of Laws*

(a) Laws Made Applicable. The following laws shall apply, as prescribed by this chapter, to the legislative branch of the Federal Government:

(1) The Fair Labor Standards Act of 1938 (29 U.S.C. 201 et seq.).

(2) Title VII of the Civil Rights Act of 1964 (42 U.S.C. 2000e et seq.).

(3) The Americans with Disabilities Act of 1990 (42 U.S.C. 12101 et seq.).

(4) The Age Discrimination in Employment Act of 1967 (29 U.S.C. 621 et seq.).

(5) The Family and Medical Leave Act of 1993 (29 U.S.C. 2611 et seq.).

(6) The Occupational Safety and Health Act of 1970 (29 U.S.C. 651 et seq.).

(7) Chapter 71 (relating to Federal service labor-management relations) of Title 5.

(8) The Employee Polygraph Protection Act of 1988 (29 U.S.C. 2001 et seq.).

(9) The Worker Adjustment and Retraining Notification Act (29 U.S.C. 2101 et seq.).

(10) The Rehabilitation Act of 1973 (29 U.S.C. 701 et seq.).

(11) Chapter 43 (relating to veterans' employment and reemployment) of Title 38.

(b) Laws Which May Be Made Applicable.

(1) In general. The Board shall review provisions of Federal law (including regulations) relating to (A) the terms and conditions of employment (including hiring, promotion, demotion, termination, salary, wages, overtime compensation, benefits, work assignments or reassignments, grievance and disciplinary procedures, protection from discrimination in personnel actions, occupational health and safety, and family and medical and other leave) of employees, and (B) access to public services and accommodations.

(2) Board report. Beginning on December 31, 1996, and every 2 years thereafter, the Board shall report on (A) whether or to what degree the provisions described in paragraph (1) are applicable or inapplicable to the legislative branch, and (B) with respect to provisions inapplicable to the legislative branch, whether such provisions should be made applicable to the legislative branch. The presiding officers of the House of Representatives and the Senate shall cause each such report to be printed in the Congressional Record and each such report shall be referred to the committees of the House of Representatives and the Senate with jurisdiction.

(3) Reports of congressional committees. Each report accompanying any bill or joint resolution relating to terms and conditions of employment or access to public services or accommodations reported by a committee of the House of Representatives or the Senate shall

(A) describe the manner in which the provisions of the bill or joint resolution apply to the legislative branch; or

(B) in the case of a provision not applicable to the legislative branch, include a statement of the reasons the provision does not apply.

On the objection of any Member, it shall not be in order for the Senate or the House of Representatives to consider any such bill or joint resolution if the report of the committee on such bill or joint resolution does not comply with the provisions of this paragraph. This paragraph may be waived in either House by majority vote of that House.

Sec. 1311. *Rights and Protections under Title VII of the Civil Rights Act of 1964, the Age Discrimination in Employment Act of 1967, the Rehabilitation Act of 1973, and Title I of the Americans with Disabilities Act of 1990*

(a) Discriminatory Practices Prohibited. All personnel actions affecting covered employees shall be made free from any discrimination based on

(1) race, color, religion, sex, or national origin, within the meaning of section 703 of the Civil Rights Act of 1964 (42 U.S.C. 2000e-2);

(2) age, within the meaning of section 15 of the Age Discrimination in Employment Act of 1967 (29 U.S.C. 633a); or

(3) disability, within the meaning of section 501 of the Rehabilitation Act of 1973 (29 U.S.C. 791) and sections 102 through 104 of the Americans with Disabilities Act of 1990 (42 U.S.C. 12112-12114).

(b) Remedy.

(1) Civil rights. The remedy for a violation of subsection (a)(1) shall be

(A) such remedy as would be appropriate if awarded under section 706(g) of the Civil Rights Act of 1964 (42 U.S.C. 2000e-5(g)); and

(B) such compensatory damages as would be appropriate if awarded under section 1977 of the Revised Statutes (42 U.S.C. 1981), or as would be appropriate if awarded under sections 1977A(a)(1), 1977A(b)(2), and, irrespective of the size of the employing office, 1977A(b)(3)(D) of the Revised Statutes (42 U.S.C. 1981a(a)(1), 1981a(b)(2), and 1981a(b)(3)(D)).

(2) Age discrimination. The remedy for a violation of subsection (a)(2) shall be

(A) such remedy as would be appropriate if awarded under section 15(c) of the Age Discrimination in Employment Act of 1967 (29 U.S.C. 633a(c)); and

(B) such liquidated damages as would be appropriate if awarded under section 7(b) of such Act (29 U.S.C. 626(b)).

In addition, the waiver provisions of section 7(f) of such Act (29 U.S.C. 626(f)) shall apply to covered employees.

(3) Disabilities discrimination. The remedy for a violation of subsection (a)(3) shall be

(A) such remedy as would be appropriate if awarded under section 505(a)(1) of the Rehabilitation Act of 1973 (29 U.S.C. 794a(a)(1)) or section 107(a) of the Americans with Disabilities Act of 1990 (42 U.S.C. 12117(a)); and

(B) such compensatory damages as would be appropriate if awarded under sections 1977A(a)(2), 1977A(a)(3), 1977A(b)(2), and, irrespective of the size of the employing office, 1977A(b)(3)(D) of the Revised Statutes (42 U.S.C. 1981a(a)(2), 1981a(a)(3), 1981a(b)(2), and 1981a(b)(3) (D)).

(c) [Omitted.]

(d) Effective Date. This section shall take effect 1 year after the date of the enactment of this Act [enacted Jan. 23, 1995].

Sec. 1312. Rights and Protections under the Family and Medical Leave Act of 1993

(a) Family and Medical Leave Rights and Protections Provided.

(1) In general. The rights and protections established by sections 101 through 105 of the Family and Medical Leave Act of 1993 (29 U.S.C. 2611 through 2615) shall apply to covered employees.

(2) Definition. For purposes of the application described in paragraph (1)

(A) the term "employer" as used in the Family and Medical Leave Act of 1993 means any employing office, and

(B) the term "eligible employee" as used in the Family and Medical Leave Act of 1993 means a covered employee who has been employed in any employing office for 12 months and for at least 1,250 hours of employment during the previous 12 months.

(b) Remedy. The remedy for a violation of subsection (a) shall be such remedy, including liquidated damages, as would be appropriate if awarded under paragraph (1) of section 107(a) of the Family and Medical Leave Act of 1993 (29 U.S.C. 2617(a)(1)).

(c) [Omitted.]

(d) Regulations.

(1) In general. The Board shall, pursuant to section 304 [2 U.S.C. §1384], issue regulations to implement the rights and protections under this section.

(2) Agency regulations. The regulations issued under paragraph (1) shall be the same as substantive regulations promulgated by the Secretary of Labor to implement the statutory provisions referred to in subsection (a) except insofar as the Board may determine, for good cause shown and stated together with the regulation, that a modification of such regulations would be more effective for the implementation of the rights and protections under this section.

(e) Effective Date.

(1) In general. Subsections (a) and (b) shall be effective 1 year after the date of the enactment of this Act [enacted Jan. 23, 1995].

(2) General Accounting Office and Library of Congress. Subsection (c) shall be effective 1 year after transmission to the Congress of the study under section 230 [2 U.S.C. §1371].

Sec. 1313. Rights and Protections under the Fair Labor Standards Act of 1938 [Equal Pay Act]

(a) Fair Labor Standards.

(1) In general. The rights and protections established by subsections (a)(1) and (d) of section 6, section 7, and section 12(c) of the Fair Labor Standards Act of 1938 (29 U.S.C. 206(a)(1) and (d), 207, 212(c)) shall apply to covered employees.

(2) Interns. For the purposes of this section, the term "covered employee" does not include an intern as defined in regulations under subsection (c).

(3) Compensatory time. Except as provided in regulations under subsection (c)(3) and in subsection (c)(4), covered employees may not receive compensatory time in lieu of overtime compensation.

(b) Remedy. The remedy for a violation of subsection (a) shall be such remedy, including liquidated damages, as would be appropriate if awarded under section 16(b) of the Fair Labor Standards Act of 1938 (29 U.S.C. 216(b)).

(c) Regulations to Implement Section.

(1) In general. The Board shall, pursuant of section 304 [2 U.S.C. §1384], issue regulations to implement this section.

(2) Agency regulations. Except as provided in paragraph (3), the regulations issued under paragraph (1) shall be the same as substantive regulations promulgated by the Secretary of Labor to implement the statutory

provisions referred to in subsection (a) except insofar as the Board may determine, for good cause shown and stated together with the regulation, that a modification of such regulations would be more effective for the implementation of the rights and protections under this section.

(3) Irregular work schedules. The Board shall issue regulations for covered employees whose work schedules directly depend on the schedule of the House of Representatives or the Senate that shall be comparable to the provisions in the Fair Labor Standards Act of 1938 [29 U.S.C. §§201 et seq.] that apply to employees who have irregular work schedules.

(4) Law enforcement. Law enforcement personnel of the Capitol Police who are subject to the exemption under section 7(k) of the Fair Labor Standards Act of 1938 (29 U.S.C. 207(k)) may elect to receive compensatory time off in lieu of overtime compensation for hours worked in excess of the maximum for their work period.

(d) [Omitted.]

(e) Effective Date. Subsections (a) and (b) shall be effective 1 year after the date of the enactment of this Act [enactment Jan. 23, 1995].

Sec. 1317. *Prohibition of Intimidation or Reprisal*

(a) In General. It shall be unlawful for an employing office to intimidate, take reprisal against, or otherwise discriminate against, any covered employee because the covered employee has opposed any practice made unlawful by this Act, or because the covered employee has initiated proceedings, made a charge, or testified, assisted, or participated in any manner in a hearing or other proceeding under this Act.

(b) Remedy. The remedy available for violation of subsection (a) shall be such legal or equitable remedy as may be appropriate to redress a violation of subsection (a).

Sec. 1361. *Generally Applicable Remedies and Limitations*

(a) Attorney's Fees. If a covered employee, with respect to any claim under this Act, or a qualified person with a disability, with respect to any claim under section 210 [2 U.S.C. §1331], is a prevailing party in any proceeding under section 405, 406, 407, or 408 [2 U.S.C. §§1405, 1406, 1407, or 1408], the hearing officer, Board, or court, as the case may be, may award attorney's fees, expert fees, and any other costs as would be appropriate if awarded under section 706(k) of the Civil Rights Act of 1964 (42 U.S.C. 2000e-5(k)).

(b) Interest. In any proceeding under section 405, 406, 407, or 408 [2 U.S.C. §§1405, 1406, 1407, or 1408], the same interest to compensate for delay in payment shall be made available as would be appropriate if awarded under section 717(d) of the Civil Rights Act of 1964 (42 U.S.C. 2000e-16(d)).

(c) Civil Penalties and Punitive Damages. No civil penalty or punitive damages may be awarded with respect to any claim under this Act.

(d) Exclusive Procedure.

(1) In general. Except as provided in paragraph (2), no person may commence an administrative or judicial proceeding to seek a remedy for the rights and protections afforded by this Act except as provided in this Act.

(2) Veterans. A covered employee under section 206 [2 U.S.C. §1316] may also utilize any provisions of chapter 43 of title 38, United States Code [38 U.S.C. §§4301 et seq.], that are applicable to that employee.

(e) Scope of Remedy. Only a covered employee who has undertaken and completed the procedures described in sections 402 and 403 [2 U.S.C. §§1402, 1403] may be granted a remedy under part A of this title [2 U.S.C. §§1311 et seq.]

(f) Construction.

(1) Definitions and exemption. Except where inconsistent with definitions and exemptions provided in this Act, the definitions and exemptions in the laws made applicable by this Act shall apply under this Act.

(2) Size limitations. Notwithstanding paragraph (1), provisions in the laws made applicable under this Act (other than the Worker Adjustment and Retraining Notification Act [29 U.S.C. §§2101 et seq.]) determining coverage based on size, whether expressed in terms of numbers of employees, amount of business transacted, or other measure, shall not apply in determining coverage under this Act.

(3) Executive branch enforcement. This Act shall not be construed to authorize enforcement by the executive branch of this Act.

Equal Pay Act

29 U.S.C. §206(d)

§206. Minimum Wage ...

(d) Prohibition of sex discrimination.

(1) [§3] No employer having employees subject to any provisions of this section shall discriminate, within any establishment in which such employees are employed, between employees on the basis of sex by paying wages to employees in such establishment at a rate less than the rate at which he pays wages to employees of the opposite sex in such establishment and for equal work on jobs the performance of which requires equal skill, effort, and responsibility, and which are performed under similar working conditions, except where such payment is made pursuant to (i) a seniority system; (ii) a merit system; (iii) a system which measures earnings by quantity or quality of production; or (iv) a differential based on any other factor other than sex: *Provided*, That an employer who is paying a wage rate differential in violation of this subsection shall not, in order to comply with the provisions of this subsection, reduce the wage rate of any employee.

(2) No labor organization, or its agents, representing employees of an employer having employees subject to any provisions of this section shall cause or attempt to cause such an employer to discriminate against an employee in violation of paragraph (1) of this subsection.

(3) For purposes of administration and enforcement, any amounts owing to any employee which have been withheld in violation of this subsection shall be deemed to be unpaid minimum wages or unpaid overtime compensation under this chapter.

(4) As used in this subsection, the term "labor organization" means any organization of any kind, or any agency or employee representation committee or plan, in which employees participate and which exists for the purpose, in whole or in part, of dealing with employers concerning grievances, labor disputes, wages, rates of pay, hours of employment, or conditions of work.

Fair Labor Standards Act

29 U.S.C. §§216–217

§216 [§16]. Penalties

(a) Fines and Imprisonment. Any person who willfully violates any of the provisions of section 215 of this title shall upon conviction thereof be subject to a fine of not more than $10,000, or to imprisonment for not more than six months, or both. No person shall be imprisoned under this subsection except for an offense committed after the conviction of such person for a prior offense under this subsection.

(b) Damages; Right of Action; Attorney's Fees and Costs; Termination of Right of Action. Any employer who violates the provisions of section 206 or section 207 of this title shall be liable to the employee or employees affected in the amount of their unpaid minimum wages, or their unpaid overtime compensation, as the case may be, and in an additional equal amount as liquidated damages. Any employer who violates the provisions of section 215(a)(3) of this title shall be liable for such legal or equitable relief as may be appropriate to effectuate the purposes of section 215(a)(3) of this title, including without limitation employment, reinstatement, promotion, and the payment of wages lost and an additional equal amount as liquidated damages. An action to recover the liability prescribed in either of the preceding sentences may be maintained against any employer (including a public agency) in any Federal or State court of competent jurisdiction by any one or more employees for and in behalf of himself or themselves and other employees similarly situated. No employee shall be a party plaintiff to any such action unless he gives his consent in writing to become such a party and such consent is filed in the court in which such action is brought. The court in such action shall, in addition to any judgment awarded to the plaintiff or plaintiffs, allow a reasonable attorney's fee to be paid by the defendant, and costs of the action. The right provided by this subsection to bring an action by or on behalf of any employee, and the right of any employee to become a party plaintiff to any such action, shall terminate upon the filing of a complaint by the Secretary of Labor in an action under section 217 of this title in which (1) restraint is sought of any further delay in the payment of unpaid minimum wages, or the amount of unpaid overtime compensation, as the case may be, owing to such employee under section 206 or section 207 of this title by an employer liable therefor under the provisions of this subsection or (2) legal or equitable relief is sought as a result of alleged violations of section 215(a)(3) of this title.

(c) Payment of Wages and Compensation; Waiver of Claims; Actions by the Secretary; Limitation of Actions. — The Secretary is authorized to supervise the payment of the unpaid minimum wages or the unpaid overtime compensation owing to any employee or employees under section 206 or 207 of this title, and the agreement of any employee to accept such payment shall upon payment in full constitute a waiver by such employee of any right he may have under subsection (b) of this section to such unpaid minimum wages or unpaid overtime compensation and an additional equal amount as liquidated damages. The Secretary may bring an action in any court of competent jurisdiction to recover the amount of the unpaid minimum wages or overtime compensation and an equal amount as liquidated damages. The right provided by subsection (b) of this section to bring an action by or on behalf of any employee to recover the liability specified in the first sentence of such subsection and of any employee to become a party plaintiff to any such action shall terminate upon the filing of a complaint by the Secretary in an action under this subsection in which a recovery is sought of unpaid minimum wages or unpaid overtime compensation under sections 206 or 207 of this title or liquidated or other damages provided by this subsection owing to such employee by an employer liable under the provisions of subsection (b) of this section, unless such action is dismissed without prejudice on motion of the Secretary. Any sums thus recovered by the Secretary of Labor on behalf of an employee pursuant to this subsection shall be held in a special deposit account and shall be paid, on order of the Secretary of Labor, directly to the employee or employees affected. Any such sums not paid to an employee because of inability to do so within a period of three years shall be covered into the Treasury of the United States as miscellaneous receipts. In determining when an action is commenced by the Secretary of Labor under this subsection for the purposes of the statutes of limitations provided in section 255(a) of this title, it shall be considered to be commenced in the case of any individual claimant on the date when the complaint is filed if he is specifically named as a party plaintiff in the complaint, or if his name did not so appear, on the subsequent date on which his name is added as a party plaintiff in such action. . . .

§217 [§17]. Injunction Proceedings

The district courts, together with the United States District Court for the District of the Canal Zone, the District Court of the Virgin Islands, and the District Court of Guam shall have jurisdiction for cause shown, to restrain violations of section 215 of this title, including in the case of violations of section 215(a)(2) of this title the restraint of any withholding of payment of minimum wages or overtime compensation found by the court to be due to employees under this chapter (except sums which employees are barred from recovering, at the time of the commencement of the action to restrain the violations, by virtue of the provisions of section 255 of this title).

Family and Medical Leave Act of 1993

29 U.S.C §§2601, 2611–2619, 2651–2654

§2601. Findings and Purposes

(a) Findings. Congress finds that—

(1) the number of single-parent households and two-parent households in which the single parent or both parents work is increasing significantly;

(2) it is important for the development of children and the family unit that fathers and mothers be able to participate in early childrearing and the care of family members who have serious health conditions;

(3) the lack of employment policies to accommodate working parents can force individuals to choose between job security and parenting;

(4) there is inadequate job security for employees who have serious health conditions that prevent them from working for temporary periods;

(5) due to the nature of the roles of men and women in our society, the primary responsibility for family caretaking often falls on women, and such responsibility affects the working lives of women more than it affects the working lives of men; and

(6) employment standards that apply to one gender only have serious potential for encouraging employers to discriminate against employees and applicants for employment who are of that gender.

(b) Purposes. It is the purpose of this Act—

(1) to balance the demands of the workplace with the needs of families, to promote the stability and economic security of families, and to promote national interests in preserving family integrity;

(2) to entitle employees to take reasonable leave for medical reasons, for the birth or adoption of a child, and for the care of a child, spouse, or parent who has a serious health condition;

(3) to accomplish the purposes described in paragraphs (1) and (2) in a manner that accommodates the legitimate interests of employers;

(4) to accomplish the purposes described in paragraphs (1) and (2) in a manner that, consistent with the Equal Protection Clause of the Fourteenth

Amendment, minimizes the potential for employment discrimination on the basis of sex by ensuring generally that leave is available for eligible medical reasons (including maternity-related disability) and for compelling family reasons, on a gender-neutral basis; and

(5) to promote the goal of equal employment opportunity for women and men, pursuant to such clause.

TITLE I — GENERAL REQUIREMENTS FOR LEAVE

§2611. *Definitions*

As used in this subchapter:

(1) Commerce. The terms "commerce" and "industry or activity affecting commerce" means any activity, business, or industry in commerce or in which a labor dispute would hinder or obstruct commerce or the free flow of commerce, and include "commerce" and any "industry affecting commerce," as defined in paragraphs (1) and (3) of section 142 of this title.

(2) Eligible employee.

(A) In general. The term "eligible employee" means an employee who has been employed—

(i) for at least 12 months by the employer with respect to whom leave is requested under section 2612 of this title; and

(ii) for at least 1,250 hours of service with such employer during the previous 12-month period.

(B) Exclusions. The term "eligible employee" does not include—

(i) any Federal officer or employee covered under subchapter V of chapter 63 of Title 5; or

(ii) any employee of an employer who is employed at a worksite at which such employer employs less than 50 employees if the total number of employees employed by that employer within 75 miles of that worksite is less than 50.

(C) Determination. For purposes of determining whether an employee meets the hours of service requirement specified in subparagraph (A)(ii), the legal standards established under section 207 of this title shall apply.

(D) Airline flight crews.

(i) Determination. For purposes of determining whether an employee who is a flight attendant or flight crewmember (as such terms are defined in regulations of the Federal Aviation Administration) meets the hours of service requirement specified in subparagraph (A)(ii), the employee will be considered to meet the requirement if —

(I) the employee has worked or been paid for not less than 60 percent of the applicable total monthly guarantee, or the equivalent, for the previous 12- month period, for or by the employer with respect to whom leave is requested under section 2612 of this title; and

(II) the employee has worked or been paid for not less than 504 hours (not counting personal commute time or time spent on vacation leave or medical sick leave) during the previous 12-month period, for or by that employer.

(ii) File. Each employer of an employee described in clause (i) shall maintain on file with the Secretary (in accordance with such regulations as the Secretary may prescribe) containing information specifying the applicable monthly guarantee with respect to each category of employee to which such guarantee applies.

(iii) Definition. In this subparagraph, the term "applicable monthly guarantee" means —

(I) for an employee described in clause (i) other than an employee on reserve status, the minimum number of hours for which an employer as agreed to schedule such employee for any given month; and

(II) for an employee described in clause (i) who is on reserve status, the number of hours for which an employer has agreed to pay such employee on reserve status for any given month, as established in this applicable collective bargaining agreement or, if none exists, in the employer's policies.

(3) Employ; Employee; State. The terms "employ," "employee," and "State" have the same meanings given such terms in subsections (c), (e), and (g) of section 209 of this title.

(4) Employer.

(A) In general. The term "employer"—

(i) means any person engaged in commerce or in any industry or activity affecting commerce who employs 50 or more employees for each working day during each of 20 or more calendar workweeks in the current or preceding calendar year;

(ii) includes—

(I) any person who acts, directly or indirectly, in the interest of an employer to any of the employees of such employer; and

(II) any successor in interest of an employer;

(iii) includes any "public agency," as defined in section 203(x) of this title; and

(iv) includes the Government Accountability Office and the Library of Congress.

(B) Public agency. For purposes of subparagraph (A)(iii), a public agency shall be considered to be a person engaged in commerce or in an industry or activity affecting commerce.

(5) Employment benefits. The term "employment benefits" means all benefits provided or made available to employees by an employer, including group life insurance, health insurance, disability insurance, sick leave, annual leave, educational benefits, and pensions, regardless of whether such benefits

are provided by a practice or written policy of an employer or through an "employee benefit plan," as defined in section 1002(3) of this title.

(6) Health care provider. The term "health care provider" means—

(A) a doctor of medicine or osteopathy who is authorized to practice medicine or surgery (as appropriate) by the State in which the doctor practices; or

(B) any other person determined by the Secretary to be capable of providing health care services.

(7) Parent. The term "parent" means the biological parent of an employee or an individual who stood in loco parentis to an employee when the employee was a son or daughter.

(8) Person. The term "person" has the same meaning given such term in section 203(a) of this title.

(9) Reduced leave schedule. The term "reduced leave schedule" means a leave schedule that reduces the usual number of hours per workweek, or hours per workday, of an employee.

(10) Secretary. The term "Secretary" means the Secretary of Labor.

(11) Serious health conditions. The term "serious health condition" means an illness, injury, impairment, or physical or mental condition that involves—

(A) inpatient care in a hospital, hospice, or residential medical care facility; or

(B) continuing treatment by a health care provider.

(12) Son or daughter. The term "son or daughter" means a biological, adopted, or foster child, a stepchild, a legal ward, or a child of a person standing in loco parentis, who is—

(A) under 18 years of age; or

(B) 18 years of age or older and incapable of self-care because of a mental or physical disability.

(13) Spouse. The term "spouse" means a husband or wife, as the case may be.

(14) Covered Active Duty. The term "covered active duty" means—

(A) in the case of a member of a regular component of the Armed Forces, a duty during the deployment of the member with the Armed Forced to a fireogn country; and

(B) in the case of a member of a reserve component of the Armed Forced, duty during the deployment of the member with the Armed Forced to a foreign country under a call or order to active duty under a provision of law referred to in section 101(a)(13)(B) of Title 10.

(15) Covered Servicemember. The term "covered servicemember" means—

(A) a member of the Armed Forces (including a member of the National Guard or Reserves) who is undergoing medical treatment, recuperation, or therapy, is otherwise in outpatient status, or is otherwise on the temporary disability retired list, for a serious injury or illness; or

(B) a veteran who is undergoing medical treatment, recuperation or therapy, for a serious injury or illness and who was a member of the Armed Forced (including a member of the National Guard of reserves) at any time during the period of 5 years preceding the date on which the veteran undergoes that medical treatment, recuperation or therapy.

(16) Outpatient Status. The term "outpatient status", with respect to a covered servicemember, means the status of a member of the Armed Forces assigned to—

(A) a military medical treatment facility as an outpatient; or

(B) a unit established for the purpose of providing command and control of members of the Armed Forces receiving medical care as outpatients.

(17) Next of Kin.—The term "next of kin," used with respect to an individual, means the nearest blood relative of that individual.

(18) Serious Injury or Illness. The term "serious injury or illness,"—

(A) in the case of a member of the Armed Forces (including a member of the National Guard or Reserves) means an injury or illness that was incurred by the member in line of duty on active duty in the Armed Forces (or existed before the beginning of the member's active duty and was aggravated by service in line of duty on active duty in the Armed Forces) and that may render the member medically unfit to perform the duties of the member's office, grade, rank, or rating; and

(B) in the case of a veteran who was a member of the Armed Forces (including a member of the National Guard or Reserves) at any time during a period described in paragraph 15(B), means a qualifying (as defined by the Secretary of Labor) injury or illness that was incurred by the member in line of duty on active duty in the Armed Forces (or existed before the beginning of the member's duty and was aggravated by service in line of duty on active duty in the Armed Forces) and that manifested itself before or after the member became a veteran.

(19) Veteran. The term "veteran" has the meaning given the term in section 101 of Title 38.

§2612. *Leave Requirement*

(a) In General.

(1) Entitlement to leave. Subject to section 2613, an eligible employee shall be entitled to a total of 12 workweeks of leave during any 12-month period for one or more of the following:

(A) Because of the birth of a son or daughter of the employee and in order to care for such son or daughter.

(B) Because of the placement of a son or daughter with the employee for adoption or foster care.

(C) In order to care for the spouse, or a son, daughter, or parent, of the employee, if such spouse, son, daughter, or parent has a serious health condition.

(D) Because of a serious health condition that makes the employee unable to perform the functions of the position of such employee.

(E) Because of any qualifying exigency (as the Secretary shall, by regulation, determine) arising out of the fact that the spouse, or a son, daughter, or parent of the employee is on covered active duty (or has been notified of an impending call or order to covered active duty) in the Armed Forces.

(2) Expiration of entitlement. The entitlement to leave under subparagraphs (A) and (B) of paragraph (1) for a birth or placement of a son or daughter shall expire at the end of the 12-month period beginning on the date of such birth or placement.

(3) Servicemember Family Leave. — Subject to section 2613, an eligible employee who is the spouse, son, daughter, parent, or next of kin of a covered servicemember shall be entitled to a total of 26 workweeks of leave during a 12-month period to care for the servicemember. The leave described in this paragraph shall only be available during a single 12-month period.

(4) Combined Leave Total. — During the single 12-month period described in paragraph (3), an eligible employee shall be entitled to a combined total of 26 workweeks of leave under paragraphs (1) and (3). Nothing in this paragraph shall be construed to limit the availability of leave under paragraph (1) during any other 12-month period.

(5) Calculation of leave for airline flight crews. The Secretary may provide, by regulation, a method for calculating the leave described in paragraph (1) with respect to employees described in section 2611(2)(D) of this title.

(b) Leave Taken Intermittently or on a Reduced Leave Schedule.

(1) In general. Leave under subparagraph (A) or (B) of subsection (a)(1) of this section shall not be taken by an employee intermittently or on a reduced leave schedule unless the employee and the employer of the employee agree otherwise. Subject to paragraph (2), subsection (e)(2) of this section, and subsection (b)(5) or (f) (as appropriate) of section 2613 of this title, leave under subparagraph (C) or (D) of subsection (a)(1) of this section or under subsection (a)(3) of this section may be taken intermittently or on a reduced leave schedule when medically necessary. Subject to subsection (e)(3) of this section and section 2613(f) of this title, leave under subsection (a)(1)(E) of this section may be taken intermittently or on a reduced leave schedule. The taking of leave intermittently or on a reduced leave schedule pursuant to this paragraph shall not result in a reduction in the total amount of leave to which the employee is entitled under subsection (a) of this section beyond the amount of leave actually taken.

(2) Alternative position. If an employee requests intermittent leave, or leave on a reduced leave schedule, under subparagraph (C) or (D) of subsection (a)(1) of this section or under subsection (a)(3) of this section, that is foreseeable based on planned medical treatment, the employer may require such employee to transfer temporarily to an available alternative position offered by the employer for which the employee is qualified and that —

(A) has equivalent pay and benefits; and

(B) better accommodates recurring periods of leave than the regular employment position of the employee.

(c) Unpaid Leave Permitted. Except as provided in subsection (d) of this section, leave granted under subsection (a) may consist of unpaid leave. Where an employee is otherwise exempt under regulations issued by the Secretary pursuant to section 213(a)(1) of this title, the compliance of an employer with this subchapter by providing unpaid leave shall not affect the exempt status of the employee under such section.

(d) Relationship to Paid Leave.

(1) Unpaid leave. If an employer provides paid leave for fewer than 12 workweeks (or 26 workweeks in the case of leave provided under subsection (a)(3) of this section), the additional weeks of leave necessary to attain the 12 workweeks (or 26 workweeks, as appropriate) of leave required under this subchapter may be provided without compensation.

(2) Substitution of paid leave.

(A) In general. An eligible employee may elect, or an employee may require the employee, to substitute any of the accrued paid vacation leave, personal leave, or family leave of the employee for leave provided under subparagraph (A), (B), (C), or (E) of subsection (a)(1) of this section, for any part of the 12-week period of such leave under such subsection.

(B) Serious health condition. An eligible employee may elect, or an employer may require the employee, to substitute any of the accrued paid vacation leave, personal leave, or medical or sick leave of the employee for leave provided under subparagraph (C) or (D) of subsection (a)(1) of this section for any part of the 12-week period of such leave under such subsection, except that nothing in this subchapter shall require an employer to provide paid sick leave or paid medical leave in any situation in which such employer would not normally provide any such paid leave. An eligible employee may elect, or an employer may require the employee, to substitute any of the accrued paid vacation leave, personal leave, family leave, or medical or sick leave of the employee for leave provided under subsection (a)(3) of this section for any part of the 26-week period of such leave under such subsection, except that nothing in this subchapter requires an employer to provide paid sick leave or paid medical leave in any situation in which the employer would not normally provide any such paid leave.

(e) Foreseeable Leave.

(1) Requirement of notice. In any case in which the necessity for leave under subparagraph (A) or (B) of subsection (a)(1) of this section is foreseeable based on an expected birth or placement, the employee shall provide the employer with not less than 30 days' notice, before the date the leave is to begin, or the employee's intention to take leave under such subparagraph, except that if the date of the birth or placement requires leave to begin in less than 30 days, the employee shall provide such notice as is practicable.

(2) Duties of employee. In any case in which the necessity for leave under subparagraph (C) or (D) of subsection (a)(1) of this section is foreseeable based on planned medical treatment, the employee—

(A) shall make a reasonable effort to schedule the treatment so as not to disrupt unduly the operations of the employer, subject to the approval of the health care provider of the employee or the health care provider of the son, daughter, spouse, or parent, or covered servicemember of the employee, as appropriate; and

(B) shall provide the employer with not less than 30 days' notice, before the date the leave is to begin, of the employee's intention to take leave under such subparagraph, except that if the date of the treatment requires leave to begin in less than 30 days, the employee shall provide such notice as is practicable.

(3) Notice for Leave Due to Covered Active Duty of Family Member. In any case in which the necessity for leave under subsection (a)(1)(E) of this section is foreseeable, whether because the spouse, or a son, daughter, or parent, of the employee is on active duty, or because of notification of an impending call or order to active duty, the employee shall provide such notice to the employer as is reasonable and practicable.

(f) Spouses Employed by Same Employer.

(1) In General. In any case in which a husband and wife entitled to leave under subsection (a) are employed by the same employer, the aggregate number of workweeks of leave to which both may be entitled may be limited to 12 workweeks during any 12-month period, if such leave is taken—

(A) under subparagraph (A) or (B) of subsection (a)(1) of this section; or

(B) to care for a sick parent under subparagraph (C) of such subsection.

(2) Servicemember Family Leave.

(A) In General. The aggregate number of workweeks of leave to which both husband and wife may be entitled under subsection (a) may be limited to 26 workweeks during the single 12-month period described in subsection (a)(3) of this section if the leave is—

(i) leave under subsection (a)(3) of this section; or

(ii) a combination of leave under subsection (a)(3) and leave described in paragraph (1).

(B) Both Limitations Applicable. If the leave taken by the husband and wife includes leave described in paragraph (1), the limitation in paragraph (1) shall apply to the leave described in paragraph (1).

§2613. *Certification*

(a) In General. An employer may require that a request for leave under subparagraph (C) or (D) of paragraph (1) or paragraph (3) of section 2612(a) of this title be supported by a certification issued by the health care provider of the eligible employee or of the son, daughter, spouse, or parent of the employee, or of the next of kin of an individual in the case of leave taken under such paragraph

(3), as appropriate. The employee shall provide, in a timely manner, a copy of such certificate to the employer.

(b) Sufficient Certification. Certification provided under subsection (a) shall be sufficient if it states—

(1) the date on which the serious health condition commenced;

(2) the probable duration of the condition;

(3) the appropriate medical facts within the knowledge of the health care provider regarding the condition;

(4)(A) for purposes of leave under section 2612(a)(1)(C) of this title, a statement that the eligible employee is needed to care for the son, daughter, spouse, or parent and an estimate of the amount of time that such employee is needed to care for the son, daughter, spouse, or parent; and

(B) for purposes of leave under section 2612(a)(1)(D) of this title, a statement that the employee is unable to perform the functions of the position of the employee;

(5) in the case of certification for intermittent leave, or leave on a reduced leave schedule, for planned medical treatment, the dates on which such treatment is expected to be given and the duration of such treatment;

(6) in the case of certification for intermittent leave, or leave on a reduced leave schedule, under section 2612(a)(1)(D) of this title, a statement of the medical necessity for the intermittent leave or leave on a reduced leave schedule, and the expected duration of the intermittent leave or reduced leave schedule; and

(7) in the case of certification for intermittent leave, or leave on a reduced leave schedule, under section 2612(a)(1)(C) of this title, a statement that the employee's intermittent leave or leave on a reduced leave schedule is necessary for the care of the son, daughter, parent, or spouse who has a serious health condition, or will assist in their recovery, and the expected duration and schedule of the intermittent leave or reduced leave schedule.

(c) Second Opinion.

(1) In general. In any case in which the employer has reason to doubt the validity of the certification provided under subsection (a) of this section for leave under subparagraph (C) or (D) of section 2612(a)(1) of this title, the employer may require, at the expense of the employer, that the eligible employee obtain the opinion of a second health care provider designated or approved by the employer concerning any information certified under subsection (b) of this section for such leave.

(2) Limitation. A health care provider designated or approved under paragraph (1) shall not be employed on a regular basis by the employer.

(d) Resolution of Conflicting Opinions.

(1) In general. In any case in which the second opinion described in subsection (c) of this section differs from the opinion in the original certification provided under subsection (a) of this section, the employer may require, at the expense of the employer, that the employee obtain the opinion

of a third health care provider designated or approved jointly by the employer and the employee concerning the information certified under subsection (b).

(2) Finality. The opinion of the third health care provider concerning the information certified under subsection (b) of this section shall be considered to be final and shall be binding on the employer and the employee.

(e) Subsequent Recertification. The employer may require that the eligible employee obtain subsequent recertification on a reasonable basis.

(f) Certification Related to Active Duty or Call to Active Duty. An employer may require that a request for leave under section 2612(a)(1)(E) of this title be supported by a certification issued at such time and in such manner as the Secretary may by regulation prescribe. If the Secretary issues a regulation requiring such certification, the employee shall provide, in a timely manner, a copy of such certification to the employer.

§2614. Employment and Benefits Protection

(a) Restoration to Position.

(1) In general. Except as provided in subsection (b) of this section, any eligible employee who takes leave under section 2612 of this title for the intended purpose of the leave shall be entitled, on return from such leave —

(A) to be restored by the employer to the position of employment held by the employee when the leave commenced; or

(B) to be restored to an equivalent position with equivalent employment benefits, pay, and other terms and conditions of employment.

(2) Loss of benefits. The taking of leave under section 2612 of this title shall not result in the loss of any employment benefit accrued prior to the date on which the leave commenced.

(3) Limitations. Nothing in this section shall be construed to entitle any restored employee to —

(A) the accrual of any seniority or employment benefits during any period of leave; or

(B) any right, benefit, or position of employment other than any right, benefit, or position to which the employee would have been entitled had the employee not taken the leave.

(4) Certification. As a condition of restoration under paragraph (1) for an employee who has taken leave under section 2612(a)(1)(D) of this title, the employer may have a uniformly applied practice or policy that requires each such employee to receive certification from the health care provider of the employee that the employee is able to resume work, except that nothing in this paragraph shall supersede a valid State or local law or a collective bargaining agreement that governs the return to work of such employees.

(5) Construction. Nothing in this subsection shall be construed to prohibit an employer from requiring an employee on leave under section 2612

to report periodically to the employer on the status and intention of the employee to return to work.

(b) Exemption Concerning Certain Highly Compensated Employees.

(1) Denial of restoration. An employer may deny restoration under subsection (a) of this section to any eligible employee described in paragraph (2) if—

(A) such denial is necessary to prevent substantial and grievous economic injury to the operations of the employer;

(B) the employer notifies the employee of the intent of the employer to deny restoration on such basis at the time the employer determines that such injury would occur; and

(C) in any case in which the leave has commenced, the employee elects not to return to employment after receiving such notice.

(2) Affected employees. An eligible employee described in paragraph (1) is a salaried eligible employee who is among the highest paid 10 percent of the employees employed by the employer within 75 miles of the facility at which the employee is employed.

(c) Maintenance of Health Benefits.

(1) Coverage. Except as provided in paragraph (2), during any period that an eligible employee takes leave under section 2612 of this title, the employer shall maintain coverage under any "group health plan" (as defined in section 5000(b)(1) of the Title 26) for the duration of such leave at the level and under the conditions coverage would have been provided if the employee had continued in employment continuously for the duration of such leave.

(2) Failure to return from leave. The employer may recover the premium that the employer paid for maintaining coverage for the employee under such group health plan during any period of unpaid leave under section 1262 of this title if—

(A) the employee fails to return from leave under section 2612 of this title after the period of leave to which the employee is entitled has expired; and

(B) the employee fails to return to work for a reason other than–

(i) the continuation, recurrence, or onset of a serious health condition that entitles the employee to leave under subparagraph (C) or (D) of section 2612(a)(1) of this title or under section 2612(a)(3) of this title; or

(ii) other circumstances beyond the control of the employee.

(3) Certification.

(A) Issuance. An employer may require that a claim that an employee is unable to return to work because of the continuation, recurrence, or onset of the serious health condition described in paragraph (2)(B)(i) be supported by—

(i) a certification issued by the health care provider of the son, daughter, spouse, or parent of the employee, as appropriate, in the case of an employee unable to return to work because of a condition specified in section 2612(a)(1)(C) of this title;

(ii) a certification issued by the health care provider of the eligible employee, in the case of an employee unable to return to work because of a condition specified in section 2612(a)(1)(D) of this title; or

(iii) a certification issued by the health care provider of the servicemember being cared for by the employee, in the case of an employee unable to return to work because of a condition specified in section 2612(a)(3) of this title.

(B) Copy. The employee shall provide, in a timely manner, a copy of such certification to the employer.

(C) Sufficiency of certification.

(i) Leave due to serious health condition of employee. The certification described in subparagraph (A)(ii) shall be sufficient if the certification states that a serious health condition prevented the employee from being able to perform the functions of the position of the employee on the date that the leave of the employee expired.

(ii) Leave due to serious health condition of family member. The certification described in subparagraph (A)(i) shall be sufficient if the certification states that the employee is needed to care for the son, daughter, spouse, or parent who has a serious health condition on the date that the leave of the employee expired.

§2615. Prohibited Acts

(a) Interference with rights.

(1) Exercise of rights. It shall be unlawful for any employee to interfere with, restrain, or deny the exercise of or the attempt to exercise, any right provided under this title.

(2) Discrimination. It shall be unlawful for any employer to discharge or in any other manner discriminate against any individual for opposing any practice made unlawful by this title.

(b) Interference With Proceedings or Inquiries. It shall be unlawful for any person to discharge or in any other manner discriminate against any individual because such individual

(1) has filed any charge, or has instituted or caused to be instituted any proceeding, under or related to this title;

(2) has given, or is about to give, any information in connection with any inquiry or proceeding relating to any right provided under this title; or

(3) has testified, or is about to testify, in any inquiry or proceeding relating to any right provided under this title.

§2616. Investigative Authority

(a) In General. To ensure compliance with the provisions of this title, or any regulation or order issued under this title, the Secretary shall have, subject to subsection (c), the investigative authority provided under section 11(a) of the Fair Labor Standards Act of 1938 (29 U.S.C. 211(a)).

(b) Obligation to Keep and Preserve Records. Any employer shall make, keep, and preserve records pertaining to compliance with this title in accordance with section 11(c) of the Fair Labor Standards Act of 1938 (29 U.S.C. 211(c)) and in accordance with regulations issued by the Secretary.

(c) Required Submissions Generally Limited to an Annual Basis. The Secretary shall not under the authority of this section require any employer or any plan, fund, or program to submit to the Secretary any books or records more than once during any 12-month period, unless the Secretary has reasonable cause to believe there may exist a violation of this title or any regulation or order issued pursuant to this title, or is investigating a charge pursuant to section 107(b).

(d) Subpoena Powers. For the purposes of any investigation provided for in this section, the Secretary shall have the subpoena authority provided for under section 9 of the Fair Labor Standards Act of 1938 (29 U.S.C. 209).

§2617. Enforcement

(a) Civil Action by Employees.

(1) Liability. Any employer who violates section 2615 shall be liable to any eligible employee affected —

(A) for damages equal to

(i) the amount of

(I) any wages, salary, employment benefits, or other compensation denied or lost to such employee by reason of the violation; or

(II) in a case in which wages, salary, employment benefits, or other compensation have not been denied or lost to the employee, any actual monetary losses sustained by the employee as a direct result of the violation, such as the cost of providing care, up to a sum equal to 12 weeks (or 26 weeks, in a case involving leave under section 2612(a)(3) of this title) of wages or salary for the employee;

(ii) the interest on the amount described in clause (i) calculated at the prevailing rate; and

(iii) an additional amount as liquidated damages equal to the sum of the amount described in clause (i) and the interest described in clause (ii), except that if an employer who has violated section 2615 of this title proves to the satisfaction of the court that the act or omission which violated section 2615 of this title was in good faith and that the employer had reasonable grounds for believing that the act or omission was not a violation of section 2615 of this title, such court may, in the discretion of the court, reduce the amount of the liability to the amount and interest determined under clauses (i) and (ii), respectively; and

(B) for such equitable relief as may be appropriate, including employment, reinstatement, and promotion.

(2) Right of action. An action to recover the damages or equitable relief prescribed in paragraph (1) may be maintained against any employer (including a public agency) in any Federal or State court of competent jurisdiction by one or more employees for and in behalf of—

(A) the employees; or

(B) the employees and other employees similarly situated.

(3) Fees and costs. The court in such an action shall, in addition to any judgment awarded to the plaintiff, allow a reasonable attorney's fee, reasonable expert witness fees, and other costs of the action to be paid by the defendant.

(4) Limitations. The right provided by paragraph (2) to bring an action by or on behalf of any employee shall terminate—

(A) on the filing of a complaint by the Secretary in an action under subsection (d) of this section in which restraint is sought of any further delay in the payment of the amount described in paragraph (1)(A) to such employee by an employer responsible under paragraph (1) for the payment; or

(B) on the filing of a complaint by the Secretary in an action under subsection (b) in which a recovery is sought of the damages described in paragraph (1)(A) owing to an eligible employee by an employer liable under paragraph (1),

unless the action described in subparagraph (A) or (B) is dismissed without prejudice on motion of the Secretary.

(b) Action by the Secretary.

(1) Administrative action. The Secretary shall receive, investigate, and attempt to resolve complaints of violations of section 2615 of this title in the same manner that the Secretary receives, investigates, and attempts to resolve complaints of violations of sections 206 and 207 of this title.

(2) Civil action. The Secretary may bring an action in any court of competent jurisdiction to recover the damages described in subsection (a)(1)(A) of this section.

(3) Sums recovered. Any sums recovered by the Secretary pursuant to paragraph (2) shall be held in special deposit account and shall be paid, on order of the Secretary, directly to each employee affected. Any such sums not paid to an employee because of inability to do so within a period of 3 years shall be deposited into the Treasury of the United States as miscellaneous receipts.

(c) Limitations.

(1) In general. Except as provided in paragraph (2), an action may be brought under this section not later than 2 years after the date of the last event constituting the alleged violation for which the action is brought.

(2) Willful violation. In the case of such action brought for a willful violation of section 2615 of this title, such action may be brought within 3 years

of the date of the last event constituting the alleged violation for which such action is brought.

(3) Commencement. In determining when an action is commenced by the Secretary under this section for the purposes of this subsection, it shall be considered to be commenced on the date when the complaint is filed.

(d) Action for Injunction by Secretary. The district courts of the United States shall have jurisdiction, for cause shown, in an action brought by the Secretary —

(1) to restrain violations of section 2615 of this title, including the restraint of any withholding of payment of wages, salary, employment benefits, or other compensation, plus interest, found by the court to be due to eligible employees; or

(2) to award such other equitable relief as may be appropriate, including employment, reinstatement, and promotion.

(e) Solicitor of Labor. The Solicitor of Labor may appear for and represent the Secretary on any litigation brought under this section.

(f) General Accountability Office and Library of Congress. In the case of the General Accountability Office and the Library of Congress, the authority of the Secretary of Labor under this subchapter shall be exercised respectively by the Comptroller General of the United States and the Librarian of Congress.

§2618. Special Rules Concerning Employees of Local Educational Agencies

(a) Application.

(1) In general. Except as otherwise provided in this section, the rights (including the rights under section 2614 of this title, which shall extend throughout the period of leave of any employee under this section), remedies, and procedures under this subchapter shall apply to —

(A) any "local educational agency" (as defined in section 7801 of Title 20) and an eligible employee of the agency; and

(B) any private elementary or secondary school and an eligible employee of the school.

(2) Definitions. For purposes of the application described in paragraph (1):

(A) Eligible employee. The term "eligible employee" means an eligible employee of an agency or school described in paragraph (1).

(B) Employer. The term "employer" means an agency or school described in paragraph (1).

(b) Leave Does Not Violate Certain Other Federal Laws. A local educational agency and a private elementary or secondary school shall not be in violation of the Individuals with Disabilities Education Act (20 U.S.C. 1400 et seq.), section 794 of this title, or title VI of the Civil Rights Act of 1964 (42 U.S.C. 2000d et seq.), solely as a result of an eligible employee of such agency or school exercising the rights of such employee under this subchapter.

(c) Intermittent Leave or Leave on a Reduced Schedule for Instructional Employees.

(1) In general. Subject to paragraph (2), in any case in which an eligible employee employed principally in an instructional capacity by any such educational agency or school requests leave under subparagraph (C) or (D) of

section 2612(a)(1) or under section 2612(a)(3) of this title that is foreseeable based on planed medical treatment and the employee would be on leave for greater than 20 percent of the total number of working days in the period during which the leave would extend, the agency or school may require that such employee elect either —

(A) to take leave for periods of a particular duration, not to exceed the duration of the planned medical treatment; or

(B) to transfer temporarily to an available alternative position offered by the employer for which the employee is qualified, and that

(i) has equivalent pay and benefits; and

(ii) better accommodates recurring periods of leave than the regular employment position of the employee.

(2) Application. The elections described in subparagraphs (A) and (B) or paragraph (1) shall apply only with respect to an eligible employee who complies with section 2612(e)(2) of this title.

(d) Rules Applicable to Periods Near the Conclusion of an Academic Term. The following rules shall apply with respect to periods of leave near the conclusion of an academic term in the case of any eligible employee employed principally in an instructional capacity by any such educational agency or school:

(1) Leave more than 5 weeks prior to end of term. If the eligible employee begins leave under section 2612 of this title more than 5 weeks prior to the end of the academic term, the agency or school may require the employee to continue taking leave until the end of such term, if—

(A) the leave is of at least 3 weeks duration; and

(B) the return to employment would occur during the 3-week period before the end of such term.

(2) Leave less than 5 weeks prior to end of term. If the eligible employee begins leave under subparagraph (A), (B), or (C) of section 2612(a)(1) of this title or under section 2612(a)(3) of this title during the period that commences 5 weeks prior to the end of the academic term, the agency or school may require the employee to continue taking leave until the end of such term, if

(A) the leave is of greater than 2 weeks duration; and

(B) the return to employment would occur during the 2-week period before the end of such term.

(3) Leave less than 3 weeks prior to end of term. If the eligible employee begins leave under subparagraph (A), (B), or (C) of section 2612(a)(1) of this title or under section 2612(a)(3) of this title during the period that commenced 3 weeks prior to the end of the academic term and the duration of the leave is greater than 5 working days, the agency or school may require the employee to continue to take leave until the end of such term.

(e) Restoration to Equivalent Employment Position. For purposes of determinations under section 2614(a)(1)(B) of this title (relating to the restoration of an eligible employee to an equivalent position), in the case of a local educational agency or a private elementary or secondary school, such determination shall be made on the basis of established school board policies and practices, private school policies and practices, and collective bargaining agreements.

(f) Reduction of the Amount of Liability. If a local educational agency or a private elementary or secondary school that has violated this title proves to the satisfaction of the court that the agency, school, or department had reasonable grounds for believing that the underlying act or omission was not a violation of this title, such court may, in the discretion of the court, reduce the amount of the liability provided for under section 2617(a)(1)(A) of this title to the amount and interest determined under clauses (i) and (ii), respectively, of such section.

§2619. Notice

(a) In General. Each employer shall post and keep posted, in conspicuous places on the premises of the employer where notices to employees and applicants for employment are customarily posted, a notice, to be prepared or approved by the Secretary, setting forth excerpts from, or summaries of, the pertinent provisions of this title and information pertaining to the filing of a charge.

(b) Penalty. Any employer that willfully violates this section may be assessed a civil money penalty not to exceed $100 for each separate offense.

§2651. Effect on Other Laws

(a) Federal and State Antidiscrimination Laws. Nothing in this Act or any amendment made by this Act shall be construed to modify or affect any Federal or State law prohibiting discrimination on the basis of race, religion, color, national origin, sex, age, or disability.

(b) State and Local Laws. Nothing in this Act or any amendment made by this Act shall be construed to supersede any provision of any State or local law that provides greater family or medical leave rights than the rights established under this Act or any amendment made by this Act.

§2652. Effect on Existing Employment Benefits

(a) More Protective. Nothing in this Act or any amendment made by this Act shall be construed to diminish the obligation of an employer to comply with any collective bargaining agreement or any employment benefit program or plan that provides greater family or medical leave rights to employees than the rights established under this Act or any amendment made by this Act.

(b) Less Protective. The rights established for employees under this Act or any amendment made by this Act shall not be diminished by any collective bargaining agreement or any employment benefit program or plan.

§2653. Encouragement of More Generous Leave Policies

Nothing in this Act or any amendment made by this Act shall be construed to discourage employers from adopting or retaining leave policies more generous than any policies that comply with the requirements under this Act or any amendment made by this Act.

§2654. Regulations

The Secretary of Labor shall prescribe such regulations as are necessary to carry out title I and this not later than 120 days after the date of the enactment of this Act [Feb. 5, 1993].

Federal Arbitration Act

9 U.S.C. §§1–16

§1. "Maritime Transactions" and "Commerce" Defined; Exceptions to Operation of Title

"Maritime transaction," as herein defined, means charter parties, bills of lading of water carriers, agreements relating to wharfage, supplies furnished vessels or repairs to vessels, collisions, or any other matters in foreign commerce which, if the subject of controversy, would be embraced within admiralty jurisdiction; "commerce," as herein defined, means commerce among the several States or with foreign nations, or in any Territory of the United States or in the District of Columbia, or between any such Territory and another, or between any such Territory and any State or foreign nation, or between the District of Columbia and any State or Territory or foreign nation, but nothing herein contained shall apply to contracts of employment of seamen, railroad employees, or any other class of workers engaged in foreign or interstate commerce.

§2. Validity, Irrevocability, and Enforcement of Agreements to Arbitrate

A written provision in any maritime transaction or a contract evidencing a transaction involving commerce to settle by arbitration a controversy thereafter arising out of such contract or transaction, or the refusal to perform the whole or any part thereof, or an agreement in writing to submit to arbitration an existing controversy arising out of such a contract, transaction, or refusal, shall be valid, irrevocable, and enforceable, save upon such grounds as exist at law or in equity for the revocation of any contract.

§3. Stay of Proceedings Where Issue Therein Referable to Arbitration

If any suit or proceeding be brought in any of the courts of the United States upon any issue referable to arbitration under an agreement in writing for such arbitration, the court in which such suit is pending, upon being satisfied that the issue involved in such suit or proceeding is referable to arbitration under such an agreement, shall on application of one of the parties stay the trial of the action until such arbitration has been had in accordance with the terms of the agreement, providing the applicant for the stay is not in default in proceeding with such arbitration.

§4. Failure to Arbitrate under Agreement; Petition to United States Court Having Jurisdiction for Order to Compel Arbitration; Notice and Service Thereof; Hearing and Determination

A party aggrieved by the alleged failure, neglect, or refusal of another to arbitrate under a written agreement for arbitration may petition any United States district court which, save for such agreement, would have jurisdiction under Title 28, in a civil action or in admiralty of the subject matter of a suit arising out of the controversy between the parties, for an order directing that such arbitration proceed in the manner provided for in such agreement. Five days' notice in writing of such application shall be served upon the party in default. Service thereof shall be made in the manner provided by the Federal Rules of Civil Procedure. The court shall hear the parties, and upon being satisfied that the making of the agreement for arbitration or the failure to comply therewith is not in issue, the court shall make an order directing the parties to proceed to arbitration in accordance with the terms of the agreement. The hearing and proceedings, under such agreement, shall be within the district in which the petition for an order directing such arbitration is filed. If the making of the arbitration agreement or the failure, neglect, or refusal to perform the same be in issue, the court shall proceed summarily to the trial thereof. If no jury trial be demanded by the party alleged to be in default, or if the matter in dispute is within admiralty jurisdiction, the court shall hear and determine such issue. Where such an issue is raised, the party alleged to be in default may, except in cases of admiralty, on or before the return day of the notice of application, demand a jury trial of such issue, and upon such demand the court shall make an order referring the issue or issues to a jury in the manner provided by the Federal Rules of Civil Procedure, or may specially call a jury for that purpose. If the jury find that no agreement in writing for arbitration was made or that there is no default in proceeding thereunder, the proceeding shall be dismissed. If the jury find that an agreement for arbitration was made in writing and that there is a default in proceeding thereunder, the court shall make an order summarily directing the parties to proceed with the arbitration in accordance with the terms thereof.

§5. Appointment of Arbitrators or Umpire

If in the agreement provision be made for a method of naming or appointing an arbitrator or arbitrators or an umpire, such method shall be followed; but if no method be provided therein, or if a method be provided and any party thereto shall fail to avail himself of such method, or if for any other reason there shall be a lapse in the naming of an arbitrator or arbitrators or umpire, or in filling a vacancy, then upon the application of either party to the controversy the court shall designate and appoint an arbitrator or arbitrators or umpire, as the case may require, who shall act under the said agreement with the same force and effect as if he or they had been specifically named therein; and unless otherwise provided in the agreement the arbitration shall be by a single arbitrator.

§6. Application Heard as Motion

Any application to the court hereunder shall be made and heard in the manner provided by law for the making and hearing of motions, except as otherwise herein expressly provided.

§7. Witnesses Before Arbitrators; Fees; Compelling Attendance

The arbitrators selected either as prescribed in this title or otherwise, or a majority of them, may summon in writing any person to attend before them or any of them as a witness and in a proper case to bring with him or them any book, record, document, or paper which may be deemed material as evidence in the case. The fees for such attendance shall be the same as the fees of witnesses before masters of the United States courts. Said summons shall issue in the name of the arbitrator or arbitrators, or a majority of them, and shall be signed by the arbitrators, or a majority of them, and shall be directed to the said person and shall be served in the same manner as subpoenas to appear and testify before the court; if any person or persons so summoned to testify shall refuse or neglect to obey said summons, upon petition the United States district court for the district in which such arbitrators, or a majority of them, are sitting may compel the attendance of such person or persons before said arbitrator or arbitrators, or punish said person or persons for contempt in the same manner provided by law for securing the attendance of witnesses or their punishment for neglect or refusal to attend in the courts of the United States.

§8. Proceedings Begun by Libel in Admiralty and Seizure of Vessel or Property

If the basis of jurisdiction be a cause of action otherwise justiciable in admiralty, then, notwithstanding anything herein to the contrary, the party claiming to be aggrieved may begin his proceeding hereunder by seizure of the vessel or other property of the other party according to the usual course of admiralty proceedings, and the court shall then have jurisdiction to direct the parties to proceed with the arbitration and shall retain jurisdiction to enter its decree upon the award.

§9. Award of Arbitrators; Confirmation; Jurisdiction; Procedure

If the parties in their agreement have agreed that a judgment of the court shall be entered upon the award made pursuant to the arbitration, and shall specify the court, then at any time within one year after the award is made any party to the arbitration may apply to the court so specified for an order confirming the award, and thereupon the court must grant such an order unless the award is vacated, modified, or corrected as prescribed in sections 10 and 11 of this title. If no court is specified in the agreement of the parties, then such application may be made to the United States court in and for the district within which such award was made. Notice of the application shall be served upon the adverse party, and thereupon the court shall have jurisdiction of such party as though he had appeared generally in the proceeding. If the adverse party is a resident of the district within which the award was made, such service shall be made upon the adverse party or his attorney as prescribed by law for service of notice of motion in an action in the same court. If the adverse party shall be a nonresident, then the notice of the application shall be served by the marshal of any district within which the adverse party may be found in like manner as other process of the court.

§10. Same; Vacation; Grounds; Rehearing

(a) In any of the following cases the United States court in and for the district wherein the award was made may make an order vacating the award upon the application of any party to the arbitration —

(1) Where the award was procured by corruption, fraud, or undue means;

(2) Where there was evident partiality or corruption in the arbitrators, or either of them;

(3) Where the arbitrators were guilty of misconduct in refusing to postpone the hearing, upon sufficient cause shown, or in refusing to hear evidence pertinent and material to the controversy; or of any other misbehavior by which the rights of any party have been prejudiced; or

(4) Where the arbitrators exceeded their powers, or so imperfectly executed them that a mutual, final, and definite award upon the subject matter submitted was not made.

(b) If an award is vacated and the time within which the agreement required the award to be made has not expired, the court may, in its discretion, direct a rehearing by the arbitrators.

(c) The United States district court for the district wherein an award was made that was issued pursuant to section 580 of title 5 may make an order vacating the award upon the application of a person, other than a party to the arbitration, who is adversely affected or aggrieved by the award, if the use of arbitration or the award is clearly inconsistent with the factors set forth in section 572 of title 5.

§11. Same; Modification or Correction; Grounds; Order

In either of the following cases the United States court in and for the district wherein the award was made may make an order modifying or correcting the award upon the application of any party to the arbitration —

(a) Where there was an evident material miscalculation of figures or an evident material mistake in the description of any person, thing, or property referred to in the award.

(b) Where the arbitrators have awarded upon a matter not submitted to them, unless it is a matter not affecting the merits of the decision upon the matter submitted.

(c) Where the award is imperfect in matter of form not affecting the merits of the controversy.

The order may modify and correct the award, so as to effect the intent thereof and promote justice between the parties.

§12. Notice of Motions to Vacate or Modify; Service; Stay of Proceedings

Notice of a motion to vacate, modify, or correct an award must be served upon the adverse party or his attorney within three months after the award is filed or delivered. If the adverse party is a resident of the district within which the award was made, such service shall be made upon the adverse party or his attorney as prescribed by law for service of notice of motion in an action in the same court. If the adverse party shall be a nonresident then the notice of the application shall be served by the marshal of any district within which the adverse party may be found in like manner as other process of the court. For the purposes of the motion any judge who might make an order to stay the proceedings in an action brought in the same court may make an order, to be served with the notice of motion, staying the proceedings of the adverse party to enforce the award.

§13. Papers Filed with Order on Motions; Judgment; Docketing; Force and Effect; Enforcement

The party moving for an order confirming, modifying, or correcting an award shall, at the time such order is filed with the clerk for the entry of judgment thereon, also file the following papers with the clerk:

(a) The agreement; the selection or appointment, if any, of an additional arbitrator or umpire; and each written extension of the time, if any, within which to make the award.

(b) The award.

(c) Each notice, affidavit, or other paper used upon an application to confirm, modify, or correct the award, and a copy of each order of the court upon such an application.

The judgment shall be docketed as if it was rendered in an action.

The judgment so entered shall have the same force and effect, in all respects, as, and be subject to all the provisions of law relating to, a judgment in an action; and it may be enforced as if it had been rendered in an action in the court in which it is entered.

§14. Contracts Not Affected

This title shall not apply to contracts made prior to January 1, 1926.

§15. Inapplicability of the Act of State Doctrine

Enforcement of arbitral agreements, confirmation of arbitral awards, and execution upon judgments based on orders confirming such awards shall not be refused on the basis of the Act of State doctrine.

§16. Appeals

(a) An appeal may be taken from
    (1) an order —
        (A) refusing a stay of any action under section 3 of this title,

  (B) denying a petition under section 4 of this title to order arbitration to proceed,

  (C) denying an application under section 206 of this title to compel arbitration,

  (D) confirming or denying confirmation of an award or partial award, or

  (E) modifying, correcting, or vacating an award;

 (2) an interlocutory order granting, continuing, or modifying an injunction against an arbitration that is subject to this title; or

 (3) a final decision with respect to an arbitration that is subject to this title.

(b) Except as otherwise provided in section 1292(b) of title 28, an appeal may not be taken from an interlocutory order —

 (1) granting a stay of any action under section 3 of this title;

 (2) directing arbitration to proceed under section 4 of this title;

 (3) compelling arbitration under section 206 of this title; or

 (4) refusing to enjoin an arbitration that is subject to this title.

42 U.S.C. §1981

§1981. Equal Rights Under the Law*

(a) All persons within the jurisdiction of the United States shall have the same right in every State and Territory to make and enforce contracts, to sue, be parties, give evidence, and to the full and equal benefit of all laws and proceedings for the security of persons and property as is enjoyed by white citizens, and shall be subject to like punishment, pains, penalties, taxes, licences, and exactions of every kind, and to no other.

(b) For purposes of this section, the term "make and enforce contracts" includes the making, performance, modification, and termination of contracts, and the enjoyment of all benefits, privileges, terms, and conditions of the contractual relationship.

(c) The rights protected by this section are protected against impairment by nongovernmental discrimination and impairment under color of State law.

---

* Sections 1981(b), (c) and 1981a were added by the Civil Rights Act of 1991.

42 U.S.C. §1981a

§1981a. Damages in Cases of Intentional Discrimination in Employment

(a) Right of Recovery.

(1) Civil rights. In an action brought by a complaining party under section 42 U.S.C. 2000e-5 or 42 U.S.C. 2000e-16 of the Civil Rights Act of 1964 against a respondent who engaged in unlawful intentional discrimination (not an employment practice that is unlawful because of its disparate impact) prohibited under section 42 U.S.C. 2000e-2, -3, or -16 of the Act, and provided that the complaining party cannot recover under 42 U.S.C. 1981 of the Revised Statutes, the complaining party may recover compensatory and punitive damages as allowed in subsection (b), in addition to any relief authorized by section 2000e-5(g) of the Civil Rights Act of 1964, from the respondent.

(2) Disability. In an action brought by a complaining party that the powers, remedies, and procedures set forth in section 2000e-5 or 2000e-16 of the Civil Rights Act of 1964 (as provided in section 42 U.S.C. 12117(a) of the Americans With Disabilities Act of 1990 and section 29 U.S.C. 794a(a)(1) of the Rehabilitation Act of 1973, respectively) against a respondent who engaged in unlawful intentional discrimination (not an employment practice that is unlawful because of its disparate impact) under section 29 U.S.C. 791 of the Rehabilitation Act of 1973 and the regulations implementing section 791, or who violated the requirements of section 791 of the Act or the regulations implementing section 791 concerning the provision of a reasonable accommodation, or section 42 U.S.C. 12112 of the Americans With Disabilities Act, or committed a violation of section 12112(b)(5) of the Act, against an individual, the complaining party may recover compensatory and punitive damages as allowed in subsection (b), in addition to any relief authorized by section 42 U.S.C. 2000e-5(g) of the Civil Rights Act of 1964, from the respondent.

(3) Reasonable accommodation and good faith effort. In cases where a discriminatory practice involves the provision of a reasonable accommodation pursuant to section 12112(b)(5) of the Americans With Disabilities Act of 1990 or regulations implementing section 791 of the Rehabilitation Act of 1973, damages may not be awarded under this section where the covered entity demonstrates good faith efforts, in consultation with the person with the disability who has informed the covered entity that accommodation is needed, to identify and make a reasonable accommodation that would provide such individual with an equally effective opportunity and would not cause an undue hardship on the question of the business.

(b) Compensatory and Punitive Damages.

(1) Determination of punitive damages. A complaining party may recover punitive damages under this section against a respondent (other than a government, government agency or political subdivision) if the complaining party demonstrates that the respondent engaged in a discriminatory practice or discriminatory practices with malice or with reckless indifference to the federally protected rights of an aggrieved individual.

(2) Exclusions from compensatory damages. Compensatory damages awarded under this section shall not include backpay, interest on backpay, or any other type of relief authorized under section 2000e-5(g) of the Civil Rights Act of 1964.

(3) Limitations. The sum of the amount of compensatory damages awarded under this section for future pecuniary losses, emotional pain, suffering, inconvenience, mental anguish, loss of enjoyment of life, and other non-pecuniary losses, and the amount of punitive damages awarded under this section, shall not exceed, for each complaining party

(A) in the case of a respondent who has more than 14 and fewer than 101 employees in each of 20 or more calendar weeks in the current or preceding calendar year, $50,000;

(B) in the case of a respondent who has more than 100 and fewer than 201 employees in each of 20 or more calendar weeks in the current or preceding calendar year, $100,000; and

(C) in the case of a respondent who has more than 200 and fewer than 501 employees in each of 20 or more calendar weeks in the current or preceding calendar year, $200,000; and

(D) in the case of a respondent who has more than 500 employees in each of 20 or more calendar weeks in the current or preceding calendar year, $300,000.

(4) Construction. Nothing in this section shall be construed to limit the scope of, or the relief available under, section 1981 of the Revised Statutes (42 U.S.C. 1981).

(c) Jury Trial. If a complaining party seeks compensatory or punitive damages under this section.

(1) any party may demand a trial by jury; and

(2) the court shall not inform the jury of the limitation described in subsection (b)(3).

(d) Definitions. As used in this section:

(1) Complaining party. The term "complaining party" means

(A) in the case of a person seeking to bring an action under subsection (a)(1), the Equal Employment Opportunity Commission, the Attorney General, or a person who may bring an action or proceeding under title VII of the Civil Rights Act of 1964; or

(B) in the case of a person seeking to bring an action under (a)(2), the Equal Employment Opportunity Commission, the Attorney General, a person who may bring an action or proceeding under section 794a(a)(1) of the Rehabilitation Act of 1973 (29 U.S.C. 794a(a)(1)), or a person who may bring an action or proceeding under title I of the Americans With Disabilities Act of 1990.

(2) Discriminatory practice. The term "discriminatory practice" means the discrimination described in paragraph (1), or the discrimination or the violation described in paragraph (2), of subsection (a).

42 U.S.C. §1983

§1983. Civil Action for Deprivation of Rights

Every person who, under color of any statute, ordinance, regulation, custom, or usage, of any State or Territory or the District of Columbia, subjects, or causes to be subjected, any citizen of the United States or other person within the jurisdiction thereof to the deprivation of any rights, privileges, or immunities secured by the Constitution and laws, shall be liable to the party injured in an action at law, suit in equity, or other proper proceeding for redress, except that in any action brought against a judicial officer for an act or omission taken in such officer's judicial capacity, injunctive relief shall not be granted unless a declaratory decree was violated or declaratory relief was unavailable. For the purposes of this section, any Act of Congress applicable exclusively to the District of Columbia shall be considered to be a statute of the District of Columbia.

42 U.S.C. §1985(3)

§1985. Conspiracy to Interfere with Civil Rights

(3) Depriving persons of rights or privileges. If two or more persons in any State or Territory conspire or go in disguise on the highway or on the premises of another, for the purpose of depriving, either directly or indirectly, any person or class of persons of the equal protection of the laws, or of equal privileges and immunities under the laws; or for the purpose of preventing or hindering the constituted authorities of any State or Territory from giving or securing to all persons within such State or Territory the equal protection of the laws; or if two or more persons conspire to prevent by force, intimidation, or threat, any citizen who is lawfully entitled to vote, from giving his support or advocacy in a legal manner, toward or in favor of the election of any lawfully qualified person as an elector for President or Vice President, or as a Member of Congress of the United States; or to injure any citizen in person or property on account of such support or advocacy; in any case of conspiracy set forth in this section, if one or more persons engaged therein do, or cause to be done, any act in furtherance of the object of such conspiracy, whereby another is injured in his person or property, or deprived of having and exercising any right or privilege of a citizen of the United States, the party so injured or deprived may have an action for the recovery of damages occasioned by such injury or deprivation, against any one or more of the conspirators.

42 U.S.C. §1988

§1988. Proceedings in Vindication of Civil Rights

(a) Applicability of Statutory and Common Law. The jurisdiction in civil and criminal matters conferred on the district courts by the provisions of Titles 13, 24, and 70 of the Revised Statutes, for the protection of all persons in the United States in their civil rights, and for their vindication, shall be exercised and enforced in conformity with the laws of the United States, so far as such laws are suitable to carry the same into effect; but in all cases where they are not adapted to the object, or are deficient in the provisions necessary to furnish suitable remedies and punish offences against law, the common law, as modified and changed by the constitution and statutes of the State wherein the court having jurisdiction of such civil or criminal cause is held, so far as the same is not inconsistent with the Constitution and laws of the United States, shall be extended to and govern the said courts in the trial and disposition of the cause, and, if it is of a criminal nature, in the infliction of punishment on the party found guilty.

(b) Attorney's Fees. In any action or proceeding to enforce a provision of sections 1981, 1981a, 1982, 1983, 1985, and 1986 of this title [42 U.S.C.], title IX of Public Law 92-318 [20 U.S.C. §§1681 et seq.], the Religious Freedom Restoration Act of 1993 [42 U.S.C. §§2000bb et seq.], the Religious Land Use and Institutionalized Persons Act of 2000 [42 U.S.C. §§2000cc et seq.], title VI of the Civil Rights Act of 1964 [42 U.S.C. §§2000d et seq.], or section 13981 of this title, the court, in its discretion, may allow the prevailing party, other than the United States, a reasonable attorney's fee as part of the costs, except that in any action brought against a judicial officer for an act or omission taken in such officer's judicial capacity such officer shall not be held liable for any costs, including attorney's fees, unless such action was clearly in excess of such officer's jurisdiction.

(c) Expert Fees. In awarding an attorney's fee under subsection (b) in any action or proceeding to enforce a provision of sections 1981 or 1981a of this title, the court, in its discretion, may include expert fees as part of the attorney's fee.

References in Text

Title 13 of the Revised Statutes, referred to in subsection (a), was in the original "this Title" meaning title 13 of the Revised Statutes, consisting of R.S. §§530 to 1093. For complete classification of R.S. §§530 to 1093 to the Code, see Tables.

Title 24 of the Revised Statutes, referred to in subsection (a), was in the original "Title 'Civil Rights,'" meaning title 24 of the Revised Statutes, consisting of R.S. §§1977 to 1991, which are classified to sections 1981 to 1983, 1985 to 1987, and 1989 to 1994 of this title. For complete classification of R.S. §§1977 to 1991 to the Code, see Tables.

Title 70 of the Revised Statutes, referred to in subsection (a), was in the original "Title 'Crimes,'" meaning title 70 of the Revised Statutes, consisting of R.S. §§5323 to 5550. For complete classification of R.S. §§5323 to 5550, see Tables.

42 U.S.C. §2000d-7

§2000d-7. *Civil Rights Remedies Equalization*

(a) General Provision.

(1) A State shall not be immune under the Eleventh Amendment of the Constitution of the United States from suit in Federal court for a violation of section 504 of the Rehabilitation Act of 1973 [29 U.S.C.A. §794], title IX of the Education Amendments of 1972 [20 U.S.C.A. §1681 et seq.], the Age Discrimination Act of 1975 [42 U.S.C.A. §6101 et seq.], title VI of the Civil Rights Act of 1964 [42 U.S.C.A. 2000d et seq.], or the provisions of any other Federal statute prohibiting discrimination by recipients of Federal financial assistance.

(2) In a suit against a State for a violation of a statute referred to in paragraph (I), remedies (including remedies both at law and in equity) are available for such a violation to the same extent as such remedies are available for such a violation in the suit against any public or private entity other than a State.

(b) Effective Date.

The provisions of subsection (a) of this section shall take effect with respect to violations that occur in whole or in part after October 21, 1986.

Genetic Information Nondiscrimination Act of 2008

Pub. L. No. 110-233, 122 Stat. 881

An Act To prohibit discrimination on the basis of genetic information with respect to health insurance and employment.

Be it enacted by the Senate and House of Representatives of the United States of America in Congress assembled,

Sec. 1. Short Title; Table of Contents

(a) SHORT TITLE. This Act may be cited as the "Genetic Information Nondiscrimination Act of 2008".

(b) TABLE OF CONTENTS. The table of contents of this Act is as follows:

Sec. 1.   Short title; table of contents.
Sec. 2.   Findings.

TITLE I—GENETIC NONDISCRIMINATION IN HEALTH INSURANCE
[not reproduced]

Sec. 101.   Amendments to Employee Retirement Income Security Act of 1974.
Sec. 102.   Amendments to the Public Health Service Act.
Sec. 103.   Amendments to the Internal Revenue Code of 1986.
Sec. 104.   Amendments to title XVIII of the Social Security Act relating to Medigap.
Sec. 105.   Privacy and confidentiality.
Sec. 106.   Assuring coordination.

TITLE II—PROHIBITING EMPLOYMENT DISCRIMINATION ON THE BASIS OF GENETIC INFORMATION

Sec. 201.   Definitions.
Sec. 202.   Employer practices.
Sec. 203.   Employment agency practices.
Sec. 204.   Labor organization practices.

Sec. 205. Training programs.
Sec. 206. Confidentiality of genetic information.
Sec. 207. Remedies and enforcement.
Sec. 208. Disparate impact.
Sec. 209. Construction.
Sec. 210. Medical information that is not genetic information.
Sec. 211. Regulations.
Sec. 212. Authorization of appropriations.
Sec. 213. Effective date.

TITLE III — MISCELLANEOUS PROVISIONS
[not reproduced]

Sec. 301. Severability.
Sec. 302. Child labor protections.

Sec. 2. Findings

Congress makes the following findings:

(1) Deciphering the sequence of the human genome and other advances in genetics open major new opportunities for medical progress. New knowledge about the genetic basis of illness will allow for earlier detection of illnesses, often before symptoms have begun. Genetic testing can allow individuals to take steps to reduce the likelihood that they will contract a particular disorder. New knowledge about genetics may allow for the development of better therapies that are more effective against disease or have fewer side effects than current treatments. These advances give rise to the potential misuse of genetic information to discriminate in health insurance and employment.

(2) The early science of genetics became the basis of State laws that provided for the sterilization of persons having presumed genetic "defects" such as mental retardation, mental disease, epilepsy, blindness, and hearing loss, among other conditions. The first sterilization law was enacted in the State of Indiana in 1907. By 1981, a majority of States adopted sterilization laws to "correct" apparent genetic traits or tendencies. Many of these State laws have since been repealed, and many have been modified to include essential constitutional requirements of due process and equal protection. However, the current explosion in the science of genetics, and the history of sterilization laws by the States based on early genetic science, compels Congressional action in this area.

(3) Although genes are facially neutral markers, many genetic conditions and disorders are associated with particular racial and ethnic groups and gender. Because some genetic traits are most prevalent in particular groups, members of a particular group may be stigmatized or discriminated against as a result of that genetic information. This form of discrimination was evident

in the 1970s, which saw the advent of programs to screen and identify carriers of sickle cell anemia, a disease which afflicts African Americans. Once again, State legislatures began to enact discriminatory laws in the area, and in the early 1970s began mandating genetic screening of all African Americans for sickle cell anemia, leading to discrimination and unnecessary fear. To alleviate some of this stigma, Congress in 1972 passed the National Sickle Cell Anemia Control Act, which withholds Federal funding from States unless sickle cell testing is voluntary.

(4) Congress has been informed of examples of genetic discrimination in the workplace. These include the use of pre-employment genetic screening at Lawrence Berkeley Laboratory, which led to a court decision in favor of the employees in that case. Norman-Bloodsaw v. Lawrence Berkeley Laboratory (135 F.3d 1260, 1269 (9th Cir. 1998)). Congress clearly has a compelling public interest in relieving the fear of discrimination and in prohibiting its actual practice in employment and health insurance.

(5) Federal law addressing genetic discrimination in health insurance and employment is incomplete in both the scope and depth of its protections. Moreover, while many States have enacted some type of genetic non-discrimination law, these laws vary widely with respect to their approach, application, and level of protection. Congress has collected substantial evidence that the American public and the medical community find the existing patchwork of State and Federal laws to be confusing and inadequate to protect them from discrimination. Therefore Federal legislation establishing a national and uniform basic standard is necessary to fully protect the public from discrimination and allay their concerns about the potential for discrimination, thereby allowing individuals to take advantage of genetic testing, technologies, research, and new therapies.

Title II — Prohibiting Employment Discrimination on the Basis of Genetic Information

Sec. 201. *Definitions*

(1) Commission. The term "Commission" means the Equal Employment Opportunity Commission as created by section 705 of the Civil Rights Act of 1964 [42 U.S.C. 2000e-4].

(2) EMPLOYEE; EMPLOYER; EMPLOYMENT AGENCY; LABOR ORGANIZATION; MEMBER.

   (A) IN GENERAL. The term "employee" means —

      (i) an employee (including an applicant), as defined in section 701(f) of the Civil Rights Act of 1964 (42 U.S.C. 2000e(f));

      (ii) a State employee (including an applicant) described in section 304(a) of the Government Employee Rights Act of 1991 (42 U.S.C. 2000e-16c(a));

(iii) a covered employee (including an applicant), as defined in section 101 of the Congressional Accountability Act of 1995 (2 U.S.C. 1301);

(iv) a covered employee (including an applicant), as defined in section 411(c) of title 3, United States Code; or

(v) an employee or applicant to which section 717(a) of the Civil Rights Act of 1964 (42 U.S.C. 2000e-16(a)) applies.

(B) EMPLOYER. The term "employer" means —

(i) an employer (as defined in section 701(b) of the Civil Rights Act of 1964 (42 U.S.C. 2000e(b)));

(ii) an entity employing a State employee described in section 304(a) of the Government Employee Rights Act of 1991;

(iii) an employing office, as defined in section 101 of the Congressional Accountability Act of 1995;

(iv) an employing office, as defined in section 411(c) of title 3, United States Code; or

(v) an entity to which section 717(a) of the Civil Rights Act of 1964 applies.

(C) EMPLOYMENT AGENCY; LABOR ORGANIZATION. The terms "employment agency" and "labor organization" have the meanings given the terms in section 701 of the Civil Rights Act of 1964 (42 U.S.C. 2000e).

(D) MEMBER. The term "member", with respect to a labor organization, includes an applicant for membership in a labor organization.

(3) FAMILY MEMBER. The term "family member" means, with respect to an individual —

(A) a dependent (as such term is used for purposes of section 701(f)(2) of the Employee Retirement Income Security Act of 1974) of such individual, and

(B) any other individual who is a first-degree, second-degree, third-degree, or fourth-degree relative of such individual or of an individual described in subparagraph (A).

(4) GENETIC INFORMATION.

(A) IN GENERAL. The term "genetic information" means, with respect to any individual, information about —

(i) such individual's genetic tests,

(ii) the genetic tests of family members of such individual, and

(iii) the manifestation of a disease or disorder in family members of such individual.

(B) INCLUSION OF GENETIC SERVICES AND PARTICIPATION IN GENETIC RESEARCH. Such term includes, with respect to any individual, any request for, or receipt of, genetic services, or participation in clinical research which includes genetic services, by such individual or any family member of such individual.

(C) EXCLUSIONS. The term "genetic information" shall not include information about the sex or age of any individual.

(5) GENETIC MONITORING. The term "genetic monitoring" means the periodic examination of employees to evaluate acquired modifications to their genetic material, such as chromosomal damage or evidence of increased occurrence of mutations, that may have developed in the course of employment due to exposure to toxic substances in the workplace, in order to identify, evaluate, and respond to the effects of or control adverse environmental exposures in the workplace.

(6) GENETIC SERVICES. The term "genetic services" means—

(A) a genetic test;

(B) genetic counseling (including obtaining, interpreting, or assessing genetic information); or

(C) genetic education.

(7) GENETIC TEST.

(A) IN GENERAL. The term "genetic test" means an analysis of human DNA, RNA, chromosomes, proteins, or metabolites, that detects genotypes, mutations, or chromosomal changes.

(B) EXCEPTIONS. The term "genetic test" does not mean an analysis of proteins or metabolites that does not detect genotypes, mutations, or chromosomal changes.

Sec. 202. *Employer Practices*

(a) DISCRIMINATION BASED ON GENETIC INFORMATION. It shall be an unlawful employment practice for an employer—

(1) to fail or refuse to hire, or to discharge, any employee, or otherwise to discriminate against any employee with respect to the compensation, terms, conditions, or privileges of employment of the employee, because of genetic information with respect to the employee; or

(2) to limit, segregate, or classify the employees of the employer in any way that would deprive or tend to deprive any employee of employment opportunities or otherwise adversely affect the status of the employee as an employee, because of genetic information with respect to the employee.

(b) ACQUISITION OF GENETIC INFORMATION. It shall be an unlawful employment practice for an employer to request, require, or purchase genetic information with respect to an employee or a family member of the employee except—

(1) where an employer inadvertently requests or requires family medical history of the employee or family member of the employee;

(2) where—

(A) health or genetic services are offered by the employer, including such services offered as part of a wellness program;

(B) the employee provides prior, knowing, voluntary, and written authorization;

(C) only the employee (or family member if the family member is receiving genetic services) and the licensed health care professional or board certified genetic counselor involved in providing such services receive individually identifiable information concerning the results of such services; and

(D) any individually identifiable genetic information provided under subparagraph (C) in connection with the services provided under subparagraph (A) is only available for purposes of such services and shall not be disclosed to the employer except in aggregate terms that do not disclose the identity of specific employees;

(3) where an employer requests or requires family medical history from the employee to comply with the certification provisions of section 103 of the Family and Medical Leave Act of 1993 (29 U.S.C. 2613) or such requirements under State family and medical leave laws;

(4) where an employer purchases documents that are commercially and publicly available (including newspapers, magazines, periodicals, and books, but not including medical databases or court records) that include family medical history;

(5) where the information involved is to be used for genetic monitoring of the biological effects of toxic substances in the workplace, but only if—

(A) the employer provides written notice of the genetic monitoring to the employee;

(B)(i) the employee provides prior, knowing, voluntary, and written authorization; or

(ii) the genetic monitoring is required by Federal or State law;

(C) the employee is informed of individual monitoring results;

(D) THE MONITORING IS IN COMPLIANCE WITH

(i) any Federal genetic monitoring regulations, including any such regulations that may be promulgated by the Secretary of Labor pursuant to the Occupational Safety and Health Act of 1970 (29 U.S.C. 651 et seq.), the Federal Mine Safety and Health Act of 1977 (30 U.S.C. 801 et seq.), or the Atomic Energy Act of 1954 (42 U.S.C. 2011 et seq.); or

(ii) State genetic monitoring regulations, in the case of a State that is implementing genetic monitoring regulations under the authority of the Occupational Safety and Health Act of 1970 (29 U.S.C. 651 et seq.); and

(E) the employer, excluding any licensed health care professional or board certified genetic counselor that is involved in the genetic monitoring program, receives the results of the monitoring only in aggregate terms that do not disclose the identity of specific employees; or

(6) where the employer conducts DNA analysis for law enforcement purposes as a forensic laboratory or for purposes of human remains identification, and requests or requires genetic information of such employer's employees, but only to the extent that such genetic information is used for analysis of DNA identification markers for quality control to detect sample contamination.

(c) PRESERVATION OF PROTECTIONS. In the case of information to which any of paragraphs (1) through (6) of subsection (b) applies, such information may not be used in violation of paragraph (1) or (2) of subsection (a) or treated or disclosed in a manner that violates section 206.

Sec. 203. Employment Agency Practices

(a) DISCRIMINATION BASED ON GENETIC INFORMATION. It shall be an unlawful employment practice for an employment agency —

(1) to fail or refuse to refer for employment, or otherwise to discriminate against, any individual because of genetic information with respect to the individual;

(2) to limit, segregate, or classify individuals or fail or refuse to refer for employment any individual in any way that would deprive or tend to deprive any individual of employment opportunities, or otherwise adversely affect the status of the individual as an employee, because of genetic information with respect to the individual; or

(3) to cause or attempt to cause an employer to discriminate against an individual in violation of this title.

(b) ACQUISITION OF GENETIC INFORMATION. It shall be an unlawful employment practice for an employment agency to request, require, or purchase genetic information with respect to an individual or a family member of the individual except —

(1) where an employment agency inadvertently requests or requires family medical history of the individual or family member of the individual;

(2) where —

(A) health or genetic services are offered by the employment agency, including such services offered as part of a wellness program;

(B) the individual provides prior, knowing, voluntary, and written authorization;

(C) only the individual (or family member if the family member is receiving genetic services) and the licensed health care professional or board certified genetic counselor involved in providing such services receive individually identifiable information concerning the results of such services; and

(D) any individually identifiable genetic information provided under subparagraph (C) in connection with the services provided under subparagraph (A) is only available for purposes of such services and shall not be disclosed to the employment agency except in aggregate terms that do not disclose the identity of specific individuals;

(3) where an employment agency requests or requires family medical history from the individual to comply with the certification provisions of section 103 of the Family and Medical Leave Act of 1993 (29 U.S.C. 2613) or such requirements under State family and medical leave laws;

(4) where an employment agency purchases documents that are commercially and publicly available (including newspapers, magazines, periodicals, and books, but not including medical databases or court records) that include family medical history; or

(5) where the information involved is to be used for genetic monitoring of the biological effects of toxic substances in the workplace, but only if —

(A) the employment agency provides written notice of the genetic monitoring to the individual;

(B)(i) the individual provides prior, knowing, voluntary, and written authorization; or

(ii) the genetic monitoring is required by Federal or State law;

(C) the individual is informed of individual monitoring results;

(D) THE MONITORING IS IN COMPLIANCE WITH

(i) any Federal genetic monitoring regulations, including any such regulations that may be promulgated by the Secretary of Labor pursuant to the Occupational Safety and Health Act of 1970 (29 U.S.C. 651 et seq.), the Federal Mine Safety and Health Act of 1977 (30 U.S.C. 801 et seq.), or the Atomic Energy Act of 1954 (42 U.S.C. 2011 et seq.); or

(ii) State genetic monitoring regulations, in the case of a State that is implementing genetic monitoring regulations under the authority of the Occupational Safety and Health Act of 1970 (29 U.S.C. 651 et seq.); and

(E) the employment agency, excluding any licensed health care professional or board certified genetic counselor that is involved in the genetic monitoring program, receives the results of the monitoring only in aggregate terms that do not disclose the identity of specific individuals.

(c) PRESERVATION OF PROTECTIONS. In the case of information to which any of paragraphs (1) through (5) of subsection (b) applies, such information may not be used in violation of paragraph (1), (2), or (3) of subsection (a) or treated or disclosed in a manner that violates section 206.

Sec. 204. Labor Organization Practices

(a) DISCRIMINATION BASED ON GENETIC INFORMATION. It shall be an unlawful employment practice for a labor organization —

(1) to exclude or to expel from the membership of the organization, or otherwise to discriminate against, any member because of genetic information with respect to the member;

(2) to limit, segregate, or classify the members of the organization, or fail or refuse to refer for employment any member, in any way that would deprive or tend to deprive any member of employment opportunities, or otherwise adversely affect the status of the member as an employee, because of genetic information with respect to the member; or

(3) to cause or attempt to cause an employer to discriminate against a member in violation of this title.

(b) ACQUISITION OF GENETIC INFORMATION. It shall be an unlawful employment practice for a labor organization to request, require, or purchase genetic information with respect to a member or a family member of the member except —

(1) where a labor organization inadvertently requests or requires family medical history of the member or family member of the member;

(2) where —

(A) health or genetic services are offered by the labor organization, including such services offered as part of a wellness program;

(B) the member provides prior, knowing, voluntary, and written authorization;

(C) only the member (or family member if the family member is receiving genetic services) and the licensed health care professional or board certified genetic counselor involved in providing such services receive individually identifiable information concerning the results of such services; and

(D) any individually identifiable genetic information provided under subparagraph (C) in connection with the services provided under subparagraph (A) is only available for purposes of such services and shall not be disclosed to the labor organization except in aggregate terms that do not disclose the identity of specific members;

(3) where a labor organization requests or requires family medical history from the members to comply with the certification provisions of section 103 of the Family and Medical Leave Act of 1993 (29 U.S.C. 2613) or such requirements under State family and medical leave laws;

(4) where a labor organization purchases documents that are commercially and publicly available (including newspapers, magazines, periodicals, and books, but not including medical databases or court records) that include family medical history; or

(5) WHERE THE INFORMATION INVOLVED IS TO BE USED FOR GENETIC MONITORING OF THE BIOLOGICAL EFFECTS OF TOXIC SUBSTANCES IN THE WORKPLACE, BUT ONLY IF

(A) the labor organization provides written notice of the genetic monitoring to the member;

(B)(i) the member provides prior, knowing, voluntary, and written authorization; or

(ii) the genetic monitoring is required by Federal or State law;

(C) the member is informed of individual monitoring results;

(D) THE MONITORING IS IN COMPLIANCE WITH

(i) any Federal genetic monitoring regulations, including any such regulations that may be promulgated by the Secretary of Labor pursuant to the Occupational Safety and Health Act of 1970 (29 U.S.C. 651 et seq.), the Federal Mine Safety and Health Act of 1977 (30 U.S.C. 801 et seq.), or the Atomic Energy Act of 1954 (42 U.S.C. 2011 et seq.); or

(ii) State genetic monitoring regulations, in the case of a State that is implementing genetic monitoring regulations under the authority of the Occupational Safety and Health Act of 1970 (29 U.S.C. 651 et seq.); and

(E) the labor organization, excluding any licensed health care professional or board certified genetic counselor that is involved in the genetic monitoring program, receives the results of the monitoring only in aggregate terms that do not disclose the identity of specific members.

(c) PRESERVATION OF PROTECTIONS. In the case of information to which any of paragraphs (1) through (5) of subsection (b) applies, such information may not be used in violation of paragraph (1), (2), or (3) of subsection (a) or treated or disclosed in a manner that violates section 206.

Sec. 205. *Training Programs*

(a) DISCRIMINATION BASED ON GENETIC INFORMATION. It shall be an unlawful employment practice for any employer, labor organization, or joint labor-management committee controlling apprenticeship or other training or retraining, including on-the-job training programs—

(1) to discriminate against any individual because of genetic information with respect to the individual in admission to, or employment in, any program established to provide apprenticeship or other training or retraining;

(2) to limit, segregate, or classify the applicants for or participants in such apprenticeship or other training or retraining, or fail or refuse to refer for employment any individual, in any way that would deprive or tend to deprive any individual of employment opportunities, or otherwise adversely affect the status of the individual as an employee, because of genetic information with respect to the individual; or

(3) to cause or attempt to cause an employer to discriminate against an applicant for or a participant in such apprenticeship or other training or retraining in violation of this title.

(b) ACQUISITION OF GENETIC INFORMATION. It shall be an unlawful employment practice for an employer, labor organization, or joint labor-management committee described in subsection (a) to request, require, or purchase genetic information with respect to an individual or a family member of the individual except—

(1) where the employer, labor organization, or joint labor-management committee inadvertently requests or requires family medical history of the individual or family member of the individual;

(2) where—

(A) health or genetic services are offered by the employer, labor organization, or joint labor-management committee, including such services offered as part of a wellness program;

(B) the individual provides prior, knowing, voluntary, and written authorization;

(C) only the individual (or family member if the family member is receiving genetic services) and the licensed health care professional or board certified genetic counselor involved in providing such services receive individually identifiable information concerning the results of such services; and

(D) any individually identifiable genetic information provided under subparagraph (C) in connection with the services provided under subparagraph (A) is only available for purposes of such services and shall not be disclosed to the employer, labor organization, or joint labor-management committee except in aggregate terms that do not disclose the identity of specific individuals;

(3) where the employer, labor organization, or joint labor-management committee requests or requires family medical history from the individual to

comply with the certification provisions of section 103 of the Family and Medical Leave Act of 1993 (29 U.S.C. 2613) or such requirements under State family and medical leave laws;

(4) where the employer, labor organization, or joint labor-management committee purchases documents that are commercially and publicly available (including newspapers, magazines, periodicals, and books, but not including medical databases or court records) that include family medical history;

(5) where the information involved is to be used for genetic monitoring of the biological effects of toxic substances in the workplace, but only if—

(A) the employer, labor organization, or joint labor-management committee provides written notice of the genetic monitoring to the individual;

(B)(i) the individual provides prior, knowing, voluntary, and written authorization; or

(ii) the genetic monitoring is required by Federal or State law;

(C) the individual is informed of individual monitoring results;

(D) THE MONITORING IS IN COMPLIANCE WITH

(i) any Federal genetic monitoring regulations, including any such regulations that may be promulgated by the Secretary of Labor pursuant to the Occupational Safety and Health Act of 1970 (29 U.S.C. 651 et seq.), the Federal Mine Safety and Health Act of 1977 (30 U.S.C. 801 et seq.), or the Atomic Energy Act of 1954 (42 U.S.C. 2011 et seq.); or

(ii) State genetic monitoring regulations, in the case of a State that is implementing genetic monitoring regulations under the authority of the Occupational Safety and Health Act of 1970 (29 U.S.C. 651 et seq.); and

(E) the employer, labor organization, or joint labor-management committee, excluding any licensed health care professional or board certified genetic counselor that is involved in the genetic monitoring program, receives the results of the monitoring only in aggregate terms that do not disclose the identity of specific individuals; or

(6) where the employer conducts DNA analysis for law enforcement purposes as a forensic laboratory or for purposes of human remains identification, and requests or requires genetic information of such employer's apprentices or trainees, but only to the extent that such genetic information is used for analysis of DNA identification markers for quality control to detect sample contamination.

(c) PRESERVATION OF PROTECTIONS. In the case of information to which any of paragraphs (1) through (6) of subsection (b) applies, such information may not be used in violation of paragraph (1), (2), or (3) of subsection (a) or treated or disclosed in a manner that violates section 206.

Sec. 206. *Confidentiality of Genetic Information*

(a) TREATMENT OF INFORMATION AS PART OF CONFIDENTIAL MEDICAL RECORD. — If an employer, employment agency, labor organization, or joint labor-management committee possesses genetic information about an employee or member, such information shall be maintained on separate forms and in separate medical files and be treated as a confidential medical record of the employee or member. An employer, employment agency, labor organization, or joint labor-management committee shall be considered to be in compliance with the maintenance of information requirements of this subsection with respect to genetic information subject to this subsection that is maintained with and treated as a confidential medical record under section 102(d)(3)(B) of the Americans With Disabilities Act (42 U.S.C. 12112(d)(3)(B)).

    (b) LIMITATION ON DISCLOSURE. — An employer, employment agency, labor organization, or joint labor-management committee shall not disclose genetic information concerning an employee or member except —

        (1) to the employee or member of a labor organization (or family member if the family member is receiving the genetic services) at the written request of the employee or member of such organization;

        (2) to an occupational or other health researcher if the research is conducted in compliance with the regulations and protections provided for under part 46 of title 45, Code of Federal Regulations;

        (3) in response to an order of a court, except that —

            (A) the employer, employment agency, labor organization, or joint labor-management committee may disclose only the genetic information expressly authorized by such order; and

            (B) if the court order was secured without the knowledge of the employee or member to whom the information refers, the employer, employment agency, labor organization, or joint labor-management committee shall inform the employee or member of the court order and any genetic information that was disclosed pursuant to such order;

        (4) to government officials who are investigating compliance with this title if the information is relevant to the investigation;

        (5) to the extent that such disclosure is made in connection with the employee's compliance with the certification provisions of section 103 of the Family and Medical Leave Act of 1993 (29 U.S.C. 2613) or such requirements under State family and medical leave laws; or

        (6) to a Federal, State, or local public health agency only with regard to information that is described in section 201(4)(A)(iii) and that concerns a contagious disease that presents an imminent hazard of death or life-threatening illness, and that the employee whose family member or family members is or are the subject of a disclosure under this paragraph is notified of such disclosure.

    (c) RELATIONSHIP TO HIPAA REGULATIONS. — With respect to the regulations promulgated by the Secretary of Health and Human Services under part C of title XI of the Social Security Act (42 U.S.C. 1320d et seq.) and section 264 of the Health Insurance Portability and Accountability Act of 1996 (42 U.S.C. 1320d-2 note), this title does not prohibit a covered entity under such regulations from any use or disclosure of health information that is authorized for the covered entity under such regulations. The previous sentence does not affect the authority of such Secretary to modify such regulations.

Sec. 207. Remedies and Enforcement

(a) EMPLOYEES COVERED BY TITLE VII OF THE CIVIL RIGHTS ACT OF 1964. —

(1) IN GENERAL. The powers, procedures, and remedies provided in sections 705, 706, 707, 709, 710, and 711 of the Civil Rights Act of 1964 (42 U.S.C. 2000e-4 et seq.) to the Commission, the Attorney General, or any person, alleging a violation of title VII of that Act (42 U.S.C. 2000e et seq.) shall be the powers, procedures, and remedies this title provides to the Commission, the Attorney General, or any person, respectively, alleging an unlawful employment practice in violation of this title against an employee described in section 201(2)(A)(i), except as provided in paragraphs (2) and (3).

(2) COSTS AND FEES. The powers, remedies, and procedures provided in subsections (b) and (c) of section 722 of the Revised Statutes of the United States (42 U.S.C. 1988), shall be powers, remedies, and procedures this title provides to the Commission, the Attorney General, or any person, alleging such a practice.

(3) DAMAGES. The powers, remedies, and procedures provided in section 1977A of the Revised Statutes of the United States (42 U.S.C. 1981a), including the limitations contained in subsection (b)(3) of such section 1977A, shall be powers, remedies, and procedures this title provides to the Commission, the Attorney General, or any person, alleging such a practice (not an employment practice specifically excluded from coverage under section 1977A(a)(1) of the Revised Statutes of the United States).

(b) EMPLOYEES COVERED BY GOVERNMENT EMPLOYEE RIGHTS ACT OF 1991.

(1) IN GENERAL. The powers, remedies, and procedures provided in sections 302 and 304 of the Government Employee Rights Act of 1991 (42 U.S.C. 2000e-16b, 2000e-16c) to the Commission, or any person, alleging a violation of section 302(a)(1) of that Act (42 U.S.C. 2000e-16b(a)(1)) shall be the powers, remedies, and procedures this title provides to the Commission, or any person, respectively, alleging an unlawful employment practice in violation of this title against an employee described in section 201(2)(A)(ii), except as provided in paragraphs (2) and (3).

(2) COSTS AND FEES. The powers, remedies, and procedures provided in subsections (b) and (c) of section 722 of the Revised Statutes of the United States (42 U.S.C. 1988), shall be powers, remedies, and procedures this title provides to the Commission, or any person, alleging such a practice.

(3) DAMAGES. The powers, remedies, and procedures provided in section 1977A of the Revised Statutes of the United States (42 U.S.C. 1981a), including the limitations contained in subsection (b)(3) of such section 1977A, shall be powers, remedies, and procedures this title provides to the Commission, or any person, alleging such a practice (not an employment practice specifically excluded from coverage under section 1977A(a)(1) of the Revised Statutes of the United States).

(c) EMPLOYEES COVERED BY CONGRESSIONAL ACCOUNTABILITY ACT OF 1995.

(1) IN GENERAL. The powers, remedies, and procedures provided in the Congressional Accountability Act of 1995 (2 U.S.C. 1301 et seq.) to the Board (as defined in section 101 of that Act (2 U.S.C. 1301)), or any person, alleging a violation of section 201(a)(1) of that Act (42 U.S.C. 1311(a)(1)) shall be the powers, remedies, and procedures this title provides to that Board, or any person, alleging an unlawful employment practice in violation of this title against an employee described in section 201(2)(A)(iii), except as provided in paragraphs (2) and (3).

(2) COSTS AND FEES. The powers, remedies, and procedures provided in subsections (b) and (c) of section 722 of the Revised Statutes of the United States (42 U.S.C. 1988), shall be powers, remedies, and procedures this title provides to that Board, or any person, alleging such a practice.

(3) DAMAGES. The powers, remedies, and procedures provided in section 1977A of the Revised Statutes of the United States (42 U.S.C. 1981a), including the limitations contained in subsection (b)(3) of such section 1977A, shall be powers, remedies, and procedures this title provides to that Board, or any person, alleging such a practice (not an employment practice specifically excluded from coverage under section 1977A(a)(1) of the Revised Statutes of the United States).

(4) OTHER APPLICABLE PROVISIONS. With respect to a claim alleging a practice described in paragraph (1), title III of the Congressional Accountability Act of 1995 (2 U.S.C. 1381 et seq.) shall apply in the same manner as such title applies with respect to a claim alleging a violation of section 201(a)(1) of such Act (2 U.S.C. 1311(a)(1)).

(d) EMPLOYEES COVERED BY CHAPTER 5 OF TITLE 3, UNITED STATES CODE.

(1) IN GENERAL. The powers, remedies, and procedures provided in chapter 5 of title 3, United States Code, to the President, the Commission, the Merit Systems Protection Board, or any person, alleging a violation of section 411(a)(1) of that title, shall be the powers, remedies, and procedures this title provides to the President, the Commission, such Board, or any person, respectively, alleging an unlawful employment practice in violation of this title against an employee described in section 201(2)(A)(iv), except as provided in paragraphs (2) and (3).

(2) COSTS AND FEES. The powers, remedies, and procedures provided in subsections (b) and (c) of section 722 of the Revised Statutes of the United States (42 U.S.C. 1988), shall be powers, remedies, and procedures this title provides to the President, the Commission, such Board, or any person, alleging such a practice.

(3) DAMAGES. The powers, remedies, and procedures provided in section 1977A of the Revised Statutes of the United States (42 U.S.C. 1981a), including the limitations contained in subsection (b)(3) of such section 1977A, shall be powers, remedies, and procedures this title provides to the President, the Commission, such Board, or any person, alleging such a practice (not an employment practice specifically excluded from coverage under section 1977A(a)(1) of the Revised Statutes of the United States).

(e) EMPLOYEES COVERED BY SECTION 717 OF THE CIVIL RIGHTS ACT OF 1964.

(1) IN GENERAL. The powers, remedies, and procedures provided in section 717 of the Civil Rights Act of 1964 (42 U.S.C. 2000e-16) to the Commission, the Attorney General, the Librarian of Congress, or any person, alleging a violation of that section shall be the powers, remedies, and procedures this title provides to the Commission, the Attorney General, the Librarian of Congress, or any person, respectively, alleging an unlawful employment practice in violation of this title against an employee or applicant described in section 201(2)(A)(v), except as provided in paragraphs (2) and (3).

(2) COSTS AND FEES. The powers, remedies, and procedures provided in subsections (b) and (c) of section 722 of the Revised Statutes of the United States (42 U.S.C. 1988), shall be powers, remedies, and procedures this title provides to the Commission, the Attorney General, the Librarian of Congress, or any person, alleging such a practice.

(3) DAMAGES. The powers, remedies, and procedures provided in section 1977A of the Revised Statutes of the United States (42 U.S.C. 1981a), including the limitations contained in subsection (b)(3) of such section 1977A, shall be powers, remedies, and procedures this title provides to the Commission, the Attorney General, the Librarian of Congress, or any person, alleging such a practice (not an employment practice specifically excluded from coverage under section 1977A(a)(1) of the Revised Statutes of the United States).

(f) PROHIBITION AGAINST RETALIATION. No person shall discriminate against any individual because such individual has opposed any act or practice made unlawful by this title or because such individual made a charge, testified, assisted, or participated in any manner in an investigation, proceeding, or hearing under this title. The remedies and procedures otherwise provided for under this section shall be available to aggrieved individuals with respect to violations of this subsection.

(g) DEFINITION. In this section, the term "Commission" means the Equal Employment Opportunity Commission.

Sec. 208. *Disparate Impact*

(a) GENERAL RULE. Notwithstanding any other provision of this Act, "disparate impact", as that term is used in section 703(k) of the Civil Rights Act of 1964 (42 U.S.C. 2000e-2(k)), on the basis of genetic information does not establish a cause of action under this Act.

(b) COMMISSION. On the date that is 6 years after the date of enactment of this Act, there shall be established a commission, to be known as the Genetic Nondiscrimination Study Commission (referred to in this section as the "Commission") to review the developing science of genetics and to make recommendations to Congress regarding whether to provide a disparate impact cause of action under this Act.

(c) MEMBERSHIP.

(1) IN GENERAL. The Commission shall be composed of 8 members, of which —

(A) 1 member shall be appointed by the Majority Leader of the Senate;

(B) 1 member shall be appointed by the Minority Leader of the Senate;

(C) 1 member shall be appointed by the Chairman of the Committee on Health, Education, Labor, and Pensions of the Senate;

(D) 1 member shall be appointed by the ranking minority member of the Committee on Health, Education, Labor, and Pensions of the Senate;

(E) 1 member shall be appointed by the Speaker of the House of Representatives;

(F) 1 member shall be appointed by the Minority Leader of the House of Representatives;

(G) 1 member shall be appointed by the Chairman of the Committee on Education and Labor of the House of Representatives; and

(H) 1 member shall be appointed by the ranking minority member of the Committee on Education and Labor of the House of Representatives.

(2) COMPENSATION AND EXPENSES. The members of the Commission shall not receive compensation for the performance of services for the Commission, but shall be allowed travel expenses, including per diem in lieu of subsistence, at rates authorized for employees of agencies under subchapter I of chapter 57 of title 5, United States Code, while away from their homes or regular places of business in the performance of services for the Commission.

(d) ADMINISTRATIVE PROVISIONS. —

(1) LOCATION. The Commission shall be located in a facility maintained by the Equal Employment Opportunity Commission.

(2) DETAIL OF GOVERNMENT EMPLOYEES. Any Federal Government employee may be detailed to the Commission without reimbursement, and such detail shall be without interruption or loss of civil service status or privilege.

(3) INFORMATION FROM FEDERAL AGENCIES. The Commission may secure directly from any Federal department or agency such information as the Commission considers necessary to carry out the provisions of this section. Upon request of the Commission, the head of such department or agency shall furnish such information to the Commission.

(4) HEARINGS. The Commission may hold such hearings, sit and act at such times and places, take such testimony, and receive such evidence as the Commission considers advisable to carry out the objectives of this section, except that, to the extent possible, the Commission shall use existing data and research.

(5) POSTAL SERVICES. The Commission may use the United States mails in the same manner and under the same conditions as other departments and agencies of the Federal Government.

(e) REPORT. Not later than 1 year after all of the members are appointed to the Commission under subsection (c)(1), the Commission shall submit to Congress a report that summarizes the findings of the Commission and makes such recommendations for legislation as are consistent with this Act.

(f) AUTHORIZATION OF APPROPRIATIONS. There are authorized to be appropriated to the Equal Employment Opportunity Commission such sums as may be necessary to carry out this section.

Sec. 209. Construction

(a) IN GENERAL. Nothing in this title shall be construed to—

(1) limit the rights or protections of an individual under any other Federal or State statute that provides equal or greater protection to an individual than the rights or protections provided for under this title, including the protections of an individual under the Americans with Disabilities Act of 1990 (42 U.S.C. 12101 et seq.) (including coverage afforded to individuals under section 102 of such Act (42 U.S.C. 12112)), or under the Rehabilitation Act of 1973 (29 U.S.C. 701 et seq.);

(2)(A) limit the rights or protections of an individual to bring an action under this title against an employer, employment agency, labor organization, or joint labor-management committee for a violation of this title; or

(B) provide for enforcement of, or penalties for violation of, any requirement or prohibition applicable to any employer, employment agency, labor organization, or joint labor-management committee subject to enforcement for a violation under—

(i) the amendments made by title I of this Act;

(ii)(I) subsection (a) of section 701 of the Employee Retirement Income Security Act of 1974 as such section applies with respect to genetic information pursuant to subsection (b)(1)(B) of such section;

(II) section 702(a)(1)(F) of such Act; or

(III) section 702(b)(1) of such Act as such section applies with respect to genetic information as a health status-related factor;

(iii)(I) subsection (a) of section 2701 of the Public Health Service Act as such section applies with respect to genetic information pursuant to subsection (b)(1)(B) of such section;

(II) section 2702(a)(1)(F) of such Act; or

(III) section 2702(b)(1) of such Act as such section applies with respect to genetic information as a health status-related factor; or

(iv)(I) subsection (a) of section 9801 of the Internal Revenue Code of 1986 as such section applies with respect to genetic information pursuant to subsection (b)(1)(B) of such section;

(II) section 9802(a)(1)(F) of such Act; or

(III) section 9802(b)(1) of such Act as such section applies with respect to genetic information as a health status-related factor;

(3) apply to the Armed Forces Repository of Specimen Samples for the Identification of Remains;

(4) limit or expand the protections, rights, or obligations of employees or employers under applicable workers' compensation laws;

(5) limit the authority of a Federal department or agency to conduct or sponsor occupational or other health research that is conducted in compliance with the regulations contained in part 46 of title 45, Code of Federal Regulations (or any corresponding or similar regulation or rule);

(6) limit the statutory or regulatory authority of the Occupational Safety and Health Administration or the Mine Safety and Health Administration to promulgate or enforce workplace safety and health laws and regulations; or

(7) require any specific benefit for an employee or member or a family member of an employee or member under any group health plan or health insurance issuer offering group health insurance coverage in connection with a group health plan.

(b) GENETIC INFORMATION OF A FETUS OR EMBRYO. Any reference in this title to genetic information concerning an individual or family member of an individual shall—

(1) with respect to such an individual or family member of an individual who is a pregnant woman, include genetic information of any fetus carried by such pregnant woman; and

(2) with respect to an individual or family member utilizing an assisted reproductive technology, include genetic information of any embryo legally held by the individual or family member.

(c) RELATION TO AUTHORITIES UNDER TITLE I. With respect to a group health plan, or a health insurance issuer offering group health insurance coverage in connection with a group health plan, this title does not prohibit any activity of such plan or issuer that is authorized for the plan or issuer under any provision of law referred to in clauses (i) through (iv) of subsection (a)(2)(B).

Sec. 210. *Medical Information That Is Not Genetic Information*

An employer, employment agency, labor organization, or joint labor-management committee shall not be considered to be in violation of this title based on the use, acquisition, or disclosure of medical information that is not genetic information about a manifested disease, disorder, or pathological condition of an employee or member, including a manifested disease, disorder, or pathological condition that has or may have a genetic basis.

Sec. 211. *Regulations*

Not later than 1 year after the date of enactment of this title, the Commission shall issue final regulations to carry out this title.

Sec. 212. *Authorization of Appropriations*

There are authorized to be appropriated such sums as may be necessary to carry out this title (except for section 208).

Sec. 213. *Effective Date*

This title takes effect on the date that is 18 months after the date of enactment of this Act.

Immigration Reform and Control Act

Immigration Reform and Control Act

8 U.S.C. §1324b

§1324b. Unfair Immigration-Related Employment Practices

(a) Prohibition of Discrimination Based on National Origin or Citizenship Status.

(1) General rule. It is unfair immigration-related employment practice for a person or other entity to discriminate against any individual (other than an unauthorized alien) with respect to the hiring, or recruitment or referral for a fee, of the individual for employment or the discharging of the individual from employment

(A) because of such individual's national origin, or

(B) in the case of a protected individual (as defined in paragraph (3)), because of such individual's citizenship status.

(2) Exceptions. Paragraph (1) shall not apply to

(A) a person or other entity that employs three or fewer employees,

(B) a person's or entity's discrimination because of an individual's national origin if the discrimination with respect to that person or entity and that individual is covered under section 703 of the Civil Rights Act of 1964, or

(C) discrimination because of citizenship status which is otherwise required in order to comply with law, regulation, or executive order, or required by Federal, State, or local government contract, or which the Attorney General determines to be essential for an employer to do business with an agency or department of the Federal, State, or local government.

(3) "Protected individual" defined. As used in paragraph (1), the term "protected individual" means an individual who

(A) is a citizen or national of the United States, or

(B) is an alien who is lawfully admitted for permanent residence, is granted the status of an alien lawfully admitted for temporary residence under section 210(1), 210A(a), or 245A(a)(1), is admitted as a refugee under section 207, or is granted asylum under section 208; but does not include (i) an alien who fails to apply for naturalization within six months of the date the alien first becomes eligible (by virtue of period of lawful permanent residence) to apply for naturalization or, if later, within six months after the date of the enactment of this section and (ii) an alien who has applied on a timely basis, but has not been naturalized as a citizen within 2 years after the date of the application, unless the alien can establish that the alien is actively pursuing naturalization, except that time consumed in the Service's processing the application shall not be counted toward the 2-year period.

(4) Additional exception providing right to prefer equally qualified citizens. Notwithstanding any other provision of this section, it is not an unfair immigration-related employment practice for a person or other entity to prefer to hire, recruit, or refer an individual who is a citizen or national of the United States over another individual who is an alien if the two individuals are equally qualified.

(5) Prohibition of intimidation or retaliation. It is also an unfair immigration-related employment practice for a person or other entity to intimidate, threaten, coerce, or retaliate against any individual for the purpose of interfering with any right or privilege secured under this section or because the individual intends to file or has filed a charge or a complaint, testified, assisted, or participated in any manner in an investigation, proceeding, or hearing under section. An individual so intimidated, threatened, coerced, or retaliated against shall be considered, for purposes of subsections (d) and (g), to have been discriminated against.

(6) Treatment of certain documentary practices as employment practices. A person's or other entity's request, for purposes of satisfying the requirements of section 274A(b) [8 U.S.C. §1324A(b)] of this title, for more or different documents than are required under such section or refusing to honor documents tendered that on their face reasonably appear to be genuine shall be treated as an unfair immigration-related employment practice if made for the purpose or with the intent of discriminating against an individual in violation of paragraph (1).

(b) Charges of Violations.

(1) In general. Except as provided in paragraph (2), any person alleging that the person is adversely affected directly by an unfair immigration-related employment practice (or a person on that person's behalf) or an officer of the Service alleging that an unfair immigration-related employment practice has occurred or is occurring may file a charge respecting such practice or violation with the Special Counsel (appointed under subsection (c)). Charges shall be in writing under oath or affirmation and shall contain such information as the Attorney General requires. The Special Counsel by certified mail shall serve a notice of the charge (including the date, place, and circumstances of the alleged unfair immigration-related employment practice) on the person or entity involved within 10 days.

(2) No overlap with EEOC complaints. No charge may be filed respecting an unfair immigration-related employment practice described in subsection

(a)(1)(A) if a charge with respect to that practice based on the same set of facts has been filed with the Equal Employment Opportunity Commission under title VII of the Civil Rights Act of 1964, unless the charge is dismissed as being outside the scope of such title. No charge respecting an employment practice may be filed with the Equal Employment Opportunity Commission under such title if a charge with respect to such practice based on the same set of facts has been filed under this subsection, unless the charge is dismissed under this section as being outside the scope of this section.

(c) Special Counsel.

(1) Appointment. The President shall appoint, by and with the advice and consent of the Senate, a Special Counsel for Immigration-Related Unfair Employment Practices (hereinafter in this section referred to as the "Special Counsel") within the Department of Justice to serve for a term of four years. In the case of a vacancy in the office of the Special Counsel the President may designate the officer or employee who shall act as Special Counsel during such vacancy.

(2) Duties. The Special Counsel shall be responsible for investigation of charges and issuance of complaints under this section and in respect of the prosecution of all such complaints before administrative law judges and the exercise of certain functions under subsection (j)(1).

(3) Compensation. The Special Counsel is entitled to receive compensation at a rate not to exceed the rate now or hereafter provided for grade GS-17 of the General Schedule, under section 5332 of title 5, United States Code.

(4) Regional offices. The Special Counsel, in accordance with regulations of the Attorney General, shall establish such regional offices as may be necessary to carry out his duties.

(d) Investigation of Charges.

(1) By special counsel. The Special Counsel shall investigate each charge received and, within 120 days of the date of the receipt of the charge, determine whether or not there is reasonable cause to believe that the charge is true and whether or not to bring a complaint with respect to the charge before an administrative law judge. The Special Counsel may, on his own initiative, conduct investigations respecting unfair immigration-related employment practices and, based on such an investigation and subject to paragraph (3), file a complaint before such a judge.

(2) Private actions. If the Special Counsel, after receiving such a charge respecting an unfair immigration-related employment practice which alleges knowing and intentional discriminatory activity or a pattern or practice of discriminatory activity, has not filed a complaint before an administrative law judge with respect to such charge within such 120-day period, the Special Counsel shall notify the person making the charge of the determination not to file such a complaint during such period and the person making the charge may (subject to paragraph (3)) file a complaint directly before such a judge within 90 days after the date of receipt of the notice. The Special Counsel's failure to file such a complaint within such 120-day period shall not

affect the right of the Special Counsel to investigate the charge or to bring a complaint before an administrative judge during such 90-day period.

(3) Time limitations on complaints. No complaint may be filed respecting any unfair immigration-related employment practice occurring more than 180 days prior to the date of the filing of the charge with the Special Counsel. This subparagraph shall not prevent the subsequent amending of a charge or complaint under subsection (e)(1) of this section.

(e) Hearings.

(1) Notice. Whenever a complaint is made that a person or entity has engaged in or is engaging in any such unfair immigration-related employment practice, an administrative law judge shall have power to issue and cause to be served upon such person or entity a copy of the complaint and a notice of hearing before the judge at a place therein fixed, not less than five days after the serving of the complaint. Any such complaint may be amended by the judge conducting the hearing, upon the motion of the party filing the complaint, in the judge's discretion at any time prior to the issuance of an order based thereon. The person or entity so complained of shall have the right to file an answer to the original or amended complaint and to appear in person or otherwise and give testimony at the place and time fixed in the complaint.

(2) Judges hearing cases. Hearings on complaints under this subsection shall be considered before administrative law judges who are specially designated by the Attorney General as having special training respecting employment discrimination and, to the extent practicable, before such judges who only consider cases under this section.

(3) Complainant as party. Any person filing a charge with the Special Counsel respecting an unfair immigration-related employment practice shall be considered a party to any complaint before an administrative law judge respecting such practice and any subsequent appeal respecting that complaint. In the discretion of the judge conducting the hearing, any other person may be allowed to intervene in the proceeding and to present testimony.

(f) Testimony and Authority of Hearing Officers.

(1) Testimony. The testimony taken by the administrative law judge shall be reduced to writing. Thereafter, the judge, in his discretion, upon notice may provide for the taking of further testimony or hear argument.

(2) Authority of administrative law judges. In conducting investigations and hearings under this subsection and in accordance with regulations of the Attorney General, the Special Counsel and administrative law judges shall have reasonable access to examine evidence of any person or entity being investigated. The administrative law judges by subpoena may compel the attendance of witnesses and the production of evidence at any designated place or hearing. In case of contumacy or refusal to obey a subpoena lawfully issued under this paragraph and upon application of the administrative law judge, an appropriate district court of the United States may issue an order requiring compliance with such subpoena and any failure to obey such order may be punished by such court as a contempt thereof.

(g) Determinations.

(1) Order. The administrative law judge shall issue and cause to be served on the parties to the proceeding an order, which shall be final unless appealed as provided under subsection (i).

(2) Orders finding violations.

(A) In general. If, upon the preponderance of the evidence, an administrative law judge determines that any person or entity named in the complaint has engaged in or is engaging in any such unfair immigration-related employment practice, then the judge shall state his findings of fact and shall issue and cause to be served on such person or entity an order which requires such person or entity to cease and desist from such unfair immigration-related employment practice.

(B) Contents of order. Such an order also may require the person or entity

(i) to comply with the requirements of section 274A(b) [8 U.S.C. §1324a(b)] with respect to individuals hired (or recruited or referred for employment for a fee) during a period of up to three years;

(ii) to retain for the period referred to in clause (i) and only for purposes consistent with section 274A(b)(5), the name and address of each individual who applies, in person or in writing, for hiring of an existing position, or for recruiting or referring for a fee, for employment in the United States;

(iii) to hire individuals directly and adversely affected, with or without back pay;

(iv)(I) except as provided in subclauses (III) through (IV), to pay a civil penalty of not less than $250 and not more than $2,000 for each individual discriminated against,

(II) except as provided in subclauses (III) and (IV), in the case of a person or entity previously subject to a single order under this paragraph, to pay a civil penalty of not less than $2,000 and not more than $5,000 for each individual discriminated against,

(III) except as provided in subclause (IV), in the case of a person or entity previously subject to more than one order under this paragraph, to pay a civil penalty of not less than $3,000 and not more than $10,000 for each individual discriminated against, and

(IV) in the case of an unfair immigration-related employment practice described in subsection (a)(6), to pay a civil penalty of not less than $100 and not more than $1,000 for each individual discriminated against;

(v) to post notices to employees about their rights under this section and employers' obligations under section 274A [8 U.S.C. §1324a];

(vi) to educate all personnel involved in hiring and complying with this section or section 274A about the requirements of this section or such section;

(vii) to remove (in an appropriate case) a false performance review or false warning from an employees personnel file; and

(viii) to lift (in an appropriate case) any restrictions on any employee's assignments, work shifts, or movements.

(C) Limitation on back pay remedy. In providing a remedy under subparagraph (B)(iii), back pay liability shall not accrue from a date more than two years prior to the date of the filing of a charge with an administrative law judge. Interim earnings or amounts earnable with reasonable diligence by the individual or individuals discriminated against shall operate to reduce the back pay otherwise allowable under such subparagraph. No order shall require the hiring of an individual as an employee or the payment to an individual of any back pay, if the individual was refused employment for any reason other than discrimination on account of national origin or citizenship status.

(D) Treatment of distinct entities. In applying this subsection in the case of a person or entity composed of distinct, physically separate subdivisions each of which provides separately for the hiring, recruiting, or referring for employment, without reference to the practices of, and not under the control of or common control with, another subdivision, each such subdivision shall be considered a separate person or entity.

(3) Orders not finding violations. If upon the preponderance of the evidence an administrative law judge determines that the person or entity named in the complaint has not engaged and is not engaging in any such unfair immigration-related employment practice, then the judge shall state his findings of fact and shall issue an order dismissing the complaint.

(h) Awarding of Attorney's Fees. In any complaint respecting an unfair immigration-related employment practice, an administrative law judge, in the judge's discretion, may allow a prevailing party, other than the United States, a reasonable attorney's fee, if the losing party's argument is without reasonable foundation in law and fact.

(i) Review of Final Orders.

(1) In general. Not later than 60 days after the entry of such final order, any person aggrieved by such final order may seek a review of such order in the United States court of appeals for the circuit in which the violation is alleged to have occurred or in which the employer resides or transacts business.

(2) Further review. Upon the filing of the record with the court, the jurisdiction of the court shall be exclusive and its judgment shall be final, except that the same shall be subject to review by the Supreme Court of the United States upon writ of certiorari or certification as provided in section 1254 of title 28, United States Code.

(j) Court Enforcement of Administrative Orders.

(1) In general. If an order of the agency is not appealed under subsection (i)(1), the Special Counsel (or, if the Special Counsel fails to act, the person filing the charge) may petition the United States district court for the district in which a violation of the order is alleged to have occurred, or in which the

respondent resides or transacts business, for the enforcement of the order of the administrative law judge, by filing in such court a written petition praying that such order be enforced.

(2) Court enforcement order. Upon the filing of such petition, the court shall have jurisdiction to make and enter a decree enforcing the order of the administrative law judge. In such a proceeding, the order of the administrative law judge shall not be subject to review.

(3) Enforcement decree in original review. If, upon appeal of an order under subsection (i)(1), the United States court of appeals does not reverse such order, such court shall have the jurisdiction to make and enter a decree enforcing the order of the administrative law judge.

(4) Awarding of attorney's fees. In any judicial proceeding under subsection (i) or this subsection, the court, in its discretion, may allow a prevailing party, other than the United States, a reasonable attorney's fee a part of costs but only if the losing party's argument is without reasonable foundation in law and fact.

(k) Termination Dates.

(1) This section shall not apply to discrimination in hiring, recruiting, referring, or discharging of individuals occurring after the date of any termination of the provisions of section 274A [8 U.S.C. §1324a], under subsection (1) of that section.

(2) The provisions of this section shall terminate 30 calendar days after receipt of the last report required to be transmitted under section 274A(j) if

(A) the Comptroller General determines, and so reports in such report that

(i) no significant discrimination has resulted, against citizens or nationals of the United States or against any eligible workers seeking employment, from the implementation of section 274A, or

(ii) such section has created an unreasonable burden on employers hiring such workers; and

(B) there has been enacted, within such period of 30 calendar days, a joint resolution stating in substance that the Congress approves the findings of the Comptroller General contained in such report. . . . *

---

* [Editor's Note: Public Law No. 99-603, which enacted these provisions, also provided in §101(b):

(b) No effect on EEOC authority. — Except as may be specifically provided in this section, nothing in this section shall be construed to restrict the authority of the Equal Employment Opportunity Commission to investigate allegations, in writing and under oath or affirmation, of unlawful employment practices, as provided in section 706 of the Civil Rights Act of 1964 or any other authority provided therein.]

Lilly Ledbetter Fair Pay Act of 2009

Pub. L. No. 111-2, 123 Stat. 5

[Editors' Note: The Lilly Ledbetter Fair Pay Act of 2009 amended a number of statutes, most notably Title VII and the ADEA. These amendments have been incorporated in the relevant statutes as they are reproduced in the Supplement. The Fair Pay Act, however, is reproduced here for ease of reference.]

Be it enacted by the Senate and House of Representatives of the United States of America in Congress assembled,

Sec. 1. Short Title

This Act may be cited as the "Lilly Ledbetter Fair Pay Act of 2009".

Sec. 2. Findings

Congress finds the following:

(1) The Supreme Court in *Ledbetter v. Goodyear Tire & Rubber Co., 550 U.S. 618 (2007),* significantly impairs statutory protections against discrimination in compensation that Congress established and that have been bedrock principles of American law for decades. The Ledbetter decision undermines those statutory protections by unduly restricting the time period in which victims of discrimination can challenge and recover for discriminatory compensation decisions or other practices, contrary to the intent of Congress.

(2) The limitation imposed by the Court on the filing of discriminatory compensation claims ignores the reality of wage discrimination and is at odds with the robust application of the civil rights laws that Congress intended.

(3) With regard to any charge of discrimination under any law, nothing in this Act is intended to preclude or limit an aggrieved person's right to introduce evidence of an unlawful employment practice that has occurred outside the time for filing a charge of discrimination.

(4) Nothing in this Act is intended to change current law treatment of when pension distributions are considered paid.

Sec. 3. Discrimination in Compensation Because of Race, Color, Religion, Sex, or National Origin

Section 706(e) of the Civil Rights Act of 1964 (*42 U.S.C. 2000e-5(e)*) is amended by adding at the end the following:

> "(3)(A) For purposes of this section, an unlawful employment practice occurs, with respect to discrimination in compensation in violation of this title, when a discriminatory compensation decision or other practice is adopted, when an individual becomes subject to a discriminatory compensation decision or other practice, or when an individual is affected by application of a discriminatory compensation decision or other practice, including each time wages, benefits, or other compensation is paid, resulting in whole or in part from such a decision or other practice.
>
> "(B) In addition to any relief authorized by section 1977A of the Revised Statutes (*42 U.S.C. 1981a*), liability may accrue and an aggrieved person may obtain relief as provided in subsection (g)(1), including recovery of back pay for up to two years preceding the filing of the charge, where the unlawful employment practices that have occurred during the charge filing period are similar or related to unlawful employment practices with regard to discrimination in compensation that occurred outside the time for filing a charge.".

Sec. 4. Discrimination in Compensation Because of Age

Section 7(d) of the Age Discrimination in Employment Act of 1967 (*29 U.S.C. 626(d)*) is amended—
> (1) in the first sentence—
>> (A) by redesignating paragraphs (1) and (2) as subparagraphs (A) and (B), respectively; and
>> (B) by striking "(d)" and inserting "(d)(1)";
> (2) in the third sentence, by striking "Upon" and inserting the following: "(2) Upon"; and
> (3) by adding at the end the following:

> "(3) For purposes of this section, an unlawful practice occurs, with respect to discrimination in compensation in violation of this Act, when a discriminatory compensation decision or other practice is adopted, when a person becomes subject to a discriminatory compensation decision or other practice, or when a person is affected by application of a discriminatory compensation decision or other practice, including each time wages, benefits, or other compensation is paid, resulting in whole or in part from such a decision or other practice.".

Sec. 5. Application to Other Laws

(a) Americans With Disabilities Act of 1990.—The amendments made by section 3 shall apply to claims of discrimination in compensation brought under title I and section 503 of the Americans with Disabilities Act of 1990 (*42 U.S.C. 12111* et seq., *12203*), pursuant to section 107(a) of such Act (*42 U.S.C. 12117(a)*), which adopts the powers, remedies, and procedures set forth in section 706 of the Civil Rights Act of 1964 (*42 U.S.C. 2000e-5*).

(b) Rehabilitation Act of 1973.—The amendments made by section 3 shall apply to claims of discrimination in compensation brought under sections 501 and 504 of the Rehabilitation Act of 1973 (*29 U.S.C. 791, 794*), pursuant to—

(1) sections 501(g) and 504(d) of such Act (*29 U.S.C. 791(g), 794(d)*), respectively, which adopt the standards applied under title I of the Americans with Disabilities Act of 1990 for determining whether a violation has occurred in a complaint alleging employment discrimination; and

(2) paragraphs (1) and (2) of section 505(a) of such Act (*29 U.S.C. 794a(a)*) (as amended by subsection (c)).

(c) Conforming Amendments.—

(1) Rehabilitation act of 1973.—Section 505(a) of the Rehabilitation Act of 1973 (*29 U.S.C. 794a(a)*) is amended—

(A) in paragraph (1), by inserting after "(*42 U.S.C. 2000e-5 (f)* through (k))" the following: "(and the application of section 706(e)(3) (*42 U.S.C. 2000e-5(e)(3)*)) to claims of discrimination in compensation)"; and

(B) in paragraph (2), by inserting after "1964" the following: "(*42 U.S.C. 2000d* et seq.) (and in subsection (e)(3) of section 706 of such Act (*42 U.S.C. 2000e-5*), applied to claims of discrimination in compensation)".

(2) Civil rights act of 1964.—Section 717 of the Civil Rights Act of 1964 (*42 U.S.C. 2000e-16*) is amended by adding at the end the following:

"(f) Section 706(e)(3) shall apply to complaints of discrimination in compensation under this section.".

(3) Age discrimination in employment act of 1967.—Section 15(f) of the Age Discrimination in Employment Act of 1967 (*29 U.S.C. 633a(f)*) is amended by striking "of section" and inserting "of sections 7(d)(3) and".

Sec. 6. *Effective Date*

This Act, and the amendments made by this Act, take effect as if enacted on May 28, 2007 and apply to all claims of discrimination in compensation under title VII of the Civil Rights Act of 1964 (*42 U.S.C. 2000e* et seq.), the Age Discrimination in Employment Act of 1967 (*29 U.S.C. 621* et seq.), title I and section 503 of the Americans with Disabilities Act of 1990, and sections 501 and 504 of the Rehabilitation Act of 1973, that are pending on or after that date.

National Labor Relations Act

29 U.S.C. §§151-169

§151. *Findings and Declaration of Policy*

The denial by some employers of the right of employees to organize and the refusal by some employees to accept the procedure of collective bargaining lead to strikes and other forms of industrial strife or unrest, which have the intent or the necessary effect of burdening or obstructing commerce by (a) impairing the efficiency, safety, or operation of the instrumentalities of commerce; (b) occurring in the current of commerce; (c) materially affecting, restraining, or controlling the flow of raw materials or manufactured or processed goods from or into the channels of commerce, or the prices of such materials or goods in commerce; or (d) causing diminution of employment and wages in such volume as substantially to impair or disrupt the market for goods flowing from or into the channels of commerce.

The inequality of bargaining power between employees who do not possess full freedom of association or actual liberty of contract, and employers who are organized in the corporate or other forms of ownership association substantially burdens and affects the flow of commerce, and tends to aggravate recurrent business depressions, by depressing wage rates and the purchasing power of wage earners in industry and by preventing the stabilization of competitive wage rates and working conditions within and between industries.

Experience has proved that protection of law of the right of employees to organize and bargain collectively safeguards commerce from injury, impairment, or interruption, and promotes the flow of commerce by removing certain recognized sources of industrial strife and unrest, by encouraging practices fundamental to the friendly adjustment of industrial disputes arising out of differences as to wages, hours, or other working conditions, and by restoring equality of bargaining power between employers and employees.

Experience has further demonstrated that certain practices by some labor organizations, their offices, and members have the intent or the necessary effect of burdening or obstructing commerce by preventing the free flow of goods in such commerce through strikes and other forms of industrial unrest or through concerted activities which impair the interest of the public in the free flow of such commerce. The elimination of such practices is a necessary condition to the assurance of the rights herein guaranteed.

It is hereby declared to be the policy of the United States to eliminate the causes of certain substantial obstructions to the free flow of commerce and to mitigate and eliminate these obstructions when they have occurred by encouraging the practice and procedure of collective bargaining and by protecting the exercise by workers of full freedom of association, self-organization, and designation of representatives of their own choosing, for the purpose of negotiating the terms and conditions of their employment or other mutual aid or protection.

§152. Definitions

When used in this subchapter

(1) The term "person" includes one or more individuals, labor organizations, partnerships, associations, corporations, legal representatives, trustees, trustees in cases under Title 11, or receivers.

(2) The term "employer" includes any person acting as an agent of an employer, directly or indirectly, but shall not include the United States or any wholly owned Government corporation, or any Federal Reserve Bank, or any State or political subdivision thereof, or any person subject to the Railway Labor Act [45 U.S.C.A. §151 et seq.], as amended from time to time, or any labor organization (other than when acting as an employer), or anyone acting in the capacity of officer or agent of such labor organization.

(3) The term "employee" shall include any employer, and shall not be limited to the employees of a particular employer, unless this subchapter explicitly states otherwise, and shall include any individual whose work has ceased as a consequence of, or in connection with, any current labor dispute or because of any unfair labor practice, and who has not obtained any other regular and substantially equivalent employment, but shall not include any individual employed as an agricultural laborer, or in the domestic service of any family or person at his home, or any individual employed by his parent or spouse, or any individual employed as a supervisor, or any individual employed by an employer subject to the Railway Labor Act, as amended from time to time, or by any other person who is not an employer as herein defined.

(4) The term "representatives" includes any individual or labor organization.

(5) The term "labor organization" means any organization of any kind, or any agency or employee representation committee or plan, in which employees participate and which exists for the purpose, in whole or in part, of dealing with employers concerning grievances, labor disputes, wages, rates of pay, hours of employment, or conditions of work.

(6) The term "commerce" means trade, tariff, commerce, transportation, or communication among the several States, or between the District of

Columbia or any Territory of the United States and any State or other Territory, or between any foreign country and any State, Territory, or the District of Columbia, or within the District of Columbia or any Territory, or between points in the same State but through any other State or any Territory or the District of Columbia or any foreign country.

(7) The term "affecting commerce" means in commerce, or burdening or obstructing commerce or the free flow of commerce, or having led or tending to lead to a labor dispute burdening or obstructing commerce or the free flow of commerce.

(8) The term "unfair labor practice" means any unfair labor practice listed in section 158 of this title.

(9) The term "labor dispute" includes any controversy concerning terms, tenure or conditions of employment, or concerning the association or representation of persons in negotiating, fixing, maintaining, changing, or seeking to arrange terms or conditions of employment, regardless of whether the disputants stand in the proximate relation of employer and employee.

(10) The term "National Labor Relations Board" means the National Labor Relations Board provided for in section 153 of this title.

(11) The term "supervisor" means any individual having authority, in the interest of the employer, to hire, transfer, suspend, lay off, recall, promote, discharge, assign, reward, or discipline other employees, or responsibly to direct them, or to adjust their grievances, or effectively to recommend such action, if in connection with the foregoing the exercise of such authority is not of a merely routine or clerical nature, but requires the use of independent judgment.

(12) The term "professional employee" means

(A) any employee engaged in work (i) predominately intellectual and varied in character as opposed to routine mental, manual, mechanical, or physical work; (ii) involving the consistent exercise of discretion and judgment in its performance; (iii) of such a character that the output produced or the result accomplished cannot be standardized in relation to a given period of time; (iv) requiring knowledge of an advanced type in a field of science or learning customarily acquired by a prolonged course of specialized intellectual instruction and study in an institution of higher learning or a hospital, as distinguished from a general academic education or from an apprenticeship or from training in the performance of routine mental, manual, or physical processes; or

(B) any employee, who (i) has completed the courses of specialized intellectual instruction and study described in clause (iv) of paragraph (A), and (ii) is performing related work under the supervision of a professional person to qualify himself to become a professional employee as defined in paragraph (A).

(13) In determining whether any person is acting as an "agent" of another person so as to make such other person responsible for his acts, the question of whether the specific acts performed were actually authorized or subsequently ratified shall not be controlling.

(14) The term "health care institution" shall include any hospital, convalescent hospital, health maintenance organization, health clinic, nursing home, extended care facility, or other institution devoted to the care of sick, infirm, or aged person.

§153. National Labor Relations Board

(a) Creation, composition, appointment, and tenure; Chairman; removal of members. The National Labor Relations Board (hereinafter called the "Board") created by this subchapter prior to its amendment by the Labor Management Relations Act, 1947, is continued as an agency of the United States, except that the Board shall consist of five instead of three members, appointed by the President by and with the advice and consent of the Senate. Of the two additional members so provided for, one shall be appointed for a term of five years and the other for a term of two years. Their successors, and the successors of the other members, shall be appointed for terms of five years each, excepting that any individual chosen to fill a vacancy shall be appointed only for the unexpired term of the member whom he shall succeed. The President shall designate one member to serve as Chairman of the Board. Any member of the Board may be removed by the President, upon notice and hearing, for neglect of duty or malfeasance in office, but for no other cause.

(b) Delegation of powers to members and regional directors; review and stay of actions of regional directors; quorum; seal. The Board is authorized to delegate to any group of three or more members any or all of the powers which it may itself exercise. The Board is also authorized to delegate to its regional directors its powers under section 159 of this title to determine the unit appropriate for the purpose of collective bargaining, to investigate and provide for hearings, and determine whether a question of representation exists, and to direct an election or take a secret ballot under subsection (c) or (e) of section 159 of this title and certify the results thereof, except that upon the filing of a request therefor with the Board by any interested person, the Board may review any action of a regional director delegated to him under this paragraph, but such a review shall not, unless specifically ordered by the Board, operate as a stay of any action taken by the regional director. A vacancy in the Board shall not impair the right of the remaining members to exercise all of the powers of the Board, and three members of the Board shall, at all times, constitute a quorum of the Board, except that two members shall constitute a quorum of any group designated pursuant to the first sentence hereof. The Board shall have an official seal which shall be judicially noticed.

(c) Annual reports to Congress and the President. The Board shall at the close of each fiscal year make a report in writing to Congress and to the President summarizing significant case activities and operations for that fiscal year.

(d) General Counsel; appointment and tenure; powers and duties; vacancy. There shall be a General Counsel of the Board who shall be appointed by the President, by and with the advice and consent of the Senate, for a term of four years. The General Counsel of the Board shall exercise general supervision over all attorneys employed by the Board (other than administrative law judges and legal assistants to Board members) and over the officers and employees in the regional offices. He shall have final authority, on behalf of the Board, in respect of the investigation of charges and issuance of complaints under section 160 of this title, and in respect of the prosecution of such complaints before the Board, and shall have such other duties as the Board may prescribe or as may be provided by law. In case of a vacancy in the office of the General Counsel the President is authorized to designate the officer or employee who shall act as General Counsel during such vacancy, but no person or persons so designated shall so act (1) for more than forty days when the Congress is in session unless a nomination to fill such vacancy shall have been submitted to the Senate, or (2) after the adjournment sine die of the session of the Senate in which such nomination was submitted.

§154. National Labor Relations Board; Eligibility for Reappointment; Officers and Employees; Payment of Expenses

(a) Each member of the Board and the General Council of the Board shall be eligible for reappointment, and shall not engage in any other business, vocation, or employment. The Board shall appoint an executive secretary, and such attorneys, examiners, and regional directors, and such other employees as it may from time to time find necessary for the proper performance of its duties. The Board may not employ any attorneys for the purpose of reviewing transcripts of hearings or preparing drafts of opinions except that any attorney employed for assignment as a legal assistant to any Board member may for such Board member review such transcripts and prepare such drafts. No administrative law judge's report shall be reviewed, either before or after its publication, by any person other than a member of the Board or his legal assistant and no administrative law judge shall advise or consult with the Board with respect to exceptions taken to his findings, rulings, or recommendations. The Board may establish or utilize such regional, local, or other agencies, and utilize such voluntary and uncompensated services, as may from time to time be needed. Attorneys appointed under this section may, at the direction of the Board, appear for and represent the Board in any case in court. Nothing in this subchapter shall be construed to authorize the Board to appoint individuals for the purpose of conciliation or mediation, or for economic analysis.

(b) All of the expenses of the Board, including all necessary traveling and subsistence expenses outside the District of Columbia incurred by the members or employees of the Board under its orders, shall be allowed and paid on the presentation of itemized vouchers therefor approved by the Board or by any individual it designates for that purpose.

§155. National Labor Relations Board; Principal Office, Conducting Inquiries Throughout Country; Participation in Decisions or Inquiries Conducted by Member

The principal office of the Board shall be in the District of Columbia, but it may meet and exercise any or all of its powers at any other place. The Board may, by one or more of its members or by such agents or agencies as it may designate, prosecute any inquiry necessary to its functions in any part of the United States.

A member who participates in such an inquiry shall not be disqualified from subsequently participating in a decision of the Board in the same case.

§156. National Labor Relations Board; Rules and Regulations

The Board shall have authority from time to time to make, amend, and rescind, in the manner prescribed by the Administrative Procedure Act, such rules and regulations as may be necessary to carry out the provisions of this subchapter.

§157. Right of Employees as to Organization, Collective Bargaining, etc.

Employees shall have the right to self-organization, to form, join, or assist labor organizations, to bargain collectively through representatives of their own choosing, and to engage in other concerted activities for the purpose of collective bargaining or other mutual aid or protection, and shall also have the right to refrain from any or all of such activities except to the extent that such right may be affected by an agreement requiring membership in a labor organization as a condition of employment as authorized in section 158(a)(3) of this title.

§158. Unfair Labor Practices

(a) Unfair labor practices by employer. It shall be an unfair labor practice for an employer

(1) to interfere with, restrain, or coerce employees in the exercise of the rights guaranteed in section 157 of this title;

(2) to dominate or interfere with the formation or administration of any labor organization or contribute financial or other support to it: Provided, That subject to rules and regulations made and published by the Board pursuant to section 156 of this title, an employer shall not be prohibited from permitting employees to confer with him during working hours without loss of time or pay;

(3) by discrimination in regard to hire or tenure of employment or any term or condition of employment to encourage or discourage membership in any labor organization: Provided, That nothing in this subchapter, or in any other statute of the United States, shall preclude an employer from making an agreement with a labor organization (not established, maintained, or assisted by any action defined in this subsection as an unfair labor practice) to require as a condition of employment membership therein on or after the thirtieth day following the beginning of such employment or the effective date of such agreement, whichever is the later, (i) if such labor organization is the representative of the employees as provided in section 159(a) of this title, in the appropriate collective-bargaining unit covered by such agreement when made, and (ii) unless following an election held as provided in section 159(e) of this title within one year preceding the effective date of such agreement, the Board shall have certified that at least a majority of the employees eligible to vote in such election have voted to rescind the authority of such labor organization to make such an agreement: Provided further,

That no employer shall justify any discrimination against an employee for nonmembership in a labor organization (A) if he has reasonable grounds for believing that such membership was not available to the employee on the same terms and conditions generally applicable to other members, or (B) if he has reasonable grounds for believing that membership was denied or terminated for reasons other than the failure of the employee to tender the periodic dues and the initiation fees uniformly required as a condition of acquiring or retaining membership.

(4) to discharge or otherwise discriminate against an employee because he has filed charges or given testimony under this subchapter.

(5) to refuse to bargain collectively with the representatives of his employees, subject to the provisions of section 159(a) of this title.

(b) Unfair labor practices by labor organization. It shall be an unfair labor practice for a labor organization or its agents

(1) to restrain or coerce (A) employees in the exercise of the rights guaranteed in section 157 of this title: Provided, That this paragraph shall not impair the right of a labor organization to prescribe its own rules with respect to the acquisition or retention of membership therein; or (B) an employer in the selection of his representatives for the purposes of collective bargaining or the adjustment of grievances;

(2) to cause or attempt to cause an employer to discriminate against an employee in violation of subsection (a)(3) of this section or to discriminate against an employee with respect to whom membership in such organization has been denied or terminated on some ground other than his failure to tender the periodic dues and the initiation fees uniformly required as a condition of acquiring or retaining membership;

(3) to refuse to bargain collectively with an employer, provided it is the representative of his employees subject to the provisions of section 159(a) of this title;

(4)(i) to engage in, or to induce or encourage any individual employed by any person engaged in commerce or in an industry affecting commerce to engage in, a strike or a refusal in the course of his employment to use, manufacture, process, transport, or otherwise handle or work on any goods, articles, materials, or commodities or to perform any services; or (ii) to threaten, coerce, or restrain any person engaged in commerce or in an industry affecting commerce, where in either case an object thereof is

(A) forcing or requiring any employer or self-employed person to join any labor or employer organization or to enter into any agreement which is prohibited by subsection (e) of this section;

(B) forcing or requiring any person to cease using, selling, handling, transporting, or otherwise dealing in the products of any other producer, processor, or manufacturer, or to cease doing business with any other person, or forcing or requiring any other employer to recognize or bargain with a labor organization as the representative of his employees unless such labor organization has been certified as the representative of such employees under the provisions of section 159 of this title: Provided,

That nothing contained in this clause (B) shall be construed to make unlawful, where not otherwise unlawful, any primary strike or primary picketing;

(C) forcing or requiring any employer to recognize or bargain with a particular labor organization as the representative of his employees if another labor organization has been certified as the representative of such employees under the provisions of section 159 of this title;

(D) forcing or requiring any employer to assign particular work to employees in a particular labor organization or in a particular trade, craft, or class rather than to employees in another labor organization or in another trade, craft, or class, unless such employer is failing to conform to an order or certification of the Board determining the bargaining representative for employees performing such work: Provided, That nothing contained in this subsection shall be construed to make unlawful a refusal by any person to enter upon the premises of any employer (other than his own employer), if the employees of such employer are engaged in a strike ratified or approved by a representative of such employees whom such employer is required to recognize under this subchapter: Provided further, That for the purposes of this paragraph (4) only, nothing contained in such paragraph shall be construed to prohibit publicity, other than picketing, for the purpose of truthfully advising the public, including consumers and members of a labor organization, that a product or products are produced by an employer with whom the labor organization has a primary dispute and are distributed by another employer, as long as such publicity does not have an effect of inducing any individual employed by any person other than the primary employer in the course of his employment to refuse to pick up, deliver, or transport any goods, or not to perform any services, at the establishment of the employer engaged in such distribution;

(5) to require of employees covered by an agreement authorized under subsection (a)(3) of this section the payment, as a condition precedent to becoming a member of such organization, of a fee in an amount which the Board finds excessive or discriminatory under all the circumstances. In making such a finding, the Board shall consider, among other relevant factors, the practices and customs of labor organizations in the particular industry, and the wages currently paid to the employees affected;

(6) to cause or attempt to cause an employer to pay or deliver or agree to pay or deliver any money or other thing of value, in the nature of an exaction, for services which are not performed or not to be performed; and

(7) to picket or cause to be picketed, or threaten to picket or cause to be picketed, any employer where an object thereof is forcing or requiring an employer to recognize or bargain with a labor organization as the representative of his employees, or forcing or requiring the employees of an employer to accept or select such labor organization as their collective bargaining representative, unless such labor organization is currently certified as the representative of such employees:

(A) where the employer has lawfully recognized in accordance with this subchapter any other labor organization and a question concerning representation may not appropriately be raised under section 159(c) of this title.

(B) where within the preceding twelve months a valid election under section 159(c) of this title has been conducted, or

(C) where such picketing has been conducted without a petition under section 159(c) of this title being filed within a reasonable period of time not to exceed thirty days from the commencement of such picketing: Provided, That when such a petition has been filed the Board shall forthwith, without regard to the provisions of section 159(c)(1) of this title or the absence of a showing of a substantial interest on the part of the labor organization, direct an election in such unit as the Board finds to be appropriate and shall certify the results thereof: Provided further, That nothing in this subparagraph (C) shall be construed to prohibit any picketing or other publicity for the purpose of truthfully advising the public (including consumers) that an employer does not employ members of, or have a contact with, a labor organization, unless an effect of such picketing is to induce any individual employed by any other person in the course of his employment, not to pickup, deliver or transport any goods or not to perform any services.

Nothing in this paragraph (7) shall be construed to permit any act which should otherwise be an unfair labor practice under this subsection.

(c) Expression of views without threat of reprisal or force or promise of benefit. The expressing of any views, argument, or opinion, or the dissemination thereof, whether in written, printed, graphic, or visual form, shall not constitute or be evidence of an unfair labor practice under any of the provisions of this subchapter, if such expression contains no threat of reprisal or force or promise of benefit.

(d) Obligation to bargain collectively. For the purposes of this section, to bargain collectively is the performance of the mutual obligation of the employer and the representative of the employees to meet at reasonable times and confer in good faith with respect to wages, hours, and other terms and conditions of employment, or the negotiation of an agreement, or any question arising thereunder, and the execution of a written contract incorporating any agreement reached if requested by either party, but such obligation does not compel either party to agree to a proposal or require the making of a concession: Provided, That where there is in effect a collective-bargaining contract covering employees in an industry affecting commerce, the duty to bargain collectively shall also mean that no party to such contract shall terminate or modify such contract, unless the party desiring such termination or modification

(1) serves a written notice upon the other party to the contract of the proposed termination or modification sixty days prior to the expiration date thereof, or in the event such contract contains no expiration date, sixty days prior to the time it is proposed to make such termination or modification;

(2) offers to meet and confer with the other party for the purpose of negotiating a new contract or a contract containing the proposed modifications;

(3) notifies the Federal Mediation and Conciliation Service within thirty days after such notice of the existence of a dispute, and simultaneously therewith notifies any State or Territorial agency established to mediate and conciliate disputes within the State or Territory where the dispute occurred, provided no agreement has been reached by that time; and

(4) continues in full force and effect, without resorting to strike or lockout, all the terms and conditions of the existing contract for a period of sixty days after such notice is given or until the expiration date of such contract, whichever occurs later.

The duties imposed upon employers, employees, and labor organizations by paragraphs (2) to (4) of this subsection shall become inapplicable upon an intervening certification of the Board, under which the labor organization or individual, which is a party to the contract, has been superseded as or ceased to be the representative of the employees subject to the provisions of section 159(a) of this title, and the duties so imposed shall not be construed as requiring either party to discuss or agree to any modification of the terms and conditions contained in a contract for a fixed period, if such modification is to become effective before such terms and conditions can be reopened under the provisions of the contract. Any employee who engages in a strike within any notice period specified in this subsection, or who engages in any strike within the appropriate period specified in subsection (g) of this section, shall lose his status as an employee of the employer engaged in the particular labor dispute, for the purposes of sections 158, 159 and 160 of this title, but such loss of status for such employee shall terminate if and when he is reemployed by such employer. Whenever the collective bargaining involves employees of a health care institution, the provisions of this subsection shall be modified as follows:

(A) The notice of paragraph (1) of this subsection shall be ninety days; the notice of paragraph (3) of this subsection shall be sixty days; and the contract period of paragraph (4) of this subsection shall be ninety days.

(B) Where the bargaining is for an initial agreement following certification or recognition, at least thirty days' notice of the existence of a dispute shall be given by the labor organization to the agencies set forth in paragraph (3) of this subsection.

(C) After notice is given to the Federal Mediation and Conciliation Service under either clause (A) or (B) of this sentence, the Service shall promptly communicate with the parties and use its best efforts, by mediation and conciliation, to bring them to agreement. The parties shall participate fully and promptly in such meetings as may be undertaken by the Service for the purpose of aiding in a settlement of the dispute.

(e) Enforceability of contract or agreement to boycott any other employer; exception. It shall be an unfair labor practice for any labor organization and any employer to enter into any contract or agreement, express or implied, whereby such employer ceases or refrains or agrees to cease or refrain from handling, using, selling, transporting or otherwise dealing with any other person, and any contract or agreement entered into heretofore or hereafter containing such an agreement shall be to such extent unenforceable and void: Provided, That nothing in this subsection shall apply to an agreement between a labor organization and an employer in the construction industry relating to the contracting or subcontracting of work to be done at the site of the construction, alteration, painting, or repair of a building, structure, or other work: Provided further, That for the purposes of this subsection and subsection (b)(4)(B) of this section the terms "any employer," "any person engaged in commerce or an industry affecting commerce," and "any person" when used in relation to the terms "any other producer, processor, or manufacturer," "any other employer," or "any other person" shall not include persons in the relation of a jobber, manufacturer, contractor, or subcontractor working on the goods or premises of the jobber or manufacturer or performing parts of an integrated process of production in the apparel and clothing industry: Provided further, That nothing in this subchapter shall prohibit the enforcement of any agreement which is within the foregoing exception.

(f) Agreement covering employees in the building and construction industry. It shall not be an unfair labor practice under subsections (a) and (b) of this section for an employer engaged primarily in the building and construction industry to make an agreement covering employees engaged (or who, upon their employment, will be engaged) in the building and construction industry with a labor organization of which building and construction employees are members (not established, maintained, or assisted by any action defined in subsection (a) of this section as an unfair labor practice) because (1) the majority status of such labor organization has not been established under the provisions of section 159 of this title prior to the making of such agreement, or (2) such agreement requires as a condition of employment, membership in such labor organization after the seventh day following the beginning of such employment or the effective date of the agreement, whichever is later, or (3) such agreement requires the employer to notify such labor organization of opportunities for employment with such employer, or gives such labor organization an opportunity to refer qualified applicants for such employment, or (4) such agreement specifies minimum training or experience qualifications for employment or provides for priority in opportunities for employment based upon length of service with such employer, in the industry or in the particular geographical area: Provided, That nothing in this subsection shall set aside the final proviso to subsection (a)(3) of this section: Provided further, That any agreement which would be invalid, but for clause (1) of this subsection, shall not be a bar to a petition filed pursuant to section 159(c) or 159(e) of this title.

(g) Notification of intention to strike or picket at any health care institution. A labor organization before engaging in any strike, picketing, or other concerted refusal to work at any health care institution shall, not less than ten days prior to such action, notify the institution in writing and the Federal Mediation and

Conciliation Service of that intention, except that in the case of bargaining for an initial agreement following certification or recognition the notice required by this subsection shall not be given until the expiration of the period specified in clause (B) of the last sentence of subsection (d) of this section. The notice shall state the date and time that such action will commence. The notice, once given, may be extended by the written agreement of both parties.

§159. Representatives and Elections

(a) Exclusive representatives; employees' adjustment of grievances directly with employer. Representatives designated or selected for the purposes of collective bargaining by the majority of the employees in a unit appropriate for such purposes, shall be the exclusive representatives of all the employees in such unit for the purposes of collective bargaining in respect of rates of pay, wages, hours of employment, or other conditions of employment. Provided, That any individual employee or a group of employees shall have the right at any time to present grievances to their employer and to have such grievances adjusted, without the intervention of the bargaining representative, as long as the adjustment is not inconsistent with the terms of a collective-bargaining contract or agreement then in effect: Provided further, That the bargaining representative has been given opportunity to be present as such adjustment.

(b) Determination of bargaining unit by Board. The Board shall decide in each case whether, in order to assure to employees the fullest freedom in exercising the rights guaranteed by this subchapter, the unit appropriate for purposes of collective bargaining shall be the employer unit, craft unit, plant unit, or subdivision thereof: Provided, That the Board shall not (1) decide that any unit is appropriate for such purposes if such unit includes both professional employees and employees who are not professional employees unless a majority of such professional employees vote for inclusion in such unit; or (2) decide that any craft unit is inappropriate for such purposes on the ground that a different unit has been established by a prior Board determination, unless a majority of the employees in the proposed craft unit vote against separate representation or (3) decide that any unit is appropriate for such purposes if it includes, together with other employees, any individual employed as a guard to enforce against employees and other persons rules to protect property of the employer or to protect the safety of persons on the employer's premises; but no labor organization shall be certified as the representative of employees in a bargaining unit of guards if such organization admits to membership, or is affiliated directly or indirectly with an organization which admits to membership, employees other than guards.

(c) Hearings on questions affecting commerce; rules and regulations.

(1) Whenever a petition shall have been filed, in accordance with such regulations as may be prescribed by the Board

(A) by an employee or group of employees or any individual or labor organization acting in their behalf alleging that a substantial number of employees (i) wish to be represented for collective bargaining and that their employer declines to recognize their representative as the representative defined in subsection (a) of this section, or (ii) assert that the individual or labor organization, which has been certified or is being currently recognized by their employer as the bargaining representative, is no longer a representative as defined in subsection (a) of this section; or

(B) by an employer, alleging that one or more individuals or labor organizations have presented to him a claim to be recognized as the representative defined in subsection (a) of this section;

the Board shall investigate such petition and if it has reasonable cause to believe that a question of representation affecting commerce exists shall provide for an appropriate hearing upon due notice. Such hearing may be conducted by an officer or employee of the regional office, who shall not make any recommendations with respect thereto. If the Board finds upon the record of such hearing that such a question of representation exists, it shall direct an election by secret ballot and shall certify the results thereof.

(2) In determining whether or not a question of representation affecting commerce exists, the same regulations and rules of decision shall apply irrespective of the identity of the persons filing the petition or the kind of relief sought and in no case shall the Board deny a labor organization a place on the ballot by reason of an order with respect to such labor organization or its predecessor not issued in conformity with section 160(c) of this title.

(3) No election shall be directed in any bargaining unit or any subdivision within which in the preceding twelve-month period, a valid election shall have been held. Employees engaged in an economic strike who are not entitled to reinstatement shall be eligible to vote under such regulations as the Board shall find are consistent with the purposes and provisions of this subchapter in any election conducted within twelve months after the commencement of the strike. In any election where none of the choices on the ballot receives a majority, a run-off shall be conducted, the ballot providing for a selection between the two choices receiving the largest and second largest number of valid votes cast in the election.

(4) Nothing in this section shall be construed to prohibit the waiving of hearings by stipulation for the purposes of a consent election in conformity with regulations and rules of decision of the Board.

(5) In determining whether a unit is appropriate for the purposes specified in subsection (b) of this section the extent to which the employees have organized shall not be controlling.

(d) Petition for enforcement or review; transcript. Whenever an order of the Board made pursuant to section 160(c) of this title is based in whole or in part upon facts certified following an investigation pursuant to subsection (c) of this section and there is a petition for the enforcement or review of such order, such certification and the record of such investigation shall be included in the transcript of the entire record required to be filed under subsection (e) or (f) of section 160 of this title, and thereupon the decree of the court enforcing, modifying, or setting aside in whole or in part the order of the Board shall be made and entered upon the pleadings, testimony, and proceedings set forth in such transcript.

(e) Secret ballot; limitation of elections.

(1) Upon the filing with the Board, by 30 per centum or more of the employees in a bargaining unit covered by an agreement between their employer and a labor organization made pursuant to section 158(a)(3) of this title, of a petition alleging they desire that such authority be rescinded, the Board shall take a secret ballot of the employees in such unit and certify the results thereof to such labor organization and to the employer.

(2) No election shall be conducted pursuant to this subsection in any bargaining unit or any subdivision within which, in the preceding twelve-month period, a valid election shall have been held.

§160. Prevention of Unfair Labor Practices

(a) Powers of Board generally. The Board is empowered, as hereinafter provided, to prevent any person from engaging in any unfair labor practice (listed in section 158 of this title) affecting commerce. This power shall not be affected by any other means of adjustment or prevention that has been or may be established by agreement, law, or otherwise: Provided, That the Board is empowered by agreement with any agency of any State or Territory to cede to such agency jurisdiction over any cases in any industry (other than mining, manufacturing, communications, and transportation except where predominantly local in character) even though such cases may involved labor disputes affecting commerce, unless the provision of the State or Territorial statute applicable to the determination of such cases by such agency is inconsistent with the corresponding provision of this subchapter or has received a construction inconsistent therewith.

(b) Complaint and notice of hearing; answer; court rules of evidence applicable. Whenever it is charged that any person has engaged in or is engaging in any such unfair labor practice, the Board, or any agent or agency designated by the Board for such purposes, shall have power to issue and cause to be served upon such person a complaint stating the charges in that respect, and containing a notice of hearing before the Board or a member thereof, or before a designated agent or agency, at a place therein fixed, not less than five days after the serving of said complaint: Provided, That no complaint shall issue based upon any unfair labor practice occurring more than six months prior to the filing of the charge with the Board and the service of a copy thereof upon the person against whom such charge is made, unless the person aggrieved thereby was prevented from filing such charge by reason of service in the armed forces, in which event the six-month period shall be computed from the day of his discharge. Any such complaint may be amended by the member, agent, or agency conducting the hearing or the Board in its discretion at any time prior to the issuance of an order based thereon. The person so complained of shall have the right to file an answer to the original or amended complaint and to appear in person or otherwise and give testimony at the place and time fixed in the complaint. In the discretion of the member, agent, or agency conducting the hearing or the Board, any other person may be allowed to intervene in the said proceeding and to present testimony. Any such proceeding shall, so far as practicable, be conducted in accordance with the rules of evidence applicable in the district courts of the United States under the rules of civil procedure for the district courts of the United States, adopted by the Supreme Court of the United States pursuant to section 2072 of Title 28.

(c) Reduction of testimony to writing; findings and orders of Board. The testimony taken by such member, agent, or agency or the Board shall be reduced to writing and filed with the Board. Thereafter, in its discretion, the Board upon notice may take further testimony or hear argument. If upon the preponderance of the testimony taken the Board shall be of the opinion that any person named in the complaint has engaged in or is engaging in any such unfair labor practice, then the Board shall state its findings of fact and shall issue and cause to be served on such person an order requiring such person to cease and desist from such unfair labor practice, and to take such affirmative action including reinstatement of employees with or without back pay, as will effectuate the policies of this subchapter: Provided, That where an order directs reinstatement of an employee, back pay may be required of the employer or labor organization, as the case may be, responsible for the discrimination suffered by him: And provided further, That in determining whether a complaint shall issue alleging a violation of subsection (a)(1) or (a)(2) of section 158 of this title, and in deciding such cases, the same regulations and rules of decision shall apply irrespective of whether or not the labor organization affected is affiliated with a labor organization national or international in scope. Such an order may further require such person to make reports from time to time showing the extent to which it has complied with the order. If upon the preponderance of the testimony taken the Board shall not be of the opinion that the person named in the complaint has engaged in or is engaging in any such unfair labor practice, then the Board shall state its findings of fact and shall issue an order dismissing the said complaint. No order of the Board shall require the reinstatement of any individual as an employee who has been suspended or discharged, or the payment to him of any back pay, if such individual was suspended or discharged for cause. In case the evidence is presented before a member of the Board, or before an administrative law judge or judges thereof, such member, or such judge; or judges as the case may be, shall issue and cause to be served on the parties to the proceeding a proposed report, together with a recommended order, which shall be filed with the Board, and if no exceptions are filed within twenty days after service thereof upon such parties, or within such further period as the Board may authorize, such recommended order shall become the order of the Board and become effective as therein prescribed.

(d) Modification of findings or orders prior to filing record in court. Until the record in a case shall have been filed in a court, as hereinafter provided, the Board may at any time upon reasonable notice and in such manner as it shall deem proper, modify or set aside, in whole or in part, any finding or order made or issued by it.

(e) Petition to court for enforcement of order; proceedings; review of judgment. The Board shall have power to petition any court of appeals of the United States, or if all the courts of appeals to which application may be made are in vacation, any district court of the United States, within any circuit or district, respectively, wherein the unfair labor practice in question occurred or wherein such person resides or transacts business, for the enforcement of such order and for appropriate temporary relief or restraining order, and shall file in the court the record in the proceedings, as provided in section 2112 of Title 28. Upon the filing of such petition, the court shall cause notice thereof to be served upon such person, and thereupon shall have jurisdiction of the proceeding and of the question determined therein, and shall have power to grant such temporary relief or restraining order as it deems just and proper, and to make and enter a decree enforcing, modifying, and enforcing as so modified, or setting aside in whole or in part the order of the Board. No objection that has not been urged before the Board, its member, agent, or agency, shall be considered by the court, unless the failure or neglect to urge such objection shall be excused because of extraordinary circumstances. The findings of the Board with respect to questions of fact if supported by substantial evidence on the record considered as a whole shall be conclusive. If either party shall apply to the court for leave to adduce additional evidence and shall show to the satisfaction of the court that such additional evidence is material and that there were reasonable grounds for the failure to adduce such evidence in the hearing before the Board, its member, agent, or agency, the court may order such additional evidence to be taken before the Board, its member, agent, or agency, and to be made a part of the record. The Board may modify its findings as to the facts or make new findings by reason of additional evidence so taken and filed, and it shall file such modified or new findings, which findings with respect to questions of fact if supported by substantial evidence on the record considered as a whole shall be conclusive, and shall file its recommendations, if any, for the modification or setting aside of its original order. Upon the filing of the record with it the jurisdiction of the court shall be exclusive and its judgment and decree shall be final, except that the same shall be subject to review by the appropriate United States court of appeals if application was made to the district court as here in above provided, and by the Supreme Court of the United States upon writ of certiorari or certification as provided in section 1254 of Title 28.

(f) Review of final order of Board on petition to court. Any person aggrieved by a final order of the Board granting or denying in whole or in part the relief sought may obtain a review of such order in any United States court of appeals in the circuit wherein the unfair labor practice in question was alleged to have been engaged in or wherein such person resides or transacts business, or in the United States Court of Appeals for the District of Columbia, by filing in such a court a written petition praying that the order of the Board be modified or set aside. A copy of such petition shall be forthwith transmitted by the clerk of the court to the Board, and thereupon the aggrieved party shall file in the court the record in the proceeding, certified by the Board, as provided in section 2112 of Title 28. Upon the filing of such petition, the court shall proceed in the same manner as in the case of an application by the Board under subsection (e) of this section, and shall have the same jurisdiction to grant to the Board such temporary relief or restraining order as it deems just and proper, and in like manner to make and enter a decree enforcing, modifying, and enforcing as so modified, or setting aside in whole or in part the order of the Board; the findings of the Board with respect to questions of fact if supported by substantial evidence on the record considered as a whole shall in like manner be conclusive.

(g) Institution of court proceedings as stay of Board's order. The commencement of proceedings under subsection (e) or (f) of this section shall not, unless specifically ordered by the court, operate as a stay of the Board's order.

(h) Jurisdiction of courts unaffected by limitations prescribed in sections 101 to 115 of this title. When granting appropriate temporary relief or a restraining order, or making and entering a decree enforcing, modifying, and enforcing as so modified, or setting aside in whole or in part an order of the Board, as provided in this section, the jurisdiction of courts sitting in equity shall not be limited by sections 101 to 115 of this title.

(i) Repealed. Pub. L. 98-620, Title IV, §402(31), Nov. 8, 1984, 98 Stat. 3360

(j) Injunctions. The Board shall have power, upon issuance of a complaint as provided in subsection (b) of this section charging that any person has engaged in or is engaging in an unfair labor practice, to petition any United States district court, within any district wherein the unfair labor practice in question is alleged to have occurred or wherein such person resides or transacts business, for appropriate temporary relief or restraining order. Upon the filing of any such petition the court shall cause notice thereof to be served upon such person, and thereupon shall have jurisdiction to grant to the Board such temporary relief or restraining order as it deems just and proper.

(k) Hearings on jurisdictional strikes. Whenever it is charged that any person has engaged in an unfair labor practice within the meaning of paragraph (4)(D) of section 158(b) of this title, the Board is empowered and directed to hear and determine the dispute out of which such unfair labor practice shall have arisen, unless, within ten days after notice that such charge has been filed, the parties to such dispute submit to the Board satisfactory evidence that they have adjusted, or agreed upon methods for the voluntary adjustment of, the dispute. Upon compliance by the parties to the dispute with the decision of the Board or upon such voluntary adjustment of the dispute, such charge shall be dismissed.

(l) Boycotts and strikes to force recognition of uncertified labor organizations, injunctions; notice; service of process. Whenever it is charged that any person has engaged in an unfair labor practice within the meaning of paragraph (4)(A), (B), or (C) of section 158(b) of this title, or section 158(e) of this title or section 158(b)(7) of this title, the preliminary investigation of such charge shall be made forthwith and given priority over all other cases except cases of like character in the office where it is filed or to which it is referred. If, after such investigation, the officer or regional attorney to whom the matter may be referred has reasonable cause to believe such charge is true and that a complaint should issue, he shall, on behalf of the Board, petition any United States district court within any district where the unfair labor practice in question has occurred, is alleged to have occurred, or wherein such person resides or transacts business, for appropriate injunctive relief pending the final adjudication of the Board with respect to such matter. Upon the filing of such petition the district court shall have jurisdiction to grant such injunctive relief or temporary restraining order as it deems just and proper, notwithstanding any other provision of law: Provided further, That no temporary restraining order shall be issued without notice unless a petition alleges that substantial and irreparable injury to the charging party will be unavoidable and such temporary restraining order shall be effective for no longer than five days and will become void at the expiration of such period: Provided further, That such officer or regional attorney shall not apply for any restraining order under section 158(b)(7) of this title if a charge against the employer under section 158(a)(2) of this title has been filed and after the preliminary investigation, he has reasonable cause to believe that such charge is true and that a complaint should issue. Upon filing of any such petition the courts shall cause notice thereof to be served upon any person involved in the charge and such person, including the charging party, shall be given an opportunity to appear by counsel and present any relevant testimony: Provided further, That for the purposes of this subsection district courts shall be deemed to have jurisdiction of a labor organization (1) in the district in which such organization maintains its principal office, or (2) in any district in which its duly authorized officers or agents are engaged in promoting or protecting the interests of employee members. The service of legal process upon such officer or agent shall constitute service upon the labor organization and make such organization a party to the suit. In situations where such relief is appropriate the procedure specified herein shall apply to charges with respect to section 158(b)(4)(D) of this title.

(m) Priority of cases. Whenever it is charged that any person has engaged in an unfair labor practice within the meaning of subsection (a)(3) or (b)(2) of section 158 of this title, such charge shall be given priority over all other cases except cases of like character in the office where it is filed or to which it is referred and cases given priority under subsection (1) of this section.

§161. *Investigatory Powers of Board*

For the purpose of all hearings and investigations, which, in the opinion of the Board, are necessary and proper for the exercise of the powers vested in it by sections 159 and 160 of this title

(1) Documentary evidence; summoning witnesses and taking testimony. The Board, or its duly authorized agents or agencies, shall at all reasonable times have access to, for the purpose of examination, and the right to copy any evidence of any person being investigated or proceeded against that relates to any matter under investigation or in question. The Board, or any member thereof, shall upon application of any party to such proceedings, forthwith issue to such party subpoenas requiring the attendance and testimony of witnesses or the production of any evidence in such proceeding or investigation requested in such application. Within five days after the service of a subpoena on any person requiring the production of evidence in his possession or under his control, such person may petition the Board to revoke, and the Board shall revoke, such subpoena if in its opinion the evidence whose production is required does not relate to any matter under investigation, or any matter in question in such proceedings, or if in its opinion such subpoena does not describe with sufficient particularity the evidence whose production is required. Any member of the Board, or any agent or agency designated by the Board for such purposes, may administer oaths and affirmations, examine witnesses, and receive evidence. Such attendance of witnesses and the production of such evidence may be

required from any place in the United States or any Territory or possession thereof, at any designated place of hearing.

(2) Court aid in compelling production of evidence and attendance of witnesses. In case of contumacy or refusal to obey a subpoena issued to any person, any district court of the United States or the United States courts of any Territory or possession, within the jurisdiction of which the inquiry is carried on or within the jurisdiction of which said person guilty of contumacy or refusal to obey is found or resides or transacts business, upon application by the Board shall have jurisdiction to issue to such person an order requiring such person to appear before the Board, its member, agent, or agency, there to produce evidence if so ordered, or there to give testimony touching the matter under investigation or in question; and any failure to obey such order of the court may be punished by said court as a contempt thereof.

(3) Repealed. Pub. L. 91-452, Title II, §234, Oct. 15, 1970, 84 Stat. 930.

(4) Process, service and return; fees of witnesses. Complaints, orders, and other process and papers of the Board, its member, agent, or agency, may be served either personally or by registered or certified mail or by telegraph or by leaving a copy thereof at the principal office or place of business of the person required to be served. The verified return by the individual so serving the same setting forth the manner of such service shall be proof of the same, and the return post office receipt or telegraph receipt therefor when registered or certified and mailed or when telegraphed as aforesaid shall be proof of service of the same. Witnesses summoned before the Board, its member, agent, or agency, shall be paid the same fees and mileage that are paid witnesses in the courts of the United States, and witnesses whose depositions are taken and the persons taking the same shall severally be entitled to the same fees as are paid for like services in the courts of the United States.

(5) Process, where served. All process of any court to which application may be made under this subchapter may be served in the judicial district wherein the defendant or other person required to be served resides or may be found.

(6) Information and assistance from departments. The several departments and agencies of the Government, when directed by the President, shall furnish the Board, upon its request, all records, papers, and information in their possession relating to any matter before the Board.

§162. Offenses and Penalties

Any person who shall willfully resist, prevent, impede, or interfere with any member of the Board or any of its agents or agencies in the performance of duties pursuant to this subchapter shall be punished by a fine of not more than $5,000 or by imprisonment for not more than one year, or both.

§163. Right to Strike Preserved

Nothing in this subchapter, except as specifically provided for herein, shall be construed so as either to interfere with or impede or diminish in any way the right to strike, or to affect the limitations or qualifications on that right.

§164. Construction of Provisions

(a) Supervisors as union members. Nothing herein shall prohibit any individual employed as a supervisor from becoming or remaining a member of a labor organization, but no employer subject to this subchapter shall be compelled to deem individuals defined herein as supervisors as employees for the purpose of any law, either national or local, relating to collective bargaining.

(b) Agreements requiring union membership in violation of State law. Nothing in this subchapter shall be construed as authorizing the execution or application of agreements requiring membership in a labor organization as a condition of employment in any State or Territory in which such execution or application is prohibited by State or Territorial law.

(c) Power of Board to decline jurisdiction of labor disputes; assertion of jurisdiction by State and Territorial courts.

(1) The Board, in its discretion, may, by rule of decision or by published rules adopted pursuant to subchapter II of chapter 5 of Title 5, decline to assert jurisdiction over any labor dispute involving any class or category of employers, where, in the opinion of the Board, the effect of such labor dispute on commerce is not sufficiently substantial to warrant the exercise of its jurisdiction: Provided, That the Board shall not decline to assert jurisdiction over any labor dispute over which it would assert jurisdiction under the standards prevailing upon August 1, 1959.

(2) Nothing in this subchapter shall be deemed to prevent or bar any agency or the courts of any State or Territory (including the Commonwealth of Puerto Rico, Guam, and the Virgin Islands), from assuming and asserting jurisdiction over labor disputes over which the Board declines, pursuant to paragraph (1) of this subsection, to assert jurisdiction.

§165. Conflict of Laws

Wherever the application of the provisions of section 672 of Title 11 conflicts with the application of the provisions of this subchapter, this subchapter shall prevail: Provided, That in any situation where the provisions of this subchapter cannot be validly enforced, the provisions of such other Acts shall remain in full force and effect.

§166. Separability

If any provision of this subchapter, or the application of such provision to any person or circumstances, shall be held invalid, the remainder of this subchapter, or the application of such provision to persons or circumstances other than those as to which it is held invalid, shall not be affected thereby.

§167. Short Title of Subchapter

This subchapter may be cited as the "National Labor Relations Act."

§168. Validation of Certificates and Other Board Actions

No petition entertained, no investigation made, no election held, and no certification issued by the National Labor Relations Board, under any of the provisions of section 159 of this title, shall be invalid by reason of the failure of the Congress of Industrial Organizations to have complied with the requirements of section 159(f), (g), or (h) of this title prior to December 22, 1949, or by reason of the failure of the American Federation of Labor to have complied with the provisions of section 159(f), (g), or (h) of this title prior to November 7, 1947: Provided, That no liability shall be imposed under any provision of this chapter upon any person for failure to honor any election or certificate referred to above, prior to October 22, 1951: Provided, however, That this proviso shall not have the effect of setting aside or in any way affecting judgments or decrees heretofore entered under section 160(e) or (f) of this title and which have become final.

§169. *Employees with Religious Convictions; Payment of Dues and Fees*

Any employee who is a member of and adheres to established and traditional tenets or teachings of a bona fide religion, body, or sect which has historically held conscientious objections to joining or financially supporting labor organization shall not be required to join or financially support any labor organization as a condition of employment; except that such employee may be required in a contract between such employees' employer and a labor organization in lieu of periodic dues and initiation fees, to pay sums equal to such dues and initiation fees to a nonreligious, nonlabor organization charitable fund exempt from taxation under section 501(c)(3) of Title 26, chosen by such employee from a list of at least three such funds, designated in such contract or if the contract fails to designate such funds, then to any such fund chosen by the employee. If such employee who holds conscientious objections pursuant to this section requests the labor organization to use the grievance-arbitration procedure on the employee's behalf, the labor organization is authorized to charge the employee for the reasonable cost of using such procedure.

Portal-to-Portal Act

29 U.S.C. §§255, 256, 260

§255 [§6]. Statute of Limitations

Any action commenced on or after May 14, 1947, to enforce any cause of action for unpaid minimum wages, unpaid overtime compensation, or liquidated damages, under the Fair Labor Standards Act of 1938, as amended, the Walsh-Healey Act, or the Bacon-Davis Act—

(a) if the cause of action accrues on or after May 14, 1947—may be commenced within two years after the cause of action accrued, and every such action shall be forever barred unless commenced within two years after the cause of action accrued, except that a cause of action arising out of a willful violation may be commenced within three years after the cause of action accrued. . . .

§256 [§7]. Determination of Commencement of Future Actions

In determining when an action is commenced for the purposes of section 255 of this title, an action commenced on or after May 14, 1947 under the Fair Labor Standards Act of 1938, as amended, the Walsh-Healey Act, or the Bacon-Davis Act, shall be considered to be commenced on the date when the complaint is filed; except that in the case of a collective or class action instituted under the Fair Labor Standards Act of 1938, as amended, or the Bacon-Davis Act, it shall be considered to be commenced in the case of any individual claimant—

(a) on the date when the complaint is filed, if he is specifically named as a party plaintiff in the complaint and his written consent to become a party plaintiff is filed on such date in the court in which the action is brought; or

(b) if such written consent was not so filed or if his name did not so appear—on the subsequent date on which such written consent is filed in the court in which the action was commenced.

§260 [§11]. Liquidated Damages

In any action commenced prior to or on or after May 14, 1947 to recover unpaid minimum wages, unpaid overtime compensation, or liquidated damages, under the Fair Labor Standards Act of 1938, as amended, if the employer shows to the satisfaction of the court that the act or omission giving rise to such action was in good faith and that he had reasonable grounds for believing that his act or omission was not a violation of the Fair Labor Standards Act of 1938, as amended, the court may, in its sound discretion, award no liquidation damages or award any amount thereof not to exceed the amount specified in section 216 of this title.

Rehabilitation Act of 1973

29 U.S.C. §§705, 791, 793, 794, 794a

§705. Definitions

For the purposes of this chapter: . . .

(6) Construction; cost of construction.

(A) Construction. The term "construction" means

(i) the construction of new buildings;

(ii) the acquisition, expansion, remodeling, alteration, and renovation of existing buildings; and

(iii) initial equipment of buildings described in clauses (i) and (ii).

(B) Cost of construction. The term "cost of construction" includes architects' fees and the cost of acquisition of land in connection with construction but does not include the cost of offsite improvements. . . .

(9) Disability. The term "disability" means

(A) except as otherwise provided in subparagraph (B), a physical or mental impairment that constitutes or results in a substantial impediment to employment; or

(B) for purposes of sections 701, 711, and 712 of this title and subchapters II, IV, V, and VII of this chapter [29 U.S.C.A. §760 et seq., and 796 et seq.], the meaning given it in section 12102 of Title 42.

(10) Drug and illegal use of drugs.

(A) Drug. The term "drug" means a controlled substance, as defined in schedules I through V of section 202 of the Controlled Substances Act [21 U.S.C. 812].

(B) Illegal use of drugs. The term "illegal use of drugs" means the use of drugs, the possession or distribution of which is unlawful under the Controlled Substances Act. Such term does not include the use of a drug taken under supervision by a licensed health care professional, or other uses authorized by the Controlled Substances Act or other provisions of Federal law. . . .

(20) Individual with a disability.

(A) In general. Except as otherwise provided in subparagraph (B), the term "individual with a disability" means any individual who

(i) has a physical or mental impairment which for such individual constitutes or results in a substantial impediment to employment; and

(ii) can benefit in terms of an employment outcome from vocational rehabilitation services provided pursuant to subchapter I, II, or VI [29 U.S.C.S. §§720 et seq., 771 et seq., or 795 et seq.].

(B) Certain programs; limitations on major life activities. Subject to subparagraphs (C), (D), (E), and (F), the term "individual with a disability" means, for purposes of sections 701, 711 and 712 of this title and subchapters I, IV, V and VII of this Act [29 U.S.C.S §760 et seq., 790 et seq.], any person who has a disability in section 12102 of Title 42.

(C) Rights and advocacy provisions.

(i) In general; exclusion of individuals engaging in drug use. For purposes of title V [29 U.S.C.S. §§790 et seq.], the term "individual with a disability" does not include an individual who is currently engaging in the illegal use of drugs, when a covered entity acts on the basis of such use.

(ii) Exception for individuals no longer engaging in drug use. Nothing in clause (i) shall be construed to exclude as an individual with a disability an individual who

(I) has successfully completed a supervised drug rehabilitation program and is no longer engaging in the illegal use of drugs, or has otherwise been rehabilitated successfully and is no longer engaging in such use;

(II) is participating in a supervised rehabilitation program and is no longer engaging in such use; or

(III) is erroneously regarded as engaging in such use, but is not engaging in such use;

except that it shall not be a violation of this chapter [29 U.S.C.A. § 720 et seq.] for a covered entity to adopt or administer reasonable policies or procedures, including but not limited to drug testing, designed to ensure that an individual described in subclause (I) or (II) is no longer engaging in the illegal use of drugs.

(iii) Exclusion for certain services. Notwithstanding clause (i), for purposes of programs and activities providing health services and services provided under titles I, II, and III [29 U.S.C.S. §§720 et seq., 760 et seq., 771 et seq.], an individual shall not be excluded from the benefits of such programs or activities on the basis of his or her current illegal use of drugs if he or she is otherwise entitled to such services.

(iv) Disciplinary action. For purposes of programs and activities providing educational services, local educational agencies may take disciplinary action pertaining to the use or possession of illegal drugs or alcohol against any student who is an individual with a disability and who currently is engaging in the illegal use of drugs or in the use of alcohol to the same extent that such disciplinary action is taken against students who are not individuals with disabilities. Furthermore, the due process procedures at section 104.36 of title 34, Code of Federal Regulations (or any corresponding similar regulation or ruling) shall not apply to such disciplinary actions.

(v) Employment; exclusions of alcoholics. For purposes of sections 793 and 794 of this title as such sections relate to employment, the term "individual with a disability" does not include any individual who is an alcoholic whose current use of alcohol prevents such individual from performing the duties of the job in question or whose employment, by reasons of such current alcohol abuse, would constitute a direct threat to property or the safety of others.

(D) Employment; exclusion of individuals with certain diseases or infections. For the purposes of sections 793 and 794 of this title, as such sections relate to employment, such term does not include an individual who has a currently contagious disease or infection and who, by reason of such disease or infection, would constitute a direct threat to the health or safety of other individuals or who, by reasons of the currently contagious disease or infection, is unable to perform the duties of the job.

(E) Rights provisions; exclusion of individuals on basis of homosexuality or bisexuality. For the purposes of sections 791, 793 and 794 of this title —

(i) for purposes of the application of subparagraph (B) to such sections, the term "impairment" does not include homosexuality or bisexuality; and

(ii) therefore the term "individual with a disability" does not include an individual on the basis of homosexuality or bisexuality.

(F) Rights provisions; exclusion of individuals on basis of certain disorders. For the purposes of sections 791, 793 and 794 of this title, the term "individual with a disability" does not include an individual on the basis of

(i) transvestism, transsexualism, pedophilia, exhibitionism, voyeurism, gender identity disorders not resulting from physical impairments, or other sexual behavior disorders;

(ii) compulsive gambling, kleptomania, or pyromania; or

(iii) psychoactive substance use disorders resulting from current illegal use of drugs.

(G) Individuals with disabilities. The term "individuals with disabilities" means more than one individual with a disability.

§791 [§501]. Employment of Individuals with Handicaps . . .

(b) Federal Agencies; Affirmative Action Program Plan. Each department, agency, and instrumentality (including the United States Postal Service and the Postal Regulatory Commission) in the executive branch and the Smithsonian

Institution shall, within one hundred and eighty days of September 26, 1973, submit to the Equal Employment Opportunity Commission and to the Committee an affirmative action program plan for the hiring, placement, and advancement of individuals with disabilities in such department, agency, or instrumentality. Such plan shall include a description of the extent to which and methods whereby the special needs of employees who are individuals with disabilities are being met. Such plan shall be updated annually, and shall be reviewed annually and approved by the Commission, if the Commission determines, after consultation with the Committee, that such plan provides sufficient assurances, procedures and commitments to provide adequate hiring, placement, and advancement opportunities for individuals with disabilities. . . .

(g) Standards used in determining violation of section. The standards used to determine whether this section has been violated in a complaint alleging non-affirmative action employment discrimination under this section shall be the standards applied under title I of the Americans with Disabilities Act of 1990 (42 U.S.C. §§12111 et seq.) and the provisions of sections 501 through 504, and 510, of the Americans with Disabilities Act of 1990 (42 U.S.C. §§12201-12204 and §12210), as such sections relate to employment.

§793 [§503]. Employment Under Federal Contracts

(a) Amount of Contracts or Subcontracts; Provision for Employment and Advancement of Qualified Individuals with Handicaps; Regulations. Any contract in excess of $10,000 entered into by any Federal department or agency for the procurement of personal property and nonpersonal services (including construction) for the United States shall contain a provision requiring that, in employing persons to carry out such contract the party contracting with the United States shall take affirmative action to employ and advance in employment qualified individuals with handicaps as defined in section 706(7) of this title. The provisions of this section shall apply to any subcontract in excess of $10,000 entered into by a prime contractor in carrying out any contract for the procurement of personal property and nonpersonal services (including construction) for the United States. The President shall implement the provisions of this section by promulgating regulations within ninety days after September 26, 1973.

(b) Administrative. Enforcement; Complaints; Investigation; Department Action. If any individual with handicaps believes any contractor has failed or refuses to comply with the provisions of his contract with the United States, relating to employment of individuals with handicaps, such individual may file a complaint with the Department of Labor. The Department shall promptly investigate such complaint and shall take such action thereon as the facts and circumstances warrant, consistent with the terms of such contract and the laws and regulations applicable thereto. . . .

§794 [§504]. Nondiscrimination Under Federal Grants and Programs; Promulgation of Rules and Regulations

(a) Promulgation of rules and regulations. No otherwise qualified individual with a disability in the United States, as defined in section 705(20) of this title, shall, solely by reason of her or his disability, be excluded from the participation in, be denied the benefits of, or be subjected to discrimination under any program or activity receiving Federal financial assistance or under any program or activity conducted by any Executive agency or by the United States Postal Service. The head of each such agency shall promulgate such regulations as may be necessary to carry out the amendments to this section made by the Rehabilitation, Comprehensive Services, and Developmental Disabilities Act of 1978. Copies of any proposed regulation shall be submitted to appropriate authorizing committees of the Congress, and such regulation may take effect no earlier than the thirtieth day after the date on which such regulation is so submitted to such committees.

(b) "Program or activity" defined. For the purposes of this section, the term "program or activity" means all of the operations of—

(1)(A) a department, agency, special purpose district, or other instrumentality of a State or of a local government; or

(B) the entity of such State or local government that distributes such assistance and each such department or agency (and each other State or local government entity) to which the assistance is extended, in the case of assistance to a State or local government;

(2)(A) a college, university, or other postsecondary institution, or a public system of higher education; or

(B) a local educational agency (as defined in section 7801 of Title 20), system of vocational education, or other school system;

(3)(A) an entire corporation, partnership, or other private organization, or an entire sole proprietorship —

(i) if assistance is extended to such corporation, partnership, private organization, or sole proprietorship as a whole; or

(ii) which is principally engaged in the business of providing education, health care, housing, social services, or parks and recreation; or

(B) the entire plant or other comparable, geographically separate facility to which Federal financial assistance is extended, in the case of any other corporation, partnership, private organization, or sole proprietorship; or

(4) any other entity which is established by two or more of the entities described in paragraph (1), (2), or (3);

any part of which is extended Federal financial assistance.

(c) Significant structural alterations by small providers; exception. Small providers are not required by subsection (a) of this section to make significant structural alterations to their existing facilities for the purpose of assuring program accessibility, if alternative means of providing the services are available. The terms used in this subsection shall be construed with reference to the regulations existing on March 22, 1988.

(d) Standards used in determining violation of section. The standards used to determine whether this section has been violated in a complaint alleging employment discrimination under this section shall be the standards applied under title I of the Americans with Disabilities Act of 1990 [42 U.S.C. §§12111 et seq.]

and the provisions of sections 501 through 504, and 510, of the Americans with Disabilities Act of 1990 [42 U.S.C. §§12201-12204 and 12210], as such sections relate to employment.

§794a [§505]. Remedies and Attorney Fees

(a)(1) The remedies, procedures, and rights set forth in section 717 of the Civil Rights Act of 1964 [42 U.S.C. §2000e-16], including the application of sections 706(f) through 706(k) [42 U.S.C. §2000e-5(f)-(k)] and the application of section 706(e)(3) [42 U.S.C. §2000e-5(e)(3)] to claims of discrimination in compensation shall be available, with respect to any complaint under section 791 of this title, to any employee or applicant for employment aggrieved by the final disposition of such complaint, or by the failure to take final action on such complaint. In fashioning an equitable or affirmative action remedy under such section, a court may take into account the reasonableness of the cost of any necessary work place accommodation, and the availability of alternatives therefor or other appropriate relief in order to achieve an equitable and appropriate remedy.

(2) The remedies, procedures, and rights set forth in title VI of the Civil Rights Act of 1964 [42 U.S.C. §2000d et seq.] (and in subsection (e)(3) of section 706 of such act [42 U.S.C. §2000e-5], applied to claims of discrimination in compensation) shall be available to any person aggrieved by any act or failure to act by any recipient of Federal assistance or Federal provider of such assistance under section 794 of this title.

(b) In any action or proceeding to enforce or charge a violation of a provision of this subchapter, the court, in its discretion, may allow the prevailing party, other than the United States, a reasonable attorney's fee as part of the costs.

Religious Freedom Restoration Act

42 U.S.C. §2000bb

§2000bb. Congressional Findings and Declaration of Purposes

(a) Findings. The Congress finds that—

(1) the framers of the Constitution, recognizing free exercise of religion as an unalienable right, secured its protection in the First Amendment to the Constitution;

(2) laws "neutral" toward religion may burden religious exercise as surely as laws intended to interfere with religious exercise;

(3) governments should not substantially burden religious exercise without compelling justification;

(4) in Employment Division v. Smith, 494 U.S. 872 (1990) the Supreme Court virtually eliminated the requirement that the government justify burdens on religious exercise imposed by laws neutral toward religion; and

(5) the compelling interest test as set forth in prior Federal court rulings is a workable test for striking sensible balances between religious liberty and competing prior governmental interests.

(b) Purposes. The purposes of this chapter are—

(1) to restore the compelling interest test as set forth in Sherbert v. Verner, 374 U.S. 398 (1963) and Wisconsin v. Yoder, 406 U.S. 205 (1972) and to guarantee its application in all cases where free exercise of religion is substantially burdened; and

(2) to provide a claim or defense to persons whose religious exercise is substantially burdened by government.

§2000bb-1. Free Exercise of Religion Protected

(a) In general. Government shall not substantially burden a person's exercise of religion even if the burden results from a rule of general applicability, except as provided in subsection (b) of this section.

(b) Exception. Government may substantially burden a person's exercise of religion only if it demonstrates that application of the burden to the person—

(1) is in furtherance of a compelling governmental interest; and

(2) is the least restrictive means of furthering that compelling governmental interest.

(c) Judicial relief. A person whose religious exercise has been burdened in violation of this section may assert that violation as a claim or defense in a judicial proceeding and obtain appropriate relief against a government. Standing to assert a claim or defense under this section shall be governed by the general rules of standing under article III of the Constitution.

§2000bb-2. Definitions

As used in this chapter—

(1) the term "government" includes a branch, department, agency, instrumentality, and official (or other person acting under color of law) of the United States, or of a covered entity;

(2) the term "covered entity" means the District of Columbia, the Commonwealth of Puerto Rico, and each territory and possession of the United States;

(3) the term "demonstrates" means meets the burdens of going forward with the evidence and of persuasion; and

(4) the term "exercise of religion" means religious exercise, as defined in section 2000cc-5 of this title.

§2000bb-3. Applicability

(a) In general. This chapter applies to all Federal law, and the implementation of that law, whether statutory or otherwise, and whether adopted before or after November 16, 1993.

(b) Rule of construction. Federal statutory law adopted after November 16, 1993 is subject to this chapter unless such law explicitly excludes such application by reference to this chapter.

(c) Religious belief unaffected. Nothing in this chapter shall be construed to authorize any government to burden any religious belief.

§2000bb-4. Establishment Clause Unaffected

Nothing in this chapter shall be construed to affect, interpret, or in any way address that portion of the First Amendment prohibiting laws respecting the establishment of religion (referred to in this section as the "Establishment Clause"). Granting government funding, benefits, or exemptions, to the extent permissible under the Establishment Clause, shall not constitute a violation of this chapter. As used in this section, the term "granting", used with respect to government funding, benefits, or exemptions, does not include the denial of government funding, benefits, or exemptions.

Residual Statute of Limitations

28 U.S.C. §1658

§1658. Time Limitations on the Commencement of Civil Actions Arising under Acts of Congress

(a) Except as otherwise provided by law, a civil action arising under an Act of Congress enacted after the date of the enactment of this section [December 1, 1990] may not be commenced later than 4 years after the cause of action accrues.

(b) Notwithstanding subsection (a), a private right of action that involves a claim of fraud, deceit, manipulation, or contrivance in contravention of a regulatory requirement concerning the securities laws, as defined in section 3(a)(47) of the Securities Exchange Act of 1934 [15 U.S.C. §78c(a)(47)], may be brought not later than the earlier of—

    (1) 2 years after the discovery of the facts constituting the violation; or

    (2) 5 years after such violation.

Title VI of the Civil Rights Act of 1964

42 U.S.C. §§2000d, 2000d-1, 2000d-3, 2000d-4(a)

§2000d [§601]. Nondiscrimination in Federally Assisted Programs

No person in the United States shall, on the ground of race, color, or national origin, be excluded from participation in, be denied the benefits of, or be subjected to discrimination under any program or activity receiving Federal financial assistance.

§2000d-1 [§602]. Federal Authority and Financial Assistance to Programs or Activities by way of Grant, Loan, or Contract Other than Contract of Insurance or Guaranty; Rules and Regulations; Approved by President; Compliance with Requirements; Reports to Congressional Committees; Effective Date of Administrative Action.

Each federal department and agency which is empowered to extend Federal financial assistance to any program or activity, by way of grant, loan, or contract other than a contract of insurance or guaranty, is authorized and directed to effectuate the provisions of section 2000d of this title with respect to such program or activity by issuing rules, regulations, or orders of general applicability which shall be consistent with achievement of the objectives of the statute authorizing the financial assistance in connection with which the action is taken. No such rule, regulation, or order shall become effective unless and until approved by the President. Compliance with any requirement adopted pursuant to this section may be affected (1) by the termination of or refusal to grant or to continue assistance under such program or activity to any recipient as to whom there has been an express finding on the record, after opportunity for hearing, of a failure to comply with such requirement, but such termination or refusal shall be limited to the particular political entity, or part thereof, or other recipient as to whom such a finding has been made and shall be limited in its effect to the particular program, or part thereof, in which such noncompliance has been so found, or (2) by any other means authorized by law: *Provided, however,* That no such action shall be taken until the department or agency concerned has advised the appropriate person or persons of the failure to comply with the requirement and has determined that compliance cannot be secured by voluntary means. In the case of any action terminating, or refusing to grant or continue, assistance because of failure to comply with a requirement, imposed pursuant to this section, the head of the Federal department or agency shall file with the committees of the House and Senate having legislative jurisdiction over the program or activity involved a full written report of the circumstances and the grounds for such action. No such action shall become effective until thirty days have elapsed after the filing of such report.

§2000d-3 [§604]. Construction of Provisions Not to Authorize Administrative Action with Respect to Employment Practices Except Where Primary Objective of Federal Financial Assistance Is to Provide Employment.

Nothing contained in this subchapter shall be construed to authorize action under this subchapter by any department or agency with respect to any employment practice of any employer, employment agency, or labor organization except where a primary objective of the Federal financial assistance is to provide employment.

§2000d-4(a) [§606]. Interpretation of "Program or Activity"

For the purposes of this title, the term "program or activity" and the term "program" mean all of the operations of—

(1)(A) a department, agency, special purpose district, or other instrumentality of a State or a local government; or

(B) the entity of such State or local government that distributes such assistance and each such department or agency (and each other State or local government entity) to which the assistance is extended, in the case of assistance to a State or local government;

(2)(A) a college, university, or other postsecondary institution, or a public system of higher education; or

(B) a local educational agency (as defined in section 7801 of Title 20), system of vocational education, or other school system;

(3)(A) an entire corporation, partnership, or other private organization, or an entire sole proprietorship—

(i) if assistance is extended to such corporation, partnership, private organization, or sole proprietorship as a whole; or

(ii) which is principally engaged in the business of providing education, health care, housing, social services, or parks and recreation; or

(B) the entire plant or other comparable, geographically separate facility to which Federal financial assistance is extended, in the case of any other corporation, partnership, private organization, or sole proprietorship; or

(4) any other entity which is established by two or more of the entities described in paragraph (1), (2), or (3);

any part of which is extended Federal financial assistance.

Title VII of the Civil Rights Act of 1964

42 U.S.C. §§2000e–2000e-17

TITLE VII

§2000e [§701]. Equal Employment Opportunity Definitions

For the purposes of this title —

(a) The term "person" includes one or more individuals, governments, governmental agencies, political subdivisions, labor unions, partnerships, associations, corporations, legal representatives, mutual companies, joint-stock companies, trusts, unincorporated organizations, trustees, trustees in bankruptcy, or receivers.

(b) The term "employer" means a person engaged in an industry affecting commerce who has fifteen or more employees for each working day in each of twenty or more calendar weeks in the current or preceding calendar year, and any agent of such a person, but such term does not include (1) the United States, a corporation wholly owned by the Government of the United States, an Indian tribe, or any department or agency of the District of Columbia subject by statute to procedures of the competitive service (as defined in section 2102 of title 5 of the United States Code), or (2) a bona fide private membership club (other than a labor organization) which is exempt from taxation under section 501(c) of the Internal Revenue Code of 1954, except that, during the first year after the date of enactment of the Equal Employment Opportunity Act of 1972, persons having fewer than twenty-five employees (and their agents) shall not be considered employers.

(c) The term "employment agency" means any person regularly undertaking with or without compensation to procure employees for an employer or to procure for employees opportunities to work for an employer and includes an agent of such a person.

(d) The term "labor organization" means a labor organization engaged in an industry affecting commerce, and any agent of such an organization, and includes any organization of any kind, any agency, or employee representation committee, group, association, or plan so engaged in which employees participate and which exists for the purpose, in whole or in part, of dealing with employees concerning grievances, labor disputes, wages, rates of pay, hours, or other terms or conditions of employment, and any conference, general committee, joint or system board, or joint council so engaged which is subordinate to a national or international labor organization.

(e) A labor organization shall be deemed to be engaged in an industry affecting commerce if (1) it maintains or operates a hiring hall or hiring office which procures employees for an employer or produces for employees opportunities to work for an employer, or (2) the number of its members (or, where it is a labor organization composed of other labor organizations or their representatives, if the aggregate number of the members of such labor organization) is (A) twenty-five or more during the first year after the date of enactment of the Equal Employment Opportunity Act of 1972, or (B) fifteen or more thereafter, and such labor organization—

(1) is the certified representative of employees under the provisions of the National Labor Relations Act, as amended, or the Railway Labor Act, as amended;

(2) although not certified, is a national or international labor organization or a local labor organization recognized or acting as the representative of employees of an employer or employers engaged in an industry affecting commerce; or

(3) has chartered a local labor organization or subsidiary body which is representing or actively seeking to represent employees of employers within the meaning of paragraph (1) or (2); or

(4) has been chartered by a labor organization representing or actively seeking to represent employees within the meaning of paragraph (1) or (2) as the local or subordinate body through which such employees may enjoy membership or become affiliated with such labor organization; or

(5) is a conference, general committee, joint or system board, or joint council subordinate to a national or international labor organization, which includes a labor organization engaged in an industry affecting commerce within the meaning of any of the preceding paragraphs of this subsection.

(f) The term "employee" means an individual employed by an employer, except that term "employee" shall not include any person elected to public office in any State or political subdivision of any State by the qualified voters thereof, or any person chosen by such officer to be on such officer's personal staff, or an appointee on the policy making level or an immediate adviser with respect to the exercise of the constitutional or legal powers of the office. The exemption set forth in the preceding sentence shall not include employees subject to the civil service laws of a State government, governmental agency, or political subdivision. With respect to employment in a foreign country, such term includes an individual who is a citizen of the United States.

(g) The term "commerce" means trade, traffic, commerce, transportation, transmission, or communication among the several States; or between a State and any place outside thereof; or within the District of Columbia, or a possession of the United States; or between points in the same State but through a point outside thereof.

(h) The term "industry affecting commerce" means any activity, business, or industry in commerce or in which a labor dispute would hinder or obstruct commerce or the free flow of commerce and includes any activity or industry "affecting commerce" within the meaning of the Labor-Management Reporting and Disclosure Act of 1959, and further includes any governmental industry, business, or activity.

(i) The term "State" includes a State of the United States, the District of Columbia, Puerto Rico, the Virgin Islands, American Samoa, Guam, Wake Island, the Canal Zone, and Outer Continental Shelf lands defined in the Outer Continental Shelf Lands Act.

(j) The term "religion" includes all aspects of religious observance and practice, as well as belief, unless an employer demonstrates that he is unable to reasonably accommodate to an employee's or prospective employee's religious observance or practice without undue hardship on the conduct of the employer's business.

(k) The terms "because of sex" or "on the basis of sex" includes, but are not limited to, because of or on the basis of pregnancy, childbirth or related medical conditions; and women affected by pregnancy, childbirth, or related medical conditions shall be treated the same for all employment-related purposes, including receipt of benefits under fringe benefit programs, as other persons not so affected but similar in their ability or inability to work, and nothing in section 2000e-2(h) of this title shall be interpreted to permit otherwise. This subsection shall not require an employer to pay for health insurance benefits for abortion, except where the life of the mother would be endangered if the fetus were carried to term, or except where medical complications have arisen from an abortion: Provided, That nothing herein shall preclude an employer from providing abortion benefits or otherwise affect bargaining agreements in regard to abortion.

(l) The term "complaining party" means the Commission, the Attorney General, or a person who may bring an action or proceeding under this title.

(m) The term "demonstrates" means meets the burdens of production and persuasion.

(n) The term "respondent" means an employer, employment agency, labor organization, joint labor-management committee controlling apprenticeship or other training or retraining program, including an on-the-job training program, or Federal entity subject to section 2000e-16 of this title.

§2000e-1 [§702]. *Application to Foreign and Religious Employment*

(a) Inapplicability of subchapter to certain aliens and employees of religious entities. This subchapter shall not apply to an employer with respect to the employment of aliens outside any State, or to a religious corporation, association, educational institution, or society with respect to the employment of individuals of a particular religion to perform work connected with the carrying on by such corporation, association, educational institution, or society of its activities.

(b) Compliance with statute as violative of foreign law. It shall not be unlawful under section 2000e-2 or 2000e-3 of this title for any employer (or a corporation controlled by an employer), labor organization, employment agency, or joint labor-management committee controlling apprenticeship or other training or retraining (including on-the-job training programs) to take any action otherwise prohibited by such section, with respect to an employee in a workplace in a foreign country if compliance with such section would cause such employer (or such corporation), such organization, such agency, or such committee to violate the law of the foreign country in which such workplace is located.

(c) Control of corporation incorporated in a foreign country.

(1) If an employer controls a corporation whose place of incorporation is a foreign country, any practice prohibited by section 2000e-2 or 2000e-3 of this title engaged in such corporation shall be presumed to be engaged in such employer.

(2) Sections 2000e-2 and 2000e-3 of this title shall not apply with respect to the foreign operations of an employer that is a foreign person not controlled by an American employer.

(3) For purposes of this subsection, the determination of whether an employer controls a corporation shall be based on—

(A) the interrelation of operations;

(B) the common management;

(C) the centralized control of labor relations; and

(D) the common ownership or financial control, of the employer and the corporation.

§2000e-2 [§703]. Discrimination Because of Race, Color, Religion, Sex, or National Origin

(a) Employer practices. It shall be an unlawful employment practice for an employer—

(1) to fail or refuse to hire or to discharge any individual, or otherwise to discriminate against any individual with respect to his compensation, terms, conditions, or privileges of employment, because of such individual's race, color, religion, sex, or national origin; or

(2) to limit, segregate, or classify his employees or applicants for employment in any way which would deprive or tend to deprive any individual of employment opportunities or otherwise adversely affect his status as an employee, because of such individual's race, color, religion, sex, or national origin.

(b) Employment agency practices. It shall be an unlawful employment practice for an employment agency to fail or refuse to refer for employment, or otherwise to discriminate against, any individual because of his race, color, religion, sex, or national origin, or to classify or refer for employment any individual on the basis of his race, color, religion, sex, or national origin.

(c) Labor organization practices. It shall be an unlawful employment practice for a labor organization —

(1) to exclude or to expel from its membership, or otherwise to discriminate against, any individual because of his race, color, religion, sex, or national origin;

(2) to limit, segregate, or classify its membership or applicants for membership or to classify or fail to refuse to refer for employment any individual, in any way which would deprive or tend to deprive any individual of employment opportunities, or would limit such employment opportunities or otherwise adversely affect his status as an employee or as an applicant for employment, because of such individual's race, color, religion, sex, or national origin; or

(3) to cause or attempt to cause an employer to discriminate against an individual in violation of this section.

(d) Training programs. It shall be an unlawful employment practice for any employer, labor organization, or joint labor-management committee controlling apprenticeship or other training or retraining, including on-the-job training programs, to discriminate against any individual because of his race, color, religion, sex, or national origin in admission to, or employment in, any program established to provide apprenticeship or other training.

(e) Business or enterprises with personnel qualified on basis of religion, sex, or national origin; educational institutions with personnel of particular religion. Notwithstanding any other provision of this title, (1) it shall not be an unlawful employment practice for an employer to hire and employ employees, for an employment agency to classify; or refer for employment any individual, for a labor organization to classify its membership or to classify or refer for employment any individual, or for an employer, labor organization, or joint labor-management committee controlling apprenticeship or other training or retraining programs to admit or employ any individual in any such program, on the basis of his religion, sex, or national origin in those certain instances where religion, sex, or national origin is a bona fide occupational qualification reasonably necessary to the normal operation of that particular business or enterprise, and (2) it shall not be an unlawful employment practice for a school, college, university, or other educational institution or institution of learning to hire and employ employees of a particular religion if such school, college, university, or other educational institution or institution of learning is, in whole or in substantial part, owned, supported, controlled, or managed by a particular religion or by a particular religious corporation, association, or society, or if the curriculum of such school, college, university, or other educational institution or institution of learning is directed toward the propagation of a particular religion.

(f) Members of Communist Party or Communist-action or Communist-front organizations. As used in this title, the phrase "unlawful employment practice" shall not be deemed to include any action or measure taken by an employer, labor organization, joint labor-management committee, or employment agency with respect to an individual who is a member of the Communist Party of the United States or of any other organization required to register as a Communist-action or

Communist-front organization by final order of the Subversive Activities Control Board pursuant to the Subversive Activities Control Act of 1950.

(g) National security. Notwithstanding any other provision of this title, it shall not be an unlawful employment practice for an employee to fail or refuse to hire and employ any individual for any position, for an employer to discharge an individual from any position, or for an employment agency to fail or refuse to refer any individual for employment in any position, or for a labor organization to fail or refuse to refer any individual for employment in any position, if—

(1) the occupancy of such position, or access to the premises in or upon which any part of the duties of such position is performed or is to be performed, is subject to any requirement imposed in the interest of the national security of the United States under any security program in effect pursuant to or administered under any statute of the United States or any Executive Order of the President; and

(2) such individual has not fulfilled or has ceased to fulfill that requirement.

(h) Seniority or merit system; quantity or quality of production; ability test; compensation based on sex and authorized by minimum wage provisions. Notwithstanding any other provision of this title, it shall not be an unlawful employment practice for an employer to apply different standards of compensation, or different terms, conditions, or privileges of employment pursuant to a bona fide seniority or merit system, or a system which measures earnings by quantity or quality or production or to employees who work in different locations, provided that such differences are not the result of an intention to discriminate because of race, color, religion, sex, or national origin; nor shall it be an unlawful employment practice for an employer to give and to act upon the results of any professionally developed ability test provided that such test, its administration or action upon the results is not designed, intended, or used to discriminate because of race, color, religion, sex, or national origin. It shall not be an unlawful employment practice under this title for any employer to differentiate upon the basis of sex in determining the amount of the wages or compensation paid to employees of such employer if such differentiation is authorized by the provisions of Section 6(d) of the Fair Labor Standards Act of 1938 as amended (29 U.S.C. 206(d)).

(i) Businesses or enterprises extending preferential treatment to Indians. Nothing contained in this title shall apply to any business or enterprise on or near an Indian reservation with respect to any publicly announced employment practice of such business or enterprise under which a preferential treatment is given to any individual because he is an Indian living on or near a reservation.

(j) Preferential treatment not to be granted on account of existing number or percentage imbalance. Nothing contained in this title shall be interpreted to require any employer, employment agency, labor organization, or joint labor-management committee subject to this title to grant preferential treatment to any individual or to any group because of the race, color, religion, sex, or national origin of such individual or group on account of an imbalance which may exist with respect to the total number of percentage of persons of any race, color, religion, sex, or national origin employed by any employer, referred or classified for employment by any employment agency or labor organization, admitted to membership or classified by any labor organization, or admitted to, or employed in, any apprenticeship or other training program, in comparison with the total number or percentage of persons of such race, color, religion, sex, or national origin in any community, State, section, or other area, or in the available work force in any community, State, section, or other area.

 (k) Burden of proof in disparate impact cases.

  (1)(A) An unlawful employment practice based on disparate impact is established under this title only if—

   (i) a complaining party demonstrates that a respondent uses a particular employment practice that causes a disparate impact on the basis of race, color, religion, sex, or national origin and the respondent fails to demonstrate that the challenged practice is job related for the position in question and consistent with business necessity; or

   (ii) the complaining party makes the demonstration described in subparagraph (C) with respect to an alternative employment practice and the respondent refuses to adopt such alternative employment practice.

  (B)(i) With respect to demonstrating that a particular employment practice causes a disparate impact as described in subparagraph (A)(i), the complaining party shall demonstrate that each particular challenged employment practice causes a disparate impact, except that if the complaining party can demonstrate to the court that the elements of a respondent's decision making process are not capable of separation for analysis, the decision making process may be analyzed as one employment practice.

   (ii) If the respondent demonstrates that a specific employment practice does not cause the disparate impact, the respondent shall not be required to demonstrate that such practice is required by business necessity.

  (C) The demonstration referred to by subparagraph (A)(ii) shall be in accordance with the law as it existed on June 4, 1989, with respect to the concept of "alternative employment practice."

  (2) A demonstration that an employment practice is required by business necessity may not be used as a defense against a claim of intentional discrimination under this title.

  (3) Notwithstanding any other provision of this title, a rule barring the employment of an individual who currently and knowingly uses or possesses a controlled substance, as defined in schedules I and II of section 102(6) of the Controlled Substances Act (21 U.S.C. 802(6)), other than the use or possession of a drug taken under the supervision of a licensed health care professional, or any other use or possession authorized by the Controlled Substances Act or any other provision of Federal law, shall be considered an unlawful employment practice under this title only if such rule is adopted or

applied with an intent to discriminate because of race, color, religion, sex, or national origin.

(l) Prohibition of discriminatory use of test scores. It shall be an unlawful employment practice for a respondent, in connection with the selection or referral of applicants or candidates for employment or promotion, to adjust the scores of, use different cutoff scores for, or otherwise alter the results of, employment related tests on the basis of race, color, religion, sex, or national origin.

(m) Impermissible consideration of race, color, religion, sex, or national origin in employment practices. Except as otherwise provided in this title, an unlawful employment practice is established when the complaining party demonstrates that race, color, religion, sex, or national origin was a motivating factor for any employment practice, even though other factors also motivated the practice.

(n) Resolution of challenges to employment practices implementing litigated or consent judgment or orders.

(1)(A) Notwithstanding any other provision of law, and except as provided in paragraph (2), an employment practice that implements and is within the scope of a litigated or consent judgment or order that resolves a claim of employment discrimination under the Constitution or Federal civil rights laws may not be challenged under the circumstances described in subparagraph (B).

(B) A practice described in paragraph (A) may not be challenged in a claim under the Constitution or Federal civil rights laws —

(i) by a person who, prior to the entry of the judgment or order described in subparagraph (A), had —

(I) actual notice of the proposed judgment or order sufficient to apprise such person that such judgment or order might adversely affect the interests and legal rights of such person and that an opportunity was available to present objections to such judgment or order by a future date certain; and

(II) a reasonable opportunity to present objections to such judgment or order; or

(ii) by a person whose interests were adequately represented by another person who had previously challenged the judgment or order on the same legal grounds and with a similar factual situation, unless there has been an intervening change in law or fact.

(2) Nothing in this subsection shall be construed to —

(A) alter the standards for intervention under Rule 24 of the Federal Rules of Civil Procedure or apply to the rights of parties who have successfully intervened pursuant to such rule in the proceeding in which the parties intervened;

(B) apply to the rights of parties to the action in which a litigated or consent judgment or order was entered, or of members of a class represented or sought to be represented in such action, or of members of a group on whose behalf relief was sought in such action by the Federal Government;

(C) prevent challenges to a litigated or consent judgment or order on the ground that such judgment or order was obtained through collusion or fraud, or is transparently invalid or was entered by a court lacking subject matter jurisdiction; or

(D) authorize or permit the denial to any person of the due process of law required by the Constitution.

(3) Any action not precluded under this subsection that challenges an employment consent judgment or order described in paragraph (1) shall be brought in the court, and if possible before the judge, that entered such judgment or order. Nothing in this subsection shall preclude a transfer of such action pursuant to section 1404 of Title 28, United States Code.

§2000e-3 [§704]. *Other Unlawful Employment Practices*

(a) Discrimination for making charges, testifying, assisting, or participating in enforcement proceedings. It shall be an unlawful employment practice for an employer to discriminate against any of his employees or applicants for employment, for an employment agency or joint labor-management committee controlling apprenticeship or other training or retraining, including on-the-job training programs, to discriminate against any individual, or for a labor organization to discriminate against any member thereof or applicant for membership, because he has opposed any practice, made an unlawful employment practice by this title, or because he has made a charge, testified, assisted, or participated in any manner in an investigation, proceeding, or hearing under this title.

(b) Printing or publication of notices or advertisements indicating prohibited preference, specification, or discrimination; occupational qualification exception. It shall be an unlawful employment practice for an employer, labor organization; employment agency, or joint labor-management committee controlling apprenticeship or other training or retraining, including on-the-job training programs, to print or cause to be printed or published any notice or advertisement relating to employment by such a labor organization, or relating to any classification or referral for employment by such an employment agency, or relating to admission to, or employment in, any program established to provide apprenticeship or other training by such a joint labor-management committee indicating any preference, limitation, specification, or discrimination, based on race, color, religion, sex, or national origin, except that such a notice or advertisement may indicate a preference, limitation, specification, or discrimination based on religion, sex, or national origin when religion, sex, or national origin is a bona fide occupational qualification for employment.

§2000e-4 [§705]. *Equal Employment Opportunity Commission*

(a) Creation; composition; political representation; Chairman and Vice Chairman; compensation of personnel. There is hereby created a Commission to be known as the Equal Employment Opportunity Commission, which shall be composed of five members, not more than three of whom shall be members of the same political party. Members of the Commission shall be appointed by the President by and with the advice and consent of the Senate for a term of five years. Any individual chosen to fill a vacancy shall be appointed only for the unexpired term of the member whom he shall succeed, and all members of the Commission shall continue to serve until their successors are appointed and qualified, except that no such member of the Commission shall continue to serve (1) for more than sixty days when the Congress is in session unless a nomination to fill such vacancy shall have been submitted to the Senate, or (2) after the adjournment sine die of the session of the Senate in which such nomination was submitted. The President shall designate one member to serve as Chairman of the Commission, and one member to serve as Vice Chairman. The Chairman shall be responsible on behalf of the Commission for the administrative operations of the Commission, and, except as provided in subsection (b), shall appoint, in accordance with the provisions of title 5, United States Code, governing appointments in the competitive service, such officers, agents, attorneys, hearing examiners, and employees as he deems necessary to assist it in the performance of its functions and to fix their compensation in accordance with the provisions of chapter 51 and subchapter III of chapter 53 of title 5, United States Code, relating to classification and General Schedule pay rates: Provided, That assignment, removal, and compensation of hearing examiners shall be in accordance with sections 3105, 3344, 5372, and 7521 of title 5, United States Code.

(b) General Counsel; appointment; term; duties; representation by attorneys and Attorney General.

(1) There shall be a General Counsel of the Commission appointed by the President, by and with the advice and consent of the Senate, for a term of four years. The General Counsel shall have responsibility for the conduct of litigation as provided in sections 706 and 707 of this title. The General Counsel shall have such other duties as the Commission may prescribe or as may be provided by law and shall concur with the Chairman of the Commission on the appointment and supervision of regional attorneys. The General Counsel of the Commission on the effective date of this Act shall continue in such position and perform the functions specified in this subsection until a successor is appointed and qualified.

(2) Attorneys appointed under this section may, at the direction of the Commission, appear for and represent the Commission in any case in court, provided that the Attorney General shall conduct all litigation to which the commission is a party in the Supreme Court pursuant to this title.

(c) Exercise of power during vacancy; quorum. A vacancy in the Commission shall not impair the right of the remaining members to exercise all the powers of the Commission and three members thereof shall constitute a quorum.

(d) Seal; judicial notice. The commission shall have an official seal which shall be judicially noticed.

(e) Reports to Congress and to President. The Commission shall at the middle and at the close of each fiscal year report to the Congress and to the President concerning the action it has taken; the names, salaries, and duties of all individuals in its employ and the moneys it has disbursed; and shall make such further reports on the cause of and means of eliminating discrimination and such recommendations for further legislation as may appear desirable.

(f) Principal and other office. The principal office of the Commission shall be in or near the District of Columbia, but it may meet or exercise any or all its powers at any other place. The Commission may establish such regional or state offices as it deems necessary to accomplish the purpose of this title.

(g) Power of Commission. The Commission shall have power—

(1) to cooperate with and, with their consent, utilize regional, state, local, and other agencies, both public and private, and individuals;

(2) to pay to witnesses whose depositions are taken or who are summoned before the Commission or any of its agents the same witness and mileage fees as are paid to witnesses in the courts of the United States;

(3) to furnish to persons subject to this title such technical assistance as they may request to further their compliance with this title or an order issued thereunder;

(4) upon the request of (i) any employer, whose employees or some of them, or (ii) any labor organization, whose members or some of them, refuse or threaten to refuse to cooperate in effectuating the provisions of this title, to assist in such effectuation by conciliation or such other remedial action as is provided by this title;

(5) to make such technical studies as are appropriate to effectuate the purposes and policies of this title and to make the results of such studies available to the public;

(6) to intervene in a civil action brought under section 706 by an aggrieved party against a respondent other than a government, governmental agency or political subdivision.

(h) Cooperation with other departments and agencies in performance of educational or promotional activities; outreach activities.

(1) The Commission shall, in any of its educational or promotional activities, cooperate with other departments and agencies in the performance of such educational and promotional activities.

(2) In exercising its powers under this title, the Commission shall carry out educational and outreach activities (including dissemination of information in languages other than English) targeted to—

(A) individuals who historically have been victims of employment discrimination and have not been equitably served by the Commission; and

(B) individuals on whose behalf the Commission has authority to enforce any other law prohibiting employment discrimination, concerning rights and obligations under this title or such law, as the case may be.

(i) Personnel subject to political activity restrictions. All officers, agents, attorneys and employees of the Commission, including the members of the Commission, shall be subject to the provisions of section 9 of the act of August 2, 1939, as amended (Hatch Act), notwithstanding any exemption contained in such section.

(j) Technical Assistance Training Institute.

(1) The Commission shall establish a Technical Assistance Training Institute, through which the Commission shall provide technical assistance and training regarding the laws and regulations enforced by the Commission.

(2) An employer or other entity covered under this title shall not be excused from compliance with the requirements of this title because of any failure to receive technical assistance under this subsection.

(3) There are authorized to be appropriated to carry out this subsection such sums as may be necessary for fiscal year 1992.

§2000e-5 [§706]. Prevention of Unlawful Employment Practices

(a) Power of Commission to prevent unlawful employment practices. The Commission is empowered, as hereinafter provided, to prevent any person from engaging in any unlawful employment practice as set forth in section 703 or 704 of this title.

(b) Charges by persons aggrieved or member of Commission of unlawful employment practices by employers, etc.; filing; allegations; notice to respondent; contents of notice; investigation by Commission; contents of charges; prohibition on disclosure of charges; determination of reasonable cause; conference, conciliation, and persuasion for elimination of unlawful practices; prohibition on disclosure of informal endeavors to end unlawful practices; use of evidence in subsequent proceedings; penalties for disclosure of information; time for determination of reasonable cause. Whenever a charge is filed by or on behalf of a person claiming to be aggrieved, or by a member of the Commission, alleging that an employer, employment agency, labor organization, or joint labor-management committee controlling apprenticeship or other training or retraining including on-the-job training programs, has engaged in an unlawful employment practice, the Commission shall serve a notice of the charge (including the date, place and circumstances of the alleged unlawful employment practice) on such employer, employment agency, labor organization, or joint labor-management committee (hereinafter referred to as the "respondent") within ten days and shall make an investigation thereof. Charges shall be in writing under oath or affirmation and shall contain such information and be in such form as the Commission requires. Charges shall not be made public by the Commission. If the Commission determines after such investigation that there is not reasonable cause to believe that the charge is true, it shall dismiss the charge and promptly notify the person claiming to be aggrieved and the respondent of its action. In determining whether reasonable cause exists, the Commission shall accord substantial weight to final findings and orders made by the State or local authorities in proceedings commenced under State or local law pursuant to the requirements of subsections (c) and (d). If the Commission determines after such investigation that there is reasonable cause to believe that the charge is true, the Commission shall endeavor to eliminate any such alleged unlawful employment practice by informal methods of conference, conciliation, and persuasion. Nothing said or done during and as a part of such informal endeavors may be made public by the Commission, its officers or employees, or used as evidence in a subsequent proceeding without the written consent of the persons concerned. Any person who makes public information in violation of this subsection shall be fined not more than $1,000 or imprisoned for not more than one year, or both. The Commission shall make its determination on reasonable cause as promptly as possible and, so far as practicable, not later than one hundred and twenty days from the filing of the charge or, where applicable under subsection (c) or (d), from the date upon which the Commission is authorized to take action with respect to the charge.

(c) State or local enforcement proceedings; notification of state or local authority; time for filing charges with Commission; commencement of proceedings. In the case of an alleged unlawful employment practice occurring in a State, or political subdivision of a State, which as a State or local law prohibiting the unlawful employment practice alleged and establishing or authorizing a State or local authority to grant or seek relief from such practice or to institute criminal proceedings with respect thereto upon receiving notice thereof, no charge may be filed under subsection (a) [Probably should be subsection (b)] by the person aggrieved before the expiration of sixty days after proceedings have been commenced under the State or local law, unless such proceedings have been earlier terminated, provided that such sixty-day period shall be extended to one hundred and twenty days during the first year after the effective date of such State or local law. If any requirement for the commencement of such proceedings is imposed by a State or local authority other than requirement of the filing of a written and signed statement of the facts upon which the proceeding is based, the proceeding shall be deemed to have been commenced for the purposes of this subsection at the time such statement is sent by registered mail to the appropriate State or local authority.

(d) State or local enforcement proceedings; notification of state or local authority; time for action on charges by Commission. In the case of any charge filed by a member of the Commission alleging an unlawful employment practice occurring in a State or political subdivision of a State which has a State or local law prohibiting the practice alleged and establishing or authorizing a State or local authority to grant or seek relief from such practice or to institute criminal proceedings with respect thereto upon receiving notice thereof, the Commission shall, before taking any action with respect to such charge, notify the appropriate State or local officials and, upon request, afford them a reasonable time, but not less than sixty days (provided that such sixty-day period shall be extended to one hundred and twenty days during the first year after the effective day of such State or local law), unless a shorter period is requested, to act under such State or local law to remedy the practice alleged.

(e) Time for filing charges; time for service of notice of charge; filing of charge by Commission with state or local agency; seniority system.

(1) A charge under this section shall be filed within one hundred and eighty days after alleged the unlawful employment practice occurred and notice of the charge (including the date, place and circumstances of the alleged unlawful employment practice) shall be served upon the person against whom such charge is made within ten days thereafter, except that in a case of an unlawful employment practice with respect to which the person aggrieved has initially instituted proceedings with a State or local agency with authority to grant or seek relief from such practice or to institute criminal

proceedings with respect thereto upon receiving notice thereof, such charge shall be filed by or on behalf of the person aggrieved within three hundred days after the alleged unlawful employment practice occurred, or within thirty days after receiving notice that the State or local agency has terminated the proceedings under the State or local law, whichever is earlier, and a copy of such charge shall be filed by the Commission with the State or local agency.

(2) For purposes of this section, an unlawful employment practice occurs, with respect to a seniority system that has been adopted for an intentionally discriminatory purpose in violation of this title (whether or not that discriminatory purpose is apparent on the face of the seniority provision), when the seniority system is adopted, when an individual becomes subject to the seniority system, or when a person aggrieved is injured by the application of the seniority system or provision of the system.

(3)(A) For purposes of this section, an unlawful employment practice occurs, with respect to discrimination in compensation in violation of this title, when a discriminatory compensation decision or other practice is adopted, when an individual becomes subject to a discriminatory compensation decision or other practice, or when an individual is affected by application of a discriminatory compensation decision or other practice, including each time wages, benefits, or other compensation is paid, resulting in whole or in part from such a decision or other practice.

(B) In addition to any relief authorized by section 1977A of the Revised Statutes (*42 U.S.C. 1981a*), liability may accrue and an aggrieved person may obtain relief as provided in subsection (g)(1), including recovery of back pay for up to two years preceding the filing of the charge, where the unlawful employment practices that have occurred during the charge filing period are similar or related to unlawful employment practices with regard to discrimination in compensation that occurred outside the time for filing a charge.

(f) Civil action by Commission, Attorney General, or person aggrieved; preconditions; procedure; appointment of attorney; payment of fees, costs, or security; intervention; stay of Federal proceedings; action for appropriate temporary or preliminary relief pending final disposition of charge; jurisdiction and venue of United States courts; designation of judge to hear and determine case; assignment of case for hearing; expedition of case; appointment of master.

(1) If within thirty days after a charge is filed with the Commission or within thirty days after expiration of any period of reference under subsections (c) or (d), the Commission has been unable to secure from the respondent a conciliation agreement acceptable to the Commission, the Commission may bring a civil action against any respondent not a government, governmental agency, or political subdivision named in the charge. In the case of a respondent which is a government, governmental agency, or political subdivision, if the Commission has been unable to secure from the respondent a conciliation agreement acceptable to the Commission, the Commission shall take no further action and shall refer the case to the Attorney General who may bring civil action against such respondent in the appropriate United States district court.

The person or persons aggrieved shall have the right to intervene in a civil action brought by the Commission or the Attorney General in a case involving a government, governmental agency, or political subdivision. If a charge filed with the Commission pursuant to subsection (b) is dismissed by the Commission, or if within one hundred and eighty days from the filing of such charge or the expiration of any period of reference under subsections (c) or (d), whichever is later, the Commission has not filed a civil action under this section or the Attorney General has not filed a civil action in a case involving a government, governmental agency, or political subdivision, or the Commission has not entered into a conciliation agreement to which the person aggrieved is a party, the Commission, or the Attorney General in a case involving a government, governmental agency, or political subdivision, shall so notify the person aggrieved and within ninety days after the giving of such notice a civil action may be brought against the respondent named in the charge (A) by the person claiming to be aggrieved or (B) if such charge was filed by a member of the Commission, by any person whom the charge alleged was aggrieved by the alleged unlawful employment practice. Upon application by the complainant and in such circumstances as the court may deem just, the court may appoint an attorney for such complainant and may authorize the commencement of the action without the payment of fees, costs, or security. Upon timely application, the court may, in its discretion, permit the Commission, or the Attorney General in a case involving a government, governmental agency, or political subdivision, to intervene in such civil action upon certification that the case is of general public importance. Upon request, the court may, in its discretion, stay further proceedings for not more than sixty days pending the termination of State or local proceedings described in subsections (c) or (d) of this section or further efforts of the Commission to obtain voluntary compliance.

(2) Whenever a charge is filed with the Commission and the Commission concludes on the basis of a preliminary investigation that prompt judicial action is necessary to carry out the purpose of this Act, the Commission, or the Attorney General in a case involving a government, governmental agency, or political subdivision, may bring an action for appropriate temporary or preliminary relief pending final disposition of such charge. Any temporary restraining order or order granting preliminary or temporary relief shall be issued in accordance with rule 65 of the Federal Rules of Civil Procedure. It shall be the duty of a court having jurisdiction over proceedings under this section to assign cases for hearing at the earliest practicable date and to cause such cases to be in every way expedited.

(3) Each United States district court and each United States court of a place subject to the jurisdiction of the United States shall have jurisdiction of actions brought under this title. Such an action may be brought in any judicial district in the State in which the unlawful employment practice is alleged to have been committed, in the judicial district in which the employment records relevant to such practice are maintained and administered, or in the judicial district in which the aggrieved person would have worked but for the alleged unlawful employment practice, but if the respondent is not found

within any such district, such an action may be brought within the judicial district in which the respondent has his principal office. For purposes of sections 1404 and 1406 of title 28 of the United States Code, the judicial district in which the respondent has his principal office shall in all cases be considered a district in which the action might have been brought.

(4) It shall be the duty of the chief judge of the district (or in his absence, the acting chief judge) in which the case is pending immediately to designate a judge in such district to hear and determine the case. In the event that no judge in the district is available to hear and determine the case, the chief judge of the district, or the acting chief judge, as the case may be, shall certify this fact to the chief judge of the circuit (or in his absence, the acting chief judge) who shall then designate a district or circuit judge of the circuit to hear and determine the case.

(5) It shall be the duty of the judge designated pursuant to this subsection to assign the case for hearing at the earliest practicable date and to cause the case to be in every way expedited. If such judge has not scheduled the case for trial within one hundred and twenty days after issue has been joined that judge may appoint a master pursuant to rule 53 of the Federal Rules of Civil Procedure.

(g) Injunctions; appropriate affirmative action; accrual of back pay; reduction of back pay; limitations on judicial orders.

(1) If the court finds that the respondent has intentionally engaged in or is intentionally engaging in an unlawful employment practice charged in the complaint, the court may enjoin the respondent from engaging in such unlawful employment practice, and order such affirmative action as may be appropriate, which may include, but is not limited to, reinstatement or hiring of employees, with or without back pay (payable by the employer, employment agency, or labor organization, as the case may be, responsible for the unlawful employment practice), or any other equitable relief as the court deems appropriate. Back pay liability shall not accrue from a date more than two years prior to the filing of a charge with the Commission. Interim earnings or amounts earnable with reasonable diligence by the person or persons discriminated against shall operate to reduce the back pay otherwise allowable.

(2)(A) No order of the court shall require the admission or reinstatement of an individual as a member of a union, or the hiring, reinstatement, or promotion of an individual as an employee, or the payment to him of any back pay, if such individual was refused admission, suspended, or expelled, or was refused employment or advancement or was suspended or discharged for any reason other than discrimination on account of race, color, religion, sex, or national origin or in violation of section 704(a).

(B) On a claim in which an individual proves a violation under section 703(m) and a respondent demonstrates that the respondent would have taken the same action in the absence of the impermissible motivating factor, the court —

(i) may grant declaratory relief, injunctive relief (except as provided in clause (ii)), and attorney's fees and costs demonstrated to be directly attributable only to the pursuit of a claim under section 703(m); and

(ii) shall not award damages or issue an order requiring any admission, reinstatement, hiring, promotion, or payment, described in subparagraph (A).

(h) Provisions of chapter 6 of title 29 not applicable to civil actions for presentation of unlawful employment practices. The provisions of the Act entitled "An Act to amend the judicial Code and to define and limit the jurisdiction of courts sitting in equity, and for other purposes," approved March 23, 1932 (29 U.S.C. 101-115), shall not apply with respect to civil actions brought under this section.

(i) Proceedings by Commission to compel compliance with judicial orders. In any case in which an employer, employment agency, or labor organization fails to comply with an order of a court issued in a civil action brought under this section the Commission may commence proceedings to compel compliance with such order.

(j) Appeals. Any civil action brought under this section and any proceedings brought under subsection (j) shall be subject to appeal as provided in sections 1291 and 1292, title 28, United States Code.

(k) Attorney's fees; liability of Commission and United States for costs. In any action or proceeding under this title the court, in its discretion, may allow the prevailing party, other than the Commission or the United States, a reasonable attorney's fee (including expert fees) as part of the costs, and the Commission and the United States shall be liable for costs the same as a private person.

§2000e-6 [§707]. *Suits by the Attorney General*

(a) Complaint. Whenever the Attorney General has reasonable cause to believe that any person or group of persons is engaged in a pattern or practice of resistance to the full enjoyment of any of the rights secured by this title, and that the pattern or practice is of such a nature and is intended to deny the full exercise of the rights herein described, the Attorney General may bring a civil action in the appropriate district court of the United States by filing with it a complaint (1) signed by him (or in his absence the Acting Attorney General), (2) setting forth facts pertaining to such pattern or practice, and (3) requesting such relief, including an application for a permanent or temporary injunction, restraining order or other order against the person or persons responsible for such pattern or practice, as he deems necessary to insure the full enjoyment of the rights herein described.

(b) Jurisdiction; hearing and determination. The district courts of the United States shall have and shall exercise jurisdiction of proceedings instituted pursuant to this section, and in any such proceeding the Attorney General may file with the clerk of such court a request that a court of three judges be convened to hear and determine the case. Such request for the Attorney General shall be accompanied by a certificate that, in the opinion, the case is of general public importance. A copy of the certificate and request for a three-judge court shall be immediately furnished by such clerk to the chief judge of the circuit (or in his absence, the presiding circuit judge of the circuit) in which the case is pending. Upon receipt of such request it shall be the duty of the chief judge of the circuit or the presiding circuit judge, as the case may be, to designate immediately three judges in such circuit, of whom at least one shall be a circuit judge and another of whom shall be a district judge of the court in which the proceeding was instituted, to hear and determine such case, and it shall be the duty of the judges so designated to assign the case for hearing at the earliest practicable date, to participate in the hearing and determination thereof, and to cause the case to be in every way expedited. An appeal from the final judgment of such court will lie to the Supreme Court.

In the event the Attorney General fails to file such a request in any such proceeding, it shall be the duty of the chief judge of the district (or in his absence, the acting chief judge) in which the case is pending immediately to designate a judge in such district to hear and determine the case. In the event that no judge in the district is available to hear and determine the case, the chief judge of the district, or the acting chief judge, as the case may be, shall certify this fact to the chief judge of the circuit (or in his absence, the acting chief judge) who shall then designate a district or circuit judge of the circuit to hear and determine the case.

It shall be the duty of the judge designated pursuant to this section to assign the case for hearing at the earliest practicable date and to cause the case to be in every way expedited.

(c) Transfer of functions to Commission. Effective two years after the date of enactment of the Equal Employment Opportunity Act of 1972, the functions of the Attorney General under this section shall be transferred to the Commission, together with such personnel, property, records, and unexpended balances of appropriations, allocations, and other funds employed, used, held, available or to be made available in connection with such functions unless the President submits, and neither House or Congress vetoes, a reorganization plan pursuant to chapter 9 of title 5, United States Code, inconsistent with the provisions of this subsection. The Commission shall carry out such functions in accordance with subsections (d) and (e) of this section.

(d) Transfer of functions, etc., not to affect suits commenced pursuant to this section prior to date of transfer. Upon the transfer of functions provided for in subsection (c) of this section, in all suits commenced pursuant to this section prior to the date of such transfer, proceedings shall continue without abatement, all court orders and decrees shall remain in effect, and the Commission shall be substituted as a party for the United States of America, the Attorney General, or the Acting Attorney General, as appropriate.

(e) Investigation and action by Commission pursuant to filing of charge of discrimination; procedure. Subsequent to the date of enactment of the Equal Employment Opportunity Act of 1972, the Commission shall have authority to investigate and act on a charge of a pattern or practice of discrimination, whether filed by or on behalf of a person claiming to be aggrieved or by a member of the Commission. All such actions shall be conducted in accordance with the procedures set forth in section 706 of this Act.

§2000e-7 [§708]. *Effect on State Laws*

Nothing in this title shall be deemed to exempt or relieve any person from any liability, duty, penalty, or punishment provided by any present or future law or any State or political subdivision of a State, other than any such law which purports to require or permit the doing of any act which would be an unlawful employment practice under this title.

§2000e-8 [§709]. Investigations

(a) Access to evidence. In connection with any investigation of a charge filed under section 706 [42 USCS §2000e-5], the Commission or its designated representative shall at all reasonable times have access to, for the purposes of examination, and the right to copy any evidence of any person being investigated or proceeded against that relates to unlawful employment practice covered by this title [42 USCS §§2000e et seq.] and is relevant to the charge under investigation.

(b) Cooperation with State and local agencies. The Commission may cooperate with State and local agencies charged with the administration of State fair employment practices laws and, with the consent of such agencies, may, for the purpose of carrying out its functions and duties under this title and within the limitation of funds appropriated specifically for such purpose, engage in and contribute to the cost of research and other projects of mutual interest undertaken by such agencies, and utilize the services of such agencies and their employees, and, notwithstanding any other provision of law, pay by advance or reimbursement such agencies and their employees for services rendered to assist the Commission in carrying out this title. In furtherance of such cooperative efforts, the commission may enter into written agreements with such State or local agencies and such agreements may include provisions under which the Commission shall refrain from processing a charge in any cases or class of cases specified in such agreements or under which the Commission shall relieve any person or class of persons in such State or locality from requirements imposed under this section. The Commission shall rescind any such agreement whenever it determines that the agreement no longer serves the interests of effective enforcement of this title.

(c) Recordkeeping; reports. Every employer, employment agency, and labor organization subject to this title shall (1) make and keep such records relevant to the determinations of whether unlawful employment practices have been or are being committed, (2) preserve such records for such periods, and (3) make such reports therefrom as the Commission shall prescribe by regulation or order, after public hearing, as reasonable, necessary, or appropriate for the enforcement of this title or the regulations or orders thereunder. The Commission shall, by regulation, require each employer, labor organization, and joint labor-management committee subject to this title which controls an apprenticeship or other training program to maintain such records as are reasonably necessary to carry out the purposes of this title, including, but not limited to, a list of applicants who wish to participate in such program, including the chronological order in which applications were received, and to furnish to the Commission upon request, a detailed description of the manner in which persons are selected to participate in the apprenticeship or other training program. Any employer, employment agency, labor organization, or joint labor-management committee which believes that the application to it of any regulation or order issued under this section would result in undue hardship may apply to the Commission for an exemption from the application of such regulation or order, and, if such application for an exemption is denied, bring a civil action in the United States district court for the district where such records are kept. If the Commission or the court, as the case may be, finds that the application of the regulation or order to the employer, employment agency, or labor organization in question would impose an undue hardship, the Commission or the court, as the case may be, may grant appropriate relief. If any person required to comply with the provisions of this subsection fails or refuses to do so, the United States district court for the district in which such person is found, resides, or transacts business, shall, upon application of the Commission, or the Attorney General in a case involving a government, governmental agency, or political subdivision, have jurisdiction to issue to such person an order requiring him to comply.

(d) Coordination with State and Federal agencies; availability of information. In prescribing requirements pursuant to subsection (c) of this section, the Commission shall consult with other interested State and Federal agencies and shall endeavor to coordinate its requirements with those adopted by such agencies. The Commission shall furnish upon request and without cost to any State or local agency charged with the administration of a fair employment practice law information obtained pursuant to subsection (c) of this section from any employer, employment agency, labor organization, or joint labor-management committee subject to the jurisdiction of such agency. Such information shall be furnished on condition that it not be made public by the recipient agency prior to the institution of a proceeding under State or local law involving such information. If this condition is violated by a recipient agency, the Commission may decline to honor subsequent requests pursuant to this subsection.

(e) Disclosure of information; penalty. It shall be unlawful for any officer or employee of the Commission to make public in any manner whatever any information obtained by the Commission pursuant to its authority under this section prior to the institution of any proceeding under this title involving such information. Any officer or employee of the Commission who shall make public in any manner whatever any information in violation of this subsection shall be guilty of a misdemeanor and, upon conviction thereof, shall be fined not more than $1,000, or imprisoned not more than one year.

§2000e-9 [§710]. Conduct of Hearings and Investigations Pursuant to Section 161 of Title 29

For the purpose of all hearings and investigations conducted by the Commission or its duly authorized agents or agencies, section 11 of the National Labor Relations Act (49 Stat. 455; 29 U.S.C. 161) shall apply.

§2000e-10 [§711]. Posting of Notices; Penalties

(a) Every employer, employment agency and labor organization, as the case may be, shall post and keep posted in conspicuous places upon its premises where notices to employees, applicants for employment and members are customarily posted a notice to be prepared or approved by the Commission setting forth excerpts from or, summaries of, the pertinent provisions of this title and information pertinent to the filing of a complaint.

(b) A willful violation of this section shall be punishable by a fine of not more than $100 for each separate offense.

§2000e-11 [§712]. Veterans' Special Rights or Preference

Nothing contained in this title shall be construed to repeal or modify any Federal, State, territorial, or local law creating special rights or preference for veterans.

§2000e-12 [§713]. Rules and Regulations

(a) The Commission shall have authority from time to time to issue, amend, or rescind suitable procedural regulations to carry out the provisions of this title. Regulations issued under this section shall be in conformity with the standards and limitations of the Administrative Procedure Act.

(b) In any action or proceeding based on any alleged unlawful employment practice, no person shall be subject to any liability or punishment for or on account of (1) the commission by such person of an unlawful employment practice if he pleads and proves that the act of omission complained of was in good faith, in conformity with, and in reliance on any written interpretation or opinion of the Commission, or (2) the failure of such person to publish and file any information required by any provision of this title if he pleads and proves that he failed to publish and file such information in good faith, in conformity with the instructions of the Commission issued under this title regarding the filing of such information. Such a defense, if established, shall be a bar to the action or proceeding, notwithstanding that (A) after such act or omission, such interpretation or opinion is modified or rescinded or is determined by judicial authority to be invalid or of no legal effect, or (B) after publishing or filing the description and annual reports, such publication or filing is determined by judicial authority not to be in conformity with the requirements of this title.

§2000e-13 [§714]. Forcibly Resisting the Commission or Its Representatives

The provisions of sections 111 and 1114, title 18, United States Code, shall apply to officers, agents, and employees of the Commission in the performance of their official duties. Notwithstanding the provisions of sections 111 and 1114 of title 18, United States Code, whoever in violation of the provisions of section 1114 of such title kills a person while engaged in or on account of the performance of his official functions under this Act shall be punished by imprisonment for any term of years or for life.

§2000e-14 [§715]. Equal Employment Opportunity Coordinating Council

The Equal Employment Opportunity Commission shall have the responsibility for developing and implementing agreements, policies and practices designed to maximize effort, promote efficiency, and eliminate conflict, competition, duplication and inconsistency among the operations, functions and jurisdictions of the various departments, agencies and branches of the Federal Government responsible for the implementation and enforcement of equal employment opportunity legislation, orders, and policies. On or before October 1 of each year, the Equal Employment Opportunity Commission shall transmit to the President and to the Congress a report of its activities, together with such recommendations for legislative or administrative changes as it concludes are desirable to further promote the purposes of this section.

§2000e-16 [§717]. Nondiscrimination in Federal Government Employment

(a) Discrimination prohibited. All personnel actions affecting employees or applicants for employment (except with regard to aliens employed outside the limits of the United States) in military departments as defined in section 102 of title 5, United States Code, in executive agencies (other than the General Accounting Office) as defined in section 105 of title 5, United States Code (including employees and applicants for employment who are paid from nonappropriated funds), in the United States Postal Service and the Postal Rate Commission, in those units of the Government of the District of Columbia having positions in the competitive service, and in those units of the legislative and judicial branches of the Federal Government having positions in the competitive service, and in the Library of Congress shall be made free from any discrimination based on race, color, religion, sex, or national origin.

(b) Role of Equal Employment Opportunity Commission; compliance of departments and agencies with rules and regulations. Except as otherwise provided in this subsection, the Equal Employment Opportunity Commission shall have authority to enforce the provisions of subsection (a) of this section through appropriate remedies, including reinstatement or hiring of employees with or without back pay, as will effectuate the policies of this section, and shall issue such rules, regulations, orders and instructions as it deems necessary and appropriate to carry out its responsibilities under this section. The Equal Employment Opportunity Commission shall —

> (1) be responsible for the annual review and approval of a national and regional equal employment opportunity plan which each department and agency and each appropriate unit referred to in subsection (a) of this section shall submit in order to maintain an affirmative program of equal employment opportunity for all such employees and applicants for employment;

> (2) be responsible for the review and evaluation of the operation of all agency equal employment opportunity programs, periodically obtaining and publishing (on at least a semiannual basis) progress reports from each such department, agency, or unit; and

> (3) consult with and solicit the recommendations of interested individuals, groups, and organizations relating to equal employment opportunity.

The head of each such department, agency, or unit shall comply with such rules, regulations, orders, and instructions which shall include a provision that an employee or applicant for employment shall be notified of any final action taken on any complaint of discrimination filed by him thereunder. The plan submitted by each department, agency, and unit shall include, but not be limited to —

(1) provision for the establishment of training and education programs designed to promote a maximum opportunity for employees to advance so as to perform at their highest potential; and

(2) a description of the qualifications in terms of training and experience relating to equal employment opportunity for the principal and operating officials of each such department, agency, or unit responsible for carrying out the equal employment opportunity program and of the allocation of personnel and resources proposed by such department, agency, or unit to carry out its equal employment opportunity program.

With respect to employment in the Library of Congress, authorities granted in this subsection to the Equal Employment Opportunity Commission shall be exercised by the Librarian of Congress.

(c) Civil action by party aggrieved. Within 90 days of receipt of notice of final action taken by a department, agency, or unit referred to in subsection 717(a), or by the Equal Employment Opportunity Commission upon an appeal from a decision or order of such department, agency, or unit on a complaint of discrimination based on race, color, religion, sex, or national origin, brought pursuant to subsection (a) of this section, Executive Order 11478 or any succeeding executive orders, or after one hundred and eighty days from the filing of the initial charge with the department, agency, or unit or with the Equal Employment Opportunity Commission on appeal from a decision or order of such department, agency, or unit, an employee or applicant for employment, if aggrieved by the final disposition of his complaint, or by the failure to take final action on his complaint, may file a civil action as provided in section 706, in which civil action the head of the department, agency, or unit, as appropriate, shall be the defendant.

(d) Application of certain provisions. The provisions of section 706(f) through (k), as applicable, shall govern civil actions brought hereunder and the same interest to compensate for delay in payment shall be available as in cases involving nonpublic parties.

(e) Continuing responsibilities of agencies and officials to assure nondiscrimination. Nothing contained in this Act shall relieve any Government agency or official of its or his primary responsibility to assure nondiscrimination in employment as required by the Constitution and statutes or of its or his responsibilities under Executive Order 11478 relating to equal employment opportunity in the Federal Government.

(f) Section 706(e)(3) shall apply to complaints of discrimination in compensation under this section.

§2000e-16a. Government Employee Rights Act of 1991

(a) Short title. This title may be cited as the "Government Employee Rights Act of 1991."

(b) Purpose. The purpose of this title is to provide procedures to protect the rights of certain government employees, with respect to their public employment, to be free of discrimination on the basis of race, color, religion, sex, national origin, age, or disability.

(c) Definition. For purposes of this title, the term "violation" means a practice that violates section 302(a) of this title [42 USCS §2000e-16b(a)].

§2000e-16b. Discriminatory Practices Prohibited

(a) Practices. All personnel actions affecting the Presidential appointees described in section 303 [2 USCS §1219] or the State employees described in section 304 [42 USCS §2000e-16c] shall be made free from any discrimination based on —

(1) race, color, religion, sex, or national origin, within the meaning of section 717 of the Civil Rights Act of 1964 (42 U.S.C. 2000e-16);

(2) age, within the meaning of section 15 of the Age Discrimination in Employment Act of 1967 (29 U.S.C. 633a); or

(3) disability, within the meaning of section 501 of the Rehabilitation Act of 1973 (29 U.S.C. 791) and sections 102 through 104 of the Americans with Disabilities Act of 1990 (42 U.S.C. 12112-14).

(b) Remedies. The remedies referred to in sections 303(a)(1) and 304(a) [2 USCS 1219(a)(1) and 42 USCS §2000e-16c(a)] —

(1) may include, in the case of a determination that a violation of subsection (a)(1) or (a)(3) has occurred, such remedies as would be appropriate if awarded under sections 706(g), 706(k), and 717(d) of the Civil Rights Act of 1964 (42 U.S.C. 2000e-5(g), 2000e-5(k), 2000e-16(d)), and such compensatory damages as would be appropriate if awarded under section 1977 or sections 1977A(a) and 1977A(b)(2) of the Revised Statutes (42 U.S.C. 1981 and 1981a(a) and (b)(2));

(2) may include, in the case of a determination that a violation of subsection (a)(2) has occurred, such remedies as would be appropriate if awarded under section 15(c) of the Age Discrimination in Employment Act of 1967 (29 U.S.C. 633a(c)); and

(3) may not include punitive damages.

§2000e-16c. Coverage of Previously Exempt State Employees

(a) Application. The rights, protections, and remedies provided pursuant to section 302 [42 USCS §2000e-16b] shall apply with respect to employment of any individual chosen or appointed, by a person elected to public office in any State or political subdivision of any State by the qualified voters thereof—

(1) to be a member of the elected official's personal staff;

(2) to serve the elected official on the policymaking level; or

(3) to serve the elected official as an immediate advisor with respect to the exercise of the constitutional or legal powers of the office.

(b) Enforcement by administrative action.

(1) In general. Any individual referred to in subsection (a) may file a complaint alleging a violation, not later than 180 days after the occurrence of the alleged violation, with the Equal Employment Opportunity Commission, which, in accordance with the principles and procedures set forth in sections 554 through 557 of title 5, United States Code, shall determine whether a violation has occurred and shall set forth its determination in a final order. If the Equal Employment Opportunity Commission determines that a violation has occurred, the final order shall also provide for appropriate relief.

(2) Referral to state and local authorities.

(A) Application. Section 706(d) of the Civil Rights Act of 1964 (42 U.S.C. 2000e-5(d)) shall apply with respect to any proceeding under this section.

(B) Definition. For purposes of the application described in subparagraph (A), the term "any charge filed by a member of the Commission alleging an unlawful employment practice" means a complaint filed under this section.

(c) Judicial review. Any party aggrieved by a final order under subsection (b) may obtain a review of such order under chapter 158 of title 28, United States Code [28 USCS §§2341 et seq.]. For the purpose of this review, the Equal Employment Opportunity Commission shall be an "agency" as that term is used in chapter 158 of title 28, United States Code [28 USCS §§2341 et seq.].

(d) Standard of review. To the extent necessary to decision and when presented, the reviewing court shall decide all relevant questions of law and interpret constitutional and statutory provisions. The court shall set aside a final order under subsection (b) if it is determined that the order was—

(1) arbitrary, capricious, an abuse of discretion, or otherwise not consistent with law;

(2) not made consistent with required procedures; or

(3) unsupported by substantial evidence.

In making the foregoing determinations, the court shall review the whole record or those parts of it cited by a party, and due account shall be taken of the rule of prejudicial error.

(e) Attorney's fees. If the individual referred to in subsection (a) is the prevailing party in a proceeding under this subsection, attorney's fees may be allowed by the court in accordance with the standards prescribed under section 706(k) of the Civil Rights Act of 1964 (42 U.S.C. 2000e-5(k)).

§2000e-17 [§718]. Special Provision with Respect to Denial, Termination and Suspension of Government Contract

No Government contract, or portion thereof, with any employer, shall be denied, withheld, terminated, or suspended, by any agency or officer of the United States under any equal employment opportunity law or order, where such employer has an affirmative action plan which has previously been accepted by the Government for the same facility within the past twelve months without first according such employer full hearing and adjudication under the provisions of title 5, United States Code, section 554, and the following pertinent sections: Provided, That if such employer has deviated substantially from such previously agreed to affirmative action plan, this section shall not apply: Provided further, That for the purposes of this section an affirmative action plan shall be deemed to have been accepted by the Government at the time the appropriate compliance agency has accepted such plan unless within forty-five days thereafter the Office of Federal Contract Compliance has disapproved such plan.

Title IX of the Education Amendments of 1972

20 U.S.C. §§1681–1688

TITLE IX

§1681. Sex

(a) Prohibition Against Discrimination; Exceptions. — No person in the United States shall, on the basis of sex, be excluded from participation in, be denied the benefits of, or be subjected to discrimination under any education program or activity receiving Federal financial assistance, except that:

(1) Classes of educational institutions subject to prohibition. — In regard to admissions to educational institutions, this section shall apply only to institutions of vocational education, professional education, and graduate higher education, and to public institutions of undergraduate higher education;

(2) Educational institutions commencing planned change in admissions. — In regard to admissions to educational institutions, this section shall not apply (A) for one year from June 23, 1972, nor for six years after June 23, 1972, in the case of an educational institution which has begun the process of changing from being an institution which admits only students of one sex to being an institution which admits students of both sexes, but only if it is carrying out a plan for such a change which is approved by the Secretary of Education or (B) for seven years from the date an educational institution begins the process of changing from being an institution which admits students of only one sex to being an institution which admits students of both sexes, but only if it is carrying out a plan for such a change which is approved by the Secretary of Education, whichever is the later;

(3) Educational institutions of religious organizations with contrary religious tenets. — This section shall not apply to an educational institution which is controlled by a religious organization if the application of this subsection would not be consistent with the religious tenets of such organization;

(4) Educational institutions training individuals for military services or merchant marine. — This section shall not apply to an educational institution

whose primary purpose is the training of individuals for the military services of the United States, or the merchant marine;

(5) Public educational institutions with traditional and continuing admissions policy. — In regard to admissions this section shall not apply to any public institution of undergraduate higher education which is an institution that traditionally and continually from its establishment has had a policy of admitting only students of one sex;

(6) Social fraternities or sororities; voluntary youth service organizations. This section shall not apply to membership practices —

(A) of a social fraternity or social sorority which is exempt from taxation under section 501(a) of Title 26, the active membership of which consists primarily of students in attendance at an institution of higher education, or

(B) of the Young Men's Christian Association, Young Women's Christian Association, Girl Scouts, Boy Scouts, Camp Fire Girls, and voluntary youth service organizations which are so exempt, the membership of which has traditionally been limited to persons of one sex and principally to persons of less than nineteen years of age;

(7) Boy or Girl conferences. — This section shall not apply to —

(A) any program or activity of the American Legion undertaken in connection with the organization or operation of any Boys State conference, Boys Nation conference, Girls State conference, or Girls Nation conference; or

(B) any program or activity of any secondary school or educational institution specifically for —

(i) the promotion of any Boys State conference, Boys Nation conference, Girls State conference, or Girls Nation conference; or

(ii) the selection of students to attend any such conference;

(8) Father-son or mother-daughter activities at educational institutions. — This section shall not preclude father-son or mother-daughter activities at an educational institution, but if such activities are provided for students of one sex, opportunities for reasonably comparable activities shall be provided for students of the other sex; and

(9) Institution of higher education scholarship awards in "beauty" pageants. — This section shall not apply with respect to any scholarship or other financial assistance awarded by an institution of higher education to any individual because such individual has received such award in any pageant in which the attainment of such award is based upon a combination of factors related to the personal appearance, poise, and talent of such individual and in which participation is limited to individuals of one sex only, so long as such pageant is in compliance with other nondiscrimination provisions of Federal law.

(b) Preferential or Disparate Treatment Because of Imbalance in Participation or Receipt of Federal Benefits; Statistical Evidence of Imbalance. — Nothing contained in subsection (a) of this section shall be interpreted to require any educational institution to grant preferential or disparate treatment to the members of one sex on account of an imbalance which may exist with respect to the total number or percentage of persons of that sex participating in or receiving the benefits of any federally supported program or activity, in comparison with the total number of percentage of persons of that sex in any community, State, section, or other area: Provided, that this subsection shall not be construed to prevent the consideration in any hearing or proceeding under this chapter of statistical evidence tending to show that such an imbalance exists with respect to the participation in, or receipt of the benefits of, any such program or activity by the members of one sex.

(c) "Educational Institution" Defined. — For purposes of this chapter an educational institution means any public or private preschool, elementary, or secondary school, or any institution of vocational, professional, or higher education, except that in the case of an educational institution composed of more than one school, college, or department which are administratively separate units, such term means each such school, college, or department.

§1682. Federal Administrative Enforcement; Report to Congressional Committees

Each Federal department and agency which is empowered to extend Federal financial assistance to any education program or activity, by way of grant, loan, or contract other than contract of insurance or guaranty, is authorized and directed to effectuate the provisions of section 1681 of this title with respect to such program or activity by issuing rules, regulations, or orders of general applicability which shall be consistent with achievement of the objectives of the statute authorizing the financial assistance in connection with which the action is taken. No such rule, regulation, or order shall become effective unless and until approved by the President. Compliance with any requirement adopted pursuant to this section may be effected (1) by the termination of or refusal to grant or to continue assistance under such program or activity to any recipient as to whom there has been an express finding on the record, after opportunity for hearing, of a failure to comply with such requirement, but such termination or refusal shall be limited to the particular political entity, or part thereof, or other recipient as to whom such a finding has been made, and shall be limited in its effect to the particular program, or part thereof, in which such noncompliance has been so found, or (2) by any other means authorized by law: Provided, however, that no such action shall be taken until the department or agency concerned has advised the appropriate person or persons of the failure to comply with the requirement and has determined that compliance cannot be secured by voluntary means. In the case of any action terminating, or refusing to grant or continue, assistance because of failure to comply with a requirement imposed pursuant to this section, the head of the Federal department or agency shall file with the committees of the House and Senate having legislative jurisdiction over the program or activity involved a full written report of the circumstances and the grounds for such action. No such action shall become effective until thirty days have elapsed after the filing of such report.

§1683. *Judicial Review*

Any department or agency action taken pursuant to section 1682 of this title shall be subject to such judicial review as may otherwise be provided by law for similar action taken by such department or agency on other grounds. In the case of action, not otherwise subject to judicial review, terminating or refusing to grant or to continue financial assistance upon a finding of failure to comply with any requirement imposed pursuant to section 1682 of this title, any person aggrieved (including any State or political subdivision thereof and any agency of either) may obtain judicial review of such action in accordance with chapter 7 of Title 5, and such action shall not be deemed committed to unreviewable agency discretion within the meaning of section 701 of that title.

§1684. *Blindness or Visual Impairment; Prohibition Against Discrimination*

No person in the United States shall, on the ground of blindness or severely impaired vision, be denied admission in any course of study by a recipient of Federal financial assistance for any education program or activity, but nothing herein shall be construed to require any such institution to provide any special services to such person because of his blindness or visual impairment.

§1685. *Authority Under Other Laws Unaffected*

Nothing in this chapter shall add to or detract from any existing authority with respect to any program or activity under which Federal financial assistance is extended by way of a contract of insurance or guaranty.

§1686. *Interpretation With Respect to Living Facilities*

Notwithstanding anything to the contrary contained in this chapter, nothing contained herein shall be construed to prohibit any educational institution receiving funds under this Act, from maintaining separate living facilities for the different sexes.

§1687. *Interpretation of "Program or Activity"*

For the purposes of this chapter, the term "program or activity" and "program" mean all of the operation of—

    (1)(A) a department, agency, special purpose district, or other instrumentality of a State or of a local government; or

        (B) the entity of such State or local government that distributes such assistance and each such department or agency (and each other State or local government entity) to which the assistance is extended, in the case of assistance to a State or local government;

    (2)(A) a college, university, or other postsecondary institution, or a public system of higher education; or

        (B) a local educational agency (as defined in section 7801 of this title), system of vocational education, or other school system;

(3)(A) an entire corporation, partnership, or other private organization, or an entire sole proprietorship —

(i) if assistance is extended to such corporation, partnership, private organization, or sole proprietorship as a whole; or

(ii) which is principally engaged in the business of providing education, health care, housing, social services, or parks and re-creation; or

(B) the entire plant or other comparable, geographically separate facility to which Federal financial assistance is extended, in the case of any other corporation, partnership, private organization, or sole pro-prietorship; or

(4) any other entity which is established by two or more of the entities described in paragraph (1), (2), or (3); any part of which is extended Federal financial assistance, except that such term does not include any operation of an entity which is controlled by a religious organization if the application of section 1681 of this title to such operation would not be consistent with the religious tenets of such organization.

§1688. Neutrality With Respect to Abortion

Nothing in this chapter shall be construed to require or prohibit any person, or public or private entity, to provide or pay for any benefit or service, including the use of facilities, related to an abortion. Nothing in this section shall be con-strued to permit a penalty to be imposed on any person or individual because such person or individual is seeking or has received any benefit or service related to a legal abortion.

Regulations

Regulations to Implement the Equal Employment Provisions of the Americans with Disabilities Act

29 C.F.R. Part 1630

§1630.1 Purpose, applicability, and construction

(a) Purpose. The purpose of this part is to implement title I of the Americans with Disabilities Act (ADA), as amended by the ADA Amendments Act of 2008 (ADAAA or Amendments Act), 42 U.S.C. 12101, et seq., requiring equal employment opportunities for individuals with disabilities. The ADA as amended, and these regulations, are intended to provide a clear and comprehensive national mandate for the elimination of discrimination against individuals with disabilities, and to provide clear, strong, consistent, enforceable standards addressing discrimination.

(b) Applicability. This part applies to "covered entities" as defined at §1630.2(b).

(c) Construction—

(1) In general. Except as otherwise provided in this part, this part does not apply a lesser standard than the standards applied under title V of the Rehabilitation Act of 1973 (29 U.S.C. 790-794a, as amended), or the regulations issued by Federal agencies pursuant to that title.

(2) Relationship to other laws. This part does not invalidate or limit the remedies, rights, and procedures of any Federal law or law of any State or political subdivision of any State or jurisdiction that provides greater or equal protection for the rights of individuals with disabilities than is afforded by this part.

(3) State workers' compensation laws and disability benefit programs. Nothing in this part alters the standards for determining eligibility for benefits under State workers' compensation laws or under State and Federal disability benefit programs.

(4) Broad coverage. The primary purpose of the ADAAA is to make it easier for people with disabilities to obtain protection under the ADA. Consistent with the Amendments Act's purpose of reinstating a broad scope of protection under the ADA, the definition of "disability" in this part shall be

469

construed broadly in favor of expansive coverage to the maximum extent permitted by the terms of the ADA. The primary object of attention in cases brought under the ADA should be whether covered entities have complied with their obligations and whether discrimination has occurred, not whether the individual meets the definition of disability. The question of whether an individual meets the definition of disability under this part should not demand extensive analysis.

§1630.2 Definitions

(a) Commission means the Equal Employment Opportunity Commission established by section 705 of the Civil Rights Act of 1964 (42 U.S.C. 2000e-4).

(b) Covered Entity means an employer, employment agency, labor organization, or joint labor management committee.

(c) Person, labor organization, employment agency, commerce and industry affecting commerce shall have the same meaning given those terms in section 701 of the Civil Rights Act of 1964 (42 U.S.C. 2000e).

(d) State means each of the several States, the District of Columbia, the Commonwealth of Puerto Rico, Guam, American Samoa, the Virgin Islands, the Trust Territory of the Pacific Islands, and the Commonwealth of the Northern Mariana Islands.

(e) Employer —

(1) In general. The term employer means a person engaged in an industry affecting commerce who has 15 or more employees for each working day in each of 20 or more calendar weeks in the current or preceding calendar year, and any agent of such person, except that, from July 26, 1992 through July 25, 1994, an employer means a person engaged in an industry affecting commerce who has 25 or more employees for each working day in each of 20 or more calendar weeks in the current or preceding year and any agent of such person.

(2) Exceptions. The term employer does not include —

(i) The United States, a corporation wholly owned by the government of the United States, or an Indian tribe; or

(ii) A bona fide private membership club (other than a labor organization) that is exempt from taxation under section 501(c) of the Internal Revenue Code of 1986.

(f) Employee means an individual employed by an employer.

(g) Definition of "disability."

(1) In general. Disability means, with respect to an individual —

(i) A physical or mental impairment that substantially limits one or more of the major life activities of such individual;

(ii) A record of such an impairment; or

(iii) Being regarded as having such an impairment as described in paragraph (l) of this section. This means that the individual has been subjected to an action prohibited by the ADA as amended because of an actual or perceived impairment that is not both "transitory and minor."

(2) An individual may establish coverage under any one or more of these three prongs of the definition of disability, i.e., paragraphs (g)(1)(i) (the "actual disability" prong), (g)(1)(ii) (the "record of" prong), and/or (g)(1)(iii) (the "regarded as" prong) of this section.

(3) Where an individual is not challenging a covered entity's failure to make reasonable accommodations and does not require a reasonable accommodation, it is generally unnecessary to proceed under the "actual disability" or "record of" prongs, which require a showing of an impairment that substantially limits a major life activity or a record of such an impairment. In these cases, the evaluation of coverage can be made solely under the "regarded as" prong of the definition of disability, which does not require a showing of an impairment that substantially limits a major life activity or a record of such an impairment. An individual may choose, however, to proceed under the "actual disability" and/or "record of" prong regardless of whether the individual is challenging a covered entity's failure to make reasonable accommodations or requires a reasonable accommodation.

Note to paragraph (g): See §1630.3 for exceptions to this definition.

(h) Physical or mental impairment means—

(1) Any physiological disorder or condition, cosmetic disfigurement, or anatomical loss affecting one or more body systems, such as neurological, musculoskeletal, special sense organs, respiratory (including speech organs), cardiovascular, reproductive, digestive, genitourinary, immune, circulatory, hemic, lymphatic, skin, and endocrine; or

(2) Any mental or psychological disorder, such as an intellectual disability (formerly termed "mental retardation"), organic brain syndrome, emotional or mental illness, and specific learning disabilities.

(i) Major life activities—

(1) In general. Major life activities include, but are not limited to:

(i) Caring for oneself, performing manual tasks, seeing, hearing, eating, sleeping, walking, standing, sitting, reaching, lifting, bending, speaking, breathing, learning, reading, concentrating, thinking, communicating, interacting with others, and working; and

(ii) The operation of a major bodily function, including functions of the immune system, special sense organs and skin; normal cell growth; and digestive, genitourinary, bowel, bladder, neurological, brain, respiratory, circulatory, cardiovascular, endocrine, hemic, lymphatic, musculoskeletal, and reproductive functions. The operation of a major bodily function includes the operation of an individual organ within a body system.

(2) In determining other examples of major life activities, the term "major" shall not be interpreted strictly to create a demanding standard for disability. ADAAA Section 2(b)(4) (Findings and Purposes). Whether an activity is a "major life activity" is not determined by reference to whether it is of "central importance to daily life."

(j) Substantially limits—

(1) Rules of construction. The following rules of construction apply when determining whether an impairment substantially limits an individual in a major life activity:

(i) The term "substantially limits" shall be construed broadly in favor of expansive coverage, to the maximum extent permitted by the terms of the ADA. "Substantially limits" is not meant to be a demanding standard.

(ii) An impairment is a disability within the meaning of this section if it substantially limits the ability of an individual to perform a major life activity as compared to most people in the general population. An impairment need not prevent, or significantly or severely restrict, the individual from performing a major life activity in order to be considered substantially limiting. Nonetheless, not every impairment will constitute a disability within the meaning of this section.

(iii) The primary object of attention in cases brought under the ADA should be whether covered entities have complied with their obligations and whether discrimination has occurred, not whether an individual's impairment substantially limits a major life activity. Accordingly, the threshold issue of whether an impairment "substantially limits" a major life activity should not demand extensive analysis.

(iv) The determination of whether an impairment substantially limits a major life activity requires an individualized assessment. However, in making this assessment, the term "substantially limits" shall be interpreted and applied to require a degree of functional limitation that is lower than the standard for "substantially limits" applied prior to the ADAAA.

(v) The comparison of an individual's performance of a major life activity to the performance of the same major life activity by most people in the general population usually will not require scientific, medical, or statistical analysis. Nothing in this paragraph is intended, however, to prohibit the presentation of scientific, medical, or statistical evidence to make such a comparison where appropriate.

(vi) The determination of whether an impairment substantially limits a major life activity shall be made without regard to the ameliorative effects of mitigating measures. However, the ameliorative effects of ordinary eyeglasses or contact lenses shall be considered in determining whether an impairment substantially limits a major life activity.

(vii) An impairment that is episodic or in remission is a disability if it would substantially limit a major life activity when active.

(viii) An impairment that substantially limits one major life activity need not substantially limit other major life activities in order to be considered a substantially limiting impairment.

(ix) The six-month "transitory" part of the "transitory and minor" exception to "regarded as" coverage in §1630.15(f) does not apply to the definition of "disability" under paragraphs (g)(1)(i) (the "actual disability" prong) or (g)(1)(ii) (the "record of" prong) of this section. The effects of an impairment lasting or expected to last fewer than six months can be substantially limiting within the meaning of this section.

(2) Non-applicability to the "regarded as" prong. Whether an individual's impairment "substantially limits" a major life activity is not relevant to coverage under paragraph (g)(1)(iii) (the "regarded as" prong) of this section.

(3) Predictable assessments —

    (i) The principles set forth in paragraphs (j)(1)(i) through (ix) of this section are intended to provide for more generous coverage and application of the ADA's prohibition on discrimination through a framework that is predictable, consistent, and workable for all individuals and entities with rights and responsibilities under the ADA as amended.

    (ii) Applying the principles set forth in paragraphs (j)(1)(i) through (ix) of this section, the individualized assessment of some types of impairments will, in virtually all cases, result in a determination of coverage under paragraphs (g)(1)(i) (the "actual disability" prong) or (g)(1)(ii) (the "record of" prong) of this section. Given their inherent nature, these types of impairments will, as a factual matter, virtually always be found to impose a substantial limitation on a major life activity. Therefore, with respect to these types of impairments, the necessary individualized assessment should be particularly simple and straightforward.

    (iii) For example, applying the principles set forth in paragraphs (j)(1)(i) through (ix) of this section, it should easily be concluded that the following types of impairments will, at a minimum, substantially limit the major life activities indicated: Deafness substantially limits hearing; blindness substantially limits seeing; an intellectual disability (formerly termed mental retardation) substantially limits brain function; partially or completely missing limbs or mobility impairments requiring the use of a wheelchair substantially limit musculoskeletal function; autism substantially limits brain function; cancer substantially limits normal cell growth; cerebral palsy substantially limits brain function; diabetes substantially limits endocrine function; epilepsy substantially limits neurological function; Human Immunodeficiency Virus (HIV) infection substantially limits immune function; multiple sclerosis substantially limits neurological function; muscular dystrophy substantially limits neurological function; and major depressive disorder, bipolar disorder, post-traumatic stress disorder, obsessive compulsive disorder, and schizophrenia substantially limit brain function. The types of impairments described in this section may substantially limit additional major life activities not explicitly listed above.

(4) Condition, manner, or duration —

    (i) At all times taking into account the principles in paragraphs (j)(1)(i) through (ix) of this section, in determining whether an individual is substantially limited in a major life activity, it may be useful in appropriate cases to consider, as compared to most people in the general population, the condition under which the individual performs the major life activity; the manner in which the individual performs the major life activity; and/or the duration of time it takes the individual to perform the major life activity, or for which the individual can perform the major life activity.

(ii) Consideration of facts such as condition, manner, or duration may include, among other things, consideration of the difficulty, effort, or time required to perform a major life activity; pain experienced when performing a major life activity; the length of time a major life activity can be performed; and/or the way an impairment affects the operation of a major bodily function. In addition, the non-ameliorative effects of mitigating measures, such as negative side effects of medication or burdens associated with following a particular treatment regimen, may be considered when determining whether an individual's impairment substantially limits a major life activity.

(iii) In determining whether an individual has a disability under the "actual disability" or "record of" prongs of the definition of disability, the focus is on how a major life activity is substantially limited, and not on what outcomes an individual can achieve. For example, someone with a learning disability may achieve a high level of academic success, but may nevertheless be substantially limited in the major life activity of learning because of the additional time or effort he or she must spend to read, write, or learn compared to most people in the general population.

(iv) Given the rules of construction set forth in paragraphs (j)(1)(i) through (ix) of this section, it may often be unnecessary to conduct an analysis involving most or all of these types of facts. This is particularly true with respect to impairments such as those described in paragraph (j)(3)(iii) of this section, which by their inherent nature should be easily found to impose a substantial limitation on a major life activity, and for which the individualized assessment should be particularly simple and straightforward.

(5) Examples of mitigating measures — Mitigating measures include, but are not limited to:

(i) Medication, medical supplies, equipment, or appliances, low-vision devices (defined as devices that magnify, enhance, or otherwise augment a visual image, but not including ordinary eyeglasses or contact lenses), prosthetics including limbs and devices, hearing aid(s) and cochlear implant(s) or other implantable hearing devices, mobility devices, and oxygen therapy equipment and supplies;

(ii) Use of assistive technology;

(iii) Reasonable accommodations or "auxiliary aids or services" (as defined by 42 U.S.C. 12103(1));

(iv) Learned behavioral or adaptive neurological modifications; or

(v) Psychotherapy, behavioral therapy, or physical therapy.

(6) Ordinary eyeglasses or contact lenses — defined. Ordinary eyeglasses or contact lenses are lenses that are intended to fully correct visual acuity or to eliminate refractive error.

(k) Has a record of such an impairment —

(1) In general. An individual has a record of a disability if the individual has a history of, or has been misclassified as having, a mental or physical impairment that substantially limits one or more major life activities.

(2) Broad construction. Whether an individual has a record of an impairment that substantially limited a major life activity shall be construed broadly to the maximum extent permitted by the ADA and should not demand extensive analysis. An individual will be considered to have a record of a disability if the individual has a history of an impairment that substantially limited one or more major life activities when compared to most people in the general population, or was misclassified as having had such an impairment. In determining whether an impairment substantially limited a major life activity, the principles articulated in paragraph (j) of this section apply.

(3) Reasonable accommodation. An individual with a record of a substantially limiting impairment may be entitled, absent undue hardship, to a reasonable accommodation if needed and related to the past disability. For example, an employee with an impairment that previously limited, but no longer substantially limits, a major life activity may need leave or a schedule change to permit him or her to attend follow-up or "monitoring" appointments with a health care provider.

(l) "Is regarded as having such an impairment." The following principles apply under the "regarded as" prong of the definition of disability (paragraph (g)(1)(iii) of this section) above:

(1) Except as provided in §1630.15(f), an individual is "regarded as having such an impairment" if the individual is subjected to a prohibited action because of an actual or perceived physical or mental impairment, whether or not that impairment substantially limits, or is perceived to substantially limit, a major life activity. Prohibited actions include but are not limited to refusal to hire, demotion, placement on involuntary leave, termination, exclusion for failure to meet a qualification standard, harassment, or denial of any other term, condition, or privilege of employment

(2) Except as provided in §1630.15(f), an individual is "regarded as having such an impairment" any time a covered entity takes a prohibited action against the individual because of an actual or perceived impairment, even if the entity asserts, or may or does ultimately establish, a defense to such action.

(3) Establishing that an individual is "regarded as having such an impairment" does not, by itself, establish liability. Liability is established under title I of the ADA only when an individual proves that a covered entity discriminated on the basis of disability within the meaning of section 102 of the ADA, 42 U.S.C. 12112.

(m) The term "qualified," with respect to an individual with a disability, means that the individual satisfies the requisite skill, experience, education and other job-related requirements of the employment position such individual holds or desires and, with or without reasonable accommodation, can perform the essential functions of such position. See §1630.3 for exceptions to this definition.

(n) Essential functions—

(1) In general. The term essential functions means the fundamental job duties of the employment position the individual with a disability holds or desires. The term "essential functions" does not include the marginal functions of the position.

(2) A job function may be considered essential for any of several reasons, including but not limited to the following:

(i) The function may be essential because the reason the position exists is to perform that function;

(ii) The function may be essential because of the limited number of employees available among whom the performance of that job function can be distributed; and/or

(iii) The function may be highly specialized so that the incumbent in the position is hired for his or her expertise or ability to perform the particular function.

(3) Evidence of whether a particular function is essential includes, but is not limited to:

(i) The employer's judgment as to which functions are essential;

(ii) Written job descriptions prepared before advertising or interviewing applicants for the job;

(iii) The amount of time spent on the job performing the function;

(iv) The consequences of not requiring the incumbent to perform the function;

(v) The terms of a collective bargaining agreement;

(vi) The work experience of past incumbents in the job; and/or

(vii) The current work experience of incumbents in similar jobs.

(o) Reasonable accommodation.

(1) The term reasonable accommodation means:

(i) Modifications or adjustments to a job application process that enable a qualified applicant with a disability to be considered for the position such qualified applicant desires; or

(ii) Modifications or adjustments to the work environment, or to the manner or circumstances under which the position held or desired is customarily performed, that enable an individual with a disability who is qualified to perform the essential functions of that position; or

(iii) Modifications or adjustments that enable a covered entity's employee with a disability to enjoy equal benefits and privileges of employment as are enjoyed by its other similarly situated employees without disabilities.

(2) Reasonable accommodation may include but is not limited to:

(i) Making existing facilities used by employees readily accessible to and usable by individuals with disabilities; and

(ii) Job restructuring; part-time or modified work schedules; reassignment to a vacant position; acquisition or modifications of equipment or devices; appropriate adjustment or modifications of examinations, training materials, or policies; the provision of qualified readers or interpreters; and other similar accommodations for individuals with disabilities.

(3) To determine the appropriate reasonable accommodation it may be necessary for the covered entity to initiate an informal, interactive process with the individual with a disability in need of the accommodation. This process should identify the precise limitations resulting from the disability and potential reasonable accommodations that could overcome those limitations.

(4) A covered entity is required, absent undue hardship, to provide a reasonable accommodation to an otherwise qualified individual who meets the definition of disability under the "actual disability" prong (paragraph (g)(1)(i) of this section), or "record of" prong (paragraph (g)(1)(ii) of this section), but is not required to provide a reasonable accommodation to an individual who meets the definition of disability solely under the "regarded as" prong (paragraph (g)(1)(iii) of this section).

(p) Undue hardship —

(1) In general. Undue hardship means, with respect to the provision of an accommodation, significant difficulty or expense incurred by a covered entity, when considered in light of the factors set forth in paragraph (p)(2) of this section.

(2) Factors to be considered. In determining whether an accommodation would impose an undue hardship on a covered entity, factors to be considered include:

(i) The nature and net cost of the accommodation needed under this part, taking into consideration the availability of tax credits and deductions, and/or outside funding;

(ii) The overall financial resources of the facility or facilities involved in the provision of the reasonable accommodation, the number of persons employed at such facility, and the effect on expenses and resources;

(iii) The overall financial resources of the covered entity, the overall size of the business of the covered entity with respect to the number of its employees, and the number, type and location of its facilities;

(iv) The type of operation or operations of the covered entity, including the composition, structure and functions of the workforce of such entity, and the geographic separateness and administrative or fiscal relationship of the facility or facilities in question to the covered entity; and

(v) The impact of the accommodation upon the operation of the facility, including the impact on the ability of other employees to perform their duties and the impact on the facility's ability to conduct business.

(q) Qualification standards means the personal and professional attributes including the skill, experience, education, physical, medical, safety and other requirements established by a covered entity as requirements which an individual must meet in order to be eligible for the position held or desired.

(r) Direct Threat means a significant risk of substantial harm to the health or safety of the individual or others that cannot be eliminated or reduced by reasonable accommodation. The determination that an individual poses a "direct threat" shall be based on an individualized assessment of the individual's present ability to safely perform the essential functions of the job. This assessment shall be based on a reasonable medical judgment that relies on the most current medical knowledge and/or on the best available objective evidence. In determining whether an individual would pose a direct threat, the factors to be considered include:

(1) The duration of the risk;

(2) The nature and severity of the potential harm;

(3) The likelihood that the potential harm will occur; and

(4) The imminence of the potential harm.

§1630.3 Exceptions to the definitions of "Disability" and "Qualified Individual with a Disability"

(a) The terms disability and qualified individual with a disability do not include individuals currently engaging in the illegal use of drugs, when the covered entity acts on the basis of such use.

(1) Drug means a controlled substance, as defined in schedules I through V of Section 202 of the Controlled Substances Act (21 U.S.C 812)

(2) Illegal use of drugs means the use of drugs the possession or distribution of which is unlawful under the Controlled Substances Act, as periodically updated by the Food and Drug Administration. This term does not include the use of a drug taken under the supervision of a licensed health care professional, or other uses authorized by the Controlled Substances Act or other provisions of Federal law.

(b) However, the terms disability and qualified individual with a disability may not exclude an individual who:

(1) Has successfully completed a supervised drug rehabilitation program and is no longer engaging in the illegal use of drugs, or has otherwise been rehabilitated successfully and is no longer engaging in the illegal use of drugs; or

(2) Is participating in a supervised rehabilitation program and is no longer engaging in such use; or

(3) Is erroneously regarded as engaging in such use, but is not engaging in such use.

(c) It shall not be a violation of this part for a covered entity to adopt or administer reasonable policies or procedures, including but not limited to drug testing, designed to ensure that an individual described in paragraph (b) (1) or (2) of this section is no longer engaging in the illegal use of drugs. (See §1630.16(c) Drug testing).

(d) Disability does not include:

(1) Transvestism, transsexualism, pedophilia, exhibitionism, voyeurism, gender identity disorders not resulting from physical impairments, or other sexual behavior disorders;

(2) Compulsive gambling, kleptomania, or pyromania; or

(3) Psychoactive substance use disorders resulting from current illegal use of drugs.

(e) Homosexuality and bisexuality are not impairments and so are not disabilities as defined in this part.

§1630.4 Discrimination prohibited

(a) In general—

(1) It is unlawful for a covered entity to discriminate on the basis of disability against a qualified individual in regard to:

(i) Recruitment, advertising, and job application procedures;

(ii) Hiring, upgrading, promotion, award of tenure, demotion, transfer, layoff, termination, right of return from layoff, and rehiring;

(iii) Rates of pay or any other form of compensation and changes in compensation;

(iv) Job assignments, job classifications, organizational structures, position descriptions, lines of progression, and seniority lists;

(v) Leaves of absence, sick leave, or any other leave;

(vi) Fringe benefits available by virtue of employment, whether or not administered by the covered entity;

(vii) Selection and financial support for training, including: apprenticeships, professional meetings, conferences and other related activities, and selection for leaves of absence to pursue training;

(viii) Activities sponsored by a covered entity, including social and recreational programs; and

(ix) Any other term, condition, or privilege of employment.

(2) The term discrimination includes, but is not limited to, the acts described in §§1630.4 through 1630.13 of this part.

(b) Claims of no disability. Nothing in this part shall provide the basis for a claim that an individual without a disability was subject to discrimination because of his lack of disability, including a claim that an individual with a disability was granted an accommodation that was denied to an individual without a disability.

§1630.5 Limiting, segregating, and classifying

It is unlawful for a covered entity to limit, segregate, or classify a job applicant or employee in a way that adversely affects his or her employment opportunities or status on the basis of disability.

§1630.6 Contractual or other arrangements

(a) In general. It is unlawful for a covered entity to participate in a contractual or other arrangement or relationship that has the effect of subjecting the covered entity's own qualified applicant or employee with a disability to the discrimination prohibited by this part.

(b) Contractual or other arrangement defined. The phrase contractual or other arrangement or relationship includes, but is not limited to, a relationship with an employment or referral agency; labor union, including collective bargaining agreements; an organization providing fringe benefits to an employee of the covered entity; or an organization providing training and apprenticeship programs.

(c) Application. This section applies to a covered entity, with respect to its own applicants or employees, whether the entity offered the contract or initiated the relationship, or whether the entity accepted the contract or acceded to the relationship. A covered entity is not liable for the actions of the other party or parties to the contract which only affect that other party's employees or applicants.

§1630.7 Standards, criteria, or methods of administration

It is unlawful for a covered entity to use standards, criteria, or methods of administration, which are not job- related and consistent with business necessity, and:

(a) That have the effect of discriminating on the basis of disability; or

(b) That perpetuate the discrimination of others who are subject to common administrative control.

§1630.8 Relationship or association with an individual with a disability

It is unlawful for a covered entity to exclude or deny equal jobs or benefits to, or otherwise discriminate against, a qualified individual because of the known disability of an individual with whom the qualified individual is known to have a family, business, social or other relationship or association.

§1630.9 Not making reasonable accommodation

(a) It is unlawful for a covered entity not to make reasonable accommodation to the known physical or mental limitations of an otherwise qualified applicant or employee with a disability, unless such covered entity can demonstrate that the accommodation would impose an undue hardship on the operation of its business.

(b) It is unlawful for a covered entity to deny employment opportunities to an otherwise qualified job applicant or employee with a disability based on the need of such covered entity to make reasonable accommodation to such individual's physical or mental impairments.

(c) A covered entity shall not be excused from the requirements of this part because of any failure to receive technical assistance authorized by section 507 of the ADA, including any failure in the development or dissemination of any technical assistance manual authorized by that Act.

(d) An individual with a disability is not required to accept an accommodation, aid, service, opportunity or benefit which such qualified individual chooses not to accept. However, if such individual rejects a reasonable accommodation, aid, service, opportunity or benefit that is necessary to enable the individual to perform the essential functions of the position held or desired, and cannot, as a result of that rejection, perform the essential functions of the position, the individual will not be considered qualified.

(e) A covered entity is required, absent undue hardship, to provide a reasonable accommodation to an otherwise qualified individual who meets the definition of disability under the "actual disability" prong (§1630.2(g)(1)(i)), or "record of" prong (§1630.2(g)(1)(ii)), but is not required to provide a reasonable accommodation to an individual who meets the definition of disability solely under the "regarded as" prong (§1630.2(g)(1)(iii)).

§1630.10 Qualification standards, tests, and other selection criteria

(a) In general. It is unlawful for a covered entity to use qualification standards, employment tests or other selection criteria that screen out or tend to screen out an individual with a disability or a class of individuals with disabilities, on the basis of disability, unless the standard, test, or other selection criteria, as used by the covered entity, is shown to be job related for the position in question and is consistent with business necessity.

(b) Qualification standards and tests related to uncorrected vision. Notwithstanding §1630.2(j)(1)(vi) of this part, a covered entity shall not use qualification standards, employment tests, or other selection criteria based on an individual's uncorrected vision unless the standard, test, or other selection criterion, as used by the covered entity, is shown to be job related for the position in question and is consistent with business necessity. An individual challenging a covered entity's application of a qualification standard, test, or other criterion based on uncorrected vision need not be a person with a disability, but must be adversely affected by the application of the standard, test, or other criterion.

§1630.11 Administration of tests

It is unlawful for a covered entity to fail to select and administer tests concerning employment in the most effective manner to ensure that, when a test is administered to a job applicant or employee who has a disability that impairs sensory, manual or speaking skills, the test results accurately reflect the skills, aptitude, or whatever other factor of the applicant or employee that the test purports to measure, rather than reflecting the impaired sensory, manual, or speaking skills of such employee or applicant (except where such skills are the factors that the test purports to measure).

§1630.12 Retaliation and coercion

(a) Retaliation. It is unlawful to discriminate against any individual because that individual has opposed any act or practice made unlawful by this part or because that individual made a charge, testified, assisted, or participated in any manner in an investigation, proceeding, or hearing to enforce any provision contained in this part.

(b) Coercion, interference or intimidation. It is unlawful to coerce, intimidate, threaten, harass or interfere with any individual in the exercise or enjoyment of, or because that individual aided or encouraged any other individual in the exercise of, any right granted or protected by this part.

§1630.13 Prohibited medical examination and inquiries

(a) Pre-employment examination or inquiry. Except as permitted by §1630.14, it is unlawful for a covered entity to conduct a medical examination of an applicant or to make inquiries as to whether an applicant is an individual with a disability or as to the nature or severity of such disability.

(b) Examination or inquiry of employees. Except as permitted by §1630.14, it is unlawful for a covered entity to require a medical examination of an employee or to make inquiries as to whether an employee is an individual with a disability or as to the nature or severity of such disability.

§1630.14 Class 1-D-E: Exemption of certain members of a reserve component or student taking military training

In Class 1- D- E shall be placed any registrant who:

(a) Is a student enrolled in an officer procurement program at a military college the curriculum of which is approved by the Secretary of Defense; or

(b) Has been enlisted in the Delayed Entry Program (DEP) at least ten days prior to his scheduled induction date; or

(c) Has been transferred to a reserve component of the Army, Navy, Air Force, Marine Corps or Coast Guard after a period of extended active duty, which was not for training only.

§1630.15 Defenses

Defenses to an allegation of discrimination under this part may include, but are not limited to, the following:

(a) Disparate treatment charges. It may be a defense to a charge of disparate treatment brought under §§1630.4 through 1630.8 and 1630.11 through 1630.12 that the challenged action is justified by a legitimate, nondiscriminatory reason.

(b) Charges of discriminatory application of selection criteria—

(1) In general. It may be a defense to a charge of discrimination, as described in §1630.10, that an alleged application of qualification standards, tests, or selection criteria that screens out or tends to screen out or otherwise denies a job or benefit to an individual with a disability has been shown to be job-related and consistent with business necessity, and such performance

cannot be accomplished with reasonable accommodation, as required in this part.

(2) *Direct threat as a qualification standard.* The term "qualification standard" may include a requirement that an individual shall not pose a direct threat to the health or safety of the individual or others in the workplace. (See §1630.2(r) defining direct threat.)

(c) *Other disparate impact charges.* It may be a defense to a charge of discrimination brought under this part that a uniformly applied standard, criterion, or policy has a disparate impact on an individual with a disability or a class of individuals with disabilities that the challenged standard, criterion or policy has been shown to be job-related and consistent with business necessity, and such performance cannot be accomplished with reasonable accommodation, as required in this part.

(d) *Charges of not making reasonable accommodation.* It may be a defense to a charge of discrimination, as described in §1630.9, that a requested or necessary accommodation would impose an undue hardship on the operation of the covered entity's business.

(e) *Conflict with other federal laws.* It may be a defense to a charge of discrimination under this part that a challenged action is required or necessitated by another Federal law or regulation, or that another Federal law or regulation prohibits an action (including the provision of a particular reasonable accommodation) that would otherwise be required by this part.

(f) *Claims based on transitory and minor impairments under the "regarded as" prong.* It may be a defense to a charge of discrimination by an individual claiming coverage under the "regarded as" prong of the definition of disability that the impairment is (in the case of an actual impairment) or would be (in the case of a perceived impairment) "transitory and minor." To establish this defense, a covered entity must demonstrate that the impairment is both "transitory" and "minor." Whether the impairment at issue is or would be "transitory and minor" is to be determined objectively. A covered entity may not defeat "regarded as" coverage of an individual simply by demonstrating that it subjectively believed the impairment was transitory and minor; rather, the covered entity must demonstrate that the impairment is (in the case of an actual impairment) or would be (in the case of a perceived impairment) both transitory and minor. For purposes of this section, "transitory" is defined as lasting or expected to last six months or less.

(g) *Additional defenses.* It may be a defense to a charge of discrimination under this part that the alleged discriminatory action is specifically permitted by §1630.14 or §1630.16.

§1630.16 *Specific activities permitted*

(a) *Religious entities.* A religious corporation, association, educational institution, or society is permitted to give preference in employment to individuals of a particular religion to perform work connected with the carrying on by that corporation, association, educational institution, or society of its activities. A religious entity may require that all applicants and employees conform to the religious tenets of such organization. However, a religious entity may not discriminate against a qualified individual, who satisfies the permitted religious criteria, on the basis of his or her disability.

(b) Regulation of alcohol and drugs. A covered entity:

(1) May prohibit the illegal use of drugs and the use of alcohol at the workplace by all employees;

(2) May require that employees not be under the influence of alcohol or be engaging in the illegal use of drugs at the workplace;

(3) May require that all employees behave in conformance with the requirements established under the Drug-Free Workplace Act of 1988 (41 U.S.C. 701 et seq.);

(4) May hold an employee who engages in the illegal use of drugs or who is an alcoholic to the same qualification standards for employment or job performance and behavior to which the entity holds its other employees, even if any unsatisfactory performance or behavior is related to the employee's drug use or alcoholism;

(5) May require that its employees employed in an industry subject to such regulations comply with the standards established in the regulations (if any) of the Departments of Defense and Transportation, and of the Nuclear Regulatory Commission, regarding alcohol and the illegal use of drugs; and

(6) May require that employees employed in sensitive positions comply with the regulations (if any) of the Departments of Defense and Transportation and of the Nuclear Regulatory Commission that apply to employment in sensitive positions subject to such regulations.

(c) Drug testing—

(1) General policy. For purposes of this part, a test to determine the illegal use of drugs is not considered a medical examination. Thus, the administration of such drug tests by a covered entity to its job applicants or employees is not a violation of §1630.13 of this part. However, this part does not encourage, prohibit, or authorize a covered entity to conduct drug tests of job applicants or employees to determine the illegal use of drugs or to make employment decisions based on such test results.

(2) Transportation employees. This part does not encourage, prohibit, or authorize the otherwise lawful exercise by entities subject to the jurisdiction of the Department of Transportation of authority to:

(i) Test employees of entities in, and applicants for, positions involving safety sensitive duties for the illegal use of drugs or for on-duty impairment by alcohol; and

(ii) Remove from safety-sensitive positions persons who test positive for illegal use of drugs or on-duty impairment by alcohol pursuant to paragraph (c)(2)(i) of this section.

(3) Confidentiality. Any information regarding the medical condition or history of any employee or applicant obtained from a test to determine the illegal use of drugs, except information regarding the illegal use of drugs, is subject to the requirements of §1630.14(b) (2) and (3) of this part.

(d) Regulation of smoking. A covered entity may prohibit or impose restrictions on smoking in places of employment. Such restrictions do not violate any provision of this part.

(e) Infectious and communicable diseases; food handling jobs—

(1) In general. Under title I of the ADA, section 103(d)(1), the Secretary of Health and Human Services is to prepare a list, to be updated annually, of infectious and communicable diseases which are transmitted through the handling of food. (Copies may be obtained from Center for Infectious Diseases, Centers for Disease Control, 1600 Clifton Road, NE., Mailstop C09, Atlanta, GA 30333.) If an individual with a disability is disabled by one of the infectious or communicable diseases included on this list, and if the risk of transmitting the disease associated with the handling of food cannot be eliminated by reasonable accommodation, a covered entity may refuse to assign or continue to assign such individual to a job involving food handling. However, if the individual with a disability is a current employee, the employer must consider whether he or she can be accommodated by reassignment to a vacant position not involving food handling.

(2) Effect on State or other laws. This part does not preempt, modify, or amend any State, county, or local law, ordinance or regulation applicable to food handling which:

(i) Is in accordance with the list, referred to in paragraph (e)(1) of this section, of infectious or communicable diseases and the modes of transmissibility published by the Secretary of Health and Human Services; and

(ii) Is designed to protect the public health from individuals who pose a significant risk to the health or safety of others, where that risk cannot be eliminated by reasonable accommodation.

(f) Health insurance, life insurance, and other benefit plans—

(1) An insurer, hospital, or medical service company, health maintenance organization, or any agent or entity that administers benefit plans, or similar organizations may underwrite risks, classify risks, or administer such risks that are based on or not inconsistent with State law.

(2) A covered entity may establish, sponsor, observe or administer the terms of a bona fide benefit plan that are based on underwriting risks, classifying risks, or administering such risks that are based on or not inconsistent with State law.

(3) A covered entity may establish, sponsor, observe, or administer the terms of a bona fide benefit plan that is not subject to State laws that regulate insurance.

(4) The activities described in paragraphs (f) (1), (2), and (3) of this section are permitted unless these activities are being used as a subterfuge to evade the purposes of this part.

Interpretive Guidance on Title I of the Americans with Disabilities Act

Appendix to Part 1630

INTRODUCTION

The Americans with Disabilities Act (ADA) is a landmark piece of civil rights legislation signed into law on July 26, 1990, and amended effective January 1, 2009. See 42 U.S.C. 12101 et seq., as amended. In passing the ADA, Congress recognized that "discrimination against individuals with disabilities continues to be a serious and pervasive social problem" and that the "continuing existence of unfair and unnecessary discrimination and prejudice denies people with disabilities the opportunity to compete on an equal basis and to pursue those opportunities for which our free society is justifiably famous, and costs the United States billions of dollars in unnecessary expenses resulting from dependency and nonproductivity." 42 U.S.C. 12101(a)(2), (8). Discrimination on the basis of disability persists in critical areas such as housing, public accommodations, education, transportation, communication, recreation, institutionalization, health services, voting, access to public services, and employment. 42 U.S.C. 12101(a)(3). Accordingly, the ADA prohibits discrimination in a wide range of areas, including employment, public services, and public accommodations.

Title I of the ADA prohibits disability-based discrimination in employment. The Equal Employment Opportunity Commission (the Commission or the EEOC) is responsible for enforcement of title I (and parts of title V) of the ADA. Pursuant to the ADA as amended, the EEOC is expressly granted the authority and is expected to amend these regulations. 42 U.S.C. 12205a. Under title I of the ADA, covered entities may not discriminate against qualified individuals on the basis of disability in regard to job application procedures, the hiring, advancement or discharge of employees, employee compensation, job training, or other terms, conditions, and privileges of employment. 42 U.S.C. 12112(a). For these purposes, "discriminate" includes (1) limiting, segregating, or classifying a job applicant or employee in a way that adversely affects the opportunities or status of the applicant or employee; (2) participating in a contractual or other arrangement or relationship that has the effect of subjecting a covered entity's qualified applicants or employees to discrimination; (3) utilizing standards, criteria, or other methods of administration that have the effect of discrimination on the basis of disability; (4) not making reasonable accommodation to the known physical or mental limitations of an otherwise qualified individual with a disability, unless the covered entity can demonstrate that the accommodation would impose an undue hardship on the operation of the business of the covered entity; (5) denying employment opportunities to a job applicant or employee who is otherwise qualified, if such denial is based on the need to make reasonable accommodation; (6) using qualification standards, employment tests or other selection criteria that screen out or tend to screen out an individual with a disability or a class of individuals with disabilities unless the standard, test or other selection criterion is shown to be job related for the position in question and is consistent with business necessity; and (7) subjecting applicants or employees to prohibited medical inquiries or examinations. See 42 U.S.C. 12112(b), (d).

As with other civil rights laws, individuals seeking protection under these anti-discrimination provisions of the ADA generally must allege and prove that they are members of the "protected class."[1] Under the ADA, this typically means they have to show that they meet the statutory definition of "disability." 2008 House Judiciary Committee Report at 5. However, "Congress did not intend for the threshold question of disability to be used as a means of excluding individuals from coverage." Id.

In the original ADA, Congress defined "disability" as (1) a physical or mental impairment that substantially limits one or more major life activities of an individual; (2) a record of such an impairment; or (3) being regarded as having such an impairment. 42 U.S.C. 12202(2). Congress patterned these three parts of the definition of disability — the "actual," "record of," and "regarded as" prongs — after the definition of "handicap" found in the Rehabilitation Act of 1973. 2008 House Judiciary Committee Report at 6. By doing so, Congress intended that the relevant case law developed under the Rehabilitation Act would be generally applicable to the term "disability" as used in the ADA. H.R. Rep. No. 485 part 3, 101st Cong., 2d Sess. 27 (1990) (1990 House Judiciary Report or House Judiciary Report); see also S. Rep. No. 116, 101st Cong., 1st Sess. 21 (1989) (1989 Senate Report or Senate Report); H.R. Rep. No. 485 part 2, 101st Cong., 2d Sess. 50 (1990) (1990 House Labor Report or House Labor Report). Congress expected that the definition of disability and related terms, such as "substantially limits" and "major life activity," would be interpreted under the ADA "consistently with how courts had applied the definition of a handicapped individual under the Rehabilitation Act" — i.e., expansively and in favor of broad coverage. ADA Amendments Act of 2008 (ADAAA or Amendments Act) at Section 2(a)(1)-(8) and (b)(1)-(6) (Findings and Purposes); see also Senate Statement of the Managers to Accompany S. 3406 (2008 Senate Statement of Managers) at 3 ("When Congress passed the ADA in 1990, it adopted the functional definition of disability from section 504 of the Rehabilitation Act of 1973, in part, because after 17 years of development through case law the requirements of the definition were well understood. Within this framework, with its generous and inclusive definition of disability, courts treated the determination of disability as a threshold issue but focused primarily on whether unlawful discrimination had occurred."); 2008 House Judiciary Committee Report at 6 & n.6 (noting that courts had interpreted this Rehabilitation Act definition "broadly to include persons with a wide range of physical and mental impairments").

That expectation was not fulfilled. ADAAA Section 2(a)(3). The holdings of several Supreme Court cases sharply narrowed the broad scope of protection Congress originally intended under the ADA, thus eliminating protection for many individuals whom Congress intended to protect. Id. For example, in Sutton v. United Air Lines, Inc., 527 U.S. 471 (1999), the Court ruled that whether an impairment substantially limits a major life activity is to be determined with reference to the ameliorative effects of mitigating measures. In Sutton, the Court also adopted a restrictive reading of the meaning of being "regarded as" disabled under the ADA's definition of disability. Subsequently, in Toyota Motor Mfg., Ky., Inc. v. Williams, 534 U.S. 184 (2002), the Court held that the terms "substantially" and "major" in the definition of disability "need to be interpreted strictly to create a demanding standard for qualifying as disabled" under the ADA, and that to be substantially limited in performing a major life activity under the ADA, "an individual must have an impairment that prevents or severely restricts the individual from doing activities that are of central importance to most people's daily lives."

As a result of these Supreme Court decisions, lower courts ruled in numerous cases that individuals with a range of substantially limiting impairments were not individuals with disabilities, and thus not protected by the ADA. See 2008 Senate Statement of Managers at 3 ("After the Court's decisions in Sutton that impairments must be considered in their mitigated state and in Toyota that there must be a demanding standard for qualifying as disabled, lower courts more often found that an individual's impairment did not constitute a disability. As a result, in too many cases, courts would never reach the question whether discrimination had occurred."). Congress concluded that these rulings imposed a greater degree of limitation and expressed a higher standard than it had originally intended, and coupled with the EEOC's 1991 ADA regulations which had defined the term "substantially limits" as "significantly restricted," unduly precluded many individuals from being covered under the ADA. Id. — ("[t]hus, some 18 years later we are faced with a situation in which physical or mental impairments that would previously have been found to constitute disabilities are not considered disabilities under the Supreme Court's narrower standard" and "[t]he resulting court decisions contribute to a legal environment in which individuals must demonstrate an inappropriately high degree of functional limitation in order to be protected from discrimination under the ADA").

Consequently, Congress amended the ADA with the Americans with Disabilities Act Amendments Act of 2008. The ADAAA was signed into law on September 25, 2008, and became effective on January 1, 2009. This legislation is the product of extensive bipartisan efforts, and the culmination of collaboration and coordination between legislators and stakeholders, including representatives of the disability, business, and education communities. See Statement of Representatives Hoyer and Sensenbrenner, 154 Cong. Rec. H8294-96 (daily ed. Sept. 17, 2008) (Hoyer-Sensenbrenner Congressional Record Statement); Senate Statement of Managers at 1. The express purposes of the ADAAA are, among other things:

(1) To carry out the ADA's objectives of providing "a clear and comprehensive national mandate for the elimination of discrimination" and "clear, strong, consistent, enforceable standards addressing discrimination" by reinstating a broad scope of protection under the ADA;

(2) To reject the requirement enunciated in Sutton and its companion cases that whether an impairment substantially limits a major life activity is to be determined with reference to the ameliorative effects of mitigating measures;

(3) To reject the Supreme Court's reasoning in Sutton with regard to coverage under the third prong of the definition of disability and to reinstate the reasoning of the Supreme Court in School Board of Nassau County v. Arline, 480 U.S. 273 (1987), which set forth a broad view of the third prong of the definition of handicap under the Rehabilitation Act of 1973;

(4) To reject the standards enunciated by the Supreme Court in Toyota that the terms "substantially" and "major" in the definition of disability under the ADA "need to be interpreted strictly to create a demanding standard for qualifying as disabled," and that to be substantially limited in performing a major life activity under the ADA "an individual must have an impairment that prevents or severely restricts the individual from doing activities that are of central importance to most people's daily lives";

(5) To convey congressional intent that the standard created by the Supreme Court in Toyota for "substantially limits," and applied by lower courts in numerous decisions, has created an inappropriately high level of limitation necessary to obtain coverage under the ADA;

(6) To convey that it is the intent of Congress that the primary object of attention in cases brought under the ADA should be whether entities covered under the ADA have complied with their obligations, and to convey that the question of whether an individual's impairment is a disability under the ADA should not demand extensive analysis; and

(7) To express Congress' expectation that the EEOC will revise that portion of its current regulations that defines the term "substantially limits" as "significantly restricted" to be consistent with the ADA as amended.

ADAAA Section 2(b). The findings and purposes of the ADAAA "give[ ] clear guidance to the courts and * * * [are] intend[ed] to be applied appropriately and consistently." 2008 Senate Statement of Managers at 5.

The EEOC has amended its regulations to reflect the ADAAA's findings and purposes. The Commission believes that it is essential also to amend its appendix to the original regulations at the same time, and to reissue this interpretive guidance as amended concurrently with the issuance of the amended regulations. This will help to ensure that individuals with disabilities understand their rights, and to facilitate and encourage compliance by covered entities under this part.

Accordingly, this amended appendix addresses the major provisions of this part and explains the major concepts related to disability-based employment discrimination. This appendix represents the Commission's interpretation of the issues addressed within it, and the Commission will be guided by this appendix when resolving charges of employment discrimination.

NOTE ON CERTAIN TERMINOLOGY USED

The ADA, the EEOC's ADA regulations, and this appendix use the term "disabilities" rather than the term "handicaps" which was originally used in the Rehabilitation Act of 1973, 29 U.S.C. 701-796. Substantively, these terms are equivalent. As originally noted by the House Committee on the Judiciary, "[t]he use of the term 'disabilities' instead of the term 'handicaps' reflects the desire of the Committee to use the most current terminology. It reflects the preference of persons with disabilities to use that term rather than 'handicapped' as used in previous laws, such as the Rehabilitation Act of 1973 * * *." 1990 House Judiciary Report at 26-27; see also 1989 Senate Report at 21; 1990 House Labor Report at 50-51.

In addition, consistent with the Amendments Act, revisions have been made to the regulations and this Appendix to refer to "individual with a disability" and "qualified individual" as separate terms, and to change the prohibition on discrimination to "on the basis of disability" instead of prohibiting discrimination against a qualified individual "with a disability because of the disability of such individual." "This ensures that the emphasis in questions of disability discrimination is properly on the critical inquiry of whether a qualified person has been discriminated against on the basis of disability, and not unduly focused on the preliminary question of whether a particular person is a 'person with a disability.'" 2008 Senate Statement of Managers at 11.

The use of the term "Americans" in the title of the ADA, in the EEOC's regulations, or in this Appendix as amended is not intended to imply that the ADA only applies to United States citizens. Rather, the ADA protects all qualified individuals with disabilities, regardless of their citizenship status or nationality, from discrimination by a covered entity.

Finally, the terms "employer" and "employer or other covered entity" are used interchangeably throughout this Appendix to refer to all covered entities subject to the employment provisions of the ADA.

The Equal Employment Opportunity Commission (the Commission or EEOC) is responsible for enforcement of title I of the Americans with Disabilities Act (ADA), 42 U.S.C. 12101 et seq. (1990), which prohibits employment discrimination on the basis of disability. The Commission believes that it is essential to issue interpretive guidance concurrently with the issuance of this part in order to ensure that qualified individuals with disabilities understand their rights under this part and to facilitate and encourage compliance by covered entities. This appendix represents the Commission's interpretation of the issues discussed, and the Commission will be guided by it when resolving charges of employment discrimination. The appendix addresses the major provisions of this part and explains the major concepts of disability rights.

The terms "employer" or "employer or other covered entity" are used interchangeably throughout the appendix to refer to all covered entities subject to the employment provisions of the ADA.

Section 1630.1 Purpose, Applicability and Construction

Section 1630.1(a) Purpose

The express purposes of the ADA as amended are to provide a clear and comprehensive national mandate for the elimination of discrimination against individuals with disabilities; to provide clear, strong, consistent, enforceable standards addressing discrimination against individuals with disabilities; to ensure that the Federal Government plays a central role in enforcing the standards articulated in the ADA on behalf of individuals with disabilities; and to invoke the sweep of congressional authority to address the major areas of discrimination faced day-to-day by people with disabilities. 42 U.S.C. 12101(b). The EEOC's ADA regulations are intended to implement these Congressional purposes in simple and straightforward terms.

Section 1630.1(b) Applicability

The EEOC's ADA regulations as amended apply to all "covered entities" as defined at §1630.2(b). The ADA defines "covered entities" to mean an employer, employment agency, labor organization, or joint labor-management committee. 42 U.S.C. 12111(2). All covered entities are subject to the ADA's rules prohibiting discrimination. 42 U.S.C. 12112.

Section 1630.1(c) Construction

The ADA must be construed as amended. The primary purpose of the Amendments Act was to make it easier for people with disabilities to obtain protection under the ADA. See Joint Hoyer-Sensenbrenner Statement on the Origins of the ADA Restoration Act of 2008, H.R. 3195 (reviewing provisions of H.R. 3195 as revised following negotiations between representatives of the disability and business communities) (Joint Hoyer-Sensenbrenner Statement) at 2. Accordingly, under the ADA as amended and the EEOC's regulations, the definition of "disability" "shall be construed in favor of broad coverage of individuals under [the ADA], to the maximum extent permitted by the terms of [the ADA]." 42 U.S.C. 12102(4)(A); see also 2008 Senate Statement of Managers at 3 ("The ADA Amendments Act * * * reiterates that Congress intends that the scope of the [ADA] be broad and inclusive."). This construction is also intended to reinforce the general rule that civil rights statutes must be broadly construed to achieve their remedial purpose. Id. at 2; see also 2008 House Judiciary Committee Report at 19 (this rule of construction "directs courts to construe the definition of 'disability' broadly to advance the ADA's remedial purposes" and thus "brings treatment of the ADA's definition of disability in line with treatment of other civil rights laws, which should be construed broadly to effectuate their remedial purposes").

The ADAAA and the EEOC's regulations also make clear that the primary object of attention in cases brought under the ADA should be whether entities covered under the ADA have complied with their obligations, not—whether the individual meets the definition of disability. ADAAA Section 2(b)(5). This means, for example, examining whether an employer has discriminated against an employee, including whether an employer has fulfilled its obligations with respect to providing a "reasonable accommodation" to an individual with a disability; or whether an employee has met his or her responsibilities under the ADA with respect to engaging in the reasonable accommodation "interactive process." See also 2008 Senate Statement of Managers at 4 ("[L]ower court cases have too often turned solely on the question of whether the plaintiff is an individual with a disability rather than the merits of discrimination claims, such as whether adverse decisions were impermissibly made by the employer on the basis of disability, reasonable accommodations were denied, or qualification standards were unlawfully discriminatory."); 2008 House Judiciary Committee Report at 6 ("An individual who does not qualify as disabled * * * does not meet th[e] threshold question of coverage in the protected class and is therefore not permitted to attempt to prove his or her claim of discriminatory treatment.").

Further, the question of whether an individual has a disability under this part "should not demand analysis." ADAAA Section 2(b)(5). See also House Education and Labor Committee Report at 9 ("The Committee intends that the establishment of coverage under the ADA should not be overly complex nor difficult. * * *").
In addition, unless expressly stated otherwise, the standards applied in the ADA are intended to provide at least as much protection as the standards applied under the Rehabilitation Act of 1973.

The ADA does not preempt any Federal law, or any State or local law, that grants to individuals with disabilities protection greater than or equivalent to that provided by the ADA. This means that the existence of a lesser standard of protection to individuals with disabilities under the ADA will not provide a defense to failing to meet a higher standard under another law. Thus, for example, title I of the ADA would not be a defense to failing to prepare and maintain an affirmative action program under section 503 of the Rehabilitation Act. On the other hand, the existence of a lesser standard under another law will not provide a defense to failing to meet a higher standard under the ADA. See 1990 House Labor Report at 135; 1990 House Judiciary Report at 69-70.

This also means that an individual with a disability could choose to pursue claims under a State discrimination or tort law that does not confer greater substantive rights, or even confers fewer substantive rights, if the potential available remedies would be greater than those available under the ADA and this part. The ADA does not restrict an individual with a disability from pursuing such claims in addition to charges brought under this part. 1990 House Judiciary Report at 69-70.

The ADA does not automatically preempt medical standards or safety requirements established by Federal law or regulations. It does not preempt State, county, or local laws, ordinances or regulations that are consistent with this part and designed to protect the public health from individuals who pose a direct threat to the health or safety of others that cannot be eliminated or reduced by reasonable accommodation. However, the ADA does preempt inconsistent requirements established by State or local law for safety or security sensitive positions. See 1989 Senate Report at 27; 1990 House Labor Report at 57.

This also means that an individual with a disability could choose to pursue claims under a State discrimination or tort law that does not confer greater substantive rights, or even confers fewer substantive rights, if the potential available remedies would be greater than those available under the ADA and this part. The ADA does not restrict an individual with a disability from pursuing such claims in addition to charges brought under this part. 1990 House Judiciary Report at 69-70.

The ADA does not automatically preempt medical standards or safety requirements established by Federal law or regulations. It does not preempt State, county, or local laws, ordinances or regulations that are consistent with this part and designed to protect the public health from individuals who pose a direct threat to the health or safety of others that cannot be eliminated or reduced by reasonable accommodation. However, the ADA does preempt inconsistent requirements established by State or local law for safety or security sensitive positions. See 1989 Senate Report at 27; 1990 House Labor Report at 57.

An employer allegedly in violation of this part cannot successfully defend its actions by relying on the obligation to comply with the requirements of any State or local law that imposes prohibitions or limitations on the eligibility of individuals with disabilities who are qualified to practice any occupation or profession. For example, suppose a municipality has an ordinance that prohibits individuals with tuberculosis from teaching school children. If an individual with dormant tuberculosis challenges a private school's refusal to hire him or her on the basis of the tuberculosis, the private school would not be able to rely on the city ordinance as a defense under the ADA.

Paragraph (c)(3) is consistent with language added to section 501 of the ADA by the ADA Amendments Act. It makes clear that nothing in this part is intended to alter the determination of eligibility for benefits under state workers' compensation laws or Federal and State disability benefit programs. State workers' compensation laws and Federal disability benefit programs, such as programs that provide payments to veterans with service-connected disabilities and the Social Security Disability Insurance program, have fundamentally different purposes than title I of the ADA.

Sections 1630.2(a)-(f) Commission, Covered Entity, etc.

The definitions section of part 1630 includes several terms that are identical, or almost identical, to the terms found in title VII of the Civil Rights Act of 1964. Among these terms are "Commission," "Person," "State," and "Employer." These terms are to be given the same meaning under the ADA that they are given under title VII. In general, the term "employee" has the same meaning that it is given under title VII. However, the ADA's definition of "employee" does not contain an exception, as does title VII, for elected officials and their personal staffs. It should further be noted that all State and local governments are covered by title II of the ADA whether or not they are also covered by this part. Title II, which is enforced by the Department of Justice, became effective on January 26, 1992. See 28 CFR part 35.

The term "covered entity" is not found in title VII. However, the title VII definitions of the entities included in the term "covered entity" (e.g., employer, employment agency, labor organization, etc.) are applicable to the ADA.

Section 1630.2(g) Disability

In addition to the term "covered entity," there are several other terms that are unique to the ADA as amended. The first of these is the term "disability." "This definition is of critical importance because as a threshold issue it determines whether an individual is covered by the ADA." 2008 Senate Statement of Managers at 6.

In the original ADA, "Congress sought to protect anyone who experiences discrimination because of a current, past, or perceived disability." 2008 Senate Statement of Managers at 6. Accordingly, the definition of the term "disability" is divided into three prongs: An individual is considered to have a "disability" if that individual (1) has a physical or mental impairment that substantially limits one or more of that person's major life activities (the "actual disability" prong); (2) has a record of such an impairment (the "record of" prong); or (3) is regarded by the covered entity as an individual with a disability as defined in §1630.2(l) (the "regarded as" prong). The ADAAA retained the basic structure and terms of the original definition of disability. However, the Amendments Act altered the interpretation and application of this critical statutory term in fundamental ways. See 2008 Senate Statement of Managers at 1 ("The bill maintains the ADA's inherently functional definition of disability" but "clarifies and expands the definition's meaning and application.").

As noted above, the primary purpose of the ADAAA is to make it easier for people with disabilities to obtain protection under the ADA. See Joint Hoyer-Sensenbrenner Statement at 2. Accordingly, the ADAAA provides rules of construction regarding the definition of disability. Consistent with the congressional intent to reinstate a broad scope of protection under the ADA, the ADAAA's rules of construction require that the definition of "disability" "shall be construed in favor of broad coverage of individuals under [the ADA], to the maximum extent permitted by the terms of [the ADA]." 42 U.S.C. 12102(4)(A). The legislative history of the ADAAA is replete with references emphasizing this principle. See Joint Hoyer-Sensenbrenner Statement at 2 ("[The bill] establishes that the definition of disability must be interpreted broadly to achieve the remedial purposes of the ADA"); 2008 Senate Statement of Managers at 1 (the ADAAA's purpose is to "enhance the protections of the [ADA]" by "expanding the definition, and by rejecting several opinions of the United States Supreme Court that have had the effect of restricting the meaning and application of the definition of disability"); id. (stressing the importance of removing barriers "to construing and applying the definition of disability more generously"); id. at 4 ("The managers have introduced the [ADAAA] to restore the proper balance and application of the ADA by clarifying and broadening the definition of disability, and to increase eligibility for the protections of the ADA."); id. ("It is our expectation that because the bill makes the definition of disability more generous, some people who were not covered before will now be covered."); id. (warning that "the definition of disability should not be unduly used as a tool for excluding individuals from the ADA's protections"); id. (this principle "sends a clear signal of our intent that the courts must interpret the definition of disability broadly rather than stringently"); 2008 House Judiciary Committee Report at 5 ("The purpose of the bill is to restore protection for the broad range of individuals with disabilities as originally envisioned by Congress by responding to the Supreme Court's narrow interpretation of the definition of disability.").

Further, as the purposes section of the ADAAA explicitly cautions, the "primary object of attention" in cases brought under the ADA should be whether entities covered under the ADA have complied with their obligations. As noted above, this means, for example, examining whether an employer has discriminated against an employee, including whether an employer has fulfilled its obligations with respect to providing a "reasonable accommodation" to an individual with a disability; or whether an employee has met his or her responsibilities under the ADA with respect to engaging in the reasonable accommodation "interactive process." ADAAA Section 2(b)(5); see also 2008 Senate Statement of Managers at 4 ("[L]ower court cases have too often turned solely on the question of whether the plaintiff is an individual with a disability rather than the merits of discrimination claims, such as whether adverse decisions were impermissibly made by the employer on the basis of disability, reasonable accommodations were denied, or qualification standards were unlawfully discriminatory."); 2008 House Judiciary Committee Report (criticizing pre-ADAAA court decisions which "prevented individuals that Congress unquestionably intended to cover from ever getting a chance to prove their case"). Accordingly, the threshold coverage question of whether an individual's impairment is a disability under the ADA "should not demand extensive analysis." ADAAA Section 2(b)(5).

Section 1630.2(g)(2) provides that an individual may establish coverage under any one or more (or all three) of the prongs in the definition of disability. However, to be an individual with a disability, an individual is only required to satisfy one prong.

As §1630.2(g)(3) indicates, in many cases it may be unnecessary for an individual to resort to coverage under the "actual disability" or "record of" prongs. Where the need for a reasonable accommodation is not at issue—for example, where there is no question that the individual is "qualified" without a reasonable accommodation and is not seeking or has not sought a reasonable accommodation—it would not be necessary to determine whether the individual is substantially limited in a major life activity (under the actual disability prong) or has a record of a substantially limiting impairment (under the record of prong). Such claims could be evaluated solely under the "regarded as" prong of the definition. In fact, Congress expected the first and second prongs of the definition of disability "to be used only by people who are affirmatively seeking reasonable accommodations * * *" and that "[a]ny individual who has been discriminated against because of an impairment—short of being granted a reasonable accommodation * * *—should be bringing a claim under the third prong of the definition which will require no showing with regard to the severity of his or her impairment." Joint Hoyer-Sensenbrenner Statement at 4. An individual may choose, however, to proceed under the "actual disability" and/or "record of" prong regardless of whether the individual is challenging a covered entity's failure to make reasonable accommodation or requires a reasonable accommodation.

To fully understand the meaning of the term "disability," it is also necessary to understand what is meant by the terms "physical or mental impairment," "major life activity," "substantially limits," "record of," and "regarded as." Each of these terms is discussed below.

Section 1630.2(h) Physical or Mental Impairment

Neither the original ADA nor the ADAAA provides a definition for the terms "physical or mental impairment." However, the legislative history of the Amendments Act notes that Congress "expect[s] that the current regulatory definition of these terms, as promulgated by agencies such as the U.S. Equal Employment Opportunity Commission (EEOC), the Department of Justice (DOJ) and the Department of Education Office of Civil Rights (DOE OCR) will not change." 2008 Senate Statement of Managers at 6. The definition of "physical or mental impairment" in the EEOC's regulations remains based on the definition of the term "physical or mental impairment" found in the regulations implementing section 504 of the Rehabilitation Act at 34 CFR part 104. However, the definition in EEOC's regulations adds additional body systems to those provided in the section 504 regulations and makes clear that the list is non-exhaustive.

It is important to distinguish between conditions that are impairments and physical, psychological, environmental, cultural, and economic characteristics that are not impairments. The definition of the term "impairment" does not include physical characteristics such as eye color, hair color, left-handedness, or height, weight, or muscle tone that are within "normal" range and are not the result of a physiological disorder. The definition, likewise, does not include characteristic predisposition to illness or disease. Other conditions, such as pregnancy, that are not the result of a physiological disorder are also not impairments. However, a pregnancy-related impairment that substantially limits a major life activity is a disability under the first prong of the definition. Alternatively, a pregnancy-related impairment may constitute a "record of" a substantially limiting impairment," or may be covered under the "regarded as" prong if it is the basis for a prohibited employment action and is not "transitory and minor."

The definition of an impairment also does not include common personality traits such as poor judgment or a quick temper where these are not symptoms of a mental or psychological disorder. Environmental, cultural, or economic disadvantages such as poverty, lack of education, or a prison record are not impairments. Advanced age, in and of itself, is also not an impairment. However, various medical conditions commonly associated with age, such as hearing loss, osteoporosis, or arthritis would constitute impairments within the meaning of this part. See 1989 Senate Report at 22-23; 1990 House Labor Report at 51-52; 1990 House Judiciary Report at 28-29.

Section 1630.2(i) Major Life Activities

The ADAAA provided significant new guidance and clarification on the subject of "major life activities." As the legislative history of the Amendments Act explains, Congress anticipated that protection under the ADA would now extend to a wider range of cases, in part as a result of the expansion of the category of major life activities. See 2008 Senate Statement of Managers at 8 n.17.

For purposes of clarity, the Amendments Act provides an illustrative list of major life activities, including caring for oneself, performing manual tasks, seeing, hearing, eating, sleeping, walking, standing, lifting, bending, speaking, breathing, learning, reading, concentrating, thinking, communicating, and working. The ADA Amendments expressly made this statutory list of examples of major life activities non-exhaustive, and the regulations include sitting, reaching, and interacting with others as additional examples. Many of these major life activities listed in the ADA Amendments Act and the regulations already had been included in the EEOC's 1991 now-superseded regulations implementing title I of the ADA and in sub-regulatory documents, and already were recognized by the courts.

The ADA as amended also explicitly defines "major life activities" to include the operation of "major bodily functions." This was an important addition to the statute. This clarification was needed to ensure that the impact of an impairment on the operation of a major bodily function would not be overlooked or wrongly dismissed as falling outside the definition of "major life activities" under the ADA. 2008 House Judiciary Committee Report at 16; see also 2008 Senate Statement of Managers at 8 ("for the first time [in the ADAAA], the category of 'major life activities' is defined to include the operation of major bodily functions, thus better addressing chronic impairments that can be substantially limiting").

The regulations include all of those major bodily functions identified in the ADA Amendments Act's non-exhaustive list of examples and add a number of others that are consistent with the body systems listed in the regulations' definition of "impairment" (at §1630.2(h)) and with the U.S. Department of Labor's non-discrimination and equal employment opportunity regulations implementing section 188 of the Workforce Investment Act of 1998, 29 U.S.C. 2801, et seq. Thus, special sense organs, skin, genitourinary, cardiovascular, hemic, lymphatic, and musculoskeletal functions are major bodily functions not included in the statutory list of examples but included in §1630.2(i)(1)(ii). The Commission has added these examples to further illustrate the non-exhaustive list of major life activities, including major bodily functions, and to emphasize that the concept of major life activities is to be interpreted broadly consistent with the Amendments Act. The regulations also provide that the operation of a major bodily function may include the operation of an individual organ within a body system. This would include, for example, the operation of the kidney, liver, pancreas, or other organs.

The link between particular impairments and various major bodily functions should not be difficult to identify. Because impairments, by definition, affect the functioning of body systems, they will generally affect major bodily functions. For example, cancer affects an individual's normal cell growth; diabetes affects the operation of the pancreas and also the function of the endocrine system; and Human Immunodeficiency Virus (HIV) infection affects the immune system. Likewise, sickle cell disease affects the functions of the hemic system, lymphedema affects lymphatic functions, and rheumatoid arthritis affects musculoskeletal functions.

In the legislative history of the ADAAA, Congress expressed its expectation that the statutory expansion of "major life activities" to include major bodily functions (along with other statutory changes) would lead to more expansive coverage. See 2008 Senate Statement of Managers at 8 n.17 (indicating that these changes will make it easier for individuals to show that they are eligible for the ADA's protections under the first prong of the definition of disability). The House Education and Labor Committee explained that the inclusion of major bodily functions would "affect cases such as U.S. v. Happy Time Day Care Ctr. in which the courts struggled to analyze whether the impact of HIV infection substantially limits various major life activities of a five-year-old child, and recognizing, among other things, that 'there is something inherently illogical about inquiring whether' a five-year-old's ability to procreate is substantially limited by his HIV infection; Furnish v. SVI Sys., Inc, in which the court found that an individual with cirrhosis of the liver caused by Hepatitis B is not disabled because liver function — unlike eating, working, or reproducing — 'is not integral to one's daily existence;' and Pimental v. Dartmouth-Hitchcock Clinic, in which the court concluded that the plaintiff's stage three breast cancer did not substantially limit her ability to care for herself, sleep, or concentrate. The Committee expects that the plaintiffs in each of these cases could establish a [substantial limitation] on major bodily functions that would qualify them for protection under the ADA." 2008 House Education and Labor Committee Report at 12. The examples of major life activities (including major bodily functions) in the ADAAA and the EEOC's regulations are illustrative and non-exhaustive, and the absence of a particular life activity or bodily function from the examples does not create a negative implication as to whether an omitted activity or function constitutes a major life activity under the statute. See 2008 Senate Statement of Managers at 8; see also 2008 House Committee on Educ. and Labor Report at 11; 2008 House Judiciary Committee Report at 17.

The Commission anticipates that courts will recognize other major life activities, consistent with the ADA Amendments Act's mandate to construe the definition of disability broadly. As a result of the ADA Amendments Act's rejection of the holding in Toyota Motor Mfg., Ky., Inc. v. Williams, 534 U.S. 184 (2002), whether an activity is a "major life activity" is not determined by reference to whether it is of "central importance to daily life." See Toyota, 534 U.S. at 197 (defining "major life activities" as activities that are of "central importance to most people's daily lives"). Indeed, this holding was at odds with the earlier Supreme Court decision of Bragdon v. Abbott, 524 U.S. 624 (1998), which held that a major life activity (in that case, reproduction) does not have to have a "public, economic or daily aspect." Id. at 639.

Accordingly, the regulations provide that in determining other examples of major life activities, the term "major" shall not be interpreted strictly to create a demanding standard for disability. Cf. 2008 Senate Statement of Managers at 7 (indicating that a person is considered an individual with a disability for purposes of the first prong when one or more of the individual's "important life activities" are restricted) (citing 1989 Senate Report at 23). The regulations also reject the notion that to be substantially limited in performing a major life activity, an individual must have an impairment that prevents or severely restricts the individual from doing "activities that are of central importance to most people's daily lives." Id.; see also 2008 Senate Statement of Managers at 5 n.12.

Thus, for example, lifting is a major life activity regardless of whether an individual who claims to be substantially limited in lifting actually performs activities of central importance to daily life that require lifting. Similarly, the Commission anticipates that the major life activity of performing manual tasks (which was at issue in Toyota) could have many different manifestations, such as performing tasks involving fine motor coordination, or performing tasks involving grasping, hand strength, or pressure. Such tasks need not constitute activities of central importance to most people's daily lives, nor must an individual show that he or she is substantially limited in performing all manual tasks.

Section 1630.2(j) Substantially Limits

In any case involving coverage solely under the "regarded as" prong of the definition of "disability" (e.g., cases where reasonable accommodation is not at issue), it is not necessary to determine whether an individual is "substantially limited" in any major life activity. See 2008 Senate Statement of Managers at 10; id. at 13 ("The functional limitation imposed by an impairment is irrelevant to the third 'regarded as' prong."). Indeed, Congress anticipated that the first and second prongs of the definition of disability would "be used only by people who are affirmatively seeking reasonable accommodations * * *" and that "[a]ny individual who has been discriminated against because of an impairment—short of being granted a reasonable accommodation * * *—should be bringing a claim under the third prong of the definition which will require no showing with regard to the severity of his or her impairment." Joint Hoyer-Sensenbrenner Statement at 4. Of course, an individual may choose, however, to proceed under the "actual disability" and/or "record of" prong regardless of whether the individual is challenging a covered entity's failure to make reasonable accommodations or requires a reasonable accommodation. The concept of "substantially limits" is only relevant in cases involving coverage under the "actual disability" or "record of" prong of the definition of disability. Thus, the information below pertains to these cases only.

Section 1630.2(j)(1) Rules of Construction

It is clear in the text and legislative history of the ADAAA that Congress concluded the courts had incorrectly construed "substantially limits," and disapproved of the EEOC's now-superseded 1991 regulation defining the term to mean "significantly restricts." See 2008 Senate Statement of Managers at 6 ("We do not believe that the courts have correctly instituted the level of coverage we intended to establish with the term 'substantially limits' in the ADA" and "we believe that the level of limitation, and the intensity of focus, applied by the Supreme Court in Toyota goes beyond what we believe is the appropriate standard to create coverage under this law."). Congress extensively deliberated over whether a new term other than "substantially limits" should be adopted to denote the appropriate functional limitation necessary under the first and second prongs of the definition of disability. See 2008 Senate Statement of Managers at 6-7. Ultimately, Congress affirmatively opted to retain this term in the Amendments Act, rather than replace it. It concluded that "adopting a new, undefined term that is subject to widely disparate meanings is not the best way to achieve the goal of ensuring consistent and appropriately broad coverage under this Act." Id. Instead, Congress determined "a better way * * * to express [its] disapproval of Sutton and Toyota (along with the current EEOC regulation) is to retain the words 'substantially limits,' but clarify that it is not meant to be a demanding standard." Id. at 7. To achieve that goal, Congress set forth detailed findings and purposes and "rules of construction" to govern the interpretation and application of this concept going forward. See ADAAA Sections 2-4; 42 U.S.C. 12102(4).

The Commission similarly considered whether to provide a new definition of "substantially limits" in the regulation. Following Congress's lead, however, the Commission ultimately concluded that a new definition would inexorably lead to greater focus and intensity of attention on the threshold issue of coverage than intended by Congress. Therefore, the regulations simply provide rules of construction that must be applied in determining whether an impairment substantially limits (or substantially limited) a major life activity. These are each discussed in greater detail below.

Section 1630.2(j)(1)(ii) Broad Construction;
not a Demanding Standard

Section 1630.2(j)(1)(i) states: "The term 'substantially limits' shall be construed broadly in favor of expansive coverage, to the maximum extent permitted by the terms of the ADA. 'Substantially limits' is not meant to be a demanding standard."

Congress stated in the ADA Amendments Act that the definition of disability "shall be construed in favor of broad coverage," and that "the term 'substantially limits' shall be interpreted consistently with the findings and purposes of the ADA Amendments Act of 2008." 42 U.S.C. 12101(4)(A)-(B), as amended. "This is a textual provision that will legally guide the agencies and courts in properly interpreting the term 'substantially limits.'" Hoyer-Sensenbrenner Congressional Record Statement at H8295. As Congress noted in the legislative history of the ADAAA, "[t]o be clear, the purposes section conveys our intent to clarify not only that 'substantially limits' should be measured by a lower standard than that used in Toyota, but also that the definition of disability should not be unduly used as a tool for excluding individuals from the ADA's protections." 2008 Senate Statement of Managers at 5 (also stating that "[t]his rule of construction, together with the rule of construction providing that the definition of disability shall be construed in favor of broad coverage of individuals sends a clear signal of our intent that the courts must interpret the definition of disability broadly rather than stringently"). Put most succinctly, "substantially limits" "is not meant to be a demanding standard." 2008 Senate Statement of Managers at 7.

Section 1630.2(j)(1)(ii) Significant or Severe Restriction Not Required; Nonetheless, Not Every Impairment Is Substantially Limiting

Section 1630.2(j)(1)(ii) states: "An impairment is a disability within the meaning of this section if it substantially limits the ability of an individual to perform a major life activity as compared to most people in the general population. An impairment need not prevent, or significantly or severely restrict, the individual from performing a major life activity in order to be considered substantially limiting. Nonetheless, not every impairment will constitute a 'disability' within the meaning of this section."

In keeping with the instruction that the term "substantially limits" is not meant to be a demanding standard, the regulations provide that an impairment is a disability if it substantially limits the ability of an individual to perform a major life activity as compared to most people in the general population. However, to be substantially limited in performing a major life activity an individual need not have an impairment that prevents or significantly or severely restricts the individual from performing a major life activity. See 2008 Senate Statement of Managers at 2, 6-8 & n.14; 2008 House Committee on Educ. and Labor Report at 9-10 ("While the limitation imposed by an impairment must be important, it need not rise to the level of severely restricting or significantly restricting the ability to perform a major life activity to qualify as a disability."); 2008 House Judiciary Committee Report at 16 (similarly requiring an "important" limitation). The level of limitation required is "substantial" as compared to most people in the general population, which does not require a significant or severe restriction. Multiple impairments that combine to substantially limit one or more of an individual's major life activities also constitute a disability. Nonetheless, not every impairment will constitute a "disability" within the meaning of this section. See 2008 Senate Statement of Managers at 4 ("We reaffirm that not every individual with a physical or mental impairment is covered by the first prong of the definition of disability in the ADA.")

Section 1630.2(j)(1)(iii) Substantial Limitation Should Not Be Primary Object of Attention; Extensive Analysis Not Needed

Section 1630.2(j)(1)(iii) states: "The primary object of attention in cases brought under the ADA should be whether covered entities have complied with their obligations, not whether an individual's impairment substantially limits a major life activity. Accordingly, the threshold issue of whether an impairment 'substantially limits' a major life activity should not demand extensive analysis."

Congress retained the term "substantially limits" in part because it was concerned that adoption of a new phrase — and the resulting need for further judicial scrutiny and construction — would not "help move the focus from the threshold issue of disability to the primary issue of discrimination." 2008 Senate Statement of Managers at 7.

This was the primary problem Congress sought to solve in enacting the ADAAA. It recognized that "clearing the initial [disability] threshold is critical, as individuals who are excluded from the definition 'never have the opportunity to have their condition evaluated in light of medical evidence and a determination made as to whether they [are] 'otherwise quali fied.'"" 2008 House Judiciary Committee Report at 7; see also id. (expressing concern that "[a]n individual who does not qualify as disabled does not meet th[e] threshold question of coverage in the protected class and is therefore not permitted to attempt to prove his or her claim of discriminatory treatment"); 2008 Senate Statement of Managers at 4 (criticizing pre-ADAAA lower court cases that "too often turned solely on the question of whether the plaintiff is an individual with a disability rather than the merits of discrimination claims, such as whether adverse decisions were impermissibly made by the employer on the basis of disability, reasonable accommodations were denied, or qualification standards were unlawfully discriminatory").

Accordingly, the Amendments Act and the amended regulations make plain that the emphasis in ADA cases now should be squarely on the merits and not on the initial coverage question. The revised regulations therefore provide that an impairment is a disability if it substantially limits the ability of an individual to perform a major life activity as compared to most people in the general population and deletes the language to which Congress objected. The Commission believes that this provides a useful framework in which to analyze whether an impairment satisfies the definition of disability. Further, this framework better reflects Congress's expressed intent in the ADA Amendments Act that the definition of the term "disability" shall be construed broadly, and is consistent with statements in the Amendments Act's legislative history. See 2008 Senate Statement of Managers at 7 (stating that "adopting a new, undefined term" and the "resulting need for further judicial scrutiny and construction will not help move the focus from the threshold issue of disability to the primary issue of discrimination," and finding that "'substantially limits' as construed consistently with the findings and purposes of this legislation establishes an appropriate functionality test of determining whether an individual has a disability" and that "using the correct standard — one that is lower than the strict or demanding standard created by the Supreme Court in Toyota — will make the disability determination an appropriate threshold issue but not an onerous burden for those seeking accommodations or modifications").

Consequently, this rule of construction makes clear that the question of whether an impairment substantially limits a major life activity should not demand extensive analysis. As the legislative history explains, "[w]e expect that courts interpreting [the ADA] will not demand such an extensive analysis over whether a person's physical or mental impairment constitutes a disability." Hoyer-Sensenbrenner Congressional Record Statement at H8295; see id. ("Our goal throughout this process has been to simplify that analysis.")

Section 1630.2(j)(1)(iv) Individualized Assessment Required, But With Lower Standard Than Previously Applied

Section 1630.2(j)(1)(iv) states: "The determination of whether an impairment substantially limits a major life activity requires an individualized assessment. However, in making this assessment, the term 'substantially limits' shall be interpreted and applied to require a degree of functional limitation that is lower than the standard for 'substantially limits' applied prior to the ADAAA."

By retaining the essential elements of the definition of disability including the key term "substantially limits," Congress reaffirmed that not every individual with a physical or mental impairment is covered by the first prong of the definition of disability in the ADA. See 2008 Senate Statement of Managers at 4. To be covered under the first prong of the definition, an individual must establish that an impairment substantially limits a major life activity. That has not changed — nor will the necessity of making this determination on an individual basis. Id. However, what the ADAAA changed is the standard required for making this determination. Id. at 4-5.

The Amendments Act and the EEOC's regulations explicitly reject the standard enunciated by the Supreme Court in Toyota Motor Mfg., Ky., Inc. v. Williams, 534 U.S. 184 (2002), and applied in the lower courts in numerous cases. See ADAAA Section 2(b)(4). That previous standard created "an inappropriately high level of limitation necessary to obtain coverage under the ADA." Id. at Section 2(b)(5). The Amendments Act and the EEOC's regulations reject the notion that "substantially limits" should be interpreted strictly to create a demanding standard for qualifying as disabled. Id. at Section 2(b)(4). Instead, the ADAAA and these regulations establish a degree of functional limitation required for an impairment to constitute a disability that is consistent with what Congress originally intended. 2008 Senate Statement of Managers at 7. This will make the disability determination an appropriate threshold issue but not an onerous burden for those seeking to prove discrimination under the ADA. Id.

Section 1630.2(j)(1)(v) Scientific, Medical, or Statistical Analysis Not Required, But Permissible When Appropriate

Section 1630.2(j)(1)(v) states: "The comparison of an individual's performance of a major life activity to the performance of the same major life activity by most people in the general population usually will not require scientific, medical, or statistical analysis. Nothing in this paragraph is intended, however, to prohibit the presentation of scientific, medical, or statistical evidence to make such a comparison where appropriate."

The term "average person in the general population," as the basis of comparison for determining whether an individual's impairment substantially limits a major life activity, has been changed to "most people in the general population." This revision is not a substantive change in the concept, but rather is intended to conform the language to the simpler and more straightforward terminology used in the legislative history to the Amendments Act. The comparison between the individual and "most people" need not be exacting, and usually will not require scientific, medical, or statistical analysis. Nothing in this subparagraph is intended, however, to prohibit the presentation of scientific, medical, or statistical evidence to make such a comparison where appropriate.

The comparison to most people in the general population continues to mean a comparison to other people in the general population, not a comparison to those similarly situated. For example, the ability of an individual with an amputated limb to perform a major life activity is compared to other people in the general population, not to other amputees. This does not mean that disability cannot be shown where an impairment, such as a learning disability, is clinically diagnosed based in part on a disparity between an individual's aptitude and that individual's actual versus expected achievement, taking into account the person's chronological age, measured intelligence, and age-appropriate education. Individuals diagnosed with dyslexia or other learning disabilities will typically be substantially limited in performing activities such as learning, reading, and thinking when compared to most people in the general population, particularly when the ameliorative effects of mitigating measures, including therapies, learned behavioral or adaptive neurological modifications, assistive devices (e.g., audio recordings, screen reading devices, voice activated software), studying longer, or receiving more time to take a test, are disregarded as required under the ADA Amendments Act.

Section 1630.2(j)(1)(vi) Mitigating Measures

Section 1630.2(j)(1)(vi) states: "The determination of whether an impairment substantially limits a major life activity shall be made without regard to the ameliorative effects of mitigating measures. However, the ameliorative effects of ordinary eyeglasses or contact lenses shall be considered in determining whether an impairment substantially limits a major life activity."

The ameliorative effects of mitigating measures shall not be considered in determining whether an impairment substantially limits a major life activity. Thus, "[w]ith the exception of ordinary eyeglasses and contact lenses, impairments must be examined in their unmitigated state." See 2008 Senate Statement of Managers at 5.

This provision in the ADAAA and the EEOC's regulations "is intended to eliminate the catch-22 that exist[ed] * * * where individuals who are subjected to discrimination on the basis of their disabilities [we]re frequently unable to invoke the ADA's protections because they [we]re not considered people with disabilities when the effects of their medication, medical supplies, behavioral adaptations, or other interventions [we]re considered." Joint Hoyer-Sensenbrenner Statement at 2; see also 2008 Senate Statement of Managers at 9 ("This provision is intended to eliminate the situation created under [prior] law in which impairments that are mitigated [did] not constitute disabilities but [were the basis for discrimination]."). To the extent cases pre-dating the 2008 Amendments Act reasoned otherwise, they are contrary to the law as amended. See 2008 House Judiciary Committee Report at 9 & nn.25, 20-21 (citing, e.g., McClure v. General Motors Corp., 75 F. App'x 983 (5th Cir. 2003) (court held that individual with muscular dystrophy who, with the mitigating measure of "adapting" how he performed manual tasks, had successfully learned to live and work with his disability was therefore not an individual with a disability); Orr v. Wal-Mart Stores, Inc., 297 F.3d 720 (8th Cir. 2002) (court held that Sutton v. United Air Lines, Inc., 527 U.S. 471 (1999), required consideration of the ameliorative effects of plaintiff's careful regimen of medicine, exercise and diet, and declined to consider impact of uncontrolled diabetes on plaintiff's ability to see, speak, read, and walk); Gonzales v. National Bd. of Med. Examiners, 225 F.3d 620 (6th Cir. 2000) (where the court found that an individual with a diagnosed learning disability was not substantially limited after considering the impact of self-accommodations that allowed him to read and achieve academic success); McMullin v. Ashcroft, 337 F. Supp. 2d 1281 (D. Wyo. 2004) (individual fired because of clinical depression not protected because of the successful management of the condition with medication for fifteen years); Eckhaus v. Consol. Rail Corp., 2003 WL 23205042 (D.N.J. Dec. 24, 2003) (individual fired because of a hearing impairment was not protected because a hearing aid helped correct that impairment); Todd v. Academy Corp., 57 F. Supp. 2d 448, 452 (S.D. Tex. 1999) (court held that because medication reduced the frequency and intensity of plaintiff's seizures, he was not disabled)).

An individual who, because of the use of a mitigating measure, has experienced no limitations, or only minor limitations, related to the impairment may still be an individual with a disability, where there is evidence that in the absence of an effective mitigating measure the individual's impairment would be substantially limiting. For example, someone who began taking medication for hypertension before experiencing substantial limitations related to the impairment would still be an individual with a disability if, without the medication, he or she would now be substantially limited in functions of the cardiovascular or circulatory system.

Evidence showing that an impairment would be substantially limiting in the absence of the ameliorative effects of mitigating measures could include evidence of limitations that a person experienced prior to using a mitigating measure, evidence concerning the expected course of a particular disorder absent mitigating measures, or readily available and reliable information of other types. However, we expect that consistent with the Amendments Act's command (and the related rules of construction in the regulations) that the definition of disability "should not demand extensive analysis," covered entities and courts will in many instances be able to conclude that a substantial limitation has been shown without resort to such evidence.

The Amendments Act provides an "illustrative but non-comprehensive list of the types of mitigating measures that are not to be considered." See 2008 Senate Statement of Managers at 9. Section 1630.2(j)(5) of the regulations includes all of those mitigating measures listed in the ADA Amendments Act's illustrative list of mitigating measures, including reasonable accommodations (as applied under title I) or "auxiliary aids or services" (as defined by 42 U.S.C. 12103(1) and applied under titles II and III). Since it would be impossible to guarantee comprehensiveness in a finite list, the list of examples of mitigating measures provided in the ADA and the regulations is non-exhaustive. See 2008 House Judiciary Committee Report at 20. The absence of any particular mitigating measure from the list in the regulations should not convey a negative implication as to whether the measure is a mitigating measure under the ADA. See 2008 Senate Statement of Managers at 9.

For example, the fact that mitigating measures include "reasonable accommodations" generally makes it unnecessary to mention specific kinds of accommodations. Nevertheless, the use of a service animal, job coach, or personal assistant on the job would certainly be considered types of mitigating measures, as would the use of any device that could be considered assistive technology, and whether individuals who use these measures have disabilities would be determined without reference to their ameliorative effects. See 2008 House Judiciary Committee Report at 20; 2008 House Educ. & Labor Rep. at 15. Similarly, adaptive strategies that might mitigate, or even allow an individual to otherwise avoid performing particular major life activities, are mitigating measures and also would not be considered in determining whether an impairment is substantially limiting. Id.

The determination of whether or not an individual's impairment substantially limits a major life activity is unaffected by whether the individual chooses to forgo mitigating measures. For individuals who do not use a mitigating measure (including for example medication or reasonable accommodation that could alleviate the effects of an impairment), the availability of such measures has no bearing on whether the impairment substantially limits a major life activity. The limitations posed by the impairment on the individual and any negative (non-ameliorative) effects of mitigating measures used determine whether an impairment is substantially limiting. The origin of the impairment, whether its effects can be mitigated, and any ameliorative effects of mitigating measures in fact used may not be considered in determining if the impairment is substantially limiting. However, the use or non-use of mitigating measures, and any consequences thereof, including any ameliorative and non-ameliorative effects, may be relevant in determining whether the individual is qualified or poses a direct threat to safety.

The ADA Amendments Act and the regulations state that "ordinary eyeglasses or contact lenses" shall be considered in determining whether someone has a disability. This is an exception to the rule that the ameliorative effects of mitigating measures are not to be taken into account. "The rationale behind this exclusion is that the use of ordinary eyeglasses or contact lenses, without more, is not significant enough to warrant protection under the ADA." Joint Hoyer-Sensenbrenner Statement at 2. Nevertheless, as discussed in greater detail below at §1630.10(b), if an applicant or employee is faced with a qualification standard that requires uncorrected vision (as the plaintiffs in the Sutton case were), and the applicant or employee who is adversely affected by the standard brings a challenge under the ADA, an employer will be required to demonstrate that the qualification standard is job related and consistent with business necessity. 2008 Senate Statement of Managers at 9.

The ADAAA and the EEOC's regulations both define the term "ordinary eyeglasses or contact lenses" as lenses that are "intended to fully correct visual acuity or eliminate refractive error." So, if an individual with severe myopia uses eyeglasses or contact lenses that are intended to fully correct visual acuity or eliminate refractive error, they are ordinary eyeglasses or contact lenses, and therefore any inquiry into whether such individual is substantially limited in seeing or reading would be based on how the individual sees or reads with the benefit of the eyeglasses or contact lenses. Likewise, if the only visual loss an individual experiences affects the ability to see well enough to read, and the individual's ordinary reading glasses are intended to completely correct for this visual loss, the ameliorative effects of using the reading glasses must be considered in determining whether the individual is substantially limited in seeing. Additionally, eyeglasses or contact lenses that are the wrong prescription or an out-dated prescription may nevertheless be "ordinary" eyeglasses or contact lenses, if a proper prescription would fully correct visual acuity or eliminate refractive error.

Both the statute and the regulations distinguish "ordinary eyeglasses or contact lenses" from "low vision devices," which function by magnifying, enhancing, or otherwise augmenting a visual image, and which are not considered when determining whether someone has a disability. The regulations do not establish a specific level of visual acuity (e.g., 20/20) as the basis for determining whether eyeglasses or contact lenses should be considered "ordinary" eyeglasses or contact lenses. Whether lenses fully correct visual acuity or eliminate refractive error is best determined on a case-by-case basis, in light of current and objective medical evidence. Moreover, someone who uses ordinary eyeglasses or contact lenses is not automatically considered to be outside the ADA's protection. Such an individual may demonstrate that, even with the use of ordinary eyeglasses or contact lenses, his vision is still substantially limited when compared to most people.

Section 1630.2(j)(1)(vii) Impairments That Are Episodic or in Remission

Section 1630.2(j)(1)(vii) states: "An impairment that is episodic or in remission is a disability if it would substantially limit a major life activity when active."

An impairment that is episodic or in remission is a disability if it would substantially limit a major life activity in its active state. "This provision is intended to reject the reasoning of court decisions concluding that certain individuals with certain conditions — such as epilepsy or post traumatic stress disorder — were not protected by the ADA because their conditions were episodic or intermittent." Joint Hoyer-Sensenbrenner Statement at 2-3. The legislative history provides: "This * * * rule of construction thus rejects the reasoning of the courts in cases like Todd v. Academy Corp. [57 F. Supp. 2d 448, 453 (S.D. Tex. 1999)] where the court found that the plaintiff's epilepsy, which resulted in short seizures during which the plaintiff was unable to speak and experienced tremors, was not sufficiently limiting, at least in part because those seizures occurred episodically. It similarly rejects the results reached in cases [such as Pimental v. Dartmouth-Hitchock Clinic, 236 F. Supp. 2d 177, 182-83 (D.N.H. 2002)] where the courts have discounted the impact of an impairment [such as cancer] that may be in remission as too short-lived to be substantially limiting. It is thus expected that individuals with impairments that are episodic or in remission (e.g., epilepsy, multiple sclerosis, cancer) will be able to establish coverage if, when active, the impairment or the manner in which it manifests (e.g., seizures) substantially limits a major life activity." 2008 House Judiciary Committee Report at 19-20.

Other examples of impairments that may be episodic include, but are not limited to, hypertension, diabetes, asthma, major depressive disorder, bipolar disorder, and schizophrenia. See 2008 House Judiciary Committee Report at 19-20. The fact that the periods during which an episodic impairment is active and substantially limits a major life activity may be brief or occur infrequently is no longer relevant to determining whether the impairment substantially limits a major life activity. For example, a person with post-traumatic stress disorder who experiences intermittent flashbacks to traumatic events is substantially limited in brain function and thinking.

Section 1630.2(j)(1)(viii) Substantial Limitation in Only One Major Life Activity Required

Section 1630.2(j)(1)(viii) states: "An impairment that substantially limits one major life activity need not substantially limit other major life activities in order to be considered a substantially limiting impairment."

The ADAAA explicitly states that an impairment need only substantially limit one major life activity to be considered a disability under the ADA. See ADAAA Section 4(a); 42 U.S.C. 12102(4)(C). "This responds to and corrects those courts that have required individuals to show that an impairment substantially limits more than one life activity." 2008 Senate Statement of Managers at 8. In addition, this rule of construction is "intended to clarify that the ability to perform one or more particular tasks within a broad category of activities does not preclude coverage under the ADA." Id. To the extent cases pre-dating the applicability of the 2008 Amendments Act reasoned otherwise, they are contrary to the law as amended. Id. (citing Holt v. Grand Lake Mental Health Ctr., Inc., 443 F. 3d 762 (10th Cir. 2006) (holding an individual with cerebral palsy who could not independently perform certain specified manual tasks was not substantially limited in her ability to perform a "broad range" of manual tasks)); see also 2008 House Judiciary Committee Report at 19 & n.52 (this legislatively corrects court decisions that, with regard to the major life activity of performing manual tasks, "have offset substantial limitation in the performance of some tasks with the ability to perform others" (citing Holt)).

For example, an individual with diabetes is substantially limited in endocrine function and thus an individual with a disability under the first prong of the definition. He need not also show that he is substantially limited in eating to qualify for coverage under the first prong. An individual whose normal cell growth is substantially limited due to lung cancer need not also show that she is substantially limited in breathing or respiratory function. And an individual with HIV infection is substantially limited in the function of the immune system, and therefore is an individual with a disability without regard to whether his or her HIV infection substantially limits him or her in reproduction.

In addition, an individual whose impairment substantially limits a major life activity need not additionally demonstrate a resulting limitation in the ability to perform activities of central importance to daily life in order to be considered an individual with a disability under §1630.2(g)(1)(i) or §1630.2(g)(1)(ii), as cases relying on the Supreme Court's decision in Toyota Motor Mfg., Ky., Inc. v. Williams, 534 U.S. 184 (2002), had held prior to the ADA Amendments Act.

Thus, for example, someone with an impairment resulting in a 20-pound lifting restriction that lasts or is expected to last for several months is substantially limited in the major life activity of lifting, and need not also show that he is unable to perform activities of daily living that require lifting in order to be considered substantially limited in lifting. Similarly, someone with monocular vision whose depth perception or field of vision would be substantially limited, with or without any compensatory strategies the individual may have developed, need not also show that he is unable to perform activities of central importance to daily life that require seeing in order to be substantially limited in seeing.

Section 1630.2(j)(1)(ix) Effects of an Impairment Lasting Fewer Than Six Months Can Be Substantially Limiting

Section 1630.2(j)(1)(ix) states: "The six-month 'transitory' part of the 'transitory and minor' exception to 'regarded as' coverage in §1630.2(l) does not apply to the definition of 'disability' under §1630.2(g)(1)(i) or §1630.2(g)(1)(ii). The effects of an impairment lasting or expected to last fewer than six months can be substantially limiting within the meaning of this section."

The regulations include a clear statement that the definition of an impairment as transitory, that is, "lasting or expected to last for six months or less," only applies to the "regarded as" (third) prong of the definition of "disability" as part of the "transitory and minor" defense to "regarded as" coverage. It does not apply to the first or second prong of the definition of disability. See Joint Hoyer-Sensenbrenner Statement at 3 ("[T]here is no need for the transitory and minor exception under the first two prongs because it is clear from the statute and the legislative history that a person can only bring a claim if the impairment substantially limits one or more major life activities or the individual has a record of an impairment that substantially limits one or more major life activities.").

Therefore, an impairment does not have to last for more than six months in order to be considered substantially limiting under the first or the second prong of the definition of disability. For example, as noted above, if an individual has a back impairment that results in a 20-pound lifting restriction that lasts for several months, he is substantially limited in the major life activity of lifting, and therefore covered under the first prong of the definition of disability. At the same time, "[t]he duration of an impairment is one factor that is relevant in determining whether the impairment substantially limits a major life activity. Impairments that last only for a short period of time are typically not covered, although they may be covered if sufficiently severe." Joint Hoyer-Sensenbrenner Statement at 5.

Section 1630.2(j)(3) Predictable Assessments

As the regulations point out, disability is determined based on an individualized assessment. There is no "per se" disability. However, as recognized in the regulations, the individualized assessment of some kinds of impairments will virtually always result in a determination of disability. The inherent nature of these types of medical conditions will in virtually all cases give rise to a substantial limitation of a major life activity. Cf. Heiko v. Columbo Savings Bank, F.S.B., 434 F.3d 249, 256 (4th Cir. 2006) (stating, even pre-ADAAA, that "certain impairments are by their very nature substantially limiting: the major life activity of seeing, for example, is always substantially limited by blindness"). Therefore, with respect to these types of impairments, the necessary individualized assessment should be particularly simple and straightforward.

This result is the consequence of the combined effect of the statutory changes to the definition of disability contained in the Amendments Act and flows from application of the rules of construction set forth in §§1630.2(j)(1)(i)-(ix) (including the lower standard for "substantially limits"; the rule that major life activities include major bodily functions; the principle that impairments that are episodic or in remission are disabilities if they would be substantially limiting when active; and the requirement that the ameliorative effects of mitigating measures (other than ordinary eyeglasses or contact lenses) must be disregarded in assessing whether an individual has a disability).

The regulations at §1630.2(j)(3)(iii) provide examples of the types of impairments that should easily be found to substantially limit a major life activity. The legislative history states that Congress modeled the ADA definition of disability on the definition contained in the Rehabilitation Act, and said it wished to return courts to the way they had construed that definition. See 2008 House Judiciary Committee Report at 6. Describing this goal, the legislative history states that courts had interpreted the Rehabilitation Act definition "broadly to include persons with a wide range of physical and mental impairments such as epilepsy, diabetes, multiple sclerosis, and intellectual and developmental disabilities * * * even where a mitigating measure — like medication or a hearing aid — might lessen their impact on the individual." Id.; see also id. at 9 (referring to individuals with disabilities that had been covered under the Rehabilitation Act and that Congress intended to include under the ADA — "people with serious health conditions like epilepsy, diabetes, cancer, cerebral palsy, multiple sclerosis, intellectual and developmental disabilities"); id. at n.6 (citing cases also finding that cerebral palsy, hearing impairments, mental retardation, heart disease, and vision in only one eye were disabilities under the Rehabilitation Act); id. at 10 (citing testimony from Rep. Steny H. Hoyer, one of the original lead sponsors of the ADA in 1990, stating that "we could not have fathomed that people with diabetes, epilepsy, heart conditions, cancer, mental illnesses and other disabilities would have their ADA claims denied because they would be considered too functional to meet the definition of disability"); 2008 Senate Statement of Managers at 3 (explaining that "we [we]re faced with a situation in which physical or mental impairments that would previously [under the Rehabilitation Act] have been found to constitute disabilities [we]re not considered disabilities" and citing individuals with impairments such as amputation, intellectual disabilities, epilepsy, multiple sclerosis, diabetes, muscular dystrophy, and cancer as examples).

Of course, the impairments listed in subparagraph 1630.2(j)(3)(iii) may substantially limit a variety of other major life activities in addition to those listed in the regulation. For example, mobility impairments requiring the use of a wheelchair substantially limit the major life activity of walking. Diabetes may substantially limit major life activities such as eating, sleeping, and thinking. Major depressive disorder may substantially limit major life activities such as thinking, concentrating, sleeping, and interacting with others. Multiple sclerosis may substantially limit major life activities such as walking, bending, and lifting.

By using the term "brain function" to describe the system affected by various mental impairments, the Commission is expressing no view on the debate concerning whether mental illnesses are caused by environmental or biological factors, but rather intends the term to capture functions such as the ability of the brain to regulate thought processes and emotions.

Section 1630.2(j)(4) Condition, Manner, or Duration

The regulations provide that facts such as the "condition, manner, or duration" of an individual's performance of a major life activity may be useful in determining whether an impairment results in a substantial limitation. In the legislative history of the ADAAA, Congress reiterated what it had said at the time of the original ADA: "A person is considered an individual with a disability for purposes of the first prong of the definition when [one or more of] the individual's important life activities are restricted as to the conditions, manner, or duration under which they can be performed in comparison to most people." 2008 Senate Statement of Managers at 7 (citing 1989 Senate Report at 23). According to Congress: "We particularly believe that this test, which articulated an analysis that considered whether a person's activities are limited in condition, duration and manner, is a useful one. We reiterate that using the correct standard—one that is lower than the strict or demanding standard created by the Supreme Court in Toyota—will make the disability determination an appropriate threshold issue but not an onerous burden for those seeking accommodations * * *. At the same time, plaintiffs should not be constrained from offering evidence needed to establish that their impairment is substantially limiting." 2008 Senate Statement of Managers at 7.

Consistent with the legislative history, an impairment may substantially limit the "condition" or "manner" under which a major life activity can be performed in a number of ways. For example, the condition or manner under which a major life activity can be performed may refer to the way an individual performs a major life activity. Thus, the condition or manner under which a person with an amputated hand performs manual tasks will likely be more cumbersome than the way that someone with two hands would perform the same tasks.

Condition or manner may also describe how performance of a major life activity affects the individual with an impairment. For example, an individual whose impairment causes pain or fatigue that most people would not experience when performing that major life activity may be substantially limited. Thus, the condition or manner under which someone with coronary artery disease performs the major life activity of walking would be substantially limiting if the individual experiences shortness of breath and fatigue when walking distances that most people could walk without experiencing such effects. Similarly, condition or manner may refer to the extent to which a major life activity, including a major bodily function, can be performed. For example, the condition or manner under which a major bodily function can be performed may be substantially limited when the impairment "causes the operation [of the bodily function] to over-produce or under-produce in some harmful fashion." See 2008 House Judiciary Committee Report at 17.

"Duration" refers to the length of time an individual can perform a major life activity or the length of time it takes an individual to perform a major life activity, as compared to most people in the general population. For example, a person whose back or leg impairment precludes him or her from standing for more than two hours without significant pain would be substantially limited in standing, since most people can stand for more than two hours without significant pain. However, a person who can walk for ten miles continuously is not substantially limited in walking merely because on the eleventh mile, he or she begins to experience pain because most people would not be able to walk eleven miles without experiencing some discomfort. See 2008 Senate Statement of Managers at 7 (citing 1989 Senate Report at 23).

The regulations provide that in assessing substantial limitation and considering facts such as condition, manner, or duration, the non-ameliorative effects of mitigating measures may be considered. Such "non-ameliorative effects" could include negative side effects of medicine, burdens associated with following a particular treatment regimen, and complications that arise from surgery, among others. Of course, in many instances, it will not be necessary to assess the negative impact of a mitigating measure in determining that a particular impairment substantially limits a major life activity. For example, someone with end-stage renal disease is substantially limited in kidney function, and it thus is not necessary to consider the burdens that dialysis treatment imposes.

Condition, manner, or duration may also suggest the amount of time or effort an individual has to expend when performing a major life activity because of the effects of an impairment, even if the individual is able to achieve the same or similar result as someone without the impairment. For this reason, the regulations include language which says that the outcome an individual with a disability is able to achieve is not determinative of whether he or she is substantially limited in a major life activity.

Thus, someone with a learning disability may achieve a high level of academic success, but may nevertheless be substantially limited in the major life activity of learning because of the additional time or effort he or she must spend to read, write, or learn compared to most people in the general population. As Congress emphasized in passing the Amendments Act, "[w]hen considering the condition, manner, or duration in which an individual with a specific learning disability performs a major life activity, it is critical to reject the assumption that an individual who has performed well academically cannot be substantially limited in activities such as learning, reading, writing, thinking, or speaking." 2008 Senate Statement of Managers at 8. Congress noted that: "In particular, some courts have found that students who have reached a high level of academic achievement are not to be considered individuals with disabilities under the ADA, as such individuals may have difficulty demonstrating substantial limitation in the major life activities of learning or reading relative to 'most people.' When considering the condition, manner or duration in which an individual with a specific learning disability performs a major life activity, it is critical to reject the assumption that an individual who performs well academically or otherwise cannot be substantially limited in activities such as learning, reading, writing, thinking, or speaking. As such, the Committee rejects the findings in Price v. National Board of Medical Examiners, Gonzales v. National Board of Medical Examiners, and Wong v. Regents of University of California. The Committee believes that the comparison of individuals with specific learning disabilities to 'most people' is not problematic unto itself, but requires a careful analysis of the method and manner in which an individual's impairment limits a major life activity. For the majority of the population, the basic mechanics of reading and writing do not pose extraordinary lifelong challenges; rather, recognizing and forming letters and words are effortless, unconscious, automatic processes. Because specific learning disabilities are neurologically-based impairments, the process of reading for an individual with a reading disability (e.g. dyslexia) is word-by-word, and otherwise cumbersome, painful, deliberate and slow — throughout life. The Committee expects that individuals with specific learning disabilities that substantially limit a major life activity will be better protected under the amended Act." 2008 House Educ. & Labor Rep. at 10-11.

It bears emphasizing that while it may be useful in appropriate cases to consider facts such as condition, manner, or duration, it is always necessary to consider and apply the rules of construction in §1630.2(j)(1)(i)-(ix) that set forth the elements of broad coverage enacted by Congress. 2008 Senate Statement of Managers at 6. Accordingly, while the Commission's regulations retain the concept of "condition, manner, or duration," they no longer include the additional list of "substantial limitation" factors contained in the previous version of the regulations (i.e., the nature and severity of the impairment, duration or expected duration of the impairment, and actual or expected permanent or long-term impact of or resulting from the impairment).

Finally, "condition, manner, or duration" are not intended to be used as a rigid three-part standard that must be met to establish a substantial limitation. "Condition, manner, or duration" are not required "factors" that must be considered as a talismanic test. Rather, in referring to "condition, manner, or duration," the regulations make clear that these are merely the types of facts that may be considered in appropriate cases. To the extent such aspects of limitation may be useful or relevant to show a substantial limitation in a particular fact pattern, some or all of them (and related facts) may be considered, but evidence relating to each of these facts may not be necessary to establish coverage.

At the same time, individuals seeking coverage under the first or second prong of the definition of disability should not be constrained from offering evidence needed to establish that their impairment is substantially limiting. See 2008 Senate Statement of Managers at 7. Of course, covered entities may defeat a showing of "substantial limitation" by refuting whatever evidence the individual seeking coverage has offered, or by offering evidence that shows an impairment does not impose a substantial limitation on a major life activity. However, a showing of substantial limitation is not defeated by facts related to "condition, manner, or duration" that are not pertinent to the substantial limitation the individual has proffered.

Sections 1630.2(j)(5) and (6) Examples of Mitigating Measures; Ordinary Eyeglasses or Contact Lenses

These provisions of the regulations provide numerous examples of mitigating measures and the definition of "ordinary eyeglasses or contact lenses." These definitions have been more fully discussed in the portions of this interpretive guidance concerning the rules of construction in §1630.2(j)(1).

SUBSTANTIALLY LIMITED IN WORKING

The Commission has removed from the text of the regulations a discussion of the major life activity of working. This is consistent with the fact that no other major life activity receives special attention in the regulation, and with the fact that, in light of the expanded definition of disability established by the Amendments Act, this major life activity will be used in only very targeted situations.

In most instances, an individual with a disability will be able to establish coverage by showing substantial limitation of a major life activity other than working; impairments that substantially limit a person's ability to work usually substantially limit one or more other major life activities. This will be particularly true in light of the changes made by the ADA Amendments Act. See, e.g., Corley v. Dep't of Veterans Affairs ex rel Principi, 218 F. App'x. 727, 738 (10th Cir. 2007) (employee with seizure disorder was not substantially limited in working because he was not foreclosed from jobs involving driving, operating machinery, childcare, military service, and other jobs; employee would now be substantially limited in neurological function); Olds v. United Parcel Serv., Inc., 127 F. App'x. 779, 782 (6th Cir. 2005) (employee with bone marrow cancer was not substantially limited in working due to lifting restrictions caused by his cancer; employee would now be substantially limited in normal cell growth); Williams v. Philadelphia Hous. Auth. Police Dep't, 380 F.3d 751, 763-64 (3d Cir. 2004) (issue of material fact concerning whether police officer's major depression substantially limited him in performing a class of jobs due to restrictions on his ability to carry a firearm; officer would now be substantially limited in brain function).

In the rare cases where an individual has a need to demonstrate that an impairment substantially limits him or her in working, the individual can do so by showing that the impairment substantially limits his or her ability to perform a class of jobs or broad range of jobs in various classes as compared to most people having comparable training, skills, and abilities. In keeping with the findings and purposes of the Amendments Act, the determination of coverage under the law should not require extensive and elaborate assessment, and the EEOC and the courts are to apply a lower standard in determining when an impairment substantially limits a major life activity, including the major life activity of working, than they applied prior to the Amendments Act. The Commission believes that the courts, in applying an overly strict standard with regard to "substantially limits" generally, have reached conclusions with regard to what is necessary to demonstrate a substantial limitation in the major life activity of working that would be inconsistent with the changes now made by the Amendments Act. Accordingly, as used in this section the terms "class of jobs" and "broad range of jobs in various classes" will be applied in a more straightforward and simple manner than they were applied by the courts prior to the Amendments Act.

Demonstrating a substantial limitation in performing the unique aspects of a single specific job is not sufficient to establish that a person is substantially limited in the major life activity of working.

A class of jobs may be determined by reference to the nature of the work that an individual is limited in performing (such as commercial truck driving, assembly line jobs, food service jobs, clerical jobs, or law enforcement jobs) or by reference to job-related requirements that an individual is limited in meeting (for example, jobs requiring repetitive bending, reaching, or manual tasks, jobs requiring repetitive or heavy lifting, prolonged sitting or standing, extensive walking, driving, or working under conditions such as high temperatures or noise levels).

For example, if a person whose job requires heavy lifting develops a disability that prevents him or her from lifting more than fifty pounds and, consequently, from performing not only his or her existing job but also other jobs that would similarly require heavy lifting, that person would be substantially limited in working because he or she is substantially limited in performing the class of jobs that require heavy lifting.

Section 1630.2(k) *Record of a Substantially Limiting Impairment*

The second prong of the definition of "disability" provides that an individual with a record of an impairment that substantially limits or limited a major life activity is an individual with a disability. The intent of this provision, in part, is to ensure that people are not discriminated against because of a history of disability. For example, the "record of" provision would protect an individual who was treated for cancer ten years ago but who is now deemed by a doctor to be free of cancer, from discrimination based on that prior medical history. This provision also ensures that individuals are not discriminated against because they have been misclassified as disabled. For example, individuals misclassified as having learning disabilities or intellectual disabilities (formerly termed "mental retardation") are protected from discrimination on the basis of that erroneous classification. Senate Report at 23; House Labor Report at 52-53; House Judiciary Report at 29; 2008 House Judiciary Report at 7-8 & n.14. Similarly, an employee who in the past was misdiagnosed with bipolar disorder and hospitalized as the result of a temporary reaction to medication she was taking has a record of a substantially limiting impairment, even though she did not actually have bipolar disorder.

This part of the definition is satisfied where evidence establishes that an individual has had a substantially limiting impairment. The impairment indicated in the record must be an impairment that would substantially limit one or more of the individual's major life activities. There are many types of records that could potentially contain this information, including but not limited to, education, medical, or employment records.

Such evidence that an individual has a past history of an impairment that substantially limited a major life activity is all that is necessary to establish coverage under the second prong. An individual may have a "record of" a substantially limiting impairment—and thus be protected under the "record of" prong of the statute—even if a covered entity does not specifically know about the relevant record. Of course, for the covered entity to be liable for discrimination under title I of the ADA, the individual with a "record of" a substantially limiting impairment must prove that the covered entity discriminated on the basis of the record of the disability.

The terms "substantially limits" and "major life activity" under the second prong of the definition of "disability" are to be construed in accordance with the same principles applicable under the "actual disability" prong, as set forth in §1630.2(j). Individuals who are covered under the "record of" prong will often be covered under the first prong of the definition of disability as well. This is a consequence of the rule of construction in the ADAAA and the regulations providing that an individual with an impairment that is episodic or in remission can be protected under the first prong if the impairment would be substantially limiting when active. See 42 U.S.C. 12102(4)(D); §1630.2(j)(1)(vii). Thus, an individual who has cancer that is currently in remission is an individual with a disability under the "actual disability" prong because he has an impairment that would substantially limit normal cell growth when active. He is also covered by the "record of" prong based on his history of having had an impairment that substantially limited normal cell growth.

Finally, this section of the EEOC's regulations makes it clear that an individual with a record of a disability is entitled to a reasonable accommodation currently needed for limitations resulting from or relating to the past substantially limiting impairment. This conclusion, which has been the Commission's longstanding position, is confirmed by language in the ADA Amendments Act stating that individuals covered only under the "regarded as" prong of the definition of disability are not entitled to reasonable accommodation. See 42 U.S.C. 12201(h). By implication, this means that individuals covered under the first or second prongs are otherwise eligible for reasonable accommodations. See 2008 House

Judiciary Committee Report at 22 ("This makes clear that the duty to accommodate . . . arises only when an individual establishes coverage under the first or second prong of the definition."). Thus, as the regulations explain, an employee with an impairment that previously substantially limited but no longer substantially limits, a major life activity may need leave or a schedule change to permit him or her to attend follow-up or "monitoring" appointments from a health care provider.

Section 1630.2(l) *Regarded as Substantially Limited in a Major Life Activity*

Coverage under the "regarded as" prong of the definition of disability should not be difficult to establish. See 2008 House Judiciary Committee Report at 17 (explaining that Congress never expected or intended it would be a difficult standard to meet). Under the third prong of the definition of disability, an individual is "regarded as having such an impairment" if the individual is subjected to an action prohibited by the ADA because of an actual or perceived impairment that is not "transitory and minor."

This third prong of the definition of disability was originally intended to express Congress's understanding that "unfounded concerns, mistaken beliefs, fears, myths, or prejudice about disabilities are often just as disabling as actual impairments, and [its] corresponding desire to prohibit discrimination founded on such perceptions." 2008 Senate Statement of Managers at 9; 2008 House Judiciary Committee Report at 17 (same). In passing the original ADA, Congress relied extensively on the reasoning of School Board of Nassau County v. Arline "that the negative reactions of others are just as disabling as the actual impact of an impairment." 2008 Senate Statement of Managers at 9. The ADAAA reiterates Congress's reliance on the broad views enunciated in that decision, and Congress "believe[s] that courts should continue to rely on this standard." Id.

Accordingly, the ADA Amendments Act broadened the application of the "regarded as" prong of the definition of disability. 2008 Senate Statement of Managers at 9-10. In doing so, Congress rejected court decisions that had required an individual to establish that a covered entity perceived him or her to have an impairment that substantially limited a major life activity. This provision is designed to restore Congress's intent to allow individuals to establish coverage under the "regarded as" prong by showing that they were treated adversely because of an impairment, without having to establish the covered entity's beliefs concerning the severity of the impairment. Joint Hoyer-Sensenbrenner Statement at 3.

Thus it is not necessary, as it was prior to the ADA Amendments Act, for an individual to demonstrate that a covered entity perceived him as substantially limited in the ability to perform a major life activity in order for the individual to establish that he or she is covered under the "regarded as" prong. Nor is it necessary to demonstrate that the impairment relied on by a covered entity is (in the case of an actual impairment) or would be (in the case of a perceived impairment) substantially limiting for an individual to be "regarded as having such an impairment." In short, to qualify for coverage under the "regarded as" prong, an individual is not subject to any functional test. See 2008 Senate Statement of Managers at 13 ("The functional limitation imposed by an impairment is irrelevant to the third 'regarded as' prong."); 2008 House Judiciary Committee Report at 17 (that is, "the individual is not required to show that the perceived impairment limits performance of a major life activity"). The concepts of "major life activities" and "substantial limitation" simply are not relevant in evaluating whether an individual is "regarded as having such an impairment."

To illustrate how straightforward application of the "regarded as" prong is, if an employer refused to hire an applicant because of skin graft scars, the employer has regarded the applicant as an individual with a disability. Similarly, if an employer terminates an employee because he has cancer, the employer has regarded the employee as an individual with a disability.

A "prohibited action" under the "regarded as" prong refers to an action of the type that would be unlawful under the ADA (but for any defenses to liability). Such prohibited actions include, but are not limited to, refusal to hire, demotion, placement on involuntary leave, termination, exclusion for failure to meet a qualification standard, harassment, or denial of any other term, condition, or privilege of employment.

Where an employer bases a prohibited employment action on an actual or perceived impairment that is not "transitory and minor," the employer regards the individual as disabled, whether or not myths, fears, or stereotypes about disability motivated the employer's decision. Establishing that an individual is "regarded as having such an impairment" does not, by itself, establish liability. Liability is established only if an individual meets the burden of proving that the covered entity discriminated unlawfully within the meaning of section 102 of the ADA, 42 U.S.C. 12112.

Whether a covered entity can ultimately establish a defense to liability is an inquiry separate from, and follows after, a determination that an individual was regarded as having a disability. Thus, for example, an employer who terminates an employee with angina from a manufacturing job that requires the employee to work around machinery, believing that the employee will pose a safety risk to himself or others if he were suddenly to lose consciousness, has regarded the individual as disabled. Whether the employer has a defense (e.g., that the employee posed a direct threat to himself or coworkers) is a separate inquiry.

The fact that the "regarded as" prong requires proof of causation in order to show that a person is covered does not mean that proving a "regarded as" claim is complex. While a person must show, for both coverage under the "regarded as" prong and for ultimate liability, that he or she was subjected to a prohibited action because of an actual or perceived impairment, this showing need only be made once. Thus, evidence that a covered entity took a prohibited action because of an impairment will establish coverage and will be relevant in establishing liability, although liability may ultimately turn on whether the covered entity can establish a defense.

As prescribed in the ADA Amendments Act, the regulations provide an exception to coverage under the "regarded as" prong where the impairment on which a prohibited action is based is both transitory (having an actual or expected duration of six months or less) and minor. The regulations make clear (at §1630.2(l)(2) and §1630.15(f)) that this exception is a defense to a claim of discrimination. "Providing this exception responds to concerns raised by employer organizations and is reasonable under the 'regarded as' prong of the definition because individuals seeking coverage under this prong need not meet the functional limitation requirement contained in the first two prongs of the definition." 2008 Senate Statement of Managers at 10; see also 2008 House Judiciary Committee Report at 18 (explaining that "absent this exception, the third prong of the definition would have covered individuals who are regarded as having common ailments like the cold or flu, and this exception responds to concerns raised by members of the business community regarding potential abuse of this provision and misapplication of resources on individuals with minor ailments that last only a short period of time"). However, as an exception to the general rule for broad coverage under the "regarded as" prong, this limitation on coverage should be construed narrowly. 2008 House Judiciary Committee Report at 18.

The relevant inquiry is whether the actual or perceived impairment on which the employer's action was based is objectively "transitory and minor," not whether the employer claims it subjectively believed the impairment was transitory and minor. For example, an employer who terminates an employee whom it believes has bipolar disorder cannot take advantage of this exception by asserting that it believed the employee's impairment was transitory and minor, since bipolar disorder is not objectively transitory and minor. At the same time, an employer that terminated an employee with an objectively "transitory and minor" hand wound, mistakenly believing it to be symptomatic of HIV infection, will nevertheless have "regarded" the employee as an individual with a disability, since the covered entity took a prohibited employment action based on a perceived impairment (HIV infection) that is not "transitory and minor."

An individual covered only under the "regarded as" prong is not entitled to reasonable accommodation. 42 U.S.C. 12201(h). Thus, in cases where reasonable accommodation is not at issue, the third prong provides a more straightforward framework for analyzing whether discrimination occurred. As Congress observed in enacting the ADAAA: "[W]e expect [the first] prong of the definition to be used only by people who are affirmatively seeking reasonable accommodations or modifications. Any individual who has been discriminated against because of an impairment—short of being granted a reasonable accommodation or modification—should be bringing a claim under the third prong of the definition which will require no showing with regard to the severity of his or her impairment." Joint Hoyer-Sensenbrenner Statement at 6.

Section 1630.2(l) Regarded as Substantially Limited in a Major Life Activity

If an individual cannot satisfy either the first part of the definition of "disability" or the second "record of" part of the definition, he or she may be able to satisfy the third part of the definition. The third part of the definition provides that an individual who is regarded by an employer or other covered entity as having an impairment that substantially limits a major life activity is an individual with a disability.

There are three different ways in which an individual may satisfy the definition of "being regarded as having a disability":

(1) The individual may have an impairment which is not substantially limiting but is perceived by the employer or other covered entity as constituting a substantially limiting impairment;

(2) The individual may have an impairment which is only substantially limiting because of the attitudes of others toward the impairment; or

(3) The individual may have no impairment at all but is regarded by the employer or other covered entity as having a substantially limiting impairment.

Senate Report at 23; House Labor Report at 53; House Judiciary Report at 29. An individual satisfies the first part of this definition if the individual has an impairment that is not substantially limiting, but the covered entity perceives the impairment as being substantially limiting. For example, suppose an employee has controlled high blood pressure that is not substantially limiting. If an employer reassigns the individual to less strenuous work because of unsubstantiated fears that the individual will suffer a heart attack if he or she continues to perform strenuous work, the employer would be regarding the individual as disabled.

An individual satisfies the second part of the "regarded as" definition if the individual has an impairment that is only substantially limiting because of the attitudes of others toward the condition. For example, an individual may have a prominent facial scar or disfigurement, or may have a condition that periodically causes an involuntary jerk of the head but does not limit the individual's major life activities. If an employer discriminates against such an individual because of the negative reactions of customers, the employer would be regarding the individual as disabled and acting on the basis of that perceived disability. See Senate Report at 24; House Labor Report at 53; House Judiciary Report at 30-31.

An individual satisfies the third part of the "regarded as" definition of "disability" if the employer or other covered entity erroneously believes the individual has a substantially limiting impairment that the individual actually does not have. This situation could occur, for example, if an employer discharged an employee in response to a rumor that the employee is infected with Human Immunodeficiency Virus (HIV). Even though the rumor is totally unfounded and the individual has no impairment at all, the individual is considered an individual with a disability because the employer perceived of this individual as being disabled. Thus, in this example, the employer, by discharging this employee, is discriminating on the basis of disability.

The rationale for the "regarded as" part of the definition of disability was articulated by the Supreme Court in the context of the Rehabilitation Act of 1973 in School Board of Nassau County v. Arline, 480 U.S. 273 (1987). The Court noted that, although an individual may have an impairment that does not in fact substantially limit a major life activity, the reaction of others may prove just as disabling. "Such an impairment might not diminish a person's physical or mental capabilities, but could nevertheless substantially limit that person's ability to work as a result of the negative reactions of others to the impairment." 480 U.S. at 283. The Court concluded that by including "regarded as" in the Rehabilitation Act's definition, "Congress acknowledged that society's accumulated myths and fears about disability and diseases are as handicapping as are the physical limitations that flow from actual impairment." 480 U.S. at 284.

An individual rejected from a job because of the "myths, fears and stereotypes" associated with disabilities would be covered under this part of the definition of disability, whether or not the employer's or other covered entity's perception were shared by others in the field and whether or not the individual's actual physical or mental condition would be considered a disability under the first or second part of this definition. As the legislative history notes, sociologists have identified common attitudinal barriers that frequently result in employers excluding individuals with disabilities. These include concerns regarding productivity, safety, insurance, liability, attendance, cost of accommodation and accessibility, workers' compensation costs, and acceptance by coworkers and customers.

Therefore, if an individual can show that an employer or other covered entity made an employment decision because of a perception of disability based on "myth, fear or stereotype," the individual will satisfy the "regarded as" part of the definition of disability. If the employer cannot articulate a non-discriminatory reason for the employment action, an inference that the employer is acting on the basis of "myth, fear or stereotype" can be drawn.

Section 1630.2(m) Qualified Individual

The ADA prohibits discrimination on the basis of disability against a qualified individual. The determination of whether an individual with a disability is "qualified" should be made in two steps. The first step is to determine if the individual satisfies the prerequisites for the position, such as possessing the appropriate educational background, employment experience, skills, licenses, etc. For example, the first step in determining whether an accountant who is paraplegic is qualified for a certified public accountant (CPA) position is to examine the individual's credentials to determine whether the individual is a licensed CPA. This is sometimes referred to in the Rehabilitation Act caselaw as determining whether the individual is "otherwise qualified" for the position. See Senate Report at 33; House Labor Report at 64-65. (See §1630.9 Not Making Reasonable Accommodation).

The second step is to determine whether or not the individual can perform the essential functions of the position held or desired, with or without reasonable accommodation. The purpose of this second step is to ensure that individuals with disabilities who can perform the essential functions of the position held or desired are not denied employment opportunities because they are not able to perform marginal functions of the position. House Labor Report at 55.

The determination of whether an individual with a disability is qualified is to be made at the time of the employment decision. This determination should be based on the capabilities of the individual with a disability at the time of the employment decision, and should not be based on speculation that the employee may become unable in the future or may cause increased health insurance premiums or workers compensation costs.

Section 1630.2(n) Essential Functions

The determination of which functions are essential may be critical to the determination of whether or not the individual with a disability is qualified. The essential functions are those functions that the individual who holds the position must be able to perform unaided or with the assistance of a reasonable accommodation.

The inquiry into whether a particular function is essential initially focuses on whether the employer actually requires employees in the position to perform the functions that the employer asserts are essential. For example, an employer may state that typing is an essential function of a position. If, in fact, the employer has never required any employee in that particular position to type, this will be evidence that typing is not actually an essential function of the position.

If the individual who holds the position is actually required to perform the function the employer asserts is an essential function, the inquiry will then center around whether removing the function would fundamentally alter that position. This determination of whether or not a particular function is essential will generally include one or more of the following factors listed in part 1630.

The first factor is whether the position exists to perform a particular function. For example, an individual may be hired to proofread documents. The ability to proofread the documents would then be an essential function, since this is the only reason the position exists.

The second factor in determining whether a function is essential is the number of other employees available to perform that job function or among whom the performance of that job function can be distributed. This may be a factor either because the total number of available employees is low, or because of the fluctuating demands of the business operation. For example, if an employer has a relatively small number of available employees for the volume of work to be performed, it may be necessary that each employee perform a multitude of different functions. Therefore, the performance of those functions by each employee becomes more critical and the options for reorganizing the work become more limited. In such a situation, functions that might not be essential if there were a larger staff may become essential because the staff size is small compared to the volume of work that has to be done. See Treadwell v. Alexander, 707 F.2d 473 (11th Cir. 1983).

A similar situation might occur in a larger work force if the workflow follows a cycle of heavy demand for labor intensive work followed by low demand periods. This type of workflow might also make the performance of each function during the peak periods more critical and might limit the employer's flexibility in reorganizing operating procedures. See Dexler v. Tisch, 660 F. Supp. 1418 (D. Conn. 1987).

The third factor is the degree of expertise or skill required to perform the function. In certain professions and highly skilled positions the employee is hired for his or her expertise or ability to perform the particular function. In such a situation, the performance of that specialized task would be an essential function.

Whether a particular function is essential is a factual determination that must be made on a case by case basis. In determining whether or not a particular function is essential, all relevant evidence should be considered. Part 1630 lists various types of evidence, such as an established job description, that should be considered in determining whether a particular function is essential. Since the list is not exhaustive, other relevant evidence may also be presented. Greater weight will not be granted to the types of evidence included on the list than to the types of evidence not listed.

Although part 1630 does not require employers to develop or maintain job descriptions, written job descriptions prepared before advertising or interviewing applicants for the job, as well as the employer's judgment as to what functions are essential are among the relevant evidence to be considered in determining whether a particular function is essential. The terms of a collective bargaining agreement are also relevant to the determination of whether a particular function is essential. The work experience of past employees in the job or of current employees in similar jobs is likewise relevant to the determination of whether a particular function is essential. See H.R. Conf. Rep. No. 101-596, 101st Cong., 2d Sess. 58 (1990) [hereinafter Conference Report]; House Judiciary Report at 33-34. See also Hall v. U.S. Postal Service, 857 F.2d 1073 (6th Cir. 1988).

The time spent performing the particular function may also be an indicator of whether that function is essential. For example, if an employee spends the vast majority of his or her time working at a cash register, this would be evidence that operating the cash register is an essential function. The consequences of failing to require the employee to perform the function may be another indicator of whether a particular function is essential. For example, although a firefighter may not regularly have to carry an unconscious adult out of a burning building, the consequence of failing to require the firefighter to be able to perform this function would be serious.

It is important to note that the inquiry into essential functions is not intended to second guess an employer's business judgment with regard to production standards, whether qualitative or quantitative, nor to require employers to lower such standards. (See §1630.10 Qualification Standards, Tests and Other Selection Criteria). If an employer requires its typists to be able to accurately type 75 words per minute, it will not be called upon to explain why an inaccurate work product, or a typing speed of 65 words per minute, would not be adequate. Similarly, if a hotel requires its service workers to thoroughly clean 16 rooms per day, it will not have to explain why it requires thorough cleaning, or why it chose a 16 room rather than a 10 room requirement. However, if an employer does require accurate 75 word per minute typing or the thorough cleaning of 16 rooms, it will have to show that it actually imposes such requirements on its employees in fact, and not simply on paper. It should also be noted that, if it is alleged that the employer intentionally selected the particular level of production to exclude individuals with disabilities, the employer may have to offer a legitimate, non-discriminatory reason for its selection.

Section 1630.2(o) *Reasonable Accommodation*

An individual with a disability is considered "qualified" if the individual can perform the essential functions of the position held or desired with or without reasonable accommodation. A covered entity is required, absent undue hardship, to provide reasonable accommodation to an otherwise qualified individual with a substantially limiting impairment or a "record of" such an impairment. However, a covered entity is not required to provide an accommodation to an individual who meets the definition of disability solely under the "regarded as" prong.

The legislative history of the ADAAA makes clear that Congress included this provision in response to various court decisions that had held (pre-Amendments Act) that individuals who were covered solely under the "regarded as" prong were eligible for reasonable accommodations. In those cases, the plaintiffs had been found not to be covered under the first prong of the definition of disability "because of the overly stringent manner in which the courts had been interpreting that prong." 2008 Senate Statement of Managers at 11. The legislative history goes on to explain that "[b]ecause of [Congress's] strong belief that accommodating individuals with disabilities is a key goal of the ADA, some members [of Congress] continue to have reservations about this provision." Id. However, Congress ultimately concluded that clarifying that individuals covered solely under the "regarded as" prong are not entitled to reasonable accommodations "is an acceptable compromise given our strong expectation that such individuals would now be covered under the first prong of the definition [of disability], properly applied"). Further, individuals covered only under the third prong still may bring discrimination claims (other than failure-to-accommodate claims) under title I of the ADA. 2008 Senate Statement of Managers at 9-10.

In general, an accommodation is any change in the work environment or in the way things are customarily done that enables an individual with a disability to enjoy equal employment opportunities. There are three categories of reasonable accommodation. These are (1) accommodations that are required to ensure equal opportunity in the application process; (2) accommodations that enable the employer's employees with disabilities to perform the essential functions of the position held or desired; and (3) accommodations that enable the employer's employees with disabilities to enjoy equal benefits and privileges of employment as are enjoyed by employees without disabilities. It should be noted that nothing in this part prohibits employers or other covered entities from providing accommodations beyond those required by this part.

Part 1630 lists the examples, specified in title I of the ADA, of the most common types of accommodation that an employer or other covered entity may be required to provide. There are any number of other specific accommodations that may be appropriate for particular situations but are not specifically mentioned in this listing. This listing is not intended to be exhaustive of accommodation possibilities. For example, other accommodations could include permitting the use of accrued paid leave or providing additional unpaid leave for necessary treatment, making employer provided transportation accessible, and providing reserved parking spaces. Providing personal assistants, such as a page turner for an employee with no hands or a travel attendant to act as a sighted guide to assist a blind employee on occasional business trips, may also be a reasonable accommodation. Senate Report at 31; House Labor Report at 62; House Judiciary Report at 39.

It may also be a reasonable accommodation to permit an individual with a disability the opportunity to provide and utilize equipment, aids or services that an employer is not required to provide as a reasonable accommodation. For example, it would be a reasonable accommodation for an employer to permit an individual who is blind to use a guide dog at work, even though the employer would not be required to provide a guide dog for the employee.

The accommodations included on the list of reasonable accommodations are generally self explanatory. However, there are a few that require further explanation. One of these is the accommodation of making existing facilities used by employees readily accessible to, and usable by, individuals with disabilities. This accommodation includes both those areas that must be accessible for the employee to perform essential job functions, as well as non-work areas used by the employer's employees for other purposes. For example, accessible break rooms, lunch rooms, training rooms, restrooms etc., may be required as reasonable accommodations.

Another of the potential accommodations listed is "job restructuring." An employer or other covered entity may restructure a job by reallocating or redistributing nonessential, marginal job functions. For example, an employer may have two jobs, each of which entails the performance of a number of marginal functions. The employer hires an individual with a disability who is able to perform some of the marginal functions of each job but not all of the marginal functions of either job. As an accommodation, the employer may redistribute the marginal functions so that all of the marginal functions that the individual with a disability can perform are made a part of the position to be filled by the individual with a disability. The remaining marginal functions that the individual with a disability cannot perform would then be transferred to the other position. See Senate Report at 31; House Labor Report at 62.

An employer or other covered entity is not required to reallocate essential functions. The essential functions are by definition those that the individual who holds the job would have to perform, with or without reasonable accommodation, in order to be considered qualified for the position. For example, suppose a security guard position requires the individual who holds the job to inspect identification cards. An employer would not have to provide an individual who is legally blind with an assistant to look at the identification cards for the legally blind employee. In this situation the assistant would be performing the job for the individual with a disability rather than assisting the individual to perform the job. See Coleman v. Darden, 595 F.2d 533 (10th Cir. 1979).

An employer or other covered entity may also restructure a job by altering when and/or how an essential function is performed. For example, an essential function customarily performed in the early morning hours may be rescheduled until later in the day as a reasonable accommodation to a disability that precludes performance of the function at the customary hour. Likewise, as a reasonable accommodation, an employee with a disability that inhibits the ability to write, may be permitted to computerize records that were customarily maintained manually.

Reassignment to a vacant position is also listed as a potential reasonable accommodation. In general, reassignment should be considered only when accommodation within the individual's current position would pose an undue hardship. Reassignment is not available to applicants. An applicant for a position must be qualified for, and be able to perform the essential functions of, the position sought with or without reasonable accommodation.

Reassignment may not be used to limit, segregate, or otherwise discriminate against employees with disabilities by forcing reassignments to undesirable positions or to designated offices or facilities. Employers should reassign the individual to an equivalent position, in terms of pay, status, etc., if the individual is qualified, and if the position is vacant within a reasonable amount of time. A "reasonable amount of time" should be determined in light of the totality of the circumstances. As an example, suppose there is no vacant position available at the time that an individual with a disability requests reassignment as a reasonable accommodation. The employer, however, knows that an equivalent position for which the individual is qualified, will become vacant next week. Under these circumstances, the employer should reassign the individual to the position when it becomes available.

An employer may reassign an individual to a lower graded position if there are no accommodations that would enable the employee to remain in the current position and there are no vacant equivalent positions for which the individual is qualified with or without reasonable accommodation. An employer, however, is not required to maintain the reassigned individual with a disability at the salary of the higher graded position if it does not so maintain reassigned employees who are not disabled. It should also be noted that an employer is not required to promote an individual with a disability as an accommodation. See Senate Report at 31-32; House Labor Report at 63.

The determination of which accommodation is appropriate in a particular situation involves a process in which the employer and employee identify the precise limitations imposed by the disability and explore potential accommodations that would overcome those limitations. This process is discussed more fully in §1630.9 Not Making Reasonable Accommodation.

Section 1630.2(p) Undue Hardship

An employer or other covered entity is not required to provide an accommodation that will impose an undue hardship on the operation of the employer's or other covered entity's business. The term "undue hardship" means significant difficulty or expense in, or resulting from, the provision of the accommodation. The "undue hardship" provision takes into account the financial realities of the particular employer or other covered entity. However, the concept of undue hardship is not limited to financial difficulty. "Undue hardship" refers to any accommodation that would be unduly costly, extensive, substantial, or disruptive, or that would fundamentally alter the nature or operation of the business. See Senate Report at 35; House Labor Report at 67.

For example, suppose an individual with a disabling visual impairment that makes it extremely difficult to see in dim lighting applies for a position as a waiter in a nightclub and requests that the club be brightly lit as a reasonable accommodation. Although the individual may be able to perform the job in bright lighting, the nightclub will probably be able to demonstrate that that particular accommodation, though inexpensive, would impose an undue hardship if the bright lighting would destroy the ambience of the nightclub and/or make it difficult for the customers to see the stage show. The fact that that particular accommodation poses an undue hardship, however, only means that the employer is not required to provide that accommodation. If there is another accommodation that will not create an undue hardship, the employer would be required to provide the alternative accommodation.

An employer's claim that the cost of a particular accommodation will impose an undue hardship will be analyzed in light of the factors outlined in part 1630. In part, this analysis requires a determination of whose financial resources should be considered in deciding whether the accommodation is unduly costly. In some cases the financial resources of the employer or other covered entity in its entirety should be considered in determining whether the cost of an accommodation poses an undue hardship. In other cases, consideration of the financial resources of the employer or other covered entity as a whole may be inappropriate because it may not give an accurate picture of the financial resources available to the particular facility that will actually be required to provide the accommodation. See House Labor Report at 68-69; House Judiciary Report at 40-41; see also Conference Report at 56-57.

If the employer or other covered entity asserts that only the financial resources of the facility where the individual will be employed should be considered, part 1630 requires a factual determination of the relationship between the employer or other covered entity and the facility that will provide the accommodation. As an example, suppose that an independently owned fast food franchise that receives no money from the franchisor refuses to hire an individual with a hearing impairment because it asserts that it would be an undue hardship to provide an interpreter to enable the individual to participate in monthly staff meetings. Since the financial relationship between the franchisor and the franchise is limited to payment of an annual franchise fee, only the financial resources of the franchise would be considered in determining whether or not providing the accommodation would be an undue hardship. See House Labor Report at 68; House Judiciary Report at 40.

If the employer or other covered entity can show that the cost of the accommodation would impose an undue hardship, it would still be required to provide the accommodation if the funding is available from another source, e.g., a State vocational rehabilitation agency, or if Federal, State or local tax deductions or tax credits are available to offset the cost of the accommodation. If the employer or other covered entity receives, or is eligible to receive, monies from an external source that would pay the entire cost of the accommodation, it cannot claim cost as an undue hardship. In the absence of such funding, the individual with a disability requesting the accommodation should be given the option of providing the accommodation or of paying that portion of the cost which constitutes the undue hardship on the operation of the business. To the extent that such monies pay or would pay for only part of the cost of the accommodation, only that portion of the cost of the accommodation that could not be recovered — the final net cost to the entity — may be considered in determining undue hardship. (See §1630.9 Not Making Reasonable Accommodation). See Senate Report at 36; House Labor Report at 69.

Section 1630.2(r) Direct Threat

An employer may require, as a qualification standard, that an individual not pose a direct threat to the health or safety of himself/herself or others. Like any other qualification standard, such a standard must apply to all applicants or employees and not just to individuals with disabilities. If, however, an individual poses a direct threat as a result of a disability, the employer must determine whether a reasonable accommodation would either eliminate the risk or reduce it to an acceptable level. If no accommodation exists that would either eliminate or reduce the risk, the employer may refuse to hire an applicant or may discharge an employee who poses a direct threat. An employer, however, is not permitted to deny an employment opportunity to an individual with a disability merely because of a slightly increased risk. The risk can only be considered when it poses a significant risk, i.e., high probability, of substantial harm; a speculative or remote risk is insufficient. See Senate Report at 27; House Report Labor Report at 56-57; House Judiciary Report at 45.

Determining whether an individual poses a significant risk of substantial harm to others must be made on a case by case basis. The employer should identify the specific risk posed by the individual. For individuals with mental or emotional disabilities, the employer must identify the specific behavior on the part of the individual that would pose the direct threat. For individuals with physical disabilities, the employer must identify the aspect of the disability that would pose the direct threat. The employer should then consider the four factors listed in part 1630:

(1) The duration of the risk;
(2) The nature and severity of the potential harm;
(3) The likelihood that the potential harm will occur; and
(4) The imminence of the potential harm.

Such consideration must rely on objective, factual evidence — not on subjective perceptions, irrational fears, patronizing attitudes, or stereotypes — about the nature or effect of a particular disability, or of disability generally. See Senate

Report at 27; House Labor Report at 56-57; House Judiciary Report at 45-46. See also Strathie v. Department of Transportation, 716 F.2d 227 (3d Cir. 1983). Relevant evidence may include input from the individual with a disability, the experience of the individual with a disability in previous similar positions, and opinions of medical doctors, rehabilitation counselors, or physical therapists who have expertise in the disability involved and/or direct knowledge of the individual with the disability.

An employer is also permitted to require that an individual not pose a direct threat of harm to his or her own safety or health. If performing the particular functions of a job would result in a high probability of substantial harm to the individual, the employer could reject or discharge the individual unless a reasonable accommodation that would not cause an undue hardship would avert the harm. For example, an employer would not be required to hire an individual, disabled by narcolepsy, who frequently and unexpectedly loses consciousness for a carpentry job the essential functions of which require the use of power saws and other dangerous equipment, where no accommodation exists that will reduce or eliminate the risk.

The assessment that there exists a high probability of substantial harm to the individual, like the assessment that there exists a high probability of substantial harm to others, must be strictly based on valid medical analyses and/or on other objective evidence. This determination must be based on individualized factual data, using the factors discussed above, rather than on stereotypic or patronizing assumptions and must consider potential reasonable accommodations. Generalized fears about risks from the employment environment, such as exacerbation of the disability caused by stress, cannot be used by an employer to disqualify an individual with a disability. For example, a law firm could not reject an applicant with a history of disabling mental illness based on a generalized fear that the stress of trying to make partner might trigger a relapse of the individual's mental illness. Nor can generalized fears about risks to individuals with disabilities in the event of an evacuation or other emergency be used by an employer to disqualify an individual with a disability. See Senate Report at 56; House Labor Report at 73-74; House Judiciary Report at 45. See also Mantolete v. Bolger, 767 F.2d 1416 (9th Cir. 1985); Bentivegna v. U.S. Department of Labor, 694 F.2d 619 (9th Cir.1982).

Section 1630.3 Exceptions to the Definitions of "Disability" and "Qualified Individual with a Disability"

Section 1630.3 (a) through (c) Illegal Use of Drugs

Part 1630 provides that an individual currently engaging in the illegal use of drugs is not an individual with a disability for purposes of this part when the employer or other covered entity acts on the basis of such use. Illegal use of drugs refers both to the use of unlawful drugs, such as cocaine, and to the unlawful use of prescription drugs. Employers, for example, may discharge or deny employment to persons who illegally use drugs, on the basis of such use, without fear of being held liable for discrimination. The term "currently engaging" is not intended to be limited to the use of drugs on the day of, or within a matter of days or weeks before, the employment action in question. Rather, the provision is intended to apply to the illegal use of drugs that has occurred recently enough to indicate that the individual is actively engaged in such conduct. See Conference Report at 64.

Individuals who are erroneously perceived as engaging in the illegal use of drugs, but are not in fact illegally using drugs are not excluded from the definitions of the terms "disability" and "qualified individual with a disability." Individuals who are no longer illegally using drugs and who have either been rehabilitated successfully or are in the process of completing a rehabilitation program are, likewise, not excluded from the definitions of those terms. The term "rehabilitation program" refers to both in-patient and out-patient programs, as well as to appropriate employee assistance programs, professionally recognized self-help programs, such as Narcotics Anonymous, or other programs that provide professional (not necessarily medical) assistance and counseling for individuals who illegally use drugs. See Conference Report at 64; see also House Labor Report at 77; House Judiciary Report at 47.

It should be noted that this provision simply provides that certain individuals are not excluded from the definitions of "disability" and "qualified individual with a disability." Consequently, such individuals are still required to establish that they satisfy the requirements of these definitions in order to be protected by the ADA and this part. An individual erroneously regarded as illegally using drugs, for example, would have to show that he or she was regarded as a drug addict in order to demonstrate that he or she meets the definition of "disability" as defined in this part.

Employers are entitled to seek reasonable assurances that no illegal use of drugs is occurring or has occurred recently enough so that continuing use is a real and ongoing problem. The reasonable assurances that employers may ask applicants or employees to provide include evidence that the individual is participating in a drug treatment program and/or evidence, such as drug test results, to show that the individual is not currently engaging in the illegal use of drugs. An employer, such as a law enforcement agency, may also be able to impose a qualification standard that excludes individuals with a history of illegal use of drugs if it can show that the standard is job-related and consistent with business necessity. (See §1630.10 Qualification Standards, Tests and Other Selection Criteria) See Conference Report at 64.

Section 1630.4 Discrimination Prohibited

Paragraph (a) of this provision prohibits discrimination on the basis of disability against a qualified individual in all aspects of the employment relationship. The range of employment decisions covered by this nondiscrimination mandate is to be construed in a manner consistent with the regulations implementing section 504 of the Rehabilitation Act of 1973.

Paragraph (b) makes it clear that the language "on the basis of disability" is not intended to create a cause of action for an individual without a disability who claims that someone with a disability was treated more favorably (disparate treatment), or was provided a reasonable accommodation that an individual without a disability was not provided. See 2008 House Judiciary Committee Report at 21 (this provision "prohibits reverse discrimination claims by disallowing claims based on the lack of disability"). Additionally, the ADA and this part do not affect laws that may require the affirmative recruitment or hiring of individuals with disabilities, or any voluntary affirmative action employers may undertake on behalf of individuals with disabilities. However, part 1630 is not intended to limit the ability of covered entities to choose and maintain a qualified workforce. Employers can continue to use criteria that are job related and consistent with business necessity to select qualified employees, and can continue to hire employees who can perform the essential functions of the job.

The Amendments Act modified title I's nondiscrimination provision to replace the prohibition on discrimination "against a qualified individual with a disability because of the disability of such individual" with a prohibition on discrimination "against a qualified individual on the basis of disability." As the legislative history of the ADAAA explains: "[T]he bill modifies the ADA to conform to the structure of Title VII and other civil rights laws by requiring an individual to demonstrate discrimination 'on the basis of disability' rather than discrimination 'against an individual with a disability' because of the individual's disability. We hope this will be an important signal to both lawyers and courts to spend less time and energy on the minutia of an individual's impairment, and more time and energy on the merits of the case—including whether discrimination occurred because of the disability, whether an individual was qualified for a job or eligible for a service, and whether a reasonable accommodation or modification was called for under the law." Joint Hoyer-Sensenbrenner Statement at 4; see also 2008 House Judiciary Report at 21 ("This change harmonizes the ADA with other civil rights laws by focusing on whether a person who has been discriminated against has proven that the discrimination was based on a personal characteristic (disability), not on whether he or she has proven that the characteristic exists.").

Section 1630.5 Limiting, Segregating and Classifying

This provision and the several provisions that follow describe various specific forms of discrimination that are included within the general prohibition of §1630.4. The capabilities of qualified individuals must be determined on an individualized, case by case basis. Covered entities are also prohibited from segregating qualified employees into separate work areas or into separate lines of advancement on the basis of their disabilities.

Thus, for example, it would be a violation of this part for an employer to limit the duties of an employee with a disability based on a presumption of what is best for an individual with such a disability, or on a presumption about the abilities of an individual with such a disability. It would be a violation of this part for an employer to adopt a separate track of job promotion or progression for employees with disabilities based on a presumption that employees with disabilities are uninterested in, or incapable of, performing particular jobs. Similarly, it would be a violation for an employer to assign or reassign (as a reasonable accommodation) employees with disabilities to one particular office or installation, or to require that employees with disabilities only use particular employer provided non-work facilities such as segregated break-rooms, lunch rooms, or lounges. It would also be a violation of this part to deny employment to an applicant or employee with a disability based on generalized fears about the safety of an individual with such a disability, or based on generalized assumptions about the absenteeism rate of an individual with such a disability.

In addition, it should also be noted that this part is intended to require that employees with disabilities be accorded equal access to whatever health insurance coverage the employer provides to other employees. This part does not, however, affect pre-existing condition clauses included in health insurance policies offered by employers. Consequently, employers may continue to offer policies that contain such clauses, even if they adversely affect individuals with disabilities, so long as the clauses are not used as a subterfuge to evade the purposes of this part.

So, for example, it would be permissible for an employer to offer an insurance policy that limits coverage for certain procedures or treatments to a specified number per year. Thus, if a health insurance plan provided coverage for five blood transfusions a year to all covered employees, it would not be discriminatory to offer this plan simply because a hemophiliac employee may require more than five blood transfusions annually. However, it would not be permissible to limit or deny the hemophiliac employee coverage for other procedures, such as heart surgery or the setting of a broken leg, even though the plan would not have to provide coverage for the additional blood transfusions that may be involved in these procedures. Likewise, limits may be placed on reimbursements for certain procedures or on the types of drugs or procedures covered (e.g. limits on the number of permitted X-rays or non-coverage of experimental drugs or procedures), but that limitation must be applied equally to individuals with and without disabilities. See Senate Report at 28-29; House Labor Report at 58-59; House Judiciary Report at 36.

Leave policies or benefit plans that are uniformly applied do not violate this part simply because they do not address the special needs of every individual with a disability. Thus, for example, an employer that reduces the number of paid sick leave days that it will provide to all employees, or reduces the amount of medical insurance coverage that it will provide to all employees, is not in violation of this part, even if the benefits reduction has an impact on employees with disabilities in need of greater sick leave and medical coverage. Benefits reductions adopted for discriminatory reasons are in violation of this part. See Alexander v. Choate, 469 U.S. 287 (1985). See Senate Report at 85; House Labor Report at 137. (See also, the discussion at §1630.16(f) Health Insurance, Life Insurance, and Other Benefit Plans).

Section 1630.6 Contractual or Other Arrangements

An employer or other covered entity may not do through a contractual or other relationship what it is prohibited from doing directly. This provision does not affect the determination of whether or not one is a "covered entity" or "employer" as defined in §1630.2.

This provision only applies to situations where an employer or other covered entity has entered into a contractual relationship that has the effect of discriminating against its own employees or applicants with disabilities. Accordingly, it would be a violation for an employer to participate in a contractual relationship that results in discrimination against the employer's employees with disabilities in hiring, training, promotion, or in any other aspect of the employment relationship. This provision applies whether or not the employer or other covered entity intended for the contractual relationship to have the discriminatory effect.

Part 1630 notes that this provision applies to parties on either side of the contractual or other relationship. This is intended to highlight that an employer whose employees provide services to others, like an employer whose employees receive services, must ensure that those employees are not discriminated against on the basis of disability. For example, a copier company whose service representative is a dwarf could be required to provide a stepstool, as a reasonable accommodation, to enable him to perform the necessary repairs. However, the employer would not be required, as a reasonable accommodation, to make structural changes to its customer's inaccessible premises.

The existence of the contractual relationship adds no new obligations under part 1630. The employer, therefore, is not liable through the contractual arrangement for any discrimination by the contractor against the contractors own employees or applicants, although the contractor, as an employer, may be liable for such discrimination.

An employer or other covered entity, on the other hand, cannot evade the obligations imposed by this part by engaging in a contractual or other relationship. For example, an employer cannot avoid its responsibility to make reasonable accommodation subject to the undue hardship limitation through a contractual arrangement. See Conference Report at 59; House Labor Report at 59-61; House Judiciary Report at 36-37.

To illustrate, assume that an employer is seeking to contract with a company to provide training for its employees. Any responsibilities of reasonable accommodation applicable to the employer in providing the training remain with that employer even if it contracts with another company for this service. Thus, if the training company were planning to conduct the training at an inaccessible location, thereby making it impossible for an employee who uses a wheelchair to attend, the employer would have a duty to make reasonable accommodation unless to do so would impose an undue hardship. Under these circumstances, appropriate accommodations might include (1) having the training company identify accessible training sites and relocate the training program; (2) having the training company make the training site accessible; (3) directly making the training site accessible or providing the training company with the means by which to make the site accessible; (4) identifying and contracting with another training company that uses accessible sites; or (5) any other accommodation that would result in making the training available to the employee.

As another illustration, assume that instead of contracting with a training company, the employer contracts with a hotel to host a conference for its employees. The employer will have a duty to ascertain and ensure the accessibility of the hotel and its conference facilities. To fulfill this obligation the employer could, for example, inspect the hotel first-hand or ask a local disability group to inspect the hotel. Alternatively, the employer could ensure that the contract with the hotel specifies it will provide accessible guest rooms for those who need them and that all rooms to be used for the conference, including exhibit and meeting rooms, are accessible. If the hotel breaches this accessibility provision, the hotel may be liable to the employer, under a non-ADA breach of contract theory, for the cost of any accommodation needed to provide access to the hotel and conference, and for any other costs accrued by the employer. (In addition, the hotel may also be independently liable under title III of the ADA). However, this would not relieve the employer of its responsibility under this part nor shield it from charges of discrimination by its own employees. See House Labor Report at 40; House Judiciary Report at 37.

Section 1630.8 Relationship or Association With an Individual With a Disability

This provision is intended to protect any qualified individual, whether or not that individual has a disability, from discrimination because that person is known to have an association or relationship with an individual who has a known disability. This protection is not limited to those who have a familial relationship with an individual with a disability.

To illustrate the scope of this provision, assume that a qualified applicant without a disability applies for a job and discloses to the employer that his or her spouse has a disability. The employer thereupon declines to hire the applicant because the employer believes that the applicant would have to miss work or frequently leave work early in order to care for the spouse. Such a refusal to hire would be prohibited by this provision. Similarly, this provision would prohibit an employer from discharging an employee because the employee does volunteer work with people who have AIDS, and the employer fears that the employee may contract the disease.

This provision also applies to other benefits and privileges of employment. For example, an employer that provides health insurance benefits to its employees for their dependents may not reduce the level of those benefits to an employee simply because that employee has a dependent with a disability. This is true even if the provision of such benefits would result in increased health insurance costs for the employer.

It should be noted, however, that an employer need not provide the applicant or employee without a disability with a reasonable accommodation because that duty only applies to qualified applicants or employees with disabilities. Thus, for example, an employee would not be entitled to a modified work schedule as an accommodation to enable the employee to care for a spouse with a disability. See Senate Report at 30; House Labor Report at 61-62; House Judiciary Report at 38-39.

Section 1630.9 Not Making Reasonable Accommodation

The obligation to make reasonable accommodation is a form of non-discrimination. It applies to all employment decisions and to the job application process. This obligation does not extend to the provision of adjustments or modifications that are primarily for the personal benefit of the individual with a disability. Thus, if an adjustment or modification is job-related, e.g., specifically assists the individual in performing the duties of a particular job, it will be considered a type of reasonable accommodation. On the other hand, if an adjustment or modification assists the individual throughout his or her daily activities, on and off the job, it will be considered a personal item that the employer is not required to provide. Accordingly, an employer would generally not be required to provide an employee with a disability with a prosthetic limb, wheelchair, or eyeglasses. Nor would an employer have to provide as an accommodation any amenity or convenience that is not job-related, such as a private hot plate, hot pot or refrigerator that is not provided to employees without disabilities. See Senate Report at 31; House Labor Report at 62.

It should be noted, however, that the provision of such items may be required as a reasonable accommodation where such items are specifically designed or required to meet job-related rather than personal needs. An employer, for example, may have to provide an individual with a disabling visual impairment with eyeglasses specifically designed to enable the individual to use the office computer monitors, but that are not otherwise needed by the individual outside of the office.

The term "supported employment," which has been applied to a wide variety of programs to assist individuals with severe disabilities in both competitive and non-competitive employment, is not synonymous with reasonable accommodation. Examples of supported employment include modified training materials, restructuring essential functions to enable an individual to perform a job, or hiring an outside professional ("job coach") to assist in job training. Whether a particular form of assistance would be required as a reasonable accommodation must be determined on an individualized, case by case basis without regard to whether that assistance is referred to as "supported employment." For example, an employer, under certain circumstances, may be required to provide modified training materials or a temporary "job coach" to assist in the training of a qualified individual with a disability as a reasonable accommodation. However, an employer would not be required to restructure the essential functions of a position to fit the skills of an individual with a disability who is not otherwise qualified to perform the position, as is done in certain supported employment programs. See 34 CFR part 363. It should be noted that it would not be a violation of this part for an employer to provide any of these personal modifications or adjustments, or to engage in supported employment or similar rehabilitative programs.

The obligation to make reasonable accommodation applies to all services and programs provided in connection with employment, and to all non-work facilities provided or maintained by an employer for use by its employees. Accordingly, the obligation to accommodate is applicable to employer sponsored placement or counseling services, and to employer provided cafeterias, lounges, gymnasiums, auditoriums, transportation and the like.

The reasonable accommodation requirement is best understood as a means by which barriers to the equal employment opportunity of an individual with a disability are removed or alleviated. These barriers may, for example, be physical or structural obstacles that inhibit or prevent the access of an individual with a disability to job sites, facilities or equipment. Or they may be rigid work schedules that permit no flexibility as to when work is performed or when breaks may be taken, or inflexible job procedures that unduly limit the modes of communication that are used on the job, or the way in which particular tasks are accomplished.

The term "otherwise qualified" is intended to make clear that the obligation to make reasonable accommodation is owed only to an individual with a disability who is qualified within the meaning of §1630.2(m) in that he or she satisfies all the skill, experience, education and other job-related selection criteria. An individual with a disability is "otherwise qualified," in other words, if he or she is qualified for a job, except that, because of the disability, he or she needs a reasonable accommodation to be able to perform the job's essential functions.

For example, if a law firm requires that all incoming lawyers have graduated from an accredited law school and have passed the bar examination, the law firm need not provide an accommodation to an individual with a visual impairment who has not met these selection criteria. That individual is not entitled to a reasonable accommodation because the individual is not "otherwise qualified" for the position.

On the other hand, if the individual has graduated from an accredited law school and passed the bar examination, the individual would be "otherwise qualified." The law firm would thus be required to provide a reasonable accommodation, such as a machine that magnifies print, to enable the individual to perform the essential functions of the attorney position, unless the necessary accommodation would impose an undue hardship on the law firm. See Senate Report at 33-34; House Labor Report at 64-65.

The reasonable accommodation that is required by this part should provide the qualified individual with a disability with an equal employment opportunity. Equal employment opportunity means an opportunity to attain the same level of performance, or to enjoy the same level of benefits and privileges of employment as are available to the average similarly situated employee without a disability. Thus, for example, an accommodation made to assist an employee with a disability in the performance of his or her job must be adequate to enable the individual to perform the essential functions of the relevant position. The accommodation, however, does not have to be the "best" accommodation possible, so long as it is sufficient to meet the job-related needs of the individual being accommodated. Accordingly, an employer would not have to provide an employee disabled by a back impairment with a state-of-the art mechanical lifting device if it provided the employee with a less expensive or more readily available device that enabled the employee to perform the essential functions of the job. See Senate

Report at 35; House Labor Report at 66; see also Carter v. Bennett, 840 F.2d 63 (DC Cir. 1988).

Employers are obligated to make reasonable accommodation only to the physical or mental limitations resulting from the disability of the individual with a disability that is known to the employer. Thus, an employer would not be expected to accommodate disabilities of which it is unaware. If an employee with a known disability is having difficulty performing his or her job, an employer may inquire whether the employee is in need of a reasonable accommodation. In general, however, it is the responsibility of the individual with a disability to inform the employer that an accommodation is needed. When the need for an accommodation is not obvious, an employer, before providing a reasonable accommodation, may require that the individual with a disability provide documentation of the need for accommodation. See Senate Report at 34; House Labor Report at 65.

PROCESS OF DETERMINING THE APPROPRIATE REASONABLE ACCOMMODATION

Once the individual with a disability has requested provision of a reasonable accommodation, the employer must make a reasonable effort to determine the appropriate accommodation. The appropriate reasonable accommodation is best determined through a flexible, interactive process that involves both the employer and the individual with a disability. Although this process is described below in terms of accommodations that enable the individual with a disability to perform the essential functions of the position held or desired, it is equally applicable to accommodations involving the job application process, and to accommodations that enable the individual with a disability to enjoy equal benefits and privileges of employment. See Senate Report at 34-35; House Labor Report at 65-67.

When the individual with a disability has requested a reasonable accommodation to assist in the performance of a job, the employer, using a problem solving approach, should:

(1) Analyze the particular job involved and determine its purpose and essential functions;

(2) Consult with the individual with a disability to ascertain the precise job-related limitations imposed by the individual's disability and how those limitations could be overcome with a reasonable accommodation;

(3) In consultation with the individual to be accommodated, identify potential accommodations and assess the effectiveness each would have in enabling the individual to perform the essential functions of the position; and

(4) Consider the preference of the individual to be accommodated and select and implement the accommodation that is most appropriate for both the employee and the employer.

In many instances, the appropriate reasonable accommodation may be so obvious to either or both the employer and the individual with a disability that it may not be necessary to proceed in this step-by-step fashion. For example, if an employee who uses a wheelchair requests that his or her desk be placed on blocks to elevate the desktop above the arms of the wheelchair and the employer complies, an appropriate accommodation has been requested, identified, and provided without either the employee or employer being aware of having engaged in any sort of "reasonable accommodation process."

However, in some instances neither the individual requesting the accommodation nor the employer can readily identify the appropriate accommodation. For example, the individual needing the accommodation may not know enough about the equipment used by the employer or the exact nature of the work site to suggest an appropriate accommodation. Likewise, the employer may not know enough about the individual's disability or the limitations that disability would impose on the performance of the job to suggest an appropriate accommodation. Under such circumstances, it may be necessary for the employer to initiate a more defined problem solving process, such as the step-by-step process described above, as part of its reasonable effort to identify the appropriate reasonable accommodation.

This process requires the individual assessment of both the particular job at issue, and the specific physical or mental limitations of the particular individual in need of reasonable accommodation. With regard to assessment of the job, "individual assessment" means analyzing the actual job duties and determining the true purpose or object of the job. Such an assessment is necessary to ascertain which job functions are the essential functions that an accommodation must enable an individual with a disability to perform.

After assessing the relevant job, the employer, in consultation with the individual requesting the accommodation, should make an assessment of the specific limitations imposed by the disability on the individual's performance of the job's essential functions. This assessment will make it possible to ascertain the precise barrier to the employment opportunity which, in turn, will make it possible to determine the accommodation(s) that could alleviate or remove that barrier.

If consultation with the individual in need of the accommodation still does not reveal potential appropriate accommodations, then the employer, as part of this process, may find that technical assistance is helpful in determining how to accommodate the particular individual in the specific situation. Such assistance could be sought from the Commission, from State or local rehabilitation agencies, or from disability constituent organizations. It should be noted, however, that, as provided in §1630.9(c) of this part, the failure to obtain or receive technical assistance from the Federal agencies that administer the ADA will not excuse the employer from its reasonable accommodation obligation.

Once potential accommodations have been identified, the employer should assess the effectiveness of each potential accommodation in assisting the individual in need of the accommodation in the performance of the essential functions of the position. If more than one of these accommodations will enable the individual to perform the essential functions or if the individual would prefer to provide his or her own accommodation, the preference of the individual with a disability should be given primary consideration. However, the employer providing the accommodation has the ultimate discretion to choose between effective accommodations, and may choose the less expensive accommodation or the accommodation that is easier for it to provide. It should also be noted that the individual's willingness to provide his or her own accommodation does not relieve the employer of the duty to provide the accommodation should the individual for any reason be unable or unwilling to continue to provide the accommodation.

REASONABLE ACCOMMODATION PROCESS ILLUSTRATED

The following example illustrates the informal reasonable accommodation process. Suppose a Sack Handler position requires that the employee pick up fifty pound sacks and carry them from the company loading dock to the storage room, and that a sack handler who is disabled by a back impairment requests a reasonable accommodation. Upon receiving the request, the employer analyzes the Sack Handler job and determines that the essential function and purpose of the job is not the requirement that the job holder physically lift and carry the sacks, but the requirement that the job holder cause the sack to move from the loading dock to the storage room.

The employer then meets with the sack handler to ascertain precisely the barrier posed by the individual's specific disability to the performance of the job's essential function of relocating the sacks. At this meeting the employer learns that the individual can, in fact, lift the sacks to waist level, but is prevented by his or her disability from carrying the sacks from the loading dock to the storage room. The employer and the individual agree that any of a number of potential accommodations, such as the provision of a dolly, hand truck, or cart, could enable the individual to transport the sacks that he or she has lifted.

Upon further consideration, however, it is determined that the provision of a cart is not a feasible effective option. No carts are currently available at the company, and those that can be purchased by the company are the wrong shape to hold many of the bulky and irregularly shaped sacks that must be moved. Both the dolly and the hand truck, on the other hand, appear to be effective options. Both are readily available to the company, and either will enable the individual to relocate the sacks that he or she has lifted. The sack handler indicates his or her preference for the dolly. In consideration of this expressed preference, and because the employer feels that the dolly will allow the individual to move more sacks at a time and so be more efficient than would a hand truck, the employer ultimately provides the sack handler with a dolly in fulfillment of the obligation to make reasonable accommodation.

Section 1630.9(b)

This provision states that an employer or other covered entity cannot prefer or select a qualified individual without a disability over an equally qualified individual with a disability merely because the individual with a disability will require a reasonable accommodation. In other words, an individual's need for an accommodation cannot enter into the employer's or other covered entity's decision regarding hiring, discharge, promotion, or other similar employment decisions, unless the accommodation would impose an undue hardship on the employer. See House Labor Report at 70.

Section 1630.9(d)

The purpose of this provision is to clarify that an employer or other covered entity may not compel the individual with a disability to accept an accommodation, where that accommodation is neither requested nor needed by the individual. However, if a necessary reasonable accommodation is refused, the individual may not be considered qualified. For example, an individual with a visual impairment that restricts his or her field of vision but who is able to read unaided would not be required to accept a reader as an accommodation. However, if the individual were not able to read unaided and reading was an essential function of the job, the individual would not be qualified for the job if he or she refused a reasonable accommodation that would enable him or her to read. See Senate Report at 34; House Labor Report at 65; House Judiciary Report at 71-72.

Section 1630.9(e)

The purpose of this provision is to incorporate the clarification made in the ADA Amendments Act of 2008 that an individual is not entitled to reasonable accommodation under the ADA if the individual is only covered under the "regarded as" prong of the definition of "individual with a disability." However, if the individual is covered under both the "regarded as" prong and one or both of the other two prongs of the definition of disability, the ordinary rules concerning the provision of reasonable accommodation apply.

Section 1630.10 Qualification Standards, Tests, and Other Selection Criteria

Section 1630.10(a)—In General

The purpose of this provision is to ensure that individuals with disabilities are not excluded from job opportunities unless they are actually unable to do the job. It is to ensure that there is a fit between job criteria and an applicant's (or employee's) actual ability to do the job. Accordingly, job criteria that even unintentionally screen out, or tend to screen out, an individual with a disability or a class of individuals with disabilities because of their disability may not be used unless the employer demonstrates that those criteria, as used by the employer, are job related for the position to which they are being applied and are consistent with business necessity. The concept of "business necessity" has the same meaning as the concept of "business necessity" under section 504 of the Rehabilitation Act of 1973.

Selection criteria that exclude, or tend to exclude, an individual with a disability or a class of individuals with disabilities because of their disability but do not concern an essential function of the job would not be consistent with business necessity.

The use of selection criteria that are related to an essential function of the job may be consistent with business necessity. However, selection criteria that are related to an essential function of the job may not be used to exclude an individual with a disability if that individual could satisfy the criteria with the provision of a reasonable accommodation. Experience under a similar provision of the regulations implementing section 504 of the Rehabilitation Act indicates that challenges to selection criteria are, in fact, often resolved by reasonable accommodation.

This provision is applicable to all types of selection criteria, including safety requirements, vision or hearing requirements, walking requirements, lifting requirements, and employment tests. See 1989 Senate Report at 37-39; House Labor Report at 70-72; House Judiciary Report at 42. As previously noted, however, it is not the intent of this part to second guess an employer's business judgment with regard to production standards. See §1630.2(n) (Essential Functions). Consequently, production standards will generally not be subject to a challenge under this provision.

The Uniform Guidelines on Employee Selection Procedures (UGESP) 29 CFR part 1607 do not apply to the Rehabilitation Act and are similarly inapplicable to this part.

Section 1630.10(b) — *Qualification Standards and Tests Related to Uncorrected Vision*

This provision allows challenges to qualification standards based on uncorrected vision, even where the person excluded by a standard has fully corrected vision with ordinary eyeglasses or contact lenses. An individual challenging a covered entity's application of a qualification standard, test, or other criterion based on uncorrected vision need not be a person with a disability. In order to have standing to challenge such a standard, test, or criterion, however, a person must be adversely affected by such standard, test or criterion. The Commission also believes that such individuals will usually be covered under the "regarded as" prong of the definition of disability. Someone who wears eyeglasses or contact lenses to correct vision will still have an impairment, and a qualification standard that screens the individual out because of the impairment by requiring a certain level of uncorrected vision to perform a job will amount to an action prohibited by the ADA based on an impairment. (See §1630.2(l); Appendix to §1630.2(l).)

In either case, a covered entity may still defend a qualification standard requiring a certain level of uncorrected vision by showing that it is job related and consistent with business necessity. For example, an applicant or employee with uncorrected vision of 20/100 who wears glasses that fully correct his vision may challenge a police department's qualification standard that requires all officers to have uncorrected vision of no less than 20/40 in one eye and 20/100 in the other, and visual acuity of 20/20 in both eyes with correction. The department would then have to establish that the standard is job related and consistent with business necessity.

Section 1630.11 Administration of Tests

The intent of this provision is to further emphasize that individuals with disabilities are not to be excluded from jobs that they can actually perform merely because a disability prevents them from taking a test, or negatively influences the results of a test, that is a prerequisite to the job. Read together with the reasonable accommodation requirement of section 1630.9, this provision requires that employment tests be administered to eligible applicants or employees with disabilities that impair sensory, manual, or speaking skills in formats that do not require the use of the impaired skill.

The employer or other covered entity is, generally, only required to provide such reasonable accommodation if it knows, prior to the administration of the test, that the individual is disabled and that the disability impairs sensory, manual or speaking skills. Thus, for example, it would be unlawful to administer a written employment test to an individual who has informed the employer, prior to the administration of the test, that he is disabled with dyslexia and unable to read. In such a case, as a reasonable accommodation and in accordance with this provision, an alternative oral test should be administered to that individual. By the same token, a written test may need to be substituted for an oral test if the applicant taking the test is an individual with a disability that impairs speaking skills or impairs the processing of auditory information.

Occasionally, an individual with a disability may not realize, prior to the administration of a test, that he or she will need an accommodation to take that particular test. In such a situation, the individual with a disability, upon becoming aware of the need for an accommodation, must so inform the employer or other covered entity. For example, suppose an individual with a disabling visual impairment does not request an accommodation for a written examination because he or she is usually able to take written tests with the aid of his or her own specially designed lens. When the test is distributed, the individual with a disability discovers that the lens is insufficient to distinguish the words of the test because of the unusually low color contrast between the paper and the ink, the individual would be entitled, at that point, to request an accommodation. The employer or other covered entity would, thereupon, have to provide a test with higher contrast, schedule a retest, or provide any other effective accommodation unless to do so would impose an undue hardship.

Other alternative or accessible test modes or formats include the administration of tests in large print or braille, or via a reader or sign interpreter. Where it is not possible to test in an alternative format, the employer may be required, as a reasonable accommodation, to evaluate the skill to be tested in another manner (e.g., through an interview, or through education license, or work experience requirements). An employer may also be required, as a reasonable accommodation, to allow more time to complete the test. In addition, the employer's obligation to make reasonable accommodation extends to ensuring that the test site is accessible. (See §1630.9 Not Making Reasonable Accommodation) See Senate Report at 37-38; House Labor Report at 70-72; House Judiciary Report at 42; see also Stutts v. Freeman, 694 F.2d 666 (11th Cir. 1983); Crane v. Dole, 617 F. Supp. 156 (D.D.C. 1985).

This provision does not require that an employer offer every applicant his or her choice of test format. Rather, this provision only requires that an employer provide, upon advance request, alternative, accessible tests to individuals with disabilities that impair sensory, manual, or speaking skills needed to take the test.

This provision does not apply to employment tests that require the use of sensory, manual, or speaking skills where the tests are intended to measure those skills. Thus, an employer could require that an applicant with dyslexia take a written test for a particular position if the ability to read is the skill the test is designed to measure. Similarly, an employer could require that an applicant complete a test within established time frames if speed were one of the skills for which the applicant was being tested. However, the results of such a test could not be used to exclude an individual with a disability unless the skill was necessary to perform an essential function of the position and no reasonable accommodation was available to enable the individual to perform that function, or the necessary accommodation would impose an undue hardship.

Section 1630.13 Prohibited Medical Examinations and Inquiries

Section 1630.13(a) Pre-employment Examination or Inquiry

This provision makes clear that an employer cannot inquire as to whether an individual has a disability at the pre-offer stage of the selection process. Nor can an employer inquire at the pre-offer stage about an applicant's workers' compensation history.

Employers may ask questions that relate to the applicant's ability to perform job-related functions. However, these questions should not be phrased in terms of disability. An employer, for example, may ask whether the applicant has a driver's license, if driving is a job function, but may not ask whether the applicant has a visual disability. Employers may ask about an applicant's ability to perform both essential and marginal job functions. Employers, though, may not refuse to hire an applicant with a disability because the applicant's disability prevents him or her from performing marginal functions. See Senate Report at 39; House Labor Report at 72-73; House Judiciary Report at 42-43.

Section 1630.13(b) Examination or Inquiry of Employees

The purpose of this provision is to prevent the administration to employees of medical tests or inquiries that do not serve a legitimate business purpose. For example, if an employee suddenly starts to use increased amounts of sick leave or starts to appear sickly, an employer could not require that employee to be tested for AIDS, HIV infection, or cancer unless the employer can demonstrate that such testing is job-related and consistent with business necessity. See Senate Report at 39; House Labor Report at 75; House Judiciary Report at 44.

Section 1630.14 Medical Examinations and Inquiries Specifically Permitted

Section 1630.14(a) Pre-employment Inquiry

Employers are permitted to make pre-employment inquiries into the ability of an applicant to perform job-related functions. This inquiry must be narrowly tailored. The employer may describe or demonstrate the job function and inquire whether or not the applicant can perform that function with or without reasonable accommodation. For example, an employer may explain that the job requires assembling small parts and ask if the individual will be able to perform that function, with or without reasonable accommodation. See Senate Report at 39; House Labor Report at 73; House Judiciary Report at 43.

An employer may also ask an applicant to describe or to demonstrate how, with or without reasonable accommodation, the applicant will be able to perform job-related functions. Such a request may be made of all applicants in the same job category regardless of disability. Such a request may also be made of an applicant whose known disability may interfere with or prevent the performance of a job-related function, whether or not the employer routinely makes such a request of all applicants in the job category. For example, an employer may ask an individual with one leg who applies for a position as a home washing machine repairman to demonstrate or to explain how, with or without reasonable accommodation, he would be able to transport himself and his tools down basement stairs. However, the employer may not inquire as to the nature or severity of the disability. Therefore, for example, the employer cannot ask how the individual lost the leg or whether the loss of the leg is indicative of an underlying impairment.

On the other hand, if the known disability of an applicant will not interfere with or prevent the performance of a job-related function, the employer may only request a description or demonstration by the applicant if it routinely makes such a request of all applicants in the same job category. So, for example, it would not be permitted for an employer to request that an applicant with one leg demonstrate his ability to assemble small parts while seated at a table, if the employer does not routinely request that all applicants provide such a demonstration.

An employer that requires an applicant with a disability to demonstrate how he or she will perform a job-related function must either provide the reasonable accommodation the applicant needs to perform the function or permit the applicant to explain how, with the accommodation, he or she will perform the function. If the job-related function is not an essential function, the employer may not exclude the applicant with a disability because of the applicant's inability to perform that function. Rather, the employer must, as a reasonable accommodation, either provide an accommodation that will enable the individual to perform the function, transfer the function to another position, or exchange the function for one the applicant is able to perform.

An employer may not use an application form that lists a number of potentially disabling impairments and ask the applicant to check any of the impairments he or she may have. In addition, as noted above, an employer may not ask how a particular individual became disabled or the prognosis of the individual's disability. The employer is also prohibited from asking how often the individual will require leave for treatment or use leave as a result of incapacitation because of the disability. However, the employer may state the attendance requirements of the job and inquire whether the applicant can meet them.

An employer is permitted to ask, on a test announcement or application form, that individuals with disabilities who will require a reasonable accommodation in order to take the test so inform the employer within a reasonable established time period prior to the administration of the test. The employer may also request that documentation of the need for the accommodation accompany the request. Requested accommodations may include accessible testing sites, modified testing conditions and accessible test formats. (See §1630.11 Administration of Tests).

Physical agility tests are not medical examinations and so may be given at any point in the application or employment process. Such tests must be given to all similarly situated applicants or employees regardless of disability. If such tests screen out or tend to screen out an individual with a disability or a class of individuals with disabilities, the employer would have to demonstrate that the test is job-related and consistent with business necessity and that performance cannot be achieved with reasonable accommodation. (See §1630.9 Not Making Reasonable Accommodation: Process of Determining the Appropriate Reasonable Accommodation).

As previously noted, collecting information and inviting individuals to identify themselves as individuals with disabilities as required to satisfy the affirmative action requirements of section 503 of the Rehabilitation Act is not restricted by this part. (See §1630.1 (b) and (c) Applicability and Construction).

Section 1630.14(b) Employment Entrance Examination

An employer is permitted to require post-offer medical examinations before the employee actually starts working. The employer may condition the offer of employment on the results of the examination, provided that all entering employees in the same job category are subjected to such an examination, regardless of disability, and that the confidentiality requirements specified in this part are met.

This provision recognizes that in many industries, such as air transportation or construction, applicants for certain positions are chosen on the basis of many factors including physical and psychological criteria, some of which may be identified as a result of post-offer medical examinations given prior to entry on duty. Only those employees who meet the employer's physical and psychological criteria for the job, with or without reasonable accommodation, will be qualified to receive confirmed offers of employment and begin working.

Medical examinations permitted by this section are not required to be job-related and consistent with business necessity. However, if an employer withdraws an offer of employment because the medical examination reveals that the employee does not satisfy certain employment criteria, either the exclusionary criteria must not screen out or tend to screen out an individual with a disability or a class of individuals with disabilities, or they must be job-related and consistent with business necessity. As part of the showing that an exclusionary criteria is job-related and consistent with business necessity, the employer must also demonstrate that there is no reasonable accommodation that will enable the individual with a disability to perform the essential functions of the job. See Conference Report at 59-60; Senate Report at 39; House Labor Report at 73-74; House Judiciary Report at 43.

As an example, suppose an employer makes a conditional offer of employment to an applicant, and it is an essential function of the job that the incumbent be available to work every day for the next three months. An employment entrance examination then reveals that the applicant has a disabling impairment that, according to reasonable medical judgment that relies on the most current medical knowledge, will require treatment that will render the applicant unable to work for a portion of the three month period. Under these circumstances, the employer would be able to withdraw the employment offer without violating this part.

The information obtained in the course of a permitted entrance examination or inquiry is to be treated as a confidential medical record and may only be used in a manner not inconsistent with this part. State workers' compensation laws are not preempted by the ADA or this part. These laws require the collection of information from individuals for State administrative purposes that do not conflict with the ADA or this part. Consequently, employers or other covered entities may submit information to State workers' compensation offices or second injury funds in accordance with State workers' compensation laws without violating this part.

Consistent with this section and with §1630.16(f) of this part, information obtained in the course of a permitted entrance examination or inquiry may be used for insurance purposes described in §1630.16(f).

Section 1630.14(c) Examination of Employees

This provision permits employers to make inquiries or require medical examinations (fitness for duty exams) when there is a need to determine whether an employee is still able to perform the essential functions of his or her job. The provision permits employers or other covered entities to make inquiries or require medical examinations necessary to the reasonable accommodation process described in this part. This provision also permits periodic physicals to determine fitness for duty or other medical monitoring if such physicals or monitoring are required by medical standards or requirements established by Federal, State, or local law that are consistent with the ADA and this part (or in the case of a Federal standard, with section 504 of the Rehabilitation Act) in that they are job-related and consistent with business necessity.

Such standards may include Federal safety regulations that regulate bus and truck driver qualifications, as well as laws establishing medical requirements for pilots or other air transportation personnel. These standards also include health standards promulgated pursuant to the Occupational Safety and Health Act of 1970, the Federal Coal Mine Health and Safety Act of 1969, or other similar statutes that require that employees exposed to certain toxic and hazardous substances be medically monitored at specific intervals. See House Labor Report at 74-75.

The information obtained in the course of such examination or inquiries is to be treated as a confidential medical record and may only be used in a manner not inconsistent with this part.

Section 1630.14(d) Other Acceptable Examinations and Inquiries

Part 1630 permits voluntary medical examinations, including voluntary medical histories, as part of employee health programs. These programs often include, for example, medical screening for high blood pressure, weight control counseling, and cancer detection. Voluntary activities, such as blood pressure monitoring and the administering of prescription drugs, such as insulin, are also permitted. It should be noted, however, that the medical records developed in the course of such activities must be maintained in the confidential manner required by this part and must not be used for any purpose in violation of this part, such as limiting health insurance eligibility. House Labor Report at 75; House Judiciary Report at 43-44.

Section 1630.15 Defenses

The section on defenses in part 1630 is not intended to be exhaustive. However, it is intended to inform employers of some of the potential defenses available to a charge of discrimination under the ADA and this part.

Section 1630.15(a) Disparate Treatment Defenses

The "traditional" defense to a charge of disparate treatment under title VII, as expressed in McDonnell Douglas Corp. v. Green, 411 U.S. 792 (1973), Texas Department of Community Affairs v. Burdine, 450 U.S. 248 (1981), and their progeny, may be applicable to charges of disparate treatment brought under the ADA. See Prewitt v. U.S. Postal Service, 662 F.2d 292 (5th Cir. 1981). Disparate treatment means, with respect to title I of the ADA, that an individual was treated differently on the basis of his or her disability. For example, disparate treatment has occurred where an employer excludes an employee with a severe facial disfigurement from staff meetings because the employer does not like to look at the employee. The individual is being treated differently because of the employer's attitude towards his or her perceived disability. Disparate treatment has also occurred where an employer has a policy of not hiring individuals with AIDS regardless of the individuals' qualifications.

The crux of the defense to this type of charge is that the individual was treated differently not because of his or her disability but for a legitimate non-discriminatory reason such as poor performance unrelated to the individual's disability. The fact that the individual's disability is not covered by the employer's current insurance plan or would cause the employer's insurance premiums or workers' compensation costs to increase, would not be a legitimate nondiscriminatory reason justifying disparate treatment of an individual with a disability. Senate Report at 85; House Labor Report at 136 and House Judiciary Report at 70. The defense of a legitimate nondiscriminatory reason is rebutted if the alleged nondiscriminatory reason is shown to be pretextual.

Section 1630.15 (b) and (c) Disparate Impact Defenses

Disparate impact means, with respect to title I of the ADA and this part, that uniformly applied criteria have an adverse impact on an individual with a disability or a disproportionately negative impact on a class of individuals with disabilities. Section 1630.15(b) clarifies that an employer may use selection criteria that have such a disparate impact, i.e., that screen out or tend to screen out an individual with a disability or a class of individuals with disabilities only when they are job-related and consistent with business necessity.

For example, an employer interviews two candidates for a position, one of whom is blind. Both are equally qualified. The employer decides that while it is not essential to the job it would be convenient to have an employee who has a driver's license and so could occasionally be asked to run errands by car. The employer hires the individual who is sighted because this individual has a driver's license. This is an example of a uniformly applied criterion, having a driver's permit, that screens out an individual who has a disability that makes it impossible to obtain a driver's permit. The employer would, thus, have to show that this criterion is job-related and consistent with business necessity. See House Labor Report at 55.

However, even if the criterion is job-related and consistent with business necessity, an employer could not exclude an individual with a disability if the criterion could be met or job performance accomplished with a reasonable accommodation. For example, suppose an employer requires, as part of its application process, an interview that is job-related and consistent with business necessity. The employer would not be able to refuse to hire a hearing impaired applicant because he or she could not be interviewed. This is so because an interpreter could be provided as a reasonable accommodation that would allow the individual to be interviewed, and thus satisfy the selection criterion.

With regard to safety requirements that screen out or tend to screen out an individual with a disability or a class of individuals with disabilities, an employer must demonstrate that the requirement, as applied to the individual, satisfies the "direct threat" standard in §1630.2(r) in order to show that the requirement is job-related and consistent with business necessity.

Section 1630.15(c) clarifies that there may be uniformly applied standards, criteria and policies not relating to selection that may also screen out or tend to screen out an individual with a disability or a class of individuals with disabilities. Like selection criteria that have a disparate impact, non-selection criteria having such an impact may also have to be job-related and consistent with business necessity, subject to consideration of reasonable accommodation.

It should be noted, however, that some uniformly applied employment policies or practices, such as leave policies, are not subject to challenge under the adverse impact theory. "No-leave" policies (e.g., no leave during the first six months of employment) are likewise not subject to challenge under the adverse impact theory. However, an employer, in spite of its "no-leave" policy, may, in appropriate circumstances, have to consider the provision of leave to an employee with a disability as a reasonable accommodation, unless the provision of leave would impose an undue hardship. See discussion at §1630.5 Limiting, Segregating and Classifying, and §1630.10 Qualification Standards, Tests, and Other Selection Criteria.

Section 1630.15(d) Defense To Not Making Reasonable Accommodation

An employer or other covered entity alleged to have discriminated because it did not make a reasonable accommodation, as required by this part, may offer as a defense that it would have been an undue hardship to make the accommodation. It should be noted, however, that an employer cannot simply assert that a needed accommodation will cause it undue hardship, as defined in §1630.2(p), and thereupon be relieved of the duty to provide accommodation. Rather, an employer will have to present evidence and demonstrate that the accommodation will, in fact, cause it undue hardship. Whether a particular accommodation will impose an undue hardship for a particular employer is determined on a case by case basis. Consequently, an accommodation that poses an undue hardship for one employer at a particular time may not pose an undue hardship for another employer, or even for the same employer at another time. Likewise, an accommodation that poses an undue hardship for one employer in a particular job setting, such as a temporary construction worksite, may not pose an undue hardship for another employer, or even for the same employer at a permanent worksite. See House Judiciary Report at 42.

The concept of undue hardship that has evolved under section 504 of the Rehabilitation Act and is embodied in this part is unlike the "undue hardship" defense associated with the provision of religious accommodation under title VII of the Civil Rights Act of 1964. To demonstrate undue hardship pursuant to the ADA and this part, an employer must show substantially more difficulty or expense than would be needed to satisfy the "de minimis" title VII standard of undue hardship. For example, to demonstrate that the cost of an accommodation poses an undue hardship, an employer would have to show that the cost is undue as compared to the employer's budget. Simply comparing the cost of the accommodation to the salary of the individual with a disability in need of the accommodation will not suffice. Moreover, even if it is determined that the cost of an accommodation would unduly burden an employer, the employer cannot avoid making the accommodation if the individual with a disability can arrange to cover that portion of the cost that rises to the undue hardship level, or can otherwise arrange to provide the accommodation. Under such circumstances, the necessary accommodation would no longer pose an undue hardship. See Senate Report at 36; House Labor Report at 68-69; House Judiciary Report at 40-41.

Excessive cost is only one of several possible bases upon which an employer might be able to demonstrate undue hardship. Alternatively, for example, an employer could demonstrate that the provision of a particular accommodation would be unduly disruptive to its other employees or to the functioning of its business. The terms of a collective bargaining agreement may be relevant to this determination. By way of illustration, an employer would likely be able to show undue hardship if the employer could show that the requested accommodation of the upward adjustment of the business' thermostat would result in it becoming unduly hot for its other employees, or for its patrons or customers. The employer would thus not have to provide this accommodation. However, if there were an alternate accommodation that would not result in undue hardship, the employer would have to provide that accommodation.

It should be noted, moreover, that the employer would not be able to show undue hardship if the disruption to its employees were the result of those employees fears or prejudices toward the individual's disability and not the result of the provision of the accommodation. Nor would the employer be able to demonstrate undue hardship by showing that the provision of the accommodation has a negative impact on the morale of its other employees but not on the ability of these employees to perform their jobs.

Section 1630.15(e) Defense — Conflicting Federal Laws and Regulations

There are several Federal laws and regulations that address medical standards and safety requirements. If the alleged discriminatory action was taken in compliance with another Federal law or regulation, the employer may offer its obligation to comply with the conflicting standard as a defense. The employer's defense of a conflicting Federal requirement or regulation may be rebutted by a showing of pretext, or by showing that the Federal standard did not require the discriminatory action, or that there was a nonexclusionary means to comply with the standard that would not conflict with this part. See House Labor Report at 74.

Section 1630.15(f) Claims Based on Transitory and Minor Impairments Under the "Regarded As" Prong

It may be a defense to a charge of discrimination where coverage would be shown solely under the "regarded as" prong of the definition of disability that the impairment is (in the case of an actual impairment) or would be (in the case of a perceived impairment) both transitory and minor. Section 1630.15(f)(1) explains that an individual cannot be "regarded as having such an impairment" if the impairment is both transitory (defined by the ADAAA as lasting or expected to last less than six months) and minor. Section 1630.15(f)(2) explains that the determination of "transitory and minor" is made objectively. For example, an individual who is denied a promotion because he has a minor back injury would be "regarded as" an individual with a disability if the back impairment lasted or was expected to last more than six months. Although minor, the impairment is not transitory. Similarly, if an employer discriminates against an employee based on the employee's bipolar disorder (an impairment that is not transitory and minor), the employee is "regarded as" having a disability even if the employer subjectively believes that the employee's disorder is transitory and minor.

Section 1630.16 Specific Activities Permitted

Section 1630.16(a) Religious Entities

Religious organizations are not exempt from title I of the ADA or this part. A religious corporation, association, educational institution, or society may give a preference in employment to individuals of the particular religion, and may require that applicants and employees conform to the religious tenets of the organization. However, a religious organization may not discriminate against an individual who satisfies the permitted religious criteria because that individual is disabled. The religious entity, in other words, is required to consider individuals with disabilities who are qualified and satisfy the permitted religious criteria on an equal basis with qualified individuals without disabilities who similarly satisfy the religious criteria. See Senate Report at 42; House Labor Report at 76-77; House Judiciary Report at 46.

Section 1630.16(b) Regulation of Alcohol and Drugs

This provision permits employers to establish or comply with certain standards regulating the use of drugs and alcohol in the workplace. It also allows employers to hold alcoholics and persons who engage in the illegal use of drugs to the same performance and conduct standards to which it holds all of its other employees. Individuals disabled by alcoholism are entitled to the same protections accorded other individuals with disabilities under this part. As noted above, individuals currently engaging in the illegal use of drugs are not individuals with disabilities for purposes of part 1630 when the employer acts on the basis of such use.

Section 1630.16(c) Drug Testing

This provision reflects title I's neutrality toward testing for the illegal use of drugs. Such drug tests are neither encouraged, authorized nor prohibited. The results of such drug tests may be used as a basis for disciplinary action. Tests for the illegal use of drugs are not considered medical examinations for purposes of this part. If the results reveal information about an individual's medical condition beyond whether the individual is currently engaging in the illegal use of drugs, this additional information is to be treated as a confidential medical record. For example, if a test for the illegal use of drugs reveals the presence of a controlled substance that has been lawfully prescribed for a particular medical condition, this information is to be treated as a confidential medical record. See House Labor Report at 79; House Judiciary Report at 47.

Section 1630.16(e) Infectious and Communicable Diseases; Food Handling Jobs

This provision addressing food handling jobs applies the "direct threat" analysis to the particular situation of accommodating individuals with infectious or communicable diseases that are transmitted through the handling of food. The Department of Health and Human Services is to prepare a list of infectious and communicable diseases that are transmitted through the handling of food. If an individual with a disability has one of the listed diseases and works in or applies for a position in food handling, the employer must determine whether there is a reasonable accommodation that will eliminate the risk of transmitting the disease through the handling of food. If there is an accommodation that will not pose an undue hardship, and that will prevent the transmission of the disease through the handling of food, the employer must provide the accommodation to the individual. The employer, under these circumstances, would not be permitted to discriminate against the individual because of the need to provide the reasonable accommodation and would be required to maintain the individual in the food handling job.

If no such reasonable accommodation is possible, the employer may refuse to assign, or to continue to assign the individual to a position involving food handling. This means that if such an individual is an applicant for a food handling position the employer is not required to hire the individual. However, if the individual is a current employee, the employer would be required to consider the accommodation of reassignment to a vacant position not involving food handling for which the individual is qualified. Conference Report at 61-63. (See §1630.2(r) Direct Threat).

Section 1630.16(f) Health Insurance, Life Insurance, and Other Benefit Plans

This provision is a limited exemption that is only applicable to those who establish, sponsor, observe or administer benefit plans, such as health and life insurance plans. It does not apply to those who establish, sponsor, observe or administer plans not involving benefits, such as liability insurance plans.

The purpose of this provision is to permit the development and administration of benefit plans in accordance with accepted principles of risk assessment. This provision is not intended to disrupt the current regulatory structure for self-insured employers. These employers may establish, sponsor, observe, or administer the terms of a bona fide benefit plan not subject to State laws that regulate insurance. This provision is also not intended to disrupt the current nature of insurance underwriting, or current insurance industry practices in sales, underwriting, pricing, administrative and other services, claims and similar insurance related activities based on classification of risks as regulated by the States.

The activities permitted by this provision do not violate part 1630 even if they result in limitations on individuals with disabilities, provided that these activities are not used as a subterfuge to evade the purposes of this part. Whether or not these activities are being used as a subterfuge is to be determined without regard to the date the insurance plan or employee benefit plan was adopted.

However, an employer or other covered entity cannot deny an individual with a disability who is qualified equal access to insurance or subject a qualified individual with a disability to different terms or conditions of insurance based on disability alone, if the disability does not pose increased risks. Part 1630 requires that decisions not based on risk classification be made in conformity with non-discrimination requirements. See Senate Report at 84-86; House Labor Report at 136-138; House Judiciary Report at 70-71. See the discussion of §1630.5 Limiting, Segregating and Classifying.

Part 1635 — Genetic Information Nondiscrimination Act of 2008

§1635.1   Purpose.
§1635.2   Definitions — General.
§1635.3   Definitions Specific to Gina.
§1635.4   Prohibited Practices — in General.
§1635.5   Limiting, Segregating, and Classifying.
§1635.6   Causing a Covered Entity to Discriminate.
§1635.7   Retaliation.
§1635.8   Acquisition of Genetic Information.
§1635.9   Confidentiality.
§1635.10   Enforcement and Remedies.
§1635.11   Construction.
§1635.12   Medical Information that Is Not Genetic Information

§1635.1 Purpose

(a) The purpose of this part is to implement Title II of the Genetic Information Nondiscrimination Act of 2008, 42 U.S.C. 2000ff, et seq. Title II of GINA:

(1) Prohibits use of genetic information in employment decision-making;

(2) Restricts employers and other entities subject to Title II of GINA from requesting, requiring, or purchasing genetic information;

(3) Requires that genetic information be maintained as a confidential medical record, and places strict limits on disclosure of genetic information; and

(4) Provides remedies for individuals whose genetic information is acquired, used, or disclosed in violation of its protections.

(b) This part does not apply to actions of covered entities that do not pertain to an individual's status as an employee, member of a labor organization, or participant in an apprenticeship program. For example, this part would not apply to:

(1) A medical examination of an individual for the purpose of diagnosis and treatment unrelated to employment, which is conducted by a health care

professional at the hospital or other health care facility where the individual is an employee; or

(2) Activities of a covered entity carried on in its capacity as a law enforcement agency investigating criminal conduct, even where the subject of the investigation is an employee of the covered entity.

§1635.1 Definitions — General.

(a) Commission means the Equal Employment Opportunity Commission, as established by section 705 of the Civil Rights Act of 1964, 42 U.S.C. 2000e-4.

(b) Covered Entity means an employer, employing office, employment agency, labor organization, or joint labor-management committee.

(c) Employee means an individual employed by a covered entity, as well as an applicant for employment and a former employee. An employee, including an applicant for employment and a former employee, is:

(1) As defined by section 701 of the Civil Rights Act of 1964, 42 U.S.C. 2000e, an individual employed by a person engaged in an industry affecting commerce who has fifteen or more employees for each working day in each of twenty or more calendar weeks in the current or preceding calendar year and any agent of such a person;

(2) As defined by section 304(a) of the Government Employee Rights Act, 42 U.S.C. 2000e-16c(a), a person chosen or appointed by an individual elected to public office by a State or political subdivision of a State to serve as part of the personal staff of the elected official, to serve the elected official on a policy-making level, or to serve the elected official as the immediate advisor on the exercise of the elected official's constitutional or legal powers.

(3) As defined by section 101 of the Congressional Accountability Act, 2 U.S.C. 1301, any employee of the House of Representatives, the Senate, the Capitol Guide Service, the Capitol Police, the Congressional Budget Office, the Office of the Architect of the Capitol, the Office of the Attending Physician, the Office of Compliance, or the Office of Technology Assessment;

(4) As defined by, and subject to the limitations in, section 2(a) of the Presidential and Executive Office Accountability Act, 3 U.S.C. 411(c), any employee of the executive branch not otherwise covered by section 717 of the Civil Rights Act of 1964, 42 U.S.C. 2000e-16, section 15 of the Age Discrimination in Employment Act of 1967, 29 U.S.C. 633a, or section 501 of the Rehabilitation Act of 1973, 29 U.S.C. 791, whether appointed by the President or any other appointing authority in the executive branch, including an employee of the Executive Office of the President;

(5) As defined by, and subject to the limitations in, section 717 of the Civil Rights Act of 1964, 42 U.S.C. 2000e-16, and regulations of the Equal Employment Opportunity Commission at 29 CFR 1614.103, an employee of a federal executive agency, the United States Postal Service and the Postal Rate Commission, the Tennessee Valley Authority, the National Oceanic and Atmospheric Administration Commissioned Corps, the Government Printing

Office, and the Smithsonian Institution; an employee of the federal judicial branch having a position in the competitive service; and an employee of the Library of Congress.

(d) Employer means any person that employs an employee defined in §1635.2(c) of this part, and any agent of such person, except that, as limited by section 701(b)(1) and (2) of the Civil Rights Act of 1964, 42 U.S.C. 2000e(b)(1) and (2), an employer does not include an Indian tribe, or a bona fide private club (other than a labor organization) that is exempt from taxation under section 501(c) of the Internal Revenue Code of 1986.

(e) Employing office is defined in the Congressional Accountability Act, 2 U.S.C. 1301(9), to mean the personal office of a Member of the House of Representatives or of a Senator; a committee of the House of Representatives or the Senate or a joint committee; any other office headed by a person with the final authority to appoint, hire, discharge, and set the terms, conditions, or privileges of the employment of an employee of the House of Representatives or the Senate; or the Capitol Guide Board, the Capitol Police Board, the Congressional Budget Office, the Office of the Architect of the Capitol, the Office of the Attending Physician, the Office of Compliance, and the Office of Technology Assessment.

(f) Employment agency is defined in 42 U.S.C. 2000e(c) to mean any person regularly undertaking with or without compensation to procure employees for an employer or to procure for employees opportunities to work for an employer and includes an agent of such a person.

(g) Joint labor-management committee is defined as an entity that controls apprenticeship or other training or retraining programs, including on-the-job training programs.

(h) Labor organization is defined at 42 U.S.C. 2000e(d) to mean an organization with fifteen or more members engaged in an industry affecting commerce, and any agent of such an organization in which employees participate and which exists for the purpose, in whole or in part, of dealing with employers concerning grievances, labor disputes, wages, rates of pay, hours, or other terms or conditions of employment.

(i) Member includes, with respect to a labor organization, an applicant for membership.

(j) Person is defined at 42 U.S.C. 2000e(a) to mean one or more individuals, governments, governmental agencies, political subdivisions, labor unions, part-nerships, associations, corporations, legal representatives, mutual companies, joint-stock companies, trusts, unincorporated organizations, trustees, trustees in cases under title 11, or receivers.

(k) State is defined at 42 U.S.C. 2000e(i) and includes a State of the United States, the District of Columbia, Puerto Rico, the Virgin Islands, American Samoa, Guam, Wake Island, the Canal Zone, and Outer Continental Shelf lands defined in the Outer Continental Shelf Lands Act (43 U.S.C. 1331 et seq.).

§1635.3 Definitions specific to GINA

(a) Family member means with respect to any individual:

(1) A person who is a dependent of that individual as the result of marriage, birth, adoption, or placement for adoption; or

(2) A first-degree, second-degree, third-degree, or fourth-degree relative of the individual, or of a dependent of the individual as defined in §1635.3(a)(1).

(i) First-degree relatives include an individual's parents, siblings, and children.

(ii) Second-degree relatives include an individual's grandparents, grandchildren, uncles, aunts, nephews, nieces, and half-siblings.

(iii) Third-degree relatives include an individual's great-grandparents, great grandchildren, great uncles/aunts, and first cousins.

(iv) Fourth-degree relatives include an individual's great-great-grandparents, great-great-grandchildren, and first cousins once-removed (i.e., the children of the individual's first cousins).

(b) Family medical history. Family medical history means information about the manifestation of disease or disorder in family members of the individual.

(c) Genetic information.

(1) Genetic information means information about:

(i) An individual's genetic tests;

(ii) The genetic tests of that individual's family members;

(iii) The manifestation of disease or disorder in family members of the individual (family medical history);

(iv) An individual's request for, or receipt of, genetic services, or the participation in clinical research that includes genetic services by the individual or a family member of the individual; or

(v) The genetic information of a fetus carried by an individual or by a pregnant woman who is a family member of the individual and the genetic information of any embryo legally held by the individual or family member using an assisted reproductive technology.

(2) Genetic information does not include information about the sex or age of the individual, the sex or age of family members, or information about the race or ethnicity of the individual or family members that is not derived from a genetic test.

(d) Genetic monitoring means the periodic examination of employees to evaluate acquired modifications to their genetic material, such as chromosomal damage or evidence of increased occurrence of mutations, caused by the toxic substances they use or are exposed to in performing their jobs, in order to identify, evaluate, and respond to the effects of, or to control adverse environmental exposures in the workplace.

(e) Genetic services. Genetic services means a genetic test, genetic counseling (including obtaining, interpreting, or assessing genetic information), or genetic education.

(f) Genetic test —

(1) In general. "Genetic test" means an analysis of human DNA, RNA, chromosomes, proteins, or metabolites that detects genotypes, mutations, or chromosomal changes.

(2) Genetic tests include, but are not limited to:

(i) A test to determine whether someone has the BRCA1 or BRCA2 variant evidencing a predisposition to breast cancer, a test to determine whether someone has a genetic variant associated with hereditary non-polyposis colon cancer, and a test for a genetic variant for Huntington's Disease;

(ii) Carrier screening for adults using genetic analysis to determine the risk of conditions such as cystic fibrosis, sickle cell anemia, spinal muscular atrophy, or fragile X syndrome in future offspring;

(iii) Amniocentesis and other evaluations used to determine the presence of genetic abnormalities in a fetus during pregnancy;

(iv) Newborn screening analysis that uses DNA, RNA, protein, or metabolite analysis to detect or indicate genotypes, mutations, or chromosomal changes, such as a test for PKU performed so that treatment can begin before a disease manifests;

(v) Preimplantation genetic diagnosis performed on embryos created using invitro fertilization;

(vi) Pharmacogenetic tests that detect genotypes, mutations, or chromosomal changes that indicate how an individual will react to a drug or a particular dosage of a drug;

(vii) DNA testing to detect genetic markers that are associated with information about ancestry; and

(viii) DNA testing that reveals family relationships, such as paternity.

(3) The following are examples of tests or procedures that are not genetic tests:

(i) An analysis of proteins or metabolites that does not detect genotypes, mutations, or chromosomal changes;

(ii) A medical examination that tests for the presence of a virus that is not composed of human DNA, RNA, chromosomes, proteins, or metabolites;

(iii) A test for infectious and communicable diseases that may be transmitted through food handling;

(iv) Complete blood counts, cholesterol tests, and liver-function tests.

(4) Alcohol and Drug Testing —

(i) A test for the presence of alcohol or illegal drugs is not a genetic test.

(ii) A test to determine whether an individual has a genetic predisposition for alcoholism or drug use is a genetic test.

(g) Manifestation or manifested means, with respect to a disease, disorder, or pathological condition, that an individual has been or could reasonably be diagnosed with the disease, disorder, or pathological condition by a health care professional with appropriate training and expertise in the field of medicine involved. For purposes of this part, a disease, disorder, or pathological condition is not manifested if the diagnosis is based principally on genetic information.

§1635.4 Prohibited practices — in general

(a) It is unlawful for an employer to discriminate against an individual on the basis of the genetic information of the individual in regard to hiring, discharge, compensation, terms, conditions, or privileges of employment.

(b) It is unlawful for an employment agency to fail or refuse to refer any individual for employment or otherwise discriminate against any individual because of genetic information of the individual.

(c) It is unlawful for a labor organization to exclude or to expel from the membership of the organization, or otherwise to discriminate against, any member because of genetic information with respect to the member.

(d) It is an unlawful employment practice for any employer, labor organization, or joint labor-management committee controlling apprenticeship or other training or retraining programs, including on-the-job training programs to discriminate against any individual because of the individual's genetic information in admission to, or employment in, any program established to provide apprenticeship or other training or retraining.

§1635.5 Limiting, segregating, and classifying

(a) A covered entity may not limit, segregate, or classify an individual, or fail or refuse to refer for employment any individual, in any way that would deprive or tend to deprive the individual of employment opportunities or otherwise affect the status of the individual as an employee, because of genetic information with respect to the individual. A covered entity will not be deemed to have violated this section if it limits or restricts an employee's job duties based on genetic information because it was required to do so by a law or regulation mandating genetic monitoring, such as regulations administered by the Occupational and Safety Health Administration (OSHA). See 1635.8(b)(5) and 1635.11(a).

(b) Notwithstanding any language in this part, a cause of action for disparate impact within the meaning of section 703(k) of the Civil Rights Act of 1964, 42 U.S.C. 2000e-2(k), is not available under this part.

§1635.6 Causing a covered entity to discriminate.

A covered entity may not cause or attempt to cause another covered entity, or its agent, to discriminate against an individual in violation of this part, including with respect to the individual's participation in an apprenticeship or other training or retraining program, or with respect to a member's participation in a labor organization.

§1635.7 Retaliation

A covered entity may not discriminate against any individual because such individual has opposed any act or practice made unlawful by this title or because such individual made a charge, testified, assisted, or participated in any manner in an investigation, proceeding, or hearing under this title.

§1635.8 Acquisition of genetic information

(a) General prohibition. A covered entity may not request, require, or purchase genetic information of an individual or family member of the individual, except as specifically provided in paragraph (b) of this section. "Request" includes conducting an Internet search on an individual in a way that is likely to result in a covered entity obtaining genetic information; actively listening to third-party conversations or searching an individual's personal effects for the purpose of obtaining genetic information; and making requests for information about an individual's current health status in a way that is likely to result in a covered entity obtaining genetic information.

(b) Exceptions. The general prohibition against requesting, requiring, or purchasing genetic information does not apply:

(1) Where a covered entity inadvertently requests or requires genetic information of the individual or family member of the individual.

(i) Requests for Medical Information:

(A) If a covered entity acquires genetic information in response to a lawful request for medical information, the acquisition of genetic information will not generally be considered inadvertent unless the covered entity directs the individual and/or health care provider from whom it requested medical information (in writing, or verbally, where the covered entity does not typically make requests for medical information in writing) not to provide genetic information.

(B) If a covered entity uses language such as the following, any receipt of genetic information in response to the request for medical information will be deemed inadvertent: "The Genetic Information Nondiscrimination Act of 2008 (GINA) prohibits employers and other entities covered by GINA Title II from requesting or requiring genetic information of an individual or family member of the individual, except as specifically allowed by this law. To comply with this law, we are asking that you not provide any genetic information when responding to this request for medical information. 'Genetic information' as defined by GINA, includes an individual's family medical history, the results of an individual's or family member's genetic tests, the fact that an individual or an individual's family member sought or received genetic services, and genetic information of a fetus carried by an individual or an individual's family member or an embryo lawfully held by an individual or family member receiving assistive reproductive services."

(C) A covered entity's failure to give such a notice or to use this or similar language will not prevent it from establishing that a particular receipt of genetic information was inadvertent if its request for medical information was not "likely to result in a covered entity obtaining genetic information" (for example, where an overly broad response is received in response to a tailored request for medical information).

(D) Situations to which the requirements of subsection (b)(1)(i) apply include, but are not limited to the following:

(1) Where a covered entity requests documentation to support a request for reasonable accommodation under Federal, State, or local law, as long as the covered entity's request for such documentation is lawful. A request for documentation supporting a request for reasonable accommodation is lawful only when the disability and/or the need for accommodation is not obvious; the documentation is no more than is sufficient to establish that an individual has a disability and needs a reasonable accommodation; and the documentation relates only to the impairment that the individual claims to be a disability that requires reasonable accommodation;

(2) Where an employer requests medical information from an individual as required, authorized, or permitted by Federal, State, or local law, such as where an employee requests leave under the Family and Medical Leave Act (FMLA) to attend to the employee's own serious health condition or where an employee complies with the FMLA's employee return to work certification requirements; or

(3) Where a covered entity requests documentation to support a request for leave that is not governed by Federal, State, or local laws requiring leave, as long as the documentation required to support the request otherwise complies with the requirements of the Americans with Disabilities Act and other laws limiting a covered entity's access to medical information.

(ii) The exception for inadvertent acquisition of genetic information also applies in, but is not necessarily limited to, situations where—

(A) A manager, supervisor, union representative, or employment agency representative learns genetic information about an individual by overhearing a conversation between the individual and others;

(B) A manager, supervisor, union representative, or employment agency representative learns genetic information about an individual by receiving it from the individual or third-parties during a casual conversation, including in response to an ordinary expression of concern that is the subject of the conversation. For example, the exception applies when the covered entity, acting through a supervisor or other official, receives family medical history directly from an individual following a general health inquiry (e.g., "How are you?" or "Did they catch it early?" asked of an employee who was just diagnosed with cancer) or a question as to whether the individual has a manifested condition. Similarly, a casual question between colleagues, or between a supervisor and subordinate, concerning the general well-being of a parent or child would not violate GINA (e.g., "How's your son feeling today?", "Did they catch it early?" asked of an employee whose family member was just diagnosed with cancer, or "Will your daughter be OK?"). However, this exception does not apply where an employer follows up a question concerning a family member's general health with questions that are probing in nature, such as whether other family members have the condition, or whether the individual has been tested for the condition, because the covered entity should know that these questions are likely to result in the acquisition of genetic information;

(C) A manager, supervisor, union representative, or employment agency representative learns genetic information from the individual or a third-party without having solicited or sought the information (e.g., where a manager or supervisor receives an unsolicited email about the health of an employee's family member from a co-worker); or

(D) A manager, supervisor, union representative, or employment agency representative inadvertently learns genetic information from a social media platform which he or she was given permission to access by the creator of the profile at issue (e.g., a supervisor and employee are connected on a social networking site and the employee provides family medical history on his page).

(2) Where a covered entity offers health or genetic services, including such services offered as part of a voluntary wellness program.

(i) This exception applies only where —

(A) The provision of genetic information by the individual is voluntary, meaning the covered entity neither requires the individual to provide genetic information nor penalizes those who choose not to provide it;

(B) The individual provides prior knowing, voluntary, and written authorization, which may include authorization in electronic format. This requirement is only met if the covered entity uses an authorization form that:

(1) Is written so that the individual from whom the genetic information is being obtained is reasonably likely to understand it;

(2) Describes the type of genetic information that will be obtained and the general purposes for which it will be used; and

(3) Describes the restrictions on disclosure of genetic information;

(C) Individually identifiable genetic information is provided only to the individual (or family member if the family member is receiving genetic services) and the licensed health care professionals or board certified genetic counselors involved in providing such services, and is not accessible to managers, supervisors, or others who make employment decisions, or to anyone else in the workplace; and

(D) Any individually identifiable genetic information provided under paragraph (b)(2) of this section is only available for purposes of such services and is not disclosed to the covered entity except in aggregate terms that do not disclose the identity of specific individuals (a covered entity will not violate the requirement that it receive information only in aggregate terms if it receives information that, for reasons outside the control of the provider or the covered entity (such as the small number of participants), makes the genetic information of a particular individual readily identifiable with no effort on the covered entity's part).

(ii) Consistent with the requirements of paragraph (b)(2)(i) of this section, a covered entity may not offer a financial inducement for individuals to provide genetic information, but may offer financial inducements for completion of health risk assessments that include questions about family medical history or other genetic information, provided the covered entity makes clear, in language reasonably likely to be understood by those completing the health risk assessment, that the inducement will be made available whether or not the participant answers questions regarding genetic information. For example:

(A) A covered entity offers $150 to employees who complete a health risk assessment with 100 questions, the last 20 of them concerning family medical history and other genetic information. The instructions for completing the health risk assessment make clear that the inducement will be provided to all employees who respond to the first 80 questions, whether or not the remaining 20 questions concerning family medical history and other genetic information are answered. This health risk assessment does not violate Title II of GINA.

(B) Same facts as the previous example, except that the instructions do not indicate which questions request genetic information; nor does the assessment otherwise make clear which questions must be answered in order to obtain the inducement. This health risk assessment violates Title II of GINA.

(iii) A covered entity may offer financial inducements to encourage individuals who have voluntarily provided genetic information (e.g., family medical history) that indicates that they are at increased risk of acquiring a health condition in the future to participate in disease management programs or other programs that promote healthy lifestyles, and/or to meet particular health goals as part of a health or genetic service. However, to comply with Title II of GINA, these programs must also be offered to individuals with current health conditions and/or to individuals whose lifestyle choices put them at increased risk of developing a condition. For example:

(A) Employees who voluntarily disclose a family medical history of diabetes, heart disease, or high blood pressure on a health risk assessment that meets the requirements of (b)(2)(ii) of this section and employees who have a current diagnosis of one or more of these conditions are offered $150 to participate in a wellness program designed to encourage weight loss and a healthy lifestyle. This does not violate Title II of GINA.

(B) The program in the previous example offers an additional inducement to individuals who achieve certain health outcomes. Participants may earn points toward "prizes" totaling $150 in a single year for lowering their blood pressure, glucose, and cholesterol levels, or for losing weight. This inducement would not violate Title II of GINA.

(iv) Nothing contained in §1635.8(b)(2)(iii) limits the rights or protections of an individual under the Americans with Disabilities Act (ADA), as amended, or other applicable civil rights laws, or under the Health Insurance Portability and Accountability Act (HIPAA), as amended by GINA. For example, if an employer offers a financial inducement for participation in disease management programs or other programs that promote healthy lifestyles and/or require individuals to meet particular health goals, the employer must make reasonable accommodations to the extent required by the ADA, that is, the employer must make "modifications or adjustments that enable a covered entity's employee with a disability to enjoy equal benefits and privileges of employment as are enjoyed by its other similarly situated employees without disabilities" unless "such covered entity can demonstrate that the accommodation would impose an undue hardship on the operation of its business." 29 CFR 1630.2(o)(1)(iii); 29 CFR 1630.9(a). In addition, if the employer's wellness program provides (directly, through reimbursement, or otherwise) medical care (including genetic counseling), the program may constitute a group health plan and must comply with the special requirements for wellness programs that condition rewards on an individual satisfying a standard related to a health factor, including the requirement to provide an individual with a "reasonable alternative (or waiver of the otherwise applicable standard)" under HIPAA, when "it is unreasonably difficult due to a medical condition to satisfy" or "medically inadvisable to attempt to satisfy" the otherwise applicable standard. See section 9802 of the Internal Revenue Code (26 U.S.C. 9802, 26 CFR 54.9802-1 and 54.9802-3T), section 702 of the Employee Retirement Income Security Act of 1974 (ERISA) (29 U.S.C. 1182, 29 CFR 2590.702 and 2590.702-1), and section 2705 of the Public Health Service Act (45 CFR 146.121 and 146.122).

(3) Where the covered entity requests family medical history to comply with the certification provisions of the Family and Medical Leave Act of 1993 (29 U.S.C. 2601 et seq.) or State or local family and medical leave laws, or pursuant to a policy (even in the absence of requirements of Federal, State, or

local leave laws) that permits the use of leave to care for a sick family member and that requires all employees to provide information about the health condition of the family member to substantiate the need for leave.

(4) Where the covered entity acquires genetic information from documents that are commercially and publicly available for review or purchase, including newspapers, magazines, periodicals, or books, or through electronic media, such as information communicated through television, movies, or the Internet, except that this exception does not apply—

(i) To medical databases, court records, or research databases available to scientists on a restricted basis;

(ii) To genetic information acquired through sources with limited access, such as social networking sites and other media sources which require permission to access from a specific individual or where access is conditioned on membership in a particular group, unless the covered entity can show that access is routinely granted to all who request it;

(iii) To genetic information obtained through commercially and publicly available sources if the covered entity sought access to those sources with the intent of obtaining genetic information; or

(iv) To genetic information obtained through media sources, whether or not commercially and publicly available, if the covered entity is likely to acquire genetic information by accessing those sources, such as Web sites and on-line discussion groups that focus on issues such as genetic testing of individuals and genetic discrimination.

(5) Where the covered entity acquires genetic information for use in the genetic monitoring of the biological effects of toxic substances in the workplace. In order for this exception to apply, the covered entity must provide written notice of the monitoring to the individual and the individual must be informed of the individual monitoring results. The covered entity may not retaliate or otherwise discriminate against an individual due to his or her refusal to participate in genetic monitoring that is not required by federal or state law. This exception further provides that such monitoring:

(i) Is either required by federal or state law or regulation, or is conducted only where the individual gives prior knowing, voluntary and written authorization. The requirement for individual authorization is only met if the covered entity uses an authorization form that:

(A) Is written so that the individual from whom the genetic information is being obtained is reasonably likely to understand the form;

(B) Describes the genetic information that will be obtained; and

(C) Describes the restrictions on disclosure of genetic information;

(ii) Is conducted in compliance with any Federal genetic monitoring regulations, including any regulations that may be promulgated by the Secretary of Labor pursuant to the Occupational Safety and Health Act of 1970 (29 U.S.C. 651 et seq.), the Federal Mine Safety and Health Act of 1977 (30 U.S.C. 801 et seq.), or the Atomic Energy Act of 1954 (42 U.S.C. 2011 et seq.); or State genetic monitoring regulations, in the case of a State that is implementing genetic monitoring regulations under the authority of the Occupational Safety and Health Act of 1970 (29 U.S.C. 651 et seq.); and

(iii) Provides for reporting of the results of the monitoring to the covered entity, excluding any licensed health care professional or board certified genetic counselor involved in the genetic monitoring program, only in aggregate terms that do not disclose the identity of specific individuals.

(6) Where an employer conducts DNA analysis for law enforcement purposes as a forensic laboratory or for purposes of human remains identification and requests or requires genetic information of its employees, apprentices, or trainees, but only to the extent that the genetic information is used for analysis of DNA identification markers for quality control to detect sample contamination and is maintained and disclosed in a manner consistent with such use.

(c) Inquiries Made of Family Members Concerning a Manifested Disease, Disorder, or Pathological Condition.

(1) A covered entity does not violate this section when it requests, requires, or purchases information about a manifested disease, disorder, or pathological condition of an employee, member, or apprenticeship program participant whose family member is an employee for the same employer, a member of the same labor organization, or a participant in the same apprenticeship program. For example, an employer will not violate this section by asking someone whose sister also works for the employer to take a post-offer medical examination that does not include requests for genetic information.

(2) A covered entity does not violate this section when it requests, requires, or purchases genetic information or information about the manifestation of a disease, disorder, or pathological condition of an individual's family member who is receiving health or genetic services on a voluntary basis. For example, an employer does not unlawfully acquire genetic information about an employee when it asks the employee's family member who is receiving health services from the employer if her diabetes is under control.

(d) Medical examinations related to employment. The prohibition on acquisition of genetic information, including family medical history, applies to medical examinations related to employment. A covered entity must tell health care providers not to collect genetic information, including family medical history, as part of a medical examination intended to determine the ability to perform a job, and must take additional reasonable measures within its control if it learns that genetic information is being requested or required. Such reasonable measures may depend on the facts and circumstances under which a request for genetic information was made, and may include no longer using the services of a health care professional who continues to request or require genetic information during medical examinations after being informed not to do so.

(e) A covered entity may not use genetic information obtained pursuant to subparagraphs (b) or (c) of this section to discriminate, as defined by §§1635.4, 1635.5, or 1635.6, and must keep such information confidential as required by §1635.9.

§1635.9 *Confidentiality*

(a) Treatment of genetic information.

(1) A covered entity that possesses genetic information in writing about an employee or member must maintain such information on forms and in medical files (including where the information exists in electronic forms and files) that are separate from personnel files and treat such information as a confidential medical record.

(2) A covered entity may maintain genetic information about an employee or member in the same file in which it maintains confidential medical information subject to section 102(d)(3)(B) of the Americans with Disabilities Act, 42 U.S.C. 12112(d)(3)(B).

(3) Genetic information that a covered entity receives orally need not be reduced to writing, but may not be disclosed, except as permitted by this part.

(4) Genetic information that a covered entity acquires through sources that are commercially and publicly available, as provided by, and subject to the limitations in, 1635.8(b)(4) of this part, is not considered confidential genetic information, but may not be used to discriminate against an individual as described in §§1635.4, 1635.5, or 1635.6 of this part.

(5) Genetic information placed in personnel files prior to November 21, 2009 need not be removed and a covered entity will not be liable under this part for the mere existence of the information in the file. However, the prohibitions on use and disclosure of genetic information apply to all genetic information that meets the statutory definition, including genetic information requested, required, or purchased prior to November 21, 2009.

(b) Exceptions to limitations on disclosure. A covered entity that possesses any genetic information, regardless of how the entity obtained the information (except for genetic information acquired through commercially and publicly available sources), may not disclose it except:

(1) To the employee or member (or family member if the family member is receiving the genetic services) about whom the information pertains upon receipt of the employee's or member's written request;

(2) To an occupational or other health researcher if the research is conducted in compliance with the regulations and protections provided for under 45 CFR part 46;

(3) In response to an order of a court, except that the covered entity may disclose only the genetic information expressly authorized by such order; and if the court order was secured without the knowledge of the employee or member to whom the information refers, the covered entity shall inform the employee or member of the court order and any genetic information that was disclosed pursuant to such order;

(4) To government officials investigating compliance with this title if the information is relevant to the investigation;

(5) To the extent that such disclosure is made in support of an employee's compliance with the certification provisions of section 103 of the Family and Medical Leave Act of 1993 (29 U.S.C. 2613) or such requirements under State family and medical leave laws; or

(6) To a Federal, State, or local public health agency only with regard to information about the manifestation of a disease or disorder that concerns a contagious disease that presents an imminent hazard of death or life-threatening illness, provided that the individual whose family member is the subject of the disclosure is notified of such disclosure.

(c) Relationship to HIPAA Privacy Regulations. Pursuant to §1635.11(d) of this part, nothing in this section shall be construed as applying to the use or disclosure of genetic information that is protected health information subject to the regulations issued pursuant to section 264(c) of the Health Insurance Portability and Accountability Act of 1996.

§1635.10 Enforcement and remedies

(a) Powers and procedures: The following powers and procedures shall apply to allegations that Title II of GINA has been violated:

(1) The powers and procedures provided to the Commission, the Attorney General, or any person by sections 705 through 707 and 709 through 711 of the Civil Rights Act of 1964, 42 U.S.C. 2000e-4 through 2000e-6 and 2000e-8 through 2000e-10, where the alleged discrimination is against an employee defined in 1635.2(c)(1) of this part or against a member of a labor organization;

(2) The powers and procedures provided to the Commission and any person by sections 302 and 304 of the Government Employees Rights Act, 42 U.S.C. 2000e-16b and 2000e-16c, and in regulations at 29 CFR part 1603, where the alleged discrimination is against an employee as defined in §1635.2(c)(2) of this part;

(3) The powers and procedures provided to the Board of Directors of the Office of Compliance and to any person under the Congressional Accountability Act, 2 U.S.C. 1301 et seq. (including the provisions of Title 3 of that act, 2 U.S.C. 1381 et seq.), where the alleged discrimination is against an employee defined in §1635.2(c)(3) of this part;

(4) The powers and procedures provided in 3 U.S.C. 451 et seq., to the President, the Commission, or any person in connection with an alleged violation of section 3 U.S.C. 411(a)(1), where the alleged discrimination is against an employee defined in §1635.2(c)(4) of this part;

(5) The powers and procedures provided to the Commission, the Librarian of Congress, and any person by section 717 of the Civil Rights Act, 42 U.S.C. 2000e-16, where the alleged discrimination is against an employee defined in §1635.2(c)(5) of this part.

(b) Remedies. The following remedies are available for violations of GINA sections 202, 203, 204, 205, 206, and 207(f):

(1) Compensatory and punitive damages as provided for, and limited by, 42 U.S.C. 1981a(a)(1) and (b);

(2) Reasonable attorney's fees, including expert fees, as provided for, and limited by, 42 U.S.C. 1988(b) and (c); and

(3) Injunctive relief, including reinstatement and hiring, back pay, and other equitable remedies as provided for, and limited by, 42 U.S.C. 2000e-5(g).

(c) Posting of Notices.

(1) Every covered entity shall post and keep posted in conspicuous places upon its premises where notices to employees, applicants for employment, and members are customarily posted a notice to be prepared or approved by the Commission setting forth excerpts from or, summaries of, the pertinent provisions of this regulation and information pertinent to the filing of a complaint.

(2) A willful violation of this requirement shall be punishable by a fine of not more than $100 for each separate offense.

§1635.11   Construction

(a) Relationship to other laws, generally. This part does not —

(1) Limit the rights or protections of an individual under any other Federal, State, or local law that provides equal or greater protection to an individual than the rights or protections provided for under this part, including the Americans with Disabilities Act of 1990 (42 U.S.C. 12101 et seq.), the Rehabilitation Act of 1973 (29 U.S.C. 701 et seq.), and State and local laws prohibiting genetic discrimination or discrimination on the basis of disability;

(2) Apply to the Armed Forces Repository of Specimen Samples for the Identification of Remains;

(3) Limit or expand the protections, rights, or obligations of employees or employers under applicable workers' compensation laws;

(4) Limit the authority of a Federal department or agency to conduct or sponsor occupational or other health research in compliance with the regulations and protections provided for under 45 CFR part 46;

(5) Limit the statutory or regulatory authority of the Occupational Safety and Health Administration or the Mine Safety and Health Administration to promulgate or enforce workplace safety and health laws and regulations; or

(6) Require any specific benefit for an employee or member or a family member of an employee or member (such as additional coverage for a particular health condition that may have a genetic basis) under any group health plan or health insurance issuer offering group health insurance coverage in connection with a group health plan.

(b) Relation to certain Federal laws governing health coverage.

(1) General: Nothing in GINA Title II provides for enforcement of, or penalties for, violation of any requirement or prohibition of a covered entity subject to enforcement under:

(i) Amendments made by Title I of GINA.

(ii) Section 701(a) of the Employee Retirement Income Security Act (29 U.S.C. 1181) (ERISA), section 2704(a) of the Public Health Service Act, and section 9801(a) of the Internal Revenue Code (26 U.S.C. 9801(a)), as such sections apply with respect to genetic information pursuant to section 701(b)(1)(B) of ERISA, section 2704(b)(1)(B) of the Public Health Service Act, and section 9801(b)(1)(B) of the Internal Revenue Code, respectively, of such sections, which prohibit a group health plan or a health insurance issuer in the group market from imposing a preexisting condition exclusion based solely on genetic information, in the absence of a diagnosis of a condition;

(iii) Section 702(a)(1)(F) of ERISA (29 U.S.C. 1182(a)(1)(F)), section 2705(a)(6) of the Public Health Service Act, and section 9802(a)(1)(F) of the Internal Revenue Code (26 U.S.C. 9802(a)(1)(F)), which prohibit a group health plan or a health insurance issuer in the group market from discriminating against individuals in eligibility and continued eligibility for benefits based on genetic information; or

(iv) Section 702(b)(1) of ERISA (29 U.S.C. 1182(b)(1)), section 2705(b)(1) of the Public Health Service Act, and section 9802(b)(1) of the Internal Revenue Code (26 U.S.C. 9802(b)(1)), as such sections apply with respect to genetic information as a health status-related factor, which prohibit a group health plan or a health insurance issuer in the group market from discriminating against individuals in premium or contribution rates under the plan or coverage based on genetic information.

(2) Application. The application of paragraph (b)(1) of this section is intended to prevent Title II causes of action from being asserted regarding matters subject to enforcement under Title I or the other genetics provisions for group coverage in ERISA, the Public Health Service Act, and the Internal Revenue Code. The firewall seeks to ensure that health plan or issuer provisions or actions are addressed and remedied through ERISA, the Public Health Service Act, or the Internal Revenue Code, while actions taken by employers and other GINA Title II covered entities are remedied through GINA Title II. Employers and other GINA Title II covered entities would remain liable for any of their actions that violate Title II, even where those actions involve access to health benefits, because such benefits are within the definition of compensation, terms, conditions, or privileges of employment. For example, an employer that fires an employee because of anticipated high health claims based on genetic information remains subject to liability under Title II. On the other hand, health plan or issuer provisions or actions related to the imposition of a preexisting condition exclusion; a health plan's or issuer's discrimination in health plan eligibility, benefits, or premiums based on genetic information; a health plan's or issuer's request that an individual

undergo a genetic test; and/or a health plan's or issuer's collection of genetic information remain subject to enforcement under Title I exclusively. For example:

(i) If an employer contracts with a health insurance issuer to request genetic information, the employer has committed a Title II violation. In addition, the issuer may have violated Title I of GINA.

(ii) If an employer directs his employees to undergo mandatory genetic testing in order to be eligible for health benefits, the employer has committed a Title II violation.

(iii) If an employer or union amends a health plan to require an individual to undergo a genetic test, then the employer or union is liable for a violation of Title II. In addition, the health plan's implementation of the requirement may subject the health plan to liability under Title I.

(c) Relationship to authorities under GINA Title I. GINA Title II does not prohibit any group health plan or health insurance issuer offering group health insurance coverage in connection with a group health plan from engaging in any action that is authorized under any provision of law noted in §1635.11(b) of this part, including any implementing regulations noted in §1635.11(b).

(d) Relationship to HIPAA Privacy Regulations. This part does not apply to genetic information that is protected health information subject to the regulations issued by the Secretary of Health and Human Services pursuant to section 264(c) of the Health Insurance Portability and Accountability Act of 1996.

§1635.12 Medical information that is not genetic information

(a) Medical information about a manifested disease, disorder, or pathological condition.

(1) A covered entity shall not be considered to be in violation of this part based on the use, acquisition, or disclosure of medical information that is not genetic information about a manifested disease, disorder, or pathological condition of an employee or member, even if the disease, disorder, or pathological condition has or may have a genetic basis or component.

(2) Notwithstanding paragraph (a)(1) of this section, the acquisition, use, and disclosure of medical information that is not genetic information about a manifested disease, disorder, or pathological condition is subject to applicable limitations under sections 103(d)(1)-(4) of the Americans with Disabilities Act (42 U.S.C. 12112(d)(1)-(4)), and regulations at 29 CFR 1630.13, 1630.14, and 1630.16.

(b) Genetic information related to a manifested disease, disorder, or pathological condition. Notwithstanding paragraph (a) of this section, genetic information about a manifested disease, disorder, or pathological condition is subject to the requirements and prohibitions in sections 202 through 206 of GINA and §§1635.4 through 1635.9 of this part.

TABLE OF CASES

Bold indicates principal cases.

14 Penn Plaza LLC v. Pyett, 30, 267

Abdullahi v. Prada USA Corp., 23
AT&T Corp. v. Hulteen, 76, 115
AT&T Mobility LLC v. Concepcion, 270
Abdullahi v. Prada USA Corp., 10
Abner v. Kan. City S. R.R. Co., 259
Adams v. Lucent Techs., Inc., 158
Adams v. O'Reilly Auto., Inc., 127
Adams v. Rice, 173
Adarand Constructors, Inc. v. Pena, 81, 91
Agro Distribution, LLC, EEOC v., 112
Aguiar v. Bartlesville Care Ctr., 130
Agusty-Reyes v. Dep't of Educ., 125, 126
Alaska v. EEOC, 254
Albemarle Paper Co. v. Moody, 88, 246
Albertson's, Inc. v. Kirkingburg, 177, 178, 184, 184
Alberty-Velez v. Corporacion de P.R. para la Difusion Publicia, 108
Alcazar v. Corp. of the Catholic Archbishop of Seattle, 138
Alicea-Hernandez v. Catholic Bishop, 138
Aliotta v. Bair, 43
Allen v. Highlands Hosp. Corp., 52, 228
Allmond v. Akal Sec. Inc., 209
Allstate Ins. Co., EEOC v., 52, 62
Alonso v. Huron Valley Ambulance Inc., 750
Alvarado v. Cajun Operating Co., 260
Alvarez v. Royal Atl. Developers, Inc., 147
Amchem Products Inc. v. Windsor, 239, 246
Ames v. Home Depot U.S.A., Inc., 209
Amini v. Oberlin College, 229
Amtrak v. Morgan, 159, 163, 165, 217, 226, 222
Anderson v. Wintco, Inc., 125
Andonissamy v. Hewlett-Packard Co., 94
Andrews v. Ohio, 147
Anza v. Ideal Steel Supply Corp., 13
Aramark Facility Servs. v. SEIU, Local 1877, 139
Arculeo v. On-Site Sales & Mktg., L.L.C., 108
Argyropoulos v. City of Alton, 148
Aron v. Quest Diagnostics Inc., 135

Arline v. School Bd. of Nassau County, 197
Aryain v. Wal-Mart Stores Tex. LP, 127
Ashcroft v. Iqbal, 25
Association of Mexican Am. Educators v. California, 64
Autozone, EEOC v., 181

Bailey v. USF Holland, Inc., 8
Baker v. Silver Oak Senior Living Mgmt. Co., 35
Baker v. Windsor Republic Doors, 213
Baldwin v. Blue Cross/Blue Shield of Ala., 127
Balint v. Carson City, Nev., 135
Barker v. Mo. Dep't of Corr., 144
Barone v. United Airlines, Inc., 6
Bates v. UPS, 201, 208
Bazemore v. Friday, 217
Beamon v. Marshall & Ilsley Trust Co., 227
Benaugh v. Ohio Civil Rights Comm'n, 206
Bennett v. Chertoff, 111
Berry v. Chi. Transit Auth., 122, 126
Beyer v. County of Nassau, 4, 6
Billings v. Town of Grafton, 121
Bisker v. GGS Info. Servs., 203
Bd. of Supervisors for Univ. of La. Sys., EEOC v., 170
Bonds v. Leavitt, 142
Bolden v. City of Topeka, 112
Boston Chapter, NAACP v. Beecher, 88, 95
Blanks v. Southwestern Bell Corp., 174
Board of Supervisors for Univ. of La. System, EEOC v., 253
Bolling v. Sharpe, 316
Brady v. Office of the Sergeant at Arms, 37
Bragdon v. Abbott, 164, 178, 183, 187
Branham v. Snow, 207
Brannum v. Mo. Dep't of Corr., 100
Breiner v. Nev. Dep't of Corr., 48, 49
Brenneman v. Famous Dave's of Am., Inc., 129
Briscoe v. City of New Haven, 104
Bridges v. City of Bossier, 195
Bright v. Hill's Pet Nutrition, Inc., 223
Bristol v. Bd. of County Comm'rs, 109, 182

Broderick v. Donaldson, 154
Brown v. City of Long Branch, 211
Brown v. General Serv. Admin., 112
Brown v. J. Katz, Inc., 108, 111
Brown v. Nucor Corp., 248
Brown v. Polk, 136
Brownfield v. City of Yakima, 211
Browning v. United States, 59
Bruno v. City of Crown Point, 6
Bruno v. Monroe County, 126
Bryant v. Aiken Reg'l Med. Ctrs., Inc., 259
Brzak v. U.N., 111
Buckley v. Mukasey, 145
Budde v. Kane County Forest Pres., 205
Burdette v. Fed. Express Corp., 134
Burlington Industries, Inc. v. Ellerth, 11
Burlington N. & S. F. R. Co. v. White, 150
Burrus v. State Lottery Comm'n of Ind., 253
Bush v. Regis Corp., 96, 134
Bush v. Vera, 92
Butler v. Ala. DOT, 144
Butler v. Round Lake Police, 203
Butts v. County of Volusia, 86

Califano v. Yamaski, 233
Carlson v. Liberty Mut. Ins. Co., 173
Collins Food Intl., Inc. v. INS, 139
Campos v. City of Blue Springs, Mo., 133
Carmona v. Sw. Airlines Co., 201
Carpenter v. Con-Way Cen. Express, Inc., 155
Cassimy v. Bd. of Educ., 196
CBOS West, Inc. v. Humphries, 141
Celestine v. Petroleos de Venezuella SA, 65
Cent. Wholesalers, EEOC v., 127
Chaloult v. Interstate Brands Corp., 126
Chamber of Commerce of the United States v.
    Whiting, 140
Chaney v. Plainfield Healthcare Ctr., 49
Chapman v. Carmike Cinemas, 128
Chapin v. Fort-Rohr Motors Inc., 156
Chase Bank USA, N.A. v. McCoy, 189
Chevron Phillips Chem. Co., EEOC v., 172
Chevron U.S.A. Inc. v. Natural Res. Def.
    Council, Inc., 187
Chicanos Por La Causa, Inc. v. Napolitano, 98
Chicago Firefighters Local 2 v. Chicago, 79
Christensen v. Harris County, 188
Christianburg Garment Co., EEOC v., 143
Clack v. Rock-Team Co., 7
Clackamas Gastroenterology Assocs. P.C. v.
    Wells, 107
Clarke v. Securities Industry Assn., 152
Clover v. Total Sys. Serv., Inc., 142
Coffman v. Indianapolis Fire Dep't, 211
Colenburg v. Starcon Int'l, Inc., 120
Collazo v. Bristol-Myers Squibb Mfg., 143
Collazo v. Nicholson, 258
Colwell v. Rite Aid Corp., 206
Commercial Office Products Co., EEOC v., 226,
    227

Community for Creative Non-Violence v.
    Reid, 107
Connecticut v. Teal, 77
Con-Way Freight, EEOC v., 7
Cook v. Rhode Island Dep't of Mental Health,
    171, 195
Cooper v. Federal Reserve Bank of Richmond,
    248, 234
Cooper v. S. Co., 248
Cornett Mgmt. Co., LLC v. Fireman's Fund Ins.
    Co., 263
Corning Glass Works v. Brennan, 55
Coulton v. Univ. of Pa., 24
Crawford v. City of Fairburn, 20
Crawford v. Carroll, 6
Crawford v. Ind. Harbor Belt R.R. Co., 22
Crawford v. Metropolitan Government of
    Nashville and Davidson County, Tennessee,
    143, 148
Croy v. COBE Labs., Inc., 225
Curay-Cramer v. Ursuline Acad. of Wilmington,
    Del., Inc., 138

D'Angelo v. Conagra Foods, 197
Darchak v. City of Chi. Bd. of Educ., 7
Dargis v. Sheahan, 201
Daubert v. Merrell Dow Pharmaceuticals, Inc.,
    235
Davidson v. Am. Online, Inc., 225
Davis v. Califano, 65
Davis v. Coca-Cola Bottling Co. Consol., 6, 65,
    225
Davis v. Town of Lake Park, Fla., 6
Davis-Dietz v. Sears, Roebuck & Co., 8
De la Rama v. Ill. Dep't of Human Servs., 6
Decaire v. Mukasey, 7
DeFreitas v. Horizon Inv. Mgmt. Corp., 133
Dehart v. Baker Hughes Oilfield Operations,
    Inc., 155
DeJohn v. Temple Univ., 131
Delaware State College v. Ricks, 220
Denman v. Davey Tree Expert Co., 211
DeRosa v. Nat'l Envelop Corp., 202
Desmond v. Mukasey, 173
Dewitt v. Proctor Hosp., 213
Dixon v. Hallmark Cos., 132
Doe v. C.A.R.S. Prot. Plus, 117
Donaldson v. CDB. Inc., 155
Donlin v. Philips Lighting N. Am. Corp., 257
Dovenmuehler v. St. Cloud Hosp., 205
Duello v. Buchanan County Bd. of Supervisors,
    202
Duncan v. Fleetwood Motor Homes of Ind., 211
Duvall v. Georgia-Pacific Consumer Prods., 204

East Tex. Motor Freight System, Inc., 233
Edelman v. Lynchburg College, 216
El Sayed v. Hilton Hotels Corp., 145
EEOC v., see name of other party
Ekstrand v. Sch. Dist. of Somerset, 204

Eisen v. Carlisle & Jacquelin, 233
Elam v. Regions Fin. Corp., 116
Elkadrawy v. Vanguard Group, Inc., 229
Ellis v. UPS, Inc., 11
Elvig v. Calvin Presbyterian Church, 137
Emory v. AstraZeneca Pharms. LP, 183
Employees Retirement System of Ohio v.
Betts, 55
Enowmbitang v. Seagate Tech., 6
Ensley Branch of NAACP v. Seibels, 88
Eshelman v. Agere Sys., Inc., 173, 197 263
Erickson v. Bartell Drug Co., 118
Exxon Co., U.S.A. v. Sofec, Inc., 13

Faiola v. APCO Graphics, Inc., 195
Fantini v. Salem State Coll., 260
Faragher v. Boca Raton, 14, 90
Farr v. St. Francis Hosp. & Health Ctrs., 128
Farrar v. Hobby, 261
Farrell v. Butler Univ., 20
Fed. Express Corp., EEOC v., 253, 259, 260
Federal Express Corp. v. Holowecki, 28, 215
Federation of African Am. Contractors v. City of
Oakland, 112
Feldman v. Law Enforcement Associates Corp.,
200
Fichman v. Media Ctr., 108, 110
Fields v. Hallsville Indep. Sch. Dist., 64
Fields v. Shelter Mut. Ins. Co., 21
Finan v. Good Earth Tools, Inc., 197
Fincher v. Depository Trust and Clearing
Corp., 155
Finnegan v. Trans World Air Lines, Inc., 52
Firebird Soc. of New Haven, Inc. v. New Haven
Bd. of Fire Comm'rs, 85
Firefighters v. Cleveland, 74
Firefighters Inst. for Racial Equality v. St. Louis,
88
Firestone Fibers & Textiles Co.,
EEOC v., 134
Fischer v. Forestwood Co., 95, 132
Fischer v. Sw. Bell Tel. Co., 258
Fiscus v. Wal-Mart Stores, Inc., 173
Fitzgerald v. Action, Inc., 38
Flitton v. Primary Residential Mortg.,
Inc., 262
Fogelman v. Mercy Hosp. Inc., 108
Formella v. U.S. Dep't of Labor, 148
Forrest v. Brinker Int'l Payroll Co., LP, 115
Fowler v. UPMC Shadyside, 25
Fox v. Vice, 261
Francis v. City of Meriden, 196
Franklin v. Local 2 of the Sheet Metal Workers
Ass'n, 147
Franks v. Bowman Transp. Co., 234, 246
Fraser v. Goodale, 173
Frederick v. Sprint/United Mgt. Co., 130
Fuller v. Fiber Glass Sys., LP, 119
Fye v. Oklahoma Corp. Comm'n, 146

Gajda v. Manhattan & Bronx Surface Transit
Operating Auth., 211
Gallagher v. C.H. Robinson Worldwide, Inc.,
112, 122
Gant v. Kash'n Karry Food Stores, Inc., 148
Garrett-Woodberry v. Miss. Bd. of Pharm., 109
Gasser v. District of Columbia, 195
Gates v. Caterpillar, Inc., 21
Gelabert-Ladenheim v. Am. Airlines, Inc., 182
General Elec. Co. v. Gilbert, 187
General Dynamic Land Systems, Inc. v.
Cline, 28
General Telephone Co. of Southwest v. Falcon,
60, 233
Geo Group, Inc., EEOC v., 134
George v. New Jersey Bd. of Veterinary Med.
Exam'rs, 64
Gilty v. Oak Park, 65
Ginger v. District of Columbia, 26
Giordano v. City of New York, 195
Gladstone, Realtors v. Village of Bellwood, 151
Glover v. S.C. Law Enf., 142
Goldsmith v. Bagby Elevator Co., 267
Gollas v. Univ. of Tex. Health Sci. Ctr. at
Houston, 146
Gomez-Perez v. Potter, 154, 255
Goodman v. NSA, Inc, 156
Gordon v. England, 228
Gorzynski v. JetBlue Airways Corp., 129
Grain v. Trinity Health, 271
Granite Rock Co. v. International Brotherhood
of Teamsters, 268
Gratzl v. Office of the Chief Judges of the 12th,
18th, 19th, and 22nd Judicial Circuits, 200
Green v. Comm'r, 263
Green v. Franklin Nat'l Bank, 127
Gribben v. UPS, 182
Griggs v. Duke Power Co., 44, 73, 84, 88 236
Groesh v. City of Springfield, 218
Gross v. FBL Financial Services, Inc., **26,** 34,
36, 37, 146, 156
Grossman v. S. Shore Pub. Sch. Dist., 132, 133
Grutter v. Bollinger, 84
Guardians Assn. of N.Y. City Police Dept. v.
Civil Serv. Comm'n, 88
Gulino v. N.Y. State Educ. Dep't, 64

Haddock v. Bd. of Dental Exam'rs, 64
Hafford v. Seidner, 26
Hall v. Forest River, Inc., 145
Hall v. Nalco Co., 117
Hall St. Assocs. v. Mattel, Inc., 271
Halpert v. Manhattan Apts., Inc., 108
Hamilton v. GE, 177
Hampton v. Ford Motor Co., 177, 265
Hankins v. Lyght, 138
Harrell v. Donahue, 135
Harris v. Boyd Tunica, Inc. 228
Harris v. Maricopa County Superior Court, 260

Harrison v. Benchmark Elecs. Huntsville, Inc., 210
Harrison v. Eddy Potash Inc., 130
Harvill v. Westward Communs., L.L.C., 121
Hasan v. Foley & Lardner LLP, 96, 133
Hatley v. Hilton Hotels Corp., 259
Hatmaker v. Mem'l Med. Ctr., 142
Hawkins v. Anheuser-Busch, Inc., 123
Hawn v. Exec. Jet Mgmt., 128
Hayes v. United Parcel Serv., Inc., 182
Hazen Paper Co. v. Biggins, 29
Head v. Glacier Northwest, Inc., 126
Heartway Corp., EEOC v., 197
Heaton v. Weitz Co., 258
Heiko v. Colombo Sav. Bank, 173
Hemni v Group, LLC v. City of New York, 13
Hennagir v. Utah Dep't of Corr., 202
Henry v. Jones, 98
Henry v. Milwaukee County, 48, 224
Henthorn v. Capitol Communs., Inc., 121
Hoffman v. Carefirst of Fort Wayne, Inc., 199
Hohider v. UPS, 252
Holcomb v. Iona College, 24
Holender v. Mut. Indus. N., Inc., 216
Holmes v State of Utah, 164, 222
Holt v. Grand Lake Mental Health Ctr., Inc., 183
Holt v. JTM Industries, 108
Horgan v. Simmons, 199
Hosanna-Tabor Evangelical Lutheran Church & Sch., EEOC v., 137
Hoyle v. Freightliner, LLC, 120, 123
Hrisinko v. N.Y. City Dep't of Educ., 6
Humphries v. Pulaski County Special Sch. Dist., 24
Huston v. Procter & Gamble Paper Prods. Corp., 94

Indergard v. Georgia-Pacific Corp., 210
International Union , UAW v. Johnson Controls, 157
Isbell v. Allstate Ins. Co., 108

Jackson v. City of Chicago, 161
Jackson v. Fedex Corporate Servs., 10
Jacques v. DiMarzio, Inc., 173
Jakubowski v. Christ Hosp., Inc., 200
Jaramillo v. Colo. Judicial Dep't., 21
Javierre v. Central Altagracia, 54
Jett v. Dallas Independent Sch. Dist., 112
Jimenez v. Wellstar Health Sys., 112
Johnson v. Ready Mixed Concrete Co., 22
Johnson v. West, 130
Jones v. Nat'l Am. Univ., 21
Jones v. Okla. City Pub. Schs., 34
Josephs v. Pacific Bell, 197
Juarez v. AGS Gov't Solution Group, 21
Justice v. Crown Cork & Seal Co., 195

Kannady v. City of Kiowa, 158
Karraker v. Rent-A-Center, Inc., 262
Kasten v. Saint-Gobain Performance Plastics Corp., 154
Kautz v. Me-Pro Corp., 20
Kaytor v. Elec. Boat Corp., 123
Keeler v. Fla. Dept. of Health, 196
Kelley v. City of Albuquerque, 146
Kellogg v. Energy Safety Services, Inc., 173
Kelly v. Metallics West, Inc., 149
Kelly Servs., EEOC v., 134
Kentucky Retirement Systems v. EEOC, 29, 42, 157
Kessler v. Westchester County Dep't of Soc. Servs., 155
King v. Hardesty, 8
Kobus v. College of St. Scholastica, Inc., 207
Kohler, Inc., EEOC v., 145
Kolstad v. American Dental Assn, 91
Kucharski v. Cort Furniture Rental, 116
Kwaauhau v. Geiger, 11

Ladd v. Grand Trunk Western R.R., 121
Lafata v. Church of Christ Home for the Aged, 206
Lake v. Yellow Transp., Inc., 18
Lam v. University of Hawaii, 26
Lampley v. Onyx Acceptance Corp., 145
Lanning v. Southeastern Pa Tansp. Auth., 95
Lauderdale v. Tex. Dep't of Crim. Justice, 129
Le Boon v. Lancaster Jewish Cmty. Ctr. Ass'n, 137
Ledbetter v. Goodyear Tire & Rubber Co., 217
Lee v. Kan. City S. Ry. Co., 40
LeGrand v. Area Res. for Cmty. & Human Servs., 121
Leibowitz v. Cornell Univ., 5
Levelle v. Penske Logistics, 196
Lewis v. Heartland Inns of Am., L.L.C., 114
Lewis v. City of Chicago, 223
Littleton v. Walmart, 173
Lombardo v. Commonwealth, 254
Lopez v. Massachusetts, 110
Lopez v. Pacific Maritime Association, 66, 209
Lorance v. AT&T Technologies, 217
Lorillard v. Pons, 55
Love v. Motiva Enters. LLC, 113
Love v. Pullman, 226
Lucero v. Nettle Creek School Corp., 6, 125, 131
Lujan v. Defenders of Wildlife, 151, 152
Lukovsky v. City & County of San Francisco, 229
Lulaj v. Wackenhut Corp., 257
Lytes v. DC Water & Sewer, 159

MacNamara v. Korean Air Lines, 111
Madden v. Chattanooga City Wide Serv. Dep't, 19

Magallanes v. Ill. Bell Tel. Co., 265
Magyar v. St. Joseph Reg'l Med. Ctr., 147
Makky v. Chertoff, 111
Mattson v. Caterpillar, Inc., 143
Markham v. Salina Concrete Products, Inc., 199
Marks v. United States, 33
Marion County Coroner's Office v. EEOC, 255
Mathews v. Denver Newspaper Agency LLP, 268
Mattenson v. Baxter Healthcare Corp., 39
Mauerhan v. Wagner Corp., 208
Mazera v. Varsity Ford Mgmg. Servs., LLC, 271
Mazumder v. Univ. of Mich., 6
McBride v. BIC Consumer Prods. Mfg. Co., 207
McClain v. Lufkin Indus., 62
McCollugh v. Univ. of Arkansas for Med. Serv., 148
McCurdy v. Arkansas State Police, 130
McDonnell Douglass Corp v. Green, 89
McDowell v. T-Mobile USA, Inc., 66
McFadden v. Ballard Spahr Andrews & Ingersoll, LLP, 204
McGovern v. City of Phila., 85
McInnis v. Fairfield Cmtys., Inc., 259
McKay v. Toyota Motor Mfg., U.S.A., Inc., 181
McKenzie v. Dovola, 146, 195
McKnight v. GMC, 156, 213
McNamara v. Yellow Transp., Inc., 269
McNary v. Schreiber Foods, Inc., 205
McWilliams v. Jefferson County, 183
McWilliams v. Latah Sanitation, Inc., 216
Meacham v. Knolls Atomic Power Laboratory, 29, **53**, 157
Medina v. Income Support Division, 114
Medlock v. UPS, Inc., 20
Mendelsohn v. Sprint/United Mgmt. Co., 66
Merritt v. Old Dominion Freight Line, Inc., 24
Mickey v. Zeidler Tool & Die Co., 145
Miller v. Johnson, 81
Mohasco Corp. v. Silver, 226
Monteagudo v. Asociacion de Empleados del Estado Libre Asociado, 129
Mora v. Jackson Mem'l Found., Inc., 35
Mosby-Grant v. City of Hagerstown, 121
Mt. Healthy City Bd. of Ed. v. Doyle, 31
Muller v. Costello, 183
Murphy v. United Parcel Serv., 184, 185, 195

Naber v. Dover Healthcare Associates, Inc., 199
Nanomantube v. Kickapoo Tribe, 111
Nash v. Jacksonville, 88
National Railroad Passenger Corp. v. Morgan, 189
Nationwide Mut. Ins. Co. v. Darden, 107
Nawrot v. CPC Int'l, 142
Nealey v. Water District No. 1, 195
Neely v. Good Samaritan Hosp., 265
Neely v. McDonald's Corp, 123
Nesbit v. Gears Unlimited, Inc., 109
New El Rey Sausage Co. v. INS, 139

Nichols v. Azteca Restaurant Enterprises, Inc., 114
Niswander v. Cincinnati Ins. Co., 143
NLRB v. Transportation Management Corp., 31
Noel v. Boeing, 219

Officers for Justice v. Civil Serv. Comm'n, 94
Opp v. Office of the State's Atty., 255
Orr v. City of Albuquerque, 89
Oscar Mayer & Co. v. Evans, 226, 227

Palmer v. Salazar, 266
Papaila v. Uniden Am. Corp., 111
Parents Involved in Community Schools v. Seattle School District No. 1, 105
Parker v. Gen. Extrusions, Inc., 258
Parra v. Bashas', Inc., 251
Patane v. Clark, 90, 122
Patterson v. Ind. Newspaper, Inc., 132
Patterson v. McLean Credit Union, 142
Paul v. Northrop Grumman Ship Systems, 90, 122
Perdue v. Kenny A., 262
Personnel Administrator of Mass. v. Feeney, 16, 90, 100
Peters v. Missouri-Pacific R. Co., 94
Philip Servs. Corp., EEOC v., 215
Phillips v. Coolings, 135
Phillips Petroleum Co. Shutts, 240
Pinkerton v. Colorado Dept. of Transp., 145
Pollard v. High's of Baltimore, Inc., 171
Porter v. Erie Foods Int'l, 128
Potter v. District of Columbia, 137
Powell v. Yellow Book USA, Inc., 136
Primes v. Reno, 6
Prowel v. Wise Bus. Forms, Inc., 114
Prospect Airport Servs., EEOC v., 123
Puente v. Ridge, 117
Pye v. Nu Aire, Inc., 147

Ragone v. Alt. Video, 269
Ramlet v. E.F. Johnson Co., 40
Randall v. Rolls-Royce Corp. 230
Randolph v. Ohio Dep't of Youth Servs., 165
Rederford v. US Airways, Inc., 264
Reeves v. C.H. Robinson Worldwide, Inc., 122
Reeves v. Sanderson Plumbing Products, Inc., 29
Rent-A-Center West, Inc. v. Jackson, 268
Reynolds v. Ethicon Endo-Surgery, 6
Rhodes v. Ill. Dep't of Transp., 125
Ricci v. DeStephano, 16, 44, 49, 52, 63, 64, **67**, 99,100
Richardson v. Comm'n on Human Rights & Opportunities, 146
Richardson v. Friendly Ice Cream Corp., 201
Richardson v. Sugg, 265
Richmond v. J. A. Croson Co., 75, 91

Ridley v. Costco Wholesale Corp., 155
Risch v. Royal Oak Police Dep't., 19
Riverate v. P.R. Aqueduct & Sewers Auth., 136
Robinson v. Lorillard Corp., 95
Robinson v. Tyson Foods, Inc., 264
Rohan v. Networks Presentation LLC, 173
Rohr v. Salt River Project Agric. Improvement
  & Power Dist., 174, 190
Roland v. United States Postal Serv., 22
Romano v. U-Haul Int'l, 258
Rossbach v. City of Miami, 195
Rothe Dev. Corp. v. DOD, 50
Rowe v. Hussmann Corp., 222
Ruiz v. County of Rockland, 18
Russell v. City of Kansas City, 128
Rweyemamu v. Cote, 139

Safeco Ins. Co. of America v. Burr, 29
Saks v. Franklin Covey Co., 117
Salamon v. Our Lady of Victory Hosp., 110
Sanders v. Southwestern Bell Tel., L.P., 8
Sanford v. Main St. Baptist Church Manor, Inc.,
  110
Sears, EEOC v., 247
Sepulveda-Villarini v. Dep't of Educ.
  of P.R., 25
Sassaman v. Gamache, 128
Serwatka v. Rockwell Automation, Inc., 35
School Board of Nassau County v. Arline, 164
Schaffer v. Weast, 29
Schroeder v. Hamilton School Dist., 95
Schiano v. Quality Payroll Sys. Inc., 121
Schroeder v. Hamilton School Dist., 131
Schuler v. Pricewaterhousecoopers, LLP, 226
Scruggs v. Garst Seed Co., 121
Seff v. Broward County, 212
Shah v. Deaconess Hosp., 110
Shapolia v. Los Alamos National Laboratory,
  132
Shollenbarger v. Planes Moving & Storage, 63
Shuler v. PricewaterhouseCoopers, LLP, 219
Simmons v. N.Y. City Transit Auth., 262
Simple v. Walgreen Co., 8
Sista v. CDC Ixis North America, Inc., 205
Skidmore v. Swift & Co., 152, 188
Skrzypczak v. Roman Catholic Diocese, 138
Smith v. City of Allentown, 35
Smith v. Hy-Vee, Inc., 113
Smith v. Riceland Foods, Inc., 108
Smith v. Xerox Corp., 35
Somoza v. Univ. of Denver, 156
Sosa v. Alvarez-Machain, 12
Sossamon v. Texas, 254
Sprint/United Management Co. v. Mendelsohn,
  38, 66
Spees v. James Marine, Inc., 116
Spencer v. World Vision Inc., 137
Stagi v. AMTRAK, 63
Standridge v. Union Pac. R.R. Co., 117
Starkman v. Evans, 138

Staub v. Proctor Hospital, 9, 146
Stewart v. County of Brown, 196
Stewart v. Miss. Transp. Comm'n, 222
Stover v. Hattiesburg Pub. Sch. Dist., 260
Stremple v. Nicholson, 257
Sturgill v. UPS, 134, 258
Sulima v. Tobyhanna Army Depot, 186
Sumitomo Shoji, America, Inc. v. Avagliano,
  111
Sun v. Bd. of Trs., 65
Sunbelt Rentals, Inc., EEOC v., 136
Sundance Rehab. Corp., EEOC v., 156
Sutherland v. Wal-Mart Stores, Inc., 127
Sutton v. United Air Lines, Inc., 130, 131, 136,
  139, 174, 175, 183, 187, **191**
Swinton v. Potomac Corp., 124
Szabo v. Bridgeport Machines, Inc., 234

Tademy v. Union Pac. Corp., 120
Talley v. Family Dollar Stores of Ohio, Inc., 206
Tamayo v. Blagojevich, 25
Taylor v. Pathmark Stores Inc., 197
Taylor v. Solis, 129
Taylor v. UPS, 228
Teamsters v. U.S., 72, 234, 237, 244, 246
Templeton v. First Tenn. Bank, 146
Theilig v. United Tech Corp., 202
Thelen v. Marc's Big Boy Corp., 168
Thomas v. Choctaw Management/Services
  Enter., 111
Thompson Contr., Grading, Paving & Utils,
  Inc, EEOC v., 135
Thompson v. North Am. Stainless, LP, 149,
  212, 228
Thompson v. Weyerhaeuser Co., 42
Thornton v. Fed. Express Corp., 127
Thornton v. McClatchy Newspapers, Inc., 181
Ticor Title Ins. Co. v. Brown, 239
Tockes v. Air-Land Transp. Serv. Inc., 196
Tomasso v. Boeing Co., 21
Tomic v. Catholic Diocese of Peoria, 138
Torgerson v. City of Rochester, 24
Townsend v. Lumbermens Mut. Cas. Co., 19
Townsend v. Shook, 254
Toyota Motor Mfg., Kentucky Inc. v.
  Williams, 127, 171, 173, **174**
Trafficante v. Metropolitan Life Ins. Co., 151
Trans World Airlines, Inc. v. Thurston, 32, 54
Trujillo v. PacfiCorp., 213
Tyler v. Univ. of Ark. Bd. of Trs., 145

Union Admin. v. First Nat. Bank & Trust Co.,
  152
United Air Lines, Inc. v. Evans, 220
United States v. Brennan, 49, 51, 100
United States v. Mead Corp., 188
Univ. of Chi. Hosps., EEOC v., 133
UPS, EEOC v., 206, 253
Upshaw v. Ford Motor Co., 18

Valentine v. City of Chi., 125
Vande Zande v. Wisconsin Dep't of Admin, 171
Vanderbroek v. PSEG Power Conn. LLC., 201
Van Koten v. Family Health Mgmt., 133
Van Voorhis v. Hillsborough County Bd. of
    County Comm'rs, 7
Vance v. Ball State, 155
Vaughn v. Epworth Villa, 146, 148
Vera v. McHugh, 121
Vincent v. Brewer Co., 40
Virts v. Consolidated Freightways Corp. of Del.,
    135
Visser v. Packer Engineering Associates, Inc., 30
Vulcan Pioneers, Inc. v. New Jersey Dept. of
    Civil Serv., 88, 96

Walsh v. National Computer Systems, 118
Walch v. Adjutant General's Dep't of Texas, 110
Wal-Mart, EEOC v., 201
Wal-Mart Stores, Inc. v. Dukes, 43, 51, 60,
    230, 256, 271
Wal-Mart., EEOC v., 151
Ward v. Int'l Paper Co., 18
Ward v. Merck & Co., 211
Wards Cove Packing Co. v. Atonio, 56, 58, 88,
    237, 245, 250
Washington v. Davis, 90
Wastak v. Lehigh Valley Health Network, 167,
    227
Watkins Motor Lines, Inc., EEOC v., 171, 253
Watson v. CEVA Logistics U.S., Inc., 119
Watson v. Fort Worth Bank & Trust, 56, 73,
    236, 244, 249
Watts v. Kroger Co., 129
Weary v. Cochran, 108
Webb v. City of Philadelphia, 134
Weber v. Strippirt, Inc., 198
Wedow v. City of Kansas, 223
West v. Ortho-McNeil Pharm. Corp., 165
West v. Tyson Foods, 127

Weyers v. Lear Operations Corp., 125
White v. Baxter Healthcare Corp., 20, 22
White v. Wyndham Vacation Ownership, Inc.,
    264
Whitten v. Fred's Inc., 124, 125
Wilkie v. Dep't of Health and Human Servs.,
    123
Wilkerson v. New Media Tech. Charter Sch.,
    Inc., 135
Will v. Michigan Dep't of State Police, 112
Williams v. Bristol-Myers Squibb Co., 6
Williams v. Excel Foundry & Machine, Inc., 183
Williams v. Giant Food, Inc., 225
Williams v. Phila. Hous. Auth. Police
    Dep't, 149
Williams v. Temple Univ. Hosp., 25
Williams v. Waste Mgmt. of Ill., Inc., 127
Willis v. Roche, 85
Wilkerson v. New Media Tech. Charter Sch.,
    Inc., 5, 135
Wilson v. Phoenix Specialty Mfg. Co., 197
Winsley v. Cook County, 125, 173
Winspear v. Cmty. Dev., Inc., 136
Witt v. Dep't of the Air Force, 114
Woodman v. WWOR-TV, Inc., 67
Wortham v. Am. Family Ins. Group, 111
Wright v. Murray Guard, Inc., 128
Wyatt v. Hunt Plywood, 129
Wygant v. Jackson Bd. of Ed., 74, 91

Xodus v. Wackenhurt Corp, 132

Young-Losee v. Graphic Packaging Int'l, Inc.,
    155
Younis v. Pinnacle Airlines, Inc. 229

Zaccagnini v. Cas. Levy Circulating Co., 21
Ziskie v. Mineta, 91, 123
Zipes v. Trans World Airlines, 228

TABLE OF SELECTED SECONDARY AUTHORITIES

Alexander, Charlotte S., Would an Opt in Requirement Fix the Class Action Settlement? Evidence from the Fair Labor Standards Act, 80 Miss. L.J. 443 (2010), 251

Anderson, Cheryl L., Comparative Evidence or Common Experience: When Does "Substantial Limitation" Require Substantial Proof Under the Americans with Disabilities Act?, 57 Am. U. L. Rev. 409 (2007), 182

Banks, Ralph Richard, & Richard Thompson Ford, (How) Does Unconscious Bias Matter?: Law, Politics, and Racial Inequality, 58 Emory L. Rev. 1053 (2009), 5

Bartlett, Katharine T., Making Good on Good Intentions: The Critical Role of Motivation in Reducing Implicit Workplace Discrimination, 95 Va. L. Rev. 1893 (2009), 4

Bauer, Jon, Buying Witness Silence: Evidence-Suppressing Settlements and Lawyers' Ethics, 87 Or. L. Rev. 481 (2008), 266

Befort, Stephen, Let's Try This Again: The ADA Amendments Act of 2008 Attempts to Reinvigorate the "Regarded As" Prong of the Statutory Definition of Disability, 2010 Utah L. Rev. 993, 199

Stephen F. Befort & Elizabeth Canney Borer, Equitable Prescription Drug Coverage: Preventing Sex Discrimination in Employer-Provided Health Plans, 70 L.a. L. Rev. 205 (2009), 118

Bent, Jason, The Telltale Sign of Discrimination: Probabilities, Information Asymmetries, and the Systemic Disparate Treatment Theory, U. of Mich. J. of L. Reform (forthcoming 2011), 43, 47

Bent, Jason R., What the Lilly Ledbetter Fair Pay Act Doesn't Do: "Discrete Acts" and the Future of Pattern or Practice Litigation, 33 Rutgers L. Rev. 31 (2009), 224

Birnbach, Rachel M., Love Thy Neighbor: Should Religious Accommodations that Negatively Affect Coworkers' Shift Preferences Constitute an Undue Hardship on the Employer Under Title VII?, 78 Fordham L. Rev. 1331(2009), 135

Bissonnette, Reagan, S., Note, Reasonably Accommodating Nonmitigating Plaintiffs After the ADA Amendments Act of 2008, 50 B.C.L. Rev. 859 (2009), 186

Borer, Elizabeth Canney, Equitable Prescription Drug Coverage: Preventing Sex Discrimination in Employer-Provided Health Plans, 70 L.A. L. Rev. 205 (2009), 118

Bowles, Tyler J., Employment Discrimination: Distinguishing Between Equitable Remedies and Compensatory Damages, 15 J. Legal Econ. 11 (2008), 256

Brake, Deborah L. & Joanna L. Grossman, The Failure of Title VII as a Rights Claiming System, 86 N.C. L. Rev. 859 (2008), 144

Brent, Jason R., Systematic Harassment, 77 Tenn. L. Rev. 151 (2009), 126

Brodin, Mark S., *Ricci v. DeStefano*: The New Haven Firefighters Case and the Triumph of White Privilege, S. Cal. Rev. L. & Soc. Justice (forthcoming 2011), 103

Canney, Tim, Note, Tax Gross-Ups: A Practical Guide to Arguing and Calculating Awards for Negative Tax Consequences in Discrimination Suits, 59 Cath. U. L. Rev. 1111 (2010), 263

Carle, Susan D., A Social Movement History of Title VII Disparate Impact Analysis, 63 Fla. L. Rev. 251 (2011), 51

Carlson, Richard R., Why The Law Still Can't Tell an Employee When It Sees One and How It Ought to Stop Trying, 22 Berkeley J. Emp. & Lab. L. 295 (2001), 108

Carlson, Richard R., The Small Firm Exemption and the Single Employer Doctrine in Employment Discrimination law, 80 St. John's L. Rev. 1197 (2006), 109

Chew, Pat K., Seeing Subtle Racism, 6 STANFORD J.C. & C.L. 183 (2011), 120

Clark, Brietta R., *Erickson v. Bartell Drug Co.*: A Roadmap for Gender Equality in Reproduction Health Care or an Empty Promise?, 23 J.I. & INEQUALITY 299 (2005), 118

Clermont, Kevin M. & Stewart J. Schwab, Employment Discrimination Plaintiffs in Federal Court: From Bad to Worse, 3 HARV. L. & POL'Y REV. 103 (2009), 40

Cole, Melissa, Beyond Sex Discrimination: Why Employers Discriminate Against Women with Disabilities When Their Employee Health Plans Exclude Contraceptives from Prescription Coverage, 42 ARIZ. L. REV. 501 (2001), 118, 170

Cole, Sarah Rudolph, Let the Grand Experiment Begin: *Pyett* Authorizes Arbitration of Unionized Employees' Statutory Discrimination Claims, 14 LEWIS & CLARK L. REV. 861 (2010), 267

Corbett, William R., Fixing Employment Discrimination Law, 62 SMU L. REV. 81 (2009), 37

Corbin, Caroline Mala, Above The Law? The Constitutionality of the Ministerial Exemption from Antidiscrimination and Sexual Abuse by Ministers, 75 FORDHAM L. REV. 1965 (2007), 138

Cox, Jeannette, "Corrective" Surgery and the Americans with Disabilities Act, 46 SAN DIEGO L. REV. 113, (2009), 186

Cox, Jeanette, Crossroads and Signposts: The ADA Amendments Act of 2008, 85 IND. L.J. 187 (2009), 159

Cox, Jeanette, Disability Stigma and Intraclass Discrimination, 62 FLA. L. REV. 429, (2010), 207

Cunningham-Parmeter, Keith, Redefining the Rights of Undocumented Workers, 58 AM U. L. REV. 1361 (2009), 141

Daniels, Troy B. & Richard A. Bales, Plus at Pretext: Resolving the Split Regarding the Sufficiency of Temporal Proximity Evidence in Title VII Retaliation Cases, 44 GONZ. L. REV. 493 (2008/2009), 145

Davis, Kenneth R., Wheel of Fortune: A Critique of the "Manifest Imbalance" Requirement for Race-Conscious Affirmative Action, 43 GEORGIA L. REV. 933 (2009), 49

Dorsey, Nicholas A., Note, Mandatory Reassignment Under the ADA: The Circuit Split and Need for a Socio-Political Understanding of Disability, 94 CORNELL L. REV. 443 (2009), 204

Duncan, Rene L., Note, The "Direct Threat" Defense Under the ADA: Posing a Threat to the Protection of Disabled Employees, 73 MO. L. REV. 1303 (2008), 207

Edmonds, Curtis D., Snakes and Ladders: Expanding the Definition of "Major Life Activity" in the Americans with Disabilities Act, 33 TEX. TECH L. REV. 321 (2002), 173

Eichhorn, Lisa, The *Chevron* Two-Step and the *Toyota* Sidestep; Dancing Around the EEOC's "Disability" Regulations Under the ADA, 39 WAKE FOREST L. REV. 532 (2000), 189

Eisenberg, Theodore & Charlotte Lanvers, Summary Judgment Rates Over Time, Across Case Categories, and Across Districts: An Empirical Study of Three Large Federal Districts, SSRN, 26

Emens, Elizabeth F., Integrating Accommodation, 156 U. PA. L. REV. 839 (2008), 203

Faigman, David L., Nilanjana Dasgupta, & Cecilia L. Ridgeway, A Matter of Fit: The Law of Discrimination and the Science of Implicit Bias, 59 HASTINGS L.J. 1389 (2008), 249

Fiske, Susan T. & Eugene Borgida, Providing Expert Knowledge in an Adversarial Context: Social Cognitive Science in Employment Discrimination Cases, 4 ANN. REV. L. & SOC. SCI. (2008), 8

Flores, Carrie L., A Disability Is Not a Trump Card: The Americans With Disabilities Act Does Not Entitle Disabled Employees to Automatic Reassignment, 43 VAL. U. L. REV. 195 (2008), 204

Gelbach, Jonah B., Jonathan Klick & Lesley Wexler, Passive Discrimination: When Does it Make Sense to Pay Too Little?, 76 U. CHI. L. REV. 797 (2009), 52

George, B. Glenn, Revenge, 83 TUL. L. REV. 439 (2008), 144

Giuliana, Laura, David I. Levine, & Jonathon Leonard, Manager Race and the Race of New Hires, 27 J. LAB. ECON. 589 (2009), 3

Goldberg, Suzanne, Discrimination by Comparison, 120 Yale L.J. 728, 742 (2011), 23

Goldin and Rouse, Orchestrating Impartiality: The Impact of "Blind" Auditions on Female Musicians, 90 AM. ECON. REV. 715, 715-16 (2000), 244

Gonzalez, Jarod S., Employment Law Remedies for Illegal Immigrants, 40 TEX. TECH L. REV. 987 (2008), 141

Gorman, Daniel, A State of Disarray: The "Knowing and Voluntary" Standard for Releasing Claims Under Title VII of the Civil Rights Act of 1964, 8 U. PA. J. LAB & EMP. L. 73 (2005), 266

Gorod, Brianne J., "Rejecting Reasonableness": A New Look at Title VII's Anti-Retaliation Provision, 56 Am. U. L. Rev. 1469 (2007), 144

Green, Tristin, Insular Individualism: Employment Discrimination Law After Ledbetter v. Goodyear, 43 Harv. C.R-C.L. L. Rev. 353 (2008), 39

Green, Tristin K., The Future of Systemic Disparate Treatment Law, 32 Berkeley. J. of Employ. & Lab. L. (forthcoming 2011), 47, 140

Green, Tristin K. & Alexandra Kalev, Discrimination-Reducing Measures at the Relational Level, 59 Hastings L.J. 1435 (2008), 48

Greenawalt, Kent, Title VII and Religious Liberty, 33 Loy. U. Chi. L. J. 1. (2001), 136

Greene, D. Wendy, Title VII: What's Hair (and Other Race-Based Characteristics) Got to Do With It?, 79 U. Colo. L. Rev. 1355 (2008), 140

Gregory, David L., Religious Harassment in the Workplace: An Analysis of the EEOC's Proposed Guidelines, 56 Mont. L. Rev. 119 (1996), 136

Gregory, David L. and Edward McNamara, Mandatory Labor Arbitration of Statutory Claims, and the Future of Fair Employment, *14 Penn Plaza v. Pyett*, 19 Cornell J. L. & Pub. Pol'y 429 (2010), 267

Griffith, Kati L., Discovering "Immployment" Law: The Constitutionality of Subfederal Immigration Regulation at Work, Yale L. & Pol'y Rev. (forthcoming 2011), 140

Greiner, James D., Causal Inference in Civil Rights Litigation, 122 Harv. L. Rev. 534 (2008), 47

Grover, Susan & Kimberely Piro, Consider the Source: When the Harasser Is the Boss, 79 Fordham L. Rev. 499 (2010), 122

Hanft, Seth, Comment, Questioning the "Presumptively Reasonable Fee" as a Substitute for the Lodestar Method, 76 U. Cin. L. Rev. 1371 (2008), 263

Harper, Michael C., The Causation Standard in Federal Employment Law: *Gross v. FBL Financial Services, Inc.*, and the Unfulfilled Promise of the Civil Rights Act of 1991, 58 Buffalo L. Rev. 69 (2010), 35

Harris, Cheryl I. and Kimberly West-Faulcon, Reading *Ricci*: White(ning) Discrimination, Race-ing Test Fairness, 58 UCLA L. Rev. 73 (2010), 104

Hart, Melissa, From *Wards Cove* to *Ricci*: Struggling Against the "Built-in-Headwinds" of a Skeptical Court, SSRN, 103

Hart, Melissa, Procedural Extremism: The Supreme Court's 2008-2009 Employment and Labor Cases, 13 Emp. Rts. & Emp. Pol'y J. 253 (2010), 35

Hart, Melissa, Retaliatory Litigation Tactics: The Chilling Effects of "After-Acquired Evidence," 40 Ariz. St. L.J. 401 (2008), 257

Hart, Melissa, Skepticism and Expertise: The Supreme Court and the EEOC, 74 Fordham L. Rev. 177 (2004), 189

Hart, Melissa & Paul M. Secunda, A Matter of Context: Social Framework Evidence in Employment Discrimination Class Actions, 78 Fordham L. Rev. 37, (2009), 249

Hébert, L. Camille, Transforming Transsexual and Transgender Rights, 15 Wm. & Mary J. Women & L. 535 (2009), 113

Hensel, Wendy, Interacting with Others: A Major Life Activity Under the Americans with Disabilities Act?, Wis. L. Rev. 1139 (2002), 174

Hersch, Joni, Profiling the New Immigrant Worker: The Effects of Skin Color and Height, 26 J. Lab. Econ., 345 (2008), 23

Hersch, Joni, Skin Color, Discrimination, and Immigrant Pay, 58 Emory L.J. 357 (2008), 23

Hickox, Stacey M., Transfer as an Accommodation: Standards from Discrimination Cases and Theory, 62 Ark. L. Rev. 195 (2009), 204

Hirsh, Elizabeth, Settling for Less? Organizational Determinants of Discrimination-Charge Outcomes, 42 L. & Soc'y Rev. 239 (2008), 40

Hubbard, Anne, Meaningful Lives and Major Life Activities, 55 Ala. L. Rev. 997 (2004), 174

Hubbard, Anne, The Major Life Activity of Belonging, 39 Wake Forest L. Rev. 217 (2004), 174

Hubbard, Anne, The Myth of Independence and the Major Life Activity of Caring, 8 J. Gender Race & Just. 327 (2004), 174

Hyde, Alan, Labor Arbitration of Discrimination Claims After *14 Penn Plaza v. Pyett*: Letting Discrimination Defendants Decide Whether Plaintiffs May Sue Them, 25 Ohio St. J. Disp. Resol. 975 (2010), 267

Ireland, Jamie L. & Richard Bales, Employment Discrimination Under Title II of the Americans with Disabilities Act, 28 N. Ill. U. L. Rev. 183 (2008), 159

Jacobi, John V., Genetic Discrimination in a Time of False Hopes, 30 Fla. St. U. L. Rev. 363 (2003), 172

Johnson, Herman N., The Evolving Strong-Basis-In-Evidence-Standard, Berkley J. Emp. & Lab. L. (forthcoming 2011), 102

Johnson, Judith I., Reasonable Factors Other Than Age: The Emerging Specter of Ageist Stereotypes, 33 Seattle Univ. L. R. 49 (2009), 59

Johnson, Margaret E., "Avoiding Harm Otherwise": Reframing Women Employees' Responses to the Harms of Sexual Harassment, 80 Temp. L. Rev. 743 (2007), 129

Jones, Jeff, Enfeebling the ADA: The ADA Amendments Act of 2008, 62 Okla. L. Rev. 667 (2010), 159

Katz, Martin J., *Gross* Disunity, 144 Penn St. L. Rev. 857 (2010), 35

Korn, Jane Byeff, Cancer and the ADA: Rethinking Disability, 74 S. Cal. L. Rev. 399 (2001), 191

Korn, Jane Byeff, Too Fat, 17 Va. J. Soc. Pol'y & L. 209 (2010), 171

Kotkin, Minna J., Diversity and Discrimination: A Look at Complex Bias, 50 Wm. & Mary L. Rev. 1439 (2009), 26

Kotkin, Minna J., Outing Outcomes: An Empirical Study of Confidential Employment Discrimination Settlements, 64 Wash & Lee L. Rev. 111 (2007), 40

Kramer, Zachary A., Heterosexuality and Title VII, 103 Nw. U. L. Rev. 205 (2009), 114

Lacy, D. Aaron, The Most Endangered Title VII Plaintiff?: Exponential Discrimination Against Black Males, 86 Neb. L. Rev. 552 (2008), 26

Larson, Dale, Comment, Unconsciously Regarded as Disabled: Implicit Bias and the Regarded-As Prong of the Americans with Disabilities Act, 56 Ucla L. Rev. 451 (2008), 197

Leonard, James, Title VII and the Protection of Minority Languages in the American Workplace: The Search for a Justification, 72 Mo. L. Rev. 745 (2007), 140

Levinson, Justin D. & Danielle Young, Implicit Gender Bias in the Legal Profession: An Empirical Study, 18 Duke L. Gender L & Pol'y 1 (2010), 3

Lewis, Harold S., & Thomas A. Eaton, The Contours of a New FRCP, Rule 68.1: A Proposed Two-Way Offer of Settlement Provision for Federal Fee-Shifting Cases, SSRN (2008), 262

Lidge, Ernest F., III, Disparate Treatment Employment Discrimination and an Employer's Good Faith: Honest Mistakes, benign Motives, and Other Sincerely Held Beliefs, 36 Okla. City U.L. Rev. 45 (2011), 18

Lidge, Ernest F., III, What Types of Employer Actions are Cognizable Under Title VII?: The Ramifications of *Burlington Northern & Santa Fe Railroad Co. v. White*, 59 Rutgers L. Rev. 497 (2007), 155

Lidge, Ernest F., III, An Employer's Exclusion of Coverage for Contraceptive Drugs Is Not Per Se Sex Discrimination, 76 Temple L. Rev. 533 (2003), 118

Lidge, Ernest F., III, The Courts' Misuse of the Similarly Situated Concept in Employment Discrimination Law, 67 Mo. L. Rev. 831 (2002), 23

Long, Alex B., Viva State Employment Law! State Law Retaliation Claims in a Post-*Crawford/ Burlington Northern* World, 77 Tenn. L. Rev. 253 (2010), 142

Long, Alex B., The Troublemaker's Friend: Retaliation Against Third Parties and the Right of Association in the Workplace, 59 Fla. L. Rev. 931 (2007), 154

Long, Alex B., (Whatever Happened to) The ADA's "Record of" Prong (?), 81 Wash. L. Rev. 669 (2006), 191

Malin, Martin H., Due Process in Employment Arbitration: The State of the Law and the Need for Self-Regulation, 11 Emp. Rts. & Emp. Pol'y J. 363, 403 (2007), 269

Malveaux, Suzette Class Actions at the Crossroads: An Answer to Wal-Mart v. Dukes, 5 Harv. L. & Pol'y Rev. (2011), 250

Malveaux, Suzette M., Front Loading and Heavy Lifting: How Pre-Dismissal Discovery Can Address the Detrimental Effect of *Iqbal* on Civil Rights Cases, 14 Lewis & Clark L. Rev. 65 (2010), 25

Malveaux, Suzette M., Is It the "Real Thing:" How Coke's One-Way Binging Arbitration May Bridge the Divide Between Litigation and Arbitration, 2009 J. Disp. Res. 77, 269

Mansfield, John H., A Tale of Two Organists: Suits Against Churches for Employment Discrimination and Sexual Abuse by Ministers, 7 Geo J. L. & Pub. Pol'y 237 (2009), 138

Martin, Natasha T., Immunity for Hire: How the Same-Actor Doctrine Sustains Discrimination in the Contemporary Workplace, 40 Conn. L. Rev. 1117 (2008), 38

Martin, Natasha T., Petext in Peril, 75 Mo. L. Rev. 313, 401 (2010), 18

McCormick, Marcia L., The Truth Is Out There: Revamping Federal Antidiscrimination Enforcement for the Twenty-First Century, 30 Berkeley J. Emp. & Lab. L. 193 (2009), 253

McCormick, Marcia L., Twisting and Turning Towards Summary Judgment, https://lawprofessors.typepad.com/laborprof_blog/2010/09/twisting-and-turning-towards-summary-judgment.html, 7

McGinley, Ann C., Creating Masculine Identities: Bullying and Harassment "Because of Sex," 79 U. Colo. L. Rev. 1151 (2008), 113

McGinley, Ann, Erasing Boundaries: Masculinities, Sexual Minorities and Employment Discrimination, 43 U. Mich J.L. Reform 713 (2010), 113

Menetrez, Frank J., Employee Status and the Concepts of Control in Federal Employment Discrimination Law 63 SMU L. Rev. 137 (2010), 109

Minow, Martha, Response, Accommodating Integration, 156 U. Pa. L. Rev. Pennumbra 165 (2008), 203

Mitchell, Gregory, Second Thoughts, 40 McGeorge L. Rev. 687 (2009), 4

Mitchell, Gregory & Philip E. Tetlock, Facts Do Matter: A Reply to Bagenstos, 37 Hofstra L. Rev. 737 (2009), 4

Modesitt, Nancy M. Reinventing the EEOC, 63 SMU L. Rev. 1237 (2010) 253

Modesitt, Nancy M. The Hundred-Years War: The Ongoing Battle Between Courts and Agencies over the Right to Interpret Federal Law, 74 Mo. L. Rev. 949 (2009), 255

Monahan, John, Laurens Walker & Gregory Mitchell, Contextual Evidence of Gender Discrimination: The Ascendance of "Social Frameworks," 2008, 94 Va. L. Rev. 1715 (2008), 235

Moses, Margaret L., Arbitration Law: Who's in Charge, Seton Hall L. Rev. (2009), 271

Moses, Margaret L., The Pretext of Textualism: Disregarding Stare Decisis in *14 Penn Plaza v. Pyett*, 14 Lewis & Clark L. Rev. 825 (2010), 267

Moss, Scott A. & Peter H. Huang, How the New Economics Can Improve Discrimination Law, and How Economics Can Survive the Demise of the "Rational Actor," 2009, 51 Wm. & Mary L. Rev. 183 (2009), 258

Murphy, Richard W., NeuroCongress, 37 Seton Hall L. Rev. 221 (2006), 16

Nagareda, Richard, Class Certification in the Age of Aggregate Proof, 84 N.Y.U. L. Rev. 97 (2009), 233

Nagareda, Richard, The Preexistence Principle and the Structure of the Class Action, 103 Colum. L. Rev. 149 (2003), 238

Nielsen, Laura Beth et al., Individual Justice or Collective Legal Mobilization? Employment Discrimination in the Post Civil Rights United States, 7 J. Emp. Stud. 175 (2010), 41

Norton, Helen, The Supreme Court's Post-Racial Turn Towards a Zero-Sum Understanding of Equality, 52 Wm. & Mary L. Rev. 197 (2010), 101

O'Gorman, Daniel P., Show Me the Money: The Applicability of Contract Law's Ratification and Tender-Back Doctrines to Title VII Releases, 84 Tul. L. Rev. 675 (2010), 266

Onwuachi-Willig, Angela, Another Hair Piece, Exploring New Strands of Analysis, 2010, 98 Geo. L. J. 1087 (2010), 115

Onwuachi-Willig, Angela, Emily Houh & Mary Campbell, Cracking the Egg: Which Came First—Stigma or Affirmative Action?, 96 Cal. L. Rev. 1299 (2009), 50

Pedersen, Natalie Bucciarel, A Legal Framework for Uncovering Implicit Bias, 79 U. Cin. L. Rev. 97 (2010), 37

Porter, Nicole B., Reasonable Burdens: Resolving the Conflict Between Disabled Employees and Their Coworkers, 34 Fla. St. U. L. Rev. 313 (2007), 204

Porter, Nicole Buonocore, Sex Plus Age Discrimination: Protecting Older Women Workers, 81 Denv. U. L. Rev. 79 (2003), 26

Primus, Equal Protection and Disparate Impact: Round 3, 117 Harv. L. Rev. 493 (2003), 80, 91

Primus, Richard, The Future of Disparate Impact, 108 Mich. L. Rev. 1314 (2010), 63

Render, Meredith M., Gender Rules, 22 Yale J. L. & Feminism 133 (2010), 115

Rosenthal, Lawrence D., Motions for Summary Judgment When Employers Offer Multiple Justifications for Adverse Employment Actions: Why the Exceptions Should Swallow the Rule, 2002 Utah L. Rev. 335, 21

Rosenthal, Lawrence D., Reading Too Much into What the Court Doesn't Write: How Some Federal Courts Have Limited Title VII's Participation Clause's Protections After *Clark County School District v. Breeden*, 83 Wash. L. Rev. 345 (2008), 143

Rosenthal, Lawrence D., Reasonable Accommodations for Individuals Regarded as Having Disabilities Under the Americans with Disabilities Act? Why "No" Should Not Be the Answer, 36 Seton Hall L. Rev. 895 (2006), 198

Rosenthal, Lawrence, Adding Insult to Injury to No Injury: The Denial of Attorney's Fees to "Victorious" Employment Discrimination and Other Civil Rights Plaintiffs, 37 Fla. St. U.L. Rev. 49 (2009), 261

Rosenthal, Lawrence, The Emerging First Amendment Law of Managerial Prerogative, 77 Fordham L. Rev. 33 (2008), 131

Ruan, Nantiya, Accommodating Respectful Religious Expression in the Workplace, 92 Marq. L. Rev. 1 (2008), 136

Ruan, Nantiya, Bringing Sense to Incentives: An Examination of Incentive Payments to Named Plaintiffs in Employment Discrimination Class Actions, 10 Emp. Rts. & Emp. Pol'y J. 395 (2006), 252

Rutherglen, George, *Ricci v. DeStefano*: Affirmative Action and the Lessons of Adversity, 2009 Sup. Ct. Rev., 100

Schwartz, David S., Mandatory Arbitration and Fairness, 84 Notre Dame L. Rev. 1247 (2009), 271

Seicshnaydre, Stacey, Is the Road to Disparate Impact Paved with Good Intentions?: Stuck on State of Mind in Antidiscrimination Law, 42 Wake Forest L. Rev. 1141 (2008), 66

Seiner, Joseph, The Failure of Punitive Damages in Employment Discrimination Cases: A Call for Change, 50 Wm. & Mary L. Rev. 735 (2008), 259

Seiner, Joseph, The Trouble with *Twombly*: A Proposed Pleading Standard for Employment Discrimination Cases, 2009 U. Ill. L. Rev 1011, 25

Seiner, Joseph A., After *Iqbal*, 45 Wake Forest L. Rev. 179 (2010), 25

Seiner, Joseph A., Pleading Disability, 51 B.C. L. Rev. (2010), 25

Selmi, Michael, The Value of the EEOC: The Agency's Role in Employment Discrimination Law, 57 Ohio St. L. J. 1 (1996), 253

Selmi, Michael, Theorizing Systemic Disparate Treatment Law, 32 Berkeley. J. of Employ. & Lab. L. (forthcoming 2011), 47

Senn, Craig Robert, Knowing and Voluntary Waivers of Federal Employment Claims: Replacing the Totality of Circumstances Test with a "Waiver Certainty" Test, 58 Fla. L. Rev. 305 (2006), 266

Senn, Craig Robert, Perception Over Reality: Extending the ADA's Concept of "Regarded as" Protection Under Federal Employment Discrimination Law, 36 Fla. St. U.L. Rev. 827 (2009), 23

Senn, Craig Robert, Proposing a Uniform Remedial Approach for Undocumented Workers Under Federal Employment Discrimination Law, 77 Fordham L. Rev. 113 (2008), 141

Shane, Richard D., Note, Teachers as Sexual Harassment Victims: The Inequitable Protections of Title VII in Public Schools, 61 Fla. L. Rev. 355 (2009), 131

Shin, Patrick, Liability for Unconscious Discrimination? A Thought Experiment in the Theory of Employment Discrimination Law, 62 Hastings L. R. 67 (2010), 4

Siegelman, Peter, Contributory Disparate Impacts in Employment Discrimination Law, 49 Wm. & Mary L. Rev. 515, 568 (2007), 62

Seiner, Joseph & Benjamin Gutman, Does *Ricci* Herald a New Disparate Impact?, 90 B. U. L. Rev. 2181 (2010), 104

Soltman, Nicholas, Comment, What About "Me (Too)"? The Case for Admitting Evidence of Discrimination against Nonparties, 76 U. Chi. L. Rev. 1875 (2009), 40

Sperino, Sandra, Judicial Preemption of Punitive Damages, 78 U. Cin. L. Rev. 227 (2009), 260

Sperino, Sandra, The "Disappearing" Dilemma: Why Agency Principles Should Now Take Center Stage in Retaliation Cases, 57 U. Kan. L. Rev. 157 (2008), 154

Sperino, Sandra F., A Modern Theory of Direct Corporate Liability for Title VII, 61 Ala. L. Rev. 773 (2010) 124

Stone, Kerri Lynn, Consenting Adults? Why Women Who Submit to Supervisory Sexual Harassment Are Faring Better in Court than Those Who Say No . . . and Why They Shouldn't, 20 Yale J.L. & Feminism 25 (2008), 125

Stone, Kerri Lynn, License to Harass: Holding Defendants Accountable for Retaining Recidivist Harassers, 41 Akron L. Rev. 1059 (2008), 126, 130

Stone, Kerri, The Unexpected Appearance of Transferred Intent in Title VII, 55 Loyola L. Rev. 752 (2010), 101

Struve, Catherine T. Shifting Burdens: Discrimination Law Through the Lens of Jury Instructions, 51 B.C. L. Rev. 279 (2010), 35

Sunstein, Cass R., Response, Caste and Disability: The Moral Foundations of the ADA, 156 U. Pa. L. Rev. Pennumbra 165 (2008), 203

Suk, Julie C., Antidiscrimination Law in the Administrative State, 2006, Ill. L. Rev. 405 (2006) 253

Suk, Julie C., Are Gender Sterotypes Bad for Women? Rethinking Antidiscrimination Law and Work-Family Conflict, 110 Colum. L. Rev. 1 (2010), 119

Sullivan, Charles A., Disparate Impact: Looking Past the Desert Palace Mirage, 47 Wm. & Mary L. Rev. 911 (2010), 41

Sullivan, Charles A., Raising the Dead: The Lilly Ledbetter Fair Pay Act, 84 Tul. L. Rev. 499 (2010), 218

Sullivan, Charles A., The Phoenix from the Ash: Proving Discrimination by Comparators, 60 Ala. L. Rev. 191 (2009), 23

Sullivan, Charles A., Plausibly Pleading Employment Discrimination, 52 Wm. & Mary L. Rev. 1613, 1622 (2011), 25

Sullivan, Charles A., *Ricci v. DeStefano*: End of the Line or Just Another Turn on the Disparate Impact Road?, 104 Nw. U. L. Rev. Colloquy 21 (2009), 103

Taylor, Lisa Durham, Adding Subjective Fuel to the Vague-Standard Fire: A Proposal for Congressional Intervention after *Burlington Northern & Santa Fe Railway Co. v. White*, 9 U. Pa. J. Lab. & Emp. L. 533 (2007), 155

Taylor, Lisa Durham, Parsing Supreme Court Dicta and the Example of Non-Workplace Harms, 57 Drake L. Rev. 75 (2008), 154

Taylor, Lisa Durham, Untangling the Web Spun by Title VII's Referral & Deferral Scheme, 59 Cath. U. L. Rev. 427 (2010) 230

Tolson, Franita, The Boundaries of Litigating Unconscious Discrimination: Firm-Based Remedies in Response to a Hostile Judiciary, 33 Del. J. Corp. L. 347, 347 (2008), 48

Tomas, Suja A., The New Summary Judgment Motion: The Motion to Dismiss Under *Iqbal* and *Twombly*, 14 Lewis & Clark L. Rev. 15 (2010), 25

Travis, Michelle A., Lashing Back at the ADA Backlash: How the Americans With Disabilities Act Benefits Americans Without Disabilities, 76 Tenn. L. Rev. 311 (2009), 203

Travis, Michelle A., Leveling the Playing Field or Stacking the Deck? The "Unfair Advantage" Critique of Perceived Disability Claims, 78 N.C.L. Rev. 901 (2000), 198

Travis, Michelle A., Perceived Disabilities, Social Cognition, and "Innocent Mistakes," 55 Vand. L. Rev. 481 (2002), 197

Travis, Michelle A., The PDA's Causation Effect: Observation of an Unreasonable Women, Yale J.L. & Feminism 51 (2009), 116

Walsh, David J., Small Change: An Empirical Analysis of the Effect of Supreme Court Precedents on Federal Appellate Court Decisions in Sexual Harassment Cases, Berkeley J. Emp. & Lab. L. 461, 130

Wax, Amy L., The Discriminating Mind: Define It, Prove It, 40 Conn. L. Rev. 979, (2008), 4

White, Rebecca Hanner, Deference and Disability Discrimination, 99 Mich. L. Rev. 532 (2000), 189

White, Rebecca Hanner, The EEOC, the Courts, and Employment Discrimination Policy: Recognizing the Agency's Leading Role in Statutory Interpretation, 1995 Utah L. Rev. 189

Widiss, Deborah A., Shadow Precedents and the Separation of Powers: Statutory Interpretation of Congressional Overrides, 84 Notre Dame L. Rev. 511 (2009), 219

Willborn, Steven & Ramona Paetzold, Statistics Is a Plural Word, 122 Harv. L. Rev. 48 (2000), 48

Williams, Joan C. & Nancy Segal, Beyond the Maternal Wall: Relief for Family Caregivers Who Are Discriminated Against on the Job, 26 Harv. Women's L.J. 77 (2003), 118

Williams, Joan C. & Stephanie Bornstein, The Evolution of FReD: Family Responsibilities Discrimination and Developments in the Law of Stereotyping and Implicit Bias, 59 Hastings L.J. 1311 (2008), 119

Williams, Joan C., Using Social Science to Litigate Gender Discrimination Cases and Defang the "Cluelessness" Defense, 7 Empl. Rts. & Employ Pol'y J. 401 (2003), 119

Yoshino, Kenji, The New Equal Protection, 124 Harv. L. Rev. F. 747 (2011), 63

Zatz, Noah, Managing the Macaw: Third-Party Harassers, Accommodation, and the Disaggregation of Discriminatory Intent, 109 COLUM. L. REV. 1357 (2009), 131

Zimmer, Michael J., A Chain of Inferences Proving Discrimination, 79 U. COLO. L. REV. 1243 (2008), 3, 7, 19, 38

Zimmer, Michael J., *Ricci's* Color-blind Standard in Race-Conscious Society: A Case of Unintended Consequences?, 2010 B.Y.U. L. REV. 1257, 101

Zimmer, Michael J., A Pro-Employee Supreme Court?: The Retaliation Decisions, 60 S.C. L. REV. 917 (2009), 154

Zisk, Nancy L., Failing the Test: How *Ricci v. DeStefano* Failed to Clarify Disparate Impact and Disparate Treatment Law, 34 HAMLINE L. REV. 27 (2011), 106